1

I had
Marvell's
'Mr Smirke' — but
use of anything from this
volume requires permission;
so I am not ~~to~~ using
any quotations — only praising
Marvell's felicity.

28/1/06

The Prose Works of Andrew Marvell

VOLUME II

Dearest Victor

Full of choice bits — sure to come in handy for socialism!

With Christmas love,
Heather
25 December 2004

THE PROSE WORKS OF

Andrew Marvell

VOLUME II
1676–1678

YALE UNIVERSITY PRESS
NEW HAVEN & LONDON

Published with assistance from the foundation established in memory of Oliver
Baty Cunningham of the Class of 1917, Yale College.

Designed by Nancy Ovedovitz and set in Caslon type by Keystone Typesetting,
Inc. Printed in the United States of America by Sheridan Books.

Library of Congress Cataloging-in-Publication Data
Marvell, Andrew, 1621–1678.
[Prose works]
The prose works of Andrew Marvell /
edited by Martin Dzelzainis and Annabel Patterson.
p. cm.
Contents: v. 2. 1676–1678
Includes index.
ISBN 0-300-09936-3 (v. 2)
I. Keeble, N. H. II. von Maltzahn, Nicholas. III. Patterson, Annabel M. IV. Title.
PR3546.A6 2003
828′.408—dc21   2003050055

A catalogue record for this book is available from the British Library.

The paper in this book meets the guidelines for permanence and durability of the
Committee on Production Guidelines for Book Longevity of the Council on
Library Resources.

10 9 8 7 6 5 4 3 2 1

Editorial Committee

Contents: Volume I

Contents: Volume II

Chronology: Marvell in the Restoration

1660

April 2	Marvell reelected to Convention parliament for Hull
April 4	Declaration of Breda
May 25	Charles II lands at Dover
October	Executions of regicides
December 17	Marvell speaks in parliament to urge Milton's release from prison
December 24	Dissolution of Convention parliament

1661

January 30	Exhumation and disgrace of Cromwell's body
May 8	Meeting of Cavalier parliament, with Marvell as member for Hull
June 27	Marvell writes to Hull about imminent passage of Act of Uniformity
June 30	Bishops restored to House of Lords
December 19	Corporation Act

1662

February 24	Roger L'Estrange becomes surveyor of the press
March	Act of Uniformity debated in parliament
March 20	Marvell quarrels with Clifford in the House
May 19	Parliament prorogued until February 18, 1663; Act of Uniformity and Licensing Act become law.

June   Marvell leaves for Holland on unspecified political
                              mission

1663
April 2   Marvell writes to Hull to announce his return to his
                              seat (*P&L*, 2:34–35)
July 20   Marvell accompanies Carlisle on embassy to Russia,
                              Sweden, and Denmark

1664
April 27   Outbreak of Second Dutch War
                              Conventicle Act (expired 1668)

1665
January   Marvell returns to parliament
June   Battle of Lowestoft
October 9   Five Mile Act
1666
April   Self-dating of *Second Advice*
June 1–4   Four Days' battle with Dutch
September 2–6   Great Fire of London
October 1   Self-dating of *Third Advice*
October 2   Marvell added to parliamentary committee to inves-
                              tigate Fire of London

1667
Spring   Locke joins Shaftesbury as his personal physician
June 10   Naval disaster at Chatham
September 4   Self-dating of *Last Instructions*
October 13   Marvell speaks in defense of Peter Pett concerning
                              Chatham disaster
November 19   Clarendon flees the country
1668
February 15   Marvell speaks intemperately against Arlington
March 13, 30   Marvell attacks proposal to renew Conventicle Act
                              Buckingham speaks in the Lords for toleration
July 24   John Darby and John Winter listed in violation of
                              Press Act

1669
February   Buckingham attacks Sir William Coventry in *The
                              Country Gentleman*
November 22   Samuel Parker's *Discourse of Ecclesiastical Politie* ad-
                              vertised for sale

December	John Owen's *Truth and Innocence Vindicated* answers Parker
1670	
March	Conventicle Act renewed
May 22	Secret Treaty of Dover signed by Clifford and Arlington
June	Samuel Parker promoted to archdeaconship of Canterbury
July	Charles sends Buckingham to negotiate cover treaty with Louis XIV
August 18	John Dryden appointed poet laureate and historiographer royal
November 21	Marvell speaks for James Hayes, prosecuted under Conventicle Act
November 22	Parker's *Defence and Continuation* advertised for sale
December/January	Locke, James Tyrrell, and others discuss Parker's *Discourse*
1671	
February 27	Speech of Lord Lucas in Commons against government (*P&L*, 2:322–23)
April 22	Parliament prorogued; Marvell perhaps begins translation of Suetonius
October	Charles cancels Buckingham's commission and transfers it to Monmouth and Ossory
December 7	First performance of Buckingham's *Rehearsal*
1672	
January 1	Stop of the Exchequer
	Marvell (?) writes *The Kings Vowes*
February	Search of all printing houses
February 7	Dryden's *Conquest of Granada*, dedicated to James, attacking commonwealth and anticipating Third Dutch War, advertised for sale
March 15	Charles's Declaration of Indulgence
March 17	Declaration of war against the Dutch
June 24	Buckingham's *Rehearsal* advertised in Term Catalogue
	Parker's *Preface* advertised in Term Catalogue; Marvell begins *RT.*
September 7	Parker's *Preface* listed in Stationers' Register

November 17	Shaftesbury becomes lord chancellor
December 2	Wardens of Stationers' Company for *RT*
	Two sheets seized by Mearne at Winter's press; Anglesey and Shaftesbury intervene
December 10	Benjamin Woodroffe writes of *RT,* "It has been stopped from spreading, but is now again allowed to be bought."
December 16	Court of Assistants orders that *RT* not be entered in Stationers' Register

1673

January 15	Arlington summons wardens to account for several printers
January 21	John Darby promises wardens to take down one of his presses
January 23	Henry Coventry deposes L'Estrange about first edition of *RT*
January 24	Wardens report three visits to Whitehall about *RT*
January 25	Coventry deposes Ponder
	Second impression of *RT,* intended for new session of parliament?
February 4	Parliament reconvenes; supply requested for Dutch war; Shaftesbury's *delendo est Carthago* speech
	Milton writes *Of true religion, haeresie, schism, toleration*
March 7	Anglesey drafts bill to exempt Protestant dissenters from legal penalties
March 8	King's speech withdraws Declaration of Indulgence
March 29	Parliament prorogued
April 22	Anglesey becomes lord privy seal
May 3	Marvell reads Parker's *Reproof* in press and declares his intention to answer it (in letter to Harley)
July 15	Thomas Blount writes to Wood concerning "great searching of the Printhouses for Marvel's Reply to Parker"
November 3	Marvell publishes *Rehearsal Transpros'd: The Second Part*
	Shaftesbury learns of secret clauses in Treaty of Dover

| November 9 | Shaftesbury dismissed from chancellorship and council by Charles, partly at request of James, and goes over to the Opposition |

1674

January 13	Buckingham attacked in Commons, dismissed from council
February 19	Treaty of Westminster ends Third Dutch War
Summer	Marvell mentioned by government spies as member of a Dutch fifth column in England
November	Marvell writes *Upon his Majesty's being made free of the City*

1675

Spring	Buckingham returns to London and begins alliance with Country party
March 1	Girolamo Alberti describes Marvell's parody of king's speech to Doge
April 13	Parliament reconvenes; Croft and five other bishops meet to discuss religious comprehension; Croft writes *Naked Truth* and has four hundred copies printed to distribute to MPs
April 22	Marvell reports to Hull on Danby's proposed test (*P&L*, 2:148–49)
May 29	*Gazette* announces setting up of king's statue in Stock Market
June 9	Parliament prorogued
July 24	Marvell describes Danby's test in a letter to Popple and comments on Buckingham's mockery of the bishops (*P&L*, 2:341–43)
Summer	Marvell writes statue poems (?)
October 13	Parliament reconvenes.
November 8	*Letter from a person of quality* ordered by Lords to be burned by the common hangman
November 9	Marvell reports this to Hull (*P&L*, 2:171–72)
November 12	Locke leaves England in haste
November 16	Buckingham drafts bill for relief of Protestant dissenters
November 18	Marvell reports "To morrow . . . a great Lord brings in a Bill into the Lords for care of dissenters"

| November 22 | Parliament prorogued; beginning of Long Proroga-tion |
| December | Marvell writes *The Royal Buss*(?) (*CSPD*, May 3, 1676) |

1676

February 7	Francis Turner's *Animadversions* on *Naked Truth* advertised in *Gazette* (no. 1066)
February 18	Evelyn reports Gunning's and Turner's answers
March 3	Wardens paid for "another search for *Naked Truth*"
March 11	Etherege's *Man of Mode* first produced at Dorset Garden
March 17	Wardens send list of printers to Henry Compton, bishop of London
April 29	Henry Oldenburg turns in his licenser's license. Marvell must have already finished *Mr. Smirke*
May 8–18	Wardens search for "Ponders Pamphlett, being part of *Mr. Smirke*"
May 10	Ponder indicted; Anglesey intervenes unsuccessfully
May 18	John Darby examined by Coventry
June 6	Thomas Blount comments on sales of *Mr. Smirke*
July 1	Marvell writes to Harley about reception of *Mr. Smirke* (*P&L*, 2:344–46)

1677

February 15	Parliament reconvenes. Buckingham's speech declares dissolution
February 16	Four lords sent to the Tower by Danby
March 27	Lords bill for educating royal children; Marvell speaks against it; named to the committee to consider it
March 29	Marvell's scuffle in the House with Sir Philip Harcourt
April	Marvell probably begins work on *Account of Growth of Popery*
July 16	Marvell in his seat; parliament adjourned to December 3
October 28	Royal proclamation postponed session to April 4
November 26	Danson's *De Causa Dei* entered in Stationers' Register

December 3	Charles moves session up to January 15
December	Premiere of Dryden's *All for Love*
	Trial of John Harrington
1678	
January 31	Wardens attend king and council at Whitehall with L'Estrange
February 8	Loose sheets of *Account* taken for stitching
February 19	Warrant for the arrest of those responsible for *Account*
February 14	Wardens seize a porter with twelve copies of *Account*
March 1	William Leach gives information about Packer's involvement
March 21	Dryden's *All for Love* appears in print, with an antirepublican dedication to Danby
March 21–25	*Gazette* advertises *All for Love* and offers a reward for the discovery of those responsible for *Account*
April 17	Marvell's *Remarks* vs. Danson licensed
May 14	L'Estrange's *Account of the Growth of Knavery* advertised for sale
June 10	Marvell writes to Popple describing search for *Account* (*P&L*, 2:357)
August 16	Marvell dies
September	Titus Oates gives first depositions about Popish Plot
1679	
March	Parliament refuses to renew Licensing Act
May	First Exclusion Bill
	Folio edition of the *Account*
May 27	Parliament prorogued, never to meet again
	Monmouth sent into exile in Holland
July 18	Wakeman acquitted; first doubts about Popish Plot
October 7	Exclusion Bill parliament prorogued before it met
November 17	Settle's antipopish pageant
1680	
Summer	Monmouth's unauthorized progress
October 15	Mary "Marvell's" dating of *Miscellaneous Poems*
October 21	Parliament reconvened
November 11	Exclusion Bill fails to pass the Lords

1681

January 10   Parliament prorogued; Narcissus Luttrell bought a
                     copy of *Miscellaneous Poems. By Andrew Marvell . . .
                     Late Member of the Honourable House of Commons.*

March 21   Oxford parliament convened, and dissolved on
                     March 28

April 8   Charles's *Declaration*

June   Dryden's *His Majesties Declaration Defended,* refers
                     to Marvell as "their deceased Judas"

July 1   Fitzharris executed

July 2   Shaftesbury arrested on charge of treason

1682

June 28   Ponder's deposition about Marvell's poverty for
                     about the last five years

Abbreviations

Account	Marvell, *An Account of the Growth of Popery and Arbitrary Government in England* ("Amsterdam") (1677)
CPW	John Milton, *The Complete Prose Works,* gen. ed., D. M. Wolfe, 8 vols. in 10 (New Haven, 1953–80)
CSPD	*Calendar of State Papers Domestic*
Censure	Samuel Parker, *A Free and Impartial Censure of the Platonick Philosophie* (Oxford, 1666)
Defence	Samuel Parker, *A Defence and Continuation of the Ecclesiastical Politie. By way of a letter to a friend in London. Together with a letter from the author of the Friendly debate* [Simon Patrick] (London, 1671)
DNB	*The Dictionary of National Biography founded in 1882 by George Smith*
Discourse	Samuel Parker, *A Discourse of Ecclesiastical Politie, Wherein The Authority of the Civil Magistrate over the Consciences of Subjects in Matters of External Religion is Asserted; The Mischiefs and Inconveniences of Toleration are Represented, And all Pretenses Pleaded in Behalf of Liberty of Conscience are Fully Answered* (London, 1669).
Essay	Marvell, *A Short Historical Essay, concerning General Councils, Creeds, and Imposition, in Matters of Religion* (London, 1676)

Grosart	*The Complete Works in Verse and Prose of Andrew Marvell M.P.*, ed. Alexander B. Grosart, 4 vols. (London, 1872–75)
Henning	Basil Duke Henning, *The House of Commons 1660–1690*, 3 vols. (1983)
HMC	Historical Manuscripts Commission
JHC	*Journal of the House of Commons, 1547–1800*, 55 vols. (1983)
JHL	*Journals of the House of Lords, beginning anno primo Henrici octavi*, 79 vols. (1771)
P&L	Andrew Marvell, *Poems and Letters*, ed. H. M. Margoliouth, 3rd ed. rev. Pierre Legouis, with the collaboration of E. E. Duncan-Jones, 2 vols. (Oxford, 1971)
POAS	*Poems on Affairs of State: Augustan Satirical Verse, 1660–1714*, vol. 1, ed. George de F. Lord (New Haven and London, 1963)
Preface	Samuel Parker, *Bishop Bramhall's Vindication of himself and the episcopal clergy, from the Presbyterian charge of popery . . . together with a preface shewing what grounds there are of Fears and Jealousies of Popery* (London, 1672).
PRO	Public Record Office
Remarks	Marvell, *Remarks Upon a Late Disingenuous Discourse, Writ by one T. D. Under the pretence De Causa Dei . . . By a Protestant.* (London, 1678)
Reproof	Samuel Parker, *A Reproof to the Rehearsal Transpros'd* (London, 1673)
RT	Marvell, *The Rehearsal Transpros'd: Or, Animadversions Upon a late Book, Intituled, A Preface Shewing what grounds there are of Fears and Jealousies of Popery* (London, 1672)
RT2	*The Rehearsal Transpros'd: The Second Part* (London, 1673)
Smirke	Marvell, *Mr. Smirke: Or, The Divine in Mode: Being Certain Annotations, upon the Animadversions on the Naked Truth.* (London, 1673)
Smith	Andrew Marvell, *The Rehearsal Transpros'd and the Rehearsal Transpros'd: The Second Part*, ed. D. I. B. Smith (Oxford, 1971)
Thompson	*The Works of Andrew Marvell, esq., Poetical, Controversial, Political, containing many Original Letters, Poems, and Tracts, never before printed. With a new life of the author*, by Capt. Edward Thompson (London, 1776)
Wood	Anthony à Wood, *Athenae Oxonienses*, ed. Philip Bliss, 5 vols. (Oxford, 1813–15)

The Prose Works of Andrew Marvell

VOLUME II

MR. SMIRKE; OR, THE DIVINE
IN MODE

AND

A SHORT HISTORICAL ESSAY
CONCERNING GENERAL
COUNCILS, CREEDS, AND
IMPOSITIONS, IN MATTERS
OF RELIGION

1676

Introduction

Annabel Patterson

There can be few publications more richly announced and situated than
Marvell's twinned pamphlets, *Mr. Smirke; or the Divine in Mode* and *A
Short Historical Essay Concerning General Councils, Creeds, and Impositions,
in Matters of Religion.* We know exactly what caused him to write them,
and the sequence of events that led both up to and down from their publication is unusually fully documented. While the two parts of the *Rehearsal
Transpros'd* can and must be located in the toleration debates of 1668–73,
there is perhaps more local information about what provoked Marvell to
return to the issue in 1676, providing us with the equivalent of what cultural
historians of an anthropological bent have termed thick description, presumably more admirable than thin.

THE CONTEXT

The local story began with Bishop Herbert Croft's decision to appeal to
the session of parliament that opened on April 13, 1675. The session had
opened with a speech by Charles II that Marvell had preemptively par-
odied, not least because it stated, against all evidence to the contrary, the
king's determination to "shew the World [his] Zeal to the Protestant Religion." The session was a heated one, involving attempts to impeach both
Lauderdale and Danby, and eventually stymied by the disputes about privilege between the two Houses in the cases of Shirley vs. Fagg and Stoughton
vs. Onslow. When not distracted by the latter issue, the Commons pursued

"effectual Ways for the Suppressing the Growth of Popery," and in general showed the coercive temper with respect to religious dissent that had forced the retraction of Charles's Declaration in 1673. Croft, bishop of Hereford, having begun as a Roman Catholic, and converted back in the 1630s to ardent Anglicanism, had by the early 1670s become one of the spokesmen for compromise, not for religious toleration or the removal of penalties for those who could not join the national church, but for comprehension within it of as many Protestants as possible by stressing what they had in common rather than the ceremonial points that divided them. In 1667 he had worked with Colonel John Birch and Sir Robert Atkins to introduce a bill for comprehension which never reached the floor of the Commons;[1] and he and Sir Edward Harley, Marvell's friend and correspondent, opposed the new and more rigorous Conventicles Act of 1670. At that time he resigned as royal chaplain. In May 1675, as the Commons floundered about with bills, on the one hand, to prevent "Papists" from sitting in Parliament, and on the other to abolish the medieval statute *de Haeretico Comburendo,* he and five other bishops attended a meeting of Anglican divines who supported some sort of comprehension, and Croft was nominated to write a pamphlet arguing this position. The result was *The Naked Truth: or, the True State of the Primitive Church.*[2] Croft must have written it in something of a hurry, trying to reach the parliament before the summer recess. It was an earnest but not particularly impressive piece of argument.

Marvell tells us in *Mr. Smirke* that Croft arranged for four hundred copies of *The Naked Truth* to be printed, intending to distribute them to "the Speakers of both Houses, and as many of the Members as [four hundred copies] could furnish." On June 9, however, Charles prorogued the parliament, as being unable to conduct its business properly, until October 13. "The Parliament rising just as the Book was delivering out and

---

[1] See Walter G. Simon, *The Restoration Episcopate* (New York, 1965), pp. 158–62. This was one of two such efforts. In February 1668, John Wilkins, shortly to become bishop of Chester, had drafted another, more realistic comprehension bill which also never reached the floor. See John Spurr, "The Church of England, Comprehension and the Toleration Act of 1689," *English Historical Review* 104 (1989), 933–35. Spurr adds in a note, "Although Wilkins appears to have initiated the proposal, it seems likely that the Duke of Buckingham and other politicians were involved in some way."

[2] Simon, *The Restoration Episcopate,* p. 172; see also Newton Key, "Comprehension and the Breakdown of Consensus in Restoration Herefordshire," in *Religion and Politics in Restoration England,* ed. T. Harris, P. Seaward, and M. Goldie (Oxford, 1990), pp. 191–215.

before it could be presented," wrote Marvell in the opening pages of his defense, Croft ordered the printer to suppress it until the next session. "Some covetous Printer in the mean time getting a Copy, surreptitiously Reprinted it, and so it flew abroad without the Authors knowledge, and against his direction" (p. 51). Both the authorized and the pirated editions were anonymous, but Croft's authorship was readily guessed. We can deduce from these statements of Marvell's that the pirated impression hit the streets in late summer or early autumn 1675. The authorized version, with a newly humble and apologetic preface, would have appeared during the short session convened on October 13, most likely in November. Between them, they caused a sensation.

John Evelyn reported in his *Diary* for February 18, 1676, one semiofficial response—a sermon by "Dr. Gunning Bish: of Elie . . . Chiefly against an Anonymous Booke called *Naked Truth,* a famous & popular Treatise against the Corruption in the Cleargie, but not sound as to its quotations; supposed to have been the Bish; Herefords: & was answered by Dr. Turner: it endeavouring to prove an Equality of Order of Bish; & Presbyter: That they were but one, from different Commissions: Dr. Gunning asserted the difference of their functions as divine & absolutely necessarie; implying that their antagonists were Sismatics." Evelyn's entry indicated that there had *already* been a published answer to Croft by Francis Turner, chaplain to the duke of York.[3] In fact, Turner's *Animadversions upon a Late Pamphlet,* also published anonymously, though it carried the imprimatur of Henry Compton, newly appointed bishop of London, dated February 23, was advertised for sale in the *Gazette* for February 3–7 (no. 1066). Since the *Gazette* was a government organ, containing only one or two advertisements for books in each issue, this meant that Turner's attack on Croft also had support in high places.

Although *Mr. Smirke* also mentions Gunning's sermon, as well as another anonymous answer that Marvell suspected to be by Gunning,[4] it was written exclusively to confute Turner, whose attack on Croft was quite

[3] Francis Turner (1638–1700) later became, under Gunning's patronage, first bishop of Rochester (1683) and the next year bishop of Ely. He delivered the coronation sermon for James II and prepared Monmouth for his execution. Although he uncharacteristically defied James on the issue of *his* Declaration of Indulgence, becoming one of the Seven Bishops who refused to promote it in their pulpits, under William he became a nonjuror and was therefore deprived of his see in 1690.

[4] *Lex Talionis: Or, The Author of Naked Truth Stript Naked* (London, 1676); also attributed to Philip Fell, fellow of Eton College.

differently focused than the sermon, and whose authorship, as Evelyn's comment shows, was the same kind of open secret as was Croft's. Self-advertised as *Animadversions,* Turner's pamphlet tore its victim apart phrase by phrase. It was also personally contemptuous in its tone, and this, along with the fact that Turner was a royal chaplain undoubtedly looking for promotion, brought Marvell into the argument. Marvell could have begun his reply, then, in the second week of February, but another incentive or inspiration was provided on March 11, when George Etherege's new play, *The Man of Mode; or, Sir Fopling Flutter* was first produced at Dorset Garden.

If these dates in February and early March 1676 conjoin to provide a starting point, a finishing point is indicated by the fact that Marvell refers in *Mr. Smirke* to "good Mr. Oldenburg" (p. 52) as someone who would be offended if Marvell decided to publish his pamphlet without a license. This teasing gesture of defiance of the unenforceable licensing law was both cryptic and revealing. Not many people would have known that Henry Oldenburg, the distinguished secretary of the Royal Society and friend of Milton, had, for barely three months, in February, March, and April of that year, held a license from Secretary of State Joseph Williamson to review political texts, presumably to enhance his always insufficient income.[5] On April 29, however, Oldenburg returned his license to Williamson "because persons have been busy to impress on Williamson's mind disquieting suspicions concerning his affection to the Government, and also because of the tenderness of the employment and the vast expense of time it requires."[6] In other words, the licenser's seat had become too hot. In letters that preceded this one, Oldenburg had been in trouble over "one unhappy amorous romance" he had been asked to license; but perhaps the heat had been further increased by the appearance of Marvell's unlicensed pamphlet, with his own name teasingly highlighted.

At any rate, Marvell must have finished *Mr. Smirke* before he learned of Oldenburg's resignation. And at the very end of the *Essay,* there is another internal dating. The *London Gazette* for May 4–8, no. 1092, advertised *Lex Talionis: Or the Author of Naked Truth Stript Naked,* and on the last page of

---

[5] See *The Correspondence of Henry Oldenburg,* ed. and trans. A. Rupert Hall and Marie Boas Hall, 13 vols. (Madison, 1965–86), 12:254–55, 263–65; Adrian Johns, *The Nature of the Book: Print and Knowledge in the Making* (Chicago, 1998), pp. 242–44.

[6] *CSPD* 1676, p. 92.

the *Essay* Marvell remarked on "a new Book fresh come out, entitled, *the Author of the Naked Truth stripp'd Naked.*" By May 8, the wardens of the Stationers' Company know of the work and are searching for it. In about two months, therefore, Marvell had put together not only his own refutation of Turner and defense of Croft, on the model of his extremely successful public disputes with Samuel Parker, but also the *Essay*, for which he had mastered the ecclesiastical history of Christianity from its origins, along with relevant materials, not so easy to locate, from the Church Fathers. Some of this reading he may have done earlier, at the time of the *Rehearsal Transpros'd*; and, as I shall argue below, the *Essay* may have been almost finished shortly before *Mr. Smirke* was quite complete; but the two works were bound, conceptually and bibliographically, too tightly together to permit of the hypothesis that the *Essay* was a separate project. Marvell was now, of course, comparatively at leisure, since the short session of 1675, convened on October 13, was prorogued by the king on November 22, 1675, not to return to work until February 15, 1677. This hiatus constituted the notorious Long Prorogation.

There is a gap of perhaps two months, then, between the likely appearance of Marvell's twin pamphlets and the famous letter he wrote describing their reception. Marvell had been keeping Sir Edward Harley, Croft's ally, informed about his tolerationist writing for some time. In May 1673, he had written to Harley about the importance, in his own eyes, of the *Rehearsal Transpros'd: The Second Part*, for which he claimed the status of "a noble and high argument."[7] On July 1, 1676, he wrote again, regaling his friend and fellow-tolerationist with very firsthand gossip:

> The book said to be Marvels makes what shift it can in the world but the Author walks negligently up & down as unconcerned. The Divines of our Church say it is not in the merry part so good as the Rehearsall Transpros'd, that it runns dreggs: the Essay they confesse is writ well enough to the purpose he intended it but that was a very ill purpose ... Dr. Turner first met it at Broom's went into a Chamber & though he were to have dined which he seldome omits nor approves of Fasting yet would not come down but read it all over in consequence. The Bp of London has carryed it in his hand at Councill severall days, showing his friends the passages he has noted but none takes notice of

---

[7] *P&L*, 2:328.

them . . . I know not what to say: Marvell, if it be he, has much staggerd me in the busnesse of the Nicene & all Councills, but had better have taken a rich Presbyterians mony that before the book came out would have bought the whole Impression to burne it.[8]

This marvelously nonchalant account of his new success, told in the prudential third person, nevertheless indicates that Marvell was alerting Harley to the conceptual daring of the *Essay* as compared to *Mr. Smirke*, much as he had signaled the difference in seriousness between the first and the second parts of the *Rehearsal Transpros'd*. The vignettes of Turner getting hold of a copy of *Mr. Smirke* at Broome's eating house and forgoing his dinner in order to find out how effective was Marvell's counterattack, and of Compton carrying his copy around trying to get the attention of his colleagues on the Privy Council, are delightful instances of thick description; but the final detail, of a rich Presbyterian attempting to stop dispersal of the pamphlets by buying up the entire stock, alerts us as well to the material life of books and booksellers.

The timing of the events here described, which surely refer to the first edition of his pamphlets, can be reconfirmed by governmental efforts to stop their circulation. In early May the Wardens' Accounts of the Stationers' Company show evidence of intensive searches for them:

May 8 Paid & spent with our master Mr. Norton &c. on a Search, & coach hire to mr. Secrty Coventry &c about Darby & Ponders Pamphlet being part of mr Smirk. 17/0 [17 shillings]
May 9 Paid & laid out in another search for the residue of mr Ponders Pamphlett with our master & others. 9/6 [9 shillings, 6 pence]
May 10 Paid for going to Whitehall to ye Councell about Ponders business in Coach hire & other expenses. 7s. [7 shillings]
May 11 Search at Thompsons & elsewhere 17/6 [17 shillings, 6 pence]
May 18 Paid & spent upon a Search at Ratcliffe & Ponders by my Lord of Londons order. 5/8 [5 shillings, 8 pence]
June 9 To Whitehall and back to speak to my Lord of London [Henry Compton]
1/-[1 shilling][9]

[8] *P&L*, 2:345–46.
[9] *Wardens' Accounts 1663–1728, Records of the Worshipful Company of Stationers*, ed. Robin Myers (Cambridge, 1985); we owe this reference to Robin Myers, via Beth Lynch.

These entries tell us several interesting things: first, that both Henry Coventry, the chief secretary of state, and Henry Compton, bishop of London (who had licensed Turner's *Animadversions* and been ironically forgiven for doing so in *Mr. Smirke*), were now trying to track down and suppress Marvell's pamphlets; second, that there was a "part of mr Smirk" in which the authorities were particularly interested, almost certainly the *Essay;* and third, that several printers were suspected of being involved in their production.

Nathaniel Ponder and John Darby were, of course, known to have been responsible for the *Rehearsal Transpros'd.* Thomas Ratcliffe was described by George Kitchin, in his biography of Sir Roger L'Estrange, as running a "large and Whiggish" printing house and was still in partnership with Nathaniel Thompson, who would soon print *The Long Parliament Dissolved.*[10] In the event, only Darby and Ponder were arrested. On May 10 Williamson recorded the indictment of Ponder "for printing Marvells book": "Owned to have had those papers from Mr. Marvell with directions from him to print them. That he, Ponder, gave them out to be printed, that he had no license for the book. Ordered to be committed. Lord Privy Seal opposed it, because the cause is bailable by statute. Lord Chancellor. That for contempt of the order of the Board made against printing without license, for the seditiousness of the matter of it &c he may be committed for it."[11] To the high-ranking officials interesting themselves in this affair, therefore, we can now add Sir Heneage Finch, the lord chancellor, and Arthur Annesley, Lord Anglesey, lord privy seal, who had in 1672 intervened successfully between Ponder and Sir Roger L'Estrange to prevent the suppression of the *Rehearsal Transpros'd* but was on this occasion overruled.

On May 18, Darby was examined before Secretary Coventry and revealed that Ponder had approached him to print a book, that he had a partner he would not name, that they intended an impression of fifteen hundred copies, and that Marvell was the author. Darby, who seems to have been a slippery fellow, testified that he had been unwilling to print the book, that he had composed only one sheet and printed none. Coventry agreed that Darby should be reexamined by L'Estrange but not punished in any way: "For then, it will be more for his Majesty's service, to make use of him, as a Wittnesse, then to punish him as a Party."[12] Amazingly, these

---

[10] George Kitchin, *Sir Roger L'Estrange: A Contribution to the History of the Press in the Seventeenth Century* (London, 1913), pp. 180, 208, 210.

[11] *CSPD* 1676, pp. 106–07.

[12] Coventry Mss. vol. ii, fol. 128.

documents have for years been misrepresented as pertaining to the publication of the *Rehearsal Transpros'd,* an error perpetrated initially by H. R. Plomer,[13] adopted by D. I. B. Smith in his edition of that work, where Darby's testimony as to the planned size of the impression of *Mr. Smirke* is cited as though it applied to the second impression of the first part of the *Rehearsal Transpros'd,*[14] and most recently reintroduced by Richard Greaves in his study of resistance activity during the Restoration as applying to the *Second Part!*[15]

The other striking fact that emerges from these documents is that Marvell's authorship of *Mr. Smirke* and the *Essay* was known virtually from the beginning, and not only to government officials. On May 23 Sir Christopher Hatton had written to his brother, "I hope Andrew Marvel will likewise be made an example for his insolence in calling Dr Turner, Chaplain to His Royal Highnesse, Chaplaine to Sr Fobling Busy, as he terms him in his scurrilous satyrical answer to his Animadversions on Naked Truth."[16] Yet apparently no action was taken against Marvell.

Indeed, there is evidence that the government was being blatantly thwarted in its efforts to shut off supplies of the pamphlets. On June 6, 1676, the Catholic antiquary Thomas Blount recorded that *Mr. Smirke* was selling "for half crowns a peece and 15 non conformists took off the whole Impression to disperse."[17] This entry is remarkable, not only for the high

[13] H. R. Plomer, *A Dictionary of the printers and booksellers . . . from 1668 to 1725* (Oxford, 1922), p. 240.

[14] D. I. B. Smith, ed., *The Rehearsal Transpros'd and the Rehearsal Transpros'd: The Second Part* (Oxford, 1971), xxiii, n.2.

[15] Richard L. Greaves, *Enemies under His Feet: Radicals and Nonconformists in Britain, 1664–1677* (Stanford, 1990), p. 232; Greaves understandably has some difficulty in explaining why a work that came out under the king's protection in 1673 should have suddenly become seditious three years later.

[16] Pierre Legouis, *P&L,* 2:394; citing *Hatton Correspondence,* 1:128; Hatton had presumably neither seen the play nor read the pamphlet, since he misnames Sir Fopling Flutter. The ascription must have been common. When Marvell died, Anthony à Wood noted him as the "author of *Rehearsal transprosed, Mr. Smirk.*" See *Life and Times,* ed. Andrew Clark, 2 vols. (Oxford, 1892), 2:414.

[17] See *The Correspondence of Thomas Blount (1618–1679); Catholic Antiquary,* ed. Theo Bongaerts (Amsterdam, 1978), p. 166. Blount was writing to Wood in a provocative mood: "But above all what say you to Mr. Smerk or the Divine in mode, if you Churchmen put up [with] so great a Joque—it will be no hard thing to prophecy, what wil become of—." The elision is significant. Blount had previously searched eagerly for a copy of the *Rehearsal Transpros'd: The Second Part* for himself (pp. 141–42).

price it records for the now-notorious Marvell pamphlets (Turner's *Animadversions* was listed in the Term Catalogue at sixpence), but also for its evidence of an organization created to protect and disseminate them—the converse of the rich Presbyterian who had offered to buy the whole impression in order to suppress it. We can infer, however, that Blount's comment did not refer to the first "impression," or edition, as Marvell's letter to Harley surely did, but rather to a second or third; which will shortly bring us to the bibliographical evidence for *three* editions of the pamphlets. Before turning to that highly technical matter, however, we can thicken still more the description of the community involved with Marvell's pamphlet: it included members of the Council who had to work together yet were divided in their responses (Finch and Coventry vs. Anglesey); courtiers, equally divided in their sympathies, like Hatton as against, presumably, Buckingham; the Anglican divines (Compton, Gunning, Turner, Burnet, and, as we shall see, Stillingfleet); the civil servants Williamson, L'Estrange, and *their* servants; and an energetic group of Nonconformists who formed a network to protect and disseminate what was probably the second edition. This community was literally buzzing with news and gossip. *Mr. Smirke* itself contains information on how both word of mouth and pamphlets spread and mentions the role of the London coffeehouses. On December 29, 1675, to still the excitement generated by *The Naked Truth* and the recent prorogation, Charles had issued a proclamation ordering the suppression of coffeehouses. A roar of protest resulted in another proclamation, on January 8, delaying the suppression until June 24 and providing for blank recognizances to be taken by the coffeehouse keepers, "to allow no scandalous papers, books or libels to be brought into their house or to be read there."[18] *Mr. Smirke* and the *Essay* therefore, like multiple resonance imaging, open a slice right through the center of Restoration culture; in part because Marvell had made sure to include so many aspects of it in his side-swipes and dancing allusions.

One of his naughtier allusions consists in rebuking Turner for having called Croft a theologian "of the second Rate." Marvell's riposte was to quote, without identifying his source, the last two lines of Rochester's *Satyr against Reason and Mankind*, as yet unpublished but circulating widely at court and among the coffeehouse constituents:

---

[18] *CSPD* 1675, p. 465; 1676, p. 510. For the importance of coffeehouses, particularly those associated with Whig and opposition groups, see *Mr. Smirke*, pp. 41–42, n. 26.

——all the subject matter of debate,
Is only who's the Knave of the First Rate. (p. 61)

The joke was not only to identify Turner himself as that First Rate Knave
and to imply that he copied his phrase from Rochester's poem, but to
involve yet another high-profile clergyman in the fracas. On February 24,
1675, Edward Stillingfleet (also royal chaplain, later to become bishop of
Worcester) preached before Charles a sermon clearly aimed at Rochester's
satire and all it stood for, especially cynicism or "wit," which he regarded as
subversive of both church and state; and Rochester had replied by adding,
after the couplet Marvell quoted, several lines of unqualified attack on the
higher clergy.[19] To continue the repartee, Stillingfleet included in his answer to Thomas Godden's *Catholicks no Idolators* a dedicatory epistle to
Henry Compton, dated May 30, 1676, in which he refuted the main positions of Marvell's *Essay*. As Marvell noted drily in the same letter to Harley
that announced the reception of his twinned pamphlets, "Dr. Stillingfleet . . . seems to have read the sheet so seditious and defamatory to
Christian Religion."[20]

To this semipublic sphere of the Privy Council, the bishops and royal
chaplains, the coffeehouse wits, and the printers, all alert to each other, we
should now add, since Marvell insisted upon it, that of the Restoration
theater. The *Rehearsal Transpros'd* had launched itself on the coattails of
Buckingham's *Rehearsal*, a topical satire on bad heroic playwriting, with
John Dryden as its new butt, no doubt because of Dryden's increasingly
evident role as a poet of the court. Marvell had substituted Samuel Parker

[19] For the bibliography on the Rochester-Stillingfleet duel, see *Mr. Smirke*, p. 61,
n. 143.

[20] *P&L*, 2:345–46. For Stillingfleet's answer, see *A Defence of the Discourse . . . in
answer to a book entituled Catholicks, no Idolaters* (London, 1676). Stillingfleet did not
mention the *Essay* explicitly but gave a definition of the early church in the time of
Theodosius the Great that contradicted Marvell's: "For that is the Age of the Church,
which our Church of England since the Reformation, comes the nearest to; Idolatry
being then suppressed by the Imperial Edicts, the Churches settled by Law under the
Government of Bishops, Publick Liturgies appointed . . . Schism discountenanced . . .
And whatever men of ill minds may suggest to the disparagement of those times, it is
really an Honour to our Church, to suffer [comparison] together with that Age . . . And
the Bishops of that time were men of that exemplary Piety . . . of that excellent Conduct
and Magnanimity, as set them above the contempt or reproach of any but Infidels and
Apostates."

for Dryden and pretended that Parker had been writing "Plays" of bad theology in the same tone of rhodomontade. *Mr. Smirke; or, the Divine in Mode* made a different sort of allusion to contemporary theater. Etherege's *The Man of Mode; or, Sir Fopling Flutter* was produced in early March but not licensed for publication until June 3, 1676, when it was authorized by Sir Roger L'Estrange himself. Instead of merely identifying his opponent as Etherege's Sir Fopling Flutter, the Man of Mode himself, Marvell cleverly conflated him with a minor character, Mr. Smirke the clergyman, who has to be hidden in a cupboard and produced at the right moment to perform the requisite marriage. Mr. Smirke has no other role in Etherege's play, and only a single line; but he was identified as "chaplain to Lady Biggot" (p. 89) a throwaway jest that must have caught Marvell's attention; "which name of Smirk he gave Dr. Turner, because in his conception he was a neat, startch'd and formal divine." So wrote Anthony à Wood, acknowledging the brilliant shift in satiric focus thereby achieved.[21] It is not now the harmless fops of Restoration society at whom one is to laugh, but the fashionable clergymen like Turner, whose convenient doctrine of enforced conformity, religion *à la mode,* is decidedly sinister.

Unlike Buckingham, Etherege was no friend to nonconformists; he could not have been pleased by this type of publicity. He dedicated the printed text of his play to the new duchess of York, Mary Beatrice, the Roman Catholic duchess of Modena, whose marriage to James had been the subject of huge protest in the Commons in 1673; and his hero, Dorimant, in his opening lines describes himself as paying his court to a now-boring woman "with as much Regret, as ever Fanatick pay'd the Royal Aid, or Church duties (p. 1). As for the name *Smirke,* it had an afterlife on the stage in Thomas Shadwell's Whig play *The Lancashire Witches,* first performed in 1681, in the heated atmosphere of the Popish Plot.[22] In that play, Smirk, defined in the cast of characters as "Foolish, Knavish, Popish, Arrogant, Insolent; yet for his Interest, Slavish," is not a minor character at all. Rather, he is the much-disliked chaplain to Sir Edward Hartfort, the typically goodhearted country gentleman, who rebukes Smirk for his intol-

---

[21] Anthony à Wood, *Athenae Oxonienses,* ed. Philip Bliss, 4 vols. (London, 1812–20), 4:546.

[22] See Susan Owen, "The Lost Rhetoric of Liberty: Marvell and Restoration Drama," in *Marvell and Liberty,* ed. Warren Chernaik and Martin Dzelzainis (London and New York, 1999) p. 350.

erance and declares, in Marvell's accents, "I will have moderation in my house."[23] As Susan Owen pointed out, Smirk's scenes were canceled by the censor in production; yet Shadwell managed to reinstate them in the published version, also 1681, with a preface explaining that all the material italicized in the text was originally censored: a brilliant marketing strategy!

Marvell's own marketing strategy in *Mr. Smirke*, beyond the provocative title, was to make further use of the innovation he had made in the dreary genre of animadversions: mixing, as he had put it in the *Rehearsal Transpros'd*, gravity with levity; that is, serious argument with various kinds of witty put-downs. "It is not every man that is qualified to sustain the Dignity of the Churches Jester" (p. 40), wrote Marvell to Turner, clearly indicating his own qualifications. But he had a tougher adversary here than in Samuel Parker, whose polemical style was self-righteous, repetitive, unimaginative bullying. What Turner had that Parker lacked was a sharp eye for Croft's logical weaknesses, a vein of quite pointed sarcasm (instead of mere shouted insult), and a gift for the telling anecdote. His allusions to the story of Antiochus and Popillius or the centurion who saved the Romans from abandoning their city, his gleeful redescription of an organ made out of cats that he had found in one of Gaspar Schott's encyclopedias, and even his dramatic extrapolation of the famous biblical scene between Philip and the eunuch, treasurer of Queen Candace of Ethiopia, made his *Animadversions* more amusing than the other answers to Croft that shortly followed. Since Marvell had learned from his victory over Parker the quite irrational effectiveness of being amusing, he had to beat Turner at his own game. "He and I," Marvell wrote, ". . . will play as well as we can in paper, at this new Game of Antiochus and Popilius. I must for this time be the Roman Senator, and he the Monarch of Asia; for by the Rules of the Play, he always that hath writ the last Book is to be Antiochus, until the other has done replying" (p. 69). He entered likewise into the spirit of the story of Philip and the Ethiopian treasurer: "suppose, for the Exposer's sake, that the Treasurer were in a Coach, discoursing, and, for all the rumbling, so dis-

---

[23] Thomas Shadwell, *The Lancashire Witches* (London, 1681), p. 4. In another short passage excised by the censor, Sir Edward asserts his values: "I am a true English man, I love the Princes Rights and Peoples Liberties . . . and dare defy the witless Plots of Papists" (p. 30). It is highly likely that Sir Edward Hartfort stands for Sir Edward Harley, who in 1681 published (anonymously) *An Humble Essay toward The Settlement of Peace and Truth in the Church* (see below, p. 23). Conversely, Smirk's creed is as follows: "Sir, I hate Parliaments, none but Phanaticks, Hobbists, and Atheists, believe the Plot" (p. 36).

tinctly and thorowly, in so short a time too," that he was completely cate-
chumenized, including in the creed of Constantinople; the only problem,
Marvell observed, was that this all happened so many hundred years before
that creed was formulated that "it must needs be an extraordinary Civility
in Philip" to have treated the treasurer to such a preview (p. 75). And at the
end of his pamphlet, Marvell tackled the tale of the organ of cats, which he
had found particularly repugnant, by citing the counteranecdote of the
fortuitously named Dr. Peter Mews ("the gentleman's name . . . is the
Monosyllable voice with which Cats do usually address themselves to us"),
whose zeal against some local Nonconformists led to his own spectacular
humiliation (pp. 112–113). *Mr. Smirke* is less rambunctious than either part
of the *Rehearsal Transpros'd,* as if Marvell felt he here encountered not a
buffoon but a worthy antagonist engaged in an unworthy cause. Nevertheless, he soon tired of animadverting itself ("I must find some more expeditious way of dealing with him, and walk faster, for really I get cold," p. 90);
and with an evident sigh of relief he handed both Turner and his larger
audience over the grander intellectual world of the *Essay.*

A SHORT HISTORICAL ESSAY
CONCERNING GENERAL COUNCILS

At this point we should remember the pseudonym Andreas Rivetus, Jr. under which both *Mr. Smirke* and the *Essay* appeared, but which applies much more directly to the latter. For this purpose, a review of the history of the early Christian church, Marvell was adopting a new persona, not that of the rakish Buckingham, but the revered Protestant theologian and combatant André Rivet, tutor to the young prince William of Orange and author of a series of scholarly critiques of Catholic patristics. Most immediately pertinent to the *Essay* was Rivet's *Histoire des choses plus notables advenues en l'eglise depuis l'envoi des Apostres jusques a nostre temps. Contenant les Entreprises des Evesques de Rome sur le spirituel & le temporel.* Published in Saumur in 1620, this work had appeared, surprisingly, with a long dedication to James I of England; and it was written in an Erastian spirit, emphasizing the role of kings as nursing-fathers of the church (A1v), a role that James had embraced. Rivet had taken his evidence from the three early church historians Eusebius, Socrates Scholasticus, and Sozomen, along with Ruffinus, and had spent some time describing the Council of Nicaea, in order to make the point that it was convened and controlled by Constantine the Great. Rivet was not interested in creeds or persecution but in jurisdiction; but his example and reputation were of use to Marvell in returning to these materials with a different set of objectives.

Marvell's objectives in the *Essay* were indeed as daring as his letter to Sir Edward Harley had intimated: to undermine the authority of all formal creeds, insofar as belief in them was mandatory, and of the general councils that had formulated them. In this he went beyond the early Reformers Luther and Calvin, who had relied on the authority of the Council of Nicaea, "the most sacred of all" councils, as ammunition against papal claims to control over church doctrine.[1] He also went beyond, though leaning upon, the position of the Thirty-Nine Articles that general councils could err and had erred in doctrine. His position was dramatically simple. The history of the early church, if demythologized, was a story of human error not quite from beginning to end, but from the moment that persecution of the church by the Roman emperors ceased and was replaced by persecution of Christians by Christians. There was, in other words, a fall

---

[1] See Manfred Schulze, "Martin Luther and the Church Fathers," in *The Reception of the Church Fathers in the West,* ed. Irena Backus, 2 vols. (Leiden, New York, Cologne, 1997), 2:598.

away from innocence, a fall more or less contemporaneous with the Council of Nicaea, whose origins Marvell describes with extraordinary narrative zest. And unlike Rivet, whose case was based upon the merits and authority of Constantine the Great, Marvell joined the crowd of those, like Milton, who saw the reign of Constantine as the beginning of a fatal collaboration between church and state. Constantine's generosity toward the church, and especially its bishops, was the direct cause of a pestilence: "It showed itself first in Ambition, then in Contention, next in Imposition, and after these Symptoms broke out at last like a Plague-sore in open Persecution" (p. 126). The successors to the early Christian bishops and their internecine struggles were, Marvell implied, all too visible in the Anglican bishops or would-be bishops of the Restoration church; Turner's mudslinging at Herbert Croft and his subsequent promotion to a bishopric of his own would make Marvell's topical point with painful exactitude.

For his material, Marvell turned to exactly the same sources as had Rivet: Eusebius, Socrates Scholasticus, and Sozomen, with an occasional glance at Ruffinus.[2] But instead of using the readily available translation by Meredith Hanmer of the first two—a translation made in the late Elizabethan era, with a strongly Protestant agenda already built in, and dedicated in its second edition to the militantly Protestant earl of Leicester[3]—Marvell decided to retranslate from a Latin intermediary. The intermediary in question was both obvious and an odd one: John Christopherson, whose three-volume Latin translation of the three Greek ecclesiastical historians had been posthumously published in Louvain in 1569. Christopherson had been Mary Tudor's personal chaplain and an ardent Counter-Reformation polemicist.[4] The Hanmer translation was clearly intended as the Protestant

[2] Ruffinus Aquileiensis, *Historiae ecclesiasticae liber decimus* (Antwerp, 1548).

[3] Meredith Hanmer, *The Auncient Ecclesiastical Histories* (London, 1577, 1587). There were five more editions before Marvell wrote his *Essay*, including one in 1663.

[4] For Christopherson's reputation, see Thomas Fuller, *History of the Worthies of England* (London, 1662), p. 101: "Grievous the persecution in this County under John Christopherson the Bishop hereof. Such his Havock in burning poor Protestants in one year, that had he sat long in that see, and continued after that rate, there needed no Iron-mill to rarify the Woods of this County, which this Bonner Junior would have done of himself. I confess the Papists admire him as a most able and profound Divine, which mindeth me of an Epigram made by one, who being a Suitor to a surly and scornfull Mistris, after he had largely praised her rare parts and Divine perfections, concluded,

She hath too much Divinity for me.

Oh! that she had some more Humanity!"

answer to this Roman Catholic interpretation of the past. It is a nice footnote to the question of the ideological valence of translations of the Fathers that the British Library copy of Christopherson's three-volume Louvain edition, bound in green velvet with gold wire and seed pearls and bearing the royal arms, with the initials E.R. on each spine, must have been the property of Mary's sister, Queen Elizabeth herself.[5] But Marvell had perhaps borrowed *his* edition from Milton, who had used instead the 1612 Geneva edition.[6]

For Marvell's purposes, since Latin was his second mother tongue, the advantages of Christopherson's version would have outweighed its lineage, of which he may not have been aware: he had access thereby to all three of the historians deployed by Rivet; and he could retranslate on his own terms, producing exactly the emphases he wanted. By a mixture of selectivity (choosing just those stories that would reflect badly on the bishops of the past), a fringe of editorial comment that ranged from the sardonic to the tragic, and a vocabulary designed to cut his subjects down to size, he launched an attack on the concept of the Church as an institution that could regulate religious belief and practice. Here is his version of an anecdote reported by Sozomen about Bishop Alexander, who was partly responsible for the Trinitarian controversy caused by Arius:

> This Alexander was the Bishop of Alexandria, and appears to have been a pious old Man, but not equally prudent, nor in Divine things of the most capable, nor in conducting the affairs of the Church, very dextrous; but he was the Bishop . . . [One day] as he was alone and looking toward the Sea side, he saw a prity way off the Boys upon the beach, at an odd Recreation, imitating it seems the Rites of the Church and office of the Bishops, and was much delighted with the sight as long as it appear'd an innocent and harmless representation: but when he observed them at last how they acted the very administration of the Sacred Mysteries, he was much troubled, and caused . . . the Boys to be taken and brought before him. He asked them par-

---

[5] Philippa Marks, curator of bookbindings at the British Library, has kindly confirmed that these volumes bear the arms of Elizabeth I, and that they came to the library as part of the gift of the Old Royal Library in 1757. The initials E.R. may have been added when the bindings were repaired.

[6] *Historiae Ecclesiasticae Scriptores Graeci* (Geneva, 1612); for the identification of this as Milton's source of ecclesiastical history, see Constance Nicholas, "The Edition of the Early Church Historians used by Milton," *Journal of English and Germanic Philology* 51 (1952), 160–62.

ticularly what kind of sport they had been at, and what the words, and
what the actions were that they had used in it. After their fear had
hindered them a while from answering, and now they were afraid of
being silent, they confessed that a Lad of their play-fellows, one
Athanasius, had baptized some of them that were not yet initiated in
those Sacred Mysteries: . . . At last, when Alexander perceiv'd by them
that his Pawn Bishop had made all his removes right, and that the
whole Ecclesiastical Order and rites had been duely observed in their
interlude, he by the advice of his Priests about him approved of that
Mock Baptism, and determined that, the boys *being once in the simplicity of their minds dipped in the Divine Grace, ought not to be Rebaptized* . . . This good natured old Bishop Alexander—was so far from
Anathemising, that he did not so much as whip the boys for profanation of the Sacrament against the Discipline of the Church, but without more doing, left them, for ought I see, as liberty to regenerate as
many more Lads upon the next Holy day as they thought convenient.
(pp. 134–35)

If we now compare this deceptively genial account with Christopherson's
Latin, we discover that the story was originally told as a tribute to Athanasius's qualifications and to demonstrate that providence intended him for a
bishopric (*non sine providentia divina ad episcopatum ascendisse*):

Cui quidem, cum nondum pubesceret, istud evenisse memorant . . .
Quem diem cum Alexander . . . solus esset, oculosque ad mare con-
vertisset, vidit longe ab se pueros in litore colludentes, & consuetudinem quodamodo episcoporum & ecclesiae ritus imitatione expri-
menter. Ubi autem in illo imitationis genere nihil inesse animadvertit
periculi, laetatus est spectaculo, & ex rebus in ludo gestis voluptatem
cepit. At tandem cum arcana mysteria imitando adumbrare inci-
perent, animo conturbatus est . . . pueros comprehendi, & ad se adduci
iubet. Percontantur ab illis de genere ludi, quibus verbis, quibusque
actionibus in eo usi sint . . . At cum quaerendo instaret Alexander,
indicarunt, Athanasium episcopum & principem ludi fuisse: pueros-
que quosdam initiatos mysteriis . . . Postremo, ubi Alexander com-
perit, universum ordinem ac ritum ecclesiasticum ab illis exquisite
servatum, consilio sacerdotum, quos circa se habebat, approbavit bap-
tismum: & pueros semel in animorum simplicitate divina gratia im-

butos, rebaptizandos non censuit, sed caeteris mysteriis, quae solis sacerdotibus fas erat obire, in illis explevit.[7]

Marvell, however, has framed it at one end with a severely qualified account of Alexander's intellectual and political limitations, and at the other with an ironic analysis of the episode's meaning that reverses Sozomen's intentions. He has increased by translation the trivializing vocabulary of theater and game: odd recreation, representation, sport, play-fellows, Pawn-bishop, [re]moves, interlude, Mock Baptism; even the phrase "a prity way off" is a playful expansion of "*longe.*" And the final sentence, hung round the neck of that personalized, judgmental, "for ought I see," has no authority in the Latin at all. The entire passage, as it were, has become playful, but inappropriately so, in order to make a serious point. The anecdote reveals the absurdity of the claims of the clergy to monopoly over the rites of the church, if children could imitate them in play and have the rituals stand as effective.

This, however, is only a preliminary and comparatively innocent example of the way the early church did business. A large part of the *Essay* is devoted to describing the immediate causes, internal politics, and systemic consequences of the Council of Nicaea, the most important of those consequences being the creation of the doctrine of *Homoousious,* the consubstantiality of the Son with the Father, and the Nicene creed by which that doctrine was mandated. In the middle of the *Essay* Marvell paused to give his own judgement of the council: "a pittiful humane business, attended with all the ill circumstances of other worldly affairs, conducted by a spirit of ambition and contention, the first and so the greatest AEcumenical blow that by Christians was given to Christianity" (p. 142). And thereafter, he argues, things go from bad to worse, with the Arians at one point reversing the defeat they had suffered and imposing matching persecutions on their former oppressors. Creeds themselves are a major part of the problem and a sign of spiritual arrogance in those who formulated them, presuming to add to what can be found in Scripture: "In those days when Creeds were most plenty and in fashion, 'twas the Bible that brought in the Reformation" (p. 144). As the *Essay* draws to a close, it reveals itself as a procedural alternative to Croft's appeal for moderation, which had been based on the insignificance of the points of dispute on ceremonial terms. Instead, Marvell has adduced "the *Naked Truth* of History" as proof that it is better,

[7] John Christopherson, *Historiae Ecclesiasticae,* 3 vols. (Louvain, 1569), 3:38.

ethically and pragmatically, for Christians to agree to disagree than to tear
each other and the Church to pieces, a process that zigzags according to the
vagaries of power. As the current representative of power is Charles II
himself, Constantine the Great, as his figurative equivalent, is alternatively
complimented for his good intentions and blamed for giving the bishops
too high an opinion of themselves.

In the *Essay* Marvell almost completely replaced literary allusion (one of
the most dazzling features of the *Rehearsal Transpros'd* and still, as we have
seen, a feature of *Mr. Smirke*) with biblical citation. The *Essay* begins with
the real life of the apostles, as told by the gospels and the Acts, and ends
(almost) with an ironic plea to the Anglican bishops that they would recommend to the clergy "the reading of the Bible." "'Tis a very good Book,"
wrote Marvell straightfacedly, "and if a man read it carefully, will make him
much wiser" (p. 173). Between them the twinned pamphlets also contain
surprisingly apposite quotations from Hilary, Chrysostom, Gregory Nazianzus, and Tertullian. The effect of these materials is not exactly to tone
down his satire, but rather to provide it with an ancient elegiac background
(of lament by the Fathers of the Church for the collapse of Christian
standards) and impeccable (indeed saintly) credentials. It was perhaps for
this reason that, as he reported to Harley, the new book was thought to be
"not in the merry part so good" as his answers to Parker; but in the vein of
gravity that Marvell equally aspired to they make their point with an often
breathtaking punch of religious sincerity. Perhaps this helps to explain the
otherwise unforeseeable move, in the 1678 *Remarks* in defense of John
Howe, to a more purely theological venture: tackling the Protestant commitment to the doctrine of predestination.

THE AFTERLIFE OF THE *ESSAY*

Despite the care with which Marvell had cemented the *Essay to Mr.
Smirke* (but because of the *Essay*'s greater conceptual daring and longer
lasting pertinence), it floated free of its topical location in the Croft-Turner
controversy and became an argument in its own right, not only for tolera-
tion as distinct from comprehension, but for still more radical positions. In
1680, a year of exceptional tension as the Popish Plot fiasco developed, the
Essay was reprinted under the following title: "*A Short Historical Essay
Touching/General Councils, Creeds, and Impositions in Matters of Religion./
Very Seasonable for Allaying the Heats of the CHURCH. Written by that
Ingenious and worthy Gentleman/Mr. ANDREW MARVELL, Who died a*

Member of Parliament." This edition was reset from A, and slightly up-dated. Marvell's reference to the "late Earth-quakes . . . here in England, thorow so many Counties" (p. 164) acquires the rider, "two years since." The parenthetical "as the Animadverter has done thorow his whole Stu-dious Chapter" is replaced by the impersonal but mysterious "as one did" (p. 36); but the previous reference to "whatsoever the Animadverter saith of the Act of Seditious Conventicles" (p. 35) escaped the reviser's attention. The final flurry of allusions back to Turner's *Animadversions* disappears, and, after the paragraph about Parker and the Walloons, the ending pro-ceeds as follows:

> But these things require a greater Time, and to enumerate all that is amiss, might perhaps be as endless as to number the People; nor are they within the ordinary sphere of my Capacity.
>
> But to the Judicious and Serious Reader, to whom I wish any thing I have said, may have given no unwelcome entertainment, I shall only so far justifie my self, that I thought it no less concerned me to vindi-cate the Laity from the Impositions that the *Few* would force upon them, than others to defend those Impositions on behalf of the Clergy. But the Reverend Mr. Hooker in his Ecclesiastical Polity, says, *The time will come when these words, uttered with Charity and Meekness, shall receive a far more blessed reward, than three thousand Volumes writ-ten with disdainful sharpnes of Wit.* And I shall conclude. *I trust in the Almighty, that with us, Contentions are now at the highest float, and that the day will come (for what cause is there of Dispair) when the passions of former enmity being allaid, men shall with ten times redoubled tokens of unfainedly reconciled Love, shew themselves to each other the same, which Joseph, and the Brethren of Joseph were at the time of their Enterview in Egypt.* And, upon this condition, let my Book also (yea, my self if it were needful) be burnt by the hand of those Enemies to the Peace and Tranquility of the Religion of England.

In other words, the revised conclusion carefully excised anything that would limit the pamphlet's application to 1676 or to a particular local quarrel. There is no evidence of who was responsible; but in the British Library copy the *Essay* immediately precedes Sir Edward Harley's 1681 pamphlet (published anonymously), *An Humble Essay toward The Settle-ment of Peace and Truth in the Church,* which was produced by Nevil and Thomas Simmons and makes the same case for toleration, though argued quite differently.[8] It is more than possible that Harley, who obviously owned a copy of Marvell's *Essay,* was behind its "seasonable" reappearance.

In 1687, shortly before the Williamite Revolution, Richard Baldwin published (and acknowledged) two separate versions of the *Essay: A Seasonable Discourse, Shewing the Unreasonableness and Mischeifs of* IMPOSITIONS In Matters of RELIGION, Recommended to Serious Consideration. By a Learned Pen; and *A Short Historical Essay touching General Councils, Creeds, and Impositions by Andrew Marvel, Esq.* There is no evidence as to which came first, or indeed why there should be two editions, but both versions follow the text of 1680 very closely, including its revisions.[9] As to its timing, on April 4 of that year James II issued his own Declaration of Indulgence, which suspended the penal laws and allowed for the peaceful meetings of Nonconformists. It is entirely possible, therefore, that Marvell's *Essay,* now out of his control, had come to serve a similar purpose as the first part of the *Rehearsal Transpros'd*—that is, to support a royal gesture toward toleration that was widely suspected of buying the support of the Nonconformists in return for what Marvell would have called the growth of popery.

But in 1703, and again in 1709, the *Essay* was returned to the service of the Whig cause. In 1703 the Commons were debating the Occasional Conformity Act, continually held off by the Whigs in the Lords but eventually passed in 1712. Despite its name, the act was intended to destroy the Williamite compromise named "occasional conformity" whereby dissenters could, by annually taking communion in the Church of England, qualify for government posts. In 1709 the country was convulsed by the reactionary sermons of Henry Sacheverell, the first preached on August 15, the second on November 5 before the lord mayor at St. Paul's, attacking ocasional conformity and the government policy of toleration in general. In 1703, accordingly, someone decided to reissue Marvell's *Essay* with a slightly adjusted title: *A Short Historical Essay Touching General Councils, Synods, Convocations, Creeds, and Impositions in Religion. By Andrew Marvel Esq.* The publisher was E. Mallet, and the text was beautifully reset from Edition A, without any of the intervening revisions. And in 1709 Marvell's *Essay* (exactly the same text as 1703 but reset less elegantly) was included in

---

[8] Though Harley leans much more heavily on the Church Fathers, he actually uses the same quotation from Tertullian's *De Coronis Militis* (p. 23) as did Marvell (p. 111), which suggests that the two pamphlets are closely related.

[9] The phrase dating the earthquakes as "two years since" makes no sense in 1687.

a collection of sermons and pamphlets by the radical Whig William Stephens, under the general title of Stephens's own pamphlet, *An Account of the Growth of Deism*, originally published in 1696. Inflected by a Marvellian irony, Stephens borrowed from the title of Marvell's *Account of the Growth of Popery* to make the case that if Deism were on the increase, the fault lay with the Anglican clergy, whose unchristian, self-interested and persecuting behavior revealed them to be not a church but a party. In the same collection, Sir Robert Howard's 1694 *History of Religion* plagiarized (pp. 321–23) part of Marvell's history of the early church, including his quotations from Hilary and Gregory Nazianzus.

The deliberate anthologizing of Marvell's *Essay* by Stephens in a Whig collection with a definite mission raises the question of what can be learned from the collecting and binding practices of earlier periods. The answer is, as might be expected, indefinite. In some instances there is a clear rationale, whereby Marvell's pamphlets are bound with those of Croft and Turner and perhaps Burnet or *Lex Talionis*. In several bound collections, however, their neighbors seem to be completely unrelated, in date or purpose. One of the most telling instances of purpose, however, is the Harvard copy of Edition A, which was donated by Thomas Hollis in 1764 and bears the inscription, in Hollis's handwriting, on the back of the title page, "By Andrew Marvell, the incorruptible." This copy bears handwritten foliations indicating that it was once part of an anthology created by Hollis which has since been dispersed into separate pamphlets.[10] Hollis also donated to Harvard a separate copy of Edition B, with the flyleaf inscription "Ex Dono Thomae Hollis, Angli, Hospit. Lincoln. . . . 9 Dec. 1767," and "The author Mr. Andrew Marvel" added to the title page. Knowing what we know of Thomas Hollis's educational and political motives,[11] these small bibliographical traces are further proof of how long and why the work was valued.

THE EDITIONS

Since Mary Pollard's 1973 article on the three copies of *Mr. Smirke* in the library of Trinity College, Dublin, it has been known that there were at least two separate editions of the pamphlet, as well as what Pollard referred

[10] One Harvard pamphlet that carries the same type of foliation is Marchamont Nedham's *Honesty's Best Policy*, an attack on Marvell's *Account of the Growth of Popery*.

[11] See Patterson, *Early Modern Liberalism* (Cambridge, 1998), pp. 27–61.

to as a variant state, but which will here be treated as a third edition.[12] The first, known here as Edition A, is instantly recognizable to persons without bibliographical expertise. Almost all known copies have two errors in the opening address "To the Captious Reader" (X1a) which have been corrected in brown ink, evidently while still in the printer's shop: in the word "tra[du]ced" the letters in brackets were added, and in the word "Laitie[s]" the incorrect plural was struck out. In addition, this preface is followed by a warning: "The Erratas are too many to be Corrected. But p. 7.1 ult. Eighth is to be struck out." On K2B, the missing "7" from the biblical citation "Zech.13.6.7." is also supplied in the same brown ink. In the second edition, designated here as B, the preface is reset in a smaller typeface and "traduced" and "Laietie" are set correctly. The statement about errata now reads: "The Errata's are too many to be Corrected; therefore the Reader is desired to pass them over, and candidly mend some of the grosest with his Pen." And the missing "7" on K2B is inserted in type.

But these are merely the most immediately obvious of the features that distinguish A from B. Closer inspection reveals that while both editions share the same physical structure: (4* A1 X1 B-F4 g4 (-g4) G-14 I4 K4, 45 leaves), the same incomplete gathering g, the same six unpaginated pages between pp. 40 and 41, and the same error in numbering p. 56 as a second p. 43,[13] Edition B was in fact completely reset. While the printer[s] of B made an effort to replicate each page, the line endings vary, the catchwords, and even the last/first lines of adjoining pages may vary, especially in the *Essay*, where for pp. 61–76 a very slightly narrower format was used. The obvi-

---

[12] In the following section of descriptive bibliography, I was much helped initially by advice from Jeremy Maule and by a then-unpublished M. Phil. thesis by his student Beth Lynch: "Printing under Pressure: A Bibliographic Account of Andrew Marvell's *Mr. Smirke . . . Together with a Short Historical Essay* (1676)." See now Lynch, *"Mr. Smirke* and 'Mr. Filth': A Bibliographic Case Study in Nonconformist Printing," *The Library*, 7th series, 1 (2000), 46–71. Although I eventually arrived at quite a different hypothesis to account for the physical peculiarities of the three major versions of Marvell's texts, Lynch's work was particularly helpful in revealing how many more copies survived than is indicated in even the revised edition of Wing. Her study of copies in Cambridge and Dr. Williams's library operates at a level of detail, including watermarks and chain-lines, which the following description does not attempt. I have endeavored to provide a description that will be readily understood by those without bibliographical expertise.

[13] Both editions make different mistakes in pagination later in the *Essay*: A has the series 64, 62, 61, 63, 64, while B has the series 64, 61, 62, 63, 64, a marginal improvement.

ous inference is that Edition B was reset from a printed copy of Edition A, the forms for Edition A no longer being available for a second impression.

Pollard identified at Dublin a variant of Edition A, which was identical with A except for gatherings F and H. In gathering F, as Pollard showed, the inner forms are identical with A, and therefore were printed from the original forms; but the outer forms have been reset, with some striking anomalies. In gathering H, even more surprisingly, the inner forms are identical with Edition B, but the outer forms again have been reset. "A variant" corrected a couple of errors, inserting (in some copies) the missing preposition in "away [by] Gods" on F4r (our p. 94) and renumbering the misnumbered page "43" to "56." But it also dropped several words from the phrase "embracing [the] Novatians and [giving them] free liberty," on H3r (our p. 130) substituted "they write or scribble" (F1r) for "they have writ or scribled" (our p. 86), and calmly altered Marvell's description of Turner's delivery boys with the "Britches stiff with the Copyes," (A version) to "Britches stuft with the Copyes," conceivably an act of prudery! Pollard, who had only one example of "A variant" (AV) to work with, did not interpret what lay behind its existence; but once one has identified a number of other identical copies (see Sigla below), the following scenario seems required.

Since almost all copies of AV also contain the brown ink corrections that characterize A, the sheets of all gatherings except F and H must have been saved in some safe place while the first edition was circulating. The existence of Edition B, reset, implies that the forms for A had been found and seized in May by L'Estrange's men. But the presence of some sheets from B in gathering H further implies that AV *follows* B chronologically. In all likelihood, B was the edition described by Thomas Blount as having been bought up in its entirety by a consortium of Nonconformists. The presence of three copies of B in Dr. Williams's Library and of six copies in the National Library of Scotland supports this hypothesis. But with B thus sold out in early June, the printers decided to try and put together a third edition, from the saved sheets of A, but with patchwork in gatherings F and H. Since only the F inner forms are identical with A, and only the H inner forms with B, it appears that the printers had found some half-printed sheets of each and made up new outer forms in each instance.

But what of the evidence that L'Estrange's men were particularly instructed to search for "part of Ponder's pamphlet," implying they had found only the other part? The initial assumption, mentioned above, is that the part in which they were so interested was the *Essay*, defined by Marvell himself as the most risky part of his project; but in Edition A, and therefore in both B and AV, the *Essay* begins on the verso of the last page of *Mr. Smirke*, (G2v, p. 44) thus making their separation between printers far from simple. Furthermore, all gatherings except one are straddled by carried-over sentences. There is, however, one marked break in the published text, at the beginning of gathering H, where the new gathering opens with a new paragraph: "But as it first was planted without the Magistrates hand." It would have been technically easy and prudent to dispatch the manuscript from this point onward, where it becomes increasingly a challenge to orthodoxy and episcopacy, to a second printer.

There remains one aberrant phenomenon: the incomplete and unnumbered gathering g. Both Pollard and Lynch speculated as to whether the missing leaves from g were used for the title page or preface (A1 or X1). Neither asked what could explain the fact that g is obviously a gathering inserted (before G) as an afterthought, with its page numbers left blank. The best hypothesis available is that Marvell was still working on *Mr. Smirke* when his manuscripts were cast off and divided. The *Essay* was complete, and he had already inserted into its conclusion (on pp. 174–76) the series of references back to Turner's *Animadversions* that tie the two pamphlets together. *Mr. Smirke* ends with a reminder that "the Printer calls: the Press is in danger" and proposes to put an end to "such stuffe" by offering Turner "this following Essay of mine." But perhaps after Marvell wrote those words he decided to expand his attack on Turner after all, an expansion which had to be accommodated by adding gathering g. In these six extra pages, Marvell dealt at length, and in high spirits, with an issue particularly close to his heart: the 1670 Act against Conventicles, and Turner's analogy between that act and one he had found in Roman history, courtesy of "the learned P. Aerodius," or Pierre Ayrault. Had it not been for that afterthought, if afterthought it was, we would have been deprived of several of Marvell's most colorful allusions: to Obeshankanogh, king of Virginia (p. 103), to the "Chocolatte Pots" of Chiapa, whereon hangs an extraordinary tale (p. 104), and to the first deployment in English of the Dutch word "snuff," which not surprisingly the printer got wrong (p. 104).

There remains the choice of copy-text. Thompson and Grosart both printed from A. As Pollard reported, however, B shows a "modernized spelling . . . and perhaps fewer literal errors," (p. 37), although it also introduces several new ones. In my view, it is also distinctly better punctuated, and the capitalization tends to be more systematic, with that feature reserved especially for abstract nouns. I therefore print from B, correcting where necessary in the light of A. Because the emphasis of this edition is on content and context, textual notes have been kept to a minimum. Variations in spelling and punctuation are not usually recorded.

Finally, this is surely the place to record my gratitude to the following special collections librarians and personnel, those who courteously supplied details of copies I was unable to see: Seth Kastan, of the Union Theological Library in New York, Margaret Kulis, of the Newberry Library in Chicago, Thomas V. Lange, of the Huntington Library in Pasadena, D. W. Riley, of the John Rylands Library, Dr. J. T. Rhodes of Durham University Library, Alexandra Rogers, of the University of Texas at Austin, Margaret Sherry, of Princeton University Library, Bruce Swann, at the University of Illinois at Urbana-Champaign, and Georgianna Ziegler, of the Folger Library in Washington, D.C.

The Editions

Title page

Mr. SMIRKE; / OR, THE / DIVINE in MODE: / BEING / Certain *Annotations*, upon the *Animad-* / *versions* on the *Naked Truth*. / Together with a Short *Historical Essay*, / concerning *General Councils, Creeds, and Im-* / *positions*, in Matters of *Religion*. // *Nuda, sed Magna est Veritas, & praevalebit*. // BY / ANDREAS RIVETUS, *Junior*. / Anagr. / *RES NUDA VERITAS*. // *Printed Anno Domini* MDCLXXVI.

Collation

4o [*X*1] B-F4 g4(-g4) G-I4 2I4 K4, 45 leaves. pp: [4] 1–40 [6] 41–55, 43, 57–64, 62, 61, 63–76 [=86]

Signatures

(4)

Contents

A 1r: T.P.; *A* 1v: blank; *X*r To the CAPTIOUS READER. *X*v Contd. *Adieu*. // *The Errata's are too many to be Corrected; But* p. 7. *l*. ult. Eighth / *is to be struck out*.

Notes

Some copies have SMIRK: e.g., Clark Library *PR3546.M61; most copies have two corrections in brown ink in the preface (*X* 1r): traced (l. 6) is corrected to traduced; Laities (ll. 10–11) is corrected to Laitie. Some copies have *the* italicized on the title page.

EDITION A VARIANT

Title page

As Edition A, with similar variations between roman and italics for "the."

Collation

As Edition A, except that p. "43" is corrected to 56.

Notes

This edition was made up from sheets of Edition A, except for gatherings F and H, which consist of a combination of new settings based on A, and, in the inner form of H, the setting from Edition B.

EDITION B

Title page

Mr. SMIRKE: / OR, THE / DIVINE in MODE / BEING / Certain *Annotations,* upon the *Animadversions* / of the *Naked Truth* / Together with a Short *Historical Essay,* / Concerning *General Councils, Creeds,* and *Impositi-* / ons, in matters of *Religion.* // *Nuda, sed Magna est Veritas, & praevalebit.* // BY / ANDREAS RIVETUS, *Junior.* / Anagr. /*RES NUDA VERITAS.* // Printed *Anno Domini* MDCLXXVI.

Collation

As in Edition A; but pp: [4], 1–40 [6] 41–55, 43, 57–64, 61–76 [=86]

Sigla

As in Edition A; but *X* 1v: *The Errata's are too many to be Corrected; therefore the Reader is / desired to pass them over, and candidly mend some of the grosest / with his Pen.*

Notes

This edition was entirely reset, though strenuous efforts were made to retain the same pagination.

EXAMPLES (copies without an asterisk have been personally inspected; those with an asterisk were described in correspondence by a special collections librarian)

EDITION A

United Kingdom *(15 copies)*

British Library: 108.d.55; 701.g.10 (14); 855.e.3
Oxford, Bodleian: Ashmolean 1231; Firth e.8 (11)
Cambridge University Library: Bb* 9.7 (10); G.10.33 (5)
Cambridge, Trinity College: Grylls 23.92 (1); K.10.59 (1)
Cambridge, St. John's College: Gg.1.12 (1)
Dr. Williams's Library, London: 3.44.18 (8)
*National Library of Scotland: L.C. 362 (1)
*Trinity College, Dublin: P.gg.21 (3)
*Durham University: Bamburgh F.5.12 (6)
*John Rylands Library, Manchester: G 988.5 (preface uncorrected)

United States *(7 copies)*

Harvard University (Houghton): EC65.M3685.676mab (gift of Thomas Hollis)
*Newberry Library, Chicago: Case C 6526.554
Folger Shakespeare Library, Washington, D.C.: M873 (preface uncorrected)
*U. of Illinois at Urbana-Champaign: C874nYm.1676; uncatalogued
*U. of Texas at Austin: HRCWJM368676M; BR757C764 1675

Canada *(2 copies)*

University of Toronto: B-10, 4297; B-10, 3620

EDITION B

United Kingdom *(14 copies)*

Oxford, Bodleian: G. Pamph. 1052 (5) (no title or preface); D12.1 Linc.
Cambridge: St. John's College: EE.4.15

Cambridge: Trinity College: K.14.21 (5)

Dr. Williams's Library, London: 1030.M.1 (3); 3008.G.6 (5); I.16.4 (6)

*National Library of Scotland: 1.48a (13); 1.172 (2); 1.180 (6); 1.186(3); 1.205 (4); Gray. 292 (2)

(this large Scottish concentration of Edition B deserves note; Gray 292 was owned by Reverend John Gray [1646–1717], who annotated his copy: "(Mr. Merveill) an Engl. presbyt: Member of the House of Commons, Droll enough & satyr too much."

*Trinity College, Dublin: LL.o.14 (6)

United States *(9 copies)*

Harvard University, Houghton: EC65 M3685.676mb (gift of Thomas Hollis)

Yale University: College Pamphlets 1071

*Princeton University: EX3850.3.364

University of California, Berkeley: BX5201.M27M5.1676

*Huntington Library: RB 16692

Folger Shakespeare Library, Washington, D.C.: 873B

*Union Theological Seminary: McAlpin 1643.575

*U. of Texas at Austin: BV646.M37 1676

*U. of Illinois at Urbana-Champaign: 261.7.C874nYm.1676 (2)

EDITION A VARIANT

United Kingdom *(7 copies)*

Oxford, Bodleian: Pamph. C.136

Cambridge University Library: Keynes W.3.12

*National Library of Scotland 1.1B (7)

*Trinity College, Dublin: GG.n.30 (4)

*John Rylands Library, Manchester: UCC B754 (2)

*University of Durham: Routh 15.C.30 (1)

*Ushaw College: XIX.G.7.3h

United States *(3 copies)*

Yale University: Z84.68m

*Clark Library, Los Angeles: PR354.1761

*Huntington Library: RB.58667

Canada *(1 copy)*

Toronto: Forbes. Pam RBSC

Mr. SMIRKE;

OR, THE

DIVINE in MODE:

BEING

Certain *Annotations,* upon the *Animadversions*
of the *Naked Truth.*
Together with a Short *Historical Essay,*
Concerning *General Councils, Creeds, and Impositions,* in matters of *Religion*

Nuda, sed Magna est Veritas, & praevalebit.

BY

ANDREAS RIVETUS, *Junior.*
Anagr.
RES NUDA VERITAS.

Printed *Anno Domini* MDCLXXVI.

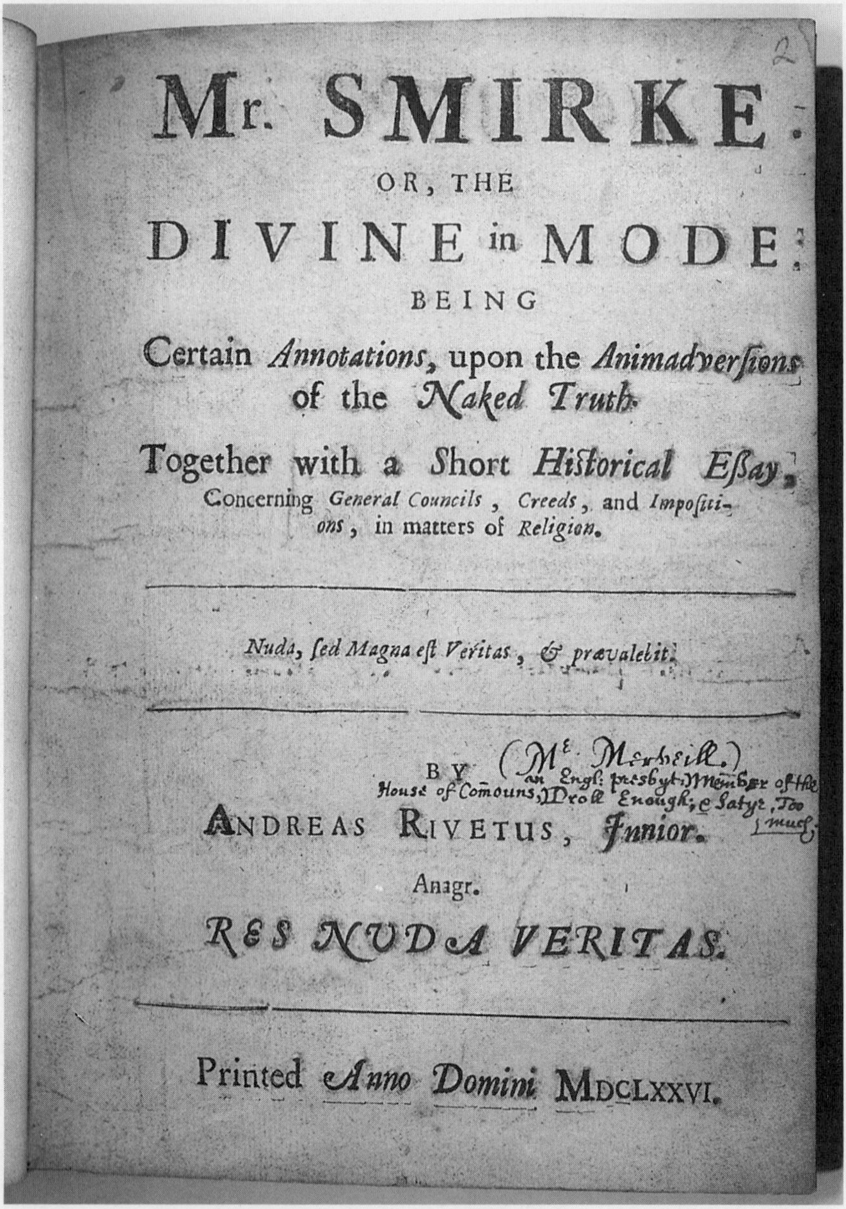

Mr. SMIRKE:

OR, THE

DIVINE in MODE:

BEING

Certain *Annotations,* upon the *Animadversions*
of the *Naked Truth.*

Together with a Short *Historical Essay,*
Concerning *General Councils,* *Creeds,* and *Impositions,* in matters of *Religion.*

Nuda, sed Magna est Veritas, & prævalebit.

BY *(Mr. Merheill.)*
*an Engl. presbyt. Member of the
House of Comouns, Droll Enough, & Satyr, Too
much.*

Andreas Rivetus, *Junior.*

Anagr.

RES NUDA VERITAS.

Printed *Anno Domini* MDCLXXVI.

Fig. 1. Title page from Mr. Smirke or, The Divine in Mode, *edition B.*

TO THE CAPTIOUS READER[1]

All that I have to require of thee is; That wheresoever my Stile or Principles Strike out, and keep not within the same Bounds, that the most judicious Author[2] of *The Naked Truth* hath all along observed; he may not therefore be traduced.[3] He could best have writ a Defence proportionable to his own Subject; had he esteemed it necessary, or that it was decent for him to have enter'd the Pit with so Scurrilous an Animadverter. But I thought it a piece of due Civility from one of the Laitie,[4] to interess myself for one of the Clergy, who had so highly obliged the people of England. And I will answer for mine own faults, I ask thee no pardon. Nor therefore is either the Author, or any other particular Person, or any Party, to be accused, or misrepresented upon my Private Account. For the rest, neither let any particular Man, or Order, enlarge my meaning against themselves, further than in Conscience they find they are guilty. Nor let the body of Chaplains think themselves affronted. None more esteems them, nor loves their Conversation better than I do. They are the succeeding hope of our Church, the Youth of our Clergy; and the Clergy are the Reserve of our Christianity. Some of them, whom I know, have indeed, and do continue daily to put very Singular Obligations upon me; but I write to a Nobler end, then to revenge my Petty Concernments.

Adieu.

The Errata's are too many to be Corrected; therefore the Reader is desired to pass them over, and candidly mend some of the grosest with his Pen.[5]

It hath been the Good Nature (and Politicians will have it the Wisdom) of most Governours to entertain the people with Publick Recreations; and therefore to incourage such as could best contribute to their

---

[1] Captious Reader: one who is disposed to make objections, caviling; cf. Thomas Fuller, *The Church History of Britain* (London, 1655), dedication to Esmé Stuart: "I conceived it best to cut off all occasions of Cavil from captious persons and dedicate it to you."

[2] Author: Herbert Croft, bishop of Hereford. See the introduction.

[3] traduced] traced A: This error is one of two in the preface that were corrected in brown ink in almost all known copies of the first edition.

[4] Laitie] Laities A; the other error corrected in brown ink.

[5] This replaces the first edition's note on errata: "The Errata's are too many to be Corrected; But p. 7.l. ult. Eighth is to be struck out." This word does not, however, appear on p. 7.

Divertisement.[6] And hence doubtless it is, that our Ecclesiastical Governours also (who as they yield to none for Prudence, so in good Humor they
exceed all others) have not disdained of late years to afford the Laity no
inconsiderable Pastime. Yea so great hath been their condescention that,
rather than fail, they have carried on the Merriment by men of their own
Faculty, who might otherwise by the gravity of their Calling, have claimed
an exemption from such Offices. They have Ordained from time to time
several of the most Ingenious and Pregnant of their Clergy, to supply the
Press continually with new Books of ridiculous and facetious argument.
Wherein divers of them have succeeded even to admiration: insomuch that
by the reading thereof, the ancient Sobriety and Seriousness of the English
Nation hath been in some good measure discussed[7] and worn out of fashion. Yet, though the Clergy have hereby manifested, that nothing comes
amiss to them; and particularly, that when they give their minds to it, no
sort of men are more proper or capable to make sport for Spectators; it hath
so happened by the Rewards and Promotions bestowed upon those who
have labour'd in this Province, that many others in hopes of the like Preferment, although otherwise by their Parts, their Complexion and Education,
unfitted for this Jocular Divinity, have in order to it wholly neglected the
more weighty cares of their Function. And from hence it proceeds, that to
the no small scandal and disreputation of our Church, a great *Arcanum*[8] of
their State hath been discovered and divulged: That, albeit Wit be not in
[1]consistent and incompatible with a Clergy-man, yet neither is it inseparable from them. So that it is of concernment to my Lords the Bishops
henceforward to repress those of 'em who have no Wit, from Writing, and
to take care that even those that have, do husband it better, as not knowing
to what exigency they may be reduced: But however, that they the Bishops
be not too forward in Licensing and prefixing[9] their venerable Names to
such Pamphlets.[10] For admitting, though I am not too positive in it, that
our Episcopacy is of Apostolic Right; yet we do not find that among all
those gifts then given to men, that which we call Wit is enumerated: nor yet
among those qualifications requisite to a Bishop. And therefore should they

[6] Divertisement: amusement, distraction.

[7] discussed: to drive away or disperse (archaic).

[8] *Arcanum:* secret; as in the phrase *arcana imperii,* secrets of state, much in use in
Stuart politics.

[9] prefixing B] perfixing A.

[10] their venerable Names: a reference to the fact that Turner's pamphlet was licensed
by Henry Compton, appointed bishop of London in 1675.

out of Complacency for an Author, or Delight in the Argument, or Facility
of their Judgments, approve of a dull Book, their own understandings will
be answerable; and irreverent people that cannot distinguish, will be ready
to think that such of them differ from men of Wit, not only in Degree, but
in Order. For all are not of my mind, who could never see any one elevated
to that Dignity, but I presently conceived a greater opinion of his Wit than
ever I had formerly. But some do not stick to affirm, that even they, the
Bishops, come by theirs not by Inspiration, not by Teaching, but even as the
poor Laity do sometimes light upon it, by a good Mother. Which has
occasioned the homely Scotch Proverb, that, *An Ounce of Mother-Wit is
worth a Pound of Clergy.*[11] And as they come by it as do other men, so they
possess it on the same condition: That they cannot transmit it by breathing,
touching, or any natural *Effluvium*[12] to other persons: not so much as to
their most Domestick Chaplain, or to the closest Residentiary.[13] That the
King himself, who is no less the Spring of That,[14] than he is the Fountain of
Honour, yet has never used the Dubbing or Creating of Wits, as a Flower
of his Prerogative: much less can the Ecclesiastical Powers[15] confer it with
the same ease as they do the Holy Orders. That whatsoever they can do of
that kind is, at uttermost, to impower men by their authority and commission, no otherwise than in the Licensing of Midwives or Physitians. But
that as to their collating[16] of any internal talent or ability, they could never
pretend to it, their grants and their prohibitions are alike invalide, and they
can neither capacitate one man to be Witty, nor hinder another from being
so, further than as the Press is at their Devotion. Which if it be the Case,
they cannot be too circumspect in their management, and should be very
exquisite, seeing this way of writing is found so necessary, in making choice
of fit Instruments. The Churches credit is more interested in an Ecclesiastical Droll,[17] than in a Lay Chancellor.[18] It is no small trust that is
reposed in him to whom the [2] Bishop shall commit *Omne & omnimodum*

[11] *Ounce . . . Clergy:* proverbial, with clergy in the sense of book learning. Marvell
found this in John Ray, *A Collection of English Proverbs* (London, 1670), p. 264.

[12] *Effluvium:* an outflow or exhalation.

[13] Residentiary: an ecclesiastic of whom residence is required.

[14] That: i.e., wit.

[15] Powers Ed.] Power A,B.

[16] collating: conferring; still used as a legal ecclesiastical term.

[17] Droll: comedian.

[18] Bishops had lay-chancellors under them who had the power to excommunicate, a
considerable grievance among the Nonconformists.

suum Ingenium tam Temporale quam Spirituale:[19] And, however it goes with Excommunication, they should take good heed to what manner of person they delegate the Keys[20] of Laughter. It is not every man that is qualified to sustain the Dignity of the Churches Jester: and, should they take as exact a scrutiny of them as of the Non-conformists thorow their Dioceses, the number would appear inconsiderable upon this Easter Visitation.[21] Before men be admitted to so important an employment, it were fit they underwent a severe Examination; and that it might appear, first, whether they have any Sense: for without that how can any man pretend, and yet they do, to be ingenious?[22] Then, whether they have any Modesty: for without that they can only be scurrilous and impudent. Next, whether any Truth: for true Jests are those that do the greatest execution. And Lastly, it were not amiss that they gave some account too of their Christianity: for the world has always hitherto been so uncivil as to expect something of that from the Clergy; in the design and stile even of their lightest and most uncanonical Writings. And though I am no rigid Imposer of a Discipline of mine own devising, yet had anything of this nature entered into the minds of other men, it is not impossible that a late Pamphlet, published by Authority, and proclaimed by the Gazette,[23] *Animadversions upon a late Pamphlet, entituled, The* Naked Truth, *or, The True State of the Primitive Church*, might have been spared.

[19] *Omne . . . Spirituale:* The bishop entrusts to the newly ordained priest "his own wisdom, complete and entire, as much temporal as spiritual."

[20] the Keys: the ecclesiastical authority conferred on bishops, especially with respect to the power of excommunication; from Christ's commitment to Peter, Matthew 16:19: "*tibi dabo claves.*"

[21] This Easter Visitation: Marvell's syntax indicates that he is writing shortly before the Easter festival of 1676. Bishops visited their dioceses at Easter and received statistics of Nonconformists and Catholic recusants.

[22] ingenious: from Latin *ingenium*, genius, intelligence; a word of high value in Marvell's vocabulary. Cf. *To his Noble Friend Mr. Richard Lovelace, upon his Poems:* "That candid Age no other way could tell / To be ingenious, but by speaking well" (ll. 5–6).

[23] the Gazette: the *London Gazette*, no. 1066; the official (and only) newspaper in England from 1665, the *London Gazette* replaced the Restoration newsletters, *Parliamentary Intelligencer* and *Mercurius Publicus*, which had been produced first by Henry Muddiman and then by Sir Roger L'Estrange. For the tone of the *Gazette*, with its tight restriction on domestic news and its new impersonality (being written by government clerks), see C. John Sommerville, *The News Revolution in England: Cultural Dynamics of Daily Information* (Oxford, 1996), pp. 57–74.

That Book so called *The Naked Truth*, is a Treatise, that, were it not for this its Opposer, needs no commendation: being writ with that Evidence and Demonstration of Spirit, that all sober men cannot but give their Assent and Consent to it, unasked. It is a Book of that kind, that no Christian scarce can peruse it without wishing himself had been the Author, and almost imagining that he is so; the Conceptions therein being of so Eternal an Idea, that every man finds it to be but the Copy of an Original in his own Mind; and though he never read it till now, wonders it could be so long before he remembered it.[24] Neither, although there be a time when as they say all truths are not to be spoken, could there ever have come forth any thing more seasonable: When the sickly Nation had been so long indisposed and knew not the Remedy, but (having taken so many things that rather did it harm then good), only longed for some Moderation, and as soon as it had tasted this, seemed to itself sensibly to recover. When their Representatives in Parliament had been of late so frequent in consultations of this nature,[25] and they the Physitians of the Nation, were ready to have received any wholsome advice for the Cure of our Malady: It appears moreover plainly that the Author is Judicious, Learned, Conscientious, a sincere Protestant, and a true [3] Son, if not a Father, of the Church of England. For the rest, the Book cannot be free from the imperfections incident to all humane indeavours, but those so small, and guarded every where with so much Modesty, that it seems there was none left for the Animadverter, who might otherwise have blush'd to reproach him. But some there were that thought Holy-Church was concerned in it, and that no true-born Son of our Mother of England, but ought to have it in detestation. Not only the Churches, but the Coffee Houses[26] rung against

[24] This description of Croft's pamphlet was all underlined in Thomas Hollis's copy of A, now at Harvard.

[25] Marvell refers to the debates about religion in the two previous sessions of parliament, beginning with the appointment of a committee on April 16, 1675, "to consider effectual Ways for the Suppressing the Growth of Popery" (*JHC* 1675, pp. 317–18). On May 7, Mr. Weld was permitted to bring in a bill to abolish the Writ *De Haeretico Comburendo*, the fifteenth-century statute that provided for the burning of heretics and that had been revived under Queen Mary (p. 332). In the short fall session, Marvell sat on a committee for a bill "to prevent Papists from sitting in either of the Houses of Parliament" (p. 363).

[26] Coffee Houses: On December 29, 1675, the London coffeehouses were closed by royal proclamation, as centers of potential sedition (*CSPD* 1675, p. 465); after much protest, they were reopened on January 8, 1676, in time for the Croft-Turner fracas. On

it, they itinerated[27] like Excise-spyes,[28] from one House to another, and some of the Morning and Evening Chaplains burnt their lips with perpetual discoursing it out of reputation, and loading the Author, whoever he were, with all contempt, malice and obloquy. Nor could this suffice them, but a lasting Pillar of Infamy must be erected to eternize his Crime and his Punishment. There must be an answer to him, in Print, and that not according to the ordinary rules of civility, or in the sober way of arguing Controversie, but with the utmost extremity of Jeer, Disdain, and Indignation: and happy the man whose lot it should be to be deputed to that performance. It was Shrove-Tuesday[29] with them; and, not having yet forgot their Boyes-play, they had set up this Cock, and would have been content some of them to have ventur'd their Coffee-Farthings,[30] yea, their Easter-pence[31] by advance, to have a fling at him. But there was this close Youth who treads always upon the heels of Ecclesiastical Preferment, but hath come nearer the heels *of the Naked Truth* than were for his Service, that rather by favour than any tolerable sufficiency, carried away this employment, as he hath done many others from them. So that being the man pitched upon, he took up an unfortunate resolution that he would be Witty. Unfortunate, I say, and no less Criminal: for I dare aver, that never any person was more manifestly guilty of the sin against Nature.[32] But however, to write a Book of that virulence, and at such a season, was very improper: even in the Holy time of Lent, when, whether upon the Sacred account, it behoved him rather to have subjugated and mortified the swelling of his passions; or whether upon the Political reason, he might well have forborn his young Wit, as but newly Pigg'd or Calv'd, in order to the growth of the yearly Summer Provisions. Yet to work he fell, not omitting first to Sum

---

the political climate of coffeehouses, see Steven Pincus, " 'Coffee Politicians does Create': Coffeehouses and Restoration Political Culture," *Journal of Modern History* 67 (1995), 822–27; and on their use as centers of news circulation, see Sommerville, *News Revolution,* pp. 74–84; and Adrian Johns, *The Nature of the Book* (Chicago, 1998), pp. 111–13.

[27] itinerated: journeyed.

[28] Excise-spyes: officers whose responsibility it was to discover tax evasion.

[29] Shrove-Tuesday: a day of festival and license before Lent.

[30] Coffee-farthings: tokens issued by coffeehouses.

[31] Easter-pence: dues paid by the parishioners to the clergy at Easter.

[32] the sin against Nature: What Marvell meant by this can only be guessed at, especially since Turner did not reply. Possibly there is a hint of the venerable transfer between simony and sodomy.

himself up in the whole wardrobe of his Function; as well because his Wit consisting wholly in his Dress, he would (and 'twas his concernment to) have it all about him; as to the end that being huff'd up in all his Ecclesiastical fluster, he might appear more formidable, and in the pride of his Heart and Habit out-*boniface*[33] an *Humble Moderator*. So that there was more to do in equipping Mr. Smirke then there is about Doriman[t];[34] and the Divine in Mode might have [4] vyed with Sir Fopling Flutter.[35] The Vestry and the Tiring-room[36] were both exhausted, and 'tis hard to say whether there went more attendants toward the Composing of Himself, or of his Pamphlet. Being thus drest up, at last forth he comes in Print. No Poet, either the First or the Third day,[37] could be more concern'd; and his little Party, like men hired for the purpose, had posted themselves at every corner, to feign a more numerous applause: but clap'd out of time, and disturb'd the whole Company.

Annotations upon his Animadversions on the Title, Dedication, &c

At first bolt in his *Animadversions on the Title, the Dedication, and the Epistle to the Reader*, he denounces sentence before inquiry,[38] but against the Book itself, forgetting already his subject, so early his brain circulates; and saith, that, *Having perused the book thorowly, he is abundantly satisfied not only from his* Stile, *which is something*[39] Enthusiastick (his speech bewrays him) *but from his* matter and Principles, *if he stick to any, that the Author is a borderer upon Fanaticism,*[40] *and does not know it.*[41] Even as the

[33] out-*boniface:* outface, with perhaps a play on Pope Boniface III, elected 607, who enjoyed a bad reputation because of his close relations with the emperor Phocas and his own decree that only the bishop of Rome could use the title of Universal Bishop.

[34] Doriman[t]: the dandyish hero of Etherege's *Man of Mode*. Dorimant admits (act I, scene I) to his valet, "I love to be well dress'd, Sir; and think it no Scandal to my understanding."

[35] Sir Fopling Flutter: the francophile fop of Etherege's play, the foil against whom Dorimant's dandyism is rendered acceptable.

[36] Tiring-room: dressing room.

[37] The dramatic poet was particularly concerned about his play's first performance because of the reviews and its third because he received its profits or a share of them.

[38] sentence before inquiry: a juridical metaphor, to pronounce the sentence against the prisoner before any evidence has been heard.

[39] *something:* Turner wrote "sometimes."

[40] *Fanaticism:* a term of abuse used against Puritanism and Nonconformity.

[41] Turner, *Animadversions*, A3r.

Animadverter is upon Wit and Reason; for I have heard that Borderers[42] for the most part, are at the greatest distance, and the most irreconcilable. What the *Stile* is of a *Title,* and what the *Principles* of a *Dedication and Epistle* to the Reader (for these, *if any,* the Animadverter ought here to have stuck to) it's indeed a weighty disquisition fit for a man of his Talent. But I have read them over, and so have others of better Judgment, and find every sentence therein poised with so much reverence, humility and judicious Piety, that from an humane pen (allowing the Reader any tolerable share too of Humanity) I know not what more could have been expected. And as to the Matter, it seems to be but a Paraphrase upon the *Principles* of the Song of the Angels; *Glory to God on high, on Earth Peace, Good Will toward men.*[43] If to speak at that rate, and upon such a subject, with so good an intention, be to have an Enthusiastick *Stile* or *Fanatical Principles,* it is the first crime of which I should be glad to be guilty. What in the mean time shall we say to these men, who out of a perverse jealousie they have of the Non-conformists, run, which few wise men do, into the contrary extream, affixing such odious names to every word or thing that is sober or serious, that with their good will they would render it impracticable for men even to discourse pertinently concerning Religion or Christianity? Put it upon this short issue: If the stile of the Epistle before the *Naked Truth* be Enthusiastick and Fanatical, the stile of the Animadverter is presumed, and so allowed of, as Spiritual, Divine, and Canonical. [5]

The first Evidence that he produces, after so hasty a sentence against the Author, is out of the Book too, not out of the Title, Dedication, or Epistle; that he has said p. 17, *In the Primitive times when the whole world of Jews and Gentiles were enemies to the Church, and not one of your Ceremonies to preserve it, the simple* Naked Truth, *without any Surplice to cover it, without any Ecclesiastical Policy to maintain it, overcame all, and so it would do now did we trust to it, and the Defender of it.* And upon this he runs division: *The Defender in Heaven,* God; *the Defender of the Faith,* His Majesty; and the many *Defenders* (among whom I suppose he reckons himself of the Principal) *who may be trusted?* This is all fooling: whereas the Author does manifestly intend it of God Almighty, and could not otherwise. For though his Majesty may well be trusted for his Reign with the Defence of the

[42] Borderers: those who live on the borders of countries, especially that between England and Scotland.

[43] the Song of the Angels . . . *Men:* the angelic chorus at the birth of Christ (Luke 2:14).

Naked Truth, yet most of us know that in the Primitive Times his Majesty was too young for that imployment,[44] and that it was God alone who could then protect it, when the *Defenders of the Faith* were all Heathens, and most of them Persecutors of Christianity. He then descants no less upon Naked Truth; *The Naked Truth of our Cause*, or *the Naked Truth of the Pamphlet*, or, *he knows what Naked Truth*. But he saith *it should have been Truth Fley'd;*[45] (so he had the Butchery of it) Which is like Pilate and no worse man, who when our Saviour told him, he came into the world, Joh. 18.37, *That he might bear witness to the Truth*, asked him, *What is Truth?* and then though he confessed *he found no evil in this man*, delivered him over, against his Conscience, to be Stripped, Scourged, *Fley'd*, and afterwards Crucified.[46] Such like also is his talking, that *this is stripping the Church to skin, nay skin and all*, and *skin for skin*.[47] so wretchedly[48] does he hunt over hedg and ditch for an University Quibble. The casual progress and leaping consequences of any mans memory are more rational then this Method of his understanding; and the Non-conformists Concordance[49] is a Discourse of more coherence than such Animadversions: I have heard a Mad-man having got a word by the end ramble after the same manner: In this only he is true to himself, and candid to the Author, having avowed that *he had scann'd the Book thorow;* this hacking and vain repetition being just like it, when we were at our

> *Montibus inquit erunt*[50] *& erant, sub montibus illis;*
> *Risit Atlantiades &, me mihi perfide prodis,*
> *Me mihi prodis, ait.*[51]

[44] too young . . . imployment: i.e., unborn, by hundreds of years.

[45] *Fley'd*: fle'd A; i.e., flayed.

[46] John 18:37–39.

[47] Turner, A3v; but the original reference is to Job 2:4.

[48] wretchedly A] wretched B.

[49] the Non-conformists Concordance: surely *A New and Useful Concordance to the Holy Bible* (London, 1671), begun by Vavasour Powell and completed by Edward Bagshaw and Thomas Hardcastle. Not only were all three ardent Nonconformists, Bagshaw and Hardcastle both being frequently imprisoned for their beliefs, but the second edition of the *Concordance* (1673) was recommended "to the studious Christian" by a preface by John Owen. Despite his implied criticism here, Marvell evidently used this *Concordance* as a tool for finding some of his biblical citations.

[50] erunt Ed., Thompson] erant A,B: Marvell or his printer has made a mistake which increases the repetition but spoils the sense by changing the tense.

[51] Ovid, *Metamorphoses*, 2:702–04: " 'They will be below those hills,' he said, and they

For as I remember, this *Scanning* was a liberal Art that we learn'd at Grammar-School; and to *Scan* verses as he does the Authors Prose, before we did, or were obliged to understand them. But his tugging all this while at *skin, and skin for skin, and all that he has* [6] *he will give for his life*,[52] meerly to hale in an ill-favor'd Jeer at the Author, and truly with some profaneness, for proposing the *Naked Truth* as necessary for the *self-preservation of our Church,* and an *expedient against Popery;* is (whatsoever the Animadverters judgment be) a wretchlesness[53] and mockery ill becoming his Character. And it savours of the Liquorishness of a Trencher-Chaplain, little concerned in the *Cura Animarum,* so he may but *Curare Cuticulam.*[54]

But as to his fastidious reproach of the Authors *seeking of God, his Fasts and his Prayers,* the Animadverter is more excusable, having doubtless writ his Pamphlet without practising any of these Fanatical Superstitions, as neither was it requisite; But if he had, 'twas such an answer to his Prayers as never before came from Heaven. The Animadverter is proof against all such Exorcismes; and although our Saviour prescribed these remedies against the most obstinate Devils, this man it seems is possessed with a superiour spirit which is not to be cast out, no not by Prayer and Fasting,[55] but sets them at defiance.

Nor had the Animadverter, when he considered himself, less reason to blame the Author for deliberating so long before he published his Book, and for doing it then with so much Modesty. These are Crimes of which the Animadverter will never be suspected or accused by any man, at least they will do him very much wrong; but however it will be impossible ever to convict him of them. But to word it too so superciliously, *This has been the Travel*[56] *of his mind, since he had these thoughts, which he has been humbly*

---

were at the bottom of those hills. Mercury laughed. 'Traitor,' he said, 'you would betray me to my face; betray me to my very face.'" Atlantiades, grandson of Atlas, is the patronym for Mercury. Thanks to Traugott Lawler for his help here.

[52] Job 2:4: "And Satan answered the Lord, and said, Skin for skin, yea, all that a man hath will he give for his life."

[53] wretchelesness: recklessness.

[54] little . . . *Cuticulam:* little concerned with the care of souls, so he may but take care of the skin.

[55] Matthew 17.21. Marvell is adapting the story of how Jesus cured the lunatic child when the disciples could not, but acknowledged that serious evil spirits of "this kind goeth not out but by prayer and fasting." Turner, presumably, is of a still worse kind.

[56] *Travel:* travail, labor.

conceiving these two years; time enough for an Elephant to bring forth in.[57] Why there is, 'tis true, a winged sort of Elephant, hath a peculiar Trunk too like the other, is not so docile and good-natured; but impudent, flying in every mans face, and sanguinary, thirsting always after blood, and as if it were some considerable Wild-Beast, makes a terrible Buzze;[58] but in conclusion 'tis a pitiful, giddy, blind, troublesome Insect, ingendered in a nights time in every Marish,[59] can but run a Pore thorow and give a Skinnewound, and the least touch of a mans finger will crush it. In the *Naked Truth* it is but a Gnat: and such is the Animadverter compared with the Author.

But in this next Paragraph the Animadverter seems to have outshot himself; that not content with having passed his own Ecclesiastical Censure upon the Author, he forges too in his mind a sentence of the Lords and Commons assembled in Parliament: who, *he believes* and *'tis probable*,[60] would have doom'd the Book to be burnt by the Hang-man. In this he hath medled beyond his Last:[61] but it is some mens property:[62] yet neither is it so likely they would have done it at the same time when they were about passing an Act for the easing all Protestant dissenters from Penalties;[63] had he vouch'd for the Convo[7]cation,[64] his Belief, or his probability might have been of more value.

But what has he to do (yet they have a singular itch to it) with Parliament

---

[57] Turner, A3v. The gestation period of the elephant, from eighteen to twenty-two months, was habitually exaggerated. But a pertinent precedent was Thomas Nashe, preface "To all Christian Readers" in *Have with you to Saffron Walden,* in *Works,* ed. R. B. McKerrow, 5 vols. (Oxford, 1966), 3:18: "like the long snouted Beast . . . carrying her yong in her wombe three yere ere she be delivered, I have been big with childe of a common place of revenge."

[58] Marvell appears to be describing the mosquito, with its long proboscis.

[59] Marish: marsh, swamp.

[60] Turner, A4r.

[61] Last: a wooden model of the foot, on which shoemakers shape shoes.

[62] Marvell alludes to the fact that Croft's book is in fact the property of a publisher, who stands to lose his investment if the edition is confiscated and burned.

[63] On April 17, 1675, Marvell reported to Hull a "motion of a member of the House concerning the growth of Popery; for giving ease to Protestant Dissenters," (*P&L,* 2:146). On November 16, Buckingham delivered a speech in the House of Lords asking permission to bring in a Bill of Indulgence to all Dissenting Protestants. The request was granted, but Parliament was prorogued six days later. Buckingham's speech was then illegally published, along with one of Shaftesbury's, with a false "Amsterdam" imprint.

[64] Convocation: an ecclesiastical assembly, summoned to debate church policy.

business? or how can so thin a skull comprehend or divine the results of the
Wisdom of the Nation? Unless he can, as in the Epilogue,

Legion his name, a People in a Man,

And, instead of Sir Fopling Flutter, he Mr Smirke,

Be Knight oth' shire and represent them all.[65]

Who knows indeed but he may, by some new and extraordinary Writ,
have been summon'd upon the Emergency of this Book, to Represent in his
peculiar person the whole Representative?[66] Yet by his leave, though he be
so, he ought not to Undertake[67] before he be Assembled. I know indeed he
may have had some late Precedents for it, and for some years continuance,
from men too of his own Profession. And if therefore he should Undertake,
and to give a good Tax for it, yet what security can he have himself, but that
there may rise such a Contest between the Lords and Commons[68] within
him, that, before they can agree about this Judicial Proceeding against the
Book, it may be thought fit to Prorogue him.[69]

[65] A quotation from Dryden's Epilogue to *The Man of Mode,* in which Sir Fopling
Flutter is defined as representative of all the follies of the audience, collected in a single
figure: "He's Knight o' th' Shire, and represents ye all. / From each he meet he culls
what e'er he can, / Legion's his Name, a People in a Man."

[66] the whole Representative: i.e., parliament.

[67] Undertake: This word acquired a pejorative meaning with respect to members of
parliament who agreed in advance to vote in a certain way. It appears first in relation to
the Addled Parliament of 1614. Cf. Sir John Holles: "A schism is cast into the House by
reason of some interlopers, whom they term undertakers, so named because they have
promised that the Parliament shall supply the King's wants to his contentment"
(H.M.C. Portland Mss. IX, p. 27).

[68] a Contest between the Lords and Commons: During the session that began on
April 13, 1675, the Commons was preoccupied with two cases, Sir Thomas Shirley vs.
John Fagg and Sir Nicholas Stoughton vs. Arthur Onslow, in each of which the first, a
member of the Lords, was suing in the upper House the second, who was a member of
the Commons. Increasingly hostile messages passed between the Houses, conferences
between them occurred, almost all other business was suspended, and on June 5 the
king sent a letter warning all parties to stop quarreling and proceed with debates on how
to deal with his financial needs. On June 9, when his message was evidently being
ignored, he prorogued the parliament for four months. Marvell deplored this un-
businesslike behavior; see *P&L,* 2:155–62, 174–76.

[69] Prorogue him: to dismiss the (one-man) parliament for a period; the alternative to
dissolution, which required a new election.

The Crimes indeed are hainous, and if the Man and Book be guilty, may, when time comes, furnish special matter for an Impeachment. That *he has made a breach upon their Glorious Act of Uniformity,*[70] *Violated their Act, their most necessary Act* (the Animadverter hath reason by this time to say so) *against Printing without a License:*[71] And I suppose he reserves another for aggravation in due time; the Act against seditious Conventicles.[72] For these three are all of a piece, and yet are the several Pieces of the Animadverters Armour: and are indeed no less, nor no more than necessary. For considering how empty of late the Church-Magazines have been of that Spiritual Armour, which the Apostle found sufficient against the assaults of whatsoever enemy,[73] even of Satan; what could men in all humane reason do less, than to furnish such of the Clergy as wanted, with these Weapons of another Warfare? But, although these Acts were the true effects of the Prudence and Piety of that season, yet it is possible (but who can provide for all cases?) that, if there have not already, there may arise thereby in a short time some notable inconvenience. For suppose that Truth should one day or other come to be Truth and every man a Lyar, (I mean of the humor of this

[70] *Act of Uniformity:* The act (14 Car. II. c. 4), under which ministers were expelled from their churches if they did not conform to Anglican church practice, took effect on August 24, 1662, the anniversary of the St. Bartholomew's Day massacre. Cf. *Third Advice to the Painter:* "O Bartlemew, Saint of their Calender! / What's worse? thy Ejection or thy Massacre?" (ll. 243–44).

[71] *Act . . . against Printing without a License:* In May 1662 Parliament voted in a new licensing act that largely reinstated the procedures instigated by Star Chamber in 1637. Printers were required to obtain licenses from a secretary of state for books on history and politics and from the archbishop of Canterbury or bishop of London for religion and philosophy. During the two sessions of 1675, the Commons was concerned about illegal publications, and just before the Long Prorogation they were about to give second reading to a "Bill for reviving and making perpetual the Act for preventing of frequent Abuses in printing seditious, treasonable and unlicensed Books and Pamphlets, and for regulating of Printers & Printing Presses" (*JHC,* November 17, 1675). Had they done so, it would not have expired in 1679.

[72] Conventicles: a technical term for outlawed religious meetings, that is, meetings of more than five persons beyond the family in whose house the meeting occurred. In 1670 the Commons passed a second act against conventicles (22 Car. II. c. 1) renewing and strengthening that of 1664. Marvell refers frequently to this new act as a matter of concern. See *P&L,* 2:89, 91, 99, 101, 316, 318 ("There is like to be a terrible Act of Conventicles"). The text of the act is given in full in Marvell's letter to Mayor Tripp of March 10, 1670 (2:101).

[73] Ephesians 6:11–17.

Parliamentum Indoctum,[74] this single Representativer, this Animadverter)
you see there is no more to be said, as the case stands at present, but
Executioner do your Office. Nor[75] therefore can it ever enter into my mind,
as to that Act particularly of Printing, that the Law-givers could thereby
intend to allow any man a promiscuous Licentiousness, and Monopoly of
Printing Pernicious Discourses [8] intending[76] to sow and increase dissention thorow the Land (of which there is but too large a crop already;) as
neither of Prohibiting Books dictated by Christian meekness and charity for
the promoting of Truth and Peace among us, and reconciling our Differences; no, nor even of such as are writ to take out the Blots of Printing-Ink,
and wipe off the Aspersions which divers of the Licensed Clergy cast upon
mens private Reputations: and yet this is the use to which the Law is
sometimes applied. And this Animadverter, who could never have any
rational confidence or pretence to the Press or Print, but by an unlucky
English saying men have,[77] or by the Text-Letters of his *Imprimatur*,[78]
arraigns this worthy Author for Printing without Allowance, as if it were a
sin against the Eleventh Commandment. Though a Samaritan perhaps
may not practise Physick without a Licence, yet must a Priest and a Levite
always pass by on the other side, and if one of them in an age, *pour oyl and wine
into the Wounds*[79] of our Church (instead of Tearing them Wider,) must he
be Cited for it into the spiritual Court, and incurr all Penalties? This high
Charge made me the more curious to inquire particularly how that Book
The Naked Truth was published, which the Animadverter himself pretends
to have got sight of with some difficulty. And I am credibly informed that
the Author caused four hundred or them and no more to be Printed against
the last Session but one of Parliament.[80] For nothing is more usual than to

[74] *Parliamentum Indoctum:* ignorant parliament; i.e., Turner.

[75] Nor A] now B.

[76] intending B] tending A, which is the catchword in both editions.

[77] an unlucky English saying men have: impossible to identify; but perhaps Marvell was
thinking of "Look high and fall into a cow turd," Ray, *Collection of English Proverbs*, p. 13.

[78] *Imprimatur:* let it be printed; the term adopted by the Spanish Inquisition for the
license to print granted by the church. In *Areopagitica* Milton sneers at the adoption of
the term by the English authorities under the 1637 decree of Star Chamber which, he
says, "besotted us to the gay imitation of a lordly *Imprimatur;* so apishly Romanizing,
that the word of command still was set downe in Latine." *CPW,* 2:504–05.

[79] *pass . . . Wounds:* an allusion to the parable of the good Samaritan and the man who
fell among thieves, Luke 10:30–37.

[80] See introduction, pp. 4–5.

Print and present to them Proposals of Revenue, Matters of Trade, or any thing of publick Convenience; and sometimes Cases and Petitions, and this, which the Animadverter calls the Authors Dedication, is his *humble Petition to the Lords and Commons assembled in Parliament:* And understanding the Parliament inclined to a Temper[81] in Religion, he prepar'd these for the Speakers of both Houses, and as many of the Members as those could furnish. But that the Parliament rising just as the Book was delivering out, and before it could be presented, the Author gave speedy order to suppress it till another Session. Some covetous Printer in the mean time getting a Copy, surreptitiously Reprinted it, and so it flew abroad without the Authors knowledg, and against his direction. So that it was not his, but the Printers fault to have put so great an obligation upon the publick. Yet because the Author has in his own Copies,[82] out of his unspeakable Tenderness and Modesty beg'd pardon of the Lords and Commons, in his Petition, for transgressing their Act against Printing without a Licence, this *Indoctum Parliamentum* mistaking the Petition as addressed to himself, will not grant it, but insults over the Author, and upbraids him the rather as a desperate offender, *that sins on,* he saith, goes on still in his wickedness, and hath done it *against his own Conscience.* Now truly if this were a sin, it was a sin of the first Impression. [9] And the Author appears so constant to the Church of England, and to its Liturgy in particular, that, having confessed four hundred times with *an humble, lowly, penitent, and obedient heart,*[83] I doubt not but in assisting at Divine Service he hath frequently since that received Absolution. It is something strange, that to publish a good Book is a sin, and an ill one a vertue; and that while one comes out with Authority; the other may not have a Dispensation.[84] So that we seem to have got an Expurgatory Press, though not an Index;[85] and the most Religious Truth must be

[81] a Temper: a compromise, moderation.

[82] his own Copies: that is, in the authorized editions. See *The Naked Truth,* ed. H. H. Henson (London, 1917), xxv, who identifies three separate editions, (a) the author's "own copyes," (b) the "first impression," with a less humble dedication, and (c) a further reprint in response to demand.

[83] with *an humble, lowly, penitent, and obedient heart:* the posture required in the Expostulation to Confession in the order for Morning Prayer.

[84] Dispensation: the relaxation or suspension of a law or duty in a particular case; especially in ecclesiastical terms.

[85] The first *Index of Prohibited Books* was issued by Pope Paul IV in 1559, with the advice of the Council of Trent. Based on the bull of Leo X (1515), it extended censorship

expung'd and suppressed in order to the false and secular interest of some of the Clergy. So much wiser are they grown by process of time than the Obsolete Apostle, that said, *We can do nothing against the Truth.*[86] But this hath been of late years the practice of these single Representers of the Church of England, to render those Peccadilloes[87] against God as few and inconsiderable as may be, but to make the sins against themselves as many as possible, and these to be all hainous and unpardonable. Insomuch that if we of the Laity would but study our Self-preservation, and learn of them to be as true to our separate interest, as these men are to theirs, we ought not to wish them any new Power for the future, but after very mature deliberation. Forasmuch as every such act does but serve, as some of them use it, to make the good people of England walk in peril of their Souls, to multiply sin and abomination thorow the Land, and by ingaging mens minds under spiritual Bondage, to lead them Canonically on into Temporal slavery. Whereas the Laity are commonly more temperate and merciful (I might say more discreet) in the exercising of any Authority they are intrusted with; and what Power they have, they will not wear it thred-bare: so that if I were to commit a fault for my life, (as suppose by Printing this without a License) I would chuse to sin against good Mr. Oldenburg.[88]

But this Animadverter is the genuine example of Ecclesiastical Clemency, who proceeding on, cannot bear that the Author should use the Title of an *Humble Moderator*[89] (he thinks him sure guilty herein *Laesae Majestatis Ecclesiasticae,*[90] and that both these Qualities[91] are incompatible with

---

to all writings, not merely theological works. The *Index* has subsequently been revised frequently and enforced where possible.

[86] 2 Corinthians 13.8: the "obsolete Apostle" is Paul.

[87] Peccadilloes Ed.] Peccadillioes, A, B; venial sins or trifling offenses.

[88] Henry Oldenburg (1615–77), philosopher and friend of Milton; one of the first elected members of the Royal Society and then its secretary. Oldenburg was briefly acting as stationer from February 22, 1676, to April 18 of that year (*Stationers' Register,* 8:16–20). During this period, he wrote to Sir Joseph Williamson exculpating himself from any wrongdoing in the attempt to publish a translation of Sebastian Bremont's *Hattige, ou Les Amours du Roy Tamerlain,* which Oldenburg assumed could be read as a reflection on Charles II (*CSPD* 1676, April 18, p. 76). See introduction, p. 6.

[89] Turner, A4r.

[90] *Laesae Majestatis Ecclesiasticae:* literally, of harm against the ecclesiastical supreme power; but in normal use, without the clerical reference, the phrase was shorthand for treason.

[91] both these Qualities: i.e., humility and moderation.

one of their Coat, and below the Dignity of any man of the Faculty) much less will he indure him when he comes, in the following Discourse, to justifie his Claim to that Title, by *letting his Moderation,* according to the Apostles precept, *be known to all men, for the Lord is at hand.*[92] But he saith that the Author *Assumes, Imposes, and Turns all upside down,* and witnesses an *Immoderate Zeal for one* (that is the Nonconformists) *Party:* than which the Animadverter could never have invented a more notorious, studied, and deliberate Falshood, to prepossess and mislead the gentle Reader. Wherein does he *Assume?* He speaks like a Man, a Creature to which Modesty and Reason are pecu-[10]liar; not like an Animadverter, that is an Animal which hath nothing Humane in it but a Malicious Grinne, that may Provoke indeed, but cannot Imitate so much as Laughter. Wherein does he *Impose?* In nothing but by declaring his Opinion against all unreasonable Imposition. And though it appears natural to him to speak with Gravity, yet he usurps not any Authority further, than as any man who speaks a Truth which he thorowly understands, cannot with all his Modesty and Humility hinder others from paying a due Reverence to his Person, and acquiescing in his Doctrine. But wherein does he *Turn all upside down?* This hath been a common Topick of Ecclesiastical Accusation. Our Saviour was accused that he would *Destroy the Temple.*[93] The first martyr Steven was stoned as a Complice.[94] And Saint Paul (as ill luck would have it) was made odious upon the same Crimination of the Animadverters, Acts 17.v.5,6. For, *certain Lewd-fellows of the baser sort, set all the City in an uproar, crying, those that have turned the world* Up-side-down *are come hither also.* And yet notwithstanding all these Calumnies, *the Naked Truth,* Christianity, hath made a shift,[95] God be thanked, to continue till this day: and there will never want those that bear testimony to it, even to the Primitive Christianity, maugre[96] all the arts that the men of Religion can contrive to

[92] Philippians 4:5.

[93] Mark 14:55–58: "And there arose certain, and bare false witness against him, saying, / 'We heard him say, "I will destroy this temple that is made with hands, and within three days I will build another made without hands.'"

[94] Complice: accomplice. The story is told in Acts 6:8–14 through 7:57–59.

[95] made a shift: managed; cf. Marvell's letter to Sir Edward Harley (see introduction, p. 7): "The book said to be Marvels makes what shift it can in the world"; and, in the *Third Advice,* the duchess of Albemarle's pun (on her previous career as a seamstress): "'Tis true I want so long the nuptiall guift, / But as I oft have don, I'le make a shift" (ll. 321–22).

[96] maugre: in spite of, notwithstanding.

misrepresent and discountenance it. But as for the *Turning all up-side-down*, the Animadverter is somewhat innocent, if by the defect of his Organs, as it fares with those whose Brain turns round, (So we vulgarly express it) he have imagined that the world is tumbling headlong with him. But as to the Prejudice, which he therefore reserved as the most effectual and taking, to undoe the Author by, that he is *Immoderately Zealous for the Non-conformists;* it is the effect of as strong a Phancy, or as Malicious an Intention as the Former; it being scarce possible to open the Book in any place without chancing upon some passage where he makes a firm Profession, or gives a clear proof of his real submission and Addiction to the Church of England: all his fault for ought I see being, that he is more Truly and Cordially concerned for our Church than some mens Ignorance is capable of, or their corrupt interest can comply with. But therefore whoever were the adviser, it is not well done to use him in this dirty manner. There is no prudence in it; nor whereas the Author, in excuse that he sets not his name, saith it is *because he is a man of great Passions, and not able to bear a Reproach* (The Animadverter had done fairer to cite the whole *or Commendations: my small Ability puts me out of danger of the last, but in great fear of the former.*)[97] Therefore to resolve thus (whereas they might have undone him you see by Commendation) the rather to Reproach him, now they have learn't his Feebleness, Holy Church, I can tell you, hath suffered upon that account so often that it were time for her to be wiser. For by exasperating [11] men of Parts, who out of an ingenious love of Truth, have temperately Writ against some abuses, She hath added Provocation to mens Wit to look still further; insomuch that at last it hath sometimes produced (then which nothing can be more dangerous to the Church) a Reformation. Therefore, though Christ hath commanded his Followers (so it be not I suppose out of his Way) that if any man press them to go one mile, they should go two;[98] yet it is not wisdom in the Church to pretend to, or however to exercise, that Power of *Angariating*[99] men further than their occasions or understandings will permit. If a man cannot go their Length, 'tis better to have his company in quiet as far as his Road lyes. For my part I take the Church of England to be very happy in having a Person of his Learning and Piety so far to comply with Her; and if my advice might be taken, She should not lose one inch more of him by handling him irreverently. For if once She

---

[97] Croft, *The Naked Truth*, "To the Reader," A4r.

[98] Matthew 5:41.

[99] *Angariating:* to angariate is to constrain men to service, to exert forced labor.

should totally lose him, God knows what an Instrument he might prove, and how much good he might do in the Nation, more than he ever yet thought of. What a shame it is to hear the Animadverter abuse him (who, by the very Character of his Stile appears no Vulgar Person and by how much he hath more of Truth, hath more of Gods Image, and should therefore have imprinted that Awe upon him that Man hath over most Brutes:) he, to trifle with so worthy a person at that rate, that one would not use the meanest Varlet,[100] the dullest School-boy, the rankest Idiot, no nor the veriest Animadverter! However he saith, *the Author hath done himself and him, the Animadverter, a great favour, by concealing his Name, in making it impossible for him to reflect upon his Person* (otherwise it seems he should have had it home)[101] *which he knows no more than the Man in the Moon.*[102] But therefore I am the rather jealous he did know him: for the Animadverter having a team of *Gnaza's*[103] always at his devotion, and being able if any one tired by the way to relieve it and draw in person,[104] never think that he would want intelligence in that Region. Come 'twas all but an affected ignorance in the Animadverter, and he had both inquired and heard as much as any of us who was the probable Author:[105] and all the Guard that he Lyes upon is, because the Author had not given him legal notice that he Writ it. And this was even as the Animadverter would have wished it. For if a Reverend Person had openly avowed it, he could not have been sawcy with so good a Grace: But under the pretence of *not knowing,* Sir, that it was you, but only, Sir, *as you were the Patron of so vile a Cause,* many a dry bob,[106] close gird,[107] and privy nip has he given him. Yet he saith, *the Author would have done well, and a piece of Justice to have named himself, so to have cleared others: for it hath been confidently layed to the charge of more then one Reverend Person* (how slily!) *who* (*I have great reason to believe, and am several ways assured*) *had no hand in it.* Truly, the Animad-[12]verter too, would have done a piece of Justice to have named himself; for there has been more than one Witty person traduced for his Pamphlet, and I believe

---

[100] Varlet: a low servant.

[101] had it home: been seriously wounded.

[102] Turner, A4r.

[103] *Gnaza's:* the printer's attempt at Gnathos, parasites, from the Terentian character of that name.

[104] person A] persons B.

[105] See introduction, p. 5.

[106] dry bob: dry taunt or stroke.

[107] close gird: a blow that comes close to its mark.

by this time he would take it for a great favour if any man would be such a
Fool as own it for him. For he very securely reproaches the Author, and yet I
have been seeking all over for the Animadverter's name, and cannot find it.
Notwithstanding that he writes forsooth in defence of the Church of England; and *against so vile a Cause,* as he stiles it, and under the Publick
Patronage. Which is most disingenuously done, as on other accounts, so in
respect of my Lord Bishop of London,[108] whom he has left in the lurch to
justifie another mans Follies with his Authority. But however that venerable Person, who has for Learning, Candor, and Piety, as he does for
Dignity also, outstripp'd his Age and his Fellows, have been drawn in to
License what certainly he cannot approve of, it was but his First Fruits,[109]
and a piece of early liberality, as is usual, upon his new Promotion, and I am
given to understand that, for the Animadverters sake, it is like to be the last
that he will allow of that nature. But this is not only a Trick of the Animadverters, but ordinary with many others of them; who, while we write at our
own peril, and perhaps set our names to it, (for I am not yet resolved
whether I can bear Reproach or Commendation) they that rail for the
Church of England, and under the Publick License and Protection, yet
leave men, as if it were at Hot-Cockles,[110] to guess blind fold who it is that
hit them. But it is possible that some of these too may lie down in their
turns. What should be the reason of it? sure theirs is not *so Vile a Cause* too
that they dare not abide by it. Or are they the Writers conscious to themselves that they are such Things *as ought not once to be Named among Christians?*[111] Or is it their own sorry performance that makes them ashamed to
avow their own Books? Or is there some secret force upon them that
obliges them to say things against their Conscience? Or would they reserve
a Latitude to themselves to turn Non-conformists again upon occasion? Or
do they in pure honesty abstain from putting a single Name to a Book,
which hath been the workmanship of the whole Diocess?

But though he know not his Name, *seeing he has vented his own Amusements to the Churches great and real prejudice,* he saith (and *that is this Case*)
he must not think to scape for the Godliness of his Stile:[112] Impious and most

[108] See p. 5 above.

[109] First Fruits: the first year's income or profits, formerly paid by each new holder of
a benefice.

[110] Hot-Cockles: a game in which a blindfolded person was struck by his fellows and
had to guess by whom.

[111] 1 Corinthians 5:1.

[112] Turner, A4v.

unmerciful! Poor David was often in this *Case*. Psal. 22, *They gaped upon him with their mouth. He trusted,* said they, *in the Lord that he would deliver him, let him deliver him, seeing he delighted in him.*[113] And Psal. 71.11, *Persecute and take him, there is none to deliver him.* And yet there are many places too in Scripture, where God spared men even for their outward Formalities, and their Hypocrisie served to delay his Judgements; and should he not still do so, the Church might re[13]ceive *greater prejudice.* But the Church, and God are two things, and are not it seems obliged to the same Measures: insomuch that even the sincerity of one Person, which might perhaps attone for a whole Order, and render them acceptable both to God and Man, yet cannot hope for his own pardon.

Neither must he think to scape for a Man of good Intentions; yet sure he is, else would not give the Devil so much more than his due, saying he would never condemn any good action though done by the Devil. As if, saith the Animadverter, *he supposed the Devil might do some such.*[114] Here he thinks he has a shrewd hit at him, and this if a man had leisure, might beget a Metaphysical Controversie: but I desire him rather to comment on that Text: *Doest thou Believe? thou doest well, the Devils also Believe and Tremble.*[115] Whereas he goeth on to mock at the Authors *Good Intentions,* and tells him pleasantly, that *Hell itself is full of such as were once full of Good Intentions:*[116] 'tis a Concluding piece of Wit, and therefore, as well as for the Rarity, should be civilly treated and incouraged; so that I shall use no further retortion[117] there, that if this be the qualification of such as go to Hell, the Animadverter hath secured himself from coming there, and so many more as were his Partners. And thus much I have said upon his *Animadversions on the Title,* &c. Wherein, he having misrepresented the Author, and prejudicated the Reader against him by all disingenuous methods, and open'd the whole Pedlers pack of his malice, which he half-p-worths[118] out in the following discourse to his petty Chapmen,[119] I could not properly say less,

---

[113] Psalm 22.8.

[114] Turner, A4v.

[115] James 2:19.

[116] Good Intentions: proverbial; cf. Ray, *Collection of English Proverbs*, p. 13, and Richard Whitlock, *Zootomia* (1654), p. 203: "It's a saying among Divines, that Hell is full of good Intentions."

[117] retortion: bending backwards; hence an answer made to an argument by converting it against its author.

[118] half-p-worths: halfpenny worths; deals with cheaply.

[119] Chapmen: itinerant salesmen, pedlars.

though it exceeds perhaps the number of his Pages. For it is scarce credible how voluminous and pithy he is in extravagance: and one of his sides in *Quarto*,[120] for Falshood, Insolence, and Absurdity, contains a Book in *Folio*.[121] Besides, the Reader may please to consider how much labour it costs to Bray[122] even a Little Thing in a Mortar: and that Calumny is like London-dirt, with which though a man may be spatter'd in an instant, yet it requires much time, pains, and Fullers-earth[123] to scoure it out again.

Annotations upon the *Animadversions* on the first Chapter, concerning *Articles of Faith.*

The Play begins. *I confess* (Do so then and make no more words) *when first I saw this Jewel of a Pamphlet, and had run over two or three pages of this Chapter, I suspected the Author for some Youngster that had been Dabling amongst the Socinian Writers,*[124] *and was ambitious of* [14] *shewing us his Talent in their way. I was quickly delivered from this Jealousie, by his Orthodox Contradictory expressions in other places.*[125] That word *Jewel* is commonly used in a good sense, and I know no reason why this Book of the Authors might not be properly enough called so, though the Animadverter hath debased the meaning of the word to deprave and undervalue the worth of the Treatise. For I perceive that, during his Chaplainship,[126] he hath learnt it in conversation with the Ladies, who translate it frequently to call Whore in a more civil and refined signification. But to say thus, that *he suspected him at first for a Socinian, yet was quickly cured of his Jealousie,* because he found the Author was Honest and *Orthodox.* Why should he *vent his own Amusements* thus, to *the great and real prejudice* of any worthy person? It is indeed a piece of second Ingenuity for a man that invents and suggests a Calumny of which he is sure to be convict in the instant, therefore with the

[120] *Quarto:* the size of a book formed by folding a sheet of paper twice.

[121] *Folio:* the size of a book made by folding a sheet of paper once; the largest size of book.

[122] Bray: pound, grind small.

[123] Fullers-earth: hydrous silicate of alumina, used in cleaning cloth.

[124] Socinian: Socinianism, the antecedent of Unitarianism, was a heresy founded by Laelius and Faustus Sozzino, uncle and nephew, sixteenth-century Italian theologians who denied the divinity of Christ. But *Socinian* is at this time perhaps the most common stigmatic term applied to anyone whose beliefs seem to diverge from orthodoxy. See also n. 267 below.

[125] Turner, p. 1.

[126] Chaplainship: Turner was chaplain to James, duke of York.

same breath to disclaim it: but it manifests in the mean time how well he was inclined, if he thought it would have pass'd upon the Author; and that could the Animadverter have secured his Reputation, he would have adventured the Falshood. What would he not have given to have made the world believe that he was a Socinian? In this beginning you have a right Pattern of the Animadverters whole Stuff, and may see what Measure the Author is to expect all thorow.

But *he finds*, he saith, *that he is one of the* Men of the second Rate,[127] (*as he takes leave to stile them) that scarce ever see to the second Consequence.*[128] At first I suspected from this expression that the Animadverter had been some Ship-Chaplain,[129] that had been *Dabling* in the Sea-Controversies,[130] a Tarpawlin[131] of the Faculty: but I was *quickly delivered from this Jealousie by his* Magisterial *Contradictions,* that shew him to be a man of more *Consequence,* one of them whose Ecclesiastical Dignities yet cannot wean them from a certain hankering after the Wit of the Laity, and applying it as their own upon (or 'tis no great matter though it be without) occasion. Yet *therefore once for all, he Protests,* too, *that he does not charge him with any of his own most obvious Consequences as his Opinions* (for who would believe the one or other that reads the Author?) *for 'tis plain that he does not* (nor any man that hath Eyes) *discern them.* This is a Candor pregnant with Contempt. But in the mean time he thinks it ingenuous to load this *second Rate-Frigat,*[132] (that was fitted out for the Kings and the Nations service) so deep, that she can scarce swim, with a whole Cargo of Consequences which are none of the Authors, but will, upon search, be all found the Animadverters proper goods and Trade, his own Inconsequences and Inanimadversions.

---

[127] Rate: class or quality; in the seventeenth century a nautical term applied to ships, according to their size or strength. In the short parliamentary session of 1675, the Commons ordered on November 6 "that One Ship of the First Rate . . . five Ships of the Second Rate shall be built" (*JHC,* p. 369).

[128] *see to the second Consequence:* understand where the logic of their arguments leads.

[129] Ship-Chaplain: Ships carried their own clergymen. In the *Third Advice to a Painter* the duchess of Albemarle advises her husband, "Look that good chaplains on each ship do wait, / Nor the sea diocese be impropriate."

[130] the sea-Controversies: the debates in the Commons as to whether to vote money to strengthen the fleet, as continually requested by Charles and his ministers since 1672.

[131] Tarpawlin: a tarpaulin is a sheet of canvas impregnated with waterproofing; in the seventeenth century a nickname for a mariner or common sailor (cf. tar).

[132] Frigat: frigate, a type of sailing vessel: formerly in a class just below ships of the line.

So men with vicious Eyes see Spiders weave from the Brim of their own Beavers.[133]

As for example, p. 1, He saith that *this Chapter does admirably serve* [15] *the turn of the rankest Sectarian. That in his two or three first pages he appeared a Socinian.* p. 12. That his *Pique at the new word* Homoousios[134] *carries such an ugly reflection upon the Nicene Creed,*[135] *that he,* the Animadverter, *scarce dares understand him.*[136] p. 6. The Author speaking against introducing new Articles of Faith, the Adversary tells him, *He hopes he does not mean all our Thirty Nine Articles;*[137] and defends them as if they were attaqued. That *he does implicitly condemn the whole Catholick Church both East and West for being so presumptuous in her Definitions.* p. 9. That *upon his Principles the Prime and most necessary Articles of Faith will be in danger. The old dormant Heresies, Monothelites,*[138] *Nestorians,*[139] *&. may safely revive again.* p. 13. That his *are the very dregs of Mr. Hobbs his Divinity,*[140] *and worse.* p. 14. That

---

[133] This brilliant phrase does not appear to be proverbial, but rather Marvell's invention.

[134] *Homoousios:* The fourth-century dispute concerning the nature of Christ was resolved by the adoption, as orthodoxy, of this term, *homoousios,* meaning of the same essence or substance (as God the Father). It was distinguished from the Arian term *homoiousios,* of similar but different identity and substance. Marvell's printers have, unsurprisingly, continued difficulties with these terms.

[135] Nicene Creed: the creed that resulted from the Council of Nicaea, convened in A.D. 325 by the emperor Constantine the Great. Nicaea was a city in Bithynia, now modern Iznik.

[136] Turner, p. 2. The original punctuation misleadingly suggests p. 6.

[137] *Thirty Nine Articles:* These were established as the basis of the English church, in belief and practice, in 1563. They represented the consolidation of a series of attempts, beginning with the Ten Articles of 1536, to define English Protestantism and were reconfirmed by Charles I in 1628. Subscription to the articles was required of all clergy as a condition of holding a parish.

[138] Monethelites: a heretical set of the seventh century that maintained that Christ has only one will.

[139] Nestorians: Following the doctrine of Nestorius, patriarch of Constantinople in the fifth century, Nestorians believed that Christ contained two distinct persons, one divine, the other human.

[140] *Hobbs . . . Divinity:* Thomas Hobbes was frequently accused of heresy on the basis of *Leviathan* (1651), in which he had advanced an unorthodox theory of the Trinity. Having excised that theory from the Latin version, published in Amsterdam in 1668, Hobbes added to it an Appendix in which he foregrounded the problems of that doctrine as expressed in the Nicene Creed. In another chapter of the Appendix, "On certain objections against *Leviathan,*" Hobbes introduced two speakers who, in di-

he would have some men live like Pagans and go to no church at all. p. 16. *So for ought we know this Author is a Jesuite,*[141] *and writes this pamphlet only to embroil us Protestants.* p. 25. That *he is guilty of unthought of Popery.* p. 33. That our Author *like her* (the foolish Woman)[142] *in the* Proverbs, *plucks down our Church with his own hands,* and that *she had need therefore to be upheld against such as he is.* Of these Inferences, which not being natural, must have required some labour, he is all along very liberal to the Author; but the vile and insolent language costs him nothing, so that he lays that on prodigally and without all reason. Now, whether a man that holds a true Opinion, or he that thus deduces ill Consequences from it, be the more blame-worthy, will prove to be the Case between the Animadverter and the Author. *And* (to shew him now from whence he borrowed his Wit of the second Rate, and at the second Hand)

> ———*all the subject matter of debate,*
> *Is only who's the Knave of the First Rate.*[143]

But he saith, because of these things, *the Mischief being done, to undo the Charm again, it is become a Duty to* Expose *him.* Alas what are they going to do with the poor man?[144] What kind of death is this *Exposing?* But sure,

---

alogue, review his contested opinions; and Speaker B, who is presumably Hobbes himself, defends a liberal position on creeds that is not dissimilar from that of Croft and Marvell, including that "the *unum necessarium* (only article of faith which the Scripture maketh simply necessary to salvation) is this: that Jesus is the Christ."

[141] *Jesuite:* a member of the Society of Jesus, an aggressively proselytizing Roman Catholic order founded by Ignatius Loyola in 1534 to assist the Counter-Reformation.

[142] the foolish Woman: see Proverbs 9:13–18: "She sitteth at the door of her house . . . / To call passengers who go right on their ways. / Whoso is simple, let him turn in here . . . / But he knoweth not that . . . her guests are in the depths of hell."

[143] *all the subject . . . First Rate:* the concluding couplet of Rochester's "Satyr against Reason and Mankind," as circulated in manuscript in 1674–75. Edward Stillingfleet targeted this poem in a sermon preached before Charles on February 24, 1675; hence some mss. allude to "Stilling fleets replies" (l. 74). Rochester replied by adding to his satire an unambiguous attack on men "blown up with vain prelatic pride." See David Trotter, "Wanton Expressions," in *Spirit of Wit: Reconsiderations of Rochester,* ed. Jeremy Treglown (Oxford, 1982), pp. 111–32; and Kristoffer Paulson, "The Reverend Edward Stillingfleet and the 'Epilogue' to Rochester's *A Satyr against Reason and Mankind,*" *Philological Quarterly* 50 (1971), 657–63.

[144] the poor man: This seems to be Marvell's way of describing Herbert Croft, which in private becomes somewhat demeaning. See his letter to Sir Edward Harley, July 1, 1676 (*Poems and Letters,* 2:345–46), where the term is used twice to refer to Croft.

considering the Executioner, it must be some Learned sort of Cruelty. Is it the *Taeda*,[145] in which they candled a Man over in Wax, and he, instead of the wick, burnt out to his lives end like a Taper, to give light to the Company? Or is it the *Scapha*,[146] wherein a man, being strip'd Naked, and Smear'd with Honey, was in the scorching Sun abandon'd to be stung and Nibled by Wasps, Hornets, and all troublesome Insects till he expired? Or is it rather *ad Bestias*,[147] turning him out unarmed to be bated, worryed, and devour'd by the wild Beasts in the Theatre? For in the Primitive Times there were these and an hundred laudable ways more to *Expose* Christians; and the Animadverter seems to have studied them. But the Crime being of Sorcery, and that there is a *Charm* which hath wrought great *Mischief, and* [16] *is not to be undone but by* Exposing *the Malefactor,* (Charme he never so wisely)[148] 'tis more probable that it may be the Punishment usual in such Cases.[149] And indeed the Animadverter hath many times in the day such Fits take him, wherein he is lifted up in the Air that six men cannot hold him down, tears, raves, and foams at the mouth, casts up all kinds of trash, sometimes speaks Greek and Latin, that no man but would swear he is bewitched: and this never happens but when the Author appears to him. And though in his *Animadversions on the Title,* &c. He hath so often scratched and got blood of him (the infallible Country Cure) yet he still[150] finds no ease by it, but is rather more tormented. So that in earnest I begin to suspect him for a Witch, or however having writ the *Naked Truth,* 'tis manifest he is a Sooth-sayer,[151] that's as bad. Many persons besides have for

---

[145] *Taeda:* pitch-pine torch; hence a kind of torture by incineration; see Juvenal, *Satires,* 1:155, where the allusion is made in the context of political censorship: "What man is there that I dare not name? . . . But mention Tigellinus [a notorious favorite of Nero] and you will blaze amidst those faggots."

[146] *Scapha:* cf. the death of Aspamitres, Ctesias, *Historicus,* 29.30, Plutarch, *Life of Artaxerxes,* 16.

[147] *ad Bestias:* thrown to the beasts; one of the most common forms of persecution of Christians in the early church.

[148] Charme . . . wisely: Psalm 58:4–5: "They are like the deaf adder that stoppeth her ear; which will not hearken to the voice of charmers, charming never so wisely."

[149] The Jacobean witchcraft statute of 1603 (1 & 2 Jac. 1.c. 12), which made invocation of spirits, etc., a felony and hence a capital crime, was still in force; but the punishment could apparently be either hanging or burning alive. In 1664 Sir Matthew Hales condemned the Suffolk witches to be burned (*State Trials,* 647).

[150] still A] not in B.

[151] Sooth-sayer: truth teller, prognosticator, or prophet; with a pun on Croft's authorship of the *Naked Truth.*

tryal run needles[152] up to the Eye in several remarkable places of his *Naked Truth,* that look like moles or warts upon his body, and yet he, though they prick never so much, feels nothing. Nay some others of the Clergy, whereof one was a Bishop,[153] have tyed him hand and foot and thrown him into the Thames betwixt Whitehall[154] and Lambeth,[155] for experiment; laying so much weight too on him as would sink any ordinary man, and nevertheless he swims still, and keeps above water. So dangerous is it to have got an Ill Name once, either for speaking Truth or for Incantation, that it comes to the same thing almost to be Innocent or Guilty: for if a man swim he is Guilty, and to be Burnt; if he sink, he is Drowned, and Innocent. But therefore this *Exposing* must surely be to condemn the Author, as he has done his Book already, to the fire (for no man stands fairer for't as being first Heretick, and now Witch by consequence) and then the Devil sure can have no more power over the Animadverter. Yet when I consider'd better, that he does not accuse him of any harm that he has suffered by him in person,[156] but that it is the *Church which may justly complain of him* and having done her so much *mischief, therefore it is become a Duty to Expose him;* I could not but imagine that it must be a severer Torment. For if our Church be bewitched, and he has done it,

> *Huic mites nimium Flammas, huic lenta putassem*
> *Flumina, fumiferi potasset nubia Peti.*[157]

Though I never heard before of a Church that was Bewitched, except that[158] of the Galatians, *Gal.* 3.1. Whom St. Paul asks, *O foolish Galatians who hath* Bewitched *you?* taking it for evident that they were so, *because* (they are his very next words) *they did not obey the Truth.*[159] (And that was a

[152] needles Ed.] needless A,B.

[153] a Bishop: one of several references to Peter Gunning's sermon against Croft. See introduction, p. 5.

[154] Whitehall: the palace which, until it burned down in 1698, was the royal residence.

[155] Lambeth: Lambeth Palace was the residence of the archbishop of Canterbury.

[156] harm . . . person: an allusion to the requirement in some witchcraft trials that the accuser show evidence of *maleficium,* actual harm that the witch has done to him or his.

[157] Unidentifiable, these lines are also difficult to translate, at least without emending "Peti" to "Pestis": "I would have thought burning too mild for him, drowning too slow, he should have snuffed up the clouds of smoky plague."

[158] that A] not in B.

[159] Cf. Reginald Scot, *The Discovery of Witchcraft* (London, 1665), p. 65. Marvell may

Naked Truth with a Witness, the Apostle teaching, that *Christ is become of none effect to them, that from their Christian Liberty returned to the Jewish Ceremonies,* Gal. 5.4) But therefore I looked over the *Canons,*[160] the *Rational,* the *Ceremonial,* the *Rubrick,*[161] imagining the *Exposing* mention'd, [17] must be some new part of our Ecclesiastical Discipline, that I had not taken notice of before, and I should find it in one or other of the Offices. But I lost my labour, and it was[162] but just I should, for being so simple, as not to understand at first that to *Expose* a man, is to write *Animadversions* upon him. For that is a crueller Torment then all the Ten Persecutors[163] (and which none but this new Clergy man[164] could have invented), To be set in the Pillory first and be dawb'd with so many Addle Eggs[165] the Animadverters own Cackle as he pelts[166] him with! How miserable then is the man that must suffer afterwards, *sub tam lento Ingenio!*[167] To be raked

---

have consulted this rationalist work for his brief foray into the penal practices against supposed witches.

[160] the *Canons:* In 1604 a collection of 141 canons or rules that had been drawn up in Latin by Richard Bancroft while bishop of London were passed by Convocation. Although never authorized by parliament, they became the permanent rules for the Anglican church on such matters as the administration of the sacrament, the duties and behavior of clerics (including the wearing of the much-contested surplice), and the treatment of nonconformity. See *Constitutions and Canons Ecclesiastical 1604,* ed. J. V. Bullard (London, 1934).

[161] the Rubrick: presumably the Ornaments Rubrick, the term for the ruling in the 1559 *Book of Common Prayer,* before the order for morning and evening prayer, that the ornaments of the church and the ministry should be those in use "by the authority of Parliament in the second year of the reign of King Edward VI." The ruling had been reenacted by parliament in 1604 and 1662.

[162] it was] 'twas B.

[163] Ten Persecutors: Orosius (fifth century) numbered ten periods of Christian persecution under, respectively, Nero, Domitian, Trajan, Marcus Aurelius, Septimus Severus, Maximus, Decius, Valerian, Aurelian, and Diocletian. Compare *RT2,* pp. 379–80: "You perhaps, because [Julian's] is not reckoned among the ten Persecutions, thought there had been no more, neither in his time, nor Pope Hildebrands, nor Bishop Bonners, nor since."

[164] new Clergy man B] "new" not in A.

[165] Addle Eggs: fertilized eggs that will never hatch; cf. the *Second Advice to a Painter,* ll. 17–20: "United Generals! sure the only spell / Wherewith United Provinces to quell. / Alas, ev'n they, though shell'd in treble Oake, / Will prove an addle Egge with double Yolke."

[166] pelts Ed.] palts A,B.

[167] *sub tam lento Ingenio:* under so slow a wit.

and harrowed thorow with so rusty a Saw! So dull a Torture that it contains all other in it, and which even the Christian Reader is scarce able to endure with all his Patience! Had he been a man of some accuteness, the pain would have been over in an instant: but this was the utmost inhumanity in whoever it was that advised (whereas several witty men were proposed that would have been glad of the imployment) to chuse out on purpose the veryest (Animadverter) in all the Faculty. This it is to which the Author is condemned. And now that I know it, and that it is an Office a Duty to which our Church it seems has advanc'd the Animadverter; I wish him joy of his new Preferment, and shall henceforth take notice of him as the Church of England's Exposer, for I can never admit him by any Analogy to be an Expositor.[168]

It is no less disingenuously, than constantly done of the Exposer in this same; *p.* 1. To concern the Author in the Non-conformists, that may have reflected any where,[169] as if there were Socinian, or Pelagian[170] Doctrines: *Allowed to be preached and maintained in the City Pulpits.* For the Author hath not in his whole book the least syllable that can be wrested to any such purpose. Only it serves the Adversaries turn,[171] as he thinks, to pre-ingage the whole Clergy and Church of England against him, if they were so simple, and by giving him an odious Badge and jumbling them altogether, to involve him in all the prejudices; which are studiously advanced against that party. But neither have I any thing to urge of that nature, further then because he will out of season mention these matters, to observe that our Church seems too remiss in the case of Socinus[172] and Volkelius,[173] who had many things to great value stolen from them by a late Plagiary,[174] but as yet have not obtained any Justice or Restitution.

[168] Expositor A] Exposer B.

[169] any where A] any were B.

[170] Pelagius, who was an ascetic teacher in Rome in the early fifth century, gave his name to the heresy that man can take the initial steps toward salvation independently of divine grace.

[171] turn A] not in B.

[172] Socinus: see n. 124.

[173] Volkelius: Johann Volkel, whose *De vera religione* was published in Amsterdam in 1641.

[174] a late Plagiary: this may be William Sherlock, later dean of St. Paul's, who in 1674 had published a *Discourse concerning the knowledge of Jesus Christ,* twice attacked for implied Socinianism: by Vincent Alsop, *Anti-Sozzo* (London, 1675), and by Thomas Danson, *A Friendly Debate between Satan and Sherlock* (London, 1676).

But seeing the Exposer is thus given to transform not only the Author, but his words and his meaning; it is requisite to state this Chapter in his own terms: as men set their Arms on their plate to prevent the nimbleness of such as would alter[175] the property. The sum of what he[176] humbly proposes is: *That nothing hath caused more mischief in the Church, than the establishing New and many Articles of Faith, and requiring men to [18] assent to them with Divine Faith. For the imposing such on Dissenters, hath caused furious Wars and lamentable Blood-shed among Christians. That it is irrational to promote the Truth of the Gospel by Imposition, which is contrary to the Laws of the Gospel, and break an evident Commandment to establish a doubtful Truth. For if such Articles be not fully expressed in Scripture words, it is Doubtful to him upon whom it is Forced, though not to the Imposer. If it be fully expressed in Scripture Words, there needs no new Articles: but if not so, and it be only Deduced from Scripture Expressions, then men that are as able and knowing as the Imposer, may think it is not clearly Deduced from Scripture. But there is nothing more fully Exprest, or that can be more clearly Deduced from Scripture, nor more suitable to Natural Reason, then that no man should be Forced to believe.[177] Because no man can Force himself to believe, no not even to believe the Scriptures. But Faith is a work of peculiar Grace, and the Gift of God. And if a man Believe what is clearly Contain'd in Scripture, he needs not believe anything else with Divine Faith. To add to, or diminish from the Scripture, is by it unlawful, and lyable to the curse in the Revelation.[178] If the Imposer answer, he requires not to believe it as Scripture, he doth, if he urge it to be believed with Divine Faith. If he say he requires it not to be Believed with Divine Faith, he does, if he makes it necessary to Salvation. There is no Command nor Countenance given in[179] the Gospel to use Force to cause men Believe. We have no Comprehensive Knowledge of the Matters declared in Scripture, that are the Prime and Necessary Articles of Faith, therefore it is not for any man to Declare one Tittle[180] more to be Believed with Divine Faith, then God hath there Declared.[181] He cannot find the least hint in the Word of God to use any Force to Compel men to the Churches established Doctrine or Discipline: and from*

175 alter A] altar B.

176 he: i.e., Croft.

177 Croft, p. 2; but cited very inexactly.

178 Revelation 22:18: "If any man shall add unto [the words . . . of this book] God shall add unto him the plagues which are written in this book."

179 in Ed.] to A,B.

180 Tittle: tiny bit.

181 Croft, p. 4.

Reason there can be no Motive to be forced beyond their Reason. To attempt any such Force, though to the True Belief, is to do Evil that Good may come of it. But the Pastor ought first by plain and sound Doctrine to stop the Mouths of Gainsayers.[182] *When the Ministers have Preached and Prayed, they have done all they can in order to mens Believing, the rest must be left to the Justice or Mercy of God. But if turbulent Spirits broach New Doctrines, Contrary to Scripture, or not Clearly Contained in the Gospel, and neither by Admonitions nor Intreaties will be stopt, the Pastors may proceed to the Exercise of the Keys.*[183] *Which if it were duely performed as in the Primitive Times, and not by Lay Chancellors and their surrogates, would be of great effect. The Magistrate ought to silence and oppose such as preach what is Contrary to, or not Clearly contained in the Gospel, and if they persevere in their perversness, he may use his power with Christian Moderation. For his power reaches to punish Evil Doers, who Publish or Practice something to subvert the Fundamentals of Religion, or to Disturb the Peace of the State, or to Injure their Neighbours: but not to Punish Evil Believers. But if the Magistrate shall conceive he hath* [19] *power also to punish Evil Believers, and on that Pretence shall punish True Believers, the Subject is bound to submit and bear it, to the loss of Goods, Liberty or Life.*[184] The Reader will excuse this one long Quotation, for it will much shorten all that follows.

But now for which of these is it that 'tis become a Duty to Expose him? What is there here that seems not at first sight, very Christian, very Rational? But however, it is all delivered in so Grave and Inoffensive manner, that there was no temptation to alter the stile into Ridicule, and Satyre. But like some Cattle, the Animadverter may Browze upon the Leaves, or Peel the Barke, but he has not teeth for the Solid, nor can hurt the Tree but by accident. Yet a man that sees not into the second, but the Thirteenth *Consequence,* that is one *of the Disputers of this World*[185] and *ought to be admitted to these Doubtfull Disputations*[186] (from which he ironically by St. Pauls rule forsooth excludes the Author) what is there that such an one, so subtile, so piercing, cannot distinguish upon and Controvert? Truth it self ought to sacrifice to him that he would be propitious; For if he appear on the other side, it will go against her unavoidably.

[182] Gainsayers: those who speak or act against some proposal; contradictors.
[183] Croft, p. 7.
[184] Croft, p. 9.
[185] 1 Corinthians 1:20.
[186] Romans 14:1.

In his 27. P. he is ravisht in Contemplation how *Rarachose*[187] it is, to *see or hear a material Question in Theology defended in the University-Schools, where one stands as a Respondent, enclos'd within the Compass of his Pen, as Popilius the Roman Embassador, made a Circle with his Wand about Antiochus, and bid him give a determinate answer before he went out of it;*[188] a most apt and learned resemblance, and which shews the Gentlemans good reading! But it is, I confess, a noble spectacle, and worthy of that Theatre which the munificence of the present Arch-bishop of Canterbury hath dedicated in one[189] (may it be too in the other) of our Universities; where no Apish *Scaramuccio,*[190] no Scenical Farces, no Combat of Wild-Beasts among themselves, or with men condemn'd, is presented to the People; but the modest Skirmish of Reason, and which is usually perform'd so well, that it turns to their great honour, and of our whole Nation. Provided, the Chaire be well filled, with an Orthodox Professor, and who does not by *Solaecismes*[191] in Latine, or mistake of the Argument, or Question, render the thing ridiculous to the By-standers. That the Pew be no less fitted with a Respondent, able to sustain and answer, in all points, the expectation of so Learned an Auditory: That the Opponent likewise exceed not the terms of Civility, nor Cavil where he should Argue; and that the Questions debated, be so discreetly chosen, as there may be no danger, by Controverting the Truth, to unsettle the minds of the Youth ever after, and innure them to a Disputable Notion about the most weighty points of our Religion; by which sort of subtilizing, the Church hath in former Ages much suffered; nor hath Ours, in the Latter, wholly escaped. [20] Now, seeing the Exposer seems to delight so much (as men use in what they excell) in this Exercise,

---

[187] *Rarachose:* a rare thing (Fr.); the *DNB* cites Marvell's usage as the only instance.

[188] Turner was unwise to introduce this famous anecdote about the encounter between Gaius Laenas Popillius (Pauly Wissowa #18), Roman praetor and consul, and Antiochus IV, head of the Seleucid empire (see Livy, 45:12ff). The story had been recycled for common use by Montaigne, "Of the Greatness of Rome." Marvell, who loved circles, was able to deploy it as a structural device to circumscribe his adversary.

[189] The Sheldonian theater in Oxford, dedicated with great ceremony on July 9, 1669. See Evelyn, *Diary,* 3:531–34.

[190] *Scaramuccio:* i.e., the Italian comedians under the leadership of Scaramouche, or Tiberio Fiorilli, whose first visit to London Marvell mentioned in the *Rehearsal Transpros'd,* p. 252. Evelyn saw them at court on May 25, 1673 (*Diary,* 4:12). They returned for a second visit and, as Marvell wrote to Popple, were playing daily at Whitehall in July 1675 (*P&L,* 2:342).

[191] *Solaecismes:* grammatical errors.

he and I, because we cannot have the conveniency of the *Schools* and *Pew,* will play as well as we can in Paper, at this new Game of Antiochus and Popilius. I must for this time be the Roman Senator, and he the Monarch of Asia: for by the Rules of the Play, he always that hath writ the last Book is to be Antiochus, until the other has done replying. And I hope to gird him up so close within his Circle, that he shall appear very slender. For I am sensible, yet could not avoid it, how much of the Readers and mine own time I have run out in examining his Levity; but now I am glad to see my labour shorten: for, having thus plumed him of that puffe of Feathers, with which he buoy'd himself up in the Air, and flew over our heads, it will, almost by the first *Consequence,* be manifest in his Argument, how little a Soul it is, and Body, that henceforward I am to deal with.

The Author having said that, *That which we commonly call the Apostles Creed, is, and was so received by the Primitive Church, as the sum Total of Christian Faith, necessary to Salvation. Why not now? Is the state of Salvation alter'd? If it be Compleat, what need other Articles?*[192] The Exposer p. 2. answers, *There may have been needful heretofore, not only other Articles, but other Creeds for the further Explication of these Articles in the Apostles Creed: and yet in those* New Creeds *not one* New Article. 'Tis safely and cautiously said, *there May,* and not *there Were* other Articles, and other Creeds needful. But the whole Clause besides is so drawn up, as if he affected the Academical glory of justifying a Paradox: nor is it for the reputation of such Creeds, whatever they be, to be maintained by the like Methods. But seeing he disdains to explicate further, how there can be a New Creed, and yet not one New Article; I will presume to understand him, and then say, that in such Creeds, whatsoever Article does either explain the Apostles Creed contrary to, or beside the Scripture, or does not contain the same Express Scriptural Authority (which only makes this that is called the Apostles Creed to be Authentick) that is a New Article to every man that cannot conceive the necessary Deduction. But then he galls[193] the Author. *The Apostles Creed is the sum of the Christian Faith True. Yet I hope he will not think the Nicene, the Constantinopolitan, and the Athanasian Creed*[194] superfluous and unnecessary.[195] First, it is not necessary to take all those Three in

---

[192] Croft, p. 1.

[193] galls: makes sore by chafing; vexes.

[194] For the texts and history of the different creeds, see J. N. D. Kelly, *Early Christian Creeds* (London, 1950), esp. pp. 215–16, 231–54, 297–98.

[195] Turner, p. 2.

the Lump, as the Exposer puts it: for perhaps a man may think but one, or but two of them to have been superfluous and unnecessary. Next it is an hard thing for the Exposer, who ought rather to have proved that they were necessary, to shift it back thus upon the Author. I have not spoke with him, nor know whether I shall as long as I live, (though I should be glad of the opportunity) to know his mind. But suppose he should think them, One, Two, or Three Unnecessary, who can help [21] it? But so much I think, upon the state or sum of this Controversie in his own words, I may adventure for him: that as Confessions of Faith he does not disapprove them, (taking it granted there is nothing in any of them flatly against the Word of God) but that if any thing be therein drawn up in such or such an exact Form of Words, not Expressed in Scripture, and required to be Believed with Divine Faith, as necessary to a Mans own Salvation; and without Believing which, he must Declare too that no Man else can be saved;[196] that this is Dangerous, and the imposing of it is unwarrantable by Reason or Scripture. He[197] adds in this same Paragraph, that *the Authors Censure upon Constantine is so bold, and upon some Godly Bishops,* (whom he conceives more Zealous then Discreet, and so do some Godly Bishops conceive of this Author)[198] *and his Pique at the new word* Homoousios,[199] *carryes such an ugly reflection upon the Creed, that he scarce dare understand him.*[200] And I on the other side take his *Fears* and his *Hopes* to be alike inconsiderable. His words[201] are p. 6. *I am confident had the most prudent and pious Constantine, the First and Best of Christian Emperours, pursued his own intention, to suppress all Disputes, and all new Questions about God the Son, both Ho-moousian, and* Homoiousian, *and commanded all to acquiesce in the very Scripture Expressions, without any addition, that the Arrian heresie had soon expired.* I note that the Exposer very disingenuously, and to make it look more ugly, takes not the least notice of his Pique against *Homoiousios* too and the Arrian Heresie. But what is there here to fright the understanding Animadverter out of his Wits, or what to make *some Godly Bishops* (who it seems must be numberless or nameless) *to conceive the Author more Zealous then Discreet?*[202] But for this Censure of the Author, as well as for the

---

[196] without . . . saved: an allusion to the postscript to the Athanasian Creed.
[197] He: i.e., Turner.
[198] and . . . Author] mistakenly italicized in original.
[199] See note 134.
[200] Turner, p. 2.
[201] His words: i.e., Croft's.
[202] Turner, p. 2.

Godliness of the Bishops, we must acquiesce it seems upon the Credit, or Gratitude of one Nameless Exposer.

He then blames the Author *p.* 3. for saying *p.* 1. that *he would have men improve in Faith rather* Intensive, *then* Extensive, *to confirm it, rather then enlarge it.*[203] Still, and alwayes, to make things a little more ugly, and of less value, he clips the Authors good English. *You would have men improve in Faith, so would I, but rather* Intensive *then* Extensive. *'Tis good to know all Gospel Truths, no doubt of that, the more the better still; but the Question is not what is Good, but what is Necessary.* This is a pious and undoubted Truth, and confirm'd by the Author out of several Places of Scripture: May I add one, Marke 9.17.[204] Where *one brought his Son, being troubled with a Dumb Spirit to our Saviour,* v. 23. *Jesus saith to the Father, if thou canst Believe, all things are possible to him that Believeth. The Father cryes out with tears, Lord I Believe, strengthen thou my Unbelief.* And this Confession of the Intensive Truth of his Faith, with his relyance upon Christ for the strengthening of it, was sufficient to co-operate with our Saviour toward a Miracle, and throwing that Dumb and [22] Deaf Spirit out of a third Person. Whoever indeed will deny this Truth, must go against the whole current of the New Testament. But the Exposer is Deaf to that, 'tis all one to him. Yet he is not Dumb, Though as good he had [been], for all he has to say to it is: *And yet it is certain that all formal and moral Hereticks, that are not Atheists, are justly condemn'd for want of due extension in their Faith.*[205] What pertinence! But there goes more Faith I see to the ejecting of a Talkative then of a Dumb Spirit. There is no need of further answer to so succinct a Bob, then that it had been well those terms of *Formal*[206] and *Mortal,*[207] and *Hereticks,*[208] and no less that of *Condemned* had in this place been thorowly explained. For we know that there was a time when the Protestants themselves were the *Formal,* and, to be sure, the *Mortal Hereticks,* even here in England,[209] and

[203] On intensive vs. extensive faith, Croft himself partly provided a definition: intensive faith deepens and strengthens belief in the fundamentals, such as the divinity of Jesus; extensive faith requires belief in more, and more complex, articles, such as the doctrine of the Trinity.

[204] Marke B] Marke the A.

[205] Turner, p. 3.

[206] *Formal:* heretical only with respect to ceremonies.

[207] *Mortal:* heretical with respect to fundamental beliefs, those upon which salvation depends.

[208] To define the term *heretic* was precisely the logical impossibility that Marvell insists on, and that the *Essay* will further document in historical terms.

[209] a time when . . . in England: during the reign of Mary Tudor.

for that very crime too, *For want of due extension in their Faith,* they were *Condemned,* whether justly or no, it is in the Exposers power to determine. For some of our Ruling Clergy, who yet would be content to be accounted good Protestants, are so loath to part with any hank[210] they have got, at what time soever over the poor Laity, or what other reason, that the Writ *de Haeretico Comburendo,*[211] though desired to be abolish'd,[212] is still kept in force to this day. So that it is of more concernment then one would at first think, how far mens *Faith* (lest afterwards for believing short their Persons and Estates) *be Extended,* and [213] taken in Execution.

He proceeds Page the 3d. and several that follow, to quarrel the Author for quoting to this purpose Acts 8.[214] and then saying, *I pray remember the Treasurer*[215] (the Exposer will do it, I warrant you, and the Chancellor too,[216] without more intreaty) *to Candace Queen of Ethiopa, whom Philip instructed with in*[217] *the Faith. His time of Catechising was very short and soon proceeded to Baptism. But Philip first required a Confession of his Faith, and the Eunuch made it, and I beseech you observe it. I believe that Jesus Christ is the Son of God, and straight way he was Baptized. How, no more than this? No more. This little Grain of Faith, being sound, believed with all his heart, purchased the Kingdom of Heaven. 'Tis not the Quantity but the Quality of our Faith God requireth.*[218] Here the Exposer, pretending now to be a learned Expositor, hopes to win his Spurrs, and layes out all his ability to prove that Philip (in a very short time for so much work as he finds him) had instructed the Treasurer thorow the whole Athanasian Creed; concerning the

---

[210] hank: hold.

[211] *de Haeretico Comburendo:* the law requiring that heretics be burned alive, enacted in 1401, in response to the spread of Wycliffe's doctrines.

[212] On May 7, 1675, the Commons ordered "that Mr. Weld have Leave to bring in a Bill to abolish the Writ *De Haeretico comburendo*" (*JHC* 1675), p. 332. After the two prorogations, the House, undeterred, returned to the issue in March 1677, and when the bill was committed on March 26, Marvell was added to the committee (*JHC* 1677), p. 406. This indicates a special interest.

[213] and B] or A.

[214] Philip's conversion of the Ethiopian treasurer (Acts 8:26–39) was an event of considerable theological importance; Turner, however, invents a long conversation that has no scriptural warrant.

[215] Treasurer A] Treasure B.

[216] Marvell means that Turner will recommend himself to Charles's treasurer, Thomas Osborne, earl of Danby, and his chancellor, Heneage Finch.

[217] with in A] within B.

[218] Croft, p. 1.

Equality, Inseparability, Co-eternity, of the three Persons in the Trinity. For saith the Exposer, *the very form of Baptism, if thorowly explained, is a perfect Creed by itself:* In the name of the Father, the Son and the Holy Ghost: *For it seems the name of the* Son, *was by a Divine Criticisme interposed between the other two Persons, whose Godhead was confest and acknowledged by the Jewish Church, rather then that of the* Word, *to denote the second Person, &c.*[219] I should [23] be glad to know where the Exposer learnt that the Jewish Church acknowledged the Godhead of the Holy Ghost, as of a Distinct Person; which if he cannot show, he is very far out in the Matter, as he is in that Expression of *Divine Criticisme.* Therefore he may do well to consider. But it is simply, to say no worse, done of him, to call that form of words as it is ordered by our Saviour himself, a *Divine Criticisme,* as if Christ had therein affected that Critical glory, which the Exposer himself in so subtile a Remarke doubtless pretends to. But the Exposer will not only have Philip to have instructed the Treasurer in this *Criticism,* but to have read him so long a Lecture upon Baptism, as must for certain have been out of the Assemblies,[220] and not Noel's Catechisme:[221] *acquainting him and instructing him abundantly, in those great Points of Faith, the Dying, Burying, and Rising again of Christ for our Justification from our sins, together with the thing signified, Death unto sin, Mortification, the New Birth unto Righteousness, then the Mystery of the First and Second Covenant, Original sin, how thereby he was a Son of Wrath, had hereby Forgiveness of sins, Adoption, being made a Child of Grace, Co-heir with Christ, to live with him in the Communion of Saints, after the Resurrection, in Life Everlasting.* I am glad to see that, at least when it serves to his purpose, this Exposer will own all the Doctrines, which another Exposer[222] would have call'd *so many Stages of Regeneration,*[223] and have thought them too many to have drove over in one days journey, but would rather have turn'd out of the Road, and lay'd short all night somewhere by the way. Here is a whole *Calvinistical Systeme* of

[219] Turner, pp. 3–4.

[220] the Assemblies [Catechism]: i.e., *The Humble Advice of the Assembly of Divines, now by authority of Parliament sitting at Westminster, concerning A Confession of Faith* (London, 1647).

[221] Alexander Nowell (1507–1607), a Marian exile and then dean of St. Paul's under Elizabeth, wrote three catechisms of various lengths. The longest was approved by Convocation in 1563, though not printed until 1670.

[222] another Exposer: i.e., Samuel Parker.

[223] *Stages of Regeneration:* cf. *RT2*, p. 386, which in turn referred back to Samuel Parker, *A Defence and Continuation of the Ecclesiastical Politie* (London, 1671), pp. 306–09.

Divinity, that, if the Treasurer had been to be Baptized in the *Lake of Geneva*,[224] more could not have been expected. And he has in a trice made him so perfect in it, that, as soon as the Christ'ning was over, he must have been fit to be received not only *ad communionem Laicam,* but the *Clericam* also,[225] if it were then come into fashion. These Exposers are notable men, they are as good as Witches, they know all things, and what was done, and what was not[226] done equally. In earnest, he has made us as formal a story of all Philip said, and the Treasurer believ'd, as if he had sat all the time in the Coach-boot;[227] and knows how long the discourse lasted, as well, as if he had set his Watch when they began, and look'd upon it just as the Spirit caught up Philip to Azotus. But (suppose, for the Exposers sake, that the Treasurer[228] were in a Coach discourse, and, for all the rumbling, so distinctly and thorowly, in so short a time too, if it had been, which is the uttermost, a days passage Catechumeniz'd)[229] it came to this short point[230] between them: The Treasurer desires to be Baptized, Philip replys; *If thou believest with all thine Heart thou mayst;* which can never signifie otherwise then with all the Intention of our Spirit, as when we are said to love God with all our Heart: The Treasurer replys, and that's all, *I believe that Jesus Christ* [24] *is the Son of God.* Now it is worth the Readers observation, that out of a desire of Cavilling, and the luxury the Exposer takes in it, he has quite forgot the matter he brought in Controversie. For the Dispute is concerning new Creeds, imposed beyond clear Scripture: the Authors Arguments and Proofs tended wholly thither; and to that purpose he urged this passage of Philip, to prove that God considers both, but rather the Quality, than Quantity of our Faith. The Exposer amuses himself and us, to tell what Philip preach'd to the Treasurer, but never minds that, let that have been as it will, and the Eunuch have believ'd all that this man can imagine, yet all the Creed demanded, and all that he professes, is no more than those formal words, believed with all his heart. *I believe that Jesus Christ is the Son of God:* Wherein the Author has clearly carried, and the

[224] Geneva: the site of Calvin's theocracy.

[225] *ad . . . Clericam* also: not only into the communion of the laiety, but of the clergy also. Also in italics in A,B.

[226] not A] no not B.

[227] Coach-boot Ed. as in Thompson's amendment] A,B: Coock-boot: a low outside compartment before or behind the body of a coach.

[228] A and B have an extra close parenthesis here.

[229] Catechumeniz'd: prepared for baptism by education.

[230] point Ed.] Print A; print B.

Exposer thus far lost the Question. And indeed Antiochus, you are much too blame to have put the Romans to all this trouble, to no purpose.[231] But anything to stuff out the Dimensions of a Book, that no man may imagine he could have said so little, in so much (which is the new way of Compendiousness found out by the Exposer) whereas he might have known, that not God only but even men always do respect the Quality of any thing, of a Book, rather than the Quantity. One Remark I must make more, before I take leave of this page; how, having thus liberally instructed both Philip and the Treasurer, he immediately chops in *p. 5*.

> *Now this Author may see what Use and Need*
> *There was of the Constantinopolitan Creed*[232]

That puts in one Baptisme for the Remission of Sins. I read it over and over, for there was something in it very surprizing, besides the Elegancy of the Verses. For the Now in that place is a word of Immediate Inference, as if it appeared necessarily, from what last preceded, that he had notably foil'd the Author in some Arguments or other; and therefore exulted over him. To any man of common sense it can signifie neither more nor less, then that (whereas I upon prospect of this spoke merrily of the Athanasian Creed, Noel's and the Assemblies Catechism, &c. wherein Philip instructed the Treasurer) the Exposer means in good earnest (if men mean what they say) that Philip having studied the Constantinopolitan Creed himself very exactly, explain'd every Article of it thorowly to the Eunuch, and in especial manner that of Baptism for the Remission of Sins: Which happening to have been so many hundred years before that Council was in being,[233] must needs be an extraordinary Civility in Philip, and which he would scarce have done, but for the particular satisfaction of so great a Personage, that had the whole manage of the Revenue of the Queen of Ethiopia. I am sure it is more than our Church will vouchsafe in Baptism, either of Infants, or those of riper years, with their God-fathers, but fobbs [25] them off[234] with the plain Apostles Creed: and truly the easier the better, if *after that*, and by

---

[231] Antiochus . . . to no purpose: i.e., forcing Rome to send an army to order him out of Egypt.

[232] Because "need" rhymes with "creed," Marvell pretends that Turner intentionally created a couplet within an ordinary sentence.

[233] The council of Constantinople, convened in 360, was notorious for adding a new chase to the creed, "I believe in one baptism for the remission of sins."

[234] off B] of A.

powring water upon them, these persons be without any more ado (*as the Priest,* according to our Rubrick, *shall then say*) Regenerate.

To as little purpose doth he trouble in this same 5.p. another Scripture, the first of John 4.2. *Every Spirit that confesses that Jesus Christ is come in the Flesh, is of God*: Which the Author urges in confirmation of what he said before concerning the intention of Faith. But, saith the Exposer, *Will a Mahumetan, or a Socinian Confession of Faith suffice?* This is I trow what they call reducing a man *ad Absurdum,*[235] and I doubt he has hamper'd the Author mischievously. No, it will not suffice in the Mahumetan or Socinian Interpretation: but a Confession according to the true sense of this, and the clear express words of Scripture in other places will do it; especially if Saint[236] John, as most men are of Opinion, writ his own Gospel. Nay, though the Exposer contends against this place, he admits another concerning Peter, that is not much more pregnant. *All the few Primary Fundamentals of Christianity,* saith he, *were vertually contained in S.*[237] *Peters short Confession of Faith,* Thou art Christ the Son of the Living God: *for which Confession he was blest, and upon which Faith Christ declared that he would build His Church as upon a Rock.*[238] In conclusion, I see Antiochus has *ex mero motu & certa scientia,*[239] and Prince-like[240] Generosity, given us the Question: For I would not suspect that he hath hunted it so long till he lost it, or let it go of necessity, because he could hold it no longer. For the Extension as well as Intention of Peter's Faith, was terminated in these few words. For it is no irreverence to take notice how plain the Apostles were under that Dispensation. The same John, the Apostle and Evangelist, *C.*14.*V.*26 and in the following Chapters, shows how little it was, and in how narrow a compass, that they knew and believed, and yet that sufficed. Insomuch that where, *C.*16.*V.*17. our Saviour promises the Holy Ghost to instruct them further, he saith only, *It is expedient for you that I go away, for if I go not away, the Comforter will not come to you.* He saith not it is necessary. For that Measure of true Belief would have sufficed for their own Salvation, but there was a larger knowledge requisite for the future work of

---

[235] *ad Absurdum:* to the point of absurdity. The *reductio ad absurdum* was a conventional rhetorical strategy, and Marvell himself uses it with zest.

[236] Saint B] St. A.

[237] S. B] St. A.

[238] Matthew 16:16–19.

[239] *ex mero motu & certa scientia:* of his own free will and certain knowledge.

[240] Prince-like B] Prince----like A; Grosart retained this sign of ellipsis, as "possibly containing a contemporary allusion and hit" (p. 427).

their Apostleship: In how many of them, and St. Peter himself as much as any, were there such *Ignorances:* I humbly use the word, in matters of Faith, that our Saviour could not but take notice of it and reprove them! As for Peter, when our Saviour was so near his Death as to be already betray'd, yet he, *Upon whose Faith he built his Church, as on a Rock,* knew not the effect of his Passion, but was ready with his Sword, against Christ's Command and Example, to have interrupted the Redemption of Mankind. And this short Confession, *in which all the Fundamentals were vertually contained* (as the Exposer here teacheth us, and so [26] hath reduced himself to that *little Grain of Faith,* against which he contends with the Author) was upon occasion of our Saviours Question, when Peter doubtless did his best to answer his Lord and Master, and told him all he knew. For that similitude, taken from so small a Grain by our Saviour, did equal the proportion of Faith then attainable and requisite. And as in a Seed, the very Plain[241] and Upright of the Plant is indiscernably express'd, though it be not branch'd out to the Eye, as when it germinates, spreads, blossoms, and bears Fruit; so was the Christian Faith seminally straitned in that vertual sincerity, vital point, and central vigour of believing with all the heart, that Jesus Christ was come in the Flesh, and was the Son of the Living God. And would men even now believe that one thing thorowly, they would be better Christians, than under all their Creeds they generally are both in Doctrine and Practice. But that Gradual Revelation, which after his Death and Resurrection shined forth in the Holy Ghost, must now determine us again within the Bounds of that Saving Ignorance by Belief according to the Scriptures, until the last and full Manifestation. And the Intention of this Faith now also, as it hath been explain'd by the Inspiration of the Holy Spirit in the Sacred Writers, is sufficient for Salvation, without the Chicanrey and[242] Conveyancing[243] of Humane Extensions. And the Controverter himself hath, if not by his own Confession, yet by his own Argument all along hitherto proved it.

In the 6. p. he saith, that where the Author charges some with introducing many and new Articles of faith, *He hopes he does not mean all our Thirty Nine Articles.* If he hopes so, why doth he raise the suspicion, for which indeed there is no cause imaginable, but for the Exposers own disingenuity;

---

[241] Plain: i.e., plan.

[242] Chicanrey and A] omitted B; chicanery means legal trickery.

[243] Conveyancing: cunning management or contrivance. Possibly B's omission of "Chicanrey" was to avoid tautology.

the Author appearing thorow his whole Book a true Subscriber to them, without that Latitude of Equivocation which some others use, or else they would not publish those Doctrines they do, and be capable nevertheless of Ecclesiastical Places? But here, as though any man had meddled with those Articles, he explicates his Learning out of Bishop Lany²⁴⁴ and of the *Communio Laica,* which is but his harping upon one string, and his usual *Scanning* on his fingers. For the Author having named *many and new Articles of faith,* the Exposer revolves over in his mind *Articles, Articles of*—and, the word not being very pregnant, he hits at last upon *the Thirty Nine Articles of the Church of England:* which yet the Exposer saith himself, *are Articles of Peace and Consent, not of Faith and Communion.* Why then does he bring them by Head and Shoulders, when the Author he knows was only upon Articles of Faith? He might as well have said *the Lords* of the *Articles.*²⁴⁵ But this, he saith, *is one, as he takes it, of our Churches greatest Ecclesiastical Policies, that she admits the many in thousands and hundred thousands, without any Subscription,*²⁴⁶ ad Communionen Laicam. Truly she [27] is very civil, and we are an hundred thousand times obliged to her. But I know not whether she will take it well of him, that he, not being content with so good an Office as that of her *Exposer,* should pretend to be her *Ecclesiastical Politian,* over another mans head²⁴⁷ that is fitter for both, and not expect the Reversion.²⁴⁸ And she cannot but be offended, that he should thus call her Fool by craft, assigning that for *her greatest Ecclesiastical Policy,* when to have done otherwise, would have been the greatest impertinence²⁴⁹ and folly. But who are these *the many,* whom she so graciously receives *[ad] Communionem Laicam* without subscription? Truly all of us whom she trusts not *with Teaching others, or with University Degrees.* The whole Body of the Laity (there again is another name for us, for we can scarce speak without affronting ourselves with some contemptuous name or other, that they (forsooth the Clergy) have affixed to us.)

²⁴⁴ Lany Ed.] Lauy A,B; Benjamin Laney, bishop of Ely from 1663 to 1674, was cited by Turner, p. 6.
²⁴⁵ the *Lords* of the *Articles:* The point is unclear. Possibly Marvell alludes to the fact that *Lord* (with its aristocratic valence) was the word selected for *God* by those who designed the articles.
²⁴⁶ *Subscription:* formally subscribing to articles of belief. The clergy were required to take an oath that they accepted the Thirty-Nine Articles; the laity were not.
²⁴⁷ Another obvious reference to Samuel Parker.
²⁴⁸ Reversion: succeeding to an office.
²⁴⁹ impertinence Ed.] Impertence A; impertinent B.

Nos Numerus sumus, the many, *et fruges consumere nati.*[250]
Even his Majesty too, God bless him, is one of the *many,* and she asks no
Subscription of him neither, although I believe he *has taken his degree in the
University.*[251] Well, we must be content to do as we may: we are *the many,*
and you are *the few,* and make your best of it. But now, though I am none of
you, yet I can tell you a greater *Ecclesiastical Policy,* than all this you have
been talking of. It is a hard word, and though it be but one Syllable, I
cannot well remember it; but by good luck it was burnt by the hand of the
Hangman, about that time that *the Naked Truth* was Printed.[252] And had
that *Policy* succeeded, *the many* must have taken not only all the *Thirty Nine
Articles,* but all the Ecclesiastical Errours and Incroachments that escaped
notice, all in the Mass[253] at once, as if they had been Articles of Faith,
Infallible, Unalterable; but the State of the Kingdom had been apparently
changed in the very Fundamentals: For *a Few* of the *Few,* for above these
forty years, have been carrying on a constant Conspiracy to turn all *Upside-
down* in the Government of the Nation:[254] but God in his mercy hath
always hitherto, and will, I hope, for ever frustrate all such Counsels.

In his 7. p. it is that he saith, *the Author in his 4. p. implicitly condemns the
whole Catholick Church, both East and West, for being so presumptuous in her
Definitions.* However if he does it but implicitly, the Exposer might have
been so Ingenuous or Prudent, as not to have explicated it further, but
conceal'd it, least it might do more harm, but at least not to have heighten'd
it so; *the whole Catholick Church,* and not only so, but, *the whole Catholick
Church, both in the East and the West too* (why did he not add in the North

---

[250] *Nos Numerus sumus et fruges consumere nati:* Horace, *Epistles,* 1.2.27: "We are but
ciphers, born to consume earth's fruits."

[251] Cf. Turner, p. 6: "All whom [the Church] recommends to the world with University Degrees, shall subscribe to these Articles as their own Opinions." How Charles II
falls into this category is unclear.

[252] the only work ordered to be burned by the hangman during 1675 concerned the
notorious *Letter from a Person of Quality to his Friend in the Country,* now attributed to
Shaftesbury. On November 9, Marvell wrote to Hull, "There being a late printed book
containing a narrative of the Test carryed on in the Lords house last session, they
yesterday voted it a Libell: and to be burnt by the hands of the Hangman & to inquire
out the Printer and Author" (*P&L,* 2:172). But in the hard word of one syllable Marvell
seems to allude to the Test itself.

[253] Mass: perhaps a punning reference to the Catholic ceremony.

[254] This conspiracy theory will be the governing premise of the *Account of the Growth
of Popery and Arbitrary Government.*

and South too?) *for being so presumptuous;* a term far beyond, and contrary to the Modesty and Deference[255] of the Authors expressions. But this is the Art and Duty of Exposing; Here it is that he brandishes the whole Dint[256] of his Disputative Faculty; and if it be not the [28] most Rational, I dare say (and yet I should have some difficulty to perswade men so) that it is the most foolish passage in the whole Pamphlet. It is impossible to clear the Dispute but by transcribing their own words. In the mean time therefore I heartily recommend myself to the Readers patience. The Author pursuing his point, how unsafe and unreasonable it is to impose new Articles of Faith drawn by humane Inferences beyond the clear Scripture expressions; instanceth in several of the prime and most necessary Principles of the Trinity, especially that of the Holy Ghost. *Are they not things,* saith he, *far above the highest Reason, and sharpest Understanding that ever man had? Yet we believe them, because God, who cannot lye, hath declared them. Is it not then a strange thing for any man to take upon him to declare one title[257] more of them than God hath declared? seeing we understand not what is declared, I mean we have no comprehensive knowledge of the matter declared, but only a believing knowledge?*[258] To which the Exposer will have it, that if the Author be here bound up to his own words, (and 'tis good reason he should) he hath said, that *we understand not that the matter is declared;* and moreover he saith, that *he is sure he has done him no wrong, in fixing this meaning to the Authors words.* No, *it is no wrong,* it seems then, to say that to understand *That,* and to comprehend *What,* is the same thing. As for example, (if our ignorance may be allowed in things so infinitely above us, to allude to things as far below us) because I understand *That* the Exposer here speaks Non-sense; I must therefore be able to comprehend *What* is the meaning of his Non sense, and be capable to raise a Rational Deduction from it. I am sure I do the Exposer right in this Inference, and shou'd be glad he only would therefore wear it for my sake, for it will fit none but him 'twas made for. But let us come down to the particular; *The Scripture,* said the Author, *plainly tells, that the Holy Ghost proceeds from the Father, and that is he sent also by the Father; that he is sent also by the Son: but whether he proceeds from the Son, or by the Son, the Scripture is silent. I grant that by Rational Deduction, and humane way of Argument, 'tis probable that the Holy Ghost proceeds from the*

---

[255] Deference A] Difference B.
[256] Dint: the sound, force, or effect of a stroke.
[257] title: tittle.
[258] Croft, p. 4.

Son, as from the Father. But we understand not What *the Procession or Mission of the Holy Ghost is, and therefore we cannot prove they are both one. And therefore to determine it, or any such Divine and high Mysteries by Humane Deductions, in Humane words, to be imposed and believed with Divine faith, is dangerous.*[259] And much more the Author adds demonstratively to the same purpose; but the Exposer Culls out,[260] by the duty of his Place, what may best serve for his, neither will that do the turn, unless he also pervert it. Here again is the *That* and the *What* the same thing: Is it the same thing to say or understand *That* the Holy Ghost is sent by the Son (which is declared in Scripture) and to understand and comprehend *What* the nature of that Mission is, or *What*[261] the Nature of Procession, that a man may [29] safely say, that he proceeds from or by the Son, as from the Father (which is not declared in Scripture, but by Humane Deduction) and exact the Divine Belief thereof under Eternal and Temporal Penalties? *Yet this is the Exposers Logick.* And away he goes with it, as if the world (as this inference is) were all his own, and knocks all on the head with a killing Instance; which that I may still open more visibly to the Readers, I must beg pardon that I am necessitated to repeat over again their own words sometimes upon occasion. The Exposer saith, *But he means we have no comprehensive knowledge. His meaning is good and true, but his Inference is stark naught, if he means therefore we understand not at all that this or that is declared.*[262] But the Author neither says nor means any such thing, and the Exposer does him, notwithstanding his averment[263] to the contrary, the most manifest wrong imaginable: for as much as he would not only fix a false meaning upon the Authors words which I first mentioned in the beginning, but upon these other words also; which contrary to their plain signification, he produces for proof against him. They are by the Exposers own relation, *If then our Reason understand not what is declared* (which is the very Equipollent[264] of what the Author had said, that we have no comprehensive knowledge of the matter declared) *how can we by reason make any deduction, by way of Argument, from that which we understand not?* No more. From whence it is

---

[259] Croft, p. 4. The issue of what was called "double Procession," whether the Holy Ghost proceeded only from the Father or also from the Son (as in the clause *filioque*) was a central issue in western trinitarianism in its battles against Arianism.

[260] Culls out: selects.

[261] *What* E] What A,B

[262] Turner, p. 7.

[263] averment: assertion.

[264] Equipollent: exact equivalent.

evident from that virtual repetition and natural reflection that every Conclusion hath of and upon its Premises, that the full sense of the words must
be—*from that which we understand not, Comprehensive.*[265] And yet he saith
that he does him no wrong; he is sure he does not in affixing this meaning
unto those words. And proceeds, *Is it even so? Then let us put the case with
reverence, that Almighty God who assuming I suppose the shape of an Angel,
treated with Abraham face to face, as a man doth with his friend; should for once
have spoken in the same manner to Arrius*[266] *or Socinus,*[267] *and made this one
Declaration, that the Catholick Churches Doctrine of the Trinity was true, and
his false: then I demand, would not this have been demonstration enough of the
Faith which we call Catholick, either to Socinus or Arrius? And yet all these
contradictory Arguments, which either of them had once fancied so insolvable,*[268]
*supposing them not answered in particular, would remain against it, and stand
as they did before any such declaration, and yet all this without giving him any
comprehensive knowledge.*[269] This instance is made in Confutation of his
own false supposition, that the Authors words, *if then our reason understand
not with comprehensive knowledge what is declared, how can we then make any
deduction, by way of Arguments, from that which we understand not,* did in
their true meaning signifie, how can we by Reason make any deduction, by
way of Argument, from that which *we understand not to have been declared,*
or, that I may put it in the furthest I can imaginable, [30] to the Exposers
purpose or service, *how can we by reason understand that it is declared,* which
is to impose a most ridiculous and impossible sense upon the Authors plain

[265] In this difficult passage, Marvell attempts to clarify Croft's meaning by continuing his sentence; unfortunately, the results do not clarify. He seems to have meant: "the
full sense of the words must be: how can we by reason deduce any comprehensive [i.e.,
full] knowledge from that of which we do not fully understand the first principles?"

[266] Arrius: Arius (c. 256–336), mid-third-century heresiarch, began his controversy
over the Trinity with his rival Alexander in 318. His heresy was a form of subordination-
ism; he denied the eternity and essential divinity of Christ. Excommunicated by the
Council of Nicaea, he was banished by Constantine but was about to be received back
into full communion in 336 when he died suddenly of a violent diarrhea, interpreted by
his enemies as God's judgment, by his friends as poison.

[267] *Socinus:* Faustus Sozzino (1539–1604), a rationalist critic of Christianity, who
taught that Christ differed from other men only in his special affinity for relationship
with God. He opposed the doctrine of the two natures of Christ. His doctrines were
translated into Latin, German, Dutch, and English, and had special influence in Poland, where they became embodied in the Racovian catechism.

[268] insolvable Ed.] insolable A,B.

[269] Turner, p. 7.

words; for if we neither understand *That* nor *What,* there is an end of all understanding. Yet admitting here, says the Exposer, I have stated you a case which proves the contrary; for here Arrius or Socinus have *no comprehensive knowledge of what is declared:* and *yet they understand that it is declared:* and doubtless the Author would say so too, without ever meaning the contrary; yea, and that this Revelation would have been *demonstrative*[270] *enough of that Faith, which we call Catholick.* But what would become of *their former Contradictory Arguments,* which the Exposer saith, *would stand as they did before,* and *remain against it.* I cannot vouch for the Author, that he would be of the same opinion. For I cannot comprehend, though God had not answered those Arguments of theirs in particular, as the Exposer puts it, that those Arguments would or could remain against it, and stand as they did before any such Declaration, to Arrius and Socinus, after they had received a sufficient Demonstration from Gods own mouth by new Revelation. They would indeed remain against it, and stand as they did before to Mr. Sherlock.[271] But when I have thus given the humorous Exposer his own will and swing in every thing, yet this superlunary[272] instance does not serve in the least to confirm his Argument that he makes against the Authors words, after his transforming them; for here Arrius and Socinus only bring their sense of hearing, and having heard this from God, do not by Reason make any *deduction by way of Argument,* but by a believing knowledge do only assent to this, second further Revelation: Nor can they then from this second Revelation make any third step of Argument to extend it beyond its own tenour, without incurring the Authors just and wise Argument again, that *seeing our Reason understands not what is declared, I mean we have no comprehensive knowledge of this Doctrine of Trinity;* (which the Exposer supposes to be declared) *how can we by Reason make any deduction, by way of Argument, from that which we understand not,* to wit, *not comprehensively?* As I have abundantly cleared. But this instance was at first extinguished, when I shewed in the beginning, that he did impertinently traduce the Authors words, and forge his meaning.

In the mean time, though he saith, *put the case with Reverence,* when the case so put cannot admit it, I cannot but at last reflect on the Exposers unpardonable indiscretion, in this more than absurd and monstrous

---

[270] demonstrative B] demonstration A.

[271] Mr. Sherlock: William Sherlock, the "plagiary" of Socinian doctrines. See n. 174 above.

[272] superlunary: over the moon.

Representation of God Almighty, assuming the shape of an Angel, as he saith he treated with Abraham face to face, as a man doth with his Friend, to discourse with Arrius and Socinus. These are small escapes with which he aptly introduces such an Inference[273] and Conference, *that he treated our father*[274] *Abraham face to face, as a man doth with his Friend:* [31] for it is true Abraham is stiled the Friend of God, and that God spoke to him; but it is never said in Scripture that God did *Treat,*[275] that is a word of Court, not of Scripture: No nor that *God spake to him face to face.* But it is said in Scripture only of Moses, *Exod.* 33.11. *The Lord spake to him face to face, as a man speaketh unto his Friend.* But that was a priviledge peculiar to Moses. Numbers 12.5. *And the Lord came down in a Pillar of Cloud, and stood in the door of the Tabernacle of the Congregation, and called Aaron and Miriam, and they both came forth, and he said, hear now my words if there be a Prophet among you, I the Lord will make my self known to him in a Vision, and will speak unto him in a Dream: my servant Moses is not so who is faithful in all my House, with him will I speak mouth to mouth, even apparently and not in dark speeches, and the similitude of the Lord shall he behold, wherefore then were not you afraid to speak against my servant Moses?* (the Exposer is not afraid to do him manifest injury) for Deut. 34.10. *And there arose not in Israel a prophet like unto Moses, whom the Lord knew face to face, &c.* And much more might be said of this matter, were the man capable of it: But I perceive he neither reads nor understands Scripture, and one *Divine Criticisme* is stock enough it seems to set up an Exposer. Neither is it so notorious an errour that he saith God assumed the shape of an Angel to treat with him. I would be glad to know of the Exposer, seeing he is so Cherubick, what is the shape of an Angel? Some humane Criticks have told me that it was the similitude of a Calf.[276] But Gods appearing in a shape to Abraham, when he treated with him face to face was in the shape of a man. Gen. 18.1. *The Lord appeared to him in the plain of Mamre*[277] *as he sate in the Tent door, and so three men stood by him, &c.* These are easie slips and he that stumbles and falls not, gains a step. Yet for one as he mocks the Author, *p.* 2. *That appears as one drop'd*

[273] Inference B] interview A; both readings have merit.

[274] father Ed.] 4th A, fourth B.

[275] Treat: negotiate.

[276] The angel in the shape of a calf: possibly a reference to the second of the four winged creatures round the throne in Revelations 4:7; but the joke is unclear.

[277] Mamre A] Mimre B.

down from Heaven, vouching himself a Son of the Church of England, teaching as one having Authority, like a Father, to trip in this manner, is something indecent. But to bring God in to so little a purpose, contrary to all rules, that I have seen one with a better grace brought down by a Machine,[278] to treat with Arrius and Socinus, no other Company, those who have contended against the Son of God and his Holy Spirit, whose Opinions have been the Pest of the Clergy for so many Ages, to have them now at last brought in as Privado's[279] to the Mysteries of Heaven, and the Trinity; what Divine in his Wits but would rather have lost an Argument! What will the Gentleman I last named[280] say, to see such a reconciliation, to behold Arrius and Socinus in so close *Communion with God,* as to be admitted even to single Revelation: He cannot then avoid thinking, what he lately Printed, and now with more Reason: *That God is all Love and Patience when he has taken his fill of Revenge, as others use to say the Devil is good when he is pleased.*[281] What a shame it is to have men like the Exposer, who are [32] dedicated to the service of the Church, and who ought, as in the place quoted by the Author in the present Argument, they of all other *to hold fast the form of sound Words*[282] thus by their rash levity administer so much occasion upon the most revered Subject, that one can scarce answer them in their own Dialect without seeming, though never so averse, to border upon their Profaneness. But these[283] are the Divines in Mode, who, being by their Dignities and Preferments plump'd up beyond Humane Proportion, do whether for their Pride or Ignorance, neither understand themselves, nor others, (men of Nonsense) much less do they[284] understand to speak of God, which ought to be their study, with any tolerable *Decorum.* These are the great Animadverters of the Times, the Church-respondents in the Pew, Men that seem to be Members only of Chelsey Colledge,[285] nothing but broken Windows,

[278] Machine A] Machin B; as in the *deus ex machina* produced in court masques.

[279] Privado's: i.e., privadoes, intimate companions or confidants.

[280] named A] name B; i.e., William Sherlock.

[281] Sherlock, *A Discourse concerning the knowledge of Jesus Christ* (London, 1674), p. 47; though Marvell quoted this accurately from Sherlock, Sherlock was deliberately distorting statements in John Owen's *Communion with God the Father, Son and Holy Ghost* (London, 1674), p. 95.

[282] 2 Timothy 1:13; the italicization of this phrase is editorial.

[283] these A,B] those A variant.

[284] understand themselves . . . do they: not in A variant.

[285] Chelsey Colledge: In 1609 James I introduced an act for the construction of

bare Walls, and rotten Timber. They with a few Villanous words, and a seared Reason, are the only Answerers of good and serious Books: but then they think a Book to be sure fully answered, when, as the Exposer has by an *Humane Criticisme,* they have writ or scribled[286] the same number of Pages. For the Authors Book of the *Naked Truth,* chancing to be of sixty six pages, the Exposer has not bated him an Ace,[287] but payed him exactly, though not in as good Billet,[288] yet in as many Notches.[289] This being done, then the Exposer ubiquits himself,[290] peeping at the Key-holes, or picking the Locks of the Bed chambers of all the Great Ministers; and though they be reading Papers of State, or at the Stool more seasonably[291] obtrudes his Pamphlet. Next he sends it by an express to his friends at the Universities, but especially to his own Colledge,[292] and can scarce refrain from recommending it to the Tutors to instruct their Pupils, reading it to them in lieu of other[293] Lectures. But they are lay'd in for Provision by the Manciple[294] and Butler, and that Quarter few escape without being sconc'd[295] for an Animadversion. The Country Cathedrals learn it latest, and arrive by slower degrees to their understanding, by the Carrier. It grows a business of

---

Chelsea College. According to Thomas Fuller, "it was intended to be a spiritual garrison, with a magazine of all books for that purpose, where learned divines should study and write in maintenance of all controversies against the papists." *The Church History of Britain,* ed. J. S. Brewer (Oxford, 1845), 5:387. James donated the land but not the funds for construction, and only one wing was ever built. Fuller, pp. 394–96, details why the project foundered. In 1654 the building was taken for the nation under Cromwell and used as a prison. In 1669 the site was given by Charles II to the Royal Society for agricultural research.

[286] have writ or scribled A,B] write or scribe AV

[287] To bate an ace was to give a competitor some start or advantage to make the race more equal.

[288] Billet: paper.

[289] Notches: a way of marking lengths or keeping score: cf. Francis Quarles, *The Shepheards Oracles* (London, 1644), Eclogue 8, p. 97, where the Nonconformist speaker, Anarchus, in dialogue with Canonicus, boasts, "We cut out doctrines, and from notch to notch / We fit our holy Stuffe."

[290] ubiquits himself: presents himself everywhere.

[291] at the Stool more seasonably: i.e., his pamphlet will be more useful to ministers on the toilet.

[292] Turner was master of St. John's College, Cambridge.

[293] other A,B] of their AV.

[294] Manciple: an officer who purchases provisions for a college or Inn of Court.

[295] sconc'd: fined by university officials for a breach of discipline.

Chapter,[296] and they admire it in body as a profound Book of Theology. Those of 'em that can confide in one another, discourse it over in private, and then 'tis odds;[297] but, before the Laity get notice of it, they first hear it Preach'd over by him whose turn it is next Sunday in the Minister;[298] the rest conceal the Fraud for the Reputation of the Diocess. After the Book is grown common, the Plagiary[299] wonders how, but that proportionable Wits jump together, the Exposer could hit so right upon his Notions.[300] But if the Dean foresee that 'tis a very vendible Book, he you may imagine forestalls the Market, and sends up for a whole Dicker[301] of 'em to retail at his best[302] advantage. All this while the little Emissaries here in Town are not idle, but hawk about from London to Westminster with their Britches stiff with the Copies,[303] and will sell them to any one for Commendation. Nor do they[304] grudge [33] this drudgery out of the hope and vision that they themselves also may, at some happy hour or other, be received into the Band of Answerers, and merit the same Applause and Advancement. But if they found it so hard a task as I do this, sure they would be better advised. 'Tis a great pain to Answer, even an Animadverter; they are much happier of the two, 'tis better by far Preaching, and a Sermon is soon Curried over.[305] Yet sometimes it happens, the Printing of a Sermon is toilsome afterwards, and hazardous: for even one that was preached before his Majesty, and by his Special Command to be Printed, is it seems making over again, there having been sure some Errour in the *Fonte*,[306] and has lay'd several Moneths in disobedience.[307] But when it shall come out new vamp'd

[296] Chapter: the body of canons of a collegiate or cathedral church, presided over by the dean.

[297] 'tis odds: wagers are laid, probably as to the authorship of the book and its likely reception.

[298] Minister: a church, especially collegiate or cathedral.

[299]the Plagiary: any person who borrows Turner's notions, for his own sermon or otherwise.

[300] Notions A,B] Motions AV.

[301] Dicker: a bundle of ten; or, casually, a large number.

[302] best A,B] last AV.

[303] stiff with the Copies A,B] stuft with the Copyes AV.

[304] they A,B] the AV.

[305] Curried over: groomed (as of a horse) or decked out smartly.

[306] *Fonte:* i.e., press font, a complete set of type of the same body and face.

[307] disobedience B] disobdience A,AV. This is surely a reference to Bishop Gunning's sermon of February 18, 1676, which Turner, Marvell, and Croft all expected would have been printed by now. See introduction, p. 5.

and refitted, it will be a Question worthy the Schools, whether it be the same Sermon, and whether he has not prevaricated against his Majesties Special Command, and *Sinn'd on,* by Printing without a License. Yet I rather expect that after all, it will incur the same Fate with that Memorable Sermon Preached before the House of Commons, at their receiving the Sacrament upon the first Opening of the Parliament; which for some dangerous Opinions there vented, was so far from ever coming forth, that one might sooner have obtain'd his Majesties Special Command against ever Printing it.[308] But to return to the Exposer, who by this impertinence has forced an occasion upon me to reflect on some *Few* who are guilty of the same, and may thank him for the favour. May not, with more reason, *p.* 1. than he saith it of the Author, *the Church justly complain of him for thrusting out such crude indigested matter, without communicating these Conceptions of his to some that would have shewed him the weak and blind sides of them?* I profess after those passages of his that I have already taken notice of, and this Egregious[309] one the last, wherein by so few lines he hath so amply molested the Judicious Reader, I do not think I owe him the patience to consider what remains with the same exactness, everything that he adds forthwith growing methodically slighter and worse, as it hastens to the Center of Levity, the Conclusion of his Pamphlet. Yet something I will reply all along, with more Justice than he practises towards the Author; for whereas he picks out here and there what he thinks tenderest in him to tire upon,[310] and render it by his affected misrepresentation obnoxious, but shuts his eyes, as not being able to endure the Resplendence of those evident Truths which he delivers with great Demonstration; I shall in the Exposer only observe and deal with what seems the least imperinent: Only I may not perhaps think him worth the transcribing so punctually as I have done hitherto, but for brevity more often refer to his own Pages.

Therefore be pleased to look on his *p.* 7. where, relating to what the Author had said *p.* 4. of the Procession of the Holy Ghost, wherein the [34] Greek Creed and ours differ, he muffles it all up with saying that *yet this*

---

[308] This was probably the sermon preached by Edward Reynolds to the Commons on Wednesday, April 25, 1660, at St. Margaret's, Westminister, for which the House officially thanked him and requested him "to print the same" (*JHC* 1660, p. 1), but which was never in fact printed.

[309] Egregious: outstanding for some quality, usually negative.

[310] tire upon: a metaphor from hawking: to pull on or tear apart with the beak.

breaks not Communion between us, the difference arising only from the Inadequation[311] of Languages.[312] Which is a Mathematical and more Civil way, either of owning his Ignorance in so weighty a point, or confessing that he cannot answer what the Author has[313] said upon it. If by reason of the *Inadequation of Lanugages,* a mystery so inexplicable could not be expressed, why did either our Church or theirs meddle in it beyond the Scripture? There is no *Inadequation between the Languages,* in speaking of it, *Dia* and *Apo,*[314] *a Patre Filioque* and *a Patre per Filium: From the Father and Son, or From the Father by the Son: Proceeding* or *Sending:* But no Language can reach the nature of Procession or Mission, nor to represent to Humane understanding how they can both be the same, or wherein they may differ. He does in this as the Arrian Bishops in their Subscription of the Nicene Creed to Jovianus Socr. 1.3.c.21. which now they said they could do with a good Conscience, understanding *neque vocabulum substantiae apud sanctos Patres ad consuetudinem Graeci Sermonis capi.*[315] 'Tis an happy thing I see to find our Church in good humour, else she might have made more ado about an Article of Faith, as she does about much lesser matters. 'Tis not strange that the Exposer finds no greater difference or distinction between terms so distant, seeing in the last Paragraph above, he was so dull that he understood not *What* is *What.* But he most aptly concludes how *Demosthenes once answered the orator AEschines, who kept much ado about an improper word. The Fortunes of Greece do not depend upon it.*[316] So trivial a thing it seems does the Exposer reckon it, to have improper words obtruded upon Christians in a Creed: without believing of which no man can be saved, and whereupon the Eastern and Western Churches divided with so much

[311] Inadequation: inadequacy.

[312] Turner, p. 7.

[313] has] hath A.

[314] *Dia* and *Apo:* Greek conjunctions, "from" and "by way of."

[315] *neque . . . Sermonis capi:* see Christopherson, 2:101v–102r; Hanmer translates: "the word substance was not used of the holy Fathers in that sense which the Graecians take it in."

[316] The original source of this quotation was Demosthenes, *De Corona,* 232; but Turner (and Marvell) would have known it from Cicero, *De Oratore,* 27: "It is easy, indeed, to criticize some flaming word . . . and to laugh at it when the passion of the moment has cooled. That is why Demosthenes in excusing himself jestingly [*jocatur*] says that the fortunes of Greece [*negat in eos positas fortunas Graeciae*] did not depend on his using this word or that."

concernment. But how proper and ingenious a contrivance was it of the Author[317] (who is the very Cannon of Concinnity)[318] to bring in Demosthenes and AEschines, as being doubtless both of the Greek Church, to decide the matter in Controversy of the Procession or Mission of the Holy Ghost between them and the West. Antiochus, whensoever you take the Pew again, be sure you forget not Demosthenes and AEschines: For it will be to you as good as current Money, which answers all things. The Exposer, though here so gentle, yet, in the very page before this was as dogged, to as good men as the Greeks some of them, the Papists, Lutherans, and Calvinists. *The Author,* he says, *may make as bold with them as he pleases, for we are none of these, I am not bound to make War in their vindication.*[319] But if he should once *Kyrie Eleison,*[320] what would become of us? Good Mother Church of England maintain this humour thorow, carry it on, but above all things make much of this thy Exposer; give him any thing, think nothing too good for him, Happy the Church that hath, and miserable that wants such a Champion! [35]

But I must find some more expeditious way of dealing with him, and walk faster, for really I get cold. The force of all that he saith in the eighth and ninth Pages,[321] is to represent the Author ridiculously and odiously; as if upon his wishing that Constantine had commanded both Parties *Homoousian,* and *Homoiousian,* to acquiess in the very Scripture Expressions, without any addition, whereby he is confident the Arrian heresie had soon expired, he did by consequence cut *Poe-dike*[322] to let in a Flood of all[323] Heresies, upon the Fens of Christianity. But the words with which he cuts the Author down, are: *Why, this was the designe of the Arrians themselves, that which they drove at Court, that silence might be imposed on both Parties.* Well, and 'twas very honestly done of them and modestly, and like Christians, if the Controversie arose, as men think, about the Imposing of a Creed, or Article concerning a Question so fine, in words so gross, which

---

[317] the Author: a slip; Marvell meant the Exposer.

[318] Concinnity: harmony, congruity.

[319] Turner, p. 6.

[320] *Kyrie Eleison* Ed.] *Elieson* A,B: "Lord have mercy"; i.e., the short petition in the liturgies of the Eastern and Western churches, as a response at the beginning of the Mass and the Anglican Communion service.

[321] the eighth and ninth Pages] the 8, and 9. pages A.

[322] *Poe-dike:* the ancient dike or embankment built in Norfolk to keep the fen waters out of Marshland.

[323] all] not in AV; perhaps an improvement.

yet a man must Believe that without Believing it *no man can be Saved;*[324] though no Humane Understanding can comprehend the Subject of the Question, nor the Scripture Expressions, as they conceived, did reach it. There is Field enough for Faith in the Scriptures, without laying out more to it; and to resign their Reason to be silenced in a Question, stirred up by others, that Peace might be established in the Church, was Ingenuity in them: and the contrary proceeding of the Church, was the occasion of many other Heresies that else had never been heard of. But the Exposer had said something, if he could have divined that they would have used this silencing the Dispute[325] by Constantine as the Arminians[326] (so they were at that time called) did the same in the Reign of his late Majesty, who procuring a Command from him to Prohibit all Writing or Preaching about those points, having thereby Gagged their Adversaries, did let the Press and the Pulpit loose more than ever to propagate their own Doctrines. That which the Exposer drops in the Ardour of this argument, p. 9. *How many terms in the Athanasian Creed, which to seek for in the Apostles Creed, or in the whole Bible, were to as much purpose as it was for the old affected Ciceronian in Erasmus, to labour and toil his Brains to turn that Creed into Ciceronian Latine.*[327] *Yet these are the terms in which the Catholick Church thought she spoke safely in these Divine matters;* is,[328] *totidem verbis,*[329] either to beg the Question, or make a Formal Resignation of it. And our Church (howsoever else he may have obliged her) has reason to resent this Indiscretion. Why was she herself so indiscreet, to admit such a Blab into her Secresies? How if no man else ought to have known it? It is an ill matter to

---

[324] without . . . *Saved:* from the postscript to the Athanasian Creed.

[325] Dispute] disputes A.

[326] Arminians: Marvell refers to the high-church clergy Robert Sibthorpe, Roger Manwaring, and Richard Montague, for example, against whom he had complained in *RT,* pp. 132–35, as contributing to the civil war by their absolutist doctrines. For discussions of Caroline Arminianism, see Nicholas Tyacke, *Anti-Calvinists: The Rise of English Arminianism c. 1590–1640* (Oxford, 1987); and its partial rebuttal by Anthony Milton, *Catholic and Reformed: The Roman and Protestant Churches in English Protestant Thought, 1600–1640* (Cambridge, 1995).

[327] Erasmus Desiderius (1469?–1536), the most famous classical scholar of his day. In his collected letters, published as *Opus Epistolarum* (Basle, 1558), book 21, pp. 792–93, a letter to Franciscus Cigalinus, on the difficulties of translating the Greek scriptures into Latin, contains the name of Athanasius in a different context.

[328] is Ed.] *is* A,B.

[329] *totidem verbis:* in so many words.

put such things in mens minds, who otherwise perhaps would never have thought of it. 'Tis enough to turn a man's Stomach that is not in strong health, not only against the Athanasian Creed, but against all others for its sake. He saith *p.* 8. scoffingly, that the Author is one of those whom St. Paul forbids *to be admitted to* [36] *any doubtful Disputations:*[330] But let the Exposer see whether it be not himself rather that is there spoken of. And withal that he make some more proper use of the place, which he warily cites not, I recommend it to him in order to his future dispute about Ceremonies:[331] 'Tis the 14. Rom. v.7, where St. Paul calls him that contends for them[332] the Weak Brother, *Weak in the Faith;* and such therefore the Apostle excludes from doubtful Disputations, so that one gone so far in Ceremony as the Exposer, had no License from him to Print Animadversions.

As to what he patches in *pag.* 10.[333] upon the matter of School-Divinity, as if the Author poured contempt upon the Fathers; I refer it to the Animadversions on the Chapter about Preaching; and should I forget, I desire him to put me in mind of it. And *page* 11, and 12. where the Author having in his 2, and 3. *p* said that, *None can force another to believe, no more than to read where the Candle does not give clear light,* and more very significantly to that purpose; the Exposer flying giddily about it, burns his wings with the very similitude of a Candle. Sure if a man went out by night on Tramelling[334] or Batfowling, or Proctoring,[335] he might catch these Exposers by Dozens. But the force of this[336] Argument is *p.* 13. Whereas the Author sayes, you can force no mans sight or his Faith,[337] he replies, *If it be not in any mans power to discern Fundamental Truths, (of which this Chapter treats) when they are laid before his eyes when there is a sufficient proposal, then it is none of his fault.* Yet this is as weak as water: For, supposing a Fundamental Truth clearly demonstrated from Scripture, though a man cannot force himself to believe it, yet there is enough to render a man inexcusable to God. *God hath not been wanting* (one of the Exposers scraps) *in necessaries:*

[330] Romans 14:1.

[331] his future dispute about Ceremonies A,B] his dispute about future Ceremonies AV.

[332] him that contends for them A,B] them that contend for him AV.

[333] *pag. 10.* B] *p. 10* A,AV.

[334] Tramelling, Ed.] traneling A; travelling B; *to trammel* is to take fish or birds with a trammel-net.

[335] Proctoring: collecting tithes or other church dues.

[336] this B] his A.

[337] or his Faith B] or his fainh A; nor his Faith AV.

But I hope he will not compel God too, but that he may dispense his saving and efficacious Influence (without which all that sufficient Proposal he speaks of will have been insufficient,) only to the minds of whom he pleases. The Animadverter in defending that a man can force himself to believe, argues against Experimental Demonstration (try it in any man, in every man) but raises only a malign ignorant and cavilling Dispute, herein to reduce the Author to *the Dreggs*, forsooth, *of Mr. Hobb's his divinity*,[338] I.c. It *is not the mans fault* saith he[339] *if he cannot believe after a sufficient Proposal.* He saith, *he is sure,* too it is not then the man's fault. (so in the Dispute lately about *That* and *What*, he said, *he was sure he did the Author no wrong*) But I desire him first to read Romans 3. the 4,5,6. verses, with the Context: But especially Romans 9. from the 13 to the 22. verse, where the Apostle introduces a man objecting in the same words to the same purpose, *Thou wilt say unto me why doth God yet find fault, &c.* And if the Exposer will not take the Apostles answer,[340] but *be sure* of the contrary, then he too cannot, it seems *force himself to be-*[37]*lieve* after what he ought to have allowed for a *sufficient Proposal.* But where the Author supposes that any man does clearly or sufficiently demonstrate a Fundamental Truth from Scipture: yet unless a mans Brains be clear it is to him no Demonstration. You suppose that all of you do clearly demonstrate, so that if they don't Believe you may justly open their Eyes with a pair of Pincers. Whereas there are some *Few* among the *Few*, such *Spermologers*,[341] that unless a grain of Faith fall down, by the by, from Heaven your Seed is Barren. I do not reckon much upon a Church Historical[342] devilish belief. Unless a thing be in the express words of Scripture, there are some of the Laity to whom a Counsel cannot demonstrate clearly, a Preacher cannot demonstrate, sneezing Powder cannot demonstrate, no Earthly [power] can do it. Christ used Clay indeed, but it was his Spittle that gave the healing quality, and cured the Blind man.[343] Alas, you are so wise in your own conceit,[344] that

[338] See note 140.

[339] saith he Ed.] *saith he* A,B,AV.

[340] the Apostles answer: Romans 9:19: "Nay, but, O man, who are thou that replies against God? Shall the thing formed say to him that formed it, 'Why didst thou make me thus?'"

[341] *Spermologers:* those who gather up seeds or pick up gossip; Marvell's usage is the only one cited by the *DNB*.

[342] Historical A] Historicol B.

[343] John 19: 1–40, especially 6.

[344] Proverbs 25:5, 12.

you cannot conceive how simple some poor men are. He saith, *the Reason which helps every man to see these Fundamental Truths, at least when they are shewed and pointed out to him* (such Truths you must conceive as the Creed Doctrines of the Trinity) *is a vulgar and popular thing* (what need then so many Disputes in the Councils?) *and sure the Author, that he may not admit any mans Hypocrisie and Wilfulness to be gross and palpable, imagins there are a world of Idiots.* So the Exposer would now cokes[345] the Lay-multitude, whom before he call'd *the hundred thousands* and *the many*, and for their simplicity *excusable from subscribing the 39 Articles*, to be grown on the sudden so very wise men, that he may with justice therefore compel them by corporal punishments or penalties to believe in spight of their Teeth or their Understandings. Alas if any men consider those Fundamental Truths, so subject he saith to vulgar and popular reason, it is one of the difficultest things in the world, and yet more to those who are most removed from being Idiots to believe them; and some men by their clear Demonstrations, by their sufficient Proposals, by their Creeds have rendered it still more difficult. Why have I wasted all this on the Exposer, who (whether it be his fault or no) yet cannot force himself to believe even *the Naked Truth,* though so clearly demonstrated from Scripture, (and the Exposer I suppose believes the Scripture) though so Consonant and obvious to the most vulgar and popular Reason, but believes his own Animadversions, against the most vulgar and popular Reason, to be a sufficient Proposal to the contrary? In the 13, and 14. *p.* speaking of that place, Gal. 5.12, which the Author understands of the Magistrates Power, but the Exposer will have to be Excommunication; I crave leave to dissent from both of them, humbly conceiving that the Word there of *Cutting off* is rather meant in the usual sense of Scripture in a multitude of places,[346] for Gods taking them off by his hand. But whatsoever it be, I desire the Exposer for his own sake to take good [38] heed, that, whether it be Executing or Punishing, or Banishing, or Excommunicating, or taking them away by[347] Gods Hand of Justice, the Apostle speaks of such as taught for Circumcision, and alluding to the Word, wishes that they were rather *cut off,* who trouble the Galatians about

---

[345] cokes: i.e., coax; but probably used in its primary sense. A "cokes" was a fool, and to "cokes" was to fool, and as this was done by wheedling, so it came to have that meaning only. Marvell says he will fool the multitude into the belief that they have grown wise (Grosart, p. 427).

[346] a multitude of places: for this information, Marvell consulted the "Nonconformist" *Concordance.* See p. 45, n. 49.

[347] away by Ed] away A,B; correct in some copies of AV.

the retaining of that, and who would oblige them contrary to *their Christian liberty* to such Jewish ceremonies.

For what he hales in of the great and notable effect, *p.* 14. of conferences, wishing that there were such held publickly or privately to satisfie the Non-conformists; truly though they be no great men, yet perhaps it were fit they were first satisfied what kind of Reception they should meet with. But I doubt such Conferences in Publick are but the Resemblance and Epitome of General Councils. For that of the Savoy,[348] in which he instances it, it might almost as well have been in Piemont.[349] A man disinteressed[350] either way, might make a pleasant story of the *Anecdota*[351] of that Meeting, and manifest how well his Majesties Gracious Declaration before his Return, and his Broad-Seal afterward were pursued.[352] But it is not my present business. But for shortness sake, as to his desire, *That he that does not believe the notable effect of them, would but read what my Lord Bishop of Winchester Printed of that Conference,*[353] *where the Adverse Party was driven immediately*

[348] that of the Savoy: The Savoy Conference sat by royal warrant at the Savoy in the Strand from April 15 to July 24, 1661, their mandate being to review the Book of Common Prayer. Led by Gilbert Sheldon, then bishop of London, it consisted of twelve bishops and twelve Presbyterian divines, who hoped, unsuccessfully, to arrive at a compromise that would allow them to retain their livings. Marvell refers several times to this and the preceding Worcester House conference in *RT* and *RT2*. See vol. 1, p. 62, n. 133.

[349] This difficult joke assumes knowledge of the close relations between the regions of the Savoy in southern France and Piedmont in northern Italy under the Roman Catholic governance of Charles Emmanuel II, duke of Savoy, and especially of the massacre of the Protestant Waldenses in Piedmont in 1655, the subject of a sonnet by Milton.

[350] disinteressed B] disintessed A,AV.

[351] *Anecdota:* the first use of this term in English; it probably indicates Marvell's knowledge of the *Anecdota* or *Secret History* of Procopius. See Patterson, *Early Modern Liberalism* (Cambridge, 1998), pp. 156–59, 187–98.

[352] Marvell means that "that Meeting," the Savoy Conference, canceled the program of religious toleration announced in the Declaration of Breda, signed by Charles on April 14, 1660. The declaration stated, that "because the passion and uncharitableness of the times have produced several opinions in religion . . . we do declare a liberty of tender consciences, and that no man shall be disquieted or called into question for differences of opinion in matter of religion, which do not disturb the peace of the kingdom."

[353] *Bishop . . . of that Conference:* George Morley (1597–1684), bishop of Worcester, and subsequently promoted to Winchester in 1662, was one of the chief spokesmen for

to assert, that whatsoever may be the occasion of sin to any must be taken away.[354] I shall as civilly as I can, though I defer much to his extraordinary veracity, tell the Exposer I do not believe him.

I come now to what he, *p.* 14, 15, 16, 17, and in other places declares to be his Judgement, as to Compulsion in matter of Faith and Religion. The Authors Opinion appears in the beginning, where I stated his own words thorow this Chapter. The Exposer does beat the Air, *p.* 14, concerning the Donatists,[355] a most[356] seditious and turbulent Sect, *who,* saith the Author (as it is objected by those that would have Force used) *some of them came to St. Augustine*[357] *and gave thanks, that the Civil Power was made use of to restrain them, confessing that was the means that brought them to consider more calmly their own former extravagant Opinions, and so brought them home to the true Church.*[358] But he quarrels the Author for his four Answers against the Magistrates using that as a Precedent. The first, *our Case is not in repressing seditious Practises, but inforcing a Confession of Faith.* I will return straight to the Exposers Answer to this. The Authors second is; *unless it can be evidenced that their hearts were changed as well as their Profession (a thing impossible to prove) all this proves nothing.* Neither does it. For the Dispute now betwixt the Author and his Adversary is, whether it be possible to compel a man to Believe. This instance proves only that those Donatists were forced to come to Church. Therefore there cannot be a more uncharitable and disingenuous thing invented, than for the Exposer to upbraid him

---

the Anglican bishops. In 1662 he published *The Bishop of Worcester's Letter to a Friend for Vindication of Himself from Mr. Baxter's Calumny,* in which he defended the conference decisions.

[354] Turner, p. 14.

[355] the Donatists: a schismatic group in the African church in the fourth and fifth centuries A.D., who formed a rigorist belief about the importance of virtue in making consecration valid. They objected to the consecration of Cecilianus, bishop of Carthage, in 311, on the grounds that his consecrator, Felix of Aptunga, had been a *traditor* under the Diocletian persecutions. The Donatists, who were often subjected to suppression (e.g., in 316, 405, and 411) were seen as a test case for the treatment of Nonconformity in England.

[356] most B] must A,AV.

[357] St. Augustine: Augustine of Hippo (354–430), teacher of rhetoric, converted to Christianity in 387 and received the see of Hippo in 395. His most famous works are the autobiographical *Confessions* and *The City of God.*

[358] Croft, p. 8. Croft's source for this anecdote was Augustine, *A Treatise concerning the correction of the Donatists,* letter 165, to Boniface, chapter 2:7 (Migne, *PL* 33:795).

with such a Retort, *for ought he knows they were Hypocrites:* (the Author does say so) *so for* [39] *ought we too*[359] *know this Author is all this while a Jesuite, and writes this Pamphlet only to imbroil us Protestants.*[360] But he must make some sputter rather than be held to the terms of the Question: and truly I perceive Antiochus is very weary, and shifts like a Crane (not to instance in a worse Bird) first one foot and then another to rest on, being tired to stand so long within so close a Circle. For thirdly, the Author answers, *Put the case their hearts were really changed, as to matter of Belief, 'tis evident their hearts were very worldly still, grovelling on earth not one step nearer Heaven:* He will not be candid without Compulsion, but leaves out what follows; *and sure their heart was evil, which was far more moved for the quiet enjoyment of this Worlds good, than for the blessed enjoyment of Christ.*[361] In earnest I begin to think an Exposer is a Rational Creature. For had he not on purpose left these last words out, he could not have cryed, *A horrible charitable saying! We may forgive the Author any thing after this;*[362] which is all the Answer he gives; so Charitable is the Exposer grown to the Donatists, for every man that will come to church is *ipso facto*[363] with him, a true Believer. But it did in truth appear to have been so, and there is not the least uncharitableness in this that the Author has said; For by those Donatists own confession, it was not any love to that which they now owned for the Truth to St. Austin, not any Conviction[364] of Conscience, not so much as even an inclination to obey the Magistrate; but meer fine force and fear of Punishment that brought them to Church, and whatsoever good came on't was by accident. Whether might not a man add, that their giving thanks for that Force, and so owning that Principle of Compulsion, was a further Evidence their heart was naught[365] still, even while they were with St. Augustine? I think a man might, until I be better informed. But the Author having given a fourth Answer, that *suppose they were now really brought over to the Truth* of the Church, of Belief, and Religion by the Magistrates severity, (I express it thus, that I may not with the Exposer trifle about the Jews care) yet St. Paul hath said, *God forbid we should do evil that good may come of it?*[366] This is

---

[359] too Ed.] to A,B,AV.
[360] Turner, p. 16.
[361] Croft, p. 8.
[362] Turner, p. 16.
[363] *ipso facto:* on the face of it.
[364] Conviction B] Convicton A,AV.
[365] naught: naughty, bad.
[366] Romans 3:8.

Answer enough for a man of understanding. For it is not lawful, suppose for St. Austin himself, to beguile any man even into Christianity; unless as St. Paul perhaps, 2 Cor.12.16. *Being crafty, caught the Corinthians with guile,* by preaching the *Gospel without being burthensome to the people.* No man ought to cheat another, though to the true belief; Not by Interlining[367] the Scripture: Not by false Quotation of Scripture, or of a Father: Not by forging a Heathen Prophesie, or altering an Author: Not by a false[368] Syllogisme: Not by telling a Lye for God. And if no *Petty Fraud,* much less can a *Pia Vis*[369] be allowed, to compel them to Faith, compel them to a Creed, seeing it were to *do evil that good may come of it;* much less to a Creed not perfectly Scriptural; and, instead of being inforced, indeed weakned [40] by compulsion, seeing it is impossible to compel a man to believe, and some Divines teach us to believe (though I suspend) that God himself cannot, or doth not Compel men to believing. But now it falls in naturally to me to be as good as my Word, to consider what the Exposer replies to the Authors first answer concerning the Donatists, that *our case is of inforcing a Confession of faith, not concerning seditious Practises, of which the Donatists were notoriously guilty, in which case he had shown before, that the civil Magistrate may proceed to punishment.*[370] Wherein the Author reasons with his usual justness, and I though a very slender accession,[371] cannot but come into him. For St. Paul, in the 13. Chapter of the Romans, laying out the Boundaries of the Duty of Christian subjects and the Magistrates power, saith, *Rulers are not* (ought not to be) *a terrour to good works, but to evil,*[372] and so forward: but to the Christian people he saith, *they must be subject not only for wrath,* as those Donatists were afterwards, *but for Conscience sake.*[373] And the subjection he defines is in doing good, walking uprightly, keeping the Moral[374] Law, fearing, honouring, and paying Tribute to the Magistrate: But not one word saith the Apostle of forbearing to Preach out of that Obedience; saying in another place, *Necessity is laid upon one, and woe is unto me if I*

[367] Interlining: interlineating (with commentary).

[368] by a false A,B] by false AV.

[369] *Pia vis:* a righteous force.

[370] Croft, p. 8.

[371] accession: addition, supplement.

[372] Romans 13:3 was one of the most cited texts during the 1640s, as the balance to Romans 13:1, "Let every soul be subject unto the higher powers." Marvell deployed it against Samuel Parker in *RT2,* p. 327.

[373] Romans 13:5.

[374] Moral A] Morral B.

Preach not the Gospel:[375] (and that supposes too meeting)[376] and as little of Compelling to hear. For in those times and a great while after there was no inforcing to Christianity. It was very long before that came in fashion: and, writing on the suddain,[377] I do not well remember whether it did ever before the dayes of Picarro and Almagro, the Apostles of the Indians,[378] yet upon recollection it was sooner. But what saith the Exposer to this of the Donatists, whom the Author allows to have been punishable onely for Seditious Practises, having before declared, that *for such as onely refuse to conform to the Churches established Doctrine and Discipline (pardon him if he say) really he cannot find any warrant, or so much as any hint from the Gospel to use any force to compel them: and from Reason sure there is no motive to use force, because as he shewed before, Force can't make a man believe your Doctrine, but only as an Hypocrite, Profess what he believes not.* I expect that the Exposer, in this place above all other, which I guess was his greatest motive to this Imployment, should ply and overlay him now with Reason, but especially with Scripture. Let us hear how he answers. *I only say this,*[379] *p.* [1]5 (for he speaks now of our Non-conformists) *the very Act against them calls them* Seditious Conventicles, *and openly to break so many Known Laws of the Land, after so many Reinforcements, is not this to be turbulent?* This now you must understand to be Reason, and not Scripture: that I suppose as the strongest is reserved for the Rear. Truly, (as far as a man can comprehend by comparing that with other Acts of this Parliament,) they did only appoint that the Penalty of Sedition should lye against those that frequent such Meetings: as in the Act against Irish Cattle,[380] if it be not in itself a Nuisance, no Law-givers can make it so. Nor can any Legislators [40a] make that to be *Sedition* which is not *Sedition* in its own nature. So Prohibitions

---

[375] *Necessity . . . Gospel:* 1 Corinthians 9:16.

[376] supposes . . . meeting: Marvell argues that if the preacher is compelled by duty to preach, the same duty requires the faithful to congregate to hear him.

[377] writing . . . suddain: confirmation that here, in the odd gathering g, Marvell is hastily inserting material.

[378] Picarro and Almagro: Francisco Pizarro and Diego de Almagro were Spanish conquerors of Peru in the early sixteenth century. See Agustín de Zárate, *Historia del Descvbrimiento y Conqvista de Peru* (Anvers, 1555). Note the irony of calling these savage imperialists apostles, on the basis of their forced conversion of the Indians to Christianity.

[379] only say this B] say only this A.

[380] Irish Cattle: On November 19, 1675, just before the Long Prorogation, the Commons discussed an act to prohibit the importation of Irish cattle (*JHC,* 1675, p. 380).

of that kind operate no more as to the intrinsique Quality, then a publick Allowance of taking away any honest mens goods by violence, and giving it another name, would extinguish the Robbery. It was the King and Parliaments prudence to make such Laws, and as long as they shall continue of that mind, it is reason the Non-conformists should lye under the Penalty, which I humbly conceive is all that could be intended. But the Exposer rivets this with Reason again, not Gospel. *And was it not ever understood so in all Religions; even in Heathen Rome? The most Learned P. AErodius tells us* (Does he so? What is it, I beseech you?) *that the Roman Senate* (the Exposer quotes it at large as a story of great use and not to be hudled over; I must be glad to contract it) *made an Act against the Conventicles of certain Innovators in their Religion;*[381] *if any particular person judged such a Sacrifice to be necessary, he must repair first to the Praetor, he to the Senate, where the* Quorum *must be an hundred, and they must not neither give him leave, if at all, to have above five persons present at the Meeting. The self same number, beside the Dissenters own family, is so far forth indur'd by an Act of this present Parliament, that there must be more then five to make it a Conventicle.*[382] This is a very subtile remarke[383] that he has made, as if it were one of those witty accidents of Fortune, or an extraordinary hand of Providence, that the Senate of Rome, and the Parliament of England should hit so pat, upon an Act of the same nature: And upon that number of five. However they are oblig'd to him, and he deserves the publick Thanks for furnishing them, so long after, with a Precedent. I confess I always wonder'd they would allow them so many as five, for fear when, not two or three, but five of 'em were gathered together, *God should hear their request:* and it seem'd therefore to me a formidable Number. But where has the example been hid so long? I believe the Exposers study has laid much this way. But this was so deep an *Arcanum*[384] that was fit for none but an Arch-Bishops Closet. I wish he have come honestly by it. But Murder, I see, and Theft will out, and so this comes to light by a blabbing Animadverter, that cannot keep counsel, but will violate the Ecclesiastical secret, rather then lose the Leachery of his Tattle, and the Vain-glory of his Pedantry. I could be glad to know what

---

[381] *P.[etrus] Aerodius:* Pierre Ayrault, *Rerum omni antiquate iudicaturum Pandecta* (Milan, 1619), book 1, p. 32: "De Fide & Religione."

[382] Turner, p. 15.

[383] remarke A] remarque B.

[384] *Arcanum:* See note 8.

complexion this Exposer is of. I am perswaded, whatsoever he may be now, he was once extream fair: for I remember since I was at School: that the Learned P. Ovidius told me, that the Crow was once a white Bird, and much in Apollo's favour till for telling of Tales,

Sperantem non falsae praemia linguae,
Inter aves albas vetuit consistere Corvum.[385]

And of another, the fairest thing that ever eyes were laid on, but for carrying of Stories, was turn'd into a Jack-daw, and grew as black as a Crow, Filching, and Kaw me, and I'le Kaw thee,[386] ever after.

And that which sure must make him more black, more a Jack-daw, and like it, worthy to be expelled from the guard, and from the protection of Minerva, and who henceforward [40b]

———*Ponatur post Noctis avem,*[387]

is that he does with open mouth proclaim the Naked design of all the *Few* that are of his party, *p.* 12. *The Jews in Rome are constrained once a week to hear a Christian Sermon.* The same *p.* 12. *We that would oblidge him to open his eyes where he will or no.* p. 14. *I can onely wish for the present, that by forcing them into our Churches, they may hear our defences.* p. 17. *I speak nothing more against them, then that they may be brought to our Churches,* &c. All this as the last result and greatest condescension of his Ecclesiastical Clemency. In conclusion he declares he would have them forced: and for what manner of force, violence, punishment[388] or penalty he leaves it all open, go as high as men will. These things still are not Scripture neither, but Reason. His first was an Heathenish Reason in one Sense, and this a Jewish in another. For I confess it is a very pregnant and *adequate* example, and of great authority for us to imitate; that *the Jews in Rome are constrained once a week to hear a Christian Sermon.* What could there[389] be more proportionable, then to

---

[385] Ovid, *Metamorphoses,* 2:631–32: "But the raven, which had hoped only for reward for his not untruthful reporting, he [Apollo] forbade to take his place among the white birds."

[386] Kaw me, and I'le Kaw thee: proverbial, i.e., You scratch my back, and I'll scratch yours. See Ray, *Collection of English Proverbs,* p. 110.

[387] Ovid, *Metamorphoses,* 2:564: "was placed after the bird of Night." The Latin should read "Ponar."

[388] punishment B] punishent A.

[389] there A] their B.

resemble the proceeding with Christians among themselves here in England, not differing in any point of Faith, with the proceeding at Rome against the Jews? But that the Exposer should *implicitly* liken and compare our Bishops to the Pope, may perhaps not be taken well by either party. So that I dare say, had he consulted with his usual prudence, he would not have disoblidged both sides at once. But for the Precedent, I have nothing to oppose to this more then the first, it being *doubtless of notable effect,* as notable as that of the[390] Piemont conference.[391] Onely out of the affection I have for him, would wish him to correct here one slip, if I be rightly informed; for some that have been abroad say, his Intelligence from Rome has failed him, for that it is not once a week, but once a year that the Jews at Rome are obliged,[392] forced, to hear a Christian Sermon: And therefore, when the *Parliamentum Indoctum*[393] sits again, I would advise him not to make his act too severe here upon this mistake, then it is against those Judaick Non-conformists at Rome.

But the next Reason would be so extraordinary troublesome to the *few* that are of the Exposers party and to himself, that if he had thorowly consider'd it, I question whether he would have been so charitable to the Fanaticks, that he would oblige them *to open their eyes whether they will or no.*[394] For it would require two of the Church of England to every Non-conformist, unless 'twere here and there one that had lost an Eye in the Service. Less would not do the business decently, and those two also must be well in order, to open the Non-conformists Eyes both at once, lest one Eye[395] should be of one and the other Eye of a contrary opinion: and then they should in humanity give them some interval for winking. Else they had as good cut off their Eye-lids, as the Episcopal Carthaginians used the Presbyterian Regulus, for keeping in the true sense to his Covenant.[396] But on the other side, it would look too bigg for a company of beggarly Fanat-

---

[390] of the A] of B.

[391] I.e., the Savoy Conference.

[392] obliged Ed.] oblidged A, oblieged B.

[393] See note 74.

[394] Turner, p. 12.

[395] Eye A] eye B.

[396] Marcus Atilius Regulus, Roman consul in 256 B.C., defeated the Carthaginians at Adys and captured Tunis but offered unacceptable peace terms. In 255 he was in turn defeated and died in captivity. The legend of his brutal murder at the hands of the Carthaginians may have been invented to balance the fact that his widow tortured two Punic prisoners in revenge for his death (Diodorus Siculus, 24.12).

icks, to be waited upon in as much Majesty as Obeshankanogh the King of Virginia,[397] that had two Squires of the Body in constant attendance, to lift up his Eye-lids [40c] as oft as he conceiv'd any man worthy to be look'd upon. But let the Exposer order it as he pleases, *I am not bound to* be any of his sight-supporters. Onely this, it would be very improper for him to chuse any one that is blind to that employment: for his several times repeated wish, *that they might be forced to come to Church to give them a fair hearing, and to hear their discourses:*[398] truly I believe they know the Lyon by the Claw,[399] there is a great part of Oratory consists in the choice of the Person that is to perswade men. And a great skill of whatsoever Orator is, to perswade the Auditory first that he himself is an honest and fair man. And then he is like to make the more impression on them too, if he be so prudent as to chuse an acceptable subject to speak on, and manage it decently, with fit arguments and good language. None but the very rabble love to hear any thing scurrilous or railing; especially if they should hear themselves rail'd on by him, they would be ready to give him the due applause of Petronius his Orator,[400] with flinging the stones about his ears, and then leaving him to be his own Auditory. Now, they have had so ample experiment of the Exposer as to all these points, in his Defence against the *Naked Truth,* that I doubt his perswasion to this comming to hear him or others, will be of little force with them, and nothing would oblige these Donatists to it, but the utmost extremity; *nor then would they find themselves one step nearer Heaven*: His Book is as good to them as a Sermon, and no doubt he has preach'd as well as printed it, and took more pains in it than

[397] Obeshankanogh the King of Virginia: This seems to be a (deliberately) garbled reference to the account of Powhatan, native king of Virginia, by Captain John Smith. See his *Description of Virginia* (1612) in *Narratives of Early Virginia, 1606–1625,* ed. L. G. Tyler (New York, 1907), p. 114: "He hath as many women as he will: whereof . . . one sitteth on his right hand, and another on his left . . . When he dineth, one of his women, before and after his meat, bringeth him water in a wooden platter to wash his hands. Another waiteth with a bunch of feathers to wipe them." The name of Opechancanough, who became king of the Ozimes and later treacherously massacred the English, appears just above this passage.

[398] Turner, p. 17.

[399] know the Lyon by the Claw: perhaps proverbial; but Marvell seems to have picked up this phrase from Vincent Alsop, *Anti-Sozzo* (1675), preface, A6v: "You shall now guess at the Lyon by his Claw."

[400] Petronius his Orator: Petronius Arbiter, *Satyricon,* 90, tells how the orator Eumolpus was stoned by his audience halfway through his recital of a dreadful imitation of the *Aeneid.*

ordinary; did his best. Must they, will they think, be compelled to make up
the pomp of his Auditory? Must they, while the good Popish Fathers
suffer'd those of Chiapa to come to church with their *Chocalatte Pots,*[401] to
comfort their hearts, be inforced to come to Church by him, to have
Snush[402] thrust up their Noses, *to clear their brains for them?* 'Tis the only
way to continue and increase the Schisme. But in good sober earnest, 'tis
happy that some or other of this *Few* chances ever and anon to speak their
minds out, to shew us plainly what they would be at. Being conscious of
their own unworthiness, and hating to be reformed, it appears that they
would establish the Christian Religion by a Mahometan way, and gather so
much force that it might be in their power, and we lye at their mercy, to
change that Religion into Heathenisme, Judaisme, Turcisme, any thing. I
speak with some emotion, but not without good reason, that I question
whether, which way soever the Church revenues were applied, such of them
would not betake themselves to that side as nimbly as the Needle to the
Load stone.[403] Have they not already, *ipso facto,*[404] renounc'd their Christianity, by avowing this Principle, so contrary to the Gospel? Why do not
they Peter Hermite it,[405] and stir up our Prince to an *Holy War* abroad; to

---

[401] See Henry Stubbe, *The Indian Nectar, or a Discourse concerning Chocolata* (London, 1662), p. 93: "The Women of Chiapa pretend much weakness and squeamishness
of Stomach, which they say is so great, that they are not able to continue in the Church,
whilst a Mass is briefly huddled over . . . unless they drink a cup of hot Chocalatte. For
this purpose it was much used by them to make their Maids bring them to Church in
the middle of Mass, or Sermon, a cup of Chocolatte, which could not be done to all, or
most of them, without a great confusion." Marvell focuses on the next phase of the
anecdote, whereby the bishop publishing an excommunication of any who ate or drank
in church, the chocolate-addicted gentlewomen deserted the cathedral, taking their
money with them, and attended instead the cloister churches, where the friars permitted the chocolate drinking. When the friars too were excommunicated, the bishop
promptly died, perhaps from a poisoned cup of chocolate, which "became afterward a
Proverb in the Country, Beware of the Chocolatte of Chiapa." Stubbe found his anecdote in Thomas Gage, *New Survey of the West Indies* (1648), which could also have been
Marvell's source.

[402] Snush: i.e., snuff, powdered tobacco for inhaling. The *OED* gives 1683 as the first
English appearance of the Dutch word, but snuff was fashionable in France at the court
of Marie de Medici in the mid-sixteenth century, and this is surely one of Marvell's
verbal imports, unknown to the printer.

[403] Load stone: magnet.

[404] *ipso facto:* from the thing itself, self-evidently.

[405] Peter the Hermit (d. 1115) was the preacher of the First Crusade, encouraging

propagate the Protestant Religion, or at least our discipline and ceremonies, and they take the Front of the Battel? No 'tis much better lurking in a
fat Benefice here, and to domineer in their own parishes above their spiritual vassals, & raise a kind of civil war at home, but that none will oppose
them: why may they not, [40d] as well as force men to Church, cram[406] the
Holy Supper too down their Throats (have they not done something not
much unlike it) and drive them into the Rivers by thousands to be baptized
or drowned? And yet this, after the King and Parliament by his, their,
Gracious Indulgence have enacted a liberty for five beside their own family
to meet together in their religious worship; and could not therefore intend
at the same time to force them to go to Church with the utmost or any
severity. What can be the end of these things, but to multiply force with
force, as one absurdity is the consequence of another, till they may again
have debased the Reason and Spirit of the Nation, to make them fit for
Ignorance and Bondage? Is it not reason, if they had care or respect to mens
souls (which they only exercise it seems the cure of, perhaps not that
neither, but evacuate[407] one residence by another) to allow that men should
address themselves to such Minister as they think best for their souls
health? Men are all infirm and indisposed in their spiritual condition.
What sick man, but if a Physician were inforced upon him, might in good
prudence suspect it were to kill him, or that, if the next Heir and Doctor
could agree, he would certainly do it? I shall conclude this reasonable
transport with remarking that although the Author did modestly challenge
any man to shew him a warrant or colour or hint from Scripture, to use
force to constrain men to the established Doctrine and worship, and offer'd
to maintain that nothing is more clear to be deduced or is more fully exprest
in Scripture, nor is more suitable to natural reason, than that no man be
forced in such cases; the Exposer took notice of it, yet hath not produced
one place of Scripture, but onely made use of force as an invincible Reason;
so that upon supposal, which none granted him, that all his *Few* do clearly

---

Pope Urban II. At the Council of Clermont of 1095 he raised an army of his own which
arrived at Constantinople ahead of the main crusade.

[406] not . . . cram A] not . . . not cram B; in B the first "not" appears only as the
catchword; therefore the typesetter may have felt he needed the second "not," which is
syntactically excessive.

[407] evacuate one residence by another: not, as might at first appear, give up one
church living for another, but in effect deprive the first of its pastor by accepting a
second *as well;* that is, to engage in pluralism.

demonstrate from Scripture, what is at best therefore but deducible from Scripture, he thinks it reasonable to oblige all men by force to come to all their Parishes. And yet he himself who does (I suppose it onely for the Cases sake) believe the Scripture, although he cannot produce one place of Scripture for using this force, and though the Author has produced so many, and urges the whole Scripture that such force is not to be used, hath his brains nevertheless so confused, or so obdurate, that he cannot force himself to believe the Author: but persists in his unchristian and unreasonable desire that men *may be compelled,* and hereby deserves to be made an Example of his own Principle. For herein he exceeds Pharaoh, who had ten *sufficient Proposals,*[408] & yet his heart was so hardned, that he'd not[409] let Israel go out of Egypt, but was *proof* against Miracles. But he only would imagine that the Israelites were idle, and would therefore force them to make Brick without Straw:[410] but the Exposers heart and brains are so hardned, that he will conceive all the Non-conformists to be *obstinate fools or hypocrites,* and therefore will *compel them* all to go to all their Parish Churches, and to make therefore faith without Reason. And hence it is not onely probable but demonstrable, if they were compelled to go and hear him and the *Few* of his Party, how well he or [40e] they would acquit themselves too in *clearly demonstrating from Scripture the Prime Articles of Faith,* as it is extended in all the Creeds, of which it was treated in this chapter that I have now done with, and truly almost with those remaining.

For I had intended to have gone Chapter by Chapter, affixing a distinct Title, as he does to every one of them (that men may believe he has animadverted thorowly without reading) except that concerning the difference between Bishops and Presbyters, which, as being the most easie to be answered, he therefore referred to a Bishop.[411] But in good earnest, after having consider'd this latter[412] chapter, so brutal whether as to force or reason, I have changed my resolution. For he argues so despicably in the rest, that even I, who am none of the best *Disputers of this world,*[413] have conceived an utter contempt for him. He is a meer Kitchin-Plunderer, and attacks but the Baggage, where even the Sutlers[414] would be too hard for

---

[408] ten *sufficient Proposals:* the ten plagues of Egypt, Exodus 7–10.

[409] he'd not B] he would not A.

[410] to make Brick without Straw: see Exodus 5:7–19.

[411] a Bishop: i.e., Gunning. See introduction, p. 5.

[412] latter B] last A.

[413] 1 Corinthians 1:20.

[414] Sutlers: small vendors, victuallers.

him. *p.* 18. Does the Exposer allow that under Constantinus Poganatus,[415] to have been a free General Council? In the same page, if the Exposer would have done anything in his *Die Ecclesiae,*[416] he should have proved that a General Council is the Church, that there can be such a General Council, or hath been; that the Church can impose new Articles of Faith beyond the Express Words of Scripture; that a General Council cannot erre in matters of Faith; That the Church of his making cannot erre in matters of faith; Whereas our Church, *Article* 19. saith thus far, *The Church of Jerusalem, Alexandria and Antioch have erred, so also the Church of Rome hath erred, not onely in their living and manner of Ceremonies, but also in matters of faith.* This is an Induction from Particulars, and remark the Title of the Article, being *of the Church.* Ours defines it, *The Visible Church of Christ is a congregation of faithful men, in which the pure Word of God is preached, and the Sacraments be duly ministred, according to Christs Ordinance in all those things that of necessity are requisite to the same.* And then, if the Reader please to look on the 20 and 21 Articles following, one *of the Authority of the Church,* the other *of the Authority of General Councils,* unless a man will industriously mis-apply and mis-construe them, those three are a Compendious and irrefragable[417] Answer, not only to what he saith here upon the *Appendix,*[418] but to his whole book, from one end to the other. *p.* 19. I ask him when the Greek Church is excommunicate by the Roman, when the Protestants left the Roman Church, when we in England are neither Papists, Lutherans, nor Calvinists, and when in Queen Maries time we returned to the Roman Church, what and where then was the Catholick Church, that was indefectible and against which the gates of Hell did not prevail? Was it not in the Savoy?[419] Moreover I ask him what hinders but a General Council may erre in matters of Faith, when we in England, that are another world,[420] that are

---

[415] Constantinus Poganatus: Eastern emperor 668–85, who convened the sixth General Council, the third at Constantinople, in 680. "Poganatus" refers to the fact that he grew a beard.

[416] *Die Ecclesiae:* in the time (day) of the church.

[417] irrefragable: incontrovertible, undeniable.

[418] the Appendix: i.e., Croft's appendix to his opening chapter on Articles of Faith.

[419] the Savoy: see note 348.

[420] Marvell alludes to the Virgilian tag *divisos ab orbe Britannos* (*Eclogues,* 1:67) frequently appropriated by the English as a compliment to their insularity. Cf. Richard Fanshawe, "An Ode upon occasion of His Majesties Proclamation in the yeare 1630," in *Il Pastor Fido* (London, 1648), p. 226: "Onely the Iland which wee sowe / (A World without the world)."

under an imperial crown, that *are none of them,* as the Exposer words it, but have a distinct Catholick Faith within our four Seas, did in the Reign before mentioned[421] (and [4of] reckon how many in that Convocation those were that dissented) again make ourselves *one of them?* unless he has a mind to do so too, which would alter the case exceedingly. *P.* 20, he quotes the Act, 1 *Eliz. cap. i.*[422] let him mind that clause in it, *by the express and plain words of Canonical Scripture;* and then tell me what service it hath done him: whether he had not better have left it alone, but that it is his Fate all along to be condemned out of his own mouth, which must alwayes succeed so, when man urges a Real Truth against a Real Truth. *P.* 23. I have reason to affirm and he will meet with it (and has already in the Author) that those General Councils howsoever called, were no *Repraesentatio totius nominis Christiani,*[423] but nominally: yea that such a Representation could not be. *P.* 22. He expounds Scriptures here, and thinks he does wonders in it, by assuming the faculties of the whole Body to the Mouth, which *Mouth,* he saith (and in some sense 'tis very true, if a man would run over the Concordance)[424] *is the Clergy.* But I know not why the Mouth of the Church should pretend to be the Brain of the Church, and Understand and Will for the whole Laity. Let every man have his word about, and 'tis Reason. We are all at the same Ordinary,[425] and pay our souls equally for the Reckoning. The Exposers *Mouth,* which is unconscionable, would not only have all the Meat, but all the Talk too, not only at Church, but at Council Table. Let him read Bishop Taylor of Liberty of Prophecy, *P.* 25.[426] The Exposer, that

[421] the Reign before mentioned: that of Mary Tudor.

[422] 1 *Eliz. cap.* i.: the Elizabethan Act of Supremacy, 1559.

[423] Turner, p. 23: "a Representative of all that are called Christians."

[424] Another sign of Marvell's use of Vavasour Powell's *Concordance,* which has a section on "Mouth."

[425] Ordinary: eating-house.

[426] Jeremy Taylor, *The Liberty of Prophesying* (London, 1647/8), written from Wales "In this great Storm which hath dasht the Vessell of the Church all in pieces," was preceded by a long dedicatory epistle to Sir Christopher Hatton offering arguments for religious toleration so liberal they anticipate Locke's. On p. 25 Marvell found: "till the time of Justinian . . . the Catholicks and Novatians had Churches indifferently permitted even in Rome it selfe, but the Bishops of Rome whose interest was much concerned in it, spoke much against it, and laboured the eradication of the Novatians . . . but it is observed by Socrates that when the first Persecution was made against them at Rome by Pope Innocent I, at the same instant the Goths invaded Italy . . . it being just in God to bring a Persecution upon them . . . who with an incompetent Authority and insufficient

always falsly *Represents* his Adversary, as an Enemy to Creeds, to Fathers, (as afterwards he does to Ceremonies, to Logick, to Mathematicks, to every thing that he judiciously speaks and allows of), here. P. 25. saith the Author (who delivers but the Church of Englands Doctrine herein, and would not have Divine Faith impos'd upon, nor things prest beyond Scripture) in this matter of General Councils is guilty of *unthought of Popery, for the Papists* (really I think he partly slanders them herein) *cannot endure Councils General and Free.*[427] They allow many a General Council more than we do. If the Pope do not, for some reason or other, delight in some that are past, or in having new ones; it does not follow that the Papists do not. I think those were Papists that ruffled the Pope too here in the West, and that at the Council of Constance burnt John Hus[428] and Hierome of Prague,[429] and resolv'd that Faith was not to be kept with Hereticks. But pray Mr. Exposer, if we must give Divine Faith[430] to General Councils, let the Author ask you in his turn which are those General Councils? How shall we know them? Why, only such as accord with Scripture. Why, then we,[431] I mean you Mr. Exposer, make ourselves, you still, Judges of the General Councils, the fault you so much condemn the Author for. But what *Popery*, thought or *unthought of,* are you, in the very next line, guilty of, that call the Popes Supremacy *the Quintessence of Popery?* So that it seems the Quintessence[432] of the Controversie betwixt our Church and theirs, is only which shall be Pope: for the Articles of Religion we do not so much differ, we need not much [41] compulsion, though the Non conformists may. I thank you, Mr. Exposer, for your News: I had often heard it before, I confess, but till now I did never, and scarce yet can, believe it; it is rather to be wish'd than hoped for, a thing so surprizingly seasonable. But for the good news, Mr. Exposer, I will give you four Bottles (which is all I

---

grounds doe persecute an errour lesse materiall, in persons agreeing with them in the profession of the same common faith."

[427] Turner, p. 25.

[428] John Hus (c. 1372–1415), Bohemian reformer and follower of Wycliffe, who was excommunicated in 1413 and burned in 1415.

[429] Jerome of Prague (c. 1370–1416), friend of Hus, who studied with Wycliffe at Oxford, returned to Prague in 1407 and was burned in 1416.

[430] Faith A] not in B.

[431] we, A] we? B.

[432] Quintessence: the fifth essence of ancient and medieval philosophy, more subtle than the four elements, and hence the material of which the heavenly bodies were supposedly composed; hence the most subtle extract of anything.

had by me, not for mine own use, but for a friend upon occasion) of the
First, Second, Third, and Fourth Essence. But the *Quintessence* I doubt
would be too strong for your Brain, especially in the morning when you are
writing Animadversions. P. 28. of Ceremonies he sports unworthily, as if
the Author spoke *Pro* and *Con*, Contradictions: while, as Moderator,[433] he
advises our Church to Condescention on the right, and the Dissenters to
submission on the left (how are men else to be brought together?) He had
as good[434] call every man, because he has two hands, an *Ambidexter*. He
would turn every mans Stomach, worse than *the Singing-mens dirty Surplices,* to hear him defend it so foolishly. P. 29, 30, 35, 36. The best of his
reasons for it are the *Apparitions in white,* in the Evangelists. The *Trans-
figuration.* The *Saints in white Linnen.* The *Purity of a Minister.* Why then
does he not wear it all the Week? The Bishop Sisynnius[435] did so, and a
Church-man asking him, why not in Black? as 'twas then the mode, he gave
the same Reasons; and I believe Gurney, the Non-conformist, if, as they
say, he[436] went to Market in it, learn'd them of him.[437] Why does not the
Exposer (there is more reason in Scripture, Col. 4.6. *Let your speech be
always seasoned with Salt, that ye may know how ye ought to answer every
man*) carry a Salt-box alwayes in his Pocket, to be tasting of? for I doubt[438]
he is of the *Salt that has lost his savour.*[439] however I am sure he is very
insipid, and this might correct it: beside it must have been of great vertue,
when he was to animadvert on *the Naked Truth,* that *he might have known
how to answer him.* See Fox, Vol. 3. p. 500, col. 2. what the Martyr, and[440]

---

[433] Moderator B] a Moderator A.

[434] as good A] not in B.

[435] Bishop Sisynnius A] of Sisynnius B: Sisynnius was a Novatian, a learned man and
a jester, who used to dress in white all the time. When asked "where he found written
that a Priest ought to wear white? Tell thou me (saith he) first where is it written that a
Bishop should wear black?" See Socrates, 6:22, trans. Hanmer, pp. 373–74.

[436] he A] not in B.

[437] Edmund Gurney, (fl. 1619–1639, d. 1648); his iconoclastic treatise was published at the Restoration: *G. Redivivus, or an appendix unto the Homily against
Images in Churches.* Marvell had heard a version of the anecdote told in the *DNB,*
in which Gurney, cited to appear before a bishop for not wearing a surplice, and
being told that he was always expected to wear it, "came home and rode a journey with
it on."

[438] doubt: in the old sense of "expect."

[439] Luke 14:34.

[440] and B] the A.

Conformable Bishop Ridley[441] saith, would not be forced to wear it, *he was no Singer.*[442] See as to all these things his beloved Tertullian,[443] *De Cor. Mil. Si ideo dicatur Coronari licere, quia non prohibeat Scriptura, aeque retorquebitur, ideo Coronari non licere, quia Scriptura non jubeat.*[444] Bishop Chrysostome:[445] *Or. i. adversus Judaeos, Ostendite eos ex Dei sententia*[446] *jejunare. Quod ni id fiat quavis ebrietate scelaratius est jejunium. Etenim*[447] *contra quod sit praeter Dei voluntatem est omnium pessimum. Non enim ipsa eorum quae fiunt natura, sed Dei voluntas ac Decretum efficit ut eadem vel bona sint vel mala.*[448] p. 33. His jeering at the Authors, *Oh my Fathers,* is inhumane and impious: *but* Oh *the pity of it that twenty such* Oh's *will not amount to one Reason.* They will, Heb. 4. 12, 13, *that day, which the Devils believe and tremble, when all things shall be bare and naked*[449] *before the word of Truth.* P. 37. he is scarce proper to come in a Pulpit, after what he saith, that the *Apostles received not the Sacrament sitting;* much less after p. 41. he has said, *We read that our Saviour kneeled in several places,* much less after p. 59. where of Preaching he saith, *He knows not what the Author means by*

[441] Bishop Ridley: Nicholas Ridley (1503–55), Protestant theologian who was burned at the stake, along with Hugh Latimer, under Queen Mary.

[442] John Foxe recorded how, in his degradation, or demotion from the priesthood, Ridley said, after they had forced the surplice on him and were now removing it, "I was never singer in all my life." See *The Ecclesiastical Historie: Containing the Acts and Monuments . . .* 3 vols. (London, 1641), 3:501.

[443] Tertullian: late second century, one of the greatest of early Christian writers in Latin. His *Apologeticus,* an appeal against the persecution of Christians, will be ammunition for Marvell in the *Essay.*

[444] Tertullian, *De Corona Militis,* chap. 2 (Migne, *Patrologia Latina,* 2:78): "If they say it is permitted to bestow the crown, because scripture does not prohibit it, it could be equally thrown back, it is not permitted to bestow the crown because scripture does not command it."

[445] Bishop Chrysostome: St. John (golden-tongued) Chrysostom (c. 345–407), most famous of the Greek Fathers of the Church.

[446] *sententia* A] *sectentia* B.

[447] *Etenim* A] *Etinim* B.

[448] Marvell cites Chrysostom from the translation by Erasmus. See Chrysostom, *Adversos Judaeos,* oration 1, in *Opera,* 6 vols. (Antwerp, 1614), 5:427. This differs considerably from the version in Migne, *Patrologia Graeca,* 48:873, where it is oration 4, and Marvell's citations are themselves fragmentary, which makes translation difficult. The gist of the passage is that one should demonstrate dietary laws only from the words of God, otherwise fasting could be worse than carousing; and that things are neither good nor evil in their own nature, but only as the will of God decrees.

[449] bare and naked B] naked and bare A; the first part of the quotation is from James 2.19.

the[450] Demonstration of [42] the Spirit, *unless to speak as he does, Magisteri-*
ally. He never read I Cor. 2.4. of *Preaching in demonstration of the Spirit;* nor
Mat. 7. 29, how Christ *taught as one having Authority:* there is such an Art if
he knew it. P. 42. He can never answer the Author upon Rom. 14. where *the*
zealous Observer of Ceremonies is the weak Brother. He whiffles, *those were the*
Jewish ceremonies. The Jews had a fairer pretence than we: for theirs were
instituted by God himself, and they knew not they were abrogate.

His intollerably ridiculous Story out of Schottus, p. 15.[451] of contriving
a pair of Organs of Cats,[452] which he had done well to have made the Pigs
at Hogs-Norton play on,[453] puts me in mind of another story to quit
it,[454] relating as his does to *screwing* the Non-conformists into Church;
and I could not possibly miss of the Rencounter, because the Gentlemans
name of whom it is told, is the Monosyllable voice with which Cats do
usually address themselves to us.[455] 'Twas (you have it as I had it) the Vice-

---

[450] the A] not in B.

[451] Actually Turner, pp. 45–46.

[452] This was one of Turner's nastiest jokes. He found it, along with the illustration, in
Gaspar Schott, *Magia Universalis Naturae et Artis* (Wurzburg, 1657), part 2, book 6,
pp. 372–73: "He describes . . . a Musical Instrument found out . . . by an Ingenious
fellow, to divert a certain great Prince from a fit of Melancholy. So he took a company of
Cats all of a different size, and consequently of a different Tone or Note all these he put
together in a kind of Chest that was fram'd for the purpose, and plac'd them so, that
their Tayls should be gently screwed up through certin holes in a board; and . . . Needles
under their Tayls so dispos'd or plac'd, that as the Musician struck the Keys, the Needles
prickt their Tayls, which so nickt the Cats, when the Organist came to play a lesson
upon them, that still as they were toucht they set up their Notes, some high, some low,
according to their several Capacities: . . . Just such a Machine of a Church would
[Croft] make us, as this Musical Instrument, if instead of our Screwing up the Non-
conformists (which we do not) or their Screwing us up (which once they did sufficiently) he could screw them into the Church, without more ado, by this Project of his
for Universal Toleration."

[453] Hogs-Norton: This unfortunately named village in Oxfordshire became proverbial for boorishness; cf. James Howell, *Lexicon Tetraglotton. With . . . Proverbs*
(London, 1660), p. 16: "I think thou was born at Hoggs-Norton where piggs play upon
the organs."

[454] to quit it: to requite or outdo it, as Chaucer's Miller's Tale "quit" the Knight's Tale.

[455] Turner's joke about cats was the perfect opportunity for Marvell to introduce
Bishop Peter Mews (1619–1702), vice-chancellor of Oxford, who became bishop of
Bath and Wells in 1672. An ardent royalist during the civil war, he was a constant
correspondent of Secretary of State Joseph Williamson during the Restoration on the
topic of Nonconformist activities.

Chancellour of one of our Universities, but now a Bishop, *Octob.* 22. 1671, and 12 *Febr.* 1669. He came to a Fanaticks House, they not being then at Worship, yet one of 'm said, *They were come to pray to the God of Heaven and Earth;* he said, *Then they were within the Act.* He would force them to church to Saint Maries, himself laid hands on 'm. *He commanded them to follow him in the Kings name.* His Beadle told them, He *would drive them thither in the Devils name.* The Vice-Chancellour said he had converted hundreds so at Reading. They spoke of Queen Maries days, he said, *He could burn them too now, if the Law required it.* There was old tugging, he had the Victory. They were placed in Saint Maries, with Beadles to attend them. As he carried them in, he quoted Luke 14. 23. *Compel them to come in.* What pity 'tis the Exposer knew not of this Text, that he might have had one Scripture for his Doctrine of Compulsion! But it chanced the Minister there preached one time Acts. 5.41.[456] the other time Mat. 10. 16.[457] Afterwards he took the penalty nevertheless for not having been at Church that same Sunday that he had hurried them thither. P. 62. He speaks of Bishop Morton,[458] whose *industrious Brain made up the fatal breach between the two Houses of York and Lancaster.* Much good do the clergy with their Lay Offices. He cogs,[459] p. [5]7. with the Bishop of Ely[460] for his short Syllogisme: he made a longer of the *Holiness of Lent.* He complements (I said he would not forget him) my Lord Chancellour,[461] *the Christian Cicero.* 'Tis true of him, but contradictorily exprest: Ps. 35.16. *With the flatterers were busie mockers, that gnashed with their teeth.* The Exposer has Commenc'd in both Faculties. But the Printer calls: the Press is in danger. I am weary of such stuff, both mine own and his. I will rather give him this following Essay of mine own to busie him, and let him take his turn of being the Popilius.

---

[456] Acts 5:41: "[The Apostles] therefore departed from the presence of the council, rejoicing that they were counted worthy to suffer dishonour for the name."

[457] Matthew 10:16: "Behold, I send you forth as sheep in the midst of wolves: be ye therefore as wise as serpents, and harmless as doves."

[458] John Morton (1420–1500), cardinal and archbishop of Canterbury, a man of enormous political skill who survived the reigns of Edward IV and Richard III to become Henry VII's lord chancellor.

[459] cog: to cheat at dice, or, here probably, to quibble.

[460] Bishop of Ely: Philip Gunning, whose tract on the holiness of Lent (1662) is objected to in *RT,* pp. 79, 119, 154.

[461] Lord Chancellour: Heneage Finch, whose speech to Parliament at the opening of the parliamentary session, April 13, 1675, Turner (p. 65) had admiringly cited as equal to Cicero's in eloquence.

A SHORT HISTORICAL ESSAY, TOUCHING GENERAL COUNCILS, CREEDS, AND IMPOSITIONS[1] IN MATTERS OF RELIGION

The Christian Religion, as first instituted by our Blessed Saviour, was the greatest security to Magistrates by the Obedience which it taught, and was fitted to enjoy no less security under them by a Practice conformable to that Doctrine. For our Saviour himself, not pretending to an Earthly Kingdom, took such care therefore to instruct his Followers in the due subjection to Governours; that while they observed his Precepts, they could neither fall under any jealousie of State, as an ambitious and dangerous Party, nor as Malefactors upon any other account deserve to suffer under the Publick Severity: So that in this only it could seem pernicious to Government, that Christianity, if rightly exercised upon its own Principles, would render all Magistracy useless. But although he, *who was Lord of all, and to whom all Power was given both in Heaven, and in Earth*[2] was nevertheless contented to come in the form of a Servant,[3] and to let the Emperours and Princes of the World alone with the use of their Dominions; he thought it good reason to retain his Religion under his own Cognizance, and exempt its Authority from their Jurisdiction. In this alone he was imperious, and did not only practice it himself against the Laws and Customs then received, and in the face of the Magistrate; but continually seasoned and hardened his Disciples in the same confidence and obstinacy. He tells them, *They shall be brought before Kings and Governours for his Name,*[4] but fear them not, he will be with them, bear them out,[5] and justifie it against all opposition. Not that he allowed them hereby to violate their duty to the Publick by any resistance in defiance of the Magistracy; but he instructed and animated them in their duty to God, in despight of suffering.

In this manner Christianity did at first set out, and accordingly found Reception. For although our Blessed Saviour, *having fulfilled all Righteousness,*[6] and the time of his Ministery being compleated, did by his Death set the Seal to his Doctrine, and shew the way toward Life and Immortality to

---

[1] Imposition: a dogma or ceremony imposed without scriptural warrant, or the act of requiring that dogma or ceremony.

[2] Matthew 28:8.

[3] Cf. Philippians 2:7.

[4] Matthew 10:18.

[5] Bear them out: back up, confirm.

[6] Romans 8:4.

such as believing imitate his Example: yet did not the Heathen Magistrate take the Government to be concerned in the point of Religion, or upon that account consent to his Execution. Pontius Pilate, then Governour of Judaea, though he were a Man unjust, and cruel by Nature, and served Tiberius,[7] the most tender, jealous, and severe, in point of State or Prerogative, of all the Roman Emperours; though he understood that great Multitudes followed him, and that he was grown the Head of a new Sect that was never before heard of in the Nation, yet did not he intermeddle. But they were the Men of Religion, the Chief Priests, Scribes and Elders, and the High-Priest Caiaphas. And yet, although they accused him falsly, That *he taught that Tribute was not to be given to Caesar,*[8] [44] that *he* was a Fifth Monarch,[9] and *made himself a King;*[10] and (as it is usual for some of the Clergy to terrifie the inferiour Magistrates out of their duty to Justice, under pretence of Loyalty to the Prince) threatned Pilate, that *if he let that Man go, he was not Caesars Friend;*[11] he understanding *that they did it out of Envy,*[12] and that the Justice and Innocence of our Saviour was what they could not bear with, would have adventured all their Informing at Court, and first have freed him, and then have exchanged him for Barrabas; saying, that *he found no fault in him.*[13] but he was overborn at last by humane weakness, and poorly imagined, that by washing his own hands he had expiated himself, and wiped off the guilt upon those alone who were the occasion. But, as for Tiberius himself, the growth of Christianity did never increase his cares of Empire at Rome, nor trouble his sleep at Capreae: but he both[14] approved of the Doctrine, and threatned the Informers with Death; nor would have staid

---

[7] Tiberius: Tiberius Claudius Nero Caesar (42 B.C.–A.D. 37), Roman emperor A.D. 14–37; notorious for his corruption and also for his retirement to the isle of Capri, leaving Rome to the mercy of his favorite, Sejanus.

[8] Luke 23:2.

[9] a Fifth Monarch: The Fifth Monarchy was the last of the five great empires referred to in Daniel 2:44. In the seventeenth century it was identified with the millennial reign of Christ predicted in the Apocalypse. For Marvell's hostile view of the Fifth Monarchists, see *RT2*, p. 427, and *First Anniversary* (*P&L* 1:305), which berates the Fifth Monarchists Christopher Feake and John Simpson, imprisoned for preaching against Cromwell in January 1654.

[10] Luke 23:2.

[11] John 19:12.

[12] Matthew 28:18.

[13] Luke 23:4.

[14] both A] hath B.

there, but attempted, according to the way of their Superstition, upon the intelligence he had from Pilate, to have received Christ into the number of their Deities. The Persecution of the Apostles after his Death, and the Martyrdom of Stephen, happened not by the interposing of the Civil Magistrate in the matter of Religion, or any disturbance occasioned by their Doctrines; but arose from the High-Priest, and his Emissaries, by suborned Witnesses, stirring up the Rabble in a brutish and riotous manner to execute their cruelty. How would the modern Clergy have taken and represented it, had they lived in the time of St. John Baptist, and seen *Jerusalem, Judaea, and all the Region round about Jordan, go out to be baptized by him!*[15] Yet that Herod,[16] for any thing we read in Scripture, though he wanted not his instillers, apprehended no Commotion: and had not Caligula banished him and his Herodias together, might in all appearance have lived without any change of Government. 'Twas she that caused John's Imprisonment for the convenience of her Incest, Herod indeed *feared him*, but rather reverenced him, *as a just man, and an holy, observed him, and when he heard him, he did many things, and heard him gladly.*[17] Nor could all her subtilty have taken off his Head, but that Herod thought himself under the Obligations of a Dance, and an Oath, and knew not in that Case they ought both to be dispensed with.[18] But *he was exeeding sorry at his death,*[19] which few Princes are, if men have lived to their jealousie or danger. The killing of James, and imprisonment of Peter by that other Herod,[20] was *because he saw he pleased the people,*[21] when the Priests had once set them on madding; a Complaisance to which the most Innocent may be exposed, but which partakes more of Guile than Civility or Wisdom.

But to find out what the disinteressed[22] and prudent Men of those days

[15] Matthew 3:13.

[16] Herod Antipas, tetrarch of Galilee, who married his niece Herodias, mother of Salome, and who, in the Gospels, consented to the death of John the Baptist.

[17] Mark 6:20.

[18] An allusion to the king's dispensing power, whereby in a particular case the law could be set aside; by extension, applied to obligations.

[19] Mark 6:26.

[20] Julius Agrippa I (10 B.C.–A.D. 44), tetrarch of parts of Galilee, grandson of Herod the Great. In the Acts of the Apostles, he is called Herod and made responsible for James's execution and Peter's imprisonment.

[21] Acts 12:3.

[22] disinteressed: disinterested, unbiased, without prejudice or personal concern in the matter.

took to be the wisest and only justifiable way for the Magistrate to proceed in upon matters of Religion, I cannot see any thing more pregnant than the concurrent Judgment of three Persons, of so different Characters, and that lived so far asunder, that there can be no danger of their having [45] corrupted one anothers Understanding in favour to Christianity. Gamaliel, the Deputy of Achaia, and the Town Clerk of Ephesus: the first a Jewish Doctor, by Sect a Pharisee, one of the Council, and of great Authority with the People, who (when the Chief-Priest had cast the Apostles in Prison, and charged them for Preaching against the Command he had before laid upon them) yet gave this advice, confirming it with several fresh Precedents: Acts 5. *That they should take heed to themselves what they intended to do with those men, and let them alone; for if this Counsel,* saith he, *or this Work be of Men, it will come to nought;* but *if it be of God, you cannot overthrow it, lest ye be found fighting with God.*[23] So that his Opinion grounded upon his best experience, was that the otherwise unblameable Sect of Christianity might safely, and ought to be left to stand or fall by Gods Providence under a free Toleration of the Magistrate. The second was Gallio, Acts 18. a Roman, and Deputy of Achaia. The Jews at Corinth hurried Paul before his Tribunal, laying the usual Charge against him, *That he perswaded Men to worship God contrary to the Law:* which Gallio looked upon as so slight, and without his Cognizance,[24] that although most Judges are willing to increase the Jurisdiction of their Courts, *He drave them away,* saving Paul the labour of a defence, and told them, *If it were a matter of wrong, or wicked lewdness, Reason would that he should bear with them; but if it be a Question of Words and Names, and of your Law, look ye to it, I will be no Judge of such matters.*[25] And when he had so said, Paul was released, but the Greeks that were present took Barrabas, and before the Judgment Seat *beat Sosthenes the Chief Ruler of the Synagogue,* and Ring-leader of the Accusers.[26] His Judg-

---

[23] Acts 5:38–39. Gamaliel's speech before the Sanhedrin was frequently cited as an authority for freedom of conscience. Sebastian Castellio invoked him in his preface to the bible of 1551 and in his controversy with Calvin. Jacques Bretagne did so in his speech of August 27, 1561, to the Estates General of France, arguing that the *permission tacite* of the 1561 Edict was insufficient. See Malcolm Smith, *Montaigne and Religious Freedom: The Dawn of Pluralism* (Geneva, 1991), pp. 191, 196–97.

[24] Cognizance: jurisdiction.

[25] Acts 18:13–15.

[26] Cf. Acts 18:17: "Then the Greeks took Sosthenes, the chief ruler of the synagogue, and beat him before the judgment seat." Barrabas has no place in this story. The 1680

ment[27] therefore was, that to punish Christians meerly for their Doctrine and Practise, unless they were Malefactors otherwise, was a thing out of the Magistrates Province, and altogether unreasonable. The third case[28] was no less remarkable: For one Demetrius, that was a Silver Smith by Trade, and made Shrines for Diana, stirred up all the Free men of his Company against Paul; and indeed he stated the matter very fairly and honestly, assigning the true Reason of most of these Persecutions: *Ye know that by this Craft we have our Wealth, but that by Paul's Preaching, that they be no Gods which are made with hands, not only our Craft is in danger to be set at naught, but also the Temple of the great Goddess, and her Magnificense, whom all Asia and the World worship, should be despised and destroyed.*[29] And it is considerable, that even the Jews, though of a contrary Religion, yet fomented, as it usually chances, this difference and egg'd the Ephesians[30] on against the Apostle and his Followers. But when they had brought Alexander, one of Paul's Companions, into the Theatre, the Recorder of Ephesus, (more temperate and wise than some would have been in that Office) would not make any *Inquisition* upon the matter, nor put Alexander upon his Tryal and Defence, (although he himself could not have born that Office without being a great Dianist, as he declared too in his discourse) he tells the people, *They had* [46] *brought those men which were neither robbers of Churches nor Blasphemers of their Goddess,* (for the Judge would not Condemn men by any inferences and Expositions of old Statutes which long after was Julian's practice[31] and since imitated)[32] *and therefore if Demetrius and his Crafts-men*

---

edition substituted Barnabas, which was ingenious but also incorrect. Thompson omitted the name. It is possible that Marvell wrote: "the Greeks . . . turned Barbarous."

[27] His Judgment: This refers back to Gallio.

[28] third case] third B.

[29] Acts 19:25.

[30] yet . . . Ephesians Ed.] yet, fomented, as it usually chances, this difference and egg'd the Ephesians A; yet, fomented, as it usually chances: this difference egg'd the Ephesians B.

[31] Julian: Flavius Claudius Julianus, Roman emperor A.D. 361–63, nicknamed "The Apostate" by Christian writers, having been brought up as a Christian under the control of his cousin Constantius, but reverting to active and coercive paganism on his accession. He is mentioned several times in *RT2* as a prototype for Samuel Parker.

[32] since imitated: This jibe is too vague to be recognizable. It could include anything from Charles I's claims to ship money to interpretations of the treason statutes in the trials of the regicides.

had any matter against them the Law was open, and it should be determined in a Lawful Assembly, but that the whole City was in danger to be called in question for that uproar, there being no cause whereby they might give account of that concourse.[33] And by this he plainly enough signified, that if Paul and his Companions had stolen Church-plate[34] they might well be indited, but that Demetrius had no more reason in Law against them, than a Chandler might have had, if by[35] Paul's Preaching Wax tapers, as well as Silver-Candlesticks had grown out of fashion. That it is matter of right and wrong betwixt man and man that the Justice of Government looks too: but that, while Christianity was according to its own Principle carried on quietly, it might so fall that the disturbers of it were guilty of a Riot, and their great City of Ephesus deserve to be fin'd for't. And taking this to have been so, he dismist the Assembly, Acts 19.

After these Testimonies which I have collected out of the History of the Acts, as of greatest Authority, I shall only add one or two more out of the same Book, wherein Paul was likewise concern'd before Heathen Magistrates of greater eminence, Acts. 23. Ananias[36] the High Priest (these alwayes were the men) having countenanc'd and instigated the Jews to a Conspiracy, in which Paul's Life was indanger'd and aim'd at, Lysias the chief Captain of Jerusalem interposes, and sends him away to Foelix then Governor of Judaea; signifying by Letter, *that he had been accused only of questions of their Law,* but he found nothing to be laid to his charge worthy of Death or of Bonds.[37] Whereof Foelix also, though the High Priest[38] was so zealous in the Prosecution that he took the journey on purpose, and had instructed an exquisite Orator, Tertullus, to harangue Paul out of his Life, as a *Pestilent fellow, a mover of Sedition, and Ring-leader of the Sect of the Nazarenes,*[39] not omitting even to charge Lysias for *rescuing him by great violence*[40] from being Murdered by them, was so well satisfied of the contrary upon full hearing, that he gave him his Liberty, and *a Centurion for his guard, with a command that none of his acquaintance should be debarr'd from*

[33] Acts 19:37–41.
[34] stolen Church-plate B] stoln the Church-Plate A.
[35] by A] not in B.
[36] Ananias A] Annanias B.
[37] Acts 23:29.
[38] High Priest A] Priest, B; a misunderstanding of the syntax.
[39] Acts 24:5.
[40] Acts 24:7.

comeing and Minstring to him.[41] But being indeed to leave his Government afterwards, *left him in Prison,*[42] partly to shew the Jews and their High-Priest another piece of complaisant Policy, which, 'tis possible they paid well for, seeing the other reason was, because though he had *sent for Paul the oftner and communed with him, in hopes that he would have given him money to be discharged,*[43] there came nothing of it. Which was so base a thing in so great a Minister, that the meanest Justice of the Peace in England would scarce have the face to do so upon the like occasion. But his Successor Festus, having called Agrippa and Bernice to hear the Cause, they all three were of Opinion that 'twas all on the Jews side Calumny and Impertinence; but [47] that Paul had *done nothing worthy of death, or of bonds, and might have been set free, but that having appeal'd to Caesar,* he must be transmitted to him in safe Custody.[44] Such was the sense of those upon whom the Emperors then relyed for the Government and security of their Provinces: and so gross were their Heathen understandings, that they could not yet comprehend how quietness was Sedition, or the Innocence of the Christian Worship could be subject to forfeiture or penalty. Nay, when Paul appear'd even before Nero[45] himself *and had none to stand by him, but all forsook him,* he was by that Emperour acquitted, and permitted a long time to follow the work of his Ministry. 'Tis true, that afterwards this Nero had the honour to be the first of the Roman Emperors that persecuted Christianity: whence it is that Tertullian in his *Apologetick* saith; *We glory in having such an one the first beginner and Author of our Punishment, for there is none that hath read of him, but must understand some great good to have been in that Doctrine, otherwise Nero would not have condemned it.*[46]

And thence forward Christianity for about three hundred years lay subject to Persecution. For the Gentile Priests could not but observe a great

---

[41] Acts 24:33.

[42] Cf. Acts 24:27; Marvell is slightly manipulating the scriptural account.

[43] Acts 24:26.

[44] Acts 25.

[45] Nero: Nero Claudius Caesar (A.D. 37–68), made emperor in A.D. 58. Though early in his reign he was a model ruler, he became a tyrant and was believed to have set the great fire of Rome (June 64) for his amusement. Fearing capture in the rebellion headed by Galba, he committed suicide.

[46] Tertullian, *Apology,* chapter 4. Marvell's source, however, was surely Eusebius, who quoted this passage, book 2, chap. 2. See John Christopherson, *Historicae Ecclesiasticae,* 3 vols. (Louvain, 1569), 1:38r.

decay in their Parishes, a neglect of their Sacrifices, and diminution of their Profits, by the daily and visible increase of that Religion. And God in his wise Providence had so ordered, that as the Jews already, so the Heathens now having fill'd up their Measure with Iniquity, *sprinkling the Blood of his Saints among their Sacrifices,*[47] and the Christians having in a severe Apprenticeship of so many Ages learned the Trade of suffering, they should at last be their own Masters, and admitted to their Freedom. Neither yet, even in those times when they lay exposed to Persecution, were they without some Intervals and catching[48] seasons of Tranquility, wherein the Churches had leisure to reap considerable advantage, and the Clergy too might have been inured, as they had been Exemplary under Affliction, so to bear themselves like Christians when they should arrive at a full prosperity. For as oft as there came a Just Heathen Emperour, and a Lover of Mankind, that either himself observed, or understood by the Governours of his Provinces the Innocence of their Religion and Practices, their readiness to pay Tribute, their Prayers for his Government and Person, their faithful Service in his Wars, but their Christian Valour and Contumacy[49] to Death, under the most Exquisite Torments, for their holy Profession, he forthwith relented; he rebated[50] the Sword of the Executioner, and could not find in his heart, or in his power, to exercise it against the exercise of that Religion: It being demonstrable, that a Religion instituted upon Justice betwixt Man and Man, Love to one another, yea even their Enemies, Obedience to the Magistrate in all Humane and Moral matters, and in Divine Worship upon a constant exercise thereof, and as constant Suffering in that Cause, without any pretence or latitude for resistance, cannot, so long as it is true to it self in these things, fall within the Magistrates Jurisdiction. [48]

But as it first was planted without the Magistrates hand, and the more they pluck'd at it, so much the more still it flourished,[51] so it will be[52] to the end of the world, and whensoever Governors have a mind to try for it, it will by the same[53] means and method sooner or later foil them; but, if they have a mind to pull up that Mandrake, it were advisable for them not to do it

---

[47] Luke 13:1.

[48] catching: either captivating or, perhaps, infectious.

[49] Contumacy to Death: resistance even unto death.

[50] rebated: repressed, blunted.

[51] flourished A,B] flouricted AV.

[52] it will be A,B] it would be AV.

[53] by the same A] be the same B,AV, corrected in Berkeley.

themselves, but to chuse out a Dog for the Imployment.[54] I confess whensoever a Christian transgresses[55] these bounds once, he is impoundable,[56] or
like a wafe[57] and stray whom Christ knows not, he falls to the Lord of the
Mannor. But otherwise he cannot suffer, he is invulnerable by the sword of
Justice: only a man may swear and damn himself to kill the first honest man
he meets, which hath been and is the case of all true Christians worshiping
God under the power and violence of their Persecutors.

But the truth is that, even in those times which some men now, as oft as
it is for their advantage, do consecrate under the name of Primitive, the
Christians were become guilty of their own punishment, and had it not
been, as is most usual, that the more Sincere Professors suffered promis-
cuously for the Sins and Crimes of those that were Carnal and Hypocrites,
their Persecutors may be look'd upon as having been the due Administra-
tors of God's Justice. For (not to go deeper) if we consider but that which is
reckoned the Tenth Persecution[58] under Dioclesian,[59] so incorrigible were
they after nine preceeding, what other could be expected when as[60] Eusebius l.3.c.I.[61] sadly laments, having related how *before that the Christians
lived in great trust and reputation in Court, the Bishops of each Church were
beloved, esteem'd and reverenced by all mankind and by the Presidents of the
Provinces, the Meetings in all the Cities were so many and numerous, that
it was necessary and allow'd them to erect in every one spacious and goodly
Churches, all things went on prosperously with them, and to such an height that
no envious man could disturb them, no Divel could hurt them, as long as*

---

[54] An allusion to the legend that uprooting a mandrake was fatal to the puller, hence a
dog should be employed in a man's stead.

[55] transgresses A,B] transgresseth AV.

[56] Impoundable: liable to be taken into custody.

[57] Waif: Wafe: wafe, a person without a home, an outcast or vagabond. Marvell is
alluding here to the strict laws against vagabondage enacted in England in the sixteenth
century.

[58] Tenth Persecution: See *Mr. Smirke*, n. 163.

[59] Dioclesian: Gaius Aurelius Valerius, abdicated in 305, died 312. His first persecu-
tory edict, February 23, 303, was designed to prevent the Christian church from func-
tioning, by requiring the burning of the Scriptures, demolition of churches, and ban-
ning of meetings for worship. Recusants were deprived of rank and made liable to
torture and summary execution.

[60] as] not in AV.

[61] Actually Eusebius, 8:1. Christopherson, 1:166v.

*walking yet worthy of those mercies they were under the Almighty's cure and
protection: after that our affair by that too much Liberty, degenerated into
Luxury and Laziness, and some prosecuted others with Hatred, Contumely,*[62]
*and almost all of us wounded our selves with the weapons of the Tongue in ill
language when Bishops set upon Bishops, and the people that belonged to one of
them stirred Sedition against the people of another; then horrible Hypocrisy and
Dissimulation sprung up to the utmost extremity of Malice, and the Judgement
of God, while yet there was liberty to meet in the Congregations, did sensibly
and by steps begin to visit us, the Persecution at first discharging it self upon our
Brethren that were in the Army. But having no feeling of the hand of God, nor
indeavouring to make our peace with him, and living as if we believed that God
did neither take notice of our Transgressions nor would visit us for them, we
heaped up Iniquity upon Iniquity. And those which seemed to be our Pastors,
kicking under foot the rules of Piety, were inflamed among themselves with
mutual Contentions, and while they minded nothing else but to exaggerate their
Quarrells, Threats, Emulation, Hatred and Enmities,*[63] *and earnestly each of
them pursued his particular Ambition in a Tyrannical manner, then indeed the
Lord, then I say, according to the voice of the Pro-*[49]*phet Jeremy,*[64] *he covered
the Daughter of Zion with a cloud in his anger,*[65] *and cast down from Heaven
unto earth the beauty of Israel; and remembered not his footstool in the day of his
anger.*[66] And so the Pious Historian Pathetically goes on, and deplores the
Calamities that insued, to the loss of all that stock of Reputation, Advantage, Liberty and Safety,[67] which Christian[68] people had by true Piety and
adhering strictly to the Rules of their Profession formerly acquired and
injoyned, but had now forfeited and smarted deservedly under Dioclesian's
persecution. And it was *a severe* one, the longest too that ever happened, ten
years from his beginning of it and continued by others: by which time one
might have thought the Church would have been sufficiently winnowed,
and nothing left but the pure Wheat, whereas it proved quite contrary, and

---

[62] Hatred, Contumely B,AV] Hatred and Contumely A.

[63] Enmities A] Enemies B,AV.

[64] A setting ends: tyrannical manner, [50] then. AV, though reset, follows B and from
l. 24 matches exactly.

[65] *in his anger* A; correct as in the scriptural text] *of his anger* B,AV.

[66] Lamentations 2:1.

[67] Safety A] Safely B,AV.

[68] Christian A] Cristian, B,AV.

the holiest and most constant of the Christians being[69] blown away by Martyrdom, it seem'd by the succeeding times as if nothing but the Chaff and the Tares remained.[70] But there was yet such a Seed left, and notwithstanding the defection of many, so internal a virtue in the Religion it self, that Dioclesian could no longer stand against it, and tired out in two years time, was glad to betake himself from rooting out Christianity, to gardening and to sow Pot-herbs at Salona. And he with his partner Maximianus, resigned the Empire to Galerius and Constantinus, the excellent Father of a more glorious and Christian son, Constantine the Great,[71] who in due season succeeded him, and by a chain of Gods extraordinary providences seemed to have been let down from Heaven to be Emperor of the whole World, and as I may say, the Universal Apostle of Christianity.

It is unexpressible the virtue of that Prince, his Care, his Indulgence, his Liberality, his own Example, every thing that could possibly tend to the promotion and incouragement of true Religion and Piety. And in order to that he thought he could not do better, nor indeed could he, then to shew a peculiar respect to the Clergy and Bishops, providing largely for their subsistence, and they too on their part behaved themselves worthy of their High Calling, are known to make right use of the advantages of his Bounty to the same ends that they were by him intended. For if the Apostle I. Tim. 5.17. requires *that an Elder,* provided *he rule well, be accounted worthy of Double Honor, especially those who labor*[72] *in the Word and Doctrine,*[73] it excludes not a Decuple[74] or any further proportion, and indeed there cannot be too high a value set[75] upon such a Person: and God forbid too that any measure of wealth should render a Clergy man Uncanonical.[76] But

---

[69] being A] bing B,AV.

[70] Tares remained B,AV] Tares had remained A.

[71] Constantine the Great: Flavius Valerius Constantinus (ca. 272–337), the founder of Constantinople; favored Christians as officials in his administration, welcomed bishops at court; summoned the Council of Nicaea in 325 to settle the Arian heresy; brought Christianity from a persecuted minority sect to near hegemony in the empire.

[72] labor Ed.] laboring A,B,AV.

[73] 1 Timothy 5:17.

[74] Decuple Ed., Thompson] Deouple A,B,AV; an amount ten times the preceding. The 1703 edition avoids the archaism by substituting "Triple."

[75] value set Ed.] value be set A,B,AV; this second, unnecessary "be" is struck out in Berkeley.

[76] Uncanonical: no longer a member of an ecclesiastical chapter.

alas, Bishops were already grown another Name and Thing, then at the
Apostles Institution; and had so altered their property, that Paul would
have had much difficulty by all the marks in[77] I Tim. 3[78] to have known
them. They were ill enough under persecution many of them, but that long
and sharp Winter under Dioclesian, being seconded by so warm a Summer
under Constantine, produced a Pestilence, which as an Infection that seizes
sometimes only one sort of Cattel, Diffused it self most remarkably thorow
the whole body of the Clergy. From his reign the most sober Historians
date that New Disease which was so [50] generally propagated then, and
ever since transmitted to some of their Successors, that it hath given reason
to inquire whether it only happened to those men as it might to others, or
were[79] not inherent to the very Function. It show'd it self first in Ambition,
then in Contention, next in Imposition,[80] and after these Symptoms broke
out at last like a Plague-sore in open Persecution. They the Bishops who
began to vouch themselves the Successors of Christ, or at least of his
Apostles, yet pretended to be Heirs and Executors of the Jewish High-
Priests and the Heathen Tyrants, and were ready to prove the Will. The
Ignorant Jews and Infidels understood not how to Persecute, had no Commission to meddle with Religion, but the Bishops had studied the Scriptures, knew better things, and the same, which was Cruelty and Tyranny in
the Heathens, if done by a Christian and Ecclesiastical hand, was hal-
lowed to be Church-Government and the care of a Diocess. But that I
may not seem to speak without book or out-run the History, I shall return
to proceed by those degrees I newly mention'd whereby the Christian Religion was usurped upon, and those things became their crime which were
their duties.

   The first was the Ambition of the Bishops, which had even before this
taken its rise when in the intervals of the former Persecutions the Piety of
the Christians had laid out ample provisions for the Church, but when
Constantine not only restored those which had been all confiscate under
Dioclesian, but was every day adding some new Possession, Priviledge, or

---

[77] in B] in the A,AV.

[78] the marks in 1 Tim.: Actually, 1 Timothy 3:1–7, where the qualifications of bishops
are defined in terms crucial to Marvell's pamphlet: "If a man desire the office of a
bishop, he desireth a good work. A bishop must be blameless, the husband of one wife,
temperate, sober-minded, of good behaviour, given to hospitality, apt to teach . . . not
greedy of filthy lucre, but patient, not a brawler, not covetous."

[79] were Ed.] where A,B,AV.

[80] Imposition: cf. the full title of the *Essay*.

Honor, a Bishoprick became very desirable, and was not only a *Good Work*[81] but a Good Thing,[82] especially when there was now no danger of paying as it was usual, formerly their First-fruits[83] to the Emperor by Martyrdom. The Arts by which Ambition climes, are Calumny, Dissimulation, Cruelty, Bribery, Adulation, all applyed in their proper places and seasons; and when the man hath attained his end he ordinarily shows himself then in his colours, in Pride, Opiniastry,[84] Contention, and all other requisite or incident ill Qualities. And if the Clergy of those times had some more dextrous and innocent way then this of managing their Ambition, it is to be lamented *inter Artes Deperditas*,[85] or lyes enviously hid by some musty Book-worm in his private Library.[86] But so much I find that both before, and then, and after, they cast such Crimes at one another, that a Man would scarce think he were reading an History of Bishops, but a Legend of Divels: and each took such care to blacken his adversary, and he regarded not how he smutted himself thereby and his own Order, to the Laughter or Horror of the by-standers. And one thing I remark particularly, that as Son of a Whore is the modern Word of Reproach among the Laity, of the same use then among the Clergy was Heretick. There were indeed Hereticks as well as there are Bastards, and perhaps it was not their fault, (neither of 'em could help it) but the Mothers or the Fathers, but they made so many Hereticks in those days, that 'tis hard to think they really believ'd them so, but adventur'd the Name only to pick a Quarrel. And one thing that makes it very suspicious is, that in the Ecclesiastical History the Ringleader[87] of any Heresy [51] was[88] for the most part accused of having a mind to be a Bishop, though it was not the way to come to it. As there[89] was the damnable Heresy of the Novatians,[90] against which Constantine, notwithstanding his

---

[81] 1 Timothy 3:1: "Faithful is the saying, If a man seeketh the office of a bishop, he desireth a good work."

[82] a Good Thing: this phrase is central to Marvell's irony.

[83] First fruits: See *Mr. Smirke*, n. 109.

[84] From the French *opiniastre*, now *opiniatre;* the condition of being opinioned; for Marvell's affection for this rare word, cf. *RT*, p. 109, and *Remarks*, p. 429.

[85] *inter Artes Deperditas* A] *Deperdetas* B,AV; corrected in Berkeley: among the lost arts.

[86] Library A] Liberary B.

[87] Ring-leader Ed., 1680, 1685, 1703] Ring-leaders A,B,AV.

[88] was Ed.] not in A,B,AV.

[89] there, A, B] here AV.

[90] The Novatians diverged from the policy of the Catholic church (which had been

Declaration of general Indulgence at his coming in,[91] was shortly after so incensed, that he published a most severe Proclamation against them; *Cognoscite jam per legem[92] hanc quae a me[93] sancita est O Novatiani[94]* &c. prohibiting all their meetings not only in Publick but in their own Private Houses, and that all such places where they assembled for their worship, should be rased[95] to the ground without delay or controversie, &c. Eus.l.3.c.62 *de vita Constantini*. Now the story the Bishops tell of Novatus the Author of that Sect, Euseb.l.6.c.42[96] is in the words of Cornelius the Bishop of Rome, the very first line. *But that you may know that this brave Novatus did even before that affect to be[97] a Bishop* (a great crime in him) *that he might conceal that petulant Ambition, he for a better cover to his arrogance, had[98] got some Confessors into his Society, &c.* and goes on calling him all to naught, *but then,* saith he, *he came with two Reprobates of his own Heresy into a little, the very least, Shire of Italy and by their means seduced three most simple high shoon[99] Bishops, wheedling them that they must with all speed go to Rome and there meeting with other[100] Bishops, all Matters should be reconciled. And when he had got thither[101] these three Silly Fellows, as I said, that were not*

---

defined by Cyprian) with respect to the finality of excommunication. While orthodox Catholicism allowed some possibility for grievous sinners or apostates to be received back into the church, Novatus argued for their permanent explusion and hence (probably) certain damnation.

[91] Declaration . . . coming in a manifest allusion to Charles II as Constantine, which sets up the analogy for what follows.

[92] *legem* A, AV] *legam* B.

[93] *a me* A,B] *in me* AV.

[94] Eusebius, *De vita Constantini*, 3:62; Christopherson, 1:285v: "O ye Novatians, know therefore by this Law which I have established . . ."

[95] rased: torn down.

[96] Eusebius, *Ecclesiastical History*, 6:43 Ed.] l 6.c.42 A; l.vi.c.42 B; l.vi.c.24 A variants: Eusebius is quoting at length the letter of Cornelius, bishop of Rome, to Fabius, bishop of Antioch.

[97] affect to be A,AV] effect to be B.

[98] *had* A,AV] *and* B.

[99] high shoon A,AV] high-shown B. Christopherson's Latin reads "*homines agrestes, rudes ac simplices*" (rustic fellows, rude and simple). Marvell's "high shoon" is an inventive translation. OED: "One who wears high shoes, as rustics did in the 17th c.", dating its use as an attribute to 1676.

[100] with other A,AV] with all other B, probably by eye-skip backwards from "all Matters."

[101] thither A] thither, B; a misunderstanding of the syntax.

aware of his cunning, he had prepared a company of Rogues like himself, that treated them in a private room very freely, and having thwack'd their bellies and heads full with meat and drink, compell'd the poor drunken Bishops by an Imaginary and vain Imposition of Hands to make Novatus also a bishop.[102] Might not one of the same Order now better have conceal'd these things had they been true, but such was the discretion. Then he tells *that one of the three returned soon after*[103] repenting it seems next morning, *and so he receiv'd him again into the Church* unto the *Laick Communion.* But for the other two he had sent Successors into their places. And yet after all this ado, and the whetting of Constantine, contrary to his own Nature and his own Declarations against the Novatians,[104] I cannot find their Heresy to have been other then that they were the Puritans of those times, and a sort of Nonconformists that could have subscribed to the Six and thirty Articles,[105] but differed only in those of Discipline: and upon some inormities therein separated, and[106] (which will always be sufficient to qualify an Heretick) they instituted Bishops of their own in most places. And yet[107] afterward in the times of the best Homotusian[108] Emperors, a sober and strictly Religious People did so constantly adhere to them, that the Bishops of the Church too found meet to give them fair quarter; for as much as *they differ'd not in Fundamentals, and therefore were of use to them against Hereticks that were more dangerous and diametrically opposite to the Religion.* Nay in so much, that even the Bishop of Constantinople, yea of Rome, notwithstanding that most tender point and interest of Episcopacy, suffered the

---

[102] G. A. Williamson, trans., *The History of the Church* (New York, 1996), p. 281n, comments on the original passage in Eusebius: "We know enough about Novatian from other sources to say that this spiteful letter gives a most unfair portrait of him." Marvell's translation is still more degrading.

[103] *returned* A,AV] not in B.

[104] Novatians A,AV] Novations B.

[105] Six and thirty Articles: for the Thirty-Nine Articles, see *Mr. Smirke,* note 137. Only three (no. 27, "Of Baptism," no. 28, "Of the Lord's Supper," and no. 34, "Of the traditions of the church") dealt with ceremonies. The Articles themselves do not, however, contain the ceremonial features to which the Nonconformists objected, i.e., kneeling as a requirement for taking communion and the use of the sign of the cross in baptism.

[106] and A,AV] not in B.

[107] yet A,AV] not in B.

[108] Homotusian, A,B,AV] 1680, 1685, 1703 emended to *homoousian,* which is probably correct; but Thompson (3:25) emended to *homoiousian*!

Novatian bishops to walk cheek by joul with them in their own Diocess; until that, as Socr. 17.c.ll. *the Roman Episcopacy having as it were passed the bounds of Priesthood, slipped into a Secular Principality, and thenceforward the Roman* [52] *Bishops would not suffer their Meetings with Security, but, though they commended them for their Consent in the same Faith with them, yet took away all their Estates.* But at Constantinople they continued to fare better, the Bishops of that Church *embracing the Novatians and giving them free liberty*[109] *to keep their Conventicles*[110] *in their Churches.*[111] What, and to have their Bishops too, Altar against Altar?[112] A Condescention which as our Non-Conformists seem not to desire or think of, so the Wisdom of these times would, I suppose, judge to be very unreasonable, but rather that it were fit to take the other course, and that whatsoever advantage the Religion might probably receive from their Doctrine and party, 'tis better to suppress them and make havock both of their Estates and Persons. But however the Hereticks in Constantine's time had the less reason to complain of ill Measure, seeing it was that the Bishops meated[113] by among themselves. I pass over that controversy betwixt Cecilianus, the Bishop of Carthage and his adherents, with another set of bishops there in Africk,[114] upon which Constantine ordered ten of each party to appear before Miltiades the Bishop[115] of Rome and others to have it desided.[116] Yet after they had given sentence Constantine found it necessary to have a Council for a review of the business, as in his Letter to Chrestus the Bishop of Syracusa, Euseb.l.10.c.6. *Whereas several have formerly separated from the Catholick Heresy*[117] (for that word was not yet so ill natured but that it might some-

---

[109] *and giving them free liberty* A,B] *and free liberty* AV.

[110] *Conventicles;* a tendentious translation; for the significance of the term, see *Mr. Smirke*, note 72.

[111] Socrates Scholasticus, 7:11. Christopherson, p. 169r.

[112] Altar against Altar: a glance back to Turner, p. 14.

[113] Meated A,B] There is a pun here on "ill Measure" and "meated by among themselves," based on Matthew 7:2: "And with what measure ye mete, it shall be measured to you again."

[114] Eusebius 10:5.

[115] the Bishop A, AV] Bishop B.

[116] desided B] deceived A, AV.

[117] It is not clear why Marvell chooses "heresy" as the term here, unless for irony's sake. Christopherson renders it "catholica Ecclesia *opinione,*" and Hanmer translates it as "opinion."

times be used in its proper and good Sense:) and then relates his Commission to the Bishop of Rome and others; *But for as much as some*[118] *having been careless of their own salvation, and forgetting the reverence due to that most holy Heresy* (again) *will not yet lay down their enmity, nor admit the sentence that hath been given, obstinately affirming that they were but*[119] *few that pronounced the Sentence, and that they did it very precipitately, before they had duly inquired of the matter: and from hence it*[120] *happened*[121] *that both they who ought to have been kept a brotherly and unanimous agreement together, do abominably and*[122] *flagitiously*[123] *dissent from one another, and such whose minds are alienated from the most holy Religion, do make a mockery both of it and them. Therefore I, &c. have commanded very many Bishops out of innumerable places to meet at Arles, that what ought to have been quieted upon the former Sentence pronounced, may now at least be determined, &c. and you to be one of them; and therefore I have ordered the Prefect of Sicily to furnish you with one of the publick Stage-Coaches and so many Servants, &c.*[124]

Such was the use then of Stage-Coaches, Post-Horses, and Councills, to the great disappointment and grievance of the *many*:[125] both Men and Horses and Leather being hackneyd, jaded and worn out upon the errand of some contentious and obstinate Bishop. So went the Affairs hitherto, and thus well disposed and prepared were the Bishops to receive the Holy Ghost a second time at the great and first general Council of Nice, which is so much Celebrated.[126] [53]

The occasions of calling it were two. The first a most important question in which the Wit and Piety of their Predecessors and now theirs[127] suc-

---

[118] *as much as some* A,AV] *as much some* B.

[119] *but* B] *but a* A,AV.

[120] *happened* B] *hath happened* A,AV.

[121] *it happened* B *it hath happened* A,AV.

[122] *and* A,B] *any* A variants.

[123] flagitiously: shamefully, atrociously.

[124] Eusebius, *Ecclesiastical History,* 10:5: "Copy of an Imperial letter commanding a second synod to be held with a view to the healing of all divisions between the bishops." Christopherson, 1:220r.

[125] Marvell's preference for the "many" vs. the "few" continues a theme of *Mr. Smirke,* p. 78.

[126] Celebrated: The Council of Nicaea (A.D. 325) usually commanded Protestant respect.

[127] theirs A] their B,AV.

cessively had been much exercised and taken up: that was upon what day they ought to keep Easter,[128] which though it were no point of Faith that it should be kept at all, yet the very calendiny[129] of it was controverted with the same zeal, and made as heavy a do in the Church as if both parties had been Hereticks. And it is reckoned by the Church Historians as one of the chief felicities of Constantines Empire to have quieted in that Councel this main controversie. The second cause of the assembling them here was indeed grown, as the Bishop had ordered it, a matter of the greatest weight and consequence to the Christian Religion, one Arrius having as is related, to the disturbance of the Church, started a most pernicious opinion in the point of the Trinity. Therefore from all parts of the Empire they met together at the City of Nice, two hundred and fifty Bishops, and better, saith Eusebius, a goodly company, three hundred and eighteen say others,[130] and the Animadverter too, with that pithy remark, *pa. 23. Equal almost to the number of servants bred up in the house of Abraham.*[131] The Emperour had accommodated them every where with the posts, or layd Horses all along for the convenience of their journey thither, and all the time they were there[132] supplied them abundantly with all sort of provision at his own charges. And when they were all first assembled in Council, in the great Hall of the Imperial Palace, he came in, having put on his best clothes to make his guests welcome; and saluted with that profound humility as if they all had been Emperour, nor would sit down in his Throne, no[133] it was a very

[128] Easter: Marvell discussed this controversy sardonically in *RT,* pp. 131–32, using John Hales' *Treatise of Schism* as his mouthpiece.

[129] calendiny A,B,AV, 1703: 1680, 1685 emend to "calendary." Grosart prints "calendiry." The *OED* records only "calendary," entering something in the calendar, and cites 1680 as the only instance. However, it also cites "calending" as the 1676 reading, which, though not attested to in any of the copies I have seen, may well be what Marvell wrote.

[130] others: Socrates Scholasticus, l.5.

[131] See Turner, p. 23, in response to Croft's appendix on councils. Turner's position was that "A General Council of Bishops is, as Tertullian styles it, *Representatio totius nominis Christiani,*" a claim that Marvell, as a parliamentarian, would have been sensitive to. Croft's (pp. 26–27) had been that it was numerically only a fraction of the universal church.

[132] there A] their B,AV.

[133] no A,B,AV] Grosart prints "tho" but Marvell is correcting his own use of "throne." For this detail, compare André Rivet, *Histoire des choses plus notables advenues in l'eglise* (Saumur, 1620), p. 134, in which the intention is to show the ritual nature of Constantine's humility and courtesy to the bishops in order to insist on his authority in convening and running the Council of Nice.

little and low stool, till they had all beckoned and made signes to him to sit down. No wonder if the first Council of Nice run in their heads ever after, and the ambitious Clergy, like those who have been long a thirst, took so much of Constantinus kindness, that they are scarce come to themselves again after so many Ages. The first thing was that he acquainted them with the causes of his summoning them thither, and in a grave and most Christian discourse *exhorted them* (to keep the peace or) *to a good agreement* as there was reason. *For* (saith Ruffin L.I.c.2.) *the Bishops being met*[134] *here almost of all parts, and as they use to do, bringing their quarrels about several matters along with them, every of them was at the Emperour, offering him Petitions, laying out one anothers faults,* (for all the good advice he had given them) *and were more intent upon these things then upon the business they were sent for. But he, considering that by these scoldings and Bickerings the main affair was frustrated, appointed a set day by which all the Bishops should bring him in whatsoever complaint they had against one another.* And they being all brought, he made them that high Asiatick complement: *God hath made you Priests, and hath given you power to judge me, and therefore it is in you to judge me righteously. But you cannot be judged by any men. It is God only can judge you, and therefore reserve all your quarrels to his Tribunal. For you are as Gods to me, and it is not convenient a man should judge of Gods, but he only of whom it is written,* God standeth in the Congregation of the Gods, and discerneth in the midst of them.[135] *And therefore setting these things* [54] *aside, apply your minds without any contention to the concernments of God's Religion.* And so *without opening or reading one Petition commanded them all together to be burnt there in his presence.*[136] An action of great Charity and excellent Wisdom, had but some of the words been spared. For doubtless, though they that would have complained of their brethren, grumbled a little; yet those that were accusable were all very well satisfied: and those expressions, *you can judge me righteously; and you cannot be judged by any man,* and *God only can judge you. You are Gods to me, &c.* were so extreamly sweet to some[137] of the Bishops palats, that they believ'd it, and could never think of them afterwards but their teeth watered; and they ruminated so long on them, that Constantine's Successors came too late to repent it. But now the

---

[134] *met* A] *meet* B,AV.

[135] Psalm 82:1.

[136] Ruffinus Aquileiensis, *Historiae ecclesiasticae liber decimus* (Antwerp, 1548), book I, chap. 2, pp. 159–60: "*De concilio apud Nicaeam congregato.*" Marvell quotes Constantine's fulsome courtesies with great exactness in order to show how they led to episcopal arrogance.

[137] to some B,AV] to most A. This alteration in B looks like a genuine correction.

Bishops, having mist of their great end of quarrelling one with another, betake themselves though somwhat aukwardly to business. And it is necessary to mine,[138] that as shortly as possible for the understanding of it, I give a cursory account of Alexander[139] and Arrius, with some few others that were the most interested in that general and first great revolution of Ecclesiastical affairs, since the dayes of the Apostles. This Alexander was the Bishop of Alexandria, and appears to have been a pious old Man, but not equally prudent, nor in Divine things of the most capable, nor in conducting the affairs of the Church, very dextrous; but he was the Bishop. This Character that I have given of him, I am the more confirmed in from some passages that follow, and all of them pertinent to the matter before me. They were used Sozom. l.2.c.16 at Alexandria to keep yearly a solemn Festival to the memory of Peter one of their former Bishops, upon the same day he[140] suffered Martyrdom; which Alexander having Celebrated at the Church with publick Devotion, was sitting after at home expecting some guests to dine with him, Sozom l.2.c.16. As he was alone and looking towards the Sea side, he saw a prity way off[141] the Boys upon the beach, at an old[142] Recreation, imitating it seems the Rites of the Church and office of the Bishops, and was much delighted with the sight as long as it appear'd an innocent and harmless representation: but when he observed them at last how they acted, the very administration of the Sacred Mysteries, he was much troubled, and sending for some of the chief of his Clergy, caused the Boys to be taken and brought before him. He asked them particularly what kind of sport they had been at, and what the words, and what the actions were that they had used in it. After their fear had hindred them a while from answering, and now they were afraid of being silent, they confessed that a Lad of their play-fellows, one Athanasius,[143] had baptized some of them that were not yet initiated in those Sacred Mysteries: Whereupon Alexander inquired the more accu-

[138] mine A] mind B,AV; an understandable, if mistaken, "correction."

[139] Alexander: St. Alexander, archbishop of Alexandria, appointed 313, d. 326. Alexander was famous primarily for his theological struggle with Arius.

[140] day he B,AV] day that he A.

[141] a prity way off: Marvell's facetious translation of "*longe.*"

[142] old B,AV] odd A, 1703: The phrase has no origin in Christopherson's Latin.

[143] Athanasius: St. Athanasius (c. 295–373) was an outstanding theologian of the Greek church, who as deacon played an influential role at Nicaea. He became bishop of Alexandria in 328, but because of the doctrinal conflicts within the church was five times deposed and exiled. Two of his exiles were to the West, to which he introduced monasticism. He developed the doctrine of the divinity and personality of the Holy Spirit, subsequently enshrined in the Athanasian Creed.

rately what the Bishop of the game had said, and what he did to the boyes he had baptized, what they also had answered or learned from him. At last, when Alexander perceiv'd by them that his[144] Pawn Bishop had made all his removes right,[145] and that the whole Ecclesiastical Order and Rites had been duely observed in their interlude, he by the advice of his Priests about him approved of that Mock Baptism, and determined that, the boys, be-[55]ing once in the simplicity of their minds dipped in the Divine Grace, ought not to be Rebaptized,[146] but he perfected it with the remaining Mysteries, which it is only lawful for Priests[147] to administer. And then he delivered Athanasius and the rest of the boys that had acted the parts of *Presbyters* and *Deacons* to their Parents, calling God to witness that they should be educated in the Ministery of the Church, that they might pass their lives in that calling which they had chosen by imitation.[148] But as for Athanasius, in a short while after Alexander took him to live with him and be his Secretary, having caused him to be carefully educated in the Schools of the best *Grammarians* and *Rhetoricians;* and he grew in the opinion of all that spoke with him a discreet and eloquent person, and will give occasion to be more[149] then once mentioned again in this Discourse, I have translated this in a manner word for word from the Author. This good natured old Bishop Alexander, that was so far from Anathemising,[150] that he did not so much as whip the boys for profanation of the Sacrament against the Discipline of the Church, but without more doing, left them, for ought I see, at liberty to regenerate as many more Lads upon the next Holy day as they thought convenient: He Socr. l.1.c.3, *being a man that lived an easy and gentle life, had*[151] *one day called his Priests and the rest of his Clergy together, and fell on Philosophysing*[152] *divinely among them, but something more subtly and curiously* (though I dare say he meant no harm) *then was usual concerning the Holy*

---

[144] his B,AV] this A.

[145] his Pawn Bishop had made all his removes right: Marvell's mocking addition.

[146] *being . . . Rebaptized:* presumably italicized as a moment of literal translation. Cf. Christopherson: "pueros semel in animorum simplicitate divina grata imbutos, rebaptizandos non censuit" (3:38v).

[147] Priests A,B] for the Priests AV.

[148] Hermias Sozomen, *Ecclesiastical History,* 2:16. Christopherson, 3:38v.

[149] be more A,AV] more B.

[150] Anathemizing: denouncing a doctrine or practice as damnable. *Anathema,* or excommunication, is a theme word of the *Essay.*

[151] had A,AV] and B.

[152] Philosphysing Ed., 1680, 1687, 1703, Berkeley correction] philosphyring A,B; philosophying AV.

Trinity. Among the rest, one Arrius a[153] Priest too of Alexandria was there present, a Man who is described to have been[154] a good Disputant, and others add, (the Capital accusation of those times) that he had a mind to have been a Bishop and bore a great pique at Alexander, for having[155] been preferr'd before him to the See of Alexandria: but more are silent of any such matter, and Sozom. l.i.c.14 saith *he was in great*[156] *esteem with his Bishop.*[157] But Arrius Socr. l.I.c.3. *hearing his discourse*[158] *about the Holy Trinity and the Unity in the Trinity, conceiv'd that, as the Bishop stated it, he had reason to suspect he was introducing afresh into the Church the Heresy of Sabellius*[159] *the African who Fatebatur unum esse Deum, & ita*[160] *in unum essentiam Trinitatem adducebat, ut assereret nullam*[161] *esse vere subjectam proprietatem personis, sed nomina mutari*[162] *pro eo atque usus poscant ut nunc de illo ut patre, nunc ut filio, nunc ut spiritu sancto disseratur.*[163] And thereupon it seems Arrius argued warmly for that opinion which was directly contrary to the Africane, driving the Bishop from one to a second, from a second to a third, seeming absurdity; which I studiously avoid the relation of, that in all these things I may not give occasion for Mens understandings[164] to work by their memories, and propogate the same errors by the same means they were first occasion'd. But hereby Arrius was himself blamed as the maintainer of those

[153] a Priest A,AV] Priest B.

[154] to have been A,AV] to be B.

[155] for having A,B] for he having AV.

[156] in great, A,B] in a great AV.

[157] Sozomen, 1:14; Christopherson, 3:18r: "Alexander eum permagni aestimare coepit."

[158] his discourse A,B] her discourse AV.

[159] Socrates, 1:3. Sabellius was active between A.D. 198 and 217 at Rome. He maintained that the three persons of the Trinity were merely different aspects or modes of manifestation of a single divine person.

[160] *ita* Ed., 1680, 1687, 1703] *eta* A,B,AV.

[161] *nullam* A,AV] *nullum* B.

[162] *mutari* A,B] *maturi* AV.

[163] *Fatebatur . . . disseratur:* "He confessed that there was one God, and put so much stress on the one essential Trinity, that he asserted there to be truly no distinct identity of person, but that the names for each changed according to need, so that now one speaks of God as the Father, now as the son, now as the Holy Spirit." The source of this passage has not been traced. It is not in Socrates or Sozomen, via Christopherson, nor in the chief source for Sabellius's doctrines, the fourth oration of Athanasius against the Arians.

[164] understandings A,AV] understanding B.

absurdities which he affixed to the Bishops opinion, as is usual in the heat[165] and wrangle of Disputation. Whereas Truth for the most part lyes in the middle, but men ordinarily seek for it in the extremities. Nor can I wonder that those ages were so fertile in what they called Heresies, when being given to meddling with the mysteries of Religion further then humane apprehension or divine revelation did or could lead them, [56] some of the Bishops were so ignorant and gross, but others so speculative, acute and refining in their conceptions, that, there being moreover a good fat Bishoprick to boot in the case, it is rather admirable to me how all the Clergy from one end to 'tother, could escape from being or being accounted Hereticks. Alexander hereupon Soz.l.i.c.14.[166] instead of stilling by more prudent Methods this new Controversie, took, doubtless with a very good intention, a course that hath seldome been successful: makes himself judge of that wherein he had first been the Party, and calling to him some others of his Clergy, would needs sit in publick to have a solemn set Disputation about the whole matter. And while Arrius was at it Tooth and Nail against his opposers, and the Arguments flew so thick that they darkened the air, and no man could yet judge which side should have the victory; the good Bishop for his part sate hay now hay,[167] neither could tell in his Conscience of a long time which had the better of it; but sometimes he lean'd on the one[168] side and then on the other, and now incouraged and commended those of one party, and presently the contrary, but at last by his own weight he cast the Scales against Arrius. And from thence forward he excommunicating Arrius for obstinacy, and Arrius writing in behalf [of himself][169] and his followers to the Bishops, each one stating his own and his adversaries case with the usual candor of such men in such matters; the Bishops too all over began to divide upon it, and after them their people. Insomuch that Constantine out of a true paternal sense and care, found necessary to send a very prudent and eminent person to Alexandria, to try if he could accomodate the matter, giving him a Letter to Alexander and Arrius, how discreet, how

---

[165] heat A,AV] heart B.

[166] Actually Sozomen 1:15; Christopherson, 3:19v.

[167] hay: in fencing, an exclamation on hitting an opponent; a home thrust. Presumably Marvell mimics the cries of a spectator at a duel. The 1703 edition of the *Essay* substitutes "was at a stand."

[168] on the one B] on one A.

[169] in behalf of himself, and his followers Ed., 1687, Grosart] in behalf, and his followers A,B,AV, 1680; in behalf of his followers 1703.

Christian-like, I never read any thing of that nature equal to it! It is too long for me here to insert, but I gladly recommend my Reader to it in the 2 Eus. *de vita Const.* c.2.67. where he begins, *I understand the foundation of the controversie to have been this, that thou Alexander didst inquire of thy Priests concerning a passage in the Scripture, nay didst ask them concerning a frivolous quillet of a question*[170] *what was each of their opinions, and thou Arrius didst inconsiderately babble what thou neither at the beginning couldst conceive, and if thou hadst conceived so, oughtest* not to have vented, &c.[171]

But the Clergy having got this once in the wind, there was no beating them off the scent. Which induced Constantine to think the convening of this Council the onely Remedy to these Disorders; and a woful ado he had with them when they were met to manage and keep them in any tollerable *decorum.* It seemed like an Ecclesiastical Cock-pit,[172] and a man might have laid wagers either way: the two parties contending in good earnest either for the truth or the victory, but the more unconcerned, like cunning Betters, sate judiciously hedging, and so ordered their matters that which side soever prevail'd, they would be sure to be the Winners; They were indeed a most venerable assembly, composed of some holy, some grave, some wise, and some of them learned Persons: and Constantine had so charitably burnt the accusations they intended against one another, which might otherwise have depopulated and dispirited the Council, that all of them may be presumed in one or other respect to have made [57] a great Character. But I observe Soz. l.I.c.16. that these great Bishops, although they only had the decisive voices, yet thought fit to bring along with them certain men that were cunning at an argument, to be auxiliary to them when it came to hard & tough Disputation;[173] beside that they had their Priests and Deacons ready at a dead lift[174] always to assist them: So that their understandings seem'd to be sequester'd,[175] and for their dayly Faith, they depended upon what their Chaplains would allow them. And in that quality Athanasius there waited

---

[170] *a frivolous quillet of a question:* Marvell's lively translation of "de inani quadam quaestionis." See Christopherson, 2:26ov.

[171] Eusebius, *De Vita Constantini,* 1:67.

[172] Cock-pit: a pit or enclosed space constructed for cockfighting.

[173] Disputation A] dispution B.

[174] at a dead lift: the pull of a horse exerting his utmost strength.

[175] Sequestered: a technical term, with several possible meanings here, both political and ecclesiastical: confiscated; isolated; imprisoned; excommunicated; to hold the income from a benefice during a vacancy for the benefit of the next incumbent. The last, if intended, would be especially witty.

upon Alexander, being his Deacon, (for as yet it seems [neither][176] Arch-bishops nor Arch-deacons[177] were[178] invented). And it is not improbable that Athanasius having so early personated the Bishop, and seeing the declining age of Alexander, would be careful that Arrius should not step betwixt him & home upon vacancy, but did his best against him to bar up his way, as it shortly after happened; Athanasius succeeding after the Council in the See of Alexandria. In the mean time you may imagine that *Hypostasis, Persona, Substantia, Subsistentia, Essentia, Coessentialis, Consubstantialis, Ante saecula Coaeturnus, &c.*[179] were by[180] so many disputants pick'd to the very bones, and those too broken afterwards to come to the marrow of Divinity. And never had Constantine in his life so hard a task as to bring them to any rational results: *meekly and patiently,* Euseb. 3 c.13 de vita Const. *list'ning to every one, taking each Man's opinion, and without the Acrimony with which it was delivered, helping each party where they disagreed, reconciling them by degrees when they were in the fiercest Contention, conferring with them a part courteously and mildly, telling them what was his own opinion of the matter.*[181] Which though some exceptious[182] persons may alledge to have been against the nature of a Free Council, yet truly unless he had taken that course, I cannot imagine how possibly he could ever have brought them to any conclusion. And thus this first great, General Council of Nice, with which the world had gone big so long, and which look'd so big upon all Christendom, at last was brought in bed, and after a very hard labor deliver'd of *Homoousios.*[183]

---

[176] neither Ed., 1703] required by sense.

[177] Arch-deacons: a gibe at Samuel Parker, archdeacon of Canterbury.

[178] were A,B] Berkeley inserts "not," to substitute for the missing "neither."

[179] These terms are all part of the theological debate about Christ's nature. *Hypostasis* and *Persona* both refer to the personality of Christ as a human person, as distinct from his *Substance. Essentia* (essence) is linked to *Coessentialis,* the state of being united in essence with another, that is, God the Father. *Consubstantialis,* similarly, means the state of being of the same essence or substance with him. *Ante saecula coaeturnus,* coeternal from before time began, refers to the belief that the Son was not created by the Father, but like him was eternal.

[180] were by A] whereby B.

[181] Eusebius, *De Vita Constantini,* 3:13; Christopherson, 1:268r; but Marvell gives a very loose translation.

[182] exceptious: disposed to make objections, caviling, captious. Cf. the prefatory address "To the captious Reader."

[183] *Homoousios:* the doctrine of Christ's identity with the Father in substance; see

They all subscribed to the New Creed, except some seventeen, who it seems had rather to be Hereticks then Bishops. For now the *Anàthema's* were published, and whoever held the contrary was to be punish'd by Deprivation and Banishment, all Arrian books to be burned, and whoever should be discover'd to conceal any of Arrius his writings, to dye for it: But it fared very well with those who were not such fools as to own his Opinion: all they were entertained by the Emperor at a magnificent Feast, receiv'd from his hand rich Presents, and were honorably dismist, with Letters recommending their great abilities and performance to the Provinces, and injoyning the Nicene Creed to be henceforth observed. With that stroke of the Pen: Socr. l.I.c.6. *For what three hundred Bishops have agreed on,* (a thing indeed extraordinary) *ought not to be otherwise conceived of then*[184] *as the decree of God Almighty, especially seeing the Holy Ghost did sit upon the minds of such and so excellent men, and opened his divine will to them.*[185] So that they went I trow with ample satisfaction; &, as they could not but take the Emperor for a very civil ge[58]nerous, and obliging Gentleman, so they thought the better of themselves from that day forward. And how budge[186] must they look when they returned back to their Dioceses, having every one of'm been a principal limn of the *AEcumenical*[187] *Apostolical, Catholick, Orthodox* Council! When the Catachrestical[188] titles of the Church and the Clergy were so appropriate to them by custome, that the Christian people had relinquished or forgotten their claim; when every Hare that crossed their way homeward was a Schismatick[189] or an Heretick, and if their

---

Mr. Smirke, note 134. Given Marvell's metaphor of parturition, it is possible he is playing with the saying (from Horace, *Ars Poetica,* l. 139): "The mountain groaned, and delivered a mouse." Cf. *RT2,* p. 223: "No Naturalist has determin'd the certain time of a Mountains pregnancy . . . but one has told us what kind of Child it always produces."

[184] *then* A, i.e., than] *them* B.

[185] Socrates, 1:6: Christopherson, 2:15v: "Nam quod trecentis episcopis visum est, non est aliud putandum quam Dei sententiam, praesertim cum in talium. & tam praeclorum mentibus sacer insideret spiritus, qui illis divinam voluntatem apernit." This passage, so important for Marvell to refute, was also quoted in French by Rivet, *Histoire,* pp. 134–35.

[186] budge: doctorally grave or stiff. Budge was lamb's fur, and, being worn by certain official dignitaries, came to signify their grave aspect. [Grosart] The 1703 edition removes the archaism but loses the point: "how big must they look," (p. 365).

[187] *AEcumenical:* ecumenical, representing the whole Christian church.

[188] Catachrestical: of words improperly used.

[189] Schismatick: a person who separates from the main body of the church. But cf. John Hales, *A Treatise of Schism* (1642), as quoted by Marvell in *RT,* p. 131: "Schism is, if

Horse stumbled with one of them, he incurr'd an Anathema. Well it was that their journeys laid so many several ways, for they were grown so cumbersome and great, that the Emperor's highway was too narrow for any two of them, and there could have been no passage without the removal of a Bishop. But soon after the Council was over, Eusebius the Bishop of Nicomedia, and Theognis the Bishop of Nice, who were already removed both by banishment and two others put in their places, were quickly restor'd upon their petition: wherein they suggested the cause of their not Signing to have been only because they thought they could not with a safe conscience subscribe the Anathema against Arrius, appearing to them both by his writings, his discourses, and Sermons that they had been auditors of, not to be guilty of those errors.[190] As for Arrius himself, the Emperor quickly wrote to him. *It is now a considerable time since I writ to your Gravity*[191] *to come to my Tents, that you might enjoy my countenance; so that I can scarce wonder sufficiently why you have so long delay'd it: therefore now take one of the publique Coaches and make all speed to my Tents, that, having had experience of my kindness and affection to you, you may return into your own Countrey. God preserve you most dear Sir.*[192] Arrius hereupon (with his comrade Euzious)[193] comes to Constantine's army, and offers him a petition, with a confession of Faith that would have passed very well before the Nicene Council,[194] and now satisfied the Emperor Socr. l.I.c.19, and 20. insomuch that he writ to Athanasius,[195] now Bishop of Alexandria, to receive him into the Church: but Athanasius[196] was of better mettle then so and absolutely refus'd it. Upon this Constantine writ him another threat-

---

we would define it, an unnecessary separation of Christians from that part of the Visible Church of which they were once members . . . Where the cause of Schism is necessary, there not he that separates, but he that is the cause of Separation is the Schismatick."

[190] Cf. Socrates, 1:10; Sozomen, 2:18.

[191] *your Gravity:* from Latin *"tuae gravitate."* Hanmer translates: "thy wisdom."

[192] Socrates, 1:19; Christopherson, 2:31v.

[193] Euzoius A] Fuzoius B.

[194] Thomas Field's copy of Hanmer's translation (1663) has a marginal note here: "equivocation." For a contemporary account of Arius's equivocation, keeping a written version of his real beliefs under his shirt while offering his spoken accommodation, see Peter Heylyn, *Cosmographie* (London, 1666), p. 931. Marvell tends to downplay the disreputable or degrading aspects of Arius's career, omitting, for example, his horrific death in a privy.

[195] Athanasius Ed.] Anathasius A,B.

[196] Athanasius Ed.] Anathanasius A,B.

ning Letter: *When you have understood hereby my pleasure,* see that you afford free entrance into the Church to all that desire it: for if I shall understand that any who desires it,[197] should be either hindred or forbidden by you, I will send some one of my Servants to remove you from your *Degree,* and place another in your stead. Yet Athanasius stood it out still, though other Churches received him into Communion: and the Heretick Novatus could not have been more unrelenting to lapsed Christians then he was to Arrius. But this, joyned with other crimes which were laid to Athanasius his charge, at the Council of Tyre, (though I suppose indeed they were forged) made Athanasius glad to flye for it, and remain the first time in exile. Upon this whole matter it is my impartial Opinion that Arrius, or whosoever else were guilty of teaching and publishing those errors whereof he was accused, deserved the utmost Severity which consists with the Christian Religion. And so willing I have been to think well of Athanasius, and [59] ill of the other, that I have on purpose avoided the reading, as I do the naming, of a book that I have hear'd tells the story quite otherwise,[198] & have only made use of the current Historians of those times, who all of them tell it against the Arrians. Only I will confess, that as in reading a particular History at adventure a Man finds himself inclinable to favor the weaker party, especially if the Conqueror appear insolent; so have I been affected in reading these Authors: which does but resemble the reasonable pitty that men ordinarily have too for those who though for an erroneous conscience suffer under a Christian Magistrate. And as soon as I come to Constantius, I shall for that reason change my compassion and be doubly ingaged on the Orthodox party. But as to the whole matter of the Council of Nice, I must crave liberty to say, that from one end to the other, though the best of the kind, it seems to me to have been a pittiful humane business, attended with all the ill circumstances of other worldly affairs, conducted by a spirit of ambition and contention, the first and so the greatest AEcumenical blow that by Christians was given to Christianity. And it is not from any sharpness of humour that I discourse thus freely of Things and Persons, much less of Orders of men otherwise venerable, but that where ought is extolled beyond reason and to the prejudice of Religion, it is necessary to depreciate

---

[197] desires it B] desires to be admitted into the Church A; B economizes intelligently.

[198] This deliberately mysterious reference is so far untraced. One possibility is Louis Maimbourg, *L'Histoire de l'Arianisme,* 3 vols. (Paris, 1673); but Maimbourg, a Jesuit, is anti-Arian. Nevertheless he makes the chief villain not Arius himself but Eusebius of Nicomedia.

it by true proportion. It is not their censure of Arianism, or the declaring of their opinion in a controverted point to the best of their understanding, (wherein to the smalness of mine they appear to have light upon the truth, had they likewise upon the measure,) that could have moved me to tell so long a story, or bring my self within the danger and aim of any captious Reader,[199] speaking thus with great liberty of mind but little concern for any prejudice I may receive, of things that are by some men Idolized. But it is their imposition of a new Article or Creed upon the Christian world, not being contained in express words of Scripture, to be believed with divine faith under spiritual & civil penalties, contrary to the priviledges of religion & their making a precedent follow'd & improv'd by all succeeding ages for most cruel persecutions, that only could animate me. In digging thus for a new deduction they undermined the fabrick of Christianity, to frame a particular Doctrine they departed from the general rule of their religion; and for their curiosity about an Article concerning Christ, they violated our Saviours first institution of a Church not subject to any Addition in matters of faith, nor liable to compulsion either in belief or in practice. Far be it from me in the event as it is from my Intention, to derogate from the just authority of any of those Creeds or[200] Confessions of Faith that are receiv'd by our Church upon clear agreement with the Scriptures: nor shall I therefore, unless some mens impertinence and indiscretion hereafter oblige me, pretend to any further knowledge of what in those particulars appears in the ancient Histories. But certainly if any Creed had been Necessary, or at least Necessary to have been Imposed, our Saviour himself would not have left his Church destitute in a thing of that moment. Or however, after the Holy Ghost, upon his departure, was descended upon the Apostles, and *They the Elders and* [60] *Brethren* (for so it was then) were assembled in a legitimate Council at Jerusalem, *it would have seemed good to the Holy Ghost and them*[201] to have saved the Council of Nice that labor, or at least the Apostle Paul 2 Cor.12.2. and 4. *who was caught up into Paradise, and heard unspeakable words, which it is not lawful for any man to utter,*[202] having thereby a

[199] Compare "To the Captious Reader."

[200] or A] for B.

[201] Cf. Acts 15:23, 25, 28: "The Apostles and elders and brethren send greeting . . . being assembled with one accord . . . For it seemed good to the Holy Ghost, and to us, to lay upon you no greater burden than these necessary things."

[202] 2 Corinthians 12:4. Paul was modestly speaking of his past experience as belonging to another.

much better opportunity then Athanasius to know the Doctrine of the Trinity, would not have been wanting, *through the abundance of that revelation*,[203] to form a Creed for the Church, sufficient to have put that business beyond controversie. Especially seeing Heresies were sprung up so early, and he foresaw others, and therefore does prescribe the method how they are to be dealt with, but no Creed that I read of.

Shall any sort of men presume to interpret those words, which to him were unspeakable, by a Gibbrish of their Imposing,[204] and force every man to Cant[205] after them what it is not lawful for any man to utter? Christ and his Apostles speak articulately enough in the Scriptures, without any Creed, as much as we are or ought to be capable of. And the Ministry of the Gospel is useful and most necessary, if it were but to press us to the reading of them, to illustrate one place by the authority of another, to inculcate those duties which are therein required, quickning us both to Faith and Practice, and showing within what bounds they are both circumscribed by our Saviour's Doctrine. And it becomes every Man to be able to give a Reason and account of his Faith, and to be ready to do it, without officiously gratifying those who demand it onely to take advantage: and the more Christians can agree in one confession of faith the better. But that we should believe ever the more for a Creed, it cannot be expected. In those days when Creeds were most plenty and in fashion, and every one had them at their fingers-ends, 'twas the Bible that brought in the Reformation. 'Tis true, a man would not stick to take two or three Creeds for a need, rather then want a Living, and if a man have not a good swallow, 'tis but wrapping them up in a Liturgy, like a wafer, and the whole dose will go down currently; especially if he wink at the

[203] 2 Corinthians 12:7.

[204] This phrase particularly inflamed Jean Daillé, in his reply to Louis du Moulin's *Short and True Account of the Several Advances the Church of England Hath made towards Rome* (London, 1680), in which Marvell (p. 88) is called a great man. In *The Lively Picture of Lewis du Moulin* (1680) Daillé responded, "This great man of his, has told the World that the *Nicene Council imposed a* NEW ARTICLE *or Creed upon the Christian world:* and called that explication which they made of the Ancient Belief, concerning the Son of God . . . *a Gibbrish of their own imposing* . . . and in plain terms represents those Fathers who were there assembled, as a company of pitiful Dunces," p. 10. Another cleric so provoked was Simon Patrick, who in *Falshood Unmaskt* (1676) attacked the anonymous author of *The Truth Unvailed* (1676) who was perhaps Arthur Annesley, earl of Anglesey. Patrick repeated "a gibberish of their own imposing" and berated his opponent for "the friendly complement of the *facetious and candid Marvel,*" p. 23.

[205] Cant: to use the current stock phrases.

same time and give his Assent and Consent without ever looking on them: But without jesting, for the matter is too serious. Every man is bound *to work out his own salvation with fear and trembling*[206] and therefore to use all helps possible for his best satisfaction: hearing, conferring, reading, praying for the assistance of God's spirit;[207] but when he hath done this, he is his own Expositor, his own both Minister and People, Bishop and Diocess, his own Council, his own Conscience excusing or condemning him, accordingly he escapes or incurs his own internal Anathema. So that when it comes once to a Creed, made and Imposed by other men as a matter of Divine Faith, the Case grows very delicate; while he cannot apprehend, though the Imposer may, that all therein is clearly contain'd in Scripture, & may fear being caught in the expressions to oblige himself to a latitude or restriction, further then comports with his own sense & judgment. A Christian of honor, when it comes to this once, will weigh every word, every syllable, nay further, if he consider that the great business of this Coun-[61]cil of Nice was but one single Letter of the Alphabet, about the inserting or omitting of[208] an Iota.[209] There must be either that exactness in the Form of such a Creed, as I dare say, no men in the world ever were or ever will be able to modulate: or else this scrupulous private judgement must be admitted, or otherwise all Creeds become meer instruments of Equivocation or Persecution. And I must confess, when I have sometimes considered with my self the dulness of the Non-conformists, and the acuteness on the contrary of the Episcopalians,[210] and the conscientiousness of both, I have thought that our Church might safely wave[211] the difference with them about Ceremonies, and try it out upon the Creeds, which were both the more honourable way, and more suitable to the method of ancient Councils, and yet perhaps might do their

---

[206] Philippians, 2:12. Milton used the same text in *Of True Religion, Haeresie, Schism, Toleration, and what best means may be us'd against the growth of Popery* (London, 1673). See *CPW,* 8:439.

[207] Cf. Milton, *Of True Religion,* 8:425: "For so long as all these profess to set the Word of God only before them as the Rule of faith and obedience; and use all diligence and sincerity of heart, by reading, by learning, by study, by prayer for Ilumination of the holy Spirit, . . . they have done what man can do."

[208] omitting of A] omiting B.

[209] Iota: the Greek letter i; that is, the difference between *homoousios* and *homoiousios.* Cf. *RT,* p. 157, where Marvell recalls this ecclesiastical quarrel as based on "the difference of one Syllable."

[210] Episcopalians Ed.] Episcoparians A,B.

[211] wave: i.e., waive.

business as effectually. For one that is a Christian in good earnest, when a Creed is imposed, will sooner eat fire then take it against his judgement. There have been Martyrs for Reason, & it was manly in them. But how much more would men be so for reason, Religionated and Christianized! But it is an inhumane and unchristian thing of those Faith-stretchers, whosoever they be, that either put mens persons or their consciences upon the torture, to rack them to the length of their notions: whereas the Bereans are made Gentlemen and Innobled by Patent in the Acts, because they would not credit Paul himself, whose writings now make so great a part of the New Testament, until *they* had *searched the Scripture daily whether those things were so and therefore many of them believed.*[212] & therefore, although where there are such Creeds, Christians may for peace and conscience sake acquiesce while there appears nothing in them flatly contrary to the words of the Scripture: yet when they are obtruded upon a man in particular, he will look very well about him, and not take them upon any Humane Authority. The greatest Pretense to Authority is in a Council. But what then? shall all Christians therefore take their Formularies[213] of Divine Worship or belief, upon trust, as writ in Tables of Stone, like the Commandments, delivered from Heaven to be[214] obey'd in the instant, not considered: because three hundred and eighteen Bishops are met in Abraham's great Hall,[215] of which most must be servants, and some Children, and they have resolv'd upon't in such a manner? No, a good Christian will not, cannot atturn[216] and indenture[217] his conscience over, to be represented by others. It is not as in secular matters, where the States of a Kingdom are deputed by their fellow Subjects to transact for them, so in spiritual: or suppose it were, yet 'twere necessary, as in the Polish constitution, that nothing should be obligatory as long as there is one Dissenter,[218] where no temporal Interests,

---

[212] Acts 17:11.

[213] Formularies A] Formularities B.

[214] to be] and to be A.

[215] A reprise of Turner, p. 23.

[216] Atturn: to assign or transfer to another.

[217] Indenture: the act of signing a deed or covenant, in this case for transfer.

[218] Marvell refers to the principle of consensus, or the *liberum veto,* of Polish *szlachta* democracy, which had been defended by Andrzej Fredro in 1660 against a campaign for reform in favor of majoritarianism. See Robert I. Frost, "'Liberty without Licence?' The Failure of Polish Democratic Thought in the Seventeenth Century," in *Polish Democratic Thought from the Renaissance to the Great Emigration: Essays and Documents,* eds. M. B. Biskupski and James S. Pula (New York, 1990).

but every man's Eternity and Salvation are concerned. The Soul is too precious to be let out at interest upon any humane security, that does or may fail, but it is onely safe when under God's custody, in its own Cabinet. But it was a General Council. A special general indeed, if you consider the proportion of three hundred and eighteen, to the body of the Christian Clergy, but much more to all Christian Mankind. But it was a general Free Council of Bishops. I do not think it possible for any Council to be free that is composed only of Bishops, [62] and where they only have the Decisive Voices.[219] Nor that a Free Council that takes away Christian Liberty. But that, as it was founded upon usurpation, so it terminated in imposition. But 'tis meant that it was free from all external impulsion. I confess that good meat and drink, and lodging, and money in a man's purse, and Coaches and Servants, and horses to attend them, did no violence to'm, nor was there any false Article in it: and discoursing now with one and then another of 'm in particular, and the Emperor telling them this is my opinion, I understand it thus, and afterwards declaring his mind frequently to them in publick, no force either. Ay! but there was a shrewd way of persuasion in it. And I would be glad to know when ever and which free general Council it was that could properly be called so: but was indeed a meer Imperial or Ecclesiastical Machine, no free agent, but wound up, set on going, and let down by the direction and hand of the Workman. A General Free Council is but a word of Art, and can never happen but under a Fifth Monarch,[220] and that Monarch too, to return from Heaven. The Animadverter will not allow the second general council of Nice to have been free, *because it was overawd by an Empress*,[221] and was guilty of a great fault (which no Council at liberty he saith could have committed) the decree for worshipping of Images. At this rate a Christian may scuffle however for one point among them, and chuse which council he likes best. But in good earnest I do not see but that Constantine might as well at this first council of Nice, have negotiated the Image worship, as to pay that superstitious adoration to the Bishops, and that prostration to their Creeds was an Idolatry more pernicious in the consequence to the Christian Faith, then that under which they so lately had suffered persecution. Nor can a council be said to have been at liberty which laid under so great and many obligations. But the Holy Ghost was present where there were three hundred and eighteen Bishops, and directed

---

[219] Voices Ed., 1703] Voces A,B, 1680, 1687.
[220] See note 9 above.
[221] See Turner, p. 24. The empress in question was Irene.

them or three hundred. Then, if I had been of their counsel, they should have sate at it all their lives, least they should never see him again after they[222] had once risen. But it concerned them to settle their *Quorum* at first by his Dictates, otherwise no Bishop could have been absent or gone forth again upon any occasion, but he let him out again: and it behoov'd to be very punctual in the Adjournments. 'Tis a ridiculous conception, and as gross as to make him of the same Substance with the Council. Nor needs there any strong argument of his absence, then their pretence to be actuated by him, and in doing such work. The Holy Spirit![223] If so many of them when they got together, acted like rational men, 'tis enough in all reason, and as much as could be expected.

But this was one affectation, among many others, which the Bishops took up so early; of the stile, priviledges, powers, and some actions and gestures peculiar & inherent to the Apostles, which they misplaced to their own behoof and usage: nay, & challenged other things as Apostolical, that were directly contrary to the Doctrine and practice of the Apostles. For so because the Holy Spirit did in an extraordinary manner preside among the Apostles at that Legitime Council of Jerusalem, Acts. 15. they, although under [64] an ordinary administration, would not go less whatever came on't: nay, whereas the Apostles, in the drawing up of their decree dictated to them by the Holy Spirit, said therefore no more but thus: *The Apostles, Elders, and Brethren, send greeting unto the Brethren of, &c. Forasmuch as, &c. It seemed good to the Holy Ghost and us to lay upon you no greater burthen then these necessary things: that ye abstain from, &c. from which if ye keep your selves, you shall do well.* Fare ye well.[224]

This Council[225] denounces every invention [not][226] of its own; (far from the Apostolic modesty, and the stile of the Holy Spirit) under no less then an Anathema. Such was their arrogating to their inferior degrees the style of *Clergy*, till custome hath so much prevailed, that we are at a loss how to speak properly either of the name or nature of their function. Whereas the *Clergy*, in the true and Apostolic sense, were only those whom they super-

[222] they A] he B; a mistaken correction.

[223] The 1703 edition here adds: "that's a fine pretence. Why if . . ." The 1709 edition continues: "Who if so tho under an ordinary Administration, would not pretend to less, whatever came on't."

[224] Acts 15:23, 28, 29.

[225] This Council: the Nicene.

[226] "Not" seems to be required to make sense.

ciliously always call the *Laity:* The word *Clerus* being never but once used in the New Testament, and in that signification, and in a very unlucky place too, Peter 1.5.3. where he admonishes the Priesthood, *that they should not Lord it or domineer over,* the Christian People, *Clerum Domini* or *the Lord's Inheritance.*[227] But having usurped the Title, I confess they did right to assume the power. But to speak of the Priest-hood in that style which they most affect, if we consider the nature too of their Function, what were the *Clergy* then but Lay-men disguis'd, drest up perhaps in another habit? Did not St. Paul himself, being a Tent-maker, rather then be idle or burthensome to his people, work of his trade, even during his Apostleship, to get his living? But did not these, that they might neglect their holy vocation, seek to compass secular imployments, and Lay-Offices? Were not very many of them, whether one respect their Vices or Ignorance, as well qualified as any other to be Laymen? Was it not usual as oft as they merited it to restore them, as in the case even of the three Bishops,[228] to the Lay-communion? And whether, if they were so peculiar from others, did the Imposition of the Bishops hands, or the lifting up of the hands of the Laity conferr more to that distinction? And Constantine, notwithstanding his complement[229] at the burning of the Bishops papers, thought he might make them and unmake them with the same power as he did his other Lay-Officers. But if the inferior degrees were the *Clergy,* the Bishops would be the Church, although that word in the Scripture-sense is proper only to a congregation of the Faithful. And being by that title the onely men in Ecclesiastical councils, then when they were once assembled they were the *Catholick Church,* and having the Holy Spirit at their devotion, whatsoever Creed they light upon, that was the *Catholick Faith, without believing of which no man can be saved.*[230] By which means there rose thenceforward so constant persecutions till this day, that, had not the little invisible *Catholick Church* and a People that always searched and believ'd the Scriptures, made a stand by their Testimonies and sufferings, the Creeds had destroyed the

[227] 1 Peter 5:2, 3: "Feed the flock of God which is among you . . . not by constraint, but willingly; not for filthy lucre, but of a ready mind; Neither as being lords over God's heritage, but being ensamples to the flock." Taken as a whole, this quotation sets up Marvell's argument in the next section.

[228] the three Bishops: see above, pp. 128–29.

[229] Complement: i.e., compliment.

[230] *Catholick . . . saved:* the phrase derives from the appendix to the Athanasian Creed, subsequently adopted by the Council of Trent as one of its articles.

Faith: and the Church had ruined the Religion. For this General council of Nice and all others of the same constitution did, and can serve to no other end or effect, than particular orders[231] of men by their usur-[61b]ping a trust upon Christianity, to make their own Price and Market of it, and deliver it up as oft as they see their own advantage.

For scarce was Constantine's head cold, but his Son Constantius succeeding his Brothers,[232] being influenced by the Bishops of the Arrian Party, turn'd the wrong side of Christianity outward, inverted the Poles of Heaven, and Faith (if I may say so) with its Heels in the Air, was forced to stand upon its[233] Head, and play Gambols, for the divertisement[234] and pleasure of the *Homoiousians.* Arrianism was the Divinity then in Mode, and he was an ignorant and ill Courtier, or Church-man, that could not dress, and would not make a new Suit for his Conscience in the Fashion.[235] And now the Orthodox Bishops (it being given to those Men to be obstinate for Power, but flexible in Faith;) began to wind about insensibly, as the *Heliotrope*[236] *Flower* that keeps its ground, but wrests its Neck in turning after the warm Sun, from Day-break to Evening. They could look now upon the Synod of Nice with more indifference, and all that Pudder[237] that had been made there betwixt *Homoousios* and *Homoiousios,* &c. began to appear to them *as a difference only arising from the Inadequation of Languages.*[238] Till by degrees they were drawn over, and rather than lose their Bishopricks, would joyn, and at last be the Head-most in the Persecution of their own former Party. But the Deacons, to be sure, that steer'd the Elephants, were thorow-paced; men to be reckon'd and relied upon in this or any other occasion, and would prick on to render themselves Capable and Episcopable,[239] upon the first Vacancy. For now the Arrians in grain,[240] scorning to come behind the Clownish *Homoousians* in any Ecclesiastical

---

[231] orders Ed.] order A,B.

[232] Constantius . . . Brothers: Flavius Julius Constantius II was the third son of Constantine.

[233] its A] his B.

[234] divertisement: diversion, amusement.

[235] A glance back at the fashion metaphor of *Mr. Smirke, or the Divine in Mode.*

[236] as the *Heliotrope:* turning to follow the sun, like marigolds or sunflowers.

[237] Pudder: dabbling in dust or mud.

[238] Turner, p. 7: "But this makes no breach of Communion between us and the Greeks, the difference arising only from the Inadequation of Languages."

[239] Episcopable: capable of being made a bishop.

[240] in grain: in nature, inclination.

Civility, were resolved to give them their full of Persecution. And it seem'd a piece of wit rather than malice, to pay them in their own Coyn, and to *Burlesque* them in earnest, by the repetition and heightning of the same severities upon them, that they had practised upon others. Had you the *Homoousians* a Creed at Nice? We will have another creed for you at Ariminum, and at Seleucia. Would you not be content with so many several Projects of Faith consonant to Scripture, unless you might thrust the new word *Homoousios* down our throats, and then tear it up again, to make us confess it? Tell us the word, ('twas *Homoiousios*) we are now upon the guard, or else we shall run you thorow. Would you Anathemize, Banish, Imprison, Execute us, and burn our Books? You shall taste of this Christian Fare, and as you relish it, you shall have more on't provided. And thus it went, Arrianism being Triumphant; but the few sincere or stomackful[241] Bishops, adhering constantly, and with a true Christian Magnanimity, especially Athanasius, thorow all sufferings unto their former Confessions, expiated so in some measure, what they had committed in the Nicene Council.

Sozomene, l.4.c.25. first tells us a story of Eudoxius, who succeeded Macedonius in the Bishoprick of Constantinople, that in the Cathedral of Sancta Sophia, being mounted in his Episcopal Throne, the first time that they assembled for its Dedication, in the very beginning of his Sermon to the People (those things were already come in Fashion) told them: *Patrem impium esse,* [61b] *Filium autem pium;* at which when they began to bustle, *Pray be quiet,* saith he, *Patrem impium esse, quia colit neminem, Filium vero Pium quia colit Patrem*[242] at which they then laughed as heartily, as before they were Angry. But this I only note to this purpose, that there were some of the greatest Bishops among the *Homoiousians,* as well as the *Homoousians,* that could not reproach one anothers Simplicity, and that it was not impossible for the *Many,* to be Wiser and more Orthodox than the *Few,* in Divine Matters. That which I cite him[243] for as most material, is, his Remark upon the Imposition then of contrary Creeds; *Which verily,* saith he, *was plainly the beginning of most great Calamities, forasmuch as hereupon there followed a Disturbance, not unlike those which we before recited over the*

[241] stomackful: brave, mettlesome.

[242] Sozomen, 4:25; Christopherson, 3:103–04: "The Father is impious, but the Son is pious"; "The Father is not pious, because He worships nobody; but the Son is pious because he worships the Father."

[243] him: i.e., Sozomen, 4:25, which concludes with the lament cited in full by Marvell here.

whole Empire; and likewise a Persecution equal almost to that of the Heathen Emperors, seized upon all of all Churches. For, although it seemed to some more gentle for what concerns the Torture of the Body, yet to Prudent Persons it appeared more bitter and severe, by reason of the Dishonour and Ignominy. For both they who stirred up, and those that were afflicted with this Persecution, were of the Christian Church. And the Grievance therefore was the greater and more ugly, in that the same things which are done among Enemies, were Executed between those of the same Tribe and Profession: but the Holy Law forbids us to carry our selves in that manner, even to those that are Without, and Aliens. And all this Mischief sprung from making of Creeds, with which the Bishops, as it were at *Tilting,* aim'd to hit one another in the Eye, and throw the opposite Party out of the Saddle. But it chanced that the weaker side were ready to yield, (for what sort of Men was there that could better manage,[244] or had their Consciences more at command at that time than the Clergy?) Then the Arrians would use a yet longer, thicker, and sharper Lance for the purpose, (for there were never Vacancies sufficient) that they might be sure to run them down, over, and thorow, and do their Business. The Creed of Ariminum was now too short for the Design, but, saith the Historian, they affix'd *further Articles like Labels to it, pretending to have made it better, and so sent it thorow the Empire with Constantius his Proclamation, that whoever would not subscribe it, should be banished.*[245] Nay, they would not admit their own beloved *Similis Substantia,* but, to do the Work throughly, the Arrians renounc'd their own Creed for Malice, and made it an Article; *Filium Patri tam substantia, quam Voluntate, Dissimilem esse.*[246] But that is a small matter with any of them, provided thereby they may do Service to the Church, that is their Party. So that one (seriously speaking) that were really Orthodox, could not then defend the Truth or himself, but by turning old Arrian,[247] if he would impugn the new ones; such was the subtilty. What shall I say more? As the Arts of Glass Coaches and Perriwigs[248] illustrate this Age, so by their Trade of Creed-making, then first Invented, we may esteem the

[244] manage: in this context, to train a horse in its paces.

[245] Socrates, 2:33; Christopherson, 2:78r.

[246] "The Son is different from the Father, as in substance, so in will."

[247] Arrian A] Arreon B.

[248] Glass Coaches and Perriwigs: periwigs, from *peruques,* French wigs. Cf. *RT2,* pp. 268–69: "e'r there was any such thing known or thought of, as Periwigs or Glass-Coaches."

Wisdom of Constantine's, and Constantius his Empire. And in a short space, as is usual among Tradesmen, where it appears Gainful, they were so many that set up of the same Profession, that they could scarce live by one another. [62b] Socr. l.2.c.32. Therefore uses these words: *But now that I have* tandem aliquando, *run through this Labyrinth of so many Creeds, I will gather up their number:*[249] And so reckons nine Creeds more, besides that of Nice, before the death of Constantius, (a blessed number.)[250] And I believe, I could for a need, make them up a Dozen, if Men have a mind to buy them so. And hence it was that Hilary,[251] then Bishop of Poictiers, represents that state of the Church pleasantly, yet sadly; *Since the Nicene Synod,* saith he, *we do nothing but write Creeds. That while we fight about words, whilst we raise Questions about Novelties, while we quarrel about things doubtful, and about Authors, while we contend in Parties, while there is difficulty in Consent, while we Anathematize one another, there is none now almost that is Christ's. What a Change there is in the last years Creed? The first Decree commands, that* Homoousios *should not be mentioned: The next does again Decree and publish* Homoousios: *The third does by Indulgence excuse the word* Ousia[252] *as used by the Fathers in their simplicity: The fourth does not excuse, but condemn it. It is come to that at last, that nothing among us, or those before us, can remain Sacred or inviolable. We Decree every Year of the Lord, a new Creed concerning God: Nay, every Change of the Moon our Faith is alter'd. We repent of our Decrees, we defend those that repent of them; we Anathemize those that we defended; and while we either condemn other Mens Opinions in our own, or our own Opinions in those of other Men, and bite at one another, we are now all of us torn in pieces.*[253] This Bishop sure was the Author of the *Naked Truth,*[254] and 'twas

---

[249] Socrates 2:32; Christopherson, 2:77r: "Nos vero tanquam labyrintho formularum tandem aliquando percurso, earum numerum iam breviter colligamus."

[250] a blessed number: nine was the heavenly number, from the number of spheres and orders of angels. Cf. Spenser, *Faerie Queene*, 2.10.22: "Nine was the circle set in heavens place."

[251] Hilary: St. Hilary, d. 368. He converted from paganism c. 350 and was raised to the episcopate of Poictiers in 353. He regarded Arianism as a deadly heresy, for which position he was exiled by Constantius. His appeal *Ad Constantium*, book 2, chap. 4, from which Marvell quotes below, was cited by both Locke and Gibbon.

[252] Ousia: Greek "substance."

[253] See Hilary, *Ad Constantium* in *Opera Complura Sancti* (Paris, 1510), 2:4, fol. 85. Marvell, who has accurately rendered the bishop's rhetorical flourishes, probably discovered this letter when searching for Hilary's treatise *De Synodis*, which he did not use.

[254] *Naked Truth:* a glance back at Croft's much maligned title.

he that *implicitly condemn'd the whole Catholick Church, both East and West, for being too presumptuous in her Definitions.*[255]

It is not strange to me, that Julian,[256] being but a Reader[257] in the Christian Church, should turn Pagan: Especially when I consider that he succeeded Emperor after Constantius. For it seems rather unavoidable, that a Man of great wit, as he was, and not having the Grace of God to direct it, and show him the Beauty of Religion, through the Deformity of its Governours and Teachers; but that he must conceive a Loathing and Aversion for it; nor could he think that he did them any injustice, when he observed that, beside all their unchristian Immorality[258] too, they practised thus, against the Institutive Law of their Galilean, the Persecution among themselves for Religion. And well might he add to his other severities, that sharpness of his Wit, both *exposing* and *animadverting* upon them, at another rate than any of the Modern Practitioners with all their study and inclination can ever arrive at. For nothing is more punishable, contemptible, and truly ridiculous, than a Christian that walks contrary to his Profession: and by how much any man stands with more advantage in the Church for Eminency, but disobeys the Laws of Christ by that Priviledge, he is thereby, and deserves to be the more Exposed. But Julian, the last Heathen Emperor, by whose Cruelty it seemed that God would sensibly admonish once again the Christian Clergy, and show them by their own smart, and an Heathen hand, the nature and odiousness of Persecution, soon died, as is usual for Men of that Imployment, not without a remarkable stroke of God's Judgment.[259] [63b]

---

[255] Turner, p. 7.

[256] Julian: see note 31 above; but here Marvell may be influenced by Montaigne, whose essay "On freedom of conscience" describes Julian's tactics as follows: "Having noted that in Constantinople the people were divided as the prelates of the Christian church were at odds with each other, he . . . stipulated that everyone without distinction or fear should practise his own religion. The reason he was so insistent on this was that he hoped this freedom would increase partisan and divisive intrigues . . . for he had found from experience of the cruelty of certain Christians that no beast in the world is as fearsome to man as is man himself." See Malcolm Smith, *Montaigne and Religious Freedom* (Geneva, 1991), p. 103.

[257] a Reader: a glance back to Turner, p. 59.

[258] Immorality A] Immortality B.

[259] not without . . . God's Judgment: Marvell is alluding to the legend, also mentioned by Montaigne (who disbelieved it) that Julian's last words were, "Thou hast conquered, Nazarene."

Yet they, as if they were only sorry that they had lost so much time upon his death, strove as eagerly to redeem it, and forthwith fell in very naturally into their former Animosities. For Jovianus[260] being chosen Emperour in Persia, and returning homeward, Socr. l.3.c.20. the Bishops of each Party, in hopes that theirs should be the Imperial Creed, strait to Horse, and rode away with Switch and Spur, as if it had been for the Plate to meet him; and he that had the[261] best Heels, made himself Cock-sure of winning the Religion.[262] The Macedonians, who dividing from the Arrians, had set up for a new Heresie concerning the Holy Ghost (and they were a Squadron of Bishops) Petition'd him that those who held *Filium Patri dissimilem,*[263] might be turned out, and themselves put in their places; which was very honestly done, and above-board. The Acacians, that were the refined Arrians, but as the Author saith, *had a notable faculty of addressing themselves to the inclination of whatsoever Emperor;* and having good intelligence that he balanced rather to the Consubstantials, presented him with a very fair insinuating Subscription,[264] of a considerable number of Bishops to the Council of Nice. But in the next Emperor's time they will be found to yield little Reverence to their own Subscription. For in matter of a Creed, a Note of their Hand, without expressing the Penalty, could not it seems bind one of their Order. But all that Jovianus said to the Macedonians was, *I hate Contention, but I lovingly imbrace and reverence those who are inclined to Peace and Concord.* To the Acacians, who had wisely given these the Precedence of Application, to try the truth of their Intelligence, he said no more (*having resolv'd by sweetness and perswasions to quiet all their Controversies*) but, *That he would not molest any Man whatsoever Creed he follow'd, but those above others he would Cherish and Honor, who should show themselves most forward in bringing the Church to a good Agreement.* He likewise call'd back all those Bishops who had been banished by Constantius and Julian, restoring them to their Sees. And he writ a Letter in particular to Athanasius, who upon Julian's death, had enter'd again upon that of Alexandria, to bid him be of good Courage. *And these things coming to the Ears of all others, did*

---

[260] Jovianus succeeded to the empire in A.D. 363; he died in 364 at the age of thirty-three, overcome, in one story, by fumes from a charcoal stove.

[261] had the] had A.

[262] strait to Horse . . . winning the Religion: Marvell's translation of the single verb "adeunt."

[263] *Filium Patri dissimilem:* The Son is different from the Father.

[264] Subscription: a petition with signatories.

wonderfully asswage the fierceness of those who were inflamed with Faction and Contention: So that the Court having declared it self of this Mind, the Church was in a short time, in all outward appearance, peaceably disposed; the Emperor by this means having wholly repressed all their violence. *Verily,* concludes the Historian, *the Roman Empire had been prosperous and happy, and both the State and the Church* (he puts them too in that order) *under so good a Prince, must have exceedingly flourished, had not an Immature death taken him away from managing the Government. For after seven Months, being seized with a Mortal Obstruction, he departed this Life.*[265] Did not this Historian, trow you, deserve to be handled, and is it not, *now the Mischief is done, to undo the Charm, become a* Duty, *to* Expose both *him* and Jovianus?[266] *By their ill chosen Principles what would have become of the Prime, and most necessary Articles of Faith? Might not the old Dormant Heresies, all of them, safely have revived?*[267] [64]

But that *Mortal Obstruction* of the Bishops, was not by his death (nor is it by their own to be) removed. They were glad he was so soon got out of their way, and God would yet further manifest their intractable spirit, which not the Persecution of the Heathen Emperour Julian, nor the gentleness of Jovianus the Christian, could allay or mitigate by their afflictions or prosperity. The Divine Nemesis executed Justice upon them, by one anothers hand: And so hainous[268] a Crime as for a Christian, a Bishop, to Persecute, stood yet [in] need, as the only equal and exemplary punishment, of being revenged with a Persecution by Christians, by Bishops. And whoever shall seriously consider all along the Succession of the Emperors, can never have taken that satisfaction in the most Judicious Representations of the Scene, which he may in this worthy Speculation of the great Order and admirable Conduct of Wise Providence, through the whole contexture of these Exteriour seeming Accidents, relating to the Ecclesiasticals of Christianity.

[265] This whole section about Jovianus derives, with some reordering, from Socrates, 3:20, 21. Christopherson, 2:101–02.

[266] Cf. Turner, p. 1. "Now since the mischief is done, to undo the Charm again it becomes a duty to Expose him [i.e., Croft]." Marvell is ironically revisiting some of Turner's most unfortunate remarks, allying Croft with Jovianus and the historian who praised him.

[267] Turner, p. 9: "For upon his measures and rules of Faith, what will become of our *Prime and most necessary Principles of Faith* . . . In the mean while the old dormant Heresies may *safely* revive again . . . their Ghosts may rise and walk and invade the Church again, under this Authors shadow."

[268] Hainous: heinous, i.e., highly criminal.

For to Jovianus succeeded Valentinian,[269] who in a short time took his Brother Valens[270] to be his Companion in the Empire. These two Brothers did as the Historian observes, *Socr. l.4.c.*I. (alike, and equally take care at the beginning, for the advantage and Government of the State) but very much disagreed, though both Christians, in matter of Religion: Valentinianus the Elder being an Orthodox, but Valens an Arrian, and they used a different method toward the Christians. For Valentinian (who chose the Western part of the Empire, and left the East to his Brother) as he imbraced those of his own Creed, so yet he did not in the least molest the Arrians: But Valens not only labour'd to increase the number of the Arrians, but afflicted those of the contrary Opinion with grievous punishments. And both of 'm, especially Valens, had Bishops for their purpose. The particulars of that heavy Persecution under Valens, any one may further satisfie himself of in the writers of those times. And yet it is observeable, that within a little space, while he pursued the Orthodox Bishops, he gave liberty to the Novatians, (who were of the same Creed, but separated from them, as I have said, upon Disciplin, *&c.*) and caused their Churches, which for a while were shut up, to be opened again at Constantinople. To be short, Valens (who out-lived his Brother, that died of a natural death,) himself in a Battle against the Goths, could not escape neither the fate of a Christian Persecutor. *For the Goths having made Application to him, he,* saith Socrates, *not well foreseeing the Consequence, admitted them to inhabit in certain places of Thracia, pleasing himself that he should by that means always have an Army ready at hand against whatsoever Enemies; and that those Forreign Guards would strike them with a greater terrour, more by far than the* Militia *of his Subjects. And so, slighting the Ancient* Veterane Militia, *which used to consist of Bodies of Men raised proportionably in every Province, and were stout Fellows that would fight Manfully; instead of them, he levied Money, rating the Country at so much for every Souldier.*[271] But these new Inmates of the Emperors soon grew troublesome, as is customary, and not only infested the Natives in Thracia, but Plunder'd even the Suburbs of Constantinople, there being no armed Force to repress them. Hereupon the [65] whole People of the City cryed out at a publick Spectacle, where Valens was present neglecting this matter,

[269] Valentinian I, Roman emperor (A.D. 321–75), became emperor in 364; a Christian, he was tolerant of pagans and most heretics.

[270] Valens was Eastern emperor 364–78. Baptized an Arian, he persecuted Christians of the opposite persuasion.

[271] Socrates, 4:28; Christopherson, 2:124.

Give us Arms, and we will manage this War our selves. This extreamly provok'd him, so that he forthwith made an Expedition against the Goths: But *threatned the Citizens if he [re]turn'd in safety, to be reveng'd on them both for those Contumelies, and for what under the Tyrant Procopius*[272] *they had committed against the Empire; and that he would Raze to the ground, and Plow up the City. Yet before his departure, out of fear of the Forreign Enemy, he totally ceas'd from persecuting the Orthodox in Constantinople. But he was kill'd in the Fight, or flying into a Village that the Goths had set on fire, he was there burnt to ashes;*[273] to the great grief of his Bishops, who, had he been Victorious, might have revived the Persecution. Such was the end of his impetuous Reign, and rash Counsels, both as to his Government of State, in matters of Peace and War, and his manage[274] of the Church by Persecution.

His death brings me to the Succession of Theodosius the Great,[275] then whom no Christian Emperor did more to make it[276] his business to Nurse up the Church, and to Lull the Bishops, to keep the House in quiet. But neither was it in his power to still their bawling, and scratching one another, as far as their Nails (which were yet more tender, but afterwards grew like Tallons) would give them leave. I shall not further vex the History, or the Reader, in recounting the particulars; taking no delight neither my self in so uncomfortable relations, or to reflect beyond what is necessary upon the Wolfishness of those which then seemed, and ought to have been, the Christian Pastors, but went on scattering their Flocks, if not devouring; and the Shepherds smiting one another. In his Reign the second General Council was called, that of Constantinople, & the Creed was there made which took its name from the place. The rest of their business, any one that is further curious, may observe in the writers. But I shall close this with a short touch concerning Gregory Nazianzen,[277] then living, than whom also

---

[272] The tyrant Procopius attacked Valentinian and was punished by being torn apart by trees. See Socrates, 4:5.

[273] Socrates, 4:31. Christopherson, 2:126r. The section "Yet before his departure . . . kill'd in the Fight" is not a quotation, but Marvell's comment. Strictly speaking, therefore, it should not have been italicized.

[274] Manage: management.

[275] Theodosius I (c. A.D. 346–95) was a pious Christian and adherent of the Nicene Creed, very severe against heretics. He became Eastern emperor in 379, and in 381 convened the Council of Constantinople, the source of the creed of that name.

[276] make it A] make B.

[277] St. Gregory Nazianzus (A.D. 329–90) was one of the four great fathers of the church. Born a pagan, he was converted by his wife and baptized at the time of the

the Christian Church had not in those times (and I question whether in any succeeding) a Bishop that was more a Christian, more a Gentleman, better appointed in all sorts of Learning requisite, seasoned under Julian's Persecution; and exemplary to the highest pitch of true Religion and Practical Piety. The Eminence of these Vertues, and in special of his Humility (the lowliest but the highest of all Christian Qualifications) raised him under Theodosius, from the Parish-like Bishoprick of Nazianzum, to that of Constantinople, where he fill'd his place in that Council. But having taken notice in what manner things were carried in that, as they had been in former Councils, & that some of the Bishops muttered at his Promotion; he of his own mind resigned that great Bishoprick, which was never of his desire or seeking, and though so highly seated in the Emperors Reverence and Favor, so acceptable to the People, and generally to the Clergy, whose unequal Abilities could not pretend or justifie an envy against him, retired back, far more content, to a solitary life to his little Nazianzum. And from thence he writes that Letter to his Friend Procopius,[278] wherein, p. 814. upon his most recollected and serious reflexion on what had faln within his observa-[66]tion, he useth these remarkable words; *I have resolved with my self (if I may tell you the* Naked *Truth,) never more to come into any Assembly of Bishops: for I never saw a good and happy end of any Council, but which rather increased than remedied the mischiefs: For their obstinate Contentions and Ambition are unexpressible.*[279]

It would require too great a Volume to deduce, from the death of

---

Council of Nicaea. A close friend and colleague of St. Basil, he vacillated constantly between the duties of his office as bishop and the desire for monastic seclusion.

[278] Procopius: praefect of Constantinople.

[279] See Migne, *Patrologia Graeca*, 37:3, p. 226: "Ego, si vera scribere oportet, hoc animo sum, ut omnem episcoporum conventum fugiam, quoniam nullius concilii finem laetum et faustum vidi, nec quod depulsionem malorum potius, quam accessionem et incrementum habuerit. Semper enim sunt contentiones, et dominandi cupiditates (ac ne me, quaeso, gravem et molestum existimes, haec scribentem), nec ullis quidem verbis explicari queunt." This was an important text for Milton, who used it in his *Apology for Smectymnuus* (*CPW,* 1:944–45) and in his correspondence with Henry Oldenburg (7:514–15). Marvell used Nazianzus's *Theologi Opera* (Paris, 1630), in which the letter to Procopius does indeed occur on p. 814. His translation makes shrewd topical use of the phrase "si vera scribere oportet." John Warly, in *The Reasoning Apostate: Or Modern Latitude-Man Consider'd, as he Opposeth the Authority of the King and Church* (London, 1677), p. 88, attacked this "partial citation" of Nazianzus as a deliberate distortion of the patriarch's "drift and design."

Theodosius, the particulars that happened in the succeeding Reigns about this matter. But the Reader may reckon, that it was as stated a Quarrel betwixt the *Homoousians,* and the *Homoiousians,* as that between the Houses of York and Lancaster:[280] And there arose now an Emperor of one Line, and then again of the other. But among all the Bishops, there was not one Morton,[281] whose *industrious Brain could or would* (for some men always reap by division) *make up the fatal Breach betwixt*[282] the two Creeds. By this means every Creed[283] was grown up to a Test, and under that pretence, the dextrous Bishops step by step hooked within their Verge[284] all the business and Power that could be catched in those Turbulences, where they mudled the water, and fished after. By this means they stalked on first to a spiritual kind of Dominion, and from that incroached upon and into the Civil Jurisdiction. A Bishop now grew terrible, and (whereas a simple Lay man might have frighted the Devil with the first words of the Apostles Creed, and *I defie thee Satan*) one Creed could not protect him from a Bishop, and it required a much longer, and a double and treble Confession, unless himself would be delivered over to Satan by an *Anathema.* But this was only an Ecclesiastical Sentence at first, with which they marked out such as sinned against them, and then whoop'd & hollow'd[285] on the Civil Magistrate, to hunt them down for their spiritual pleasure. They crept at first by Court-insinuations and flattery into the Princes favour, till those generous Creatures suffered themselves to be backed and ridden by them, who would take as much of a Free Horse as possible; but in Persecution, the Clergy as yet wisely interposed the Magistrate betwixt themselves & the People, not

[280] An allusion to the Wars of the Roses during the fifteenth century.

[281] See *Mr. Smirke,* note 458.

[282] Turner, p. 62: "No men were greater Blessings to their times, even in those times of Popery when they sat at the Helm, than the Bishops. 'Twas Bishop Morton's Industrious Brain that made up the Fatal breach, and United the two Houses of York and Lancaster."

[283] every Creed A] ital. B.

[284] Verge: generally, boundary; but see also the technical meaning: the area subject to the jurisdiction of the lord high steward, within a twelve-mile radius from the king's court.

[285] Cf. *RT,* p. 116: " 'Tis true, that being distracted betwixt his desire that the Consciences of men should be persecuted, and his anger at Princes that will not be advised, [Parker] confounds himself every where in his reasonings, that you can hardly distinguish which is the *Whoop* and which is the *Holla.* " Marvell returned to this game, for which Buckingham's *Rehearsal* gave him the idea, several times.

caring so their end were attained, how odious they rendred him. And you may observe that for the most part hitherto, they stood crouching, and shot either over the Emperors back, or under his belly. But in process of time they became bolder and open fac'd, and persecuted before the Sun at Mid-day. Bishops grew worse, but Bishopricks every day better and better. There was now no Eusebius left to refuse the Bishoprick of Antiochia, whom therefore Constantine told, *That he deserv'd the Bishoprick of the whole World for that Modesty.* They were not such fools as Ammonius Parotes, I warrant you, in the time[286] of Theodosius. *He,* Socr. l.6.c.30. *being seized upon by some that would needs make him a Bishop, when he could not perswade them to the contrary, cut off one of his Ears, telling them that now should he himself desire to be a Bishop, he was by the Law of Priesthood incapable: but when they observed that those things only obliged the Jewish Priesthood, and that the Church of Christ did not consider whether a Priest were*[287] *sound or perfect in Limb of Body, but only that he were intire in his manners, they return'd to seize on him again: But when he saw them coming, he swore with a solemn Oath, that if to Conse-[67]crate him a Bishop they laid violent hands upon him, he would cut out his Tongue also; whereupon they, fearing he would do it, de-sisted.*[288] What should have been the matter, that a man so Learned and Holy, should have such an aversion to be promoted in his own Order; that rather than yield to be a compelled or compelling Bishop, he would inflict upon himself as severe a Martyrdom, as any Persecutor could have done for him? Sure he saw something more in the very Constitution, than some do at present. But this was indeed an example too rigid, and neither fit to have been done, nor to be imitated, as there was no danger. For[289] from this they followed the Precedent rather of Damasus, and Ursinus, which last, *Socr. l.4.c.24. In Valentinians time, perswaded certain obscure and abject Bishops* (for there were it seems of all sorts and sizes) *to create him Bishop in a Corner, and then*[290] (so early) he and Damasus, who was much the better Man, waged War for the Bishoprick of Rome, to the great scandal of the Pagan Writers, who made Remarks for this and other things upon their Christianity, and

---

[286] in the time A] in time B.

[287] were A] wore B.

[288] The reference should be not to Socrates but to Sozomen, 6:30, where the entire story as retold here is to be found. Cf. Christopherson, 3:155v–156r. Marvell alluded to Ammonius also in *RT2*, p. 287, where he appears as the antithesis of Samuel Parker.

[289] For] far A.

[290] Socrates, 4:24; Christopherson, 2:121v–122r.

to the bloodshed and death of a multitude of the Christian People. But this last I mention'd, only as a weak and imperfect Essay in that time, of what it came to in the several Ages after, which I am now speaking of, when the Bishops were given, gave themselves over to all manner of Vice, Luxury, Pride, Ignorance, Superstition, Covetousness, and Monopolizing of all secular imployments and Authority. Nothing could escape them: They medled, troubled themselves and others with many things, every thing, forgetting that *one only needful.*[291] Insomuch that I could not avoid wondring often, that among so many Churches that with Paganick Rites they dedicated to Saint Mary, I have met with none to Saint[292] Martha. But above all, Imposition and Cruelty became Inherent in them, & the power of Persecution was grown so good & desirable a thing, that they thought the Magistrate scarce worthy to be trusted with it longer, and a meer Novice at it, and either wrested it out of his hands, or gently eased him of that and his other burdens of Government. The sufferings of the Laity were become the Royalties[293] of the Clergy; and being very careful Christians, the Bishops, that not a word of our Saviours might fall to the ground, because he had foretold how Men should be persecuted for his Names sake, they undertook to see it done effectually in their own Provinces, and out of pure Zeal of doing him the more Service of this kind, inlarged studiously their Dioceses beyond all proportion. Like Nostradamus his Son, that to fulfil his Fathers Prediction of a City in France that should be burned, with his own hands set it on fire.[294] All the calamities of the Christian World, in those Ages, may be derived from them, while they warm'd themselves at the flame; and like Lords of Missrule,[295] kept a perpetual *Christmas.* What in

[291] Luke 10:43. The allusion is to the story of Mary and Martha, Martha being "careful and troubled about many things," but Mary being focused only on Christ. Marvell expands sardonically on his allusion in the next sentence. Milton used the same text in *Of True Religion, CPW,* 8:434.

[292] Saint A] St. B.

[293] Royalties: royal prerogatives or rights, especially in respect of jurisdiction, granted by the sovereign to individuals or groups.

[294] Nostradamus: Michel de Notredame, a French prophet, astronomer, and physician who became personal physician to Charles IX, but was primarily famous for his *Centuries,* a book of arcane prophecies published at Lyons in 1555. One of his sons, Michel le Jeune, in 1574 set fire to the town of Pouzin, which was beseiged by the royal troups, but it was his own prophecy (in imitation of his father) that he intended to fulfill. He was caught in the act and killed by the commander of the beseiging army.

[295] Lords of Missrule: In an inversion ritual, a Lord of Misrule was chosen by the lord of a manor to preside over the Christmas games and festivities.

the Bishops name is the matter? How came it about that Christianity, which approved itself under all Persecutions to the Heathen Emperors, and merited their Favor so far, till at last it regularly succeeded to the Monarchy, should under those of their own Profession be more distressed? Were there some Christians then too, that feared still lest Men should be Christians, and for whom *it was* [68] *necessary,* not for the Gospel reason, *that there should be Heresies.*[296] Let us collect a little now also in the Conclusion what[297] at first was not particulariz'd, how the Reason of State, and Measure of Government, stood under the Roman Emperors, in aspect to them. I omit Tiberius, mention'd in the beginning of this Essay. Trajane,[298] after having persecuted them, and having used Pliny the second[299] in his Province to that purpose, upon his relation that they lived in conformity to all Laws, but that which forbad their Worship, and in all other things were blameless, and good men, straitly by his Edict commanded that none of them should be farther enquired after. Hadrian,[300] in his Edict to Minutius Fundanus, Pro-consul of Asia, commands him that, *If any accuse the Christians, and can prove it, that they commit any thing against the State, that then he punish them according to their Crime: but if any man accuse them meerly for calumny and vexation, as Christians, then I'faith let him suffer for't, and take you care that he feel the smart of it.*[301] Antoninus Pius[302] writ his Edict very remarkable, if there were place here to recite it, to the States of Asia assembled at Ephesus; wherein he takes notice of his Fathers Command, that *unless the Christians were found to act any thing against the Roman Empire, they should not be molested;* and then Commands, *that if any man*

---

[296] I Corinthians 11–19: "For there must be heresies among you, that they which are approved may be made manifest among you."

[297] what A] which B.

[298] Trajan (Marcus Ulpius Trajanus) was Roman emperor from A.D. 98 to 117, succeeding Nerva, whose brief reign succeeded the long persecution of Domitian (A.D. 81–96). His reputation was primarily that of a military conqueror, and he constructed the Forum of Trajan in Rome to commemorate his campaigns.

[299] Pliny the Younger, nephew of the elder Pliny, author of a famous collection of letters, held a series of offices under Trajan, including the governorship of Bithynia c. A.D. 111 till his death in 113.

[300] Hadrian (Publius Aelius Hadrianus) was Roman emperor A.D. 117–38. An accomplished Hellenist, he founded c. 135 the Athenaeum at Rome and completed at Athens the temple of Zeus begun by Pisistratus.

[301] Marvell found this in Eusebius, 4:9; Christopherson, 1:70v.

[302] Antoninus Pius was Roman emperor from A.D. 138 to 161, when he was succeeded by Marcus Aurelius. Marvell is working his way through the emperors chronologically.

thereafter shall continue to trouble them, tanquam quales, *as Christians, for their Worship, in that case he that is the Informer should be exposed to punishment, but the accused should be free and discharged.* I could not but observe that among other things in this Edict, where he is speaking, *It is desirable to them that they may appear, being accused, more willing to die for their God than to live,* he adds, *It would not be amiss to admonish you concerning the Earthquakes which have, and do now happen, that when you are afflicted at them, you would compare our affairs with theirs. They are thereby so much the more incouraged to a confidence and Reliance upon God, but you all the while go on in your ignorance, and neglect both other Gods, and the Religion towards the Immortal, and banish and persecute them unto death.*[303] Which words of the Emperours fall in so naturally with what, it seems, was a common observation about Earthquakes, that I cannot but to that purpose take further notice, how also Gregory Nazianzen, in Or. 2d. *contra Gentiles,* tells, besides the breakings in of the Sea in several places, and many fires that happened, of the Earthquakes in particular, which he reckons as Symptomes of Julian's Persecution.[304] And to this I may add, *Socr. l.3.c.10.* who in the Reign of Valens, that notorious Christian Persecutor, saith, at the same time there was an Earthquake in Bithynia, which ruined the City of Nice, (that same in which that General Councel was held under Constantine) and a little while after there was another. *But although these so happened, the minds of Valens, and of Eudoxius, the Bishop of the Arrians, were not at all stirred up unto Piety, and a right opinion of Religion:* For *nevertheless they never ceased, made no end of persecuting those who in their Creed dissented from them. Those Earthquakes seemed to be certain Indications of tumult in the Church.*[305] All which put together, could not but make me reflect upon the late Earth-[69]quakes, great by how much more unusual, here in England, thorow so many Counties since *Christmas,*[306] at the same time when the

---

[303] Eusebius, 4:12; Christopherson, 1:71.

[304] The reference should be not to *contra Gentiles,* an oration Nazianzus never wrote, but to his second oration *contra Julianum.* See Migne, *Patrologia Graeca,* 35:667–71.

[305] Actually, Socrates 4:10; Christopherson, 2:107v.

[306] I can find no other contemporary references to earthquakes in England in January 1676. But cf. *A Chronological and Historical Account of the most Memorable Earthquakes That have happened in the world . . . With an Appendix, containing A distinct Series of those that have been felt in England* (Cambridge, 1750), p. 58: "In the year 1677, in Christmas-time, about eleven at Night, was an Earthquake in Staffordshire . . . It was considerable about Willenhall near Wolverhampton, but very short . . . The same Earthquake was felt also at Hanbury upon the confines of Derbyshire." Perhaps this anonymous chron-

Clergy, some of them, were so busie in their Cabals,[307] to promote this (I would give it a modester name then) Persecution, which is now[308] on foot against the Dissenters; at so unseasonable a time, & upon no occasion administred by them, that those who comprehend the reasons, yet cannot but wonder at the wisdom of it. Yet I am not neither one of the most credulous Nickers or Applyers of Natural Events to humane transactions: but neither am I so secure as the Learned Dr. Spencer,[309] nor can walk along the world without having some eye to the Conjunctures of God's admirable Providence. Neither was Marcus Aurelius[310] (that I may return to my matter) negligent as to this particular. But he observing, as Antoninus had the Earthquakes, that in an Expedition against the Germans and Sarmatians, his Army being in despair almost for want of water, the Melitine (afterwards from the event called the *Thundring*)[311] Legion, which consisted of Christians, kneel'd down in the very heat of their thirst and fight, praying for Rain; which posture the Enemies wondring at, immediately there brake out such a Thundring and Lightning, as together

---

icler wrote 1677 for 1676. Alternatively, since in the 1680 edition of the *Essay* (and hence also in 1687, which copies 1680) "since Christmas" is replaced by "two years since," 1677 may be correct, and hence the referent for the 1680 edition.

[307] Cabals: Two *OED* definitions intertwine here: "A private intrigue of a sinister character formed by a small body of persons"; and "Applied in the reign of Charles II to a small committee of the Privy Council." Supposedly the term was also an acronym, from the names of Clifford, Arlington, Buckingham, Ashley, and Lauderdale. Cf. *Last Instructions*, ll. 120–21: "The close Cabal mark'd how the Navy eats, / And thought all lost that goes not to the Cheats."

[308] The topical reference of this "now" in reference to clerical cabals and attacks on the Dissenters obviously varies, without losing its strength, from 1676 through 1680 to 1703 and 1709.

[309] Marvell refers to Dr. John Spencer, dean of Ely, *A discourse concerning prodigies* (London, 1663, 1665), whose agenda was to discourage the political interpretation of natural phenomena like earthquakes; especially, of course, interpretations hostile to the Restoration government.

[310] Marcus Aurelius (A.D. 121–80), became emperor in 161 and was revered as a philosopher-ruler. The episode Marvell describes occurred in 172, in a campaign against the Marcomanni. It is shown on the Aurelian column in Rome.

[311] The term derived from Apolinarius, writing just after the event to Marcus Aurelius. Williamson, trans. *The History of the Church*, p. 207, notes that inscriptions show that in Nero's time the legion had been entitled "Fulminata," or "Thunderstruck" and suggests that Marcus Aurelius, to commemorate the event, renamed the legion "Fulminatrix," "Hurler of the Thunderbolt."

with the Christian Valor, routed the adverse Army; but so much Rain fell therewith, as refreshed Aurelius his Forces that were at the last gasp for thirst: he thenceforward commanded by his Letters, *that upon pain of death none should inform against the Christians,* as Tertullian in his Apology for the Christians witnesses.[312] But who would have believed that even Commodus,[313] so great a Tyrant otherwise, should have been so favourable as to make a Law, *that the Informers against Christians should be punished with death?* Yet he did, and the Informer against Apollonius was by it executed. Much less could a man have thought, that that Prodigy of cruelty[314] Maximine,[315] and who exercised it so severely upon the Christians, should, as he did, being struck with God's hand, publish when it was too late, Edict after Edict, in great favour of the Christians. But above all, nothing could have been less expected, then that after those Heathen Emperors, the first Christian Constantine should have been seduced by the Bishops, to be, after them, the first occasion of Persecution, so contrary to his own excellent inclination:[316] 'Twas then that he spake his own mind, when he said, Eus. *de vita Consti.* 69. *You ought to retain within the bounds of your private thoughts those things, which you cunningly and subtilly seek out concerning most frivolous questions.*[317] And then much plainer, c. 67. where he saith so wisely. *You are not ignorant that the Philosophers all of them do agree in the profession of the same Discipline, but do oftentimes differ in some part of the Opinions which they dogmatize in; but yet, although they do dissent about the Discipline that each several Sect observeth, they nevertheless reconcile themelves again for the sake of that common Profession to which they have concurred.* But against compulsion in Religious matters so much every where, that it is needless to insert one passage. And he being of this disposition, and universally famous for his care and countenance of the Christian Religion: Eusebius saith [70] these words: *While the People of God did glory and heighten it self in the doing of good things, and all fear from without was taken away, and the Church as*

[312] Again, Marvell mentions Tertullian, but his source is Eusebius, 5:5; Christopherson, 1:96r.

[313] Commodus was Roman emperor from A.D. 180 to 192.

[314] cruelty A] cruel B.

[315] Maximin was Roman emperor from A.D. 235 to 238. For his illness and his remorseful edict, see Eusebius, 8:15, 16.

[316] inclination: another allusion to Charles II's instincts for toleration, as Marvell strategically interpreted them.

[317] Eusebius, *De Vita Constantini,* 2:67; Christopherson, 1:261.

fortifi'd, as I may say, on all sides by a peaceable and illustrious tranquility, then Envy lying in wait against our prosperity, craftily crept in, and began first to dance in the midst of the company of Bishops.[318] So goes on, telling the History of Alexander and Arrius. I have been before large enough in that relation, wherein it appeared, that contrary to that great Emperours Pious Intention, whereas *Envy began to dance among the Bishops first,* the good Constantine brought them the Fiddles.[319] But it appear'd likewise how soon he was weary of the Ball, and toward his latter end, as Princes often do upon too late experience, would have redressed all, and returned to his natural temper. Of the other Christian Emperors I likewise discoursed, omitting, that I might insert it in this place, how the great Heathen Philosopher Themistius,[320] in his Consular Oration, celebrated Jovianus for having given that tolleration in Christian Religion, and therby defeated the *flattering* Bishops; which sort of men, said he wittily, *do not worship God, but the Imperial Purple.*[321]

It was the same Themistius, that only out of an upright natural apprehension of things, made that Excellent Oration afterward to Valens, which is in Print,[322] exhorting him to cease Persecution; wherein he chances upon, and improves the same notion with Constantine's, and tells him, *That he should not wonder at the Dissents in Christian Religion, which were very small, if compared with the multitude and crowd of Opinions among the Gentile Philosophers; for there were at least three hundred differences, and a very great dissention among them there was about their resolutions, unto which each several Sect was as it were necessarily bound up and obliged: and that God seemed to intend more to illustrate his own glory by that divers and unequal variety of Opinions, to the end every each one might therefore so much the more Reverence his Divine Majesty, because it is not possible for any one accurately to know him.*[323] And

---

[318] Eusebius, *De Vita Constantini*, 2:60; Christopherson, 1:259.

[319] Compare *RT,* p. 104: "Where the Horses are . . . taught to dance, the Enemy need only learn the Tune and bring the Fiddles."

[320] Themistius: rhetorician of Paphlagonia, fl. A.D. 360; he lived at Constantinople as a pagan but advanced toleration of other religious beliefs.

[321] Socrates, 3:21. Thomas Field, in his copy of Hanmer's translation, added at this point this marginal note: "They worship not the K. of Heaven, but the earthly crowne & Scepter."

[322] An edition of Themistius's *Orationes* was published in Paris in 1618. Marvell could have seen a copy in Anglesey's library.

[323] Socrates, 4:27; Christopherson, 2:123v. Thomas Field annotates this passage: "300

this had a good effect upon Valens, for the mitigating in some measure his severities against his Fellow Christians. So that after having cast about, in this Summary again, (whereby it plainly appears, that according to natural right, and the apprehension of all sober Heathen Governours, Christianity, as a Religion, was wholly exempt from the Magistrates Jurisdiction or Laws, farther than any particular person among them immorally[324] transgressed, as others, the common rules of human society) I cannot but return to the question with which I begun. What was the matter? How came it about that Christianity, which approved it self under all Persecutions to the Heathen Emperours, and merited their favour so far, till at last it regularly succeeded to the Monarchy, should, under those of their own Profession be more distressed? But the Answer is now much shorter and certainer, and I will adventure boldly to say, the true and single cause then was the Bishops. And they were the cause against Reason. For what Power had the Emperors by growing Christians, more than those had before them? None. What obligation were Christian [71] Subjects under to the Magistrate more than before? None. But the Magistrates Christian Authority was, what the Apostle describ'd it while Heathen, *not to be a terror to good works, but to evil.*[325] What new Power had the Bishops acquired, whereby they turned every Pontificate into a Caiaphat?[326] None neither? 2 Cor. 10.8. Had they been Apostles, *The Lord had but given them Authority for Edification, not for Destruction.*[327] They, of all other, ought to have preached to the Magistrate the terrible Denunciations in Scripture against usurping upon, and persecuting of Christians. They, of all others, ought to have laid before them the horrible examples of Gods ordinary Justice against those that exercised Persecution. But, provided they could be the swearers of the Prince to do all

---

opinions among Philosophers." Its value for tolerationists may be compared with St. Paul's statement in 1 Corinthians 11:19 about the necessity of heresies for the emergence of truth.

[324] immorally A] immortally B; this repeats an earlier mistake, though it is more plausible here.

[325] Romans 13:3. See *Mr. Smirke,* p. 98.

[326] Caiaphat Ed., 1680, 1687, 1703] Caiaphas, A,B: the kind of ecclesiastical government initiated by Caiaphas, the high-priest of Jerusalem who headed the trial of Christ, which was held illegally at night and deployed false witnesses. In Matthew 26:65, Caiaphas "rent his clothes, saying, He hath spoken blasphemy; what further need have we of witnesses?"

[327] 2 Corinthians 10:8. Paul is actually asserting his spiritual authority, and the phrase quoted by Marvell is only a slight adjustment to the claim.

due Allegiance to the Church, & to preserve the Rights and Liberties of the Church, however they came by them, they would give him as much scope as he pleased in matter of Christianity, and would be the first to solicit him to break the Laws of Christ, & ply him with hot places of Scripture, in order to all manner of Oppression and Persecution in Civils and Spirituals. So that the whole business how this unchristian Tyranny came, and could entitle it self among Christians, against the Christian priviledges, was only the case in Zech.13.6,7. *And one shall say unto him, what are these wounds in thy hands? then he shall answer, those with which I was wounded in the house of my friends.*[328] Because they were all Christians, they thought forsooth they might make the bolder with them, make bolder with Christ, and wound him again in the hands and feet of his Members. Because they were friends they might use them more coursly,[329] and abuse them, against all common Civility, in their own house, which is a Protection to strangers. And all this to the end that a Bishop might sit with the Prince in a *Junto*,[330] to consult wisely how to preserve him from those people that never meant him any harm, and to secure him from the Sedition and Rebellion of men that seek, nor think any thing more, but to follow their own Religious Christian Worship. It was indeed as ridiculous a thing to the Pagans to see that work, as it was afterwards in England to strangers, where Papists and Protestants went both to wrack at the same instance, in the same Market; and when Erasmus said wittily, *Quid agitur in Anglia? Consulitur* he might have added, though not so elegantly *Comburitur de Religione.*[331] Because they knew that Christian Worship was free by Christs Institution, they procured the Magistrate to make Laws in it concerning things unnecessary; as the Heathen Persecutor Julian introduced some bordering Pagan Ceremonies, and arguing with themselves in the same manner as he did, Soz. l.5.c.16. That *if Christians should obey those Laws, they should be able to bring them about to something further which they had designed: But if they would not, then*

---

[328] Zechariah, 13:6. The erroneous citation of verse 7, however, would have taken the reader in a different direction: "Awake, O sword, against my shepherd, and against the man that is my fellow, saith the Lord of hosts."

[329] Corsely: coarsely, rudely.

[330] *Junto:* a clique, faction, or cabal.

[331] For Erasmus, see *Mr. Smirke*, note 327. Marvell is slightly misremembering a standard grammar text paradigm of question and anwer. See, for example, Charles Hook, *The Latine Grammar fitted for the Use of Schools* (London, 1651), pp. 198–99: "What is now adoing in England? They consult about Religion. Quid rerum nunc geritur in Anglia? Consulitur de Religione."

they might proceed against them without any hope of pardon, as breakers of the Laws of the Empire, and represent them as turbulent & dangerous to the Government.[332] Indeed, whatsoever the Animadverter saith[333] of the Act of Seditious Conventicles here in England, as if it were Anvill'd after another of the Roman Senate,[334] the Chri-[72]stians of those Ages, had all the finest tools of Persecution out of Julian's Shop, and studied him then as curiously as some do now Machiavel.[335] These Bishops it was, who because the Rule of Christ was incompatible with the Power that they assumed, and the Vices they practised, had no way to render themselves necessary or tolerable to Princes, but by making true Piety difficult, by Innovating Laws to revenge themselves upon it, and by turning Make-bates[336] between Prince and People, instilling dangers of which themselves were the Authors. Hence it is, that having awakened this jealousie once in the Magistrate against Religion, they made both the Secular and the Ecclesiastical Government so uneasie to him, that most Princes began to look upon their Subjects as their Enemies, and to imagine a reason of State different from the Interest of their People; and therefore to weaken themselves by seeking unnecessary and grievous supports to their Authority. Whereas if men could have refrain'd this cunning, and from thence forcible governing of Christianity, leaving it to its own simplicity, and due liberty, but causing them in all other things to keep the King's and Christ's Peace among themselves, & towards others, all the ill that could have come of it would have been, that such kind of Bishops should have proved less implemental;[337] but the good that must have thence risen to the Christian Magistrate, and the Church, then and ever after, would have been inexpressible.

But this discourse having run in a manner wholly upon the Imposition of Creeds, may seem not to concern (and I desire that it may not reflect upon) our Clergy, nor the Controversies which have so unhappily vex'd our Church, ever since the Reign of Edward the Sixth,[338] unto this day. Only, if

---

[332] Sozomen, 5:16; Christopherson, 3:122.

[333] In both the editions of 1703 and 1709, this phrase became: "whatsoever some may say of the Act."

[334] Turner, p. 15.

[335] Niccolò Machiavelli (1469–1527), Florentine statesman and political writer. His *Il Principe* (1513) and his commentary on Livy became virtually textbooks, though of opposite persuasions, for political theorists in the seventeenth century.

[336] Make-bates: makers of strife.

[337] implemental: effective, being able to implement their designs.

[338] Edward VI, only son of Henry VIII, who succeeded to the throne at ten years of

there might something be pick'd out of it towards the Compromising of those differences (which I have not from any performance of mine the vanity to imagine) it may have use as an Argument *a Majori ad Minus*[339] their Disputes having risen only from that of Creeds, ours from the Imposition only of Ceremonies, which are of much inferior consideration. Faith being necessary, but Ceremonies dispensable. Unless our Church should lay the same weight upon them as the Animadverter has done thorow his whole Studious Chapter on that Subject, and because p.34. *this is the time of her settlement, that there is a Church at the end of every Mile, that the Sovereign Powers spread their Wings to cover and protect her, that Kings and Queens are her Nursing Fathers, and Nursing Mothers, that she hath stately Cathedrals,*[340] there be so many Arguments now to make Ceremonies necessary; which may all be answered with one Question that they use to ask Children; *Where are you proud?*[341] But I should rather hope from the Wisdom and Christianity of the present Guides of our Church, that they will (after an age and more, after so long a time almost as those Primitive Bishops I have spoke of, yet suffered the Novatian Bishops in every Diocess) have mercy on the Nation, that hath been upon so slender a matter as the Ceremonies and Liturgy so long, so miserably harass'd. That they will have mercy upon the King, whom they know against his Natural Inclination, his Royal In-[72]tention, his many Declarations,[342] they have induced to more severities, than all the Reigns since the Conquest will contain, if summ'd up together:

---

age and died at sixteen. Under Protector Somerset and other Protestant magnates, Edward instituted the first genuinely Protestant regime in England, which was reversed by his death and the accession of Mary Tudor in 1653.

[339] *a Majori ad Minus:* from the greater premise to the less.

[340] Turner, p. 34: "First, I demand, Is it Reason the Church should be as Unceremonious now in the times of her Settlement, as then in the days of her Persecution? Now that there is a Church at the end of almost every mile, as then when there was hardly one in twenty miles? Now when the Soveraign Powers of the World spread their wings to cover and protect her, as then when *they stretcht out their Arms to vex her?* Now when *kings* and *Queens, her Nursing-fathers, and Nursing mothers,* bid her quit her Cave and shew her *beauteous* face in stately Cathedrals, as then when she was fain to hide her self *in the Wilderness* and her Members were forc'd to *wander about in Sheep skins?*"

[341] *Where are you proud?:* this does not seem to be either proverbial or catechistical.

[342] His many Declarations: Marvell refers to the Declaration of Breda (April 1660), whereby Charles promised an amnesty and liberty of conscience, and which Marvell considered him to have betrayed, and the Declaration of Indulgence of 1672, which parliament had forced him to withdraw in 1673.

who may, as Constantine among his Private Devotions, put up one Collect to the Bishops. Euseb. *de vita Const.* c.20. *Date*[343] *igitur mihi Dies tranquillos & Noctes curarum expertes.* And it runs thus almost together *verbatim*[344] in that Historian. *Grant, most merciful Bishop and Priest, that I may have calm days and nights, free from care and molestation, that I may live a peaceable life in all godliness and honesty for the future by your good agreement; which unless you vouchsafe me, I shall waste away my Reign in perpetual sadness and vexation. For as long as the People of God stands divided by so unjust and pernicious a Contention, how can it be that I can have any ease in my own Spirit. Open therefore by your good agreement the way to me, that I may continue my Expedition towards the East; and grant that I may see both you, and all the rest of my people, having laid aside your Animosities, rejoycing together, that we may all with one voice give Laud and Glory, for the Common good Agreement and Liberty, to God Almighty for ever.*[345] Amen. But if neither the People, nor his Majesty enter into their consideration; I hope it is no unreasonable request, that they will be merciful unto themselves, and have some reverence at least for the *Naked Truth* of History, which either in their own times will meet with them, or in the next Age overtake them: That they, who are some of them so old, that, as Confessors, they wore[346] the Scars of the former Troubles; others of them so young, that they are free from all the Motives of Revenge and Hatred, should yet joyn in reviving the former Persecution upon the pretences, yea even themselves in a turbulent, Military, and uncanonical manner execute Laws of their own procuring, and depute their Inferior Clergy to be the Informers. I should rather hope to see not only that Controversie so scandalous abolished, but that also upon so good an occasion as the Author of the *Naked Truth* had administred them, they will inspect their Clergy, and cause many things to be corrected, which are far more ruinous in the Consequence, than the dispensing with a Surplice.[347] I shall mention some too confusedly, as they occur to my Pen at present, reserving much more for better leasure.[348]

[343] *Date* A] *dat* B.

[344] *verbatim:* word for word.

[345] Eusebius, *De Vita Constantini*, 2:70; Christopherson, 1:262.

[346] wore the scars Ed.] were the scars A,B.

[347] Surplice: a loose garment of white linen, worn, usually over a cassock, by clerics during church services. The requirement that the clergy wear surplices was one of the issues most hotly contended by Croft and defended by Turner. Cf. *Mr. Smirke,* pp. 110–11.

[348] better leasure: a sign that Marvell intended to write more on this topic.

Methinks it might be of great edification, that those of them who have ample Possessions, should be in a good sense.[349] *Multas inter opes inopes.*[350] That they would inspect the Canons of the Ancient Councils, where are many excellent ones for the regulation of the Clergy. I saw one, looking but among those of the same Council of Nice, against any Bishops removing from a less Bishoprick to a greater, nor that any of the Inferiour Clergy should leave a less living for a fatter. That is methinks the most natural use of General, or any Councils to make Canons, as it were By-Laws for the ordering of their own Society, but they ought not to take out, much less forge any Patent to invade and prejudice the Community. It were good that the greater Church-men relied more upon themselves, and their own direction, not building too much upon Stripling Chaplains; that men may not suppose the Master (as one that has a good Horse, or a Fleet hound) [74] attributes to himself the vertues of his Creature. That they inspect the Morals of the Clergy: the Moral Hereticks do the Church more harm, than all the Non-conformists can do, or can wish it. That before they admit men to subscribe the Thirty Nine Articles for a Benefice, they try whether they know the meaning. That they would recommend to them the reading of the Bible. 'Tis a very good Book, and if a man read it carefully, will make him much wiser. That they would advise them to keep the Sabbath: if there were no Morality in the day, yet there is a great deal of prudence in the observing it.[351] That they would instruct those that came for Holy Orders and Livings, that it is a terrible Vocation they enter upon, but that has indeed the greatest reward. That to gain a Soul is beyond all the Acquists[352] of Traffick,[353] and to convert an Atheist more glorious that all the Conquests of the Souldier. That, betaking themselves to this Spiritual Warfare, they ought to disintangle from the World. That they do not ride for a Benefice, as it were for a Fortune, or a Mistress; but there is more in it. That they take the Ministry up not as a Trade, and because they have heard of

[349] in a good sense: sane.

[350] A misquotation of Horace, *Carmina*, 3:16:28: "magnas inter opes inops" (a beggar in the midst of great wealth).

[351] This alludes to the sabbatarian controversy, mentioned briefly in *RT* pp. 139–40, where Marvell appeared to accept the "morality" of the seventh day; but he was perhaps by now aware of the antisabbatarian views of French and Dutch Protestants, including André Rivet. See Anthony Milton, *Catholic and Reformed: The Roman and Protestant Churches in English Protestant Thought 1600–1640* (Cambridge, 1995), pp. 410–12.

[352] Acquists: acquisitions, profits.

[353] Traffick: trade, business.

Whittington,[354] in expectation that the Bells may so Chime, that they come in their turns to be Lord Mayors of Lambeth.[355] That they make them understand, as well as they can, what is the Grace of God. That they do not come into the Pulpit too full of Fustian, or Logick, a good Life is a Clergy-mans best Syllogism, and the quaintest Oratory: and till they out-live'm, they will never get the better of the Fanaticks, nor be able to Preach with Demonstration of Spirit, or with any effect or Authority. That they be lowly minded, and no Railers.

And particularly, that the Archdeacon of Canterbury[356] being in ill humor upon account of his *Ecclesiastical Policy*, may not continue to revenge himself upon the Innocent Walloons[357] there, by ruining their Church which subsists upon the Ecclesiastical Power of his Majesty, and so many of his Royal Predecessors.

But these things require greater time, and to enumerate all that is amiss, might perhaps be as endless as to number the People: nor are they within the ordinary Sphaere of my Capacity; and our Exposer will think I have forgot him. I shall take my leave of him for the present, being only troubled to find out a Complement[358] for so Civil a Person. It must be thus.

I will not say as Popilius said to Antiochus,[359] nor as Demosthenes said to AEschines,[360] nor as the most Learned P. AErodius,[361] or the Jesuite Gaspar Schottus[362] said to the Animadverter, nor as Dolubella said to Cicero,[363] nor as the Christian Cicero said to the English Parliament,[364]

---

[354] Since 1605, when a completely fictional tale of him began to circulate in plays and ballads, everyone had heard of "Dick Whittington," lord mayor of London, who was supposed to have risen from being a poor orphan to the mayoralty with the help of his cat. In fact, Richard Whittington (d. 1423) came of a wealthy merchant family and became, under Richard II, the last of the great medieval mayors, before the Wars of the Roses seriously retrenched the powers of the city magnates.

[355] Lambeth: the palace of the archbishop of Canterbury.

[356] Archdeacon of Canterbury: Samuel Parker.

[357] Walloons: In *RT2*, p. 435, Marvell alluded to the fact that a community of Dutch and German Protestants in the reign of Edward VI had the Church in Austin-Friars in Canterbury assigned to them for a place of worship. Exiled during Mary's reign, they returned to Canterbury in Elizabeth's. [S]

[358] Complement: i.e., compliment.

[359] For Popilius and Antiochus, see Turner, p. 27, and *Mr. Smirke*, p. 68.

[360] For Demosthenes' rebuke to Aeschines, see Turner, p. 7, and *Mr. Smirke*, p. 89.

[361] For P. Aerodius, see Turner, p. 15, and *Mr. Smirke*, p. 100.

[362] For Gaspar Schott, see *Mr. Smirke*, p. 112.

[363] Dolabella, Cicero's son-in-law, who had joined Caesar's camp, wrote to Cicero

nor as the Roman Centurion said to the Roman Ensign:[365] but I will say something like what Leonas (that presided from Constantius at the Council of Seleucia, when they made an endless Disputing to no purpose) said to them: not, *Abite igitur & in Ecclesia nugas agite*,[366] but, good Mr. Exposer, what do you Loytering like an idle Schollar, and Animadverting here in Town? Get you home again, or it were better for you, and Expose and Animadvert, as long as you will, at your own Colledge. [75]

But as to a new Book fresh come out, Intitled, *the Author of the Naked Truth stripp'd Naked*[367] (to the *Fell*, or to the skin) that Hieroglyphical Quibble of the *Great Gun*,[368] on the Title Page, will not excuse Bishop Gunning:[369] For his Sermon is still expected.[370]

But to the Judicious and Serious Reader, to whom I wish any thing I have said may have given no Unwelcom Entertainment; I shall only so far

---

during the blockade of Dyrrachium, encouraging him to abandon Pompey and go over to Caesar: "There was nothing left, but to be, where the Republic itself now was, rather than by following that ancient one, to be in none at all." See *Epistolae Familiares*, 9.9. Turner, pp. 45–46, had cited this statement (in Latin) as an example of political disloyalty and negativity.

[364] as the Christian Cicero said to the English Parliament: see Turner, p. 65, and *Mr. Smirke*, p. 113, both of which refer to the speech by Chancellor Heneage Finch to both houses of Parliament, April 13, 1675, subsequently published. Finch had said (p. 22), "What the Romans scornd to do after the Battle of Cannae, What the Venetians never did when they had lost all their *Terra firma*, That Men are now Taught to think a Vertue, and the Sign of a Wise and good Man, Desperare de Republica."

[365] as the Roman Centurion said to the Roman Ensign: see Turner, pp. 65–66, citing Livy, 5:55:2: "Signifer statue Signum. Sta Miles: hic optime manebimus" (Standard-bearer, plant your standard. Soldier, stay. It will be best if we remain here). Turner applied the quotation, attributed to Camillus, to the state of the Anglican church.

[366] See Socrates, 2.32. Hanmer p. 288, translates as follows: "The next day after, when they made sute for proroguing of the Council, he would not sit with them again, but told them flatly, that the Emperor had sent him to be present at an uniform and peaceable Council, but insomuch that divers of them be at discord and debate among themselves, I cannot away (saith he) with your company. Go your wayes therefore, dally and brawle ye at home in your own Churches."

[367] fresh come out: the *Gazette* for May 4–8, 1676 (no. 1092), advertised the publication of *Lex Talionis: Or the Author of Naked Truth stript Naked*.

[368] *Gun* B] *Gunn* A.

[369] For Bishop Peter Gunning, see introduction, p. 5. Marvell here equivocates between two theories of who wrote *Lex Talionis*, Gunning or Philip Fell of Eton.

[370] The last of many references to Gunning's as-yet-unpublished sermon.

justifie my self, that I thought it no less concerned me to vindicate the Laity from the Impositions that the *Few* would force upon them, than him to defend those Impositions on behalf of the Clergy. And moreover, I judged my self most proper for the work, it not being fit that so slight a Pamphlet as his should be answered by any Man of great abilities. For the rest, I take the *Naked Truth* to have been part of that effect which Reverend Mr. Hooker[371] foretold, *Praef. to Eccl. Policy*, p. 10. The *time will come when three words, uttered with Charity and Meekness, shall receive a far more blessed Reward, than three thousand Volumes written with disdainful sharpness of Wit.*[372] And I shall conclude with him in his close; *I trust in the Almighty, that with us Contentions are now at the highest float, and that the day will come (for what cause is there of Despair) when the Passions of former Enmity being allaid, men shall with ten times redoubled tokens of unfainedly reconciled Love, shew themselves each to other the same which Joseph, and the Brethren of Joseph, were at the time of their Enterview in Egypt.*[373] And upon this condition, *let my Book also* (yea my self if it were needful) *be burnt by the hand of the* Animadverter.

---

[371] Reverend Mr. Hooker: Richard Hooker (1554–1600), great Elizabethan theologian, who wrote his *Laws of Ecclesiastical Polity* in response to public debates on church government between himself and the puritan Walter Travers. The first four books were published in 1593. They supplied the Elizabethan settlement of the church with a philosophical basis.

[372] This matches the tenth unnumbered page of the 1639 edition of Richard Hooker's *Laws of Ecclesiastical Polity*, B5r, slightly misquoted.

[373] Hooker, *Laws*, e5r.

AN ACCOUNT OF THE GROWTH

OF POPERY AND ARBITRARY

GOVERNMENT IN ENGLAND

1677

Introduction

Nicholas von Maltzahn

From 1660 until his death in 1678, Andrew Marvell was a member of parliament for his native Yorkshire constituency of Kingston-upon-Hull. It was his experience as parliamentarian that made him the author of *An Account of the Growth of Popery and Arbitrary Government,* which work led to his posthumous reputation as "a famous Sticler about the French Popish & Court interest."[1] This was Andrew Marvell "the incorruptible,"[2] of "Patriot fame,"[3] celebrated as an exemplary MP in the eighteenth century. Of all his writings, the *Account* most contributed to contemporary politics and to the rich Whig tradition that sprang from them.

PARLIAMENT AND PUBLICATION

Parliament was the central forum for public debate in late seventeenth-century England. Such debate followed from the role of parliament in domestic and also foreign affairs. The House of Commons shared with the House of Lords responsibility for legislation, the Commons being the

---

[1] Newsletter of Sept. 2, 1678, Oxford, Bodleian, MS Carte 103, f. 225r.

[2] Thus *The Craftsman* 482 (Sept. 27, 1735), quoted in Patterson, "Marvell and Secret History," p. 40; likewise, the inscription by the republican Thomas Hollis (1720–74) in a copy of *Mr. Smirke* donated to the Harvard College Library (shelfmark *EC65.M3685.676mab).

[3] William Mason, "To Independency," quoted in E. S. Donno, *Andrew Marvell: The Critical Heritage* (London, 1978), p. 114.

source of bills of taxation and of redress of grievances. Yielding supplies to the Crown—monies crucial for administering the kingdom, and especially for funding army and navy—might thus be delayed as long as politically possible in order that other public and private bills could be passed before the next adjournment of the House. The lack of cooperation between the Crown and both Houses, and between the Houses themselves, had by the mid-1670s become a chronic problem.

The strain followed in part from England's role in continental politics. In Europe, the convulsions of the Thirty Years War in the first half of the century had left a legacy of contest between the empires old and new, Spanish and French. The Stuart sympathy for the French, and secret acceptance of subsidies from them in return for pro-French and pro-Catholic policies, were increasingly at odds with public suspicions of the French and widespread English anti-Catholicism. In the 1670s the French threat to the Spanish Netherlands was a source of special concern. In the Low Countries, the Dutch had freed themselves from Spanish rule a century before; now, faced with French designs on their neighbor, they made common cause with their former oppressors. The French threat led the Dutch and Spanish to lobby for English support, claiming that the protection of the Spanish Netherlands was also very much in the English interest. Marvell's secret services to the Dutch in the earlier 1670s show a sympathy with their position, and again in 1677 he energetically supported policies directed against the French.[4]

England's relations with Holland and France played a significant part in domestic politics between the Second Anglo-Dutch War (1665–67) and the Popish Plot (1678). Fears of French dominion increasingly displaced earlier concerns about the economic and political threat of the Dutch.[5] Such opinion, voiced in public debate, and in parliament particularly, questioned

---

[4] Marvell's earlier work for the Dutch had culminated in his appointment (Feb. 3, 1673/4) "for the only time in his parliamentary career . . . to draw up reasons for a conference with the Lords about an address for peace" with Holland (K. H. D. Haley, *William of Orange and the English Opposition, 1672–4* (Oxford, 1953), pp. 57–58; Basil Henning, *The House of Commons, 1660–1690* (London, 1983), 3:26); he seems unlikely to have been the sponsor of the republication of his satire *The Character of Holland* in 1672. The wider political context in 1677 is described in K. H. D. Haley, "The Anglo-Dutch Rapprochement of 1677," *English Historical Review* 43 (1958), 614–48.

[5] Steven Pincus, "From Butterboxes to Wooden Shoes: The Shift in English Popular Sentiment from anti-Dutch to anti-French in the 1670s," *Historical Journal* 38 (1995), 333–61.

the apparent allegiance of the English Crown to France in the 1670s. Royal ambitions met with successive setbacks from parliamentary opposition, in debates, in votes, and eventually in public agitation. This rivalry between the court and its opponents shaped Marvell's later career in parliament and occasioned the *Account*.

Mindful of the midcentury revolution, Restoration governments with some success attempted to exert controls on the pulpit and university, and also if with less success on the press and on that newer center of communication, the coffeehouse. Over parliament itself, the Crown exerted increasing power in the 1670s, this through the Lords especially, with its loyal complement of bishops, and also through the increasing number of placemen in the Commons. Now too, through more frequent adjournments and prorogations of parliament, the Crown often postponed unwelcome legislation or frustrated it altogether. These developments were pronounced enough to elicit countermeasures from MPs in defense, as they put it, of English liberties. They sought support for their tactics within the House of Commons by courting public opinion. Marvell's *Account* explained national affairs to parliament. It also explained parliamentary affairs to the nation. The *Account* was a considerable success on both fronts, both in the short and in the longer term. It contributed to the development of a form of historical writing centered in parliamentary records, interwoven with affairs of state at home and abroad.

The *Account* has too often been described as a work written chiefly against "popery," a mistake in emphasis compounded by the frequent abbreviation of the title to *An Account of the Growth of Popery*. But Marvell early and late can be shown more tolerant of that confession than has been allowed.[6] The "character of popery" with which the work begins is plainly

---

[6] His support for the Declaration of Indulgence (1672) is unqualified in the *Rehearsal Transpros'd,* and a contemporary Catholic writer could appreciate Marvell's toleration, qv. Martin Dzelzainis, "Marvell and the Earl of Castlemaine," in *Marvell and Liberty,* ed. Warren Chernaik and Martin Dzelzainis (London, 1999), pp. 290–312. Late in his studies of Cambridge, Marvell may have briefly converted to Rome, and even in the *Account* he is less immoderate than many of his contemporaries, controverting more as if in sorrow than in anger William Lloyd's position distinguishing the church from the court of Rome (pp. 291–92 below). Relatively eirenic, especially for that season, are his comments in the *Remarks* (1678), pp. 142–43 (see pp. 481–82 below). His correspondence with the Hull Corporation also shows him reluctant at this date to provoke antipopery and conscious of its evil potential for popular disturbance (*P & L,* 2:230).

something of an interpolation, related to but distinct from the burden of political analysis that follows.[7] It is the second term in Marvell's title that is the more revealing. For he soon condemns popery especially owing to its association with arbitrary government, to which the work then turns at length. Popery gains a less confessional and more secular sense; in sum, the work is written not against Rome but against France. It synthesizes for public debate issues in national policy centered in the growth of French power.

Not least for political publications, there was still a very seasonal aspect to London publishing in the late seventeenth century. Their timing was very much determined by the next sitting of parliament, for, as Marvell had observed, "nothing is more usual then to Print and present to them Proposals of Revenue, Matters of Trade, or any thing of Publick Convenience; and sometimes Cases and Petitions."[8] This practice increased owing to the lack of elections for the duration of the Restoration Long Parliament. The frequent and sometimes lengthy adjournments afforded leisure to political writers, some members of parliament among them, and encouraged their efforts through publication to influence parliament when it did meet. These factors intensified the print activity in preparation for new sessions, and in the 1670s we encounter a number of such sessional publications with a broader impact than any in the preceding decade. In these oppositional pamphlets publicizing high politics for a wider readership, authors sought to sway public opinion and help it shape parliamentary debate. There is much in common between the pro-Dutch *Englands Appeal* (1673), the comparable *Relation of the Most Material Matters Handled in Parliament* (1673), the *Letter From a Person of Quality, To His Friend In the Country* (1675) which appeared from the earl of Shaftesbury's circle, and Marvell's *Account* (1677).

At issue was the role in government of parliament, and in Marvell's case especially the role of the Commons. Parliamentary publication had flourished in the 1640s and 1650s; "after the Restoration, by a species of self-censorship, parliamentary printing disappeared again."[9] But the demand for

---

[7] See pp. 209, 227 below. That it might for its tone be set against the more serious parliamentary argument of the *Account* appears from Roger L'Estrange's excerpting of it to discredit the whole work, *Account of the Growth of Knavery* (1678), pp. 65, 65–72.

[8] *Mr. Smirke,* pp. 50–51 above.

[9] Sheila Lambert, *Printing for Parliament, 1641–1700*, List and Index Society, Special Series, vol. 20 (London, 1984), p. i.

such news had not been extinguished by the events of 1660. Instead, the
dissemination of parliamentary news now reverted in great part to scribal
publication, a practice of long standing.[10] Early and late, it is plain that the
work of the clerks of the Houses was supplemented by a significant number
of other records, from inside the House and out. Complaints issued against
"all those loose idle New[s] Mongers who have always been soe close
hangers on upon the Parliament Lobby."[11] Debates, individual speeches,
parliamentary addresses, and royal proclamations were widely communicated in newsletters and scribal "separates."[12] As an MP, Marvell himself
was very much involved in the dissemination of parliamentary news. The
Hull Corporation having hitherto paid Gilbert Mabbott for such "intelligence," Marvell was quick to propose himself as a replacement when
Mabbott went to Ireland.[13] He promised weekly newsletters "as long as I
continue here in Town," and this service he in considerable part performed,
although the frequency of correspondence was tied to levels of parliamentary business.[14] At first he cooperated with his fellow MPs from Hull, first
of all John Ramsden in the Convention Parliament (1660), and then Colonel Anthony Gilby (1661–78), with whom, however, he soon fell out. Thereafter he wrote alone. He often turned to such correspondence after the close
of the day's business, tired and hungry, in "haste" struggling to catch the
post and even writing in the Post House adjacent to parliament in order to
do so. His usual reserve in such communication to the Hull Corporation
contrasts with his greater freedom with other correspondents—the Thompsons of York, for example, and Sir Edward Harley, and especially his
nephew William Popple. Marvell's assiduity also lay in sending the printed
acts and proclamations as these became available, singly and gathered
in books. It was through these that the government publicized laws and

---

[10] This has been better charted for Jacobean than for later Stuart parliaments, especially in Wallace Notestein and Frances Helen Relf, *Commons Debates for 1629* (Min-
neapolis, 1921).

[11] R. Tempest to E. Poley, Feb. 15, 1680/1, Poley Papers, Osborn Collection, Yale,
quoted in Timothy Crist, "Francis Smith and the Opposition Press in England, 1660–
1688" (Cambridge diss., 1977), p. 179.

[12] Harold Love, *Scribal Publication in Seventeenth-Century England* (Oxford 1993),
pp. 9–22.

[13] Letter to the Hull Corporation (hereafter LHC), Jan. 12, 1660/1 (*P & L*, 2:17).

[14] LHC, Nov. 8, 1670 (*P & L*, 2:112). The Hull Corporation had another "intelligencer" in the metropolis, Robert Stockdale, with whom Marvell sometimes cooperated (*P & L*, 2:363).

measures. In his constituency letters he often cites delays in their publication. But even when the publication of a speech was prohibited he can promise "a written copy" to the corporation.[15] In the *Account* too, for example with Lord Keeper Bridgeman's speech (1670) and the Bishops' Bill of March 1677, he shows himself adept as an MP and committee member at gathering materials published scribally rather than in print.

Marvell on several occasions mentions his notes as the basis for his parliamentary newsletters. In the hectic session of the spring of 1670, for example, he in one letter to the corporation apologizes that business forbids his usual communication, "but I have given to Mr Stockdale my notes who I doubt not will informe you particularly of what hath passed this week." A few weeks later, in excusing himself he adds, "I have besides communicated my notes to Mr Stockdale."[16] Such habits as a reporter contributed to his success as an MP. Although no record has surfaced of Marvell as a full-blown parliamentary diarist like Anchitell Grey, Sir Edward Dering, or Daniel Finch,[17] he seems to have kept track of points in debates. On his and others' recollections he was to draw in the *Account*, where he notes how proudly MPs might recall their speeches ("and that they may be thought some body, often arrogating where they cannot be disproved, another mans Conception to their own honour"—p. 324 below). But he could also resort to the Clerks in Parliament, whose notes toward the official journals and whose committee minutes might document proceedings more fully. And there were a number of fellow-MPs with substantial records of parliament: none more so than his friend John Rushworth,[18] a former clerk and the great parliamentary chronicler of the seventeenth century. On points of common political interest, members and Lords might resort to considerable documentary accumulations, official and private. Marvell was well placed to make the most of them and in the last third of the *Account* depends on them very heavily.

---

[15] LHC, Nov. 1, 1670 (*P & L*, 2:111).

[16] LHC, Mar. 5 and Apr. 2, 1669/70 (*P & L*, 2:99, 105).

[17] Anchitell Grey, *Debates of the House of Commons*, 10 vols. (London, 1763); *The Diaries and Papers of Sir Edward Dering, Second Baronet, 1644 to 1684*, ed. Maurice F. Bond (London, 1975), especially pp. 21, 180–82, and compare *The Parliamentary Diary of Sir Edward Dering, 1670–1673*, ed. B. D. Henning (New Haven, 1940); Daniel Finch worked his notes of the debates into a fuller summary of the session of 1676/77 (Leicestershire Record Office, Finch Papers, P.P. 42).

[18] *P & L*, 2:335 (also 254); Caroline Robbins, *Absolute Liberty*, ed. Barbara Taft (Hamden Conn., 1982), p. 86.

1677: THE DATE OF THE ACCOUNT

There were two main stages to the composition of the *Account,* the first and major one at some time between April and October 1677, the second around the end of the year. After the Easter adjournment of April 16, 1677, Marvell had time to write his history of the late session, and again after the further adjournment of May 28. His discomfiture in parliament late that March (see below) may have helped animate him to attempt the work. Perhaps already in May 1677, a government informer heard news of a work expected at the press that may well have been the *Account.*[19] An October date for the completion of the first stage of the work allows for the time needed for printing its almost twenty sheets—156 pages quarto in the first edition—in preparation for the parliamentary session expected to begin on December 3.[20] How much of this six-month period he needed is uncertain, since Marvell can at one point note of his composition "the Progress made in so few weeks" (p. 241); long parts of the work, moreover, had some separate origin and were ready to be pieced into the parliamentary narrative he supplies. These include perhaps the introductory "character of popery" and certain other documents including the Bishops' Bill and some extant summaries of the debates about war with France in March–April and in May 1677. These materials form almost half the work. Marvell scarcely altered them.

That summer he was "much out of Towne," although he was in attendance for the parliamentary meeting of July 16, 1677, when the further adjournment that had been expected was commanded, until December 3.[21] But late in October, by which time Marvell should have had the work ready for the press, a royal proclamation on the twenty-eighth then unexpectedly

[19] PRO, SP 29/401/321: the oppositional publications in prospect included a "Discourse reflecting upon the Duke of York, and the Lord Treasurer concerning a design to bring in Popery." This testimony was taken from L'Estrange on August 9, 1677, reporting information given him ca. July 28: it cites the attempt of a "Nonconformist Minister" Smith to enlist a printer for works that appear to include J.E., *A Narrative of the Cause and Manner of the Imprisonment of the Lords,* to which Marchamont Nedham was already responding in May 1677, *Second Pacquet of Advices* (London, 1677), p. 55–76—Nedham's pamphlet dates itself May 7 (p. 3), but these last pages may well have been written while the work was in the press that month.

[20] Some preparation for the press by October may also be reflected in the 1677 date of the imprint.

[21] LHC, July 17, 1677, and Marvell to Harley, July 17 and Aug. 7, 1677 (*P & L,* 2:205–06, 353–56).

postponed the sitting of parliament still further, to April 4, 1678, as had been agreed between Charles II and France.[22] This postponement took any haste out of the publication, since the *Account* was designed in part for an audience in parliament. There would have been disadvantage in publishing too soon, since this allowed court writers time for a response before the parliamentary session in prospect, or early enough into the session for their rebuttals to be influential.[23] Some postponement or interruption of the presswork for the *Account* may therefore be supposed at the end of October. By mid-November, Marvell writes to Sir Edward Harley that he has no further installment to send of what may have been the *Account*. If so, this may well have been some part of the manuscript already printed, since those manuscript pages thus made redundant were likelier to have been ventured by post or other carrier than any printed sheets.[24] At this point, whatever the conditions of his private life, Marvell must have anticipated more of the leisure that instead invited his now writing against Thomas Danson's *De Causa Dei*. That provocation, now from a Presbyterian disciplinarian rather than the Anglican one he had confronted in *Mr. Smirke*, likely came to hand in late November.[25] In choosing to controvert Danson, Marvell could, with most of the *Account* written, expect four months before its publication against the proposed April session. Marvell must have been surprised, then, by the about-face from the crown, when in an interim meeting came "a written Message from his *Majesty* on the 3d. December, of a contrary effect . . . That the Houses *should be Adjourned* only to the 15. of January 1677[/78]."[26] Now the rest of the *Account* needed printing right away. Impelled by the sudden deadline and a necessary secrecy, the press-

[22] J. J. Jusserand, *Recueil des Instructions Données aux Ambassadeurs et Ministres de France . . . Angleterre*, 2 vols. (Paris, 1929), 2:240, 249–50.

[23] The practice is noted in an earlier letter to Marvell from Herbert Croft, bishop of Hereford, who cites a polemic that an antagonist "hath certainly printed but keeps very close to put forth I suppose the next approaching session of parliament when there cannot be time to make a reply" (*P & L*, 2:347).

[24] "I have not further of what I last inclosed." Nov. 17, 1677 (*P & L*, 2:357). No other evidence has surfaced of the precirculation of the tract.

[25] Nov. 26, 1677 is the date *De Causa Dei* was registered with the Stationers; Oct. 31, 1677, the date of Danson's preface to this work of eight sheets (qv. below p. 393).

[26] P. 373 below [*Account* 77a, pp. 152–53, *Account* 77b, p. 140]; LHC, Dec. 4, 1677 (*P & L*, 2:207–8). Even the French were taken aback by this breach of the arrangements they had agreed upon with Charles (Jusserand, *Recueil*, 2:255–56).

work shows every sign of haste, with almost no correction of its many errors and only a minimal listing of errata. And Marvell needed to finish writing the *Account*.

Marvell in a letter later in 1678 says that the *Account* "came out, about Christmass last."[27] His approximation allows time for presswork as late as, say, Epiphany. A second and much briefer stage of composition generated the last pages of the work. They are plainly written later, since they refer to the December call for a January session and supply a coda of December date that revisits the argument of the book as a whole and answers some possible objections to it.[28] In this coda, Marvell ascribes to one Captain Elsdon the seditious sentence, "*Si Rebellio evenerit in Regno, & non accideret fore, contra omnes tres Status, Non est Rebellio.*" This sentence had featured centrally in Elsdon's testimony against Marvell's associate John Harrington in Harrington's December 1677 trial; it was part of Harrington's rebuttal of the charges against him to impugn Elsdon's evidence as manufactured. Hence the bitter wit of Marvell's present attribution of this sentence to Elsdon himself.[29] If the publication was indeed ready for the mid-January sitting, its release may then again have been briefly delayed when the session proper was postponed another fortnight to January 29, 1677/8.

To publish the *Account,* Marvell depended on the Baptist printer John Darby, who had previously been involved in the publication of *The Rehearsal Transpros'd* and *Mr. Smirke.* Some doubtful testimony from a government informer indicates that, as with *Mr. Smirke* where "15 non conformists took off the whole Impression to disperse," the same Presbyterian group was again at work in the summer of 1677. The Baptist bookseller Francis Smith seems to have been their chief agent, and the politician who "appear'd most" in the business was that leading supporter of the

[27] Marvell to William Popple, June 10, 1678 (*P & L,* 2:357).

[28] Pp. 372–77 below.

[29] "Our Government is by three Estates, and to raise armes unless it be against all three Estates is no Rebellion." *Mr. Harringtons Case* (4° [1678]), p. 6. This apologetic pamphlet makes a particular point of denying Elsdon's attribution of those words to Harrington; its publication is closely associated with that of the *Account* (as in the stationer Joseph Leigh's affidavit, March 26, 1678, PRO, 29/402/192, and in Goodman Atwood's report, March 21, 1677/8, PRO, SP 29/405/189). Although it seems to have had a different printer (the fonts and paper-stocks differ), the style recalls Marvell's, and to the French translation of the *Account* (*Relation de l'Accroissement* . . . 1680) is appended the "Procès de Mr. Harrington" (pp. 231–45).

Presbyterians, Philip, fourth baron Wharton. He had been Marvell's friend for a decade or more.[30] The Amsterdam imprint of the *Account* was intended to mislead. The title page does not of course name the printer. But the same distinctive watermarks appear in a number of contemporary Amsterdam tracts of a similar political cast,[31] and the same mix of paperstocks features in other contemporary Darby imprints. Most of Darby's Amsterdam titles concern the long prorogation of 1675 to 1676/7 and the question whether the length of that prorogation did not amount to a dissolution of the House, requiring the new election for which the Crown's opponents hoped.[32] Others amplify the complaints of the *Account*, publicizing French depredations on English shipping and the corruption of MPs.[33] The *Account* was printed on two presses: the typesetting and paperstocks show some separation of the presswork—gatherings A-H and T-U2 on the one, and gatherings I-S on the other. But the two presses are likely to have been under the same roof.[34] Darby at this date had two presses, and

---

[30] PRO, SP 29/401/321—the informer seems to have specified to L'Estrange only one "Mr. Smith a NonConformist Minister" rather than Francis Smith the bookseller, but the latter "was 'teacher' to a congregation of 400 or 500" Baptists in Goswell Street; see Richard Greaves and Robert Zaller, ed., *Biographical Dictionary of British Radicals in the Seventeenth Century*, 3 vols (Brighton, 1982–84), 3:184. Thomas Blount to Anthony à Wood, 6 June 1676 (Bodleian, MS Wood F40, f.214); *P & L*, 2:309–10.

[31] For his mapping of the watermarks in the *Account* and some related works, I am much indebted to Edward Holberton, who generously shared his pioneering description of these materials with me.

[32] Compare especially *Some Considerations upon the Question, Whether the Parliament is Dissolved* (1676), *A Seasonable Question, and an Usefull Answer* (1676), and the two distinct editions of *The Long Parliament Dissolved* (1676), as well as J. E., *A Narrative of the Cause and Manner of the Imprisonment of the Lords Now Closed Prisoners in the Tower of London* (1677). This context of the prorogation tracts explains a telling slip in the first edition of the *Account* (pp. 16–17), where it proposes to narrate "the meeting of Parliament the 15 of Febr. 1675": it is of course the session beginning February 1676/7 that is meant, but the printer had worked on a number of pamphlets looking back to the preceding session. Marvell had been unimpressed by the argument of these tracts, which seemed to him "a Cavill" (letter to Edward Thompson, Dec. 2, 1676, *P & L*, 2:350).

[33] *A List of Several Ships Belonging to English Merchants* (1677); *A Seasonable Argument To Perswade All the Grand Juries in England, to Petition for A New Parliament* (1677).

[34] Copies of the related *List of Several Ships* reveal that two stocks of paper that seem to have been used entirely separately in printing the *Account* are now combined in at least the L-gathering of the *List:* in these L-gatherings, compare the three-circles watermark in Cambridge University Library, Syn 5.66.7 (which mark predominates in

four or five persons in his household able to work them.[35] The coda of the *Account,* including the materials from December 1677, begins about halfway through the T-gathering (T2^v = p. 148 in the first edition). That this additional material was printed in a way continuous with the main narrative indicates that the printing was hurried and late.

The first report of the dissemination of the printed *Account* resulted from the discovery that loose sheets had been taken for stitching around February 8. On February 19 came the first official reaction to the publication, in a warrant for the discovery and arrest of those responsible for it. Two days later a dozen copies of the printed tract were seized by the stationer William Whitwood.[36]

THE ORIGINS OF THE ACCOUNT

Why such an official reaction to the publication of the *Account?* The answer lies in some fiercely disputed issues in earlier parliamentary sessions and now especially those of 1677 and 1678. These parliamentary contests expressed themselves in personal as well as factional ways. In particular, the *Account* seems to have had its inception in Marvell's discomfiture in parliament at the hands of the Speaker, Sir Edward Seymour, and Arlington's protégé the secretary of state Sir Joseph Williamson. The discomfiture came in an episode in Marvell's career in which not the prudence for which he was later famed but rather imprudence is the most notable feature. On March 29, 1677, it is reported, "Mr Marvell, coming up the House to his place, stumbling at Sir Philip Harcourt's foot, in recovering himself, seemed to give Sir Philip a box on the ear." Seymour, that most peremptory of Speakers, acquainted the House, "that he saw a box on the ear given, and 'twas his duty to inform the House of it." In the debate that followed, Marvell and his Country allies tried to save him from the rebuke of the House for this breach of decorum, Harcourt himself claiming that "Marvell had

---

the A-H gatherings of the *Account 77a*) with the mark of a fleur-de-lys over a quatrefoil in Newberry Library U. 545 .514 and British Library 1508/1457 (which mark predominates in the I-N gatherings of the *Account 77a*).

[35] John Hetet, "A Literary Underground in Restoration England: Printers and Dissenters in the Context of Constraints 1660–1689" (diss. Cambridge, 1987), pp. 181–82.

[36] Stationers' Company, Wardens' Accounts, Feb. 24, 1678. Two of these impounded copies have come to light, with their seizure dated Feb. 21, 1678: Oxford, Queen's College, Z.b.17 (1), and British Library, C.55 d. 20.

some kind of a stumble, and mine was only a thrust; and the thing was accidental." On the other hand, Court MPs sought to make the affront instead a cause for censure, and the wily Williamson retreated only after the point had been well made.[37] Whatever the later Patriot legend of Marvell as parliamentarian, the whole episode is strangely in keeping with other evidence of Marvell's parliamentary performances. Almost a decade before, he had in 1668 been called to account in the House after "reflecting on Lord Arlington, [when Marvell] somewhat transportedly said" harsh things against the failings of secretaries of state under the present regime, with Arlington himself noting "that Mr. Marvel hath struck hard at me."[38] But it is Marvell's "transportedness" that already stands out. Now in 1677 his first reaction to the Speaker's calling him to account was defiance. He claimed that his and Harcourt's "great acquaintance and familiarity" were their own business. Moreover, since the Speaker had spoken ill of Marvell "yesterday, when he was out of the House . . . he hopes, that, as the Speaker keeps us in Order, he [the Speaker] will keep himself in Order for the future." Thus to impugn the Speaker was of course a bridge too far, and the wrath of the House then descended on Marvell, leading to his belated apology that "he seldom speaks to the House, and if he commit an error, in the manner of his Speech, being not so well tuned, he hopes it is not an Offence. Whether out, or in, the House, he has a respect to the Speaker." But this had plainly not been the case.

Why should this episode prove such a flashpoint? Here the personal and the partisan are linked. The speech came only two days after what was surely Marvell's longest speech in the House, indeed one of the longer speeches recorded in the parliamentary diary for that time. In that address too he had become self-conscious about his public speaking. He excused himself by saying, "He is not used to speak here, and therefore speaks with abruptness." The abruptness must have lain in the manner rather than the length of the speech, which has been styled a "rambling" one.[39] But it had been a remarkable intervention. Marvell had broken the silence of the Country party to speak against the bill designed to provide for the bishops' "education of children of the royal family in Protestant religion," which had come down from the Lords, where the bishops now had considerable sway. This was a late episode in Marvell's long battle for a Comprehension of the

---

[37] Grey, *Debates*, 4:321–31; British Library, Egerton MS 3345, f. 41.

[38] Grey, *Debates*, 1:70–71; James Ralph, *The History of England* (London, 1744), 1:171.

[39] Henning, *House of Commons*, 3:26.

Presbyterians into the national church. It was also one of the major early skirmishes in the emerging Exclusion or Succession Crisis. Here Marvell and others were seeking to prevent an accommodation whereby the education of the children of James duke of York would be given to the bishops, in exchange, as it were, for James's being allowed as a Catholic to succeed to the throne. Opponents of such compromise, and especially the earl of Shaftesbury, sought to prevent such episcopal mediation of the growing crisis and became notably kinder to royal power where it was opposed to episcopal pretensions.[40] Conveniently for the bishops, and not coincidentally, the great lords Shaftesbury and Buckingham were imprisoned in the Tower at this point; Shaftesbury had in earlier sessions of parliament sponsored a more severe version of such a bill.[41] But the Bishops' Bill was now exposed to opposition in the Commons. Despite Marvell's intervention— "'tis an ill thing, and let us be rid of it as soon as we can. He could have wished it had perished at the first reading rather than have been revived by a second"—the bill went to committee, a committee to which he was named. There the bill foundered.[42]

Marvell could redress his failings as a speaker in parliament through his flair as a writer in print. This invited the dangerous expedient of publishing parliamentary proceedings, with those presented at every turn to partisan advantage. The March episode plainly rankled with him. The *Account* offered an opportunity for revenge. There, for example, on pages 89 to 100 of the first edition, he returns at huge length to the Bishops' Bill, the egregious "Act for further securing the Protestant Religion, by Educating the Children of the Royal Family therein," supplying the unpublished text in full. This was to preserve a copy for the record and perhaps even for indignant royal eyes; by contrast, Marvell rather passes over the other episcopal bill for religion, which must have had considerable appeal for the king, but which the Commons had let lapse because too lenient against recusants. The length of the Bishops' Bill massively disrupts the unfolding of the narrative of the *Account.* But its inclusion has the virtue of making Marvell's argument against French power also into an antiepiscopal tract.

---

[40]Mark Goldie, "Danby, the Bishops and the Whigs," in *The Politics of Religion in Restoration England,* ed. T. Harris, P. Seaward, and M. Goldie (Oxford, 1990), pp. 75–105.

[41] *Historical Manuscripts Commission, 9th report,* 2:82.

[42] *JHC* 9:407. Also on the committee was Daniel Finch, in whose papers two drafts of the bill survive (Leicestershire RO, Finch MSS, P.P. 44).

Again, as in other poetry and prose in which Marvell attacks episcopal presumption, his irritation is extreme. In the *Account,* the longer the bill goes on, page after page, the more demented seems the bishops' fantasy in making every kind of provision for their own role or rule. For as Marvell had complained in Parliament, "whether this Bill will prevent Popery, or not, this will secure the Promotions of the Bishops; 'twill make them certain."[43] The effect is enhanced in the first edition by some surprises in the typesetting, perhaps unprompted by the author, which introduce into the tedious formulae of such legislation some references to the power of a "Bishop-prick" and a fortiori of an "Arch-bishop-prick."

Moreover, the *Account* allowed Marvell more widely to condemn the Court party. With Lord Keeper Sir Heneage Finch there had been difficulties already when *Mr. Smirke* was published; the *Account* takes the opportunity to asperse his "Eloquence and Veracity" and dwells on his imprudence.[44] Among the damned, however, the lowest circle was reserved for the Speaker, Sir Edward Seymour.[45] He had once been of Buckingham's party—"daring Seymour" as Marvell had named him in *Last Instructions*—and Marvell never forgave his apostasy. Directing at him some of its fiercest wit, the *Account* rages against his misgovernment and the subversions he attempts against English liberties. This leads to the climactic description of Seymour's arbitrary and perhaps treasonable irregularities as Speaker.[46] Others involved in Marvell's discomfiture were not spared, especially Sir Joseph Williamson and Sir Robert Holmes. Williamson features as notorious for his greed and manipulation in seeking a share in "all the Great or Small Offices in the Kingdom."[47] But Marvell indicates that Williamson

[43] Grey, *Debates,* 4:320, the Bishops' Bill (March 1676/7) was viewed with suspicion by MP Michael Malet, because "it will blow up the Government, it states an *interregnum* and an Oligarchy. 'Tis now a Thesis amongst some Churchmen, that the King is not King but by their magical Unction—He knows not what the Bill is—No interregnum can be by Law—It sets up nine Mitres above the Crown—*Monstrum horrendum!*" Likewise Edward Vaughan (4:320–21), who concluded "The Bill is fatal to the Crown, and so little in it to be retained, and so much to be rejected, that he would throw it out."

[44] See below pp. 274–75, 282–84, 295.

[45] For Seymour see Henning, *House of Commons,* and Marvell, *Last Instructions,* ll. 257–58, and Marvell to William Popple, Nov. 28, 1670 (*P & L,* 2:318); *A Seasonable Argument* (1677), p. 19, notes that he "had for four year 2000 l. Pension to betray the Country Party."

[46] Below, pp. 289, 309, 368–73.

[47] Below, p. 279.

also has a more central part in the conspiracy afoot, as shown by William-son's denunciation of the patriot John Harrington, the Shaftesburian[48] whistle-blower who had brought to the Crown's reluctant notice the violent pressing of Scots to serve in France, an impressment contrary to parliamen-tary address and royal proclamation. Marvell also disparages Holmes, whose base violations against the Dutch in the 1660s seemed again to com-mend him for new evils in the Anglo-Dutch War of 1672–74. Holmes was, Marvell observes with bitter irony, "the person for understanding, experi-ence and courage, fittest for a design of this or any higher nature," and there is further dark comment about "Sir Roberts" jealous guard over "the Spoile of Honour or Profit."[49] Other echoes can be heard of the dispute over Mar-vell's embarrassing incident with Harcourt. For example, that debate had been concluded by a country MP's claim that "by our long sitting together, we lose, by our familiarity and acquaintance, the decencies of the House." Marvell in the *Account* now moralizes likewise: "By this long haunting so together they are grown too so familiar among themselves, that all rever-ence of their own Assembly is lost, that they live together not like Parlia-ment men, but like so many Good-fellows, met together in a Publick House to make merry."[50] Marvell also is loyal in his praises in the *Account*, especially of the patriot Harrington. For personal and partisan reasons alike, he celebrates the virtues of the duke of Buckingham and the earl of Shaftesbury.

For Marvell had more than just personal scores to settle. His earlier discomfiture had been occasioned in the first place by the rift that ran deep through parliament and English politics in the 1670s. His *Account* presents itself as a contribution to mending that rift, although in fact, and in effect, it was anything but eirenic. Under attack was the Court party, and that part of it which might be described as favoring the French at the expense of the English interest. On this point the success of the *Account* follows from its insistent allusions to the "Conspirators," and its evocation of a conspiracy never quite defined but everywhere felt. These conspirators, like Sallust's

[48] K. H. D. Haley, *The First Earl of Shaftesbury* (Oxford, 1978), pp. 424–26, 521n, 665. Harrington was plainly associated with 'his Cozen Shaftsbury' (PRO, SP 29/392/21); in the present context, his Shaftesbury connections appear from his errand to the Stationers' Company, Feb. 7, 1677, where he claims on Shaftesbury's behalf to seek the suppression of Marchamont Nedham's *A Pacquet of Advices . . . to the Men of Shaftesbury* (Stationers' Company, Court Books, Liber D, f. 273r–v).

[49] See below p. 256.

[50] Grey, *Debates,* 4:331 (Sir Thomas Meres); cf. below p. 304.

infamous *coniuratores*, seem at once malignant and unresting in their work of destruction. The effect is enhanced by Marvell's talent for ironic sympathy. The *Account* presents the conspirators almost as they might see them themselves—as if high-minded, and not just high-handed—only then to expose such deceit as scarcely veiling the most naked private interest. Privately conducted for private ends, the conspiracy is contrasted with public debate in the public interest, conducted by the opposition in parliament and at large. This was to invert the logic of attacks on the Country party that described it as faction; now the real faction to be exposed is that in the councils of the king.

The most hotly contested issues in the *Account* are those that had been raised by the first earl of Shaftesbury and the parliamentary opposition he came to lead. So much does the *Account* speak to these that the "thrice-worthy" Marvell seems to have moved into Shaftesbury's sphere of influence.[51] Bishop Thomas Barlow, not an unknowledgeable contemporary, even attributed the *Account* to "My Ld. Shaftesbury," who, Barlow notes, "is believed, and (as 'tis said) knowne to be the Author of it"; in his view it was "certaine Mr Marvell neither did, nor could compose" the *Account*.[52] Barlow's observation is instructive, although his doubts about Marvell's authorship were misplaced. The *Account* did present the fullest synthesis yet of the Shaftesburian analysis of the history of the last decade. Where other Shaftesburian pamphlets presented pieces of the puzzle, or his arguments in brief, this one explained recent events in a much more complete and coherent way, in a way directed to Shaftesbury's agenda. It did so, however, with a Commons voice distinct from baronial populism.

Barlow's doubts about Marvell's authorship also reflect the contrast between, on the one hand, the partisan and unrelenting argument of the *Account* and, on the other, Marvell's fame hitherto as the "buffooning champion," as Anthony à Wood termed him, of dissent, the celebrated wit who had vanquished Samuel Parker in a famous "pen-combat" a few years before.[53] Although the introductory "character of popery" is facetious in

---

[51] K. H. D. Haley, "Shaftesbury's List of the Lay Peers and Members of the Commons, 1677–8," *Bulletin of the Institute of Historical Research* 43 (1970), 103; there may be some truth in Dryden's allegation that Marvell had a pension from this quarter, *Works*, 17:213, and n427 (*His Majesties Declaration Defended*, 1681).

[52] Barlow on the title page of Marvell's *Account* (1679), Oxford, Queen's College, 6 B. 17 (11).

[53] The contest was famous for "much smart, cutting and satyrical wit on both sides,"

the way of *The Rehearsal Transpros'd* and *Mr. Smirke*, in the main the *Account* is far from such "sportive and jeering buffoonry." Never in his prose works had Marvell spoken so directly the language of the times. But the wit is still alive in the narrative of the *Account*, and that to a different degree than in related productions from Shaftesbury and the Shaftesburians. Irony is Marvell's hallmark, in his poetry and prose alike, and the *Account* often reveals the distance between its professed and real intentions. What might be said was so different from what might be thought. In his parliamentary speeches the difference may have been a handicap to Marvell. In his writings, however, his lack of personal authority could be made good by the virtuosity of his ironies. In historical narration, his use of wit and ambiguity produces a constant pressure on the reader toward complicity in Marvell's politics. The effect can be as broad as sarcasm: Marvell refers, for example, to Danby's notorious corruption as his "farre more effectual way of Perswasion with the Commons" (p. 295 below). But subtler intimations, and a more playful wit, energize Marvell's handling even of parliamentary commonplaces. These are encountered at every turn in the *Account* and show a parliamentarian's discipline in exploiting the decorum required of addresses to the Crown. At its most innocuous Marvell's voice can prove surprisingly inflected. When he loyally observes of the king, for example, that "so forward are his Peoples affections to give even to superfluity, that a Forainer (or English man that hath been long abroad) would think they could neither will nor chuse, but that the asking of a supply, were a meer formality, it is so readily granted" (p. 226 below), the apparent compliment is thick with ambiguities. Had supplies been too generously given in the past? Certainly they were now given much more reluctantly. Likewise, foreigners, and perhaps especially the French, might indeed think supply "a meer formality," but this shows their ignorance of the role of English parliaments. An "English man that hath been long abroad" might think the same but only because he would recall the more serviceable meetings of parliament earlier in Charles II's reign. Now an Englishman closer to home would know all too well the wranglings over votes for money. Or perhaps Charles himself and some of his ministers might be held to have lost their constitutional bearings owing to their having been too "long abroad" in the Interregnum. That these sallies were felt is obvious from the initial reaction to the tract of those against whom it was written, as recorded in Roger

---

in which "the odds and victory [were held to lie] on Marvell's side." Anthony à Wood, *Athenae . . . Fasti*, ed. P. Bliss (London, 1813–20), 4:230–31.

L'Estrange's response to the difference here between the apparent civility and real polemic: "There's scarce a Page where the Poyson has not eaten quite thorough the Vernish."[54]

1678-: RECEPTION

The timing of Marvell's publication was designed to give it the greatest influence on the first parliamentary session of 1678. It was an incendiary tract for that purpose. Now Marvell was more than ever before tapping the widest mood, within parliament and without. As a result it can be difficult to distinguish between his response to present concerns and his influence on them, so much does the language of "popery and arbitrary government" find common expression in 1678. The session that winter was remarkably acrimonious from the start, with increasingly heated debates especially about war with France and the impossibility of supplies to the Crown without public commitment to such a war. In the teeth of royal disapproval, the voting of supply was linked to alliances with the Dutch and against "the power of the French King."[55] The winter session of 1678 also proved the eclipse of the extravagant Seymour as speaker.[56] Charles professed surprise at these reversals, but his dissatisfaction did not deflect the beleaguered opposition in the Commons. The influence of the *Account* in these debates may be supposed, which put heavy pressure on the Crown to follow what had become, in effect, the Shaftesburian prescriptions that Marvell articulated.[57] Thus one parliamentary correspondent reports at the end of February that the Crown's request for supplies

> stirred up a very cloudy and ungrateful repetition of things passed, shewing all along our partiality to France, the breach of the Triple Alliance, the engaging with France against Holland, our aiding of France when we seemed to leave the war, and by all these ways and provocations so affronting the Spaniard and running counter to our own interest, that it was no wonder to see them so distrustful and suspicious as they are represented; that this news from Flanders is not matter of surprise, nor to hear that all the rest is gone, since it was

[54] *Account of the Growth of Knavery* (1678), p. 5.

[55] LHC, Feb. 5, 1678 (*P & L*, 2:213).

[56] Henning, *House of Commons*, 3:415.

[57] Bodleian, MS Carte 221, f. 128, letter from Arlington to Ormonde, about the debate of Feb. 14/15, 1678.

foretold years past by the repeated addresses of that House. That still they are kept in the dark touching the contents of that alliance, which being now said to be ratified also by Holland must be supposed known to the States-General and the States that sent them, and yet thought fit to be still made a secret to the House. That until they saw a war declared against France they could not tell how to interpret anything, or to what purpose the money intended should be given; and that if His Majesty were in earnest there ought to be some other demonstrations than the language of necessity and irreparable damage now impending, for he ought to make examples of those who had been authors of these miscarriages, and not expect to get out of them by the same hands that [ ] the frequent prorogations were here also thrown in to aggravate the account.[58]

The correspondent then notes, "There are two wicked libels come out. The one is a book shewing (or pretending to shew) the growth of Popery in the management of the late Councils; and the other [the *Seasonable Argument*] is to persuade all the Grand Juries in England to petition for a new Parliament by giving a list of all those who vote for the Court as labourers in the great design of Popery and arbitrary power." Less than a week later he reports that he cannot think the *Account* the marquis of Halifax's work, as is rumored, adding darkly that "many also do guess at Mr. Mervin [*sic*], who surely knows how to employ his time much better."[59] The immediate influence of the *Account* appears unmistakably in the great debate in mid-March on the state of the nation.[60]

The government's reaction to the *Account* was severe. In an anonymous letter to his nephew, Marvell himself observed, "There have been great Rewards offered in private, and considerable in the Gazette, to any who could inform of the Author or Printer, but not yet discovered. Three or four

---

[58] Sir Robert Southwell to Ormonde (HMC Ormonde, NS 4:407–8).

[59] Sir Robert Southwell to Ormonde (HMC Ormonde, NS 4:411)—although Mervin seems a likely mistranscription of Mervill, Marvell's name was often enough thus mistaken.

[60] Such indebtedness appears even in specific turns of wit: on March 16, 1677/8, for example, a parliamentary newsletter reports speeches against the king's ministers, which include complaint about the prorogation the previous May, when "they were sent home with shame & reproaches for their boldnes, and put into the Gazet ignominiously, with run away servants, and lost Dogs" (Bodleian, MS Carte 72, f. 361v). Compare p. 369 below.

printed Books since have described, as near as it was proper to go, the Man being a Member of Parliament, Mr. Marvell to have been the author; but if he had, surely he should not have escaped being questioned in Parliament, or some other Place."[61] Danby's writers were quick to controvert the tract in print. Almost immediately, in February 1678, Marchamont Nedham incorporates some response to the *Account* late in a work then in press.[62] In March, he published *Honesty's best Policy,* a pamphlet triumphing belatedly over Shaftesbury's forced submission to the House of Lords and the king the year before and providing a lively rebuttal of the *Account.* Without naming Marvell, Nedham impugns the "Recorder . . . of the Faction" as having produced "a Treasonous Libellous Pamphlet, industriously now spread and dispersed into all hands about the Kingdom." He responds to the *Account* in some detail, aiming at every turn to refute its claims about government in the 1670s and the implications of this "virulent Scribe."[63] That this refutation might reassure those loyal to the court appears in a diary of the day, in which the writer had plainly been unsettled by Marvell's "most infamous libell."[64] From John Dryden, too, another of Marvell's sometime colleagues in the Protectoral government, a rebuttal of sorts was forthcoming in the dedication to Danby of *All for Love.* Dryden's play was advertised in the official *Gazette* right below the prize offer for information leading to the detection of the author and publishers of the *Account.*[65] And even as L'Estrange as surveyor of the press sought their discovery, he was also writing his "confutation and censure" of Marvell's and other Shaftesburian publications. L'Estrange's *Account of the Growth of Knavery* had appeared by mid-April, when a Court MP could commend it as "writ by a

[61] Marvell to William Popple, June 10, 1678 (*P & L,* 2:357); he had once similarly referred in the third person to "Marvels" *Mr. Smirke,* in a letter to Sir Edward Harley (*P & L,* 2:346).

[62] *Christianissimus Christianandus* (London, 1678), cites those "Authors" of discontents (pp. 73–74), who revive just before a new meeting of parliament and who speak in terms of the "Confederates" (p. 76). This title is registered with the Stationers on Jan. 25, 1678, at which point its text need not have been complete; its publication is advertised Feb. 28, 1678 (Term Catalogues, 1:302).

[63] Marchamont Nedham, *Honesty's best Policy* (London, 1678), pp. 9–12, 18.

[64] Edmund Bohun, *The Diary and Autobiography,* ed. S. Wilton Rix (Beccles, 1853), pp. 40–41.

[65] *London Gazette,* no. 1288 (March 21–25, 1678); Dryden, *All for Love* (London, 1678); James Winn, *John Dryden and His World* (New Haven, 1987), pp. 305–06, 588–89.

good smart pen."[66] A few days later there appeared a spurious *Letter from Amsterdam to a friend in England* attacking Marvell by name in connection with the *Account*, this also from Nedham's printer, and soon republished.[67]

Another index of the influence of the *Account*, and official fears of its effectiveness in persuading the political population of its anti-French argument, is the effort to suppress its publication and republication and prosecute those involved in its dissemination. A second quarto edition, hitherto unnoted by students of Marvell, was forthcoming, with a third edition in folio appearing in 1679, after the lapse of the Licensing Act. That some further dissemination of the text was expected after the first edition appears from the steps the authorities took to discover its publishers and to prevent more such publication. The vigilance of the investigators was thwarted despite the boasts of informants that it would be possible to surprise the press doing similar work again. The printer Cartwright, so the informants explained, worked "below staires" in a house in Bethnal Green and employed a silk weaver at the front of the house so that the noise of the presswork might be concealed by that of the loom. Such precautions were of course necessary for illegal printing, whether seditious or in breach of copyright or of the protected Stock of the Stationers' Company. The stationers' informant knew to associate such illicit printing with money-clipping (a corruption of coinage that was a capital crime) and claimed of Cartwright's establishment that "they are Printing, and Dollaring, and the Divell and all." With disbursements coming their way, the informants seem repeatedly to have postponed the success of the investigation, and a subsequent search of the suspected premises yielded nothing for a prosecution.[68]

The urgency in the printing of the *Account* appears in the extraordinary number of errors in the first edition, with almost no corrections made in press. The work featured the Amsterdam imprint common in Darby's opposition publications of this date. No one seems to have been fooled. The warrant issued to search for this "scandalous pamphlet" soon led to the seizure of some copies, for which their discoverer, the stationer William

[66] Sir Robert Southwell to Ormonde, April 16, 1678 (HMC Ormonde, NS 4:423).

[67] *Letter from Amsterdam* (London, 1678), pp. 4–5. Dated to April 18, 1678 in *CSPD 1678*, pp. 121–23. This shares paper-stock with copies of *Christianandus* and *Honesty's Best Policy*, and of *A Letter from a Gentleman in Ireland* (London, printed and to be sold by Langley Curtis, 1677).

[68] PRO, SP 29/402/192-3, affidavit of stationer Joseph Leigh, March 26, 1678.

Whitwood, later sought reward.[69] A bounty for the discovery of the printer (worth fifty pounds) or author (worth a hundred) of the *Account* was soon offered in the *London Gazette*, with still greater rewards promised to anyone in the print trade whose information led to a prosecution; before long, the reward could be cited as "worth two or three hundred pound to the Discoverer."[70] The pamphlet was under review by the House of Lords, which was urged to give it the "most severe inquisition."[71] Surveyor of the Press L'Estrange, trying to find author and publisher, was quick to relate the *Account* to the parliamentary session of March the year before, and in particular to other libels circulating at that time.[72] He sought permission to gain access to them, presumably to check on evidence of their common origin.

Soon the investigations into who had published the *Account* began to yield results. First a stationer, William Leach, revealed having been asked to arrange stitching a copy of that work. The next step was to track down the man who had brought it to him, Samuel Packer, a clerk in the Poultry Counter. After the initial seizure of the work, however, Packer was discovered only a month later.[73] He had hidden himself the more carefully

[69] Warrant: Feb. 19, 1678 (PRO, SP 44/334/457); seizure: "on the 21th: of February last William Whitwood of London Staconer did apprehend One Thomas Bedwell who was by his Majesty in Councell Comitted to Newgate for Publishing and Offering to Sale a Seditious booke Entituled Consideracons of the Growth of Popery and Arbitrary Government in England Twelve of the said Bookes he did likewise seize from the said Bedwell." (Warden Thomas Vere's certificate to Williamson, annexed to the latter's certificate of April 13, 1678, PRO, SP 29/403/38–40)—see also note 36 above; reminder to Williamson in June 1678, PRO, SP 29/404/297. Bedwell was discharged upon his mother's petition (May 3, 1678, PRO, PC 2/66/319).

[70] *London Gazette*, no. 1288 (March 21–25, 1678). Roger L'Estrange, *An Account of the Growth of Knavery* (London, 1678), pp. 4, 6; L'Estrange, *The Parallel or, An Account of the Growth of Knavery* (London, 1679), sig. A2r–v.

[71] Nedham, *Honesty's best Policy*, p. 17. It was one of several for which searches were under way, another being *Mr Harringtons Case*.

[72] Feb. 25, 1678: *LJ* xiii. 161.

[73] Goodman Atwood (deputy marshall of the King's Bench) to the Lord Treasurer [Danby], PRO, SP 29/405/189 (bound out of sequence, but endorsed March 21, 1677/8); this followed the earlier information of stationer William Leach to Joseph Williamson (March 1, 1678): "Mr. Samuel Packer one of the clerks of the Poultry Counter about three weeks since came to [Leach's] shop and brought a booke or pamphlet intitled the growth of popery and of Arbitrary government in England, to stitch up for him, and to the best of his remembrance the said Packer tould him that it

since he believed that "A Thousand Pounde is bidd for me." Only in July was he prosecuted for taking the "treasonable and seditious Libell Entituled An Account of the Growth of Popery etc. to be stitched in order to the dispersing thereof, for which he is now under Restraint."[74] His subsequent death in King's Bench Prison shows what he had to fear.[75] Searches were ordered, including one of the house and warehouse of one Axtel (son of the regicide), with his arrest ordered too.[76] A month or so later, L'Estrange had "with much difficulty" found out that inveterate oppositional bookseller and long-standing associate of Darby's, the widow Ann Brewster, to whom he traced a number of the pamphlets in question, including the *Account*. But now L'Estrange faced a new problem with his prosecution, for notwithstanding his success in running Brewster to ground, "if she be questiond, probably shee will cast the whole, upon Mr Marvell." And Marvell, the frustrated official reports, "is lately dead; and there the Enquiry ends."[77]

By whom and when in this period was the *Account* reprinted in quarto? The provenance of this second quarto edition remains uncertain. Its printer plainly worked from the first quarto edition, sometimes following it page for page, but he or she remains unidentified (nor does the mix of papers in the second quarto edition match other Darby imprints of the day). The title page retains the date 1677 in order not to advertise that this was indeed a second edition. There was considerable incentive to reprint the work already in

---

was presented him that morning, and was very unwilling this Informant should see the title, that the said Packer hath since absented himselfe from his Employment in the Poultry Compter" (PRO, SP 29/401/337).

[74] The Privy Council order is dated July 12 (PRO, PC 2/66/370, see also SP 29/405/96). Packer's examination before Williamson (PRO, SP 29/405/168: July 19? or 22) included review of his notes to his wife Ann when he had been in hiding; he had then planned to see her when "their Rage is A little over" (PRO, SP 29/405/190–194: March ?–21, 1678).

[75] MS note on British Library, C. 55 d. 20, *Account* (1677a), t-p; this seems to have followed from his prosecution for some later sedition, cf. Folger Library MS L.c. 1429 (Sept. 6, 1683).

[76] PRO, SP 44/334/514 and 518 (July 6 and 8, 1678); PRO, SP 29/405/116 and 44/334/522 (July 16, 1678).

[77] PRO, SP 29/406/49 (Aug. 23, 1678). A month later, another informant sends the same information: "since the death of our friend Mr. uxhmbz [*sic*] the Wrighting of that booke of the growth of etc was said to be donne by him." PRO, SP 29/405/189 (Sept. 22, 1678).

1678, despite the risks, and there were plainly official suspicions that it was again in press in the spring or summer of 1678. That the bookseller Francis Smith was involved in its distribution is consistent with his role in oppositional publishing in 1677–78 and with the authorities' repeated investigation of his premises early in July 1678. A few years later he maintained in print that they had found nothing in that search "reflecting on Church or State."[78] This needs to be set against his much later complaint that his losses included as many copies of "The Growth of Popery and Arbitrary Government . . . burnt by the Common Hangman, as would have yielded above 150 1." The latter represents a massive destruction of perhaps an entire print run of a tract this size.[79] If Smith may be taken at his word, such a book burning could explain why the second quarto edition (of which only three copies have been located) survives in notably smaller numbers than the first (over twenty-five copies located). Smith prudently did not press this claim before the Revolution of 1688/9 and in earlier days failed to cite this great damage in any specific way.[80] But on July 16, 1678, the bishop of London did indeed order that such of Smith's books as were "not fitt for Damaskeing . . . [should] be burnt in their garden adjoyneing to their [the Stationers'] Common Hall,"[81] and the order may have been performed on the *Account* especially.[82] If so, the question remains why Smith in 1681

[78] *An Account of the Injurious Proceedings* (London, [Feb. 1] 1680/1), p. 19; the Privy Council ordered the search of his warehouse July 12, 1678 (PRO, PC 2/66/370), qv. Timothy Crist, "Francis Smith and the Opposition Press in England, 1660–1688" (diss., Cambridge, 1977), pp. 102–03.

[79] *The Speech of a Noble Peer of this Realm* (London, 1689), p. 2; BL, Add. MS 71446, ff. 107v–105v. I am grateful to Hilton Kelliher for guidance on this point.

[80] *An Impartial Account of the Tryal of Francis Smith* (London, 1680), and *An Account of the Injurious Proceedings* (1680/1), p. 19, citing 50 pounds' worth of publications lost to damasking owing to the Stationers' warden Samuel Mearne's raid of July 1678, but compare p. 22 which recalls Mearne's seizing books from Smith in 1676 only to reprint them himself (qv. Williamson's notes of Dec. 20, 1676, PRO, SP 29/366/132) and again "a second seizure two or three years after," which losses Smith values at 210 pounds.

[81] C. R. Rivington, *A Brief Account of the Worshipful Company of Stationers* (London, 1921), p. 6g.

[82] Such punishment might have attracted wider comment from this date than seems to have survived, although in February 1684 John Locke less specifically cites the burning of "The History of the Growth of Popery" as if a current enough example, without further revealing the date or which edition or part of the *Account* was involved, *Correspondence of John Locke,* ed. E. S. De Beer, 8 vols. (Oxford, 1976–89), 2:609.

would invite flat contradiction in claiming his earlier innocence on this score. The explanation may instead lie with the second quarto edition having been published in this quarter but later than 1678. If so, it is most likely to date from 1682–83 when the publication of *The Second Part of The Growth of Popery and Arbitrary Government* (1682) invited some such republication of the *Account* itself. The second quarto edition seems to have been a separate venture from *The Second Part*, however, whose pagination and signatures follow from the first edition and whose mix of paper-stocks is quite distinct from that in the second quarto edition. In the summer of 1683, at the time of the discovery of the Rye House Plot, the book burning to which Smith later alludes might more easily have gone unspecified in reports of the prosecution of *The Second Part*. As yet, however, the evidence for Smith's involvement with the second quarto edition remains stronger than that for one date or the other.

Marvell's death on August 16, 1678, freed the way for him to be named on the title page of the third edition, which appeared late in 1679[83] to help explain the Popish Plot. In that still greater political upheaval, the new imprint recommended the work "to the Reading of all English Protestants." It was a more imposing folio, printed from the first edition with many minor editorial corrections. That the author of such a tract should be thus named was unusual and helped raise Andrew Marvell, Esquire, to his posthumous prominence as an author in the company of Shaftesbury, Buckingham, and the like. Now his account of the pro-French conspiracy was caught up in confessional politics in which popery soon outweighed arbitrary government. For "Popery" now profoundly animated and enlarged the political nation, to a degree not seen since the turbulent days of the 1640s. Now came the breach in the Court's defenses marked by the fall of Danby; by various impeachments, including that of Seymour; by new elections, at last proving this "Immortal" parliament mortal after all; and by the intensifying Exclusion (or Restoration) Crisis from late in 1678 to the winter of 1681. Amid these excitements, the *Account* was not forgotten. It found translation into French as the *Relation de l'Accroissement . . .* (1680), which perhaps spurious Huguenot imprint from Hamburg may conceal an Amsterdam publication for a continental audience; appended to this is a translation also of *Mr Harringtons Case*. The success of the *Account* was reflected in publications of the Exclusion Crisis, especially in further

---

[83] This undated imprint is commonly styled 1678, but the publication is much more likely to be from the following year (see pp. 216–17 below).

publications indebted to Marvell's work, as in an electoral call to arms where we are warned of "approaching ruine"—"Think how the French King shakes his Fasces over us, when at the same time the Treacherous Papist renders us naked to his correction!"[84]—or in the sequel to Marvell's work, *The Second Part of The Growth of Popery and Arbitrary Government* (1682), probably by Robert Ferguson, the Whig "Plotter" who carried the story from 1678 to 1682.[85]

Printed attacks on the *Account* also persisted. John Nalson observed of the clamor against arbitrary government that "Andrew Marvel, Oliver's Latin Secretary, leads the Van," and a Tory *The Third Part of the Growth of Popery an Arbitrary Government in England* further argues that it is instead the contempt of magistracy that leads "to Arbitrary Government, when Men will cast off the Yoke of lawful obedience, and be governed only by their own Arbitrary Wills."[86] After the discovery of the Rye House Plot (1683), L'Estrange would in his counterattack against "fanatics" seek to show that the Shaftesburians had already been conspiring before the Popish Plot. Marvell was now useful because he had been named on Shaftesbury's famous parliamentary list of the worthy and the vile, which L'Estrange presented as a list of plotters and their projected victims; owing to the date of Marvell's death in 1678, this list could thus be shown to predate "Oates's" Plot. But L'Estrange also sought to demonstrate that Marvell had played a more sinister part in the "Republican" machinations, owing to the way that "Marvel Dreamt of a Popish Plot, and Otes Expounded it."[87] The *Ac-*

---

[84] "Philolaus," *A Character of Popery and Arbitrary Government, With a Timely Caveat and Advice to all the Freeholders, Citizens and Burgesses, how they may prevent the same, By choosing Good Members To Serve in this New Parliament* (1679?), p. 2.

[85] "Philo-Veritas," *The Second Part of the Growth of Popery and Arbitrary Government: Beginning Where the Former left, viz. From the Year 1677. unto the Year 1682* ("Cologne: Printed for Philliotus," 1682). Here the signatures and pagination follow from those of the first quarto edition. Some question remains whether the author may have been John Culliford, who suffered in the prosecution of this publication.

[86] John Nalson, *The Complaint of Liberty & Property against Arbitrary Government* (London, 1681), p. 5; *The Third Part of the Growth of Popery and Arbitrary Government in England* (London, 1683), A3v–A4r. See also the hostile notices in [George Savile, marquis of Halifax?], *A Seasonable Address To both Houses of Parliament Concerning the Succession; The Fears of Popery, and Arbitrary Government* (London, 1681), p. 10 (among "many scandalous Pamphlets . . . one in particular"), and Edmund Bohun, *An Address to the Free-men and Free-holders of the Nation* (London, 1682), p. 39 ("a damnable Libel").

[87] *Observator*, 2d ser., nos. 13–17 (Feb. 6–17, 1683/4).

count also met with a belated riposte from Marvell's old antagonist Samuel Parker, whose *History of His Own Time* introduces the narrative of the Popish Plot with a Sallustian account of the tavern-haunting conspirators who came boldly to disclose themselves as the Green-Ribbon club, amongst which "lewd Revilers, the lewdest was one whose name was Marvel." This *History*, then, rebuts at length the history retailed in the *Account*, in large part along the anti-Shaftesburian lines that had been set out by Nedham, emphasizing the inconsistencies between Shaftesbury's politics before and after his move into opposition in 1673.[88]

The success of the *Account* appears variously thereafter. Its history of the 1670s would prove influential at the Revolution of 1688/9, when the energetic Whig bookseller Richard Baldwin triumphantly reprinted it in the *State Tracts* of 1689 and 1693, which we may think of as a Shaftesburian anthology.[89] Baldwin also soon published *Mr Andrew Marvell's Character of Popery* (licensed Jan. 17, 1689), a quarto pamphlet extracting the anti-Catholic marrow of Marvell's argument in order now to wish good riddance to the last of the Stuart kings.[90] Marvell was here characterized as "a Person of no less Piety and Learning then Sharpness of Wit and Soundness of Judgment," whose attack on "the Popish Religion" was "his last Legacy to this Nation."[91] At the Revolution, Marvell's work might lend itself to Whig constitutional claims on one hand and on the other to resentments against Stuart Catholicism.[92] Together with the *Collection[s] of Poems on Affairs of State*, which promoted Marvell as a primary author of such satires since the 1660s, these editions of the *Account* confirmed Marvell as the Patriot hero of later legend. In the *State Tracts*, the prefatory note to the reader by the bookseller summarizes the Shaftesburian line as adumbrated by Marvell, and the *Account* supplies a narrative that gives the other Whig pieces there collected a context. The publication offers a verdict on Stuart

---

[88] Samuel Parker, *Bishop Parker's History of His Own Time*, trans. Thomas Newlin (London, 1727), pp. 330–49.

[89] Leona Rostenberg, *Literary, Political . . . Publishing, Printing and Bookselling in England, 1551–1700* (New York, 1965), pp. 369–400.

[90] The extract is from the *Account* (1677a), pp. 5–11.

[91] *Mr. Andrew Marvell's Character of Popery* (London, 1689), sig. A2r.

[92] British Library, C. 55 d. 20: this copy of the *Account* (1677a) features significant early marginalia by a John Lands, reflecting a great Whig interest in English liberties and the role of parliament, not least in supply, as well as the problems with indulging recusants (dated 1691, from note in *The Second Part . . .* [BL, C. 55 d. 20*], p. 319).

absolutist claims more generally. It supplies a constitutional argument about the limits of monarchy and thus seeks also to explain in more radical Whig terms the present revolution.[93] Moreover, it was also a tract for later times in favoring an alliance with the Dutch and Spanish against the French. On the eve of the War of the Spanish Succession, the debates of 1677 favoring war with the French and alliance with the Spanish and Dutch could find separate publication;[94] on the eve of the Peace of Utrecht, an abbreviated version of the *Account* could again present its historical narrative and its version of the debate about war with France.[95] Historiographically, the *Account* showed how to combine parliamentary history with a larger narrative of national and international affairs. Later historians would return to this example, if usually with a less inflected or ironic thrust. Later Whigs, moderate and radical, would draw on the *Account* freely to explain the politics of the 1670s: Roger Coke, White Kennett, John Oldmixon, James Ralph, Thomas Hollis, Richard Chandler, Catherine Macaulay, Charles McCormick, and William Cobbett and John Wright, among others. And so persuasive was Marvell's history of that decade that even those, like David Hume, who sought to correct the Whig historians could not easily free themselves from his version of those events.[96]

When Captain Thompson published the first complete edition of Marvell's prose and poetry in 1776, the *Account* still served to justify the end of Stuart rule and the Hanoverian Succession. The succession had long been decided, however; more pressing now was the cause of reform and parliamentary independence of court management. The eighteenth century valued Marvell's work for its indictment of parliamentary corruption, where it might still prove a tract for the times. English historiography then and since shows just how influential Marvell's description of French interference in English affairs had been. He had given Shaftesburian and coun-

[93] *State Tracts: Being a Collection of Several Treatises Relating to the Government. Privately Printed in the Reign of K. Charles II* (London, 1689), sig. A2r especially.

[94] *Private Debates in the House of Commons, In the Year 1677. In Relation to a War with France, and an Alliance with Holland, &c.* (London, 1702), pp. 1–96.

[95] *The History of the Peace with France and War with Holland In the Year 1672. & Seq. . . . The whole written by a Member of the then House of Commons* (London, 1712).

[96] Their basic strategy was to blame the Cabal ministry (1668–72), and Shaftesbury in particular, for the misdeeds of which the Whigs accused the Crown and court more generally. David Hume, *History of England*, ed. William Todd (Indianapolis, 1983), 6:243–308.

try politics the history of the 1670s that it needed. To a remarkable degree, English historiography thereafter remained persuaded of that history as presented in his *Account*.

TEXT

The *Account* as an Assembled Text

The copy-text for the present edition is the second quarto edition (*77b*), based on a comparison of the three copies discovered to date.[97] That text was set from a slightly corrected copy of the first edition (*77a*). *77b* is in its spellings and accidentals rather kinder than *77a* to the modern eye. Moreover, *77a* is in these respects sufficiently distinct from the example of Marvell's holograph letters and state papers to indicate that in the transmission of text, whether at the stage of manuscript transcription or of print composition, his example was not much respected. If haste marred the production, secrecy too may have contributed to practices of transcription likely to obscure authorial copy.[98] Variations in orthography and accidentals arose also from the *Account* being in some part an assembly of preexisting documents, which it organizes into its fuller narrative. This origin as an assembled text further diminishes the value of the first edition as copy-text, owing to its incorporation of a number of separates of parliamentary speeches and addresses, as well as the full text of an unsuccessful bill, and of extracts from the Commons Journal and other notes or journals of Commons debates, some of which were substantial. These documents are not peculiar to Marvell, nor likely in a number of instances to have been transcribed by him. The *Account* also refers to a separate register of English

[97] Chicago, Newberry Library, Case J 5454 .551 (1); Harry Ransom Center, University of Texas, Aj.M368.677aa (1); and Yale University, Beinecke Library, By46 408.

[98] Of Ann Brewster, who brought related "Libells to the Presse in Manuscript," L'Estrange claimed, "She is in the House of a person formerly an officer under Cromwell [presumably Col. Henry Danvers]: one that writes Three or Foure very good Hands, and owns to have been Employed in Transcribing things for a Counsellor in the Temple [presumably Joseph Browne]. From which Circumstances one may fayrly presume that all those Delicate Copyes, which Brewster carried to the Presse, were written by Brewsters LandLord, and Copyd by him, from the Author. Beside that it is very probable, that the late Libells concerning the Growth of Popery, and the List of the Members of Parlmt past through the same hands." August 23, 1678 (PRO, SP 29/406/49).

shipping taken by the French, which is to be "annexed" to the tract. More-over, even the introductory excursus on popery seems of an origin some-what separate from the surrounding text.

It remains unclear how sequential this work of assembly and composi-tion was. If some preliminary version was being undertaken already in May 1677, Marvell had much opportunity thereafter to add materials to it. The author describes his work of composition in a way that suggests that the narrative of the parliamentary session of 1676/7 was written first (*77a*, pp. 70–121),[99] followed by further assembly and the addition of the longer retrospective of the history of the previous decade. There are also points in the retrospective first half of the *Account* where issues from the 1676/7 session, yet to be encountered in the narration, already obtrude upon the earlier history.[100] Lacking the manuscript(s) of the *Account,* we are fortu-nate to have for comparison another MP's manuscript summary of the session of 1677. Daniel Finch supplies an account of "the most consider-able transactions," which narrative includes intermittent references to an appended series of transcribed documents—royal speeches, parliamentary addresses, Harrington's petition, and the like.[101] With the *Account,* such separates may well have been incorporated into the manuscript without transcription, since their punctuation and orthography seem less anoma-lous than those in much of the narrative as printed in *77a.* The printer regularly anticipates them as separate documents, to be set off distinctly, often on a new page; at one point, his anticipation leads to a significant catchword error (*77a*, pp. 87–88, with which compare p. 89). With the separate of "a written Copy of the Lord Bridgmans speech," which the author had acquired "not without much labour," the typesetting again indi-cates that the distinct document was pieced in during printing (*77a*, pp. 19,

---

[99] The cues are the reference to the "Progress made in so few weeks" (p. 241 below) [*77a:* 17], and "Thus are we at length arrived at this much controverted and as much expected Session. And though the way to it hath proved much longer than was in-tended in the entry of this discourse . . ." (p. 294) [*77a:* 70].

[100] Especially the somewhat obscure remark, "So Legal was it in this Session to Distinguish between the King of Englands Personal, and his Parliamentary Authority" (p. 269 below) [*77a:45*], explained by the reference to the lord chancellor's speech of Feb. 15, 1676/7, in which he urged, "*Away with that ill meant distinction between the Natural and the Politique Capacity*" of the king (p. 283) [*77a:59*].

[101] Leicestershire RO, OG 7, P.P. 42. Finch's headings bear noting: "the prorogacion for 15 months," "bills against popery," "money bills," "some of the publick bills," "Grei-vances," and "French Grandeur" (p. 1).

20–26, 26–27).[102] More significant still is the derivation from independent sources of the debates regarding war with France in March–April and May 1677, the basis for much of the last part of the *Account*. Other versions of these appear in manuscript, and the May "Private Debates" were published separately at the time of the War of the Spanish Succession (1702); the different texts witness an original summary of this debate that the *Account* only lightly rewrites.[103]

Thus the following scheme suggests itself for the assembly of the *Account*, although this numbering of the main parts of the narrative may well differ from the order of their composition. The dozen or more separates here listed with alphabetical references have not in every case survived independently in manuscript. Because some features of the first edition reflect the assembled character of the manuscript, its pagination is supplied.

1.1 [77a: 3–5] Introduction (constitutionalist). [Pp. 225–27 below]

A. [77a: 5–14] Satirical character of "popery," beginning as if an awkward interpolation, "That Popery is such a thing as cannot, but for want of a word to express it, be called a Religion . . ."; and continuing to " . . . to maintain the established Protestant Religion." [Pp. 227–37 below]

1.2 [77a: 14–16] Transition relating this religious issue to the constitutional one, with reference to the "Conspirators": "And yet, all this notwithstanding, there are those men among us, who have undertaken, and do make it their business, under so Legal and perfect a Government, to introduce a French slavery, and instead of so pure a Religion, to establish the Roman Idolatry: both and either of which are Crimes of the highest nature . . ."; and continuing to " . . . Inclination and Interest." [Pp. 237–41]

2.1 [77a: 16–17] Transitional paragraph: "And now, should I enter into a particular retail of all former and latter Transactions, relating to this affaire, there would be sufficient for a just Volume of History. But my intention is only to write a naked Narrative of some the most considerable passages in the meeting of Parliament the 15. of Febr. 1675 [=1676/7]. . . . Yet, that I may not be too abrupt, and leave the Reader wholely destitute of a thread to guide himself by thorow so intreaguing a Labyrinth, I shall summarily, as

---

[102] The anomaly appears on the inner forme of the D-gathering (*77a:* D1v–D2r). Elsewhere some inconsistent spacing of the paragraphs reveals comparable practices, especially in both forms of the G-gathering (and the short G1r, *77a:* 49), with the pagination error "65" for 56 looking beyond the H-gathering to I1r (= p. 65 proper).

[103] For March–April 1677, see BL, Add. MS 35865, ff. 135–56; for May, see BL, Add. MS 72603, ff. 48–59, BL, Stowe MS 182, ff. 56–66, and *Private Debates in the House of Commons, In the year 1677. In Relation to a War with France . . .* (London, 1702).

short, as so copious and redundant a matter will admit, deduce the order of affairs both at home and abroad, as it led into the Session." [P. 241 below]

2.2 [*77a:* **17–19**] The political prehistory needed to explain the course of the parliamentary session of 1677, beginning with the Second Anglo-Dutch War (1665). [Pp. 241–44 below]

B. [*77a:* **20–26**] Interpolation of Lord Bridgeman's speech (October 24, 1670) from "a written Copy." This may have been provided in a copy that went to the printer untranscribed, since in the first edition this interpolated text appears in a distinct and larger font on pp. 20–26 (sig. C2r-D1r), as if there had been some mistaking the space required for it. [Pp. 245–49 below]

2.3 [*77a:* **27–69**] The main narrative of English political history from 1667 to 1676 resumes and is presented in the smaller font that had been used earlier, before it was interrupted by Bridgeman's speech (set thus from the top of page 27 [sig. D2r]). Especially regarding the Declaration of Indulgence (1672), the narrative features less concern about religion than about the suspension of law, as if popery were less at issue than arbitrary government.

C. [*77a:* **69**] Interpolation of "A short account of some Ammunition, &c. Exported from the Port of London to France," a short list that serves as an appendix in the conclusion of the pre-1677 narrative, followed by brief final comment. [Pp. 249–94 below]

3.1 [*77a:* **70–82/82–85**] The narrative of the 1677 session begins: "Thus are we at length arrived at this much controverted, and as much expected Session. And though the way to it hath proved much longer then was intended in the entry of this discourse, yet is it very short of what the matter would have afforded, but is past over to keep within bounds of this Volumn." The story starts with the contest over the length of the preceding prorogation and the imprisonment of the four lords; there follows a digression on the character of this long parliament, and then the narrative resumes with the prosecution of one concerned in the prorogation pamphlets and with the details of the case of John Harrington [82–85]. [Pp. 294–308]

3.2 [*77a:* **85–88**] "And now to proceed, rather according to the Coherence of the matters, than to the particular Date of every days action . . . " There is a conspicuous catchword error in *77a* pp. 87/88 (sig. L4r–v), of "*An*" for "*And,*" which shows that the printer was looking ahead not to the next page of manuscript narrative—which is Marvell's notice of the fate of the first of the Bishops' Bills, as noted in Commons Journal, and then his admonitory "defence" of the bishops—but instead to the next separate, the extended text of the second Bishops' Bill, which starts on the new gathering M

(p. 89); hence also his ending p. 87 early to set off that new document to follow, whereas the text of Marvell's narrative requires no such gap at this point. This error then induced the further error of introducing the next paragraph with the additional word "And," which finds manuscript correction in two copies[104] and in *77b*. [Pp. 308–13 below]

D.   [*77a:* **89–100**] Double-rule heading to set off the text of the Bishops' Bill, "An Act for further securing the Protestant Religion . . . ," supplied in full (sig. M1r–N2v). [Pp. 313–23 below]

3.3   [*77a:* **100**] Followed by two paragraphs: one of further comment on the Bishops' Bill; another resuming the narrative, "Henceforward another scene opens . . . " The page ends short (sig. N2v), suggesting that the following materials from a separate source were set from another document.

E.1   [*77a:* **101–07**] Extended summary of the debates and addresses about a war with France, March–April 1677, which with some abbreviation, some narrative framing, and other local rewriting pieces into the *Account* a separate "Journall touching the Engageing the King to joyne with the Confederates in a Warr against France" (British Library, Add. MS 35865, ff. 135–56) or more likely some common source. These "Proceedings of the Parliament against the growing Power of France" begin with extracts from the Commons Journal, March 6–29, 1677 (*77a:* 101–03). They then summarize the ensuing debates, March 30, 1677, organized as pro (*77a:* 103–04) and contra (*77a:* 104–07) the French (court) interest. [Pp. 323–30 below]

3.4   [*77a:* **107**] Marvell briefly resumes historical narration with reference to parliament, in a paragraph set off from the preceding summary of debates; this links those debates to the next passage from "A Journall touching the Engageing the King to joyne with the Confederates in a Warr against France" (BL, Add. MS 35865, ff. 144r–), heralded by the extra gap at the bottom of p. 107. [P. 330 below]

E.2   [*77a:* **108–19**] Following "A Journall" (BL, Add. MS 35865, ff. 144r–52v) or their common source, the narrative supplies the royal address of April 11, 1677, set off with a rule at the top of the page, after which come the responses to King's Speech, with reference first to adjournment (*77a:* 108–09), then at greater length to foreign affairs (*77a:* 109–15); the summary of debate is organized into alternating claims for and against the Court position, with the much more extensive "answers" being the Country position.

[104] Bodleian Library, G. Pamph. 1359 (22) and Chicago, Newberry Library, Case J 5454.55.

The resulting "Answer to the King," April 13, 1677, is set on a single page (*77a:* 116 [=sig. P2v]; cf. BL, Add. MS 35865, ff. 152v–53v); briefly framed, the royal response of April 16, 1677 comes next (*77a:* 117; cf. BL, Add. MS 35865, ff. 154r–v). Still following "A Journall," the parliamentary response is then summarized (*77a:* 117–18), issuing in the parliamentary address, set on a single, very full page (*77a:* 119 [= sig. P4r]; cf. BL, Add. MS 35865, ff. 155v–56v). [Pp. 330–41 below]

3.5   [*77a:* 120–21] Summary of parliamentary business and French progress on the Continent, leading to Marvell's attack on *A Second Pacquet of Advices.* [Pp. 341–3 below]

F.   **[*77a:* 122–48]** Extended description of the brief parliamentary session of May 21–28, 1677, with special reference to the debate over the war with France. This lightly rewrites a summary of those debates, of which other copies survive in British Library, Add. MS 72603, ff. 48–59, and Stowe MS 182, ff. 56–66. The version in the Stowe MS later finds publication as *Private Debates in the House of Commons, In the Year 1677. In relation to a War with France* (London, 1702).[105] In the first edition of the *Account,* the separates of particular royal speeches and parliamentary addresses are now no longer set off on new pages, as had so often been the case in its earlier sections: this also shows the prior integration of the narrative with such documents.

At page 145, the beginning of the T-gathering, the paper-stock shifts back to that predominating in the A–H gatherings; this argues continuity in the printing of the main text of the *Account* and the following coda referring to events of December 1677. [Pp. 343–68 below]

4.   [*77a:* 148–52] Reports the appalled response of the House and its highhanded adjournment by the Speaker; this then extends into a more expansive summary, including the verdict that, whatever the Commons' failings,

---

[105] There is some variation between these texts, but the manuscripts and *Private Debates* very consistently agree against the evident rewriting in the *Account.* Where there is variation between the former, Add. MS 72603 (from the Trumbull papers) is consistently closer to Marvell's text, whereas Stowe is very close to 1702. In these copies of the "Private Debates," the phrasing is simpler, the punctuation lighter (especially in Add. MS 72603), and the paragraphing more frequent and sometimes differently distributed than in the *Account.* There is an extra sentence on p. 61 not in the *Account* (p. 360 below); an extra phrase on p. 68 indicating a case of eyeslip in the *Account* (p. 362 below); and extra references to works by Bacon and by Boccalini (pp. 345, 348 below). Marvell reincorporates the royal speeches and the parliamentary address omitted from the "Private Debates."

parliament had addressed and debated "against the French power and progresse." Continues with the story of summer adjournments, and wider perspective including the ongoing incarceration of the four lords, and note of the release of Buckingham, Salisbury, and Wharton. [Pp. 368–73 below]

5. **[77a: 152–56]** Conclusion, as of December 3, 1677, and unexpected shortening of adjournment to only January 15, 1677/8: "And here it is time to fix a period, if not to them [this "immortal" parliament], yet to this Narrative . . . " Wider summary, exculpating his majesty, indicting his bad ministers. Errata (very limited sampling, through only to p. 133). [Pp. 373–77]

[**G.** *A List of Several Ships Belonging to English Merchants Taken by French Privateers* . . . (Amsterdam, 1677). The *Account* itself advertises "the Paper at the end [/69] of this Treatise annexed . . . returned by some Members of the Privy Council to his Majesties Order, to which was also adjoyned a Register of so many of the *English* Ships as then came to notice which the *French* had taken." The list declares its origin as the report of the Committee on Trade, August 4, 1676, complaining of French depredations and the difficulty of winning reparations. The same day, it seems, Shaftesbury's associate John Harrington was publicizing the outrage: "takeing a Coppy of the affidavits of such masters whose ships were taken by the French, he read and show'd them to as many as he cold upon and about the Exchange in reflecion upon the Goverment."[106] Its publication the next year as *A List of Several Ships Belonging to English Merchants Taken by French Privateers* . . . features a 1677 Amsterdam imprint like that of the *Account,* and as Edward Holberton has shown, it is printed on two of the same paper-stocks as the *Account.* Unlike the *Account,* however, this quarto is in pairs (A–L2 = 44 pp.), and this unusual format, resulting from half-sheet imposition, indicates haste in the production or constraints on type or both. The *List* includes several addenda extending the scroll of ships taken by French privateers to as late as September 4, 1676; a last catchword suggests that yet another such addendum might have been planned. Access to the text may have followed from Marvell's parliamentary service, especially to the shipping interests represented by Trinity House, in Hull and in London; or from his cooperation with Harrington.

The distinct origin and character of the *List* have led to its omission from this edition. Despite the reference within the *Account* to this tract, the shipping list was published independently from *77a,* and the one example of

---

[106] PRO, SP 29/392/21.

their being bound together in a large composite volume shows that they had at first been separately stitched and were put together only after the fact.[107] The list is omitted from *77b*. L'Estrange's early notices of the *Account* show that he did not find it bound with the *List;* the 1680 French translation of the *Account* omits it; and the signatures and pagination of the 1682 *Second Part of the Growth of Popery and Arbitrary Government: Beginning Where the Former left* . . . (Cologne [= London], 1682) also follow directly from those of *77a* proper. But it is included as an appendix integral to the 1679 edition and to the editions in the *State Tracts* (1689, 1693), and excerpts from it are also included in Grosart's edition (1875), vol. 4, pp. 415–24. Darby's publication of the list as a politically charged state paper deserves notice as not very remote from the assembly that is the *Account* itself.

SUMMARY OF EDITIONS

77a = 1677a: first edition, quarto, Wing M860. An Account of the / GROWTH / OF / POPERY, / AND / Arbitrary Government / IN / ENGLAND. / More Particularly, from the Long *Prorogation,* / of *November,* 1675, Ending the 15*th.* of / *February* 1676, till the Last Meeting of / *Parliament,* the 16*th.* of *July* 1677. / [rule] / *AMSTERDAM*, Printed in the Year 1677. [all framed with a double rule]

Collation

4^0: A–T^{4}U^2 = 78 leaves (t.-p., blank, pp. 3–156). Pagination errors: 65 for 56, 119 for 122; 108 for 127. Several copies have title page inscriptions indicating that they were seized in the initial prosecution of those associated with the publication in February 1678.[108] Comparison of seventeen copies indicates that except for tightening some loosening type there was next to no correction in press, despite many errors, of which only a few are noted in the errata at the end of the final page of the edition. The division of printing between two presses shows in the change of paper-stocks between the gatherings A-H on one hand, and on the other the gatherings I-S, with a final reversion to the earlier stock for T-U^2; and there are some related anomalies in the typesetting, also owing to the printers' approximations in casting off the manuscript copy.

[107] Bodleian Library, G. Pamph. 1120 (4–5).
[108] Oxford, Queen's College, Z.b.17 (1); British Library, C. 55 d. 20.

Copies consulted

Bodleian Library: Ashmole 733 (3); G. Pamph. 1120(4); G. Pamph. 1359
(22); Pamph. C 138 (12); Fairfax deposit copy, M860 (present location
unknown).

British Library: Ashley 1104; C.55.d.20; 702.e.4(2) [= the copy micro-
filmed in *Early English Books, 1641–1700*, reel 216:12, reproduced in Early
English Books Online].

Cambridge University Library: Syn. 7.67.56; Keynes W.3.14 (2).

Cambridge, Christ's College Library: I.6.6 (3).

Chicago, Newberry Library: Case J 5454.55.

Chicago, University of Chicago, Regenstein Library: Special Collection,
DA 448. M395

Durham University Library: Routh. 51.E.10 (1).

Folger Shakespeare Library, Washington, D.C.: M860.

Huntington Library, San Marino, California: 92421.

Kingston upon Hull Local Studies Library, Marvell Collection.

77b = 1677b: second quarto edition, Wing M860A. An Account of the /
GROWTH / OF / POPERY / AND / Arbitrary   Government / IN /
ENGLAND. / [rule] / More Particularly, from the Long *Prorogation*
of / *November,* 1675. Ending the 15*th.* of *February,* / 1676, till the last
Meeting of *Parliament,* the 16 / of *July* 1677. / [rule] / *AMSTERDAM,*
Printed in the Year, 1677.

Collation

$4^{0:}$ A–S^4 = 72 leaves (t.-p., blank, pp. 3–144). Pagination errors, 30 for 32;
103 for 130. This title page may be readily distinguished from that of the first
edition, since it conspicuously lacks the double border of *77a,* and in the
imprint now has a comma before the date. Comparison of three copies
indicates next to no correction in press, despite some errors.[109] *77b* is plainly
set from *77a,* to which the typesetting often corresponds line for line, and
even page for page. Most of the errors of *77a* have been corrected, however,
and *77b* shows extensive modernization of orthography and punctuation,
and some anglicization of foreign words. *77b* also incorporates the two
significant manuscript corrections found as yet only in two copies of *77a*

---

[109] The correction of the catchword "wich" (Texas) to "which" (Chicago, Yale) on
p. 41 is the exception.

(pp. 230, 312 below).[110] Some new errors[111] are introduced in turn, however, and there are additional paragraph breaks late in *77b*, in order that the text better fill out the pages of the final gathering.

Copies consulted

Chicago, Newberry Library: Case J 5454 .551 (1).
Harry Ransom Center, University of Texas: Aj.M368.677aa(1).
Yale University, Beinecke Library: By46 408.

79 = 1679: first folio edition, Wing M86. AN / ACCOUNT / OF THE / GROWTH / OF / POPERY, / AND / Arbitrary GOVERNMENT / IN / ENGLAND. / More Particularly from the Long *Prorogation*, of *No-* / *vember*, 1675, Ending the 15*th*. of *February*, 1676, / till the Last Meeting of *Parliament*, the 16*th*. of / *July*, 1677. / [rule] / By *Andrew Marvel*, Esq; / [rule] / [ornaments] / Printed at *Amsterdam*, And Recommended to the Reading of / all *English* Protestants. [all framed with a double rule]

Collation

2⁰: A–S² = 36 leaves (t.-p., blank, pp. 3–8, 5–68), of which the *Account* comprises A–P1v; *A List of Several Ships* P2r–S2v. The major pagination error falls at C1r, where there is also a change to a smaller font, which with the change in watermarks (from bunch of grapes to foolscap) suggests a division of the presswork. Since Marvell is named on the title, the folio may be assumed to be a posthumous publication (he died on August 16, 1678), and this undated imprint is dated 1678 by Alexander Grosart (*Complete Prose Works of Andrew Marvell* [1875], 4:246), by Donald Wing (*Short-Title Catalogue*), and by many library catalogues; a publication after the disclosures of the Popish Plot seems reflected in the added emphasis of its imprint, which drops the publication date of the first edition and instead

---

[110] *77a*, pp. 8, 88 = Bodleian, G. Pamph. 1359 (22) and Chicago, Newberry, Case J. 5454.55; cf. *77b*, pp. 8, 79.

[111] For example, "*claves non errant*" (*77b*, p. 7) instead of "*clave non errante*" (p. 230) as per the errata of the first edition, or the similar failures to correct as per the errata "a Grand French Ambassador" (*77a*, p. 120; *77b*, p. 108) to "*Embassade*" (p. 341), and "the 15 of Feb. 1675" (*77a*, p. 17; *77b*, p. 16) to "1676" (p. 241); or now "condemned too, as they" (*77b*, p. 10) for *recte* "condemned to, as they" (*77a* 10; p. 233 below); or now "Transubstantiation" (*77b*, 6) losing the wit of "Transubstantiall" (*77a*, p. 7; p. 229 below); or now the omission of the word "last" from "should have the last opportunity" (*77a*, p. 152; *77b*, p. 139; p. 372 below).

recommends the tract "to the Reading of all English Protestants." But there are strong grounds for dating it to later in 1679. The first of the Popish Plot catalogues thus dates it (*A Compleat Catalogue of all the Stitch'd Books and Single Sheets Printed since the First Discovery of The Popish Plot*, 1680), where among the folios is listed, p. 5: "Growth of Popery. 1679." in 18 sheets; and in a letter of November 8, 1679, Francis Gwyn can observe to Lord Conway that he has supplied "the most considerable pamphlets I can pick up, that caled the Growth of Popery is only a new eddition of the Former without any additions to it" (PRO, SP 29/412/77). At this date, too, a newsletter cites it among works "Complained Against" and to be prosecuted (Folger Library, MS L.c. 850, Oct. 18, 1679) and the Privy Council is reported to have deemed the *Account* to "have Treasonable matter" in it (October 20, 1679, Oxford, All Souls MS 171, f. 76r). Only late in 1679 (a November advertisement, *Term Catalogues* 1:374) does L'Estrange answer this folio *Account* with a second edition in folio of his response to it, now retitled *The Parallel or, An Account of the Growth of Knavery*, remarking with suspicion the attempt now to make of Marvell the prophet of the Popish Plot (sig. A2r-v). The folio *Account* is set from *77a*, with some correction—notably of the phrase "to the great injury of the Divels" (cf. *77a*, p. 8, with *79*, p. 5; p. 230 below)—and much modernization of orthography and punctuation, and with some new errors added.

Copies consulted

Bodleian Library: C 11.15 (7) Th.
British Library: 4707.h.12; T.88* (11).
Cambridge University Library: Sel.3.239 (21). (The Narcissus Luttrell copy.)
Durham University Library: Bamb. H 3.26 (12).
Folger Shakespeare Library, Washington, D.C.: M861.
Harvard University Library: *fEC65.M3685.677ab.
Huntington Library, San Marino, California: 12889 [= the copy micro-filmed in *Early English Books, 1641–1700*, reel 324:8, reproduced in Early English Books Online].
Kingston upon Hull Local Studies Library, Marvell Collection.
London, Middle Temple Library, Ashley Collection, Tracts on the Popish Plot, no. 1.
Oxford, Queen's College: 6 B.17 (11).
University of Toronto Library: E-10/1040.
Yale University, Beinecke Library: By46 040.

1680 = *Relation de l'Accroissement de la Papauté Et du Gouvernement Absolu en Angleterre, Particulierement Depuis la longue Prorogation de Novembre 1675. laquelle a fini le 15. Fevrier 1676. jusques à present. Traduit en François de la Copie Angloise.* A Hambourgh, Chez Pierre Pladt, Libraire, 1680. Duodecimo, 245pp., of which 228 pp. for the translation of the *Account,* and 15 pp. for that of *Mr Harringtons Case.*

A French translation based on the *77a* text, the *Relation* very much respects the original, except on a few points of idiom—for example, "by cursing one Prince or other upon every Maunday Thursday" here becomes "anathematisant un Prince ou un autre tout les *Lundys* & les *Mardys*" (p. 12). There are also a few expansions in order to make plain some points in the more laconic English original. The Hamburg imprint of the *Relation* may be a deception: other evidence of a Pierre Pladt working in that city has not emerged, and this could instead be an instance of the fictitious attribution of controversial Amsterdam publications to printers or booksellers in free cities elsewhere. But like London, Marvell's Hull was connected to Hamburg by significant trading interests.

1689a = excerpt in *Mr. Andrew Marvell's Character of Popery.* London, Printed for Richard Baldwin, next the Black Bull, in the Old-Bailey. MDCLXXXIX. (Licensed by Robert Midgly January 17, 1688/89). Wing M866. This single-sheet quarto pamphlet (t.p., blank, pp. 3–8) extracts the anti-Catholic marrow of Marvell's argument in order now to wish good riddance to the last of the Stuart kings. A page and a half of introduction drawing from the *Account* frames the extract proper, which runs from "And as we are thus happy in the Constitution of our State, so are we yet more blessed in that of our Church; being free from that Romish Yoak . . . " to "than when the Bramine, by having the first night of the Bride, assures himself of her Devotion for the future, and makes her more fit for the Husband" (pp. 227–34 below). Microfilm in *Early English Books, 1641–1700,* reel 216:14.

89 = 1689: included in *State Tracts: Being a Collection of Several Treatises Relating to the Government. Privately Printed in the Reign of K. Charles II.* London: Printed in the Year, 1689. Wing S5329. The sixth tract included in this folio collection is "An Account of the Growth of Popery, and Arbitrary Government in England. More particularly from the Long Prorogation, of November, 1675. Ending the 15th. of February, 1676. till the Last Meeting of Parliament, the 16th. of July, 1677. By Andrew Marvel, Esq; First Printed in the Year 1677." (sig. T1r–Ii2r [pp. 69–123]), to which is appended *A List of Several Ships* (sig. Ii2v–Mm2r [pp. 124–35]). The text of the *Account* follows that of *79*. Published in the revolutionary year 1689, this edition of the *Account* in effect supplies a scathing Whig denunciation of the Stuart submission to France and of the constitutional breakdown this occasioned. The collection as a whole variously expounds the Shaftesburian line as adumbrated by Marvell, whose work is much the longest here included. Microfilm in *Early English Books, 1641–1700*, reel 926:18.

93 = 1693: included in new edition of *State Tracts: Being a Collection of Several Treatises Relating to the Government. Privately Printed in the Reign of K. Charles II.* London, Printed in the year 1693. Wing S5330. Set from *89*, with some incidental changes, chiefly of punctuation. Microfilm in *Early English Books, 1641–1700*, reel 1493:7. This edition of *State Tracts* also was issued with *State Tracts: Being a farther Collection* (1692) under a common title page, *State-Tracts. In Two Parts* . . . London: Printed, and are to be sold by Richard Baldwin, near the Oxford-Arms in Warwick-Lane. MDCXCIII. Wing S5332. Microfilm in *Early English Books, 1641–1700*, reel 1411:1.

1712 = excerpts composing *The History of the Peace with France and War with Holland In the Year 1672. & Seq. Containing the Secret Intreagues between the Courts of England and France, and the Debates in Parliament thereupon. The whole written by a Member of the then House of Commons. To which is added a Preface relating to the Present Times.* London, Printed for A. Baldwin in Warwick Lane, MDCCXII. This octavo pamphlet (t.p., pp. i–vii, 1–71) supplies much of Marvell's historical narrative in the *Account,* and especially the passages of the debate about the war with France, in order now to warn against present Tory compromises with that enemy. The *History* runs from "It is well known, were it as well remembred, what the provocation was, and what the success of the War begun by the English in the Year 1665 . . . " to the end of Marvell's tract (pp. 241–377 below). Seven pages of introduction frame these extracts from the *Account,* which amount to about 40 percent of Marvell's work.

1776 = included in the great three-volume "Thompson" edition of Marvell's collected works, in very large quarto: *The Works of Andrew Marvell, Esq. Poetical, Controversial, and Political, Containing Many Original Letters, Poems, and Tracts, never before printed. With a New Life of the Author, By Capt. Edward Thompson.* Epigraph from Thomson's *Liberty,* "By these three Virtues be the Frame sustain'd, / Of British Freedom . . . [etc.]" Printed for the editor, by Henry Baldwin, and sold by Dodsley [et al.: thirteen more booksellers named]. Vol. I, pp. 439–648: "An Account of the Growth of Popery and Arbitrary Government in England. More particularly from the long Prorogation of November, 1675, ending the 15th of February 1676, till the last Meeting of Parliament the 16th of July 1677. By ANDREW MARVELL. Printed at Amsterdam in the Year M.DC.LXXVII."

1872–75 = *The Complete Works in Verse and Prose of Andrew Marvell . . .* Ed. Alexander B. Grosart. 4 vols. London: Robson, 1872–75. Volume 4, pp. 245–414. Appends a much abbreviated *List of Several Ships . . .* 4: 415–24. Grosart's four volumes are also available in photoreprint (New York: AMS Press, 1966).

1971 = facsimile of *77a*, ed. Gamini Salgado, with four-page introduction (does not specify the original copy from which this facsimile was made). Farnsborough, U.K.: Gregg International Publishers Limited, 1971.

CONVENTIONS

In keeping with the norms of the present edition, there has been considerable modernizing of this text from that of the first edition on the authority of the second edition, *77b*, which has been used for copy-text. Variations have been noted from *77a*; these are only at the level of word and a few phrases. For present purposes the text has, where more plausible, adopted other readings from *77a*, and in a few instances from *79*; in these cases the readings from *77b* are noted. Some of the variations in font of *77a* and *77b* have been omitted; in particular, italicization has not been kept for the distinction of personal or place names, for nationalities, for days and months, or for initial letters of nouns (where this intermittent usage in *77a* notably increases in *77b*). Modern usage governs the regularization of spellings involving u/v, i/j, and the expansion of æ and &. There is much silent correction of typographical errors and transpositions—some u/n and e/c confusions, and also mistakings of e/o, e/s, t/r, t/c, a/n, n/m, and foul case—and also of some awkward omissions or alterations in *77b* of more intelligent punctuation from *77a*, and upper for lower case. There are losses as well as gains from using *77b*, the chief loss being the more deliberate effect of the heavier punctuation in the first edition. But the punctuation in *77a* is so heavy and sometimes placed in ways so unlike Marvell's practice elsewhere, especially in his state papers 1657–59, that it is worth abandoning for present purposes. There are also abbreviations in the second edition that seem driven by convenience in typesetting: here I have kept with *77a*. Likewise, where extra paragraphing is introduced late in *77b* in order to fill out the final sheet, I have instead followed the example of *77a*. Pagination of *77a* is marked at the end of each page in {braces}; pagination of *77b* likewise in [square brackets].

I am very grateful to my research assistant Angela Woollam for her intelligent and patient help and am glad to acknowledge our support by the University of Ottawa Research Fund. My warm thanks also to Edward Holberton for sharing with me his mapping of watermarks in the *Account;* to Blair Worden, Mark Knights, and Hilton Kelliher for their timely and generous assistance; and to my fellow editors for their advice and encouragement.

An Account of the

GROWTH

OF

POPERY

AND

Arbitrary Government

IN

ENGLAND.

More Particularly, from the Long *Prorogation* of
November, 1675. Ending the 15*th*. of *February*,
1676, till the last Meeting of *Parliament*, the 16
of *July* 1677.

AMSTERDAM, Printed in the Year, 1677.

An Account of the

GROWTH

OF

POPERY

AND

Arbitrary Government

IN

ENGLAND.

More Particularly, from the Long *Prorogation* of *November*, 1675. Ending the 15th. of *February*, 1676, till the laſt Meeting of *Parliament*, the 16 of *July* 1677.

AMSTERDAM, Printed in the Year, 1677.

Fig. 2. Title page from An Account of the Growth of Popery, *edition 1677b.*

An Account of the / GROWTH / of / POPERY / and / Arbitrary Government / in / ENGLAND. / [rule] / More Particularly, from the Long *Prorogation* of / *November,* 1675. Ending the 15th. of *February,* / 1676, till the last Meeting of *Parliament,* the 16 / of *July* 1677. / [rule] / *AMSTERDAM*, Printed in the Year, 1677. [verso blank]

An account of the Growth of POPERY, and Arbitrary Government in England, &c.

There has now for divers Years, a design been carried on, to change the Lawful Government of England into an Absolute Tyranny, and to convert the established Protestant Religion into down-right Popery: than both which, nothing can be more destructive or contrary to the Interest and Happiness, to the Constitution and Being of the King and Kingdom.[1]

For if first we consider the State, the Kings of England Rule not upon the same terms with those of our neighbour Nations, who having by force or by address usurped that due share which their people had in the Government, are now for some Ages in possession of an Arbitrary Power, (which yet no prescription can make Legal) and exercise it over their persons and estates in a most Tyrannical manner. But here the Subjects retain their proportion in the Legislature; the very meanest Commoner of England is represented in *Parliament,* and is a party to those Laws by which the Prince is sworn to Govern himself and his people. {3} No money is to be levied but by the common consent. No man is for life, limb, goods, or liberty at the Soveraigns discretion: but we have the same Right (modestly understood) in our Propriety that the Prince hath in his Regality; and in all Cases where the King is concerned, we have our just remedy as against any private person of the neighbourhood, in the Courts of Westminster Hall,[2] or in the High Court of *Parliament.* His very Prerogative is no more then what the Law has determined. His Broad Seal,[3] which is the Legitimate stamp of his pleasure, yet is no longer currant, than upon the Tryal it is found to be

---

[1] The censorious Roger L'Estrange found this introduction too much like the Grand Remonstrance (Dec. 15, 1641) in thus beginning "with a General Charge upon Ill Ministers," and he resented its claims about the coordination of the estates. *Account of the Growth of Knavery* (London, 1678), pp. 10–11, 44, 46; also *The Observator,* vol. I, no. 188, August 14, 1682.

[2] Courts of Westminster Hall: where sit the courts of Common Pleas, King's Bench, Chancery, and Exchequer.

[3] Broad Seal: the Great Seal used by English monarchs since the eleventh century.

Legal. He cannot commit any person by his particular warrant. He cannot himself be witness in any cause: the Ballance of publick Justice being so delicate, that not the hand only but even the breath of the [3] Prince would turn the scale. Nothing is left to the Kings will, but all is subjected to his Authority: by which means it follows that he can do no wrong, nor can he receive wrong,[4] and a King of England, keeping to these measures, may without arrogance be said to remain the only Intelligent Ruler over a Rational People. In recompence therefore and acknowledgment of so good a Government under his influence, his Person is most sacred and inviolable; and whatsoever excesses are committed against so high a trust, nothing of them is imputed to him, as being free from the necessity or temptation, but his Ministers only are accountable for all and must answer it at their perills. He hath a vast Revenue constantly arising from the Hearth of the Housholder, the Sweat of the Labourer,[5] the Rent of the Farmer, the Industry of the Merchant, and consequently out of the estate of the Gentleman: a large competence to defray the ordinary expense of the Crown, and maintain its lustre. And if any extraordinary occasion happen, or be but with any probable decency pretended, the whole Land at whatsoever season of the year does yield him a plentiful Harvest. So forward are his Peoples affections to give even {4} to superfluity, that a Forainer (or English man that hath been long abroad) would think they could neither will nor chuse, but that the asking of a supply, were a meer formality, it is so readily granted. He is the Fountain of all Honours,[6] and has moreover the distribution of so many profitable Offices of the Houshold, of the Revenue, of State, of Law, of religion, of the Navy (and since his present Majesties time, of the Army) that it seems as if the Nation could scarce furnish honest men enow[7] to supply all those imployments. So that the Kings of England are in nothing inferiour to other Princes, save in being more abridged[8] from injuring their

[4] That the king "cannot err" was a common maxim, but L'Estrange bridled at this last constitutional formula limiting monarchy, *Account of the Growth of Knavery*, 42–3.

[5] Laboures *77a*] Labourers *77b*] The more plausible "Labourer" appears in the version of this passage in Thomas Hollis's edition of Algernon Sidney, *Discourses Concerning Government* (London, 1763), "Apology" p. 197n.

[6] Fountain of all Honours: common epithet, e.g., Francis Bacon, *An Essay of a King* (London, 1642), p. 3, or Edmund Hickeringill, *Gregory Father-Greybeard* (London, 1673), p. 172.

[7] enow: enough. A characteristic Marvellian irony at the expense of contemporary corruptions.

[8] abridged: restrained.

own subjects: But have as large a field as any of external felicity, wherein to exercise their own Virtue and so reward and incourage it in others. In short, there is nothing that comes nearer in Government to the Divine Perfection, then where the Monarch, as with us, [4] enjoys a capacity of doing all the good imaginable to mankind, under a disability to all that is evil.

And as we are thus happy in the Constitution of our State so are we yet more blessed in that of our Church; being free from the *Romish Yoak,*[9] which so great a part of Christendom do yet draw and labour under, That *Popery* is such a thing as cannot, but for want of a word to express it, be called a *Religion,* nor is it to be mentioned with that civility which is otherwise decent to be used, in speaking of the differences of *Human Opinion* about *Divine Matters.* Were it either open *Judaism,* or plain *Turkery,*[10] or honest *Paganism,* there is yet a certain *Bona fides*[11] in the most extravagant Belief, and the sincerity of an erroneous Profession may render it more pardonable; but this is a compound of all the three, an extract of whatsoever is most ridiculous and impious in them, incorporated with more peculiar absurdities of its own, in which those were deficient; and all this deliberately contrived, knowingly carried on by the bold imposture of *Priests* under the name of *Christianity.* The wisdom of this fifth *Religion,*[12] this last and insolentest attempt {5} upon the credulity of Mankind seems to me (though not ignorant otherwise of the times, degrees and methods of its progresse)[13] principally to have consisted in their owning the *Scriptures* to be *The Word of God,* and the *Rule of Faith* and *Manners,* but in prohibiting at the same time their common use, or the reading of them in *publick Churches* but in a *Latin Translation* to the vulgar:[14] there being no better or more rational way to frustrate the very design of the great *Institutor* of *Christianity,*

---

[9] *Romish Yoak:* Complaints against "the Romish yoke" were commonplace in attacks on Catholicism, e.g., Isaac Penington, *Some Considerations proposed to this distracted Nation of England* (London, 1659).

[10] *Turkery:* Islam. During the Turkish siege of Vienna a few years later, when Christianity itself seemed under threat, L'Estrange was quick to recall Marvell's discreditable preference for Jews, pagans, or Turks to Roman Catholics, *The Observator,* vol. 1, nos. 189, 204, 399 (Aug. 15, Sept. 1682; Sept. 6, 1683).

[11] *Bona fides:* good faith.

[12] fifth *Religion:* after paganism, Judaism, Christianity, and Islam (e.g. "Turk-Christian-Pagan-Jew," in "The Character of Holland," l. 70).

[13] This may point back to Marvell's research for the *Short Historical Essay.*

[14] to the vulgar: to an unlearned audience.

who first planted it by the extraordinary Gift of *Tongues*,[15] then to forbid the use even of the ordinary Languages. For having thus a book which is universally avowed to be of Divine Authority, but sequestring it only into such hands as were intrusted in the cheat,[16] they had the opportunity to vitiate, suppress or interpret to their own profit those *Records* by which the poor People hold their Salvation. And this necessary point being once gained, there was thence [5] forward nothing so monstrous to reason, so abhorring from *Morality,* or so contrary to *Scripture* which they might not in prudence adventure on. The Idolatry (for alas it is neither better nor worse) of adoring and praying to Saints and Angels, of worshipping Pictures, Images and Reliques, Incredible Miracles and palpable Fables to promote that veneration. The whole Liturgy and Worship of the Blessed Virgin. The saying of *Pater Nosters* and Creeds, to the honour of Saints, and of *Ave Mary's* too, not to her honour, but of others.[17] The Publick Service, which they can spare to God among so many competitors, in an unknown tongue; and intangled with such Vestments, Consecrations, Exorcismes, Whisperings, Sprinklings, Censings, and Phantastical Rites, Gesticulations, and Removals, so unbeseeming a Christian Office, that it represents rather the pranks and ceremonies of Juglers and Conjurers. The refusal of the Cup to the Laity.[18] The necessity of the Priests intention to make any of their Sacraments effectual. Debarring their Clergy from marriage. Interdicting of {6} meats.[19] Auricular Confession and Absolution,[20] as with

[15] *Institutor* of *Christianity . . . Tongues:* the Holy Spirit gave Jesus' disciples the gift of tongues at Pentecost (Acts 2:1–21).

[16] cheat: a robbery or fraud, also recalling the legal term *escheat* for property that falls to the lord of the fee by way of forfeit ("Upon Appleton House," l. 274).

[17] Catholics are charged with idolatry for using formal prayers—specifically the Lord's Prayer, the Confession of Faith, and the Hail Mary—to venerate saints.

[18] This list, from the "Publick Service," specifies ceremonial and doctrinal aspects of the Catholic mass: "Whisperings" refers to priestly prayers recited by the celebrant alone in the name of the whole assembly; "Sprinklings" to blessings made through the casting about of holy water; "Censings" to the burning of incense; "The Refusal of the Cup to the laity" to the practice of receiving the Eucharist through consuming the consecrated bread only, and not the wine (since Christ might be wholly present under either species).

[19] Interdicting of meats: days of abstention from meat in commemoration of the Passion of Christ.

[20] Auricular Confession: voicing one's confession in the presence of a priest. "Auricular . . . Absolution": the verbal absolution of the priest who administers the sacrament in the name of Christ and the Church.

them practised, Penances, Pilgrimages, Purgatory, and Prayer for the dead. But above all their other devices, that Transubstantiall solacisme,[21] whereby that glorifyed Body, which at the same time they allow to be in Heaven, is sold again and crucified dayly upon all the Altars of their Communion. For God indeed may now and then do a miracle, but a Romish Priest can, it seems, work in one moment a thousand Impossibilities. Thus by a new and antiscriptural Belief, compiled of Terrours to the Phancy, Contradictions to Sense, and Impositions on the Understanding their Laity have turned Tenants for their Souls, and in consequence Tributary[22] for their Estates to a more then omnipotent Priesthood.

I must indeed do them that right to avow that, out of an equitable consideration and recompense of so faithful a slavery, they have discharged the People from all other services and dependance, infranchised[23] them from all duty to [6] *God* or *Man;* insomuch that their severer and more learned *Divines,* their *Governours* of *Conscience,* have so well instructed them in all the arts of *Circumventing* their *Neighbour,* and of colluding with Heaven, that, were the Scholars as apt as their Teachers, there would have been long since an end of all either true Piety or common Honesty; and nothing left among them but authorized *Hypocrisie, Licentiousness* and *Knavery;* had not the natural worth of the better sort, and the good Simplicity of the meaner, in great measure preserved them. For nothing indeed but an extraordinary temper and ingenuity of spirit, and that too assisted by a diviner influence, could possibly restrain those within any the terms[24] or Laws of *Humanity,* who at the same time own the Doctrine of their *Casuists*[25] or the *Authority* of the *Pope,* as it is by him claimed and exercised. He by his *Indulgences*[26] delivers souls out of the pains of the other world: So that who would refuse to be vicious here, upon so good {7} security. He by his *Dispensation* annuls *Contracts* betwixt man and man, dissolves Oaths between *Princes,* or betwixt them and their People, and gives allowance in

---

[21] Transubstantion solacism *77b*] Transubstantiall solacisme *77a*] disparaging the Roman Catholic belief that in the Eucharist the bread and wine are transformed into the actual body and blood of Christ.

[22] Tributary: providing subsidiary supplies or aid.

[23] infranchised: set free.

[24] terms: bounds.

[25] *Casuists:* those who resolve cases of conscience or doubtful questions regarding duty or conduct; often used pejoratively.

[26] *Indulgences:* privileges granted by the Roman Catholic Church to remit punishment due to forgiven sin, abuses of which had given impetus to the Reformation.

cases which God and nature prohibites. He, as Clerk of the spiritual *Market,* hath set a rate upon all crimes: the more flagitious[27] they are and abominable, the better *Commodities,* and men pay only a higher price as for greater rarities. So that it seems as if the commands of God had been invented meerly to erect an Office for the *Pope;* the worse *Christians* men are, the better *Customers,* and this Rome does by the same policy people its Church, as the Pagan Rome did the City, by opening a *Sanctuary* to all Malefactors. And why not, if his power be indeed of such vertue and extent as is by him challenged? That he is the *Ruler* over Angels, Purgatory and Hell.[28] That his Tribunal and Gods are all one. That all that God, he can do, *clave non errante,*[29] and what he does is as God and not as man. That he is the Universal Head of the *Church,* The sole *Interpreter* of *Scripture,* and *Judge* of *Controversy.* That he is above *General Councils.* That his *Power* is absolute, and his *Decrees* infallible. [7] That he can change the very nature of things, making what is *Just* to be *Unjust,* and what is *Vice* to be *Vertue.* That all Laws are in the Cabinet of his Breast. That he can dispense with the new Testament to the great injury of the Divels.[30] That he is Monarch[31] of this *World* and that he can dispose of *Kingdoms* and *Empires* as he pleases. Which things being granted, that stile[32] of *Optimum, Maximum & su-*

---

[27] flagitious: extremely wicked, villainous.

[28] In this and the following "That . . . " clauses, Marvell seems to work through claims for the papacy promulgated by the Council of Trent (this first the decree concerning purgatory, from the twenty-fifth session, Dec. 4, 1563) and more generally the canon law.

[29] *clave non errante* (as per *77a* errata, correcting *errant* in the text; miscorrected to *claves non errant* in *77b*): Marvell turns against infallibility ("the key not erring") the canon law claim that "the key not turn the wrong way." The key symbolizes ecclesiastical authority, held by Roman Catholics to have been conferred on St. Peter by Christ (Matt. 16:19) and transmitted to the popes as his successors.

[30] to the great injury of the Divels *77a, 1689a, 1776*]. This phrase is crossed out in some copies of *77a* (Bodleian, G. Pamph. 1359 (22); Newberry Library, Case J 5454.55; Kingston upon Hull Local Studies Library: Marvell Collection) and is omitted in *77b, 79, 89, 93,* perhaps as too horrible (also suggested by the extra scoring out of "Divels" in the Newberry copy), or too puzzling. Compare Milton's *Treatise of Civil Power:* "The papist exacts our beleef as to the church due above scripture" (*CPW* 7:254); Marvell's additional charge is that the papacy presumes its own ecclesiastical authority of greater effect than that of the gospel and not just than that of the Old Testament as per canon law.

[31] still Monarch *77a,* corrected in errata]; this common Protestant complaint had recently been voiced anew by Milton in *Of True Religion* (*CPW* 8:429).

[32] stile: an introductory formula (last *OED* 1648–49), or title, ceremonial designation.

premum numen in terris,[33] or that of *Dominus, Deus noster, Papa,*[34] was no such extraordinary stroke of *Courtship,*[35] as we reckoned: but it was rather a great clownishness in him that treated so mighty a *Prince* under the simple Title of *Vice Deus.*[36] The exercise of his Dominion is in all points suitable to this his pretence. He antiquates[37] the precepts of Christ as things only of good advice, not commanded; but makes it a mortal sin even to doubt of any part of his own *Religion,* {8} and demands under pain of damnation the subjection of all *Christians* to his *Papal Authority:* the denying of two things so reasonable as blind Obedience to this power, and an Implicite Faith to his Doctrine, being the most unpardonable crime, under his *Dispensation.* He has indeed of late been somewhat more retentive than formerly as to his faculty of *Disposing of Kingdoms,* the thing not having succeded well with him in some Instances, but he lays the same claim still, continues the same inclination, and though velvet headed[38] hath the more itch to be pushing. And however in order to any occasion he keeps himself in breath always by cursing one Prince or other upon every Maunday Thursday.[39] Nor is their any, whether Prince or Nation, that dissents from his Usurpations, but are marked out under the notion of *Hereticks* to ruine and destruction whensoever he shall give the signal.[40] That word of *Heresy* misapplyed, hath served him for so many Ages to Justifie all the Executions, Assassinations, Wars, Massacres, and Devastations, whereby his Faith hath been propagated; of which our times also have not wanted Examples, and more is to be expected for the future. For by how much any thing is more false and unreasonable, it requires more cruelty to establish it: and to intro-[8]duce that which is absurd, there must be somewhat done that is barbarous. But nothing of any sect in Religion can be more recommended by all these

---

[33] *Optimum, Maximum & supremum numen in terris:* best, greatest, and highest deity on earth.

[34] *Dominus, Deus noster, Papa:* Lord, our God, Pope.

[35] Courtship: courtesy to a dignitary, flattery.

[36] *Vice Deus:* in the place of God, with wordplay likely on "vice."

[37] antiquates: makes obsolete.

[38] velvet headed: refers to the head of a deer while the horns are still covered with velvet, often applied contemptuously to a person. The specific reference here is to the red velvet *camauro,* the ermine-trimmed cap reserved to the pope in place of the *biretta.*

[39] Maundy Thursday: the Thursday before Easter (mistaken for "tout les Lundys & les Mardys" in translation of *1680,* p. 12).

[40] Against the abuse of the term *heresy* see also the *Essay,* pp. 127–28 above, and Milton's *Treatise of Civil Power* and *Of True Religion* (CPW 7:247–54, 8:421–23).

qualities than the *Papacy*. The *Pagans* are excusable by their natural dark-
ness, without Revelation. The *Jews* are tolerable, who see not beyond the
Old *Testament*. Mahomet was so honest as to own what he would be at, that
he himself was the greatest Prophet, and that his was a Religion of the
Sword.[41] So that these were all, as I may say, of another Allegiance and if
Enemies, yet not Traitors: But the Pope avowing Christianity by profession
doth in Doctrine and Practise renounce it: And presuming to be the only
Catholick,[42] does persecute those to {9} the death, who dare worship the
Author of their Religion instead of his pretended Vice-gerent.[43]

And yet there is nothing more evident, notwithstanding his most notorious forgeries and falsification of all Writers, then that the Pope was for
several Hundred of Years an honest Bishop as other men are, and never so
much as dreamed upon the Seven Hills[44] of that universal power which he
is now come to, nay was the first that opposed any such pretension. But
some of them at last, growing wiser, by foisting a counterfeit Donation of
Constantine,[45] and wresting another Donation from our Saviour, advanced
themselves in a weak, ignorant, and credulous Age, to that Temporal and
Spiritual Principality that they are now seised of. *Tu es Petrus, & super hanc
Petram, aedificabo Ecclesiam meam.*[46] Never was a Bishoprick and a Verse of
Scripture so improved by good management. Thus, by exercising in the
quality of Christs Vicar the publick function under an invisible Prince, the
Pope, like the Mairs of the Palace,[47] hath set his Master aside and delivered
the Government over to a new Line of Papal Succession. But who can,

[41] Mahomet . . . Religion of the Sword: the prophet of Islam, Muhammad, and the
Jihad, as found in the "sword verses" of the Koran and in the *hadith*.

[42] only *Catholick*: "catholic" meaning "universal" or "general." The contradiction in
terms satirized in "only Catholick" had long amused Marvell, as in "The Character of
Holland," ll. 75–76.

[43] Vice-gerent: appointed by a ruler to act in his place; a title often applied to kings
and magistrates as representatives of God.

[44] Seven Hills: on which Rome is set.

[45] Donation of Constantine: an eighth-century document claimed to be the record of
the Roman emperor Constantine's (d. 337) conversion to and profession of his Christian
faith, and of the wide privileges he conferred on the papacy; the forgery was proven in
the fifteenth century.

[46] Matt. 16:18, "Thou art Peter, and upon this rock I will build my church."

[47] Mairs of the Palace: French *maire du palais*, from medieval Latin *major domus* or
maior palatii, the title borne by the prime ministers of the Frankish kingdoms.

unless wilfully, be ignorant what wretched doings, what Bribery, what Ambition there are, how long the Church is without an Head upon every Vacancy, till among the crew of bandying[48] Cardinals the Holy Ghost have declared for a Pope of the French or Spanish Fa-[9]ction.[49] It is a succession like that of the Egyptian Ox[50] (the living Idol of that Country) who dying or being made away by the Priests, there was solemn and general mourning for want of a Deity; until in their Conclave they had found out another Beast with the very same marks as the former, whom then they themselves adored and with great Jubilee brought forth to the People to worship. Nor was that Election a grosser reproach to human Reason than this is also to Christianity. Surely it is the greatest Miracle of the Romish Church that it should still continue, and that in all this time the Gates of Heaven should not prevail against it. {10}

It is almost unconceivable how Princes can yet suffer a Power so pernicious, and Doctrine so destructive to all Government. That so great a part of the Land should be alienated and condemned to, as they call it, Pious Uses. That such millions of their People as the Clergy, should, by remaining unmarried, either frustrate human Nature if they live chastly, or, if otherwise, adulterate it. That they should be privileged from all labour, all publick Service, and exempt from the power of all Secular Jurisdiction. That they, being all bound, by strict Oaths and Vows of Obedience to the *Pope*, should evacuate the Fealty[51] due to the Soveraign. Nay, that not only the Clergy but their whole People, if of the Romish perswasion, should be obliged to rebel at any time upon the *Popes* pleasure.[52] And yet how many of the Neighbouring Princes are content, or do chuse to reign, upon those Conditions; which being so dishonourable and dangerous, surely some great and more weighty reason does cause them submit to. Whether it be out of personal fear, having heard perhaps of several attempts which the

[48] bandying: a tennis-like hitting back and forth, or contention.

[49] Faction: perhaps recalling the long contest issuing in the election of Clement X (1670) and his uneasy papacy, or the more recent reluctance of the French to support the election of Innocent XI (1676).

[50] *Egyptian* Ox: the ox-god Apis, recalling also the golden calf of Aaron's making (Exodus 32), sign of the Israelites' apostasy.

[51] evacuate the Fealty: annul the feudal obligation to a lord.

[52] Here L'Estrange ends the extended extract from the *Account* with which he concludes his *Account of the Growth of Knavery*, pp. 65–72, aiming to misrepresent Marvell's work as mere witty excess.

blind Obedience of *Popish Zealots* hath executed against their Princes. Or, whether aiming at a more absolute and tyrannical Government, they think it still to be the case of Boniface and Phocas[53] (an usurping Emperor and an usurping Bishop) and that, as other cheats, this also is best to be managed by Confederacy. But, as far as I can apprehend, there is [10] more of Sloth then Policy on the Princes side in this whole matter: and all that pretense of inslaving men by the assistance of Religion more easily, is neither more nor less than when the *Bramine,* by having the first night of the Bride assures himself of her devotion for the future, and makes her more fit for the husband.[54]

This reflection upon the state of our Neighbours, in aspect to Religion, doth sufficiently illustrate our happiness, and spare me the labour of describing it further, then by the Rule of Contraries: Our Church standing upon all points {11} in a direct opposition to all the forementioned errours. Our Doctrine being true to the Principles of the first Christian Institution, and Episcopacy being formed upon the primitive Model,[55] and no Ecclesiastical Power jostling the Civil, but all concurring in common Obedience

[53] Phocas (ca. 547–610), tyrannical Byzantine emperor (602–10); Boniface III, pope from February 19 to November 12, 607. Phocas addressed an edict to Boniface III in which he recognized the Church of Rome as the head of all Churches, and thus contested the title "ecumenical patriarch" that had recently been assumed by the patriarch of Constantinople.

[54] *Bramine . . .* husband: the 1689 extract from the *Account,* styled *Mr. Andrew Marvell's Character of Popery* (London: for Richard Baldwin), ends with this as its parting shot (p. 8). A concern regarding contamination from hymeneal blood might recommend the Hindu priest in this role, qv. Jan Huygen van Linschoten, . . . *his Discours of Voyages into the Easte and West Indies* (London, 1598) p. 64, cf. 29, 70, 79, and Thomas Herbert, *Some Years Travels into Divers Parts of Africa, and Asia the Great,* 4th ed. (London, 1677), p. 337; compare Henry Neville, *The Isle of Pines* (London, 1668), pp. 27–28. Marvell may here recall also the more familiar slur against "those unchristian Bramins, the Cardinal Confessors," when Catholics "jeer one another, that their Children are *Fils de Prestre*" (William Lawrence, *Marriage by the Morall Law of God Vindicated* (1680), p. 53); he himself was a minister's son and may even while in Italy have astonished the clergy there by professing himself "the sonne of a Priest in England," John Raymond, *An Itinerary Contayning a Voyage Made through Italy, In the yeare 1646, and 1647* (London, 1648), Introduction, p. [3].

[55] Episcopacy . . . primitive Model: the system of church government by bishops was commonly related to the apostolate instituted by Christ, but the claim here may be more prescriptive than normative.

to the Soveraign.[56] Nor therefore is there any, whether Prince or Nation, that can with less probability be reduced back to the *Romish* perswasion, than ours of England.

For, if first we respect our Obedience to God, what appearance is there that, after so durable and general an enlightning of our minds with the sacred Truth, we should again put out our own Eyes, to wander thorow the palpable darkness[57] of that gross Superstition? But forasmuch as most men are less concerned for their Interest in Heaven than on Earth, this seeming the nearer and more certain, on this account also our alteration from the *Protestant Religion* is the more impossible. When beside the common ill Examples and consequences of *Popery* observable abroad, whereby we might grow wise at the expence of our Neighbours, we cannot but reflect upon our own Experiments at home, which would make even fools docible.[58] The whole Reign of Queen Mary, in which the *Papists* made Fewel[59] of the *Protestants*. The Excommunicating and Deprivation of Queen Elizabeth by the *Pope*, pursued with so many *Treasons* and attempts upon her Person, by her own Subjects, and the Invasion in *Eighty Eight* by the Spanish.[60] The two *Breves*[61] of the *Pope*, in [11] order to exclude King James from the Succession to the Crown, seconded by the *Gunpowder Treason*.[62] In the time of his late Majesty, King Charles the first, (besides what they contributed to the Civil War in England) the Rebellion and horrid Massacre in Ireland, and, which was even worse than that, their pretending that it was done by the Kings Commission,[63] and vouching the *Broad Seal* for

[56] Soveraign: this appears an ironic as well as a strongly Erastian claim, until a less secular reading is suggested by the first sentence of the next paragraph, where the phrase is recalled in "Obedience to God."

[57] thorow the palpable darkness: through the "thick darkness," recalling Exodus 10:22.

[58] docible: teachable.

[59] Queen Mary . . . Fewel: the Catholic Mary Tudor (1516–58), queen of England 1553–58, in whose reign Protestants were burned for heresy.

[60] Queen Elizabeth by the *Pope* . . . Subjects . . . *Spanish:* the excommunication of Elizabeth by Pope Pius V was proclaimed in his bull *Regnans in Excelsis* (1570); the treasons were especially those of the Northern Rising (1569–70), in which the Catholic earls of Northumberland and Westmorland rebelled; in 1588, Philip II of Spain sent the Armada in an unsuccessful attempt to invade England.

[61] *Breves:* letters of authority.

[62] *Gunpowder Treason:* the Catholic plot to blow up the Houses of Parliament on November 5, 1605, when the king, Lords and Commons were there assembled.

[63] *77a*] Kings Commishon *77b*]: Charles I's order or command.

their Authority. The *Popes Nuncio*[64] assuming nevertheless and exercising there the Temporal as well as Spiritual Pow-{12}er, granting out Commissions[65] under his own Hand, breaking the Treaties of Peace between the King, and, as they then styled themselves, the *Confederate Catholicks;* heading two Armies against the Marquess of Ormond, then Lord Lieutenant, and forcing him at last to quit the Kingdom: all which ended in the ruine of His Majesties Reputation, Government and Person; which but upon occasion of that Rebellion, could never have happened.[66] So that we may reckon the Reigns of our late Princes, by a succession of the *Popish Treasons* against them. And, if under his present Majesty we have as yet seen no more visible effects of the same spirit than the *Firing* of London (acted by Hubert, hired by Pieddelou two French men) which remains a Controversie,[67] it is not to be attributed to the good nature or better Principles of that Sect, but to the wisdom of his *Holyness;*[68] who observes that we are not of late so dangerous *Protestants* as to deserve any special mark of his Indignation, but that we may be made better use of to the weakning of those that are of our own Religion, and that if he do not disturb us, there are those among our selves, that are leading us into a fair way of Reconciliation with him.

But those continued fresh Instances, in relation to the Crown, together

[64] *Nuncio:* an official representative of the Roman Catholic Church at a foreign court.

[65] granting out Commissions: granting warrants conferring authority.

[66] In the course of the Irish Rebellion (1641–53), James Butler, twelfth earl and first duke of Ormonde, negotiated a truce between the English and the Catholic Confederates in September 1643, a peace that lasted until the nuncio Giovanni Rinuccini arrived in Ireland in 1645, insisting on full recognition of the Catholic faith and further compromises from Charles I, whose ties with the Confederates then helped seal his fate.

[67] *Firing* of London . . . Controversie: The Great Fire of London ravaged the city on September 2–6, 1666; investigation of the disaster yielded a confession from Robert Hubert, a French watchmaker, that he had started the fire in a French plot led by Stephen Pedilow (also Peidloe), for which Hubert was executed. The controversy followed from his then recanting his mad claim and his proving to have arrived in England from Sweden two days after the fire began (*Londons Flames* [London, 1667], pp. [2–3], 8–9; *The Diary of Samuel Pepys,* ed. R. C. Latham and W. Matthews [London, 1970–93], 8:81n). Marvell was on the committee of inquiry into the fire: *Londons Flames,* p. 7, republished by William Bedloe in *A Narrative and Impartial Discovery of the Horrid Popish Plot: Carried on for the Burning and Destroying the Cities of London and Westminster* (London, 1679), pp. 4, 8; qv. Nigel Smith and Maureen Bell, "Andrew Marvell and the 'femina periculosa,'" *Times Literary Supplement* 5104 (Jan. 26, 2001), pp. 14–15.

[68] Sect . . . his *Holyness:* Catholics and the pope.

with the *Popes* claim of the Temporal and immediate Dominion of the Kingdoms of England and Ireland, which he does so challenge, are a sufficient caution to the *Kings* of England, and of the People, there is as little hopes to seduce them, the *Protestant Religion* being so interwoven [12] as it is with their secular Interest. For the Lands that were formerly given to superstitious uses, having first been applyed to the Publick Revenue, and afterward by severall Alienations and Contracts distributed into private possession, the alteration of Religion would necessarily introduce a change of Property.[69] *Nullum tempus occurrit Ecclesiae*,[70] it would make a general Earth-quake over the Nation, and even now the *Romish* Clergy on the other side of the {13} water, snuffe up the savoury odour[71] of so many rich *Abbies* and *Monasteries* that belonged to their Predecessors. Hereby no considerable Estate in England but must have a piece torn out of it upon the Title of Piety, and the rest subject to be wholly forfeited upon the account of *Heresy*. Another *Chimny mony*[72] of the old *Peter pence*[73] must again be payed, as tribute to the Pope, beside that which is established on his Majesty: and the People, instead of those moderate Tithes[74] that are with too much difficulty payed to their Protestant Pastors, will be exposed to all the exactions of the Court of Rome, and a thousand artifices by which in former times they were used to draine away the wealth of ours more then any other Nation. So that in conclusion, there is no Englishman that hath a Soul, a Body, or an Estate to save, that Loves either God, his King, or his Country, but is by all those Tenures bound, to the best of his Power and Knowledge, to maintain the established *Protestant Religion*.

And yet, all this notwithstanding, there are those men among us, who

[69] a change of Property: There was lasting concern in England that lands confiscated from the Roman church at the Reformation (which claim of sacrilege Marvell mocks in "Upon Appleton House," ll. 85–280) might need to be restored upon any future return to that religion.

[70] *Nullum tempus occurrit Ecclesiae:* "time does not bar the church's right"; i.e., there is no statute of limitations.

[71] Cf. Milton, *Paradise Lost* 10.268–73, "taste / The savour of death . . . / . . . with delight he snuffed the smell of mortal change on earth."

[72] *Chimny mony:* the Hearth Tax of two shillings a year on every fire-hearth in England and Wales, imposed in 1662, which "taxing our smoke" occasioned long resentments ("A Dialogue Between Two Horses," l. 88, *POAS* 1:279).

[73] the old *Peter pence:* annual tax of a penny on householders, paid to the see at Rome; it was discontinued in England in 1534.

[74] Tithes: taxes of "tenth" portions for the church.

have undertaken, and do make it their business, under so Legal and perfect a Government, to introduce a French slavery, and instead of so pure a Religion, to establish the Roman Idolatry: both and either of which are Crimes of the highest nature.[75] For, as to matter of Government, if to murther the King be, as certainly it is, a Fact so horrid, how much more hainous is it to assassinate the Kingdom? And as none will deny, that to alter our *Monarchy* into a *Common wealth* were *Treason,* so by the same Fundamental Rule, the Crime is no less to make that *Monarchy Absolute.* [13]

What is thus true in regard of the State, holds as well in reference to our Religion. Former Parliaments have made it Treason in whosoever shall attempt to seduce any one, the meanest of the Kings subjects, to the Church of Rome: And this Parliament hath, to all penalties by the Common or Statute Law, added incapacity for any man who shall pre-{14}sume to say that the King is a Papist or an Introducer of Popery. But what lawless and incapable miscreants[76] then, what wicked Traytors are those wretched men, who endeavour to pervert our whole Church, and to bring that about in effect, which even to mention is penal, at one Italian stroke attempting to subvert the Government and Religion, to kill[77] the Body and damn the Soul of our Nation.

Yet were these men honest old Cavaliers[78] that had suffered in his late Majesties service, it were allowable in them, as oft as their wounds brake out at Spring or Fall, to think of a more Arbitrary Government, as a soveraign Balsom for their Aches, or to imagine that no Weapon-salve[79]

---

[75] This first sentence after the introductory "character of popery" marks a departure in which hostility against the French soon overtakes that against Rome. L'Estrange views the shift with particular suspicion, *Account of the Growth of Knavery,* p. 45.

[76] miscreants: villains (perhaps with some of its original meaning of heretic or unbeliever).

[77] *77a*] kil *77b*].

[78] Cavaliers: those who fought for Charles I in the civil wars of the 1640s. However ironic, this moderates the Shaftesburian line against "the Old Cavalier" in *A Letter from a Person of Quality* (London, 1675), p. 1; Marvell had been more openly cynical about the courting of "the whole old Cavalier Party" in earlier correspondence with William Popple, July 24, 1675 (*P & L,* 2:341).

[79] Weapon-salve: ointment believed to heal through sympathetic agency when applied to the weapon that had caused the injury; compare Milton's letter to Emeric Bigot, March 24, 1656/7, *Joannis Miltoni Angli, Epistolarum Familiarum Liber Unus* (London, 1674), p. 50, citing "the example of King Telephus of the Mysians, who was

but of the Moss that grows on an Enemies Skul could cure them. Should they mistake this Long *Parliament*[80] also for Rebels, and that, although all Circumstances be altered, there were still the same necessity to fight it all over again in pure Loyalty, yet their Age and the Times they have lived in, might excuse them. But those worthy Gentlemen are too generous, too good Christians and Subjects, too affectionate to the good English Government, to be capable of such an Impression. Whereas these Conspirators are such as have not one drop of *Cavalier Blood,* or no *Bowels* at least of a *Cavalier* in them; but have starved them, to Revel and Surfet upon their Calamities,[81] making their Persons, and the very Cause, by pretending to it themselves, almost Ridiculous.

Or, were these *Conspirators* on the other side but avowed *Papists,* they were the more honest, the less dangerous, and the Religion were answerable for the Errours they might commit in order to promote it. Who is there but must [14] acknowledge, if he do not commend the Ingenuity[82] (or by what better Name I may call it) of Sir Thomas Strickland,[83] Lord Bellassis,[84] the late Lord Clifford[85] and others, eminent in their several

---

not unwilling to be later healed by the weapon which wounded him" (*CPW,* 7:497); and the skeptical discussion in John Hales, *Golden Remains* (London, 1673), pp. 281–91 (oo1r-pp2r).

[80] this Long *Parliament:* a common mock against the duration of the present Parliament (e.g., *The Long Parliament Dissolved,* 1676), which first sat in May 8, 1661; the term recalls its infamous counterpart of the 1640s and 1650s.

[81] to Revel and Surfet upon their Calamities: to make merry and feast gluttonously upon their afflictions. That those who had been loyal to the House of Stuart might go unrewarded in the Restoration was a frequent complaint; the *Account* displaces onto the courtiers a blame that had in the 1660s more often attached to the Presbyterians.

[82] Ingenuity: simple honesty.

[83] Sir Thomas Strickland (1621–94), another Yorkshire MP, and a moderate Cavalier, whose conversion to Rome was of uncertain date (Henning 3:504–06).

[84] Bellassis: John, Baron Belasyse (1614–89), soon to be one of the Catholic lords imprisoned in the Popish Plot. He was a Yorkshireman, Cavalier, and sometime governor of Hull (1667–72) and thus often features in Marvell's correspondence; in 1657, Marvell had celebrated in "Two Songs . . . " Belasyse's nephew's marriage to Mary, daughter of Oliver Cromwell.

[85] Lord Clifford: Thomas Clifford, Baron Clifford of Chudleigh (1630–73), a dynamic MP and servant of the Crown, with whom Marvell had once come to blows in the House (Mar. 18, 1662, Henning 2:91–94; cf. "The Last Instructions," ll. 17–18). His successes led eventually to knighthood and his promotion as lord treasurer (1672), but

stations? These, having so long appeared the most zealous Sons of our Church, yet, as soon as the late {15} Test against *Popery*[86] was inacted, took up the Cross,[87] quitted their present Imployments and all hopes of the future, rather than falsify their opinion; though otherwise men for Quality, Estate and Abilities whether in War or Peace, as capable and well deserving (without disparagement) as others that have the art to continue in Offices. And above all his Royal Highness[88] is to be admired for his unparallelled magnanimity on the same account; there being in all History perhaps no Record of any *Prince* that ever changed his Religion in his Circumstances. But these persons, that have since taken the work in hand, are such as lye under no temptation of Religion: secure men, that are above either Honour or Conscience but obliged by all the most sacred tyes of Malice and Ambition to advance the ruine of the King and Kingdom, and quallified much better than others, under the name of good Protestants, to effect it.

And because it was yet difficult to find Complices[89] enough at home, that were ripe for so black a design, but they wanted a Back for their Edge;[90] therefore they applyed themselves to France, that King[91] being indowed with all those qualityes, which in a Prince, may pass for vertues; but in any private man, would be capital;[92] and moreover so abounding in wealth that no man else could go to the price of their wickedness: To which considerations, adding that he is the Master of *Absolute Dominion*, the *Presumptive*

---

with the Test Act (see note below) he spectacularly fell from power the next year and soon died, perhaps making "himself away, after an extraordinary melancholy" (Evelyn, *Diary*, Aug. 18, 1673).

[86] Test against *Popery:* The purpose of the Test Act of 1673 was to bar Roman Catholics from holding governmental offices, sitting in parliament, or serving in the military. All men had to perform a number of tests, consisting of oaths of supremacy and allegiance, communion in the Church of England, and rejection of the doctrine of transubstantiation.

[87] took up the Cross: bore the trial for Christ's sake with patience (e.g., Matt. 10:38, 16:24).

[88] Royal Highness: James, duke of York, no longer much disguised his Catholicism by late 1672 and, after the Test Act, resigned the admiralty in 1673.

[89] Complices: accomplices.

[90] a Back for their Edge: as in a knife.

[91] that King: of France.

[92] capital: punishable by death.

Monarch of *Christendom*, the declared *Champion* of *Popery*, and the heredi-
tary, natural, inveterate *Enemy* of our *King* and *Nation* he was in all respects
the most likely (of all earthly powers) to reward and support them in a
Project every way suitable to his own Inclination and Interest.

And now, should I enter into a particular retail of all [15] former and
latter Transactions, relating to this affair, there would be sufficient for a just
Volume of History. But my intention is only to write a naked Narrative of
some the most considerable passages in the meeting of *Parliament* {16} the
15. of Feb. 1676.[93] Such as have come to my notice which may serve for
matter to some stronger Pen and to such as have more leisure and further
opportunity to discover and communicate to the Publick. This in the mean
time will by the Progress made in so few weeks, demonstrate at what rate
these men drive over the necks of King and People, of Religion and Government; and how near they are in all human Probability to arrive Triumphant at the end of their Journey. Yet, that I may not be too abrupt, and
leave the Reader wholly destitute of a thread to guide himself by thorow so
intreaguing a Labyrinth, I shall summarily as short, as so copious and
redundant a matter will admit, deduce the order of affairs both at home and
abroad, as it led into this Session.[94]

It is well known,[95] were it as well remembred, what the provocation was,
and what the success of the War begun by the English in the Year 1665.
against Holland:[96] what vast supplies were furnished by the Subject for
defraying it, and yet after all, no Fleet set out, but the Flower of all the
Royal Navy burnt or taken in Port to save charges.[97] How the French,
during that War, joyned themselves in assistance of Holland against us, and

[93] I.e., 1676/7. In the errata to the first edition, this is corrected from "1675" (uncorrected in *77b*): the error seems to have sprung from the related tracts that the printer
Darby had been publishing, which centered on the length of the prorogation of parliament since 1675. The narrative here promised will begin only on p. 294 below.

[94] Session: the period between the opening of Parliament and its prorogation.

[95] Here begins the main political narrative of the *Account,* from which lengthy extracts were republished in *The History of the Peace with France and War with Holland*
(London, 1712).

[96] against Holland: the Second Anglo-Dutch War (1665–67).

[97] Navy burnt . . . save charges: The Dutch in forcing their way to Chatham dock
(June 13, 1667) destroyed or towed away two flagships and a number of other warships.
The fleet had been in large part laid up in the spring of 1667 to economize in expecta-
tion of peace with the Dutch and French. Qv. "The Last Instructions," ll. 523–760.

yet, by the credit he had with the Queen Mother,[98] so far deluded his Majesty, that upon assurance the Dutch neither would have any Fleet out that Year, he forbore to make ready, and so incurred that notable loss, and disgrace at Chatham. How (after this fatal conclusion of all our Sea-*Champaynes*)[99] as we had been obliged to the French for that War, so we were glad to receive the Peace from his favour which was agreed at Breda betwixt England, France and Holland.[100]

His Majesty was hereby now at leisure to remark how the French had in the year 1667. taken the time of us and [16] while we were imbroiled and weakned had in violation of all the most solemn and sacred Oaths and Treaties invaded and taken a great part of the Spanish Nether-Land,[101] which had {17} always been considered as the natural Frontier of England. And hereupon he judged it necessary to interpose, before the flame that consumed his next neighbour should throw its sparkles over the water. And therefore, generously slighting all punctilioes[102] of ceremony or peeks of animosity, where the safety of his people and the repose of Christendom were concerned, he sent first into Holland, inviting them to a nearer Alliance, and to enter into such further Counsels as were most proper to quiet this publick disturbance which the French had raised. This was a work wholely of his Majesties designing and (according to that felicity which hath always attended him, when excluding the corrupt Politicks of others he hath followed the dictates of his own Royal wisdom) so well it succeeded. It is a thing scarce credible, though true, that two Treaties of such weight, intricacy, and so various aspect as that of the *Defensive League* with Holland, and the other for repressing the further progress of the French in the Spanish Nether-Land, should in five days time, in the year 1668 be concluded.[103] Such was the expedition and Secresy then used in prosecut-

[98] Queen Mother: Henrietta Maria (1609–69), youngest child of Marie de Medici and Henri IV of France, married Charles I and was mother of Charles II. Her brother became Louis XIII, her nephew Louis XIV.

[99] Sea campaigns.

[100] the Peace . . . Holland: The Treaty of Breda was signed on July 21, 1667.

[101] Spanish Nether-Land: comprising largely what is today Belgium.

[102] punctilioes: minutiae of conduct, nice points of ceremony; but also, in a sense that plays with "peeks" (picque, peak) in the next phrase, the highest point or apex.

[103] Treaties . . . in five days time . . . concluded: *Englands Appeal*, p. 7, "within five days"—the first compact made between England and the Netherlands was to defend each other from France; their second to mediate the settlement between France and Spain. These were signed at The Hague on Jan. 13/23, 1668.

ing his Majesties particular Instructions, and so easy a thing is it for Princes, when they have a mind to it, to be well served. The Swede too shortly after made the third in this concert; whether wisely judging that in the minority of their King reigning over several late acquired Dominions, it was their true interest to have an hand in all the Counsels that tended to peace and[104] undisturbed Possession, or, whether indeed those Ministers, like ours, did even then project in so glorious an Alliance to betray it afterward to their own greater advantage. From their joyning in it was called the Triple Alliance.[105] His Majesty with great sincerity continued to sollicite other Princes according to the seventh Article to come into the Guaranty of this Treaty, and delighted himself in cultiva-[17]ting by all good means what he had planted. But in a very short time these Counsels, which had taken effect with so great satisfaction to the Nation and {18} to his Majestyes eternal honour, were all changed and it seemed that Treaties, as soon as the Wax is cold, do lose their virtue.[106] The King in June 1670 went down to Dover to meet after a long absence, *Madam*,[107] his only remaining sister: where the days were the more pleasant, by how much it seldomer happens to Princes then private persons to enjoy their Relations, and when they do, yet their kind interviews are usually solemnized with some fatality and disaster, nothing of which here appeared. But upon her first return into France she was dead,[108] the Marquis of Belfons[109] was immediately sent hither, a Person, of great Honour[110] dispatched thither;[111] and before ever the inquiry and grumbling at her death could be abated, in a trice there was

[104] pease an *79*].

[105] Triple Alliance: the Anglo-Dutch alliance to which Sweden agreed conditionally in January and then fully in May 1668; the aim was to contest French ambitions, especially to the Spanish succession.

[106] virtue: force.

[107] *Madam:* Henriette-Anne, duchesse d'Orléans (1644–1670), who had in 1661 married Louis XIV's brother, Philippe, duc d'Orléans ("Monsieur"). She served as an intermediary between Charles II and Louis XIV and assisted the negotiations at Dover that led to the Secret Treaty between those kings (May 22, 1670, cf. below). She landed May 16, 1670.

[108] Henriette is thought to have died of acute peritonitis, but there were wide suspicions that Monsieur had had her poisoned.

[109] Marquess of Belfons: Bernardin Gigault, maréchal de Bellefonds, sent to Charles II in London on a mission of condolence, July 1670.

[110] Person, of great Honour: the duke of Buckingham, Charles II's representative at the funeral.

[111] hither *77b*].

an invisible League,[112] in prejudice of the Triple one, struck up with France, to all the height of dearness and affection, as if upon dissecting the Princess[113] there had some state Philtre[114] been[115] found in her bowels, or the reconciliation with France were not to be celebrated with a less sacrifice then of the Blood Royal of England: The sequel will be suitable to so ominous a beginning. But as this Treaty was a work of Darkness, and which could never yet be understood or discovered but by the effects, so before those appeared it was necessary that the Parliament should after the old wont be gulld to the giving of mony.[116] They[117] met the 24th Oct. 1670.[118] and it is not without much labor that I have been able to recover a written Copy of the Lord Bridgmans[119] speech, none being printed, but forbidden, doubtless lest so notorious a Practice as certainly was never before, tho there have indeed been many put upon the Nation, might remain publick.[120]

---

[112] an invisible League: Something like the secret Treaty of Dover, already negotiated and ratified between Charles II and Louis XIV in May, is here inferred; it required a second, less secret version in order to conceal Charles's pledge to convert to Rome and Louis's promise of French troops to quell any English reaction to that conversion. Also concealed in the more public treaty (signed Dec. 21, 1670) was the perpetual alliance agreed upon between France and England, and their joining in war against the Dutch.

[113] Princes 77b].

[114] Philtre: potion.

[115] being 77b].

[116] gulld . . . mony: duped, deceived. The king "and the Keeper [Sir Orlando Bridgeman], spoke of Nothing but to have Mony," Marvell to William Popple, Nov. 28, 1670 (P & L, 2:318).

[117] They: the House of Commons and Lords, JHC 9:158.

[118] Oct. 24, 1670 77b].

[119] Lord Bridgman: Sir Orlando Bridgeman (1606–74), the "talking fool" of the satire "Nostradamus's Prophecy" (P & L, 1:179, line 35). In 1660 he became lord chief justice of the Court of Common Pleas, and in 1667 lord keeper and hence the mouthpiece of Charles II to the parliament. He was discharged from office on Nov. 17, 1672, and replaced by Shaftesbury.

[120] forbidden . . . publick: In constituency letters Marvell had reported the speech "as well as I can remember," promising "if it be printed (there is some doubt of it) I shall send you one" (Oct. 25, 1670, LHC 126; P & L, 2:110), with Arlington's prohibition of its publication then leading to the promise that "you will nevertheless receive a written copy" (Nov. 1, 1670, P & L, 2:111). Marvell writes to Popple, "Both Speeches forbid to be printed, for the King said very little, and the Keeper, it was thought, too much in his politic simple Discourse of foreign Affairs" (Nov. 28, 1670, P & L, 2:318); the speech was seen as evidence of royal support for the Triple Alliance to a degree that led the French ambassador Colbert to request its suppression (CSPV 1669–70, p. xxvi).

Altho that honourable Person cannot be presumed to have been accessary to what was then intended, but was in due time, when the Project ripened and grew hopeful, discharged from his Office, and he, the Duke of Ormond,[121] the late Secretary Trevor,[122] with the Prince Rupert,[123] discarded together out of the Committee for the Foreign Affairs,[124] he spoke thus. {19} [18] My Lords, and you the Knights, Citizens and Burgesses[125] of the House of Commons.[126]

When the two Houses were last Adjourned, this Day, as you well know, was perfixed[127] for your Meeting again. The Proclamation since issued requiring all your attendances at the same time shewed not only his Majesties belief that his business will thrive best when the Houses are fullest, but the importance also of the Affairs for which you are so called: and important they are. You cannot be

[121] Duke of Ormond: James Butler, twelfth earl and first duke of Ormonde, had been viceroy of Ireland in the 1660s, but with Clarendon's fall he was exposed to Arlington and Buckingham's displeasure and was only made viceroy again in 1677.

[122] Secretary Trevor: Sir John Trevor (1626–72), rose to become a secretary of state (Sept. 1668) after the fall of Clarendon and became a supporter of Buckingham. Like Marvell, who may have approved Trevor's part in the "governing Cabal" of that spring of 1670 (letter to Popple Apr. 14, 1670, *P & L*, 2:317), he strongly favored the Triple Alliance and opposed the Conventicles Act; he was viewed by the duke of York as "of the republican or Cromwellian stamp" (Henning 3:603).

[123] Prince Rupert: Third son of Charles I's sister Elizabeth, queen of Bohemia, and the Elector Palatine, Prince Rupert served Charles I in the 1640s and was a prominent courtier in the Restoration. Vice-admiral and then admiral in the Second and Third Anglo-Dutch Wars, his growing links with the Country Party in the 1670s give some credence to the later story of "the great Regard Prince Rupert always had to [Marvell's] Counsels. It is reported of that Prince, whenever he voted according to the Sentiments of Marvell, which he often did, it was a Saying with the adverse Party, He has been with his Tutor. The Intimacy betwixt him and Mr. Marvell was so great, that when it was unsafe for the latter to have it known where he lived, for Fear of losing his Life by Treachery, which was often the Case, his royal Friend would frequently renew his Visits in the Habit of a private Person," *The Works of Andrew Marvell Esq.*, ed. Thomas Cooke (London, 1726), pp. 10–11.

[124] Committee for the Forreign Affairs: the change marking the emergence of the governing Cabal (Clifford, Arlington, Buckingham, Ashley, Lauderdale).

[125] Burgesses: members of parliament representing boroughs, corporate towns, or the universities.

[126] Speech in *JHL* 12:352 (almost word for word if with different punctuation from *77a* and *77b*), "which, being in Writing, was also read to the House" of Commons (*JHC* 9:158).

[127] perfixed: determined. The Houses had adjourned on April 11, 1670.

ignorant of the great Forces both for Land and Sea-service which our Neigh-bours of France and the Low-Countries have raised, and have now in actual Pay; nor of the great Preparations which they continue to make in Levying of Men, Building of Ships, filling their Magazines and Stores with immense quantities of all sorts of Warlike Provisions. Since the beginning of the last Dutch War,[128] *the French have increased the Greatness and Number of their Ships so much, that their strength by Sea is thrice as much as it was before. And since the end of it, the Dutch have been very diligent also in augmenting their Fleets. In this conjuncture, when our Neighbours Arm so potently, even common prudence requires that his Majesty should make some suitable* {20} *preparations; that he may at least keep pace with his Neighbours, if not out-go them in Number and Strength of Shipping. For this being an Island,*[129] *both our Safety, our Trade, our Being, and our Well-Being depend upon our Forces at Sea.*

His Majesty *therefore, of his* Princely Care *for the* Good *of his* People, *hath given order for the fitting out of* Fifty Sail *of his* Greatest Ships, *against the* Spring,[130] *besides those which are to be for* Security *of our* Merchants *in the* Mediterranean: As *foreseeing, if he should not have a considerable* Fleet, *whilst his* Neighbours *have such* Forces *both at* Land *and* Sea, *Temptation might be given to those who seem not now to intend it, to give us an* Affront, *at least, if not to do us a* Mischief.

To which may be added, That his Majesty, by the Leagues which he hath made, for the Common Peace of Christen-[19]dom, and the good of his Kingdoms, is obliged to a certain Number of Forces in case of Infraction thereof, as also for the Assistance of some of his Neighbours, in case of Invasion. *And his* Majesty *would be in a very ill condition to perform his part of the* Leagues *(if whilst the Clouds are gathering so thick about us) he should, in hopes that the Wind will disperse them, omit to provide against the Storm.*

My Lords *and* Gentlemen, *Having named the* {21} Leagues *made by his* Majesty, *I think it necessary to put you in mind, That since the Close of the late War, his* Majesty *hath made several* Leagues, *to his own great* Honour, *and infinite* Advantage *to the* Nation.

One known by the Name of the *Tripple Alliance,* wherein his *Majesty,* the Crown of Sweden and the States of the United Provinces[131] are ingaged to

---

[128] *the last Dutch War:* Second Anglo-Dutch War (1665–67).

[129] *a Island 77b*].

[130] *against the* Spring: outfitting in readiness for the next spring.

[131] States of the United Provinces: the Netherlands, chiefly Holland.

preserve the *Treaty* of Aix la Chapelle,[132] concerning a Peace between the two warring Princes, which Peace produced that effect, that it quenched the Fire which was ready to have set all Christendom in a Flame. *And besides other great* Benefits *by it, which she still enjoyes, gave opportunity to transmit those* Forces *against the* Infidels,[133] *which would otherwise have been imbrued in* Christian Blood.

Another between his Majesty and the said States, for a Mutual Assistance, with a certain number of Men and Ships in case of Invasion by any others.[134]

Another between his Majesty *and the* Duke *of Savoy,*[135] *Establishing a* Free Trade *for his* Majesties Subjects *at Villa Franca, a* Port *of his own upon the Mediterranean, and through the* Dominions *of that* Prince; *and thereby opening a* Passage *to a Rich part of Italy, and part of Germany, which will be {22} of a very great advantage for the* Vending of Cloth *and other our home* Commodities, *bringing back* Silk *and other* Materials *for* Manifactures *here.*[136]

Another between his Majesty *and the* King *of Denmark,*[137] *whereby those other* Impositions *that were lately laid upon our* Trade *there, are taken off, and as great* Priviledges *granted* [20] *to our* Merchants, *as ever they had in former Times, or as the* Subjects *of any other* Prince *or* State *do now enjoy.*

And another League *upon a* Treaty of Commerce *with* Spain,[138] *whereby*

---

[132] Treaty of Aix la Chapelle: agreement made at Aix-la-Chapelle (Aachen) on May 2, 1668, forced on France by members of the Triple Alliance (Britain, Sweden, Netherlands), with France returning the Franche-Comté to Spain and retaining conquests in Flanders and in the Spanish Netherlands. This treaty temporarily ended the War of Devolution (1667–68), fought over Louis XIV's claims to the Spanish Netherlands.

[133] Especially against the Turks in the Cretan theater.

[134] The Treaty of Peace and Alliance with the Netherlands, signed at Breda on July 21/31, 1667.

[135] Duke *of Savoy:* Carlo Emanuele (1634–75). The Treaty of Friendship and Commerce with Savoy, signed at Florence on Sept. 9/19, 1669, gave English ships access to Villefranche.

[136] than here *77a, 77b, 79, 1776*] only *89* and *93*, p. 76, omit the nonsensical "than" here, in keeping with *LJ* 12:353.

[137] *King of Denmark:* Christian V (1646–99). The recent Treaty of Alliance and Commerce with Denmark, signed at Copenhagen on July 1/11, 1670.

[138] Under the Treaty of Madrid (Godolphin's Treaty, July 8/18, 1670), the two nations renounced piracy, and Spain recognized England's possession of Jamaica, which had been captured by Cromwell's navy in 1655.

there is not only a Cessation *and giving up to his* Majesty *of all their Preten-sions to Jamaica, and other* Islands *and* Countries *in the West-Indies, in the Possession of his* Majesty *or his* Subjects, *but with all, free Liberty is given to his* Majesties Subjects, *to enter their* Ports *for* Victuals *and* Water, *and safety of* Harbour *and* Return, *if* Storm *or other* Accidents *bring them thither;* Priviledges *which were never before granted*[139] *by them to the English or any others.*

Not to mention the Leagues *formerly made with* Sweden[140] *and* Portugal,[141] *and the* Advantages *which we enjoy thereby; nor those* Treaties *now depending between his* Majesty *and France, or his* Majesty *and the States of the United Provinces touching* Commerce, *wherein his* Majesty *will have a singular re-{23}gard to the* Honour *of this* Nation, *and also to the* Trade *of it, which never was greater than now it is.*[142]

In a word, Almost all the Princes *in Europe do seek his* Majesties Friend-ship, *as acknowledging they cannot secure, much less* Improve *their present condition without it.*

His Maiesty is confident that you will not be contented to see him deprived of all the advantages which he might procure hereby to his own Kingdoms, nay even to all Christendom, in the Repose and Quiet of it. *That you will not be content abroad to see your Neighbours strengthening themselves in* Shipping, *so much more than they were before, and at Home to see the* Government *struggling every year with* Difficulties; *and not able to keep up our* Navies *equal with theirs. He finds that by his Accounts from the year* 1660 *to the* Late War, *the ordinary Charge of the* Fleet Communibus Annis*[143] came to about 500000 l.*[144] *a year, and it cannot be supported with less.*

If that particular alone take up so much, add to it the other constant Charges *of the* Government, *and the* Revenue *(although the* Commissioners *of the* Treasury *have manag'd it with all imaginable* Thrift*) will in no degree suffice to take of the Debts due* [21] *upon* Interest, *much less give him a* Fond[145] *for the*

---

[139] *77a] never granted 77b*].

[140] Treaties of alliance and commerce (Whitehall, Oct. 21, 1661; Stockholm, Mar. 1, 1665 and Feb. 16, 1666).

[141] Especially the marriage treaty of Charles II with the Infanta Catherina of Portugal (1661).

[142] Although "now depending," nothing came of these.

[143] Communibus Annis: on annual average.

[144] *l.:* abbreviates *libra,* a pound of money.

[145] Fond: fund.

fitting out of this Fleet,[146] *which by common Estimation thereof* {24} *cannot cost less than* 800000 *l. His* Majesty, *in his most gratious Speech, hath expressed the great sence he hath of your zeal and affection for him and as he will ever retain a grateful memory of your former readiness to supply him in all Ex-igences,*[147] *so he doth with particular thanks acknowledg* your frank and chear-ful Gift of the New Duty[148] upon Wines, *at your last* Meeting: *But the same is likely to fall very short in value of what it was conceived to be worth and should it have answered expectation, yet far too short to ease and help him upon these Occasions. And therefore such a Supply as may enable him to take off his* Debts *upon Interest, and to set out this* Fleet *against the* Spring, *is that which he desires from you, and recommends it to you, as that which concerns the* Honour *and support of the* Government, *and the* Welfare *and* Safety *of your* Selves *and the whole* Kingdom.

My Lords *and* Gentlemen, *You may perceive by what his* Majesty *hath already said, that he holds it requisite that an* End *be put to this* Meeting *before* Christmas. *It is so not only in reference to the* Preparation *for his* Fleet, *which must be in readiness in the* Spring, *but also to the Season of the* Year. *It is a time when you would be willing to be in your* Countries, *and your* Neighbours *would be glad to see you there, and pertake of your* Hospitality *and* Charity, *and you* {25} *thereby endear your selves to them, and keep up that* Interest *and* Power *among them, which is necessary for the service of your* King *and* Country, *and a* Recess *at that time, leaving your business unfinished till your* Return, *cannot either be convenient for you, or* suitable *to the condition of his* Majesties Affairs, *which requires your* Speedy, *as well as* Affectionate Consideration. {26}[149] [22]

There needed not so large a Catalogue of past, present and future Leagues and Treaties, for even Villa Franca sounded so well (being besides so considerable a Port, and that too upon the Mediterranean (another remote word of much efficacy) and opening moreover a passage to a rich part of Italy, and a part of Germany, &c.) that it alone would have sufficed to charm the more ready Votes of the Commons into a supply, and to justifie

---

[146] Fliet *77b*].

[147] *Exigences:* urgent needs.

[148] Duty: tax.

[149] In *77a* there are here two rules and a long space to the end of the page, which anomalous spacing seems to reflect the compositor's working from a separate of Bridge-man's speech.

the necessity of it in the noise of the Country. But indeed the making of that *Tripple League,* was a thing of so good a report and so generally acceptable to the Nation, as being a hook in the French nostrils, that this Parliament (who are used, whether it be War or Peace, to make us pay for it) could not have desired a fairer pretence to colour their liberality.[150]

And therefore after all the immense summs lavished in the former War with Holland, they had but in April last, 1670, given the *Additional* Duty upon Wines for 8 years, amounting to 560000 and confirmed the sale of the *Fee Farm Rents,*[151] which was no less their gift, being a part of the publick Revenue, to the value of 1800000 l.[152] Yet upon the telling of this Story by the *Lord Keeper,* they could no longer hold but gave with both hands now again a Subsidy of 1 *s.* in the pound to the real value of all Lands, and other Estates proportionably, with several more beneficial Clauses into the bargain, to begin the 24th of June 1671, and expire the 24 of June 1672.[153] Together with this, they granted the *Additional Excise* upon *Beer, Ale, &c.* for six years, to reckon from the same 24 of June 1671, And lastly, the *Law-Bill*[154] commencing from the first of *May* 1671, and at nine years end to determine. These three Bills summed up therefore cannot be estimated at less than two millions and an half.[155]

So that for the *Tripple League,* here was also *Tripple Supply,* and the Subject had now all reason to believe that this Alliance, which had been fixed at first by the *Publick Interest, Safety and Honour* (yet, should any of those give way) was {27} by these *Three Grants,* as with three *Golden*

---

[150] liberality: "The House was thin and obsequious" (Marvell to Popple, Nov. 28, 1670, *P & L,* 2:318); "And those false Men the Sovereign People Sent / Give Taxes to the King and Parliament" ("Nostradamus's Prophecy," ll. 11–12; *P & L,* 1:178).

[151] *Fee Farm Rents:* a fixed perpetual income from lands.

[152] Qv. Marvell's constituency letters of Feb.-Apr. 1670 (*P & L,* 2:97–107); *JHC* 9:153–7.

[153] *JHC* 9:159, 171–74; Grey 1:327, Dec. 15–17, 1670; LHC Nov. 8, 1670: "I heare there was an intention that same day to have moved for the 20th part of every mans estate"; also LHC Nov. 17, 1670, "Yesterday the King & the Treasurers farmd the Customs with the 8 years on Wine & Wine licenses for 600000 li per an for 5 years" (*P & L,* 2:112–15); also letters to Edward Thompson, Dec. 17, 1670, and William Popple, ca. Jan. 24, 1670/71 (*P & L,* 2:320, 321).

[154] *Law-Bill:* "The House hath orderd another bill of imposition upon all proceedings in all the Law Courts" (LHC 8 Dec. 1670, *P & L,* 2:120).

[155] The corruption of MPs that was needed to secure the bills' passage found comment from Marvell that following summer (letter to Thomas Rolt, Aug. 9, 1671; *P & L,* 2:324–5).

Nailes,[156] suffici-[23]ently clenched and reivetted.[157] But now therefore was the most proper time and occasion for the Conspirators, I have before described, to give demonstration of their fidelity to the French *King,* and by the forfeiture of all these obligations to their King and Countrey, and other Princes, and at the expence of all this Treasure given to contrary uses, to recommend themselves more meritoriously to his patronage.

The *Parliament* having once given this Money, were in consequence Prorogued,[158] and met not again till the 24th of February 1672, that there might be a competent scope for so great a work as was desined, and the Architects of our Ruine might be so long free from their busie and odious inspection till it were finished. Henceforward, all the former applications made by his Majesty to induce Forraign Princes into the *Guarranty* of the Treaty of an Aix la Chapelle ceased, and on the contrary, those who desired to be admitted into it, were here refused. The Duke of Lorrain, who had alwaies been a true friend to his Majesty, and by his affection to the *Tripple League* had incurred the French *Kings* displeasure, with the loss of his whole Territory, seized in the year 1669, against all Laws not only of *Peace* but *Hostility,* yet was by means of these men rejected, that he might have no Interest in the Alliance, for which he was sacrificed.[159] Nay even the Emperour,[160] though he did his Majesty the honour to Address voluntarily to him, that himself might be received into that *Tripple League,* yet could not so great a Prince prevail but was turned off with blind Reason, and most frivolous Excuses. So far was it now from fortifying the Alliance by the

---

[156] three *Golden Nailes:* The crucifixion of Christ was commonly symbolized by three nails. It was disputed just how "golden" these "three bills of additionall Excise" were, as Marvell reports in a constituency letter of Dec. 10, 1670 (*P & L,* 2:121).

[157] reivetted: rivetted.

[158] were . . . Prorogued: session terminated by royal proclamation, Apr. 22, 1671 (*JHC* 9:244–5); at that time, Marvell gave a reason for the prorogation nearer the official one, citing irreconcilable differences between Lords and Commons (*LHC* Apr. 22, 1671, *P & L,* 2:140; letter to Thomas Rolt, Aug. 9, 1670, *P & L,* 2:325).

[159] Lorrain . . . sacrificed: "In 1669 [1670], they hunted the poor Duke of Lorraine [Charles, 1625–75] out of his Dutchy, and to this day possess it all," Pierre Du Moulin, *Englands Appeale* (London, 1673), p. 10; in a personal letter, Marvell complained of the situation at the time, observing "We truckle to France in all Things, to the Prejudice of our Alliance and Honour" (Marvell to Thomas Rolt, Aug. 9, 1671; *P & L,* 2:325).

[160] the Emperour: the emperor of the Holy Roman Empire, Leopold I, of the House of Habsburg.

Accession of other Princes, that Mr. Henry Coventry[161] went now to Sweden expressly, as he affirmed at his departure hence, to dissolve the *Tripple League.* And he did so much towards it, cooperating in that Court with the *French* Ministers, that Sweden never (after it came to a Rupture) did assist or prosecute effectually the ends of the {28} *Alliance,* but only arming it self at the expence of the *League,* did first, under a disguised *Mediation,* Act the French *Interest,* [24] and at last threw off the *Vizard,*[162] and drew the Sword in their Quarrel. Which is a matter of sad reflexion, that he, who in his *Embassy* at Breda, had been so happy an Instrument to end the first unfortunate War with Holland, should now be made the *Toole* of a second, and of breaking that threefold Cord, by which the Interest of England and all Christendom was fastned. And, what renders it more wretched, is, that no man better than he understood both the *Theory* and *Practrick of Honour;* and yet, could in so eminent an Instance, forget it. All which can be said in his excuse, is, that upon his return he was for this service made Secretary of State (as if to have remained the same *Honest Gentleman,* had not been more necessary and less dishonourable).[163] Sir William Lockyard[164] and several others were dispatched to other Courts upon the like errand.

All things were thus far well disposed here towards a War with Holland; only all this while there wanted a Quarrel, and to pick one required much Invention. For the Dutch although there was a *si quis*[165] to find out complaints, and our East India Company[166] was summoned to know whether they had any thing to object against them, had so punctually complied with all the Conditions of the Peace at Breda, and observed his Majesty with

[161] Mr. Henry Coventry: In 1667, Coventry (1619–86) was sent with Lord Holles to negotiate peace with the Dutch, which resulted in the Treaty of Breda; in 1671, Coventry was sent on an embassy to Stockholm to persuade the Swedes to join against the Dutch (on his return he was appointed secretary of state).

[162] threw off the *Vizard:* dispensed with the disguise.

[163] .] no punctuation after the parenthesis in any of the early editions.

[164] Sir William Lockyard: In 1671, Lockhart (1621–76) was sent to Brandenburg and Lüneburg to attempt to secure their cooperation or neutrality in the alliance with France against Holland; afterward he was reappointed to the embassy in France.

[165] *si quis:* "if anyone," the opening words of a public notice requesting information, and thus a name for such an advertisement (also in *RT2,* 1:248.)

[166] East India Company: This company had been founded at the end of the sixteenth century in order to compete with the Dutch merchants; its members thus had a special interest in the successive Anglo-Dutch Wars and in whether the peace conditions were being met.

such respect (and in paying the due Honour of the *Flagg*, particularly as it was agreed in the 19*th*. Article)[167] that nothing could be alledged, and as to the *Tripple League*, their *Fleet* was then out, riding near their own Coasts, in prosecuting of the ends of that *Treaty*. Therefore, to try a new experiment and to make a Case[168] which had never before happened or been imagined, a sorry *Yatch*, but bearing the English *Jack*,[169] in August 1671. sails into the midst of their *Fleet*, singled out the *Admiral*, shooting twice as they call it, sharp upon him. Which must sure have appeared as ridiculous and unnatural as for a *Lark* to dare the Hobby.[170] {29} [25] Nevertheless their Commander in Chief, in deference to his Majesties Colours,[171] and in consideration of the Amity betwixt the two Nations, payed our Admiral of the *Yatch* a visit, to know the reason; and learning that it was because he and his whole Fleet had failed to strike Saile to his small-craft, the Dutch *Commander* civily excused it as a matter of the first instance,[172] and in which he could have no Instructions,[173] therefore proper to be referred to their Masters, and so they parted. The *Yatch* having thus acquitted it self, returned, fraught with the Quarrel she was sent for, which yet was for several moneths passed over here in silence without any Complaint or demand of satisfaction, but to be improved afterwards when occasion grew riper. For there was yet one thing more to be done at home to make us more capable of what was shortly after to be executed on our Neighbours.

The *Exchequer* had now for some years by excessive gain decoy'd in the wealthy *Goldsmiths*, and they the rest of the Nation by due payment of Interest, till the King was run (upon what account I know not) into debt of above two Millions: which served for one of the pretences in my Lord *Keepers Speech* above recited, to demand and grant the late Supplies, and

---

[167] 19th. Article: "That the ships and vessels of the said United Provinces, as well men of war as others, meeting any men of war of the said King of Great Britain's in the British seas, shall strike the flag, and lower the top-sail."

[168] Case: a cause or suit brought into court for decision.

[169] English *Jack:* ship's flag used to indicate the nationality at sea, flown from the jack-staff at the bow of the vessel.

[170] *Lark* to dare the Hobby: A hobby is a small falcon, flown at larks and small birds; Marvell seems also to recall that the name of the adventurous yacht was the *Merlin*, another species of small falcon, and may allude to Dryden's similar characterization of the beaten Dutch fleet in *Annus Mirabilis*, l. 780.

[171] his Majesties Colours: the flag on the ship (i.e., the English Jack).

[172] matter of the first instance: a first case.

[173] Instructions: previous directions from his superiors.

might have sufficed for that work, with peace and any tolerable good husbandry. But as if it had been perfidious to apply them to any one of the Purposes declared, it was instead of payment privately resolved to shut up the *Exchequer*,[174] least any part of the money should be legally expended, but that all might be appropriate to the Holy War in project, and those further pious uses to which the Conspirators had dedicated it.

This affair was carried on with all the secresy of so great Statesmen, that they might not by venting it unseasonably spoile the wit and malice of the business. So that all on the suddain, upon the first of January 1671, to the great astonishment, ruine and despaire of so many interested persons, and to the terrour of the whole Nation, by so Arbitrary a {30} [26] Fact, the Proclamation issued whereby the Crown, amidst the confluence of so vast Aides and Revenue, published it self Bankrupt, made price[175] of the Subject, and broke all Faith and Contract at home in order to the breaking of them abroad[176] with more advantage.

There remained nothing now but that the Conspirators, after this exploit upon our own Countrymen, should manifest their impartiality to Forainers, and avoid on both sides the reproach of injustice by their equality in the distribution. They had now started the dispute about the Flag upon occasion of the Yatch, and begun the discourse of Surinam,[177] and somwhat of *Pictures and Medalls*,[178] but they handled these matters so nicely[179] as men not less afraid of receiving all satisfaction therein from the Hollanders,

[174] shut up the *Exchequer:* By the Stop of the Exchequer (Jan. 1671/2), which closed the office that received and disbursed royal revenues, the bankers (from the guild of goldsmiths) lost their income from loans to the Crown; thus the Crown could now avail itself of the supplies that had just been voted for servicing that debt. Verse satires of the day made much of the "Lombard Street break," including some later attributed to Marvell: "Nostradamus's Prophecy," ll. 13–14; "Statue in Stocks-Market," l. 4; "Upon his Majesties being made free of the City," ll. 43–48; "A Dialogue between the Two Horses," l. 36 (*P & L,* 1:178, 188, 191, 209).

[175] made price] made prize 79, 89, 93]: seized or captured, as in war.

[176] abroad: i.e., the breach of foreign alliances.

[177] discourse of Surinam: The English had settled the mouth of the Surinam River (northeast South America) in 1651; the Dutch took the settlement in 1657, which led to a lasting grievance against that nation, compounded when the settlement was awarded to Holland in the Treaty of Breda.

[178] *Pictures and Medalls:* especially of the triumphant De Witt, with the English fleet burning in the background (*Poems and Letters,* 1:188, 396n), but the Dutch flair for such satire had long been an annoyance.

[179] nicely: precisely, fastidiously.

then of giving them any umbrage of[180] arming against them upon those pretences. The Dutch therefore, not being conscious to themselves of any provocation given to England, but of their readiness, if there had been any, to repair it, and relying upon that faith of Treaties and Alliances with us, which hath been thought sufficient security, not only amongst *Christians* but even with *Infidels,* persued their Traffick and Navigation thorow our Seas without the least suspicion. And accordingly a great and rich Fleet of Merchantmen from Smyrna[181] and Spain, were on their Voyage homeward near the Isle of Wight, under a small Convoy of five or six of their men of War. This was the Fleet in contemplation of which the conspirators had so long deferred the War to plunder them in peace; the wealth of this was that which by its weight turned the Ballance of all Publick Justice and Honour; with this Treasure they imagined themselves in stock for all the wickedness of which they were capable, and that they should never, after this addition, stand in need again or fear of a Parliament. Therefore they had with great stilness[182] and expedition equipped early in the year, so many of the Kings Ships as might without jealousy of the number, yet be of compe-{31} [27]tent strength for the intended action, but if any thing should chance to be wanting, they thought it abundantly supplyed by virtue of the Commander. For Sir Robert Holmes[183] had with the like number of Ships in the year 1661, even so timely commenced the first Hostility against Holland, in time of Peace; seizing upon Cape Verde, and other of the Dutch-Forts on the Coast of Guiny, and the whole New Netherlands, with great success: in defence of which Conquests, the English undertook, 1665, the first War against Holland. And in that same War, he with a proportionable Squadron signalized[184] himself by burning the Dutch Ships and Village of Brandaris at Schelling, which was unfortunately revenged upon us at Chatham.

[180] umbrage of: reason for suspicion.

[181] Smyrna: chief port of Asia Minor.

[182] stilness] stillness 79]: secrecy.

[183] Sir Robert Holmes: see introduction above (p. 193). Holmes (1622–92) had in the early 1660s been sent to support the Royal Africa Company against Dutch depredations, with a success that in 1664 also included the taking of New Amsterdam on the other side of the Atlantic; his prosperity in the Second Anglo-Dutch War led to his promotion to admiral and to Dryden's claim that his "name shal live in Epique Song" (*Annus Mirabilis*, l. 687). *A Seasonable Argument* ("Amsterdam," 1677), pp. 8–9, styles him "first an Irish Livery Boy, then a High-way-man, now Bashaw of the Isle of Wight . . . The Cursed Beginner of the two Dutch Wars."

[184] signalized: distinguished.

So that he was pitched upon[185] as the person for understanding, experience and courage, fittest for a design of this or any higher nature; and upon the 14th. of March 1672. as they sailed on, to the number of 72 Vessels in all, whereof six the Convoy; near our Coast, he fell in upon them with his accustomed bravery, and could not have failed of giving a good account of them, would he but have joyned fortunes, Sir Edward Spraggs[186] Assistance to his own Conduct: For Sr. Edward was in sight at the same time with his Squadron, and Captain Legg[187] making sail towards him, to acquaint him with the design, till called back by a Gun from his Admiral, of which several persons have had their conjectures. Possibly Sir Robert Holmes, considering that Sir Edward had sailed all along in consort with the Dutch in their voiage, and did but now return from bringing the Pirates of Algier[188] to reason, thought him not so proper to ingage in this enterprice before he understood it better. But it is rather believed to have proceeded partly from that Jealousy (which is usuall to marshall spirits; like Sir Roberts) of admitting a Companion to share with him in the Spoil of Honour or Profit;[189] and partly out of too strict a regard to preserve the secret of his Commission. However, by this means the whole affair miscarried. For the Mer-{32}chant Men themselves, and their little Convoy did so bestir [28] them, that Sir Robert, although he shifted his Ship, fell foul on his best Friends, and did all that was possible, unless he could have multiplied himself, and been every where, was forced to give it over, and all the Prize that was gotten, sufficed not to pay the Chirurgeons and Carpenters.

To descend to the very bottom of their hellish Conspiracy, there was yet one step more; that of Religion. For so pious and just an Action as Sir Robert Holmes was imployed upon, could not be better accompanied than by

[185] pitched upon: chosen.

[186] Sir Edward Spragg: admiral (d. 1673), whose role at sea in the Second Anglo-Dutch War earned him Marvell's kindness as "practic'd in the Sea command" ("The Last Instructions," l. 561), and Dryden's praise "as bountiful as brave" (*Annus Mirabilis*, l. 693).

[187] Legg: George Legge (c. 1647–91), captain of the *Fairfax*, later first baron Dartmouth and, under James II, admiral and commander in chief of the fleet; also an MP, he was "supposed to be a papist" in *A Seasonable Argument* (1677), p. 20.

[188] Pirates of Algier: Spragg's striking success against the Barbary pirates (May 1671).

[189] This dark construction of Holmes's action may have originated with Marvell, R. C. Anderson, ed., *Journals and Narratives of the Third Dutch War* (London, 1946), pp. 6–7.

the Declaration of *Liberty of Conscience*[190] (unless they should have expected[191] till he had found that pretious Commodity in plundering the
Hoale[192] of some Amsterdam Fly-boat).[193] Accordingly, while he was trying his Fortune in Battle with the Smyrna Merchant-Men, on the *thirteenth*
and *fourteenth* of March, *One thousand six hundred seventy two*,[194] the *Indulgence* was Printing off here in all haste, and was Published on the *fifteenth*, as
a more proper means than *Fasting* and *Prayer* for propitiating Heaven to
give Success to his Enterprise, and to the War that must second it.

Hereby all the Penal *Laws* against *Papists*, for which former *Parliaments*
had given so many Supplies, and against *Nonconformists*,[195] for which this
Parliament had payed more largely, were at one Instant Suspended, in order
to defraud the Nation of all that *Religion* which they had so dearly purchased, and for which they ought at least, the Bargain being broke, to have
been reimbursed.

There is, I confess, a measure to be taken in those things, and it is indeed
to the great reproach of Humane Wisdom, that no man has for so many
Ages been able or willing to find out the due temper of Government in
Divine Matters. For it appears at the first sight, that men ought to enjoy the
same Propriety and Protection in their Consciences, which they have in
their Lives, Liberties, and Estates: But that to take away these in Penalty
for the other, is meerly a more Legal {33} [29] and Gentile way of Padding[196] upon the Road of Heaven, and that it is only for want of Money and
for want of Religion that men take those desperate Courses.[197]

Nor can it be denied that the *Original Law* upon which Christianity at

---

[190] Declaration of *Liberty of Conscience:* The second Declaration of Indulgence, 1672,
suspended penal laws and permitted all Protestants freedom to worship in public and
Roman Catholics freedom to worship in private. The declaration was soon withdrawn
and followed by the Test Act.

[191] expected: waited.

[192] Hoale: hold (of a ship).

[193] Fly-boat: a Dutch flat-bottomed boat used for rapid transport.

[194] Now Marvell links Holmes's attack on the Dutch Smyrna convoy as it passed
through the English Channel with the timing of the Declaration of Indulgence the
next day.

[195] *Nonconformists:* After the Act of Uniformity in 1662, Nonconformist was the
name given to Protestants who were not members of the Church of England.

[196] Gentile . . . Padding: genteel way of robbing (on the highway).

[197] desperate Courses: of action.

the first was founded, does indeed expressly provide against all such severity; And it was by the Humility, Meekness, Love, Forbearance and Patience
which were part of that excellent Doctrine,[198] that it became at last the
Universal Religion, and can no more by any other means be preserved, than
it is possible for another Soul to animate the same Body.

But, with shame be it spoken, the Spartans obliging themselves to
Lycurgus[199] his Laws, till he should come back again, continued under his
most rigid Discipline, above twice as long as the Christians did endure
under the gentlest of all Institutions, though with far more certainty expecting the return of their Divine Legislator.[200] Insomuch that it is no great
Adventure to say, That the World was better ordered under the Antient
Monarchies and Common wealths, that the number of Vertuous men was
then greater, and that the Christians found fairer quarter[201] under those,
than among themselves, nor hath there any advantage acrued unto mankind from that most perfect and practical Moddel of Humane Society,
except the Speculation of a better way to future Happiness, concerning
which the very Guides disagree, and of those few that follow, it will suffer
no man to pass without paying at their Turn-pikes.[202] All which had proceeded from no other reason, but that men instead of squaring their Governments by the Rule of Christianity; have shaped Christianity by the
Measures of their Government, have reduced that streight Line by the
crooked, and bungling Divine and Humane things together, have been
always hacking and hewing one another, to frame an irregular Figure of
Political Incongruity.

For wheresoever either the Magistrate, or the Clergy, or {34} [30] the
People could gratify their Ambition, their Profit, or their Phansie by a Text

---

[198] *Original Law* . . . excellent Doctrine: fundamentally the two great commandments, Matt. 22:37–40.

[199] Lycurgus: legendary legislator of Sparta, perhaps ninth or eighth century B.C.,
whose excellent laws the Spartans promised to observe until his return from Delphi.
When the oracle foretold that Sparta would thrive as long as those laws were followed,
Lycurgus sent along that message without ever returning himself.

[200] Divine Legislator: Christians await the second coming of Christ.

[201] quarter: protection. This is Marvell's argument in the *Essay.*

[202] Turn-pikes: tollgates. In the next sentence, Marvell may echo his own "Dialogue
between the Soul and Body," where "Architects do square and hew / Green Trees that in
the Forest grow" (*P & L*, 1: 23, ll. 43–44; noted in Nigel Smith, " 'Courtesie is fatal': The
Civil and Visionary Poetics of Andrew Marvell," *Proceedings of the British Academy* 101
[1998], p. 188).

improved or misapplyed,[203] that they made use of though against the consent, sense and immutable precepts of *Scripture,* and because Obedience for Conscience sake was there prescribed, the less Conscience did men make in Commanding; so that several Nations have little else to shew for their Christianity (which requires Instruction only and Example) but a parcel of severe Laws concerning Opinion or about the Modes of Worship, not so much in order to the Power of Religion as over it.[204] Nevertheless because Mankind must be governed some way and be held up to one Law or other, either of Christs or their own making, the vigour of such Human Constitutions is to be preserved until the same Authority shall upon better reason revoke them; and as in the mean time no privat Man may without the guilt of Sedition or Rebellion resist, so neither by the Nature of the English Foundation can any publick Person suspend them without committing an Error which is not the less for wanting a legal name to express it. But it was the *Master-piece* therefore of boldness and contrivance in these Conspirators to issue this Declaration, and it is hard to say wherein they took the greater felicity, whither in suspending hereby all the Statutes against Popery, that it might thence forward passe like current *Money*[205] over the Nation, and no man dare to refuse it, or whether gaining by this a President[206] to suspend as well all other Laws that respect the Subjects Propriety, and by the same power to abrogate and at last inact what they pleased, till there should be no further use for the Consent of the *People in Parliament.*[207]

Having been thus true to their great design and made so considerable a progress, they advanced with all expedition. It was now high time to Declare the War, after they had begun it; and therefore by a *Manifesto* of the seventeenth of March 1672, the pretended Causes were made publick {35} [31] which were. The not having Vailed Bonnet[208] to the English Yatch: though the Dutch had all along, both at home and here as carefully

---

[203] Text improved or misapplyed: Marvell now finds nearer to home the same religious self-aggrandizement he had earlier imputed to Rome ("Never was a Bishoprick and a Verse of Scripture so improved by good management," above p. 232).

[204] not much . . . as over it: not so much with reference to the power of religion as above and beyond it.

[205] current *Money:* neither outdated nor counterfeit.

[206] President: precedent.

[207] By contrast, Marvell had supported the Declaration of Indulgence in the *Rehearsal Transpros'd* (1672).

[208] Vailed Bonnet: doffed the cap, with common nautical sense of striking sail by way of salute.

endeavoured to give, as the English Minister to avoid the receiving of all satisfaction, or letting them understand what would do it, and the Council Clock[209] was on purpose set forward, lest their utmost Compliance in the Flag, at the hour appointed, should prevent the Declaration of War by some minutes. The detaining of some few English families (by their own consent) in Surinam after the Dominion of it was by Treaty surrendred up to the Hollander, in which they had likewise constantly yielded to the unreasonable demands that were from one time to another extended from hence to make the thing impracticable, till even Banister[210] himself, that had been imployed as the Agent and Contriver of this misunderstanding, could not at the last forbear to cry shame of it. And moreover to fill up the measure of the Dutch iniquity, they are accused of Pillars, Medalls, and Pictures:[211] a Poet indeed, by a dash of his Pen, having once been the cause of War against Poland;[212] but this certainly was the first time that ever a *Painter* could by a stroke of his Pencil occasion the Breach of a Treaty. But considering the weakness and invalidity of those other allegations, these indeed were not unnecessary, the Pillars to add strength, the Meddals Weight, and the Pictures Colour to their Reasons.

[209] Council Clock: that of the Privy Council.

[210] Banister: Major Banister had been sent to Surinam to bring back English settlers and was under instructions from the duke of York to accept no satisfaction on points of difference with the Dutch. Abraham de Wicquefort, *Histoire des Provinces Unies des Pais Bas,* 4 vols. (Amsterdam, 1861–74), 4:238.

[211] Pillars, Medalls, and Pictures: "A portrait of Cornelius de Wit, brother to the pensionary, painted by order of certain magistrates of Dort, and hung up in a chamber of the town-house" included "some ships on fire in a harbour . . . construed to be Chatham" *OPH* 4:500; for this and the mottoes on the offending medals, see Wicquefort, *Histoire des Provinces Unies,* 4:109–10, 115–16, 230–38; the mold for the medals had been broken in 1670, F. A. M. Mignet, *Négociations relatives à la succession d'Espagne* (Paris, 1835–42), 3:427.

[212] Poet . . . war against Poland: the bizarre *casus belli* claimed by the exceptionally proud "Duke of Muscovy" found notice in *Mercurius Politicus,* no. 204 (May 4–11, 1654), although Marvell's connection to the English embassy to Sweden that yielded this news may have given him more direct knowledge of this lasting grievance, which was deplored by some sixteen Russian embassies to Poland since the 1630s, with complaints also to Denmark (1653) and the Empire (1654)—my thanks to Maria Unkovskaya for assistance on this point. Marvell also referred to it in *RT2,* 1:258; he himself had fallen foul of the Muscovite obsession with protocol in 1664, when in service to the earl of Carlisle's embassy, Guy Miège, *A Relation of Three Embassies* (London, 1669), pp. 194–95.

But herein they had however observed Faith with France though on all other sides broken, having capitulated to be the first that should do it. Which as it was no small piece of French Courtesy in so important an action to yield the English the Precedence,[213] so was it on the English part as great a Bravery in accepting to be the formost to discompose the State of all *Christendom,* and make themselves principal to all the horrid Destruction, Devastation, Ravage and Slaugh-{36}[32]ter, which from that fatal *seventeenth* of March, *One thousand six hundred seventy two,* has to this very day continued.[214]

But that which was most admirable in the winding up[215] of this *Declaration,* was to behold these Words,

And whereas we are engaged by a Treaty to support the Peace made at Aix la Chapelle: We do finally Declare, that, notwithstanding the Prosecution of this War, We will maintain the true intent and scope of the said Treaty; and that, in all Alliances, which We have, or shall make in the progress of this War, We have, and will take care, to preserve the ends thereof inviolable, unless provoked to the contrary.

And yet it is as clear as the Sun, that the French had by that Treaty of Aix la Chapelle, agreed to acquiess in their former Conquests in Flanders, and that the English, Swede and Hollander, were reciprocally bound to be aiding against whomsoever should disturb that Regulation, (besides the League Offensive and Defensive, which his Majesty had entered into with the States General of the United Provinces) all which was by this Conjunction with France to be broken in pieces. So that what is here declared, if it were reconcileable to Truth, yet could not consist with Possibility (which two do seldom break company) unless by one only Expedient, that the English, who by this new League with France, were to be the Infractors[216] and Aggressors of the Peace of Aix la Chapelle (and with Holland) should to fulfill their Obligations to both Parties, have sheathed the Sword in our own Bowels.

But such was the Zeal of the Conspirators, that it might easily transport them either to say what was untrue, or undertake what was impossible, for the French Service. {37}

---

[213] Precedence: the privilege of going first.

[214] The date of the English declaration of war on Holland, starting the Third Dutch War (1672–74).

[215] winding up: conclusion.

[216] Infractors: violators, breakers (of the treaty).

That King having seen the English thus engaged beyond a Retreat, comes now into the War according to agreement. But he was more Generous and Monarchal than to assign Cause, true or false, for his Actions. He therefore, on the *27th.* of March 1672,[217] publishes a Declaration of War without any Reasons. Only, *The ill satisfaction which his Majesty* [33] *hath of the Behaviour of the States General towards him, being risen to that degree, that he can no longer, without diminution to his Glory dissemble his Indignation against them, &c. Therefore he hath resolved to make War against them both by Sea and Land, &c. And commands all his Subjects, Courir sus,*[218] upon the Hollanders. (a Metaphor which, out of respect to his own Nation, might have been spared) *For such is our pleasure.*

Was ever in any Age or Nation of the World, the Sword drawn upon no better Allegation? A stile so far from being *Most Christian,* that nothing but some vain French Romance can parallel or justify the Expression. How happy were it could we once arrive at the same pitch, and how much credit and labour had been saved, had the Compilers of our Declaration, instead of the mean English way of giving Reasons, contented themselves with that of the Diminution of the English *Honour,* as the French of his *Glory!* But nevertheless, by his Embassador to the *Pope,*[219] he gave afterwards a more clear account of his Conjunction with the English, and that he had not undertaken this War against the Hollanders, but for extirpating[220] of Heresie. To the Emperour,[221] That the Hollanders were a People who had forsaken God, were Hereticks, and that all good Christians were in duty bound to associate for their extirpation, and ought to pray to God for a blessing upon so pious an enterprise. And to other Popish Princes,[222] that it was a War of Religion and in order to the Propagation of the Catholick Faith.

And in the second Article of his Demands afterward from the Hollanders,[223] it is in express words contained, *That from* {38} *thence forward*

---

[217] Marvell translates this independently of the published English version, *The Most Christian Kings Declaration of Warr Against the States Generall of the United Provinces* (London, 1672), p. 1 (the date of the original declaration being April 6, 1672 NS).

[218] *Courir sus:* to fall upon, attack.

[219] Embassador to the *Pope:* Supporting the duke of Estrées, his brother César d'Estrées (1628–1714) was in effect French ambassador to Clement X.

[220] extirpating: rooting out.

[221] The Emperour: Leopold I, of the Holy Roman Empire.

[222] other Popish Princes: the rulers of Catholic nations.

[223] For a full list of Louis XIV's conditions, see Add. MS. 72758, ff. 14r–15v. Marvell translates closely from the French.

there shall be not only an intire Liberty, but a Publick Exercise of the Catholick Apostolick Romane Religion throughout all the United Provinces. So that wheresoever there shall be more than one Church, another shall be given to the Catholicks. That where there is none, they shall be permitted to build one: and till that be finished, to exercise their Divine Service publickly in such Houses as they shall buy, or hire for that purpose. That the States General, or each Province in particular, shall [34] appoint a reasonable Salary for a Curate[224] *or Priest in each of the said Churches, out of such Revenues as have formerly appertained to the Church, or otherwise.* Which was conformable to what he published now abroad, that he had entered into the War only for Gods Glory; and that he would lay down Armes streightwayes, would the Hollanders but restore the True Worship in their Dominions.

But he made indeed twelve Demands more, and notwithstanding all this devotion, the Article of Commerce, and for revoking their *Placaets*[225] against Wine, Brandy, and French manufactures was the first, and took place of the *Catholick Apostolick Romane Religion.* Whether all these were therefore only words of course,[226] and to be held or let lose according to his occasions, will better appear when we shall have heard that he still insists upon the same at Nimegen,[227] and that, although deprived of our assistance, he will not yet agree with the Dutch but upon the termes of restoring the *True Worship.* But, whatever he were, it is evident that the English were sincere and in good earnest in the Design of Popery; both by that Declaration above mentioned of Indulgence to the Recusants,[228] and by the Negotiation of those of the English Plenipotentiaries[229] (whom for their honour

---

[224] Curate: a clergyman who has the care of a parish.

[225] *Placaets:* placets, permissions from council (Lat. *placet,* "it pleases").

[226] of course: belonging to ordinary procedure; to be expected.

[227] Nimegen: Nijmegen, in the eastern Netherlands, in 1677 site of the current peace congress between France and Holland.

[228] Declaration . . . of Indulgence to the Recusants: The royal Declaration of Indulgence (1672) offered toleration to nonconformist Protestants and to Catholics; the latter were termed recusants (Lat. *recusare,* to refuse) because they refused to acknowledge the Act of Uniformity (1559) and to attend Church of England services.

[229] Plenipotentiaries: from the Latin *pleni* (full) *potentia* (power), denoting diplomats who are invested with full authority—here the earl of Arlington and duke of Buckingham first of all, who arrived in The Hague on June 25/July 5, 1672, soon followed by George Savile, at this date viscount Halifax, and the duke of Monmouth. Marvell must have been especially reluctant to name Buckingham, in view of his praises of him below (p. 275–76, 285, 296–97) and possible debts for information about these English nego-

I name not) that being in that year sent into Holland, pressed that Article among the rest upon them, as without which they could have no hope of Peace with England. And the whole processe of affaires will manifest further, that both here and there it was all of a piece, as to the project of Religi-{39} on and the same threed ran throw the Web of the English and French Counsels, no less in relation to that, then unto Government.

Although the issuing of the French Kings Declaration, and the sending of our English *Plenipotentiaries* into Holland be involved together in this last period, yet the difference of time was so small that the anticipation is inconsiderable. For having declared the War but on the 27th of March, 1672. He struck so home and followed his blow so close, that by July following, it seemed that Holland could no longer stand [35] him, but that the swiftness and force of his motion was something supernatural. And it was thought necessary to send over those *Plenipotentiaries,* if not for Interest yet at least for Curiosity. But it is easier to find the Marks than Reasons of some mens Actions, and he that does only know what happened before, and what after might perhaps wrong them by searching for further Intelligence.[230]

So it was, that the English and French Navies being joined, were upon the *Twentieighth* of May, *One thousand six hundred seventy two,* Attaqued in Soule Bay by De Ruyter,[231] with too great advantage. For while his Royal Highness, then *Admiral,* did all that could be expected, but *Monsieur* d'Estree, that commanded the French, did all that he was sent for, Our English *Vice-Admiral,* Montague, was sacrificed; and the rest of our Fleet so mangled, that there was no occasion to boast of Victory.[232] So that being here

---

tiations with the Dutch. With Savile too he may have had a longer association, Pauline Burdon, "Marvell after Cambridge," *British Library Journal* 4 (1978), 42–48.

[230] Intelligence: information or news.

[231] De Ruyter: Admiral Michael Adrianzoon de Ruyter (1607–76) had long been one of the most accomplished naval commanders in Europe; his successes in the earlier Anglo-Dutch wars of 1652–54 and 1665–67 were now crowned by this resilient defense of the Dutch Mediterranean merchant fleet. Marvell had come close to celebrating "the Ravisher De-Ruyter's" triumph over the English in 1667, in "The Last Instructions," ll. 523–50, 758.

[232] The Battle of Sole Bay took place on May 28, 1672. The English fleet commanded by Vice-Admiral Edward Montague (1625–72) and the Admiral, James, duke of York, allied with the French fleet commanded by Vice-Admiral Jean d'Estrées, met the smaller Dutch fleet commanded by de Ruyter. The battle proved a setback for the English-French alliance, and Montague drowned after his ship, the *Royal James,*

still on the losing hand, 'twas fit some body should look to the Betts on the other side of the Water; least that Great and Lucky Gamster, when he had won all there, and stood no longer in need of the Conspirators, should pay them with a Quarrel for his Mony, and their ill Fortune. Yet were they not conscious to themselves of having given him by any *Behaviour* of theirs, any cause of *Dissatisfaction,* but that they had dealt with him in all things most frankly; That, notwithstanding all the Expressions in my Lord Keeper Bridgmans Speech, {40} of the *Treaty between* France *and his Majesty concerning Commerce, wherein his Majesty will have a singular regard to the Honour and also to the Trade of this Nation,* and notwithstanding the intollerable oppressions upon the English *Traffick* in France ever since the Kings Restauration, they had not in all that time made one step towards a Treaty of Commerce or Navigation with him; no not even now when the English were so necessary to him, that he could not have begun this War without them, and might probably therefore in this conjuncture have condescended to some equality. But they knew how tender that King was on that point, and to preserve and encrease the Trade of his Subjects, [36] and that it was by the *Diminution* of that Beam of his *Glory,* that the Hollanders had raised his *Indignation.* The Conspirators had therefore the more to gratify him, made it their constant Maxime,[233] to burden the English Merchant here with one hand, while the French should load them no less with the other, in his Teritories; which was a parity of trade indeed, though something an extravagant one, but the best that could be hoped from the prudence and integrity of our States-men; insomuch, that when the Merchants have at any time come down from London to represent their grievances from the French, to seek redress, or offer their humble advice, they were Hector'd,[234] Brow-beaten, Ridiculed, and might have found fairer audience even from *Monsieur* Colbert.[235]

They knew moreover, that as in the matter of Commerce, so they had more obliged him in this War. That except the irresistable bounties of so great a Prince in their own particular, and a frugal Subsistance-money for the Fleet, they had put him to no charges, but the English Navy Royal

---

blew up.

[233] Maxime: rule of conduct.

[234] Hector'd: bullied, threatened.

[235] *Monsieur* Colbert: Charles Colbert de Croissy, French ambassador to England in 1668–74.

serv'd him, like so many *Privateers*,[236] No *Purchase*, No *Pay*. That in all things they had acted with him upon the most abstracted[237] Principles of Generosity. They had tyed him to no {41} terms, had demanded no Partition of Conquests, had made no humane Condition; but had sold all to him for those *two* Pearls of price,[238] the *True Worship*, and the *True Government*. Which disinteressed proceeding of theirs, though suited to Forraine Magnanimity; yet, should we still lose at Sea, as we had hitherto, and the French Conquer all at Land, as it was in prospect, might at one time or other breed some difficulty in answering for it to the King and Kingdom: However this were, it had so hapned before the arrival of the *Plenipotentiaries*, that, whereas here in England, all that brought applications[239] from Holland were treated as Spies and Enemies, till the French *King* should signify his pleasure; he on the contrary, without any communication here, had received Addresses from the Dutch *Plenipotentiaries*, and given in to them the sum of his Demands (not once mentioning his Majesty or his [37] Interest, which indeed he could not have done unless for mockery, having demanded all for himself, so that there was no place left to have made the English any satisfaction) and the French Ministers therefore did very candidly acquaint those of Holland, that, upon their accepting those Articles, there should be a firm Peace, and Amity restored: But as for England, the States, their Masters, might use their discretion, for that France was not obliged by any Treaty to procure their advantage.

This manner of dealing might probably have animated, as it did warrant the English *Plenipotentiaries*, had they been as full of Resolution as of Power, to have closed with the Dutch, who, out of aversion to the French, and their intollerable demands, were ready to have thrown themselves into his Majesties Armes, or at his Feet, upon any reasonable conditions; But it wrought clean otherwise: For, those of the English *Plenipotentiaries*, who were, it seems, intrusted with a fuller Authority, and the deeper Secret, gave in also the English Demands to the Hollanders, consisting in eight Articles, but at last the Ninth saith,[240] {42}

---

[236] Privateers: armed vessels owned by private persons, and often holding a commission from the government authorizing their operations against a hostile nation.

[237] abstracted: without concrete embodiment, disinterested.

[238] *Pearls* of price: mocking recollection of Matthew 13:45–46.

[239] applications: appeals, requests, petitions.

[240] For a full list of the English terms to the Dutch, see Add. MS 72578, f. 13r–v.

Although his Majesty contents himself with the foregoing Conditions, so that they be accepted within ten days, after which his Majesty understands himself to be no further obliged by them. He declares nevertheless precisely, that albeit they should all of them be granted by the said States, yet they shall be of no force, nor will his Majesty make any Treaty of Peace or Truce, unless the Most Christian King *shall have received satisfaction from the said States in his particular.* And by this means they made it impossible for the Dutch, however desirous, to comply with England, excluded us from more advantagious terms, than we could at any other time hope for, and deprived us of an honest, and honourable evasion out of so pernicious a War, and from a more dangerous Alliance. So that now it appeared by what was done that the Conspirators securing their own fears at the price of the Publick Interest, and Safety, had bound us up more strait then ever, by a new Treaty,[241] to the French Project. [38]

The rest of this year passed with great successe to the French, but none to the English. And therefore the hopes upon which the War was begun, of the Smyrna and Spanish Fleet, and Dutch Prizes, being vanished, the slender Allowance from the French not sufficing to defray it, and the ordinary Revenue of the King, with all the former Aides being (as was fit to be believed) in less than one years time exhausted, The Parliament by the Conspirators good leave, was admitted again to sit at the day appointed, the 4th. of February 1672.[242]

The War was then first communicated to them, and the Causes, the Necessity, the Danger, so well Painted out, that the Dutch abusive Historical Pictures, and False Medalls (which were not forgot to be mentioned) could not be better imitated or revenged; Onely, there was one great omission of their False Pillars, which upheld the whole Fabrick of the Eng. Declaration; Upon this signification, the House of Commons (who had never failed the Crown hitherto up-{43}on any occasion of mutual gratuity) did now also, though in a War contrary to former usuage, begun without their Advice, readily Vote, no less a summe than 1250000 *l*. But for better Colour,[243] and least they should own in words, what they did in effect,

---

[241] "Treaty for a strict Union of Interests between Lewis XIV. King of France, and Charles II. King of England . . . Done at the Camp of Hesurick [Heeswick], July 16, 1672," *A General Collection of Treatys*, 4 vols. (London, 1732), 4:441–43.

[242] 1672/3.

[243] for better Colour: to give a better appearance, to conceal the truth.

they would not say it was for the War, but for the Kings Extraordinary Occasions.[244]

And because the Nation began now to be aware of the more true Causes, for which the War had been undertaken, they prepared an Act[245] before the Money-Bill[246] slipt thorrow their Fingers, by which the Papists were obliged, to pass thorow a new State Purgatory,[247] to be capable of any Publick Imployment; whereby the House of Commons, who seem to have all the Great Offices of the Kingdom in Reversion, could not but expect some Wind-falls.[248]

Upon this Occasion it was, that the Earl of Shaftsbury,[249] though then Lord Chancellour of England, yet Engaged so far in Defence of that ACT, and of the PROTESTANT RELIGION, that in due time it cost him his Place, and was the first moving Cause of all those Misadventures, and [39] Obloquy,[250] which since he lyes (ABOVE, not) *Under*.

The Declaration also of Indulgence was questioned, which, though his MAJESTY had out of his Princely, and Gracious Inclination, and the memory

---

[244] A royal contingency fund.

[245] Act: the Test Act, passed into law on March 29, 1673, denying public office to those who refused to take the oaths of allegiance and supremacy and who would not subscribe to a declaration against transubstantiation.

[246] the Money-Bill: ordered to be engrossed on March 15, 1672/3 (*JHC* 9:269), an eighteen months' assessment to raise £1,238,750.

[247] State Purgatory: ironic invocation of Roman Catholic description of spiritual purification, wherein the souls of the dead that have had eternal punishment remitted by the grace of God suffer and become purged of sins committed.

[248] Wind-falls: unexpected acquisitions or advantages.

[249] Earl of Shaftsbury: Anthony Ashley Cooper, first earl of Shaftesbury (1621–83), whose long, active political service included court promotions to chancellor of the Exchequer (1661–72) and lord chancellor (1672–73), but who when forced from high office turned to a career in opposition, increasingly focused on resistance to the French interest and against the succession to the throne of the duke of York. Marvell's work as a controversialist won Shaftesbury's political protection and then perhaps also his financial support. Shaftesbury's support of protestant dissenters was perhaps the most consistent feature of his career, and here Marvell very generously makes this the defining feature of his lord chancellorship, overlooking his role in breaking the Triple League and encouraging the Third Anglo-Dutch War. In 1677 Shaftesbury was one of the four lords imprisoned in the Tower for maintaining the long prorogation of 1675–77 as a dissolution of parliament; he was not released until February 1678.

[250] Obloquy: evil-speaking, slander.

of some former Obligations[251] granted, yet upon their Representation of the Inconveniencies, and at their humble Request, he was pleased to Cancel, and Declare, that it should be no President for the Future: For otherwise some succeeding Governour, by his single Power Suspending Penal Laws, in a favourable matter, as that is of Religion, might become more dangerous to the Government, than either Papists or Fanaticks,[252] and {44} make us *Either*, when he pleased: So Legal was it in this Session to Distinguish between the King of Englands Personal, and his Parliamentary Authority.

But therefore the further sitting being grown very uneasie to those, who had undertaken for the Change of Religion, and Government, they procured the Recess so much sooner, and a Bill sent up by the Commons in favour of Dissenting Protestants, not having passed thorow the Lords preparation, the Bill concerning Papists, was enacted in Exchange for the Money, by which the Conspirators, when it came into their management, hoped to frustrate, yet the effect of the former. So the Parliament was dismissed[253] till the *Twenty seventh* of October, *One thousand six hundred seventy three.*

In the mean time therefore they strove with all their might to regain by the War, that part of their Design, which they had lost by Parliament; and though several honourably forsook their Places rather than their Consciences, yet there was never wanting some double-dyed Son of our Church, some Protestant in grain,[254] to succeed upon the same Conditions. And the difference was no more, but that their Offices, or however their Counsels, were now to be administred by their Deputies, such as they could confide in.

The business of the Land Army was vigourously carried on, in appearance to have made some descent in Holland, but though the Regiments were Compleated and kept Imbodyed,[255] [40] it wanted effect,

---

[251] Declaration . . . former Obligations: Parliament rescinded the Declaration of Indulgence in 1673, in part for the reasons to which Marvell now turns, and Charles II was forced to withdraw it and pass the Test Act.

[252] Fanaticks: Marvell adopts the seventeenth-century pejorative for Protestant nonconformists in order to reflect the thinking of the Cavalier Parliament.

[253] further sitting . . . dismissed: Marvell imputes to the "Conspirators" a trade-off accepting the Test Act in order to secure supply, while frustrating by the adjournment of March 29, 1673, the progress of the bill to ease Protestant dissenters.

[254] double-dyed . . . in grain: deeply stained (often figurative), dyed in the Kermes or scarlet grain, used contemptuously.

[255] Imbodyed: organized into a military array, marshaled.

and therefore gave cause of suspition: The rather, because no English-man, among so many well-disposed, and qualified for the work, had been thought capable, or fit to be trusted with Chief Command of those Forces, but that *Monsieur* Schomberg[256] a French Protestant, had been made General, and Colonel Fitsgerald,[257] an Irish Papist, Major General, as more proper for the Secret; the first of advancing the French Government, the second of promoting the Irish Religion.{45}

And therefore the dark hovering of that Army so long at Black-Heath,[258] might not improbably seem the gatherings of a Storm to fall upon London; But the ill successes which our Fleet met withal this Year also at Sea, were sufficient, had there been any such design at home, to have quasht[259] it: for such Gallantries are not to be attempted, but in the highest raptures of Fortune.

There were three several Engagements of ours against the Dutch *Navy* in this one Summer; but while nothing was Tenable at Land, against the French, it seem'd that to us at Sea every thing was impregnable; which is not to be attributed to the want of Courage or Conduct, either the former Year under the Command of his Royal Highness, so Great a Souldier, or this Year under the Prince Rupert;[260] But is rather to be imputed to our

[256] *Monsieur* Schomberg: Frederick Herman Schomberg, duke of Schomberg (1615–90). Born at Heidelberg, he became a French subject in 1664, and on July 3, 1673 became a commander of English troops, under Prince Rupert. He encamped with his army around Yarmouth, but the plan to invade Holland was dashed by the English setback in the sea battle off Texel, after which his unpopularity in England led him to return to France that November.

[257] Colonel Fitsgerald: Colonel John Fitzgerald, formerly deputy-governor of Tangier, commanded an Irish regiment and was notorious as a Catholic who had nonetheless taken the test (*P & L*, 1:422–23nn; *Letters Addressed from London to Sir Joseph Williamson*, ed. W. D. Christie [London, 1874], 1:21).

[258] Black-Heath: The perceived threat found satirical comment in the verse "History of Insipids" (possibly by Marvell himself, Lord, *POAS*, 1:243–51): "Our Blackheath host, without dispute / (Rais'd, put on board, why, no man knows) / Must Charles have render'd absolute / Over his subjects or his foes . . ."

[259] quasht: put an end to.

[260] the Prince Rupert: *77a, 79, 89* Robert]; on August 15, 1672, Rupert was appointed vice-admiral of England. After the duke of York resigned, Prince Rupert became general at sea and land (April 26, 1673) and admiral of the fleet (June 16, 1673). The "three several Engagements . . . against the Dutch Navy in this one Summer" are the two battles fought against the Dutch off Schoneveldt, May 28 / June 7 and June 4/14, and the Battle of the Texel on August 11/21, in which Dutch success proved the

unlucky Conjunction with the French, like the disasters that happen to men by being in ill Company.

But besides it was manifest that in all these Wars, the French meant nothing less than really to assist us: He[261] had first practised the same Art at Sea, when he was in League with the Hollander against us, his Navy never having done them any service, for his business was only to see us Batter one another. And now he was on the English side, he only studied to sound our *Seas,* to spy our *Ports,* to learn our *Building,* to contemplate our way of *Fight,* to consume ours, and preserve his own *Navy,* to encrease his *Commerce,* and to order all so, that the two great Naval Powers of Europe, being crushed together, he might remain sole Arbitrator of the Ocean, and by consequence Master of all the Isles and Continent. To [41] which purposes the Conspirators furnished him all possible opportunities. Therefore it was that *Monsieur* d'Estree, though a Person otherwise of tryed Courage and Prudence, yet never did worse than in the third and last Engagement; and because brave *Monsieur* d'Martel[262] did better, and could not endure a thing that looked like Cowar-{46}dise or Treachery, though for the Service of his Monarch, commanded him in, rated[263] him, and at his return home he was, as then was reported, discountenanced and dismissed from his Command, for no other crime, but his breaking of the French measures,[264] by adventuring one of those sacred Ships in the English, or, rather his own Masters Quarrel.

---

frustration of the English invasion of the Netherlands. The allied French fleet was commanded by d'Estrées.

[261] He: personifies "the French" in this and the next sentence. Bitter suspicions of the French, and especially of d'Estrées, were voiced after the Texel standoff and then influentially by Prince Rupert himself. J. C. Davies, *Gentlemen and Tarpaulins* (Oxford, 1991), pp. 172–74.

[262] *Monsieur* d'Martel: the marquis de Martel, who had brought support from the Mediterranean fleet and had become French second-in-command by the time of the Battle of the Texel; he soon "published a statement confirming Rupert's charges against d'Estrées in every particular." Anderson, ed., *Journals and Narratives of the Third Dutch War,* pp. 54–55; Davies, *Gentlemen and Tarpaulins,* p. 174.

[263] rated: berated. "The wits of the Town tell us, that when the fight was done the Count D'Estrées sent for Martell, and told him when he came home he would have him hanged for dareing to hazard the King's Ship." Robert Yard newsletter to Sir Joseph Williamson, Sept. 5, 1673 (*Letters Addressed from London to Sir Joseph Williamson,* ed. Christie, 2:9).

[264] measures: plan or course of action.

His Royal Highnesse (by whose having quitted the Admiralty, the Sea service thrived not the better) was now intent upon his Marriage, at the same time the parliament was to reassemble the 27th of October 1673, The Princess of Modena, his Consort,[265] being upon the way for England, and that business seemed to have passed all impediment. Nor were the Conspirators who (to use the French phrase) made a considerable Figure[266] in the Government, wholly averse to the Parliaments meeting: For if the House of Commons had after one years unfortunate War, made so vast a Present to his Majesty of 1250000 *l.* but the last February, it seemed the argument would now be more pressing upon them, that by how much the ill successes, of this year had been greater, they ought therefore to give a yet more liberal Donative.[267] And the Conspirators as to their own particular reckoned, that while the Nation was under the more distress and hurry they were themselves safer from Parliament, by the Publick Calamity.

A supply therefore was demanded with much more importunity and assurance then ever before, and that it should be a large one and a speedy: They were told that it was now *Pro Aris & Focis*,[268] all was at stake. And yet besides all this, the Payment of the Debt to the Banckers upon shutting the Exchequer was very civilly recommended to them. And [42] they were assured that his Majesty would be constantly ready to give them all proofs of his Zeal for the true Religion and the Laws of the Realm, upon all occasions. But the House of Commons not having been sufficiently prepared for such demands, nor well satisfied in several matters of {47} Fact, which appeared contrary to what was represented, took check; and first interposed in that tender point of his Royal Highnesse's Match, although she was of his own Religion, which is a redoubled sort of Marriage, or the

---

[265] Princess of Modena, his Consort: Mary Beatrice of Modena (1658–1718), daughter of Alfonso IV, duke of Modena, second wife of James II (whose first wife, Anne Hyde, had died in 1671). A marriage ceremony uniting James (by proxy) and the Catholic Mary Beatrice was performed on September 30, 1673. Parliament called upon Charles II to declare the proxy marriage void, but the king would not comply; and Mary Beatrice met James at Dover on November 21, where the ceremony was performed again.

[266] made . . . Figure: the Gallicism is *faire figure.*

[267] Donative: financial supply, perhaps with some classicizing irony recalling imperial Rome.

[268] *Pro Aris & Focis:* "For altars and hearths," or, figuratively, "for God and country" (Cicero *Pro Roscio Amerino,* V; Sallust, *Catiline,* LIX), here also with ironic reference to the Declaration of Indulgence and to the Hearth Tax granted previously.

more spiritual part of its Happiness. Besides, that she had been already solemnly married by the Dukes Proxcy, so that unless the Parliament had been Pope, and Claimed a power of Dispensation,[269] it was now too late to avoid it. His Majesty by a short Prorogation of six days, when he understood their intention, gave them opportunity to have desisted: But it seems they judged the National Interest of Religion so far concerned in this matter, that they no sooner meet again, but they drew up a second request by way of Address to his Majesty with their Reasons against it. That for his Royal Highness to marry the Princess of Modena, or any other of that Religion, had very dangerous consequences: That the minds of his Majesties Protestant subjects will be much disquieted, thereby filled with infinite discontents and Jealousies. That his Majesty would thereby be linked into such a foraine Alliance, which will be of great disadvantage and possibly to the Ruine of the Protestant Religion. That they have found by sad experience how such marriages have always increased Popery, and incouraged Priests and Jesuits to prevert his Majesties subjects: That the Popish party already lift up their heads in hopes of his marriage: That they fear it may diminish the affection of the people toward his Royal Highness, who is by bloud so near related to the Crown: That it is now more then one Age,[270] that the subjects have lived in continual apprehensions of the increase of Popery, and the decay of the Protestant Religion: Finally that she having many Kindred and Relations in the Court of Rome, by this means their enterprises [43] here might be facilitated, they might pierce into the most secret Counsels of his Majesty, and discover the state of the Realm. That the most learned men are of opinion, that Marriages no further Proceeded in, {48} may lawfully be Dissolved: And therefore they beseech his Majesty to Annul the Consummation of it, and the Rather, because they have not yet the Happiness to see any of his Majestyes own Linage to Succeed in his Kingdoms.

These Reasons, which were extended more amply against his Royal Highnesses Marriage, obtained more weight, because most men are apt to Judge of things by Circumstances, and to attribute what happens by the Conjuncture of Times, to the Effect of Contrivance. So that it was not

---

[269] power of Dispensation: the granting of a license by the pope, archbishop, or bishop to a person to nullify or "avoid" what is enjoined by ecclesiastic law or solemn obligation.

[270] one Age: a lifetime (presumably going back at least to Charles I's marriage to Henrietta Maria).

difficult to Interpret what was in his Royal Highness, an ingagement only of Honour and Affection, as proceeding from the Conspirators Counsels, seeing it made so much to their purpose.

But the business was too far advanced to retreat, as his Majesty with great reason had replyed, to their former Address, the Marriage having been celebrated already, and confirmed by his Royal Authority, and the House of Commons though sitting when the Duke was in a Treaty for the Arch Dutchess of Inspruck,[271] one of the same Religion, yet having taken no notice of it.

Therefore while they pursued the matter thus, by a second Address, it seemed an easier thing, and more decent, to Prorogue the Parliament, than to Dissolve the Marriage. And, which might more incline his Majesty to this Resolution, the House of Commons had now bound themselves up by a Vote that having considered the present State of the Nation, they would not take into {49} Deliberation, nor have any further Debate upon any other Proposals of Aid, or any Surcharge upon the Subject,[272] before the payment of the *Twelve hundred and fifty thousand pounds,* in *eighteen Months,* which was last granted, were expired, or at least till they should evidently see that the Obstinacy of the Hollanders should oblige them to the contrary, nor till after the kingdom should be effectually [44] secured against the dangers of Popery, and Popish Counsellors, and that Order be taken against other present Misdemeanours.

There was yet another thing, the Land-Army, which appearing to them expensive, needless, and terrible to the People, they addressed to his Majesty also, that they might be disbanded. All which things put together, his Majesty was induced to Prorogue the Parliament again for a short time, till the *seventh* of January, *One thousand six hundred seventy three.*[273] That in the mean while the Princess of Modena arriving, the Marriage might be consummated without further interruption.

That Session was opened with a large deduction also, by the new Lord *Keeper,*[274] this being his first Experiment in the Lords House of his Elo-

---

[271] Arch Dutchess of Inspruck: Archduchess Claudia Felicitas. In the summer of 1672 negotiations with Leopold I, Holy Roman emperor, for a marriage between James and Claudia Felicitas broke down.

[272] Surcharge upon the Subject: further taxation.

[273] I.e., 1674 new style.

[274] the new Lord *Keeper:* Sir Heneage Finch (1621–82) had succeeded Shaftesbury after the latter's resignation of the chancellorship, Nov. 9, 1673, but only with the title of

quence and Veracity, of the Hollanders averseness to Peace or Reason, and their uncivil and indirect dealing in all Overtures of Treaty[275] with his Majesty, and a Demand was made therefore and re-inforced as formerly, of a proportionable and speedy Supply. But the Hollanders that had found themselves obstructed alwayes hitherto, and in a manner excluded from all Applications, and that whatever means they had used was still misinterpreted, and ill represented, were so industrious, as by this time (which was perhaps the greatest part of their Crime) to have undeceived the generality of the Nation in those particulars. {50}

The House of Commons therefore not doubting, but that if they held their hands in matter of money, a Peace would in due time follow, grew troublesome rather to several of the great Ministers of State, whom they suspected to have been Principal in the late pernicious Counsels. But instead of the way of Impeachment,[276] whereby the Crimes might have been brought to Examination, Proof and Judgment, they proceeded Summarily within themselves, noting them only with an ill Character, and requesting his Majesty to remove them from his Counsels, his Presence, and their Publick Imployments. Neither in that way of handling were they Impartial. [45]

Of the three which were questioned, the Duke of Buckingham[277] seemed to have much the more favourable Cause, but had the severest Fortune. And

---

lord keeper. His long speech appears in the *Lords Journal* (12:595–98). Marvell had identified Finch as first in "th' Lawyers Mercenary Band" in "The Last Instructions," ll. 185–86, and the present observations at his expense are already implied in *Mr. Smirke;* they may now have been sharpened by Finch's part in the prosecution of *Mr. Smirke* (see p. 9 above).

[275] Overtures of Treaty: negotiations preparatory to peace.

[276] Impeachment: prosecution for treason or other high crime, brought by the House of Commons before the House of Lords.

[277] Duke of Buckingham: George Villiers, second duke of Buckingham (1628–87), prominent politician, miscellaneous writer, and owner of great properties in Yorkshire. Marvell's praise for Buckingham may have stemmed from an association dating back to the 1640s (Edward Chaney, *The Grand Tour and the Great Rebellion* [Geneva, 1985], pp. 347–50); Buckingham had in 1657 married Marvell's former pupil, Mary, daughter of the great parliamentary general Lord Fairfax; and there are signs in the 1670s of Marvell's part in what may be termed the Buckingham circle (Hertfordshire RO, MSS D/EP F.37, passim, and p. 262; Harold Love, "How Personal Is a Personal Miscellany? Sarah Cowper, Martin Clifford and the 'Buckingham Commonplace Book,'" in *Order and Connexion,* ed. R. C. Alston [Cambridge, 1997], p. 118); see also *P & L,* 1:379–80.

this whole matter not having been managed in the solemn Methods of National Justice, but transmitted to his Majesty, it was easily changed into a Court Intrigue, where though it be a Modern *Maxime,*

That no State Minister ought to be punished, but, *especially not upon Parliamentary Applications.*

Yet other Offenders thought it of security to themselves, in a time of Publick Discontent, to have one Man sacrificed, and so the Duke of Buckingham having worse Enemies, and as it chanced worse Friends than the rest, was after all his Services abandoned, they having only heard the sound, while he felt all the smart of that Lash from the House of Commons.

But he was so far a Gainer, that with the loss of his Offices, and dependance, he was restored to the Freedom of his own Spirit, to give thenceforward those admirable {51} Proofs of the Vigour, and Vivacity of his better Judgment, in Asserting, (though to his own Imprisonment,) the due Liberties of the English Nation.

This manner of proceeding in the House of Commons, was a new way of negotiating the Peace with Holland, but the most effectual; the Conspirators living all the while under continual apprehensions of being called to further account for their Actions, and no mony appearing, which would either have perpetuated the War, or might in case of a Peace, be misapplied to other uses then the building of Ships, insinuated by the Lord Keeper.

The Hollanders Proposalls, by this means, therefore, began to be thought more reasonable, and the *Marquis* del Fresno,[278] the Spanish Minister in this Court, laboured so well, that his Majesty thought fit to Communicate the overture to both Houses; and though their advice had not been asked to the War, yet not to make the Peace without it. There was not much difficulty in their Resolutions; For the general bent of the Nation was against the War; the French now had by [46] their ill behaviour at Sea, in all the Engagements, raised also the English Indignation; their pernicious Counsels were visible in their book of the *Politique Francoise,*[279] tending by frequent levyes of men, and mony, to exhaust and weaken our Kingdom, and by their conjunction with us, on set purpose, to raise betwixt the King and his People, a rational Jealousy of Popery, and French Government, till we

---

[278] *Marquis* del Fresno: Pedro Fernandez de Jovar Velasco, the marqués del Fresno, Spanish ambassador, had arrived on March 2, 1671/2.

[279] *Politique Francoise:* a hostile evaluation of French ambitions by François Paul de Lisola, *Le Politique du Temps ou le Conseil Fidelle sur les Mouvemens de la France. Tiré des evenemens passez pour servir d'instruction à la Triple Ligue* (Charleville, 1671), pp. 164–71.

should insensibly devolve into[280] them by Inclination or Necessity: As men of ill conversation, pin themselves maliciously on persons more sober, that if they can no otherwise debauch them, they may blast their Reputation by their society, and so oblige them to theirs, being suspected by better Company. {52}

Besides all which the very reason of Traffick, which hath been so long neglected by our greater Statesmen was now of some consideration, for as much as by a Peace with the Hollander the greatest part of the Trade and Navigation of Europe as long as the French King disturbed it, would of course fall into the English management. The Houses therefore gave their humble advice to his Majesty for a just and honourable Peace with the States General,[281] which when it could be no longer resisted, was concluded.

In the seventh Article of this Treaty[282] it is said.

That the Treaty which was made at Breda in the yeare 1667, as also all the others which are by this present Treaty confirmed, shall by the present be renewed, and shall continue in their full force and vigour, as far as they shall not be contrary unto this said present Treaty.

Which words are the more to be taken notice of, that they may be compared afterwards with the effects that follow, to see how well on the English part that Agreement hath been observed.

The business of the Peace thus being once over, and this Parliament still lowring upon[283] the Ministers of State, or bogling at[284] the Land Forces (whereof the eight new raised Regiments were upon the request of the Commons at last disbanded) or imployed in further Bills against Popery, and for [47] the Education, and Protestant Marriage henceforward of those of the Royal Family; the necessity of their further sitting seemed not so urgent, but that they might have a repose till the tenth of November 1674. following.

The Conspirators had hitherto failed of the accomplishing their design,

---

[280] devolve into: roll or flow on to or into some condition (thus cited in *OED*).

[281] Marvell had been employed by the Dutch toward this end, and on Feb. 3, 1674, "for the only time in his parliamentary career, he was appointed to draw up reasons for a conference with the Lords about an address for peace" with Holland (Henning, 3:26; Haley, *William of Orange*, 57–58).

[282] The Treaty of Westminster agreeing peace between England and the Netherlands was signed at Westminster on Feb. 19, 1674, bringing the Third Dutch War to a close. Marvell's wording differs only slightly from that in the version published in 1686.

[283] lowring upon: frowning or scowling at.

[284] bogling at: taking alarm at, or stickling over.

by perpetual disappointments, and which {53} was most grievous to them, foresaw, that the want of mony would still necessitate the frequent sitting of Parliament, which danger they had hoped long ere this to have conquered. In this state of their affairs the French King therefore was by no means to be further disobliged, he being the Master of their secret, and the only person which if they helped him at this plunge, might yet carry them thorow. They were therefore very diligent to profit themselves of all the advantages to this purpose that their present posture could afford them. They knew that his Majesty being now disengaged from War, would of his Royal Prudence interpose for Peace by his Mediation, it being the most glorious Character that any Prince can assume, and for which he was the more proper, as being the most Potent, thereby to give the sway, and the most disinteressed whereby to give the Equity requisite to such a Negotiation; and the most obliged in Honour, as having been the occasion by an unforeseen conse-quence of drawing the sword of all this part of Europe. But if they feared any propension[285] in his Majesty to one party, it was toward Spain, as knowing how that Crowne (as it is at large recited, and acknowledged, in the preamble of the last Treaty between England and Holland)[286] had been the only instrument of the happy Peace which after that pernicious War we now injoyed.

Therefore they were resolved by all their influence, and industry (though the profit of the War did now wholly, redound to the English Nation, and however in case of peace it was our interest, that if any, France should be depressed to any equality) to labour that by this Mediation France might be the onely gainer, and having all quiet about him, might be at perfect leisure to attend their project upon England. And one [48] of these our Statesmen being pressed, solved all Arguments to the contrary with an oraculous French question {54}

Faut il que tout se fasse par Politique, rien par Amitie?

Must all things be done by Maxims or Reasons of State; nothing for Affection?

Therefore that such an absurdity as the ordering of Affairs abroad, ac-cording to the Interest of our Nation might be avoided, the English, Scotch

---

[285] propension: inclination, tendency.

[286] Westminster Treaty, Feb. 9/19, 1674, which preamble cited how "especially the most Serene Queen Regent of Spain, out of regard to that antient Union and Friend-ship which has subsisted between the Crowns of Great Britain and Spain, has us'd her Endeavours that Peace might be the sooner restor'd, by the removing of all manner of Disputes between the Kingdom of Great Britain and the Provinces of the United Netherlands."

and Irish Regiments, that were already in the French Service, were not only to be kept in their full Complement, but new numbers of Souldiers daily transported thither, making up in all, (as is related) at least a constant Body of *Ten thousand Men,* of his Majesties Subjects, and which oftentimes turned the Fortune of Battle on the French side by their Valour.

How far this either consisted with the Office of a Mediatour, or how consonant it was to the seventh Article above mentioned, of the last Treaty with Holland; It is for them to demonstrate who were the Authors. But it was indeed a good way to train up an Army, under the French *Discipline* and *Principles,* who might be ready seasoned upon occasion in England, to be called back and execute the same Counsels.

In the mean time, they would be trying yet what they could do at home. For the late proceedings of *Parliament,* in quashing the Indulgence, in questioning Ministers of State, in Bills against *Popery,* in not granting Money whensoever asked, were Crimes not to be forgiven, nor (however the Conspirators had provided for themselves) named in the Act of General Pardon.[287]

They began therefore after fifteen Years to remember that there were such a sort of men in England as the Old Cavalier Party;[288] and reckoned, that by how much the more generous, they were more credulous than others, and so more fit to be again abused. These were told, that all {55} was at Stake, Church and State (How truly said! But meant, how falsly!) That the Nation was running again into *Fourty One,*[289] That this was the time to refresh their antient merit, and [49] receive the Recompence double of all their Loyalty, and that hence forward the Cavaliers should have the Lottery[290] of all the Great or Small Offices in the Kingdom, and not so much as Sir Joseph Williamson[291] to have a share in it.

---

[287] Act of General Pardon: recalling that by Charles II in 1660, as if now a further Restoration after another parliamentary usurpation.

[288] Old Cavalier Party: Marvell's bid to divide royalist parliamentarians from the court invited this consideration for their grievances; he had written in a letter to William Popple that the efforts to forge an "Episcopal Cavalier Party" included discourse "of none having any beneficial Offices but Cavaliers, or Sons of Cavaliers" (July 24, 1675, *P & L,* 2:341).

[289] running again into *Fourty One:* reverting to the conditions of 1641, a commonplace for fears of a civil war.

[290] Lottery: this was a recent vogue.

[291] Sir Joseph Williamson (1633–1701) had emerged as a busy secretary of state in the 1660s, when he enjoyed the patronage of Arlington. Among the lucrative benefits was

By this means they indeed designed to have raised a Civil War, for which they had all along provided, by new Forts, and standing Forces, and to which they had on purpose both in England and Scotland given all provocation if it would have been taken, that so they might have a *Rase Campagne*[292] of Religion, Government, and Propriety: or they hoped at least by this means to fright the one party, and incourage the other, to give henceforward Money at pleasure, and that money on what title soever granted, with what stamp coyned, might be melted down for any other service or uses. But there could not have been a greater affront and indignity offered to those Gentlemen, (and the best did so resent it) then whether these hopes were real, to think them men that might be hired to any base action, or whether as hitherto but imaginary, that by erecting the late Kings Statue that whole Party might be rewarded in Effigie.[293]

While these things were upon the Anvill[294] the tenth of November was come for the Parliaments sitting, but that was put of till the 13th. of April 1675. And in the mean time, which fell out most opportune for the Conspirators, these Counsels were matured, and something further to be contrived, that was yet wanting: The Parliament accordingly meeting, and the House of Lords, as well as that of the Commons, being in deliberation of several wholesome Bills, such as the present state of the Nation required, the great Design came out in a Bill unexpectedly offered one morning in

---

his commission to run the Royal Oak lottery; his official newsletters became first the *Oxford Gazette* in 1665, and later the profitable *London Gazette*. Elected to parliament in 1669, he helped orchestrate the Court Party in the 1670s, and often joined in debate on the part of the Crown. For his discomfiture of Marvell in the winter-spring session of 1677, see the introduction above (p. 190). His career as a statesman suffered irreversible setbacks in the Popish Plot, and he was relegated to a more modest role as secretary and MP in the years that followed, although he found his way to serving as a court Whig in the 1690s (Henning, 3:736–40).

[292] *Rase Campagne:* flat and empty country. In debate on February 6, 1678, Marvell's Country ally Sir Thomas Meres makes some play with the word: "I desire your excuse, if I make use of a French word, *Campagne*, to be better understood in an English Parliament. We are forced to send out children into France to learn that language, to be better understood here. Therefore I would know the charge of this *Campagne*" (Grey, *Debates* 5:106).

[293] Compare the satires "The Statue at Charing Cross" and "A Dialogue between the Two Horses," sometimes attributed to Marvell (*POAS*, 1:270–83); "for more Pageantry, the old King's Statue on Horseback, of Brass, was bought, and to be set up at Charing Cross" (Marvell to Popple, July 24, 1675, *P & L*, 2:341).

[294] upon the Anvill: in preparation.

the House of Lords, whereby all such as injoyed any {56} beneficial Office, or Imployment, Ecclesiastical, Civil, or Military, to which was added, Privy Counsellors, Justices of the Peace, and Members of Parliament, were under a Penalty to take the Oath, and make the Declaration, and Abhorrence, insuing,[295] [50]

I A. B. *Do declare, That it is not Lawful upon any pretence whatsoever to take up Armes against the King, and that I do abhorre that Traiterous position, of taking Armes by his Authority against his Person, or against those that are Commissioned by him in Pursuance of such Commission. And I do swear, that I will not at any time Indeavour the Alteration of the Government either in Church or State. So help me God.*

This same Oath had been brought into the House of Commons, in the Plague year[296] at Oxford, to have been imposed upon the Nation; but there, by the assistance of those very same persons, that now introduce it,[297] 'twas thrown out, for fear of a General Infection of the Vitales[298] of this Kingdom: And though it passed then in a particular Bill, known by the name of the *Five-mile Act,*[299] because it only concerned the Non-conformist Preachers, yet even in that, it was throughly opposed by the late Earl of Southampton,[300] whose Judgement might well have been reckoned for the *Standard of Prudence and Loyalty.* It was indeed happily said, by the Lord Keeper, in the opening of this Session; *No Influences of the Starrs, no Configuration of the Heavens, are to be feared, so long as these two Houses stand in a Good Disposition to each other, and both of them in a happy Conjunction, with*

[295] Declaration . . . insuing: An oath opposing alterations in government, the Non-Resisting Test was brought into the Lords on May 17, 1675 (discussion of which episode is central to *A Letter from a Person of Quality*, 1675); in the Commons its progress faltered, until prorogation put an end to the matter. Marvell ironizes at the expense of this "politic Test" in a letter to William Popple, July 24, 1675 (*P & L*, 2:341).

[296] Plague year: during the Great Plague in 1665 parliament met at Oxford, with Marvell in attendance.

[297] very same persons, that now introduce it: "Lord Lindsay brought in the bill, and Danby seconded—these two, with Lord Lindsay's brother, being the three whose votes caused a rejection of similar test in the Oxford Session of 1665" (Grosart, 4:429).

[298] Vitales] vitals *79, 89*]: parts of the body upon which life depends.

[299] *Five-mile Act:* prevented Nonconformist ministers who had not sworn the oath of nonresistance from visiting their former congregations (1665).

[300] Earl of Southampton: Thomas Wriothsley, fourth earl of Southampton (1608–67), who with Marvell's friend Lord Wharton and Shaftesbury had then opposed the oath, *A Letter from a Person of Quality* (1675), p. 3.

their Lord and Soveraign. But if he had so early this Act in his prospect, the same *Astrology* might have taught him, that there is nothing more porten-tous, and of worse *Omen*, then when such an Oath hangs over a Nation, like a New *Comet* forboding the Alteration of Religion, or Govern-{57}ment: Such was the *Holy League* in France[301] in the Reign of Henry *the third.* Such in the time of Philip *the second,* the Oath in the Netherlands.[302] And so the Oaths in our late Kings time taught the Fanaticks, because they could not swear, yet to Covenant.[303] Such things therefore are, if ever, not needlessely thought for good fortune sake only to be attempted, and when was there any thing less necessary? No King of England had ever so great a Treasure of this Peoples Affections except what those ill men have, as they have done all the rest, consumed; whom but out of an excess of Love to [51] his Person, the Kingdom would never (for it never did formerly) so long have suffered: The Old Acts of Allegiance and Supremacy[304] were still in their full Vigour, unless against the Papists, and even against them too of late, whensoever the way was to be smoothed for a liberal Session of Parliament. And moreover to put the Crown in full security, this Parliament had by an Act of theirs determined a Question which the wisdom of their Ancestors had never decided, that the King hath the sole power of the *Militia.* And therefore my Lord Keeper[305] did by his patronizing this Oath, too grossely prevaricate,[306] against two very good *State Maximes,* in his *Harangue* to the Parliament, for which he had consulted not the *Astrologer,* but the *Historian,*[307] advising them first, That they should not *Quieta movere,*[308] that is, said he, *when men*

---

[301] the *Holy League* in France: an association of Roman Catholics formed during the French Wars of Religion in the late sixteenth century, first to oppose Henry III's granting of a concession to Protestants (Huguenots).

[302] the Oath in the Netherlands: the reenactment of the Edict of 1550 by Philip II in 1556 contributed to the unrest that led to the Dutch Revolt.

[303] to Covenant: recalling especially the Presbyterians' rebellious Solemn League and Covenant (1643).

[304] Old Acts of Allegiance and Supremacy: to the king as supreme head of the Church of England (1534, 1559).

[305] Sir Heneage Finch. His speech after the king's, opening the session of April 13, 1675, notably warned of "Two Symptoms which are dangerous in every State, and of which the Historian had long since given us Warning" (*JHL* 12:653–55), on which maxims Marvell now seizes at Finch's expense.

[306] prevaricate: deviate, go astray.

[307] the *Historian:* particularly Sallust and Tacitus.

[308] *Quieta movere:* "disturb the peace" (Sallust, *Catiline* 21.1; and also proverbial in law).

stirre those things or Questions which are, and ought to be in peace. And secondly, That they should not *Res parvas magnis motibus agere:*[309] That is, saith he againe, *when as much weight is laid upon a new and not always necessary Proposition, as if the whole summe of affaires depended upon it.*

And this Oath, it seems was the little thing he meant of, being forsooth but a *Moderate Security to the Church and Crown,* as he called it, but which he and his party *layd so much weight on, as if the whole sum of Affairs did depend upon it.* {58}

But as to the *Quieta movere,* or stirring of those things or Questions which are and ought to be in Peace, was not this so, of taking Armes against the King upon any pretence whatsoever? And was not that also in Peace, of the *Traiterous Position* of taking Armes by his Authority against his Person? Had not the three Acts of *Corporations,* of *Militia,* and the *Five Miles,* sufficiently quieted it? Why was it further *stirred?* But being stirred, it raises in mens thoughts many things more; some less, others more to the purpose.

Sir Walter Tirrells Arrow grazed upon the Deer it was shot at, but by that chance kill'd King William Rufus;[310] Yet so far was it that Sir Walter should for that chance shot be adjudged of Treason, that we do not perceive he underwent any [52] other Tryal like that of *Manslaughter:* But which is more to the point, it were difficult to instance a Law either in this or other Country, but that a private Man, if any king in Christendom assault him, may having retreated to the Wall,[311] stand upon his Guard; and therefore, if this matter as to a particular man be dubious, it was not so prudent to *stirre* it in the General,[312] being so well setled. And as to all other things, though since Lord *Chancellour,*[313] he have in his Speech of the 15 of Feb. *One thousand six hundred seventy six,* said (to testify his own abhorrency) *Away with that ill meant distinction between the Natural and the Politique Capacity.*[314] He is too well read to be ignorant that without that Distinction there would be no Law nor Reason of Law left in England; To which end it was,

---

[309] *Res parvas magnis motibus agere:* do little things with great disturbance. Marvell further alters Finch's more Tacitean formulation regarding troubled times, when "parvae quoque res magnis motibus agebantur" (even little things give rise to great excitements) (Tacitus, *Histories* 2:10.1).

[310] William Rufus: William II (1057–1100), king of England 1087–1100, was killed while deer hunting by a stray arrow thought to have been shot by Walter Tyrrell.

[311] retreated to the Wall: having given way.

[312] the General: population at large.

[313] Lord *Chancellour:* Sir Heneage Finch had belatedly gained this title, Dec. 19, 1675.

[314] *JHL* 13:38–39 (Feb. 15, 1676/7).

and to put all out of doubt, that it is also required in this *Test,* to declare mens abhorrency as of a *Traiterous Position,* to take Armes against those that are Commissioned by him, in pursuance of such Commission; and yet neither is the Tenour,[315] or Rule, of any such Commission specified, nor the Qualification of those that shall be armed with such Commissions, expressed or limited. Never was so much sence contained in so few words. No Conveyancer[316] could ever in more Compendious or binding terms have {59} drawn a Dissettlement of the whole Birth-right of England.

For as to the Commission, if it be to take away any mans Estate, or his Life by force, yet it is the Kings Commission: Or if the Person Commissionate,[317] be under never so many Dissabilities by Acts of Parliament, yet his taking this Oath, removes all those Incapacities, or his Commission makes it not Disputable. But if a man stand upon his Defence, a good Judge for the purpose, finding that the Position is *Traiterous,* will declare that by this Law, he is to be Executed for Treason.

These things are no Nicetyes,[318] or remote Considerations (though in making of Laws, and which must come afterwards under Construction of Judges; *Durante Bene-placito,*[319] all Cases are to be put and imagined) but there being an Act in Scotland for *Twenty thousand Men* to March into England [53] upon Call,[320] and so great a Body of English Souldiery[321] in France, within Summons, besides what *Forainers* may be obliged by Treaty to furnish; and it being so fresh in memory, what sort of persons had lately been in Commission among us, to which add the many Books then Printed by Licence, Writ, some by Men of the *Black,* one of the *Green-Cloath,*[322]

---

[315] Tenour: the means of proceeding.

[316] Conveyancer: a lawyer who prepares documents for the conveyance of property.

[317] Commissionate: commissioned.

[318] Nicetyes *77a, 77b*] Niceties *79, 89.*

[319] *Durante Bene-placito:* "during good pleasure," i.e., as long as it is wished. By this tenure the judges of England held their seats at the will of the sovereign, rather than as after the Act of Settlement (1700), when they did so *quamdiu se bene gesserint,* "as long as they should conduct themselves well."

[320] Act in Scotland: the Scottish Act ordering the militia (June 25, 1672), "so that on all occasions the King may have 20,000 foot and 2,000 horse well manned and ready for service" (*CSPD 1672,* p. 288).

[321] Souldery *77b*].

[322] Men of the *Black,* one of the *Green-Cloath:* men of the black cloth are clergy— Marvell has in view especially his earlier antagonist Samuel Parker; the green cloth was a department of the royal household—here the offender is Winston Churchill, who in *Divi*

wherein the Absoluteness of the *English* Monarchy is against all Law asserted.

All these Considerations put together, were sufficient to make any honest and well-advised man, to conceive indeed, that upon the passing of this Oath and Declaration, *the whole sum of Affairs depended.*

It grew therefore to the greatest contest, that has perhaps ever been in Parliament, wherein those Lords, that were against this Oath, being assured of their own Loyalty and Merit, stood up now for the English Liberties with the same Genius, Virtue and Courage, that their Noble Ancestors had formerly defended the *Great Charter of* England,[323] but with so much greater Commendation, in that they had here a fairer {60} Field, and the more Civil way of Decision: They fought it out under all the disadvantages imaginable: They were overlaid by Numbers, the noise of the House, like the Wind was against them, and if not the Sun, the Fireside[324] was alwayes in their Faces; nor being so few, could they, as their Adversaries, withdraw to refresh themselves in a whole days Ingagement: Yet never was there a clearer Demonstration how dull a thing is humane Eloquence, and Greatness, how little, when the bright Truth discovers all things in their proper Colours and Dimensions, and shining shoots its Beams thorow all their Fallacies. It might be injurious where all of them did so excellently well, to attribute more to any one of those Lords than another, unless because the Duke of Buckingham, and the Earl of Shaftsbury, have been the more reproached for this brave Action, it be requisite by a double proportion of Praise, to set them two on equal terms with the rest of their Companions in Honour. The particular Relation of this Debate, which lasted many days with great eagerness [54] on both sides, and the Reasons but on one, was in the next Session burnt by Order of the Lords, but the Sparkes of it will eternally fly in their Adversaries faces.[325]

Britannici (London, 1675) had notoriously "publisht in Print That the King may raise Money without his Parliament." *Seasonable Argument* (1677), pp. 7–8; Henning 2:72.

[323] *Great Charter of* England: the Magna Carta, reluctantly signed by King John in 1215, was a charter of English liberties, recognizing the people's right to justice.

[324] Fire-side: where the king might stand in the Lords. Marvell seems to recall the famous passage in Milton's *Areopagitica* describing how the warrior for truth "calls out his adversary into the plain, offers him the advantage of wind and sun" (*CPW,* 2:562), qv. Annabel Patterson, *Marvell: The Writer in Public Life* (Harlow, 2000), pp. 151–52; in Marvell's erotic lyric "The Fair Singer," by contrast, the lover is finally vanquished, "She having gained both the Wind and Sun" (*P & L,* 1:33).

[325] The House of Lords condemned the Shaftesburians' *Letter from a Person of*

Now before this *Test* could in so vigorous an opposition pass the House of Peers,[326] there arose unexpectedly a great Controversy betwixt the two Houses, concerning their Priviledges on this occasion; The Lords according to their undoubted Right, being the Supream Court of Judicature in the Nation, had upon Petition of Doctor Shirley, taken cognizance of a Cause between him and *Sir* John Fagg, a Member of the House of Commons,[327] and of other Appeales from the Court of Chancery, which the Commons, whether in good earnest, which I can hardly believe; or rather some crafty Parliament men among them, having an eye upon the *Test,* and to prevent the hazard of its coming among them, presently took hold of, and blew the Coales to such a degree, that there was no quenching them. {61}

In the House of Peers both Partyes, as in a point of their own Priviledge, easily united, and were no less inflamed against the Commons, and to uphold their own ancient Jurisdiction; wherein nevertheless both the Lords for the *Test,* and those against it, had their own particular reasons, and might have accused each-other perhaps of some artifice; The matter in conclusion was so husbanded[328] on all sides, that any longer converse betwixt the two Houses grew impracticable, and his Majesty Prorogued them therefore till the 13th of October 1675 following: And in this manner that fatal *Test* which had given so great disturbance to the minds of our Nation, dyed the *Second Death*[329] which in the language of the Divines, is as much as to say, it was *Damned.*

The House of Commons had not in that Session been wanting to Vote

---

Quality (1675) in the autumn session (*JHL,* 13:13, 14; Nov. 8–9, 1675). Cf. Francis Bacon, *A Wise and Moderate Discourse* (London, 1641), p. 11: "Forbidden writing is thought to be a certaine sparke of truth that flieth up in the faces of them that seeke to choke and tread it out," quoted by Milton in *Areopagitica* (*CPW,* 2:542; Patterson, *Marvell: The Writer in Public Life,* 152).

[326] House of Peers: House of Lords.

[327] Doctor Shirley . . . John Fagg: Thomas Shirley M.D. (1638–78) was heir to his father's estate, but it had been granted to Sir John Fagg (d. 1701) during the civil war. Shirley endeavored to recover his lost inheritance, but his suit was unsuccessful. Because he brought an appeal to the House of Lords in 1675, he was ordered into custody for breach of privilege, since Fagg was a member of parliament. A dispute between the Houses erupted over the matter, and Charles took the opportunity to prorogue the parliament on November 22, 1675.

[328] husbanded: carefully managed.

[329] dyed the *second Death:* utter destruction (cf. Rev. 2:11; 20:6, 14; and 21:8), since a prorogation marked an end to any pending legislation.

300000 *l.* towards the building of Ships, and to draw a Bill for appropriating the Ancient *Tunnage* and *Poundage*,[330] amounting to 400000 *l.* yearly to the use of the Navy, as it ought in Law already, and had been granted formerly upon that special Trust and Confidence; but neither did that [55] 300000 *l.* although Competent at present, and but an earnest for future meeting, seem considerable, and had it been more, yet that Bill of appropriating any thing to its true use, was a sufficient cause to make them both miscarry, but upon pretense of the quarrel between the Lords and Commons in which the Session thus ended.

The Conspirators had this interval to reflect upon their own affairs. They saw that the King of France (as they called him) was so busy abroad, that he could not be of farther use, yet, to them here, then by his directions, while his Armies were by assistance of the English Forces, several times saved from ruines. They considered that the *Test* was defeated, by which the Papists hoped to have had *Reprisals* for that of *Transubstantiation*,[331] and the Conspirators {62} to have gained Commission, as extensive and arbitrary, as the malice of their own hearts could dictate: That herewith they had missed of a Legality to have raised mony without Consent of Parliament, or to imprison or execute whosoever should oppose them in *pursuance of such their Commission.* They knew it was in vain to expect that his Majesty in that want, or rather opinion of want, which they had reduced him to, should be diverted from holding this Session of Parliament: nor were they themselves for this once wholly averse to it. For they presumed either way to find their own account, that if money were granted it should be attributed to their influence, and remain much within their disposal, but if not granted, that by joining this with other accidents of Parliament, they might so represent things to his Majesty as to incense him against them, and distrusting all Parliamentary Advice to take Counsel from themselves, from France, and from Necessity.

And in the mean time they fomented all the Jealousies which they caused. They continued to inculcate *Forty and One*[332] in Court and Country.

Those that refused all the mony they demanded, were to be the only

---

[330] Ancient *Tunnage* and *Poundage:* long-established customs, per ton of wine imported and per pound's worth of merchandise imported or exported, granted to the Crown at the beginning of each reign.

[331] *Reprisalls* for that of *Transubstantiation:* i.e., the Test Act against Roman Catholics was to have been answered by the (unsuccessful) Non-Resisting Test.

[332] *Forty and One:* 1641 again.

Recusants, and all that asserted the Liberties of the Nation, were to be reckoned in the *Classis* of *Presbyterians.*[333] [56]

The 13*th*. of October came, and his Majesty now asked not only a Supply for his building of Ships, as formerly, but further, to take off the *Anticipation* upon his *Revenue.*

The House of Commons took up again such Publick Bills as they had on foot in their former sitting, and others that might either Remedy Present, or Prevent Future Mischiefs.

The Bill for *Habeas Corpus.*[334]

That against sending men Prisoners beyond Sea. {63}

That against raising Money without Consent of Parliament.

That against Papists sitting in either House.

Another Act for speedier convicting of Papists.

That for recalling his Majestyes Subjects out of the French service, *&c.* And as to his Majestyes supply, they proceeded in their former Method of the two Bills. One for raising 300000 *l.* and the other for Appropriating the *Tunnage* and *Poundage* to the use of the Navy.

And in the Lords House there was a good disposition toward things of Publick Interest: But 300000 *l.* was so insipid a thing to those who had been continually regaled[335] with Millions, and that Act of Appropriation,[336] with some others, went so much against stomack that there wanted only an opportunity to reject them, and that which was readiest at hand was the late quarrel betwixt the House of Lords and the Commons. The House of Commons did now more peremptorily then ever, oppose the Lords Jurisdiction in Appeals:[337] The Lords on the other side were resolved not to depart from so essential a Priviledge and Authority, but to proceed in the Exercise of it: So that this Dispute was raised to a greater Ardure[338] and

[333] Recusants . . . *Classis* of *Presbyterians:* In mocking the court's desperation for supply, Marvell imagines another more secular Test Act. A classis is a local unit in Presbyterian church organization.

[334] *Habeas Corpus:* "you shall have the body," a legal writ issued by a court which orders those who hold a person in custody to produce that person before the court, thus protecting personal liberty against official authority. This "Bill" developed into the historic Habeas Corpus Act of 1679, checking illegal imprisonments.

[335] regaled: feasted, gratified.

[336] Act of Appropriation: for taxation.

[337] Jurisdiction in Appeals: another contest over the respective authority and functions of the Houses.

[338] Ardure: ardor.

Contention then ever, and there appeared no way of accomodation. Hereupon the Lords were in consultation for an Address to his Majesty, containing many weighty Reasons for his Majestyes dissolving this Parliament, deduced from the nature and behaviour of the present House of Commons: But his Majesty, although the transaction between the two Houses was at present become impracticable, Judging that this House might at some other [57] time be of use to him, chose only to Prorogue the Parliament; The blame of it was not only laid, but aggravated, upon those in both Houses, but especially on the Lords House, who had most vigorously opposed the French and Popish Interest. But those who were present at the Lords, and observed the conduct of the Great Ministers {64} there, conceived of it otherwise; And as to the House of Commons, who in the heat of the Contest had Voted,

That whosoever shall Sollicite or prosecute any Appeal against any Commoner of England, from any Court of Equity[339] before the House of Lords, shall be deemed and taken a betrayer of the Rights and Liberties of the Commons of England, and shall be proceeded against accordingly.

Their Speaker, going thorow Westminster-Hall to the House, and looking down upon some of those Lawyers, commanded his Mace[340] to seize them, and led them up Prisoners with him, which it is presumed, that he being of his Majesties Privy-Councill, would not have done, but for what some men call his Majesties *Service;* And yet it was the highest, this, of all the Provocations which the Lords had received in this Controversie. But however,[341] this fault ought to be divided, there was a greater committed in Proroguing the Parliament, from the 22th.[342] of November 1675. unto the 15th. of February 1676.[343] And holding it after that dismission, there being no Record of any such thing done since the being[344] of Parliaments in England, and the whole Reason of Law no less then the Practise and Custome holding Contrary.

This vast space betwixt the meetings of Parliament cannot more properly be filled up, then with the coherence of those things abroad and at home,

[339] *Court of Equity:* Court of Chancery.

[340] Mace: Sergeant of Mace, sent with this staff of office for authority to arrest.

[341] The comma might better be omitted here, with "however" qualifying "ought to be divided."

[342] the 22th. *77a, 77b, 79, 78, 89*] "the 22" *93.*

[343] I.e., Feb. 15, 1677. That the prorogation was more than a year long occasioned sharp doubts about its constitutionality.

[344] beginning *89, 93*].

that those that are intelligent may observe whether the Conspirators found any interruption, or did not rather sute[345] this event also to the Continuance of their Counsels. The Earl of Northampton[346] is not to be esteemed as one engaged in those Counsels, being a person of too great Honour, though the advancing of him to be [58] *Constable of the Tower,*[347] was the first of our Domestick occurrents.[348] But if they could have any hand in it, {65} 'tis more probable that lest he might perceive their Contrivances, they apparelled him in so much Wall[349] to have made him insensible. However men conjectured even then by the Quality of the Keeper, that he was not to be disparaged with any mean and vulgar Prisoners. But another thing was all along very remarkable, That during this Inter-Parliament, there were five Judges places either fell, or were made vacant (for it was some while before that Sir Francis North had been created Lord Chief Justice of the Common Pleas) the five that succeeded, were Sir Richard Rainsford, Lord Chief Justice of the *Kings Bench.* Mountague, Lord Chief Baron of the Exchequer. Vere Bartie, Barrister at Law, one of the Barons of the *Exchequer.* Sir William Scroggs, one of the Justices of the *Commons Pleas.* And Sir Thomas Jones, one of the Justices of the *Kings Bench.*[350] Concerning all whom there is something too much to be said; and it is not out of a figure of speech, but for meer reverence of their Profession that I thus pass it over, considering also humane infirmity, and that they are all by

[345] sute *77a, 77b*] suit[e] *79, 89, 93.*

[346] Earl of Northampton: James Compton, third earl of Northampton (1622–81).

[347] *Constable of the Tower:* the warden governing the garrison of the Tower of London.

[348] occurrents: happenings, occurrences, events.

[349] apparelled him in so much Wall: The Tower of London is indeed massive, and this may also recall Snout's costume as Wall in *Midsummer Night's Dream,* III.i (proposed) and V.i (performed), which role Marvell had cited in *RT2,* 1:224.

[350] Sir Francis North, Lord Guilford (1637–85) became chief justice of Common Pleas on Jan. 23, 1674/5. Sir Richard Rainsford (1605–80) succeeded Matthew Hale as chief justice of the King's Bench on Apr. 12, 1676. William Montague (c. 1619–1707) became chief baron of the Exchequer on Apr. 12, 1676. Vere Bertie (ent. Middle Temple 1654–d. 1680) became a baron of the Exchequer on June 4, 1675. Sir William Scroggs (1623–83) was appointed a justice of the Common Pleas on Oct. 23, 1676; his harsh judgments in the Popish Plot did not save him from later parliamentary impeachment (1680–81). Sir Thomas Jones (c. 1612–92) became a judge of the King's Bench on Apr. 13, 1676.

their Pattens,[351] *Durante Bene Placito,* bound as it were to their[352] Good Behaviour. And it is a shame to think what trivial, and to say the best of them, obscure persons have and do stand next in prospect, to come and sit by them. Justice Atkins[353] also by Warping[354] too far towards the Laws, was in danger upon another pretense to have made way for some of them, but upon true Repentance and Contrition, with some *Almes Deeds,*[355] was admitted to Mercy; And all the rest of the Benches will doubtless have profited much by his, and some other example. Alas the Wisdom and Probity of the Law went of for the most part with good Sir Matthew Hales,[356] and Justice is made a meer property. This poysonous Arrow strikes to the very heart of Government, and could come from no Quiver but that of the Conspirators. What French Counsel, what standing Forces, what Parliamentary Bribes, what National Oaths, and all the other Machinations of wicked men have [59] not yet {66} been able to effect, may be more compendiously Acted by twelve Judges in Scarlet.[357]

The next thing considerable that appeared preparatory for the next session, was a Book that came out by publick Authority, intituled, *Considerations touching the true way to suppress Popery, &c.*[358] A very good design, and writ, I believe, by a very good man, but under some mistakes, which are not to be passed over. One in the Preface, wherein he saith, *The Favour here proposed in behalf of the Romanists, is not more than they enjoy*

---

[351] Pattens: patents, documents issued by a sovereign or a person in authority, here issued to record the contract entered into by judges.

[352] their *79, 89*] "the" *77a, 77b*

[353] Justice Atkins: Sir Robert Atkyns (1621–1709) became judge of the Court of Common Pleas in 1672.

[354] Warping: hauling himself laboriously toward (from the nautical usage).

[355] *Almes Deeds:* charity to the poor, here used ironically of his compliance.

[356] Sir Mathew Hale (1609–76) became chief justice of King's Bench in 1671, presiding with distinction until his death; he had played an important part in successive efforts to draft legislation for the comprehension of moderate Presbyterians into the national church.

[357] twelve Judges in Scarlet: the High Court judges—the Country complaint against Danby and Finch's handling of legal appointments was now gathering force, Lionel Glassey, *Politics and the Appointment of Justices of the Peace 1675–1720* (Oxford, 1979), pp. 32–38.

[358] William Lloyd, *Considerations Touching the True way to suppresse Popery in this Kingdom: By making a Distinction between Men of Loyal and Disloyal Principles In that Communion* (London, 1677).

among Protestants abroad at this day.[359] This I take not to be true either in Denmark or Sweden and some other Countries where Popery is wholey suppressed; and therefore if that have been effected there, in ways of prudence and consisting with Christianity, it ought not to have been in so general words misrepresented.

Another is, *p.* 59. and 60. a thing ill and dangerously said, concluding, *I know but one Instance, that of David in Gath, of a man that was put to all these straits, and yet not corrupted in his principles.* When there was a more Illustrious Example[360] near him, and more obvious.

What else I have to say in passing, is, as to the Groundwork of his whole design, which is to bring men nearer, as by a distinction betwixt the Church and Court of Rome,[361] a thing long attempted, but ineffectually, it being the same thing as to distinguish betwixt the Church of England, and the English Bishops, which cannot be separated. But the intention of the Author, was doubtless very honest, and the English of that Profession, are certainly of all *Papists* the most sincere and most worthy of favour; but this seemed no proper time to negotiate further then the Publick Convenience.

There was another Book likewise that came out by Authority, towards the Approach of the Session, intitled, A *Packet of Advice to the Men of Shaftsbury, &c.*[362] But the name of the Author was concealed, not out of any spark of mo-{67}desty, but that he might with more security exercise his impudence, not so much against those Noble Lords, as against all publick [60] Truth and Honesty. The whole composition is nothing else but an Infusion of Malice, in the Froath of the Town, and the Scum of the *University,* by the Prescription of the Conspirators. Nor therefore did the Book deserve naming, no more then the Author, but that they should rot together in their own Infamy, had not the first events of the following

---

[359] Lloyd, *Considerations,* sig. A4v.

[360] *David in Gath* . . . Example: Marvell's point is tellingly ambiguous because when David, in flight from Saul, sought refuge with Achish, king of Gath, he is in one episode or version not well received and escapes by feigning madness (1 Sam. 21), but in another is welcomed and enters the service of Gath (1 Sam. 27–29); hence the example of Charles II and France.

[361] Lloyd, *Considerations,* esp. 136 ff.

[362] *A Packet of Advice:* Marchamont Nedham, *A Pacquet of Advices and Animadversions* . . . (London, 1676). Williamson and Roger L'Estrange supported this publication, for which with other such services Needham was richly compensated by Danby (receiving as much as £1000, Chicago, Newberry Library, J5454.71, flyleaf, and title pages nos. 3–5). Marvell's view is noted by Wood, 3:1187.

Session made it remarkable, that the Wizard dealt with some Superior Intelligence.

And on the other side, some scattering papers straggled out in Print,[363] as is usual for the information of Parliament men, in the matter of Law concerning Prorogation, which all of them, it is to be presumed, understood not, but was like to prove therefore a great Question.

As to matters abroad from the year 1674. That the Peace was concluded betwixt England and Holland; the French King, as a mark of his displeasure, and to humble the English *Nation*, let Loose his Privateers among our Merchant men: There was thenceforth no security of Commerce or Navigation, notwithstanding the publick Amity betwixt the two Crowns, but at Sea they Murthered, Plundred, made Prize and Confiscated those they met with. Their Picaroons[364] laid before the mouth of our Rivers, hoverd all along the Coast, took our Ships in the very Ports, that were in a manner blocked up by Water. And if any made application at his Soveraign *Port* for Justice, they were insolently baffled, except some few, that by Sir Ellis Leightons[365] Interest, who made a second prize of them, were redeemed upon easier Composition.[366] In this manner it continued from 1674, till the latter end of 1676 without remedy, even till the time of the Parliaments Sitting: so that men doubted whether even the Conspirators were not Complices also in the matter; and found partly their own account in it. For evidence of what is said, formerly, the Paper at the end {68} of this Treatise annexed[367] may serve, returned by some Members of the Privy-Council to his Majesties Order, to which was also adjoined a Register of so

[363] Especially other John Darby publications such as *The Long Parliament Dissolved* (1676); *A Seasonable Question, and an Usefull Answer* (1676); and *Some Considerations upon the Question, Whether the Parliament is Dissolved* (1676). *JHL* 13:42, Feb. 16, 1676/7: a committee was appointed in the Lords to find author and printer of *Some Considerations*.

[364] Picaroons: small pirate ships.

[365] Sir Ellis Leightons: Sir Elisha Leighton (d. 1685). In 1675 he went on embassy to France and accepted many bribes while arranging for the restitution of vessels captured by French privateers; in the summer of 1677 he was under renewed prosecution for that corruption, PRO, SP 44/334/407-8 (August 6, 1677).

[366] Composition: an agreement for the payment of a sum of money in lieu of the discharge of some other obligation, or in a different way from that required by the initial contract.

[367] the Paper . . . annexed: For the Trinity House shipping list and the report of this Committee on Trade, see introduction above, pp. 213–14.

many of the English Ships as then came to [61] notice which the French had taken, (and to this day cease not to treat our Merchants at the same rate.) And yet all this while that they made these intolerable and barbarous Piracyes, and depredations[368] upon his Majesties Subjects, from hence they were more diligently then ever supplied with Recruits, and those that would go voluntarily into the French service were incouraged, others that would not, pressed, imprisoned, and carried over by maine force, and constraint, even as the Parliament here was ready to sit down; notwithstanding all their former frequent applications to the Contrary. And his Majesties Magazins[369] were daily emptied, to furnish the French with all sorts of Ammunition, of which the following note contains but a small parcel, in comparison of what was daily conveyed away, under colour of Cockets for Jarsy,[370] and other places:

A short account of some Ammunition, &c. Exported from the Port of London to France, from June 1675. to June 1677.

Granadoes without number, Shipt off under the colour of unwrought *Iron*.

Lead Shot	21 Tuns.
Gunpowder	7134 Barrels.
Iron Shot	18 Tun, 600 Weight.
Match	88 Tun, 1900 Weight.

Iron Ordinance 441. Quantity, 292 Tuns, 900 Weight.

Carriages, Bandileirs, Pikes,[371] &c. uncertain.

Thus was the French King to be gratified for undoing us by Sea with contributing all that we could rap and rend[372] of Men, or Amunition at Land, to make more potent against us, and more formidable. {69}

Thus are we at length arrived at this much controverted, and as much expected Session. And though the way to[373] it hath proved much longer then was intended in the entry of this discourse, yet is it very short of what the matter would have afforded, but is past over to keep within bounds of

---

[368] depredations: plunders, pillages.

[369] Magazins: buildings which store supplies of arms, ammunition, and military provisions.

[370] Cockets for Jarsy: Cockets were documents sealed by the Customs House and delivered to merchants to certify that their merchandise had been entered and duty paid. *Jarsy* is an archaic form of Jersey, largest of the Channel Islands.

[371] Carriages, Bandileirs: A carriage is the wheeled support on which a piece of artillery is carried (e.g., a gun carriage); a bandoleer is a box containing musket-charges.

[372] rap and rend: seize and snatch.

[373] to *77a*] of *77b*.

this [62] Volumn. The 15*th* of February 1676 came, and that very same day the French King appointed his March for Flanders. It seemed that his motions were in Just *Cadence,* and that as in a *Grand Balet,* he kept time with those that were tuned here to his measure. And he thought it a becoming *Galantrie,* to take the rest of Flanders our natural out work in the very face of the King of England and his *Petites Maisons*[374] of Parliament.

His Majesty demanded of the Parliament in his Speech at the opening of the Sessions, a *Supply for building of Ships, and the further continuance of the Additional Excise upon Beer and Ale,* which was to expire the 24*th.* of June 1677, and *recommended earnestly a good correspondence between the two Houses, representing their last Differences as the reason of so long a Proroga-tion,* to allay them.[375] The Lord Chancellor,[376] as is usuall with him, spoiled all, which the King had said so well, with straining to do it better; For indeed the mischances of all the Sessions since he had the Seales, may in great part be ascribed to his indiscreet and unlucky Eloquence. And had not the Lord Treasurer a farre more effectual way of Perswasion[377] with the Commons, there had been the same danger of the ill success of this Meet-ing, as of those formerly. Each House being now seated, the case of this long Prorogation[378] had taken place so far without doors, and was of that consequence to the Constitution of all Parliaments, and the Validity of all proceedings in this Session, that even the Commons, though sore against their inclination, could not pass it over. But they handled it so tenderly, as if they were afraid to touch it.

The first day, instead of the Question, Whether the Par-{70}liament were by this unpresidented Prorogation indeed *Dissolved;* it was proposed,

---

[374] *Petites Maisons:* literally "little houses," but also the insane asylum or "Bedlam" of Paris, *The Royal Dictionary* (1700).

[375] Marvell summarizes the King's Speech, to the Lords and Commons assembled, Feb. 15, 1676/7, of which a copy was again read to the House of Commons (*JHL* 13:36–37; *JHC* 9:382–3).

[376] The Lord Chancellor: Sir Heneage Finch enlarged on the peace of the church and peace abroad and emphasized "the strange Diffidence and Distrust, which, like a general infection, begins to spread itself into almost all the Corners of the Land," and which might be cured by a greater compliance by parliament to the Crown's agenda (*JHL* 13:37–9, Feb. 15, 1676/7).

[377] the Lord Treasurer . . . Perswasion: Sir Thomas Osborne, earl of Danby (1631–1712), with reference to his notorious briberies.

[378] the case of this long Prorogation: much debated in the press and in the Lords; cf. LHC 15, Feb. 17, 1676/7, *P & L,* 2:177–78, 179; *JHL* 13:39; *JHC* 9:383.

something ridiculously, Whether this *Prorogation* were *not an Adjourn-ment?* And this Debate too, they Adjourned till the next day, and from thence they put it off till the Munday morning. Then those that had proposed it, yet before they would enter upon the Debate, asked, Whether they might have liberty? as if that had not been [63] more then implied before, by Adjourning the Debate, and as if Freedom of speech, were not a Concession of Right, which the King grants at the first opening of all Parliaments. But by this faintness, and half-counsel, they taught the House to deny them it. And so all that matter was wrapped up in a cleanly Question, Whether their grand Committees should sit, which involving the Legitimacy of the Houses Sitting, was carried in the Affirmative, as well as their own hearts could wish: But in the Lords House it went otherwise. For the first day, as soon as the Houses were separate, the Duke of Buckingham, who usually saith what he thinks, argued by all the Laws of Parliament, and with great strength of Reason, that this *Prorogation* was Null, and this Parliament consequently Dissolved, offering moreover to maintain it to all the Judges, and desiring as had been usuall in such Cases, but would not here be admitted, that even they might give their opinions. But my Lord Frechwell[379] as a better Judge of so weighty a point in Law, did of his great Courtship move, That the Duke of Buckingham might be called to the Barr,[380] which being opposed by the Lord Salisbury,[381] as an extravagant motion; but the Duke of Buckinghams proposal asserted, with all the *Cecilian* height[382] of Courage and Reason, the Lord Arundell of Trerise[383] a Peer of no less consideration, and Authority then my Lord Frechwell, and as much out of order, as if the Salt had been thrown down, or an Hare[384] had crossed his way, Opening, renewed the motion for calling the Duke to the Barr; But there were yet too many Lords between, {71} and the *Couriers* of the House of Commons brought up advice every moment,

---

[379] John Frescheville (1607–82), Cavalier and Court supporter (Henning 2:367–68).

[380] called to the Barr: the bar or barrier in either House, dividing the floor from the more public space near the door, and the threshold to which members were called when required to submit to the assembly.

[381] James Cecil, third earl of Salisbury (d. 1683). Frescheville moves to call Buckingham to the bar, which is opposed by Salisbury, who further supports Buckingham's proposal, only for Arundell of Trerice to renew Frescheville's motion.

[382] *Cecilian* height: in keeping with Salisbury's dignity, and that of his family.

[383] Richard, Lord Arundell of Trerice (c. 1616–87), very much a Cavalier and a consistent supporter of the Court (Henning 1:551).

[384] Salt . . . Hare: miserable portents.

that the matter was yet in agitation among them; So that the Earl of Shaftsbury had opportunity to appear with such extraordinary vigour, in what concerned both the Duke of Buckingham's person and his Proposal, that as the Duke of Buckingham might have stood single in any rational contest, so the Earl of Shaftsbury was more properly another Principal, than his Second. The Lord *Chancellour* therefore in answer undertook on the contrary, to make the [64] *Prorogation* look very formal, laying the best colours upon it, after his manner when Advocate, that the Cause would bear (and the worst upon his Opponents) but such as could never yet endure the Day-light. Thus for five or six hours it grew a fixed Debate, many arguing it in the regular method,[385] till the expected news came, that the Commons were rose without doing any thing; whereupon the greater number called for the Question, and had it in the Affirmative, that the Debate should be laid aside.[386]

And being thus flushed, but not satisfied with their Victory, they fell upon their Adversaries in cool blood, questioning such as they thought fit, that same night, and the morrow after, sentencing them; the Duke of Buckingham, the Earl of Salisbury, the Earl of Shaftsbury, and the Lord Wharton[387] to be committed to the Tower, under the notion of Contempt,[388] during his Majesties, and the Houses pleasure. That Contempt, was their refusing to recant their Opinion, and ask pardon of the King, and the House of Lords. Thus a *Prorogation* without President was to be warranted by an Imprisonment without Example. A sad Instance and whereby the Dignity of Parliaments, and especially of the House of Peers, did at present much suffer, and may probably more for the future; For nothing but Parliament can destroy Parliament, If a House shall once be Felon of it self[389] and stop its own breath, taking away that Liberty of speech,{72}

---

[385] regular method: by contrast with the less parliamentary thrust by Frescheville, whose motion Shaftesbury opposed as extravagant (*OPH* 4:824).

[386] Cf. *JHL* 13:39.

[387] Lord Wharton: Marvell's friend Philip, fourth Baron Wharton (1613–96) with only some remission remained in prison longer than all but Shaftesbury, until July 29, 1677. He had been close to Cromwell and remained an influential supporter of Presbyterians in the 1660s and 1670s. Marvell writes to Wharton in a personal vein in letters dating from 1667 to 1674, and by the early 1670s might stay at one of Wharton's houses (in Buckinghamshire) over the Christmas season (*P & L*, 2:309, 326–27, 382–83, 386; Bodl. MS Rawl. letters 51, f. 218).

[388] Contempt: disobedience or disrespect to the authority of the legislative body.

[389] be felon of it self: from the Anglo-Norman *Felo-de-se*, "felon of himself," meaning

which the King verbally, and of course allows them, (as now they had done in both Houses) to what purpose is it coming thither? But it was now over, and by the weakness in the House of Commons, and the Force in the House of Lords, this Presumptuous[390] Session was thus farre settled and confirmed; so that henceforward men begun to wipe their Mouths, as if nothing had been, and to enter upon the Publick Business.

And yet it is remarkable that shortly after, upon occasion of a discourse among the Commons, concerning *Libells* and *Pamphlets,* first one Member of them stood up, and in the face of their House, said, *That it was affirmed to him, by a person* [65] *that might be spoke with, that there were among them, thirty, forty, fifty (God knows how many) outlawed. Another* thereupon rose, and told them: *It was reported too, that there were diverse of the Members Papists;* A third, *That a multitude of them were Bribed, and Pensioners.*[391] And yet all this was patiently hushed up by their House, and digested, being it seems, a thing of that Nature, which there is no Reply to; which may very well administer, and deserve a serious Reflexion, how great an opportunity this House of Commons lost, of ingratiating themselves with the Nation, by acknowledging in this Convention their invalidity to proceed in Parliament, and by addressing to his Majesty as being *Dissolved* for a *Dismission.* For were it so, that all the Laws of England require, and the very Constitution of our Government, as well as Experience, teaches the necessity of the frequent Meeting, and change of *Parliaments,* and suppose that the Question concerning this *Prorogation,* were by the Custom of *Parliaments* to be justified, (which hath not been done hitherto) yet who that desires to maintain the reputation of an honest man, would not have layed hold upon so plausible an occasion, to break company when it was

---

suicide. Likewise, in a prorogation paper of the day, "the law cannott admitt of prorogations exceeding the Compasse of a yeare for that were to make the law felo de se, and to Divest it selfe of capacity to take effect or to be executed" (Bodl. MS. Eng. hist. c. 710, f. 16); also Shaftesbury, "upon the debate of appointing a Day for hearing Dr: Shirleys Cause, 20th October 1675" begged that "our house may not be Felo de se" Huntington MS EL8416, p. [19].

[390] Presumptuous: with a hint of the etymological root "to take before," thus anticipative, assumed beforehand.

[391] These claims likewise surface in the conclusion to *A Seasonable Argument To Perswade All the Grand Juries in England, to Petition for A New Parliament* ("Amsterdam," 1677), also printed by John Darby. Thompson included this tract in his edition of Marvell's works (1776), 2:555–83.

grown so Scandalous. For it is too notorious to be concealed, that near a third part of the House have bene-{73}ficial Offices under his Majesty, in the Privy Councill, the Army, the Navy, the Law, the Household, the Revenue both in England and Ireland, or in attendance on his Majesties person.[392] These are all of them indeed to be esteemed Gentlemen of Honor, but more or less according to the quality of their several imploy-ments under his Majesty, and it is to be presumed that they brought along with them some Honour of their own into his service, at first to set up with. Nor is it fit that such an Assembly should be destitute of them to inform the Commons of his Majesties affairs, and communicate his Counsels, so that they do not by irregular procuring of Elections in place where they have no proper interest, thrust out the Gentlemen that have, and thereby disturb the several Countreys;[393] Nor that they croude into the House in numbers be-[66]yond modesty, and which instead of giving a Temper to their delib-erations, may seem to affect the Predominance. For although the House of Peers, besides their supream and sole Judicature, have an equal power in the Legislature with the House of Commons, and as the second Thoughts in the Government have often corrected their errours: yet it is to be confessed, that the Knights, Citizens and Burgesses there assembled, are the Repre-senters of the People of England, and are more peculiarly impowred by them to transact concerning the Religion, Lives, Liberties, and the Pro-priety of the Nation. And therefore no Honorable person, related to his Majesties more particular service, but will in that place and opportunity suspect himself, least his Gratitude to his Master, with his self-interest should tempt him beyond his obligation there to the Publick. The same excludes him that may next inherit from being Guardian to an Infant, not but there may the same affection and integritie be found in those of the Fathers side as those on the Mothers, but out of decent and humane caution, and in like manner however his Majesties Officers may be of, as sound and untainted reputation, as the {74} best, yet common Discretion would teach them not to seek after, and ingross such different Trusts in those bordering Interests of the King and Countrey, where from the People they have no Legal advantage, but so much may be gained by betraying them. How im-proper would it seem for a Privy Counsellour, if in the House of Commons

---

[392] *A Seasonable Argument* (1677) supplies a detailed list of MPs enjoying such patronage.

[393] Countreys: counties.

he should not justify the most arbitrary Proceedings of the Councill Table,[394] represent affairs of State with another face, defend any misgovernment, patronize the greatest Offenders against the Kingdom, even though they were too his own particular enemies, and extend the supposed Prerogative on all occasions, to the detriment of the Subjects certain and due Liberties! What self-denyal were it in the Learned Counsel at Law, did they not vindicate the Misdemeanours of the Judges, perplex all Remedies against the Corruptions and Incroachment of Courts of Judicature, Word all Acts towards [67] the Advantage of their own Profession, palliate[395] unlawful Elections, extenuate and advocate Publick Crimes, where the Criminal may prove considerable: step into the chair of a Money Bill, and pen the Clauses so dubiously, that they may be interpretable in Westminster-Hall beyond the Houses intention, mislead the House, not only in point of Law, but even in matter of Fact, without any respect to *Veracity*, but all to his own further Promotion! What Souldier in Pay, but might think himself fit to be cashiered,[396] should he oppose the increase of Standing Forces, the Depression of Civil Authority, or the Levying of Money by whatsoever means or in what Quantity? Or who of them ought not to abhor that Traiterous Position, of taking Armes by the Kings Authority against those that are Commissionated by him in pursuance of such Commission?[397] What Officer of the Navy, but takes himself under Obligation to magnify the expence, extol the management, conceal the neglect, increase the Debts and press the Necessity, rigging and unrigging it to the House in the same moment, and repre-{75}senting it all at once in a good and a bad condition? should any Member of Parliament and of the Exchequer omit to transform the Accounts, conceal the Issues,[398] highten the Anticipations,[399] and in despight of himself oblige whosoever chance to be the Lord Treasurer; might not his Reversioner[400] justly expect to be put into present Possession of the Office? Who that is either concerned in the Customs, or of their Brethren of the Excise, can with any decency refuse, if they do not invent,

[394] Councill Table: of the Privy Council.

[395] palliate: represent an evil as less than it really is, excuse.

[396] cashiered: dismissed permanently from service in disgrace.

[397] Marvell harks back to the terms of the Non-Resisting Test (see note 295 above).

[398] Issues: profits from lands, tenements, or fines.

[399] Anticipations: the sums of money dealt with in advance, before they are actually disposed.

[400] Reversioner: one who succeeds to an office after the death or retirement of the previous incumbent.

all further Impositions upon Merchandise, Navigation, or our own domestick Growth and Consumption; and if the Charge be but Temporary, to perpetuate it? Hence it shall come that instead of relieving the Crown by the good old and certain way of Subsidies, wherein nothing was to be got [but] by the House of Commons, they devised this Foraine course of Revenue, to the great Grievance and double charge of the People, that so many of the Members might be gratified in the Farmes or Commissions.[401] [68]

But to conclude this digression whatsoever other Offices have been set up for the use of the Members, or have been extinguished upon occasion, should they have failed at a Question, did not they deserve to be turned out? Were not all the Votes as it were in *Fee Farme*,[402] of those that were intrusted with the sale? Must not Surinam be a sufficient cause of quarrel with Holland, to any Commissioner of the Plantations? Or who would have denied Mony to continue the War with Holland, when he were a Commissioner of Prizes, of Sick and Wounded, of Transporting the English, or of Starving the Dutch Prisoners? How much greater then would the hardship be for those of his Majesties Houshold, or who attend upon his Royal Person, to forget by any chance Vote, or in being absent from the House, that they are his Domestick servants? Or that all those of the capacity abovementioned are to be lookt upon as a distinct Body {76} under another Discipline;[403] and whatsoever they may commit in the House of Commons against the National Interest, they take themselves to be justified by their Circumstances, their hearts indeed are, they say, with the Country, and one of them[404] had the boldness to tell his Majesty, That he was come from Voting in the House *Against his Conscience.*

And yet these Gentlemen being full, and already in Imployment, are more good natured and less dangerous to the Publick, than those that are hungry and out of Office, who may by probable computation, make another Third part of this House of Commons. Those are such as having observed by what steps, or rather leaps and strides, others of their House have ascended into the highest Places of the Kingdom, do upon measuring their own Birth, Estates, Parts, and Merit, think themselves as well and

[401] Farmes or Commissions: A farm was a fixed yearly amount payable as rent or tax; a commission was an office, usually a profitable one.

[402] *Fee Farme:* see note 151 above.

[403] Discipline: system of rules for conduct.

[404] This was John Hervey, vice chamberlain; the story is told more fully in *Bishop [Gilbert] Burnet's History of His Own Time,* ed. O. Airy, 2 vols. (Oxford, 1897–1900), 2:80–81.

better qualified in all respects as their former Companions. They are generally men, who by speaking against the French, inveighing against the Debauches of Court, talking of the ill management of the Revenue, and such Popular flourishes, have cheated the Countreys into Electing them, and when they come up, if [69] they can speak in the House, they make a faint attaque or two upon some great Minister of State, and perhaps relieve some other that is in danger of Parliament, to make themselves either way considerable.

In matters of money they seem at first difficult, but having been discourst with[405] in private, they are set right, and begin to understand it better themselves, and to convert their Brethren: For they are all of them to be bought and sold, only their Number makes them cheaper, and each of them doth so overvalue himself, that sometimes they outstand or let slip their own Market.[406] {77}

It is not to be imagined, how small things in this case, even Members of great Estates will stoop at, and most of them will do as much for Hopes, as others for Fruition, but if their patience be tired out, they grow at last mutinous, and revolt to the Country, till some better occasion offer.

Among these are some men of the best understanding, were they of equal integrity, who affect to ingross all business, to be able to quash any good motion by Parliamentary skill, unless themselves be the Authors, and to be the leading men of the House, and for their natural Lives to continue so. But these are men that have been once fooled, most of them, and discovered, and slighted at Court, so that till some turn of State shall set them in their Adversaries Place, in the mean time they look Sullen, make big Motions, and contrive specious Bills for the Subject, yet only wait the opportunity to be the Instruments of the same Counsels, which they oppose in others.

There is a Third Part still remaining, but as contrary in themselves as Light and Darkness; Those are either the worst, or the best of Men; The first are most profligate[407] persons, that have neither Estates, Consciences, nor good Manners, yet are therefore picked out as the necessary men, and whose Votes will go furthest; The charges of their Elections are defrayed, whatever they amount to, Tables are kept for them at White-Hall,[408] and

---

[405] discourst with *77a, 77b, 1776*] discoursed with *79, 89, 93*.

[406] outstand or let slip their own Market: misjudge their selling out.

[407] profligate: reckless, licentious.

[408] White-Hall: the palace in Westminster of the royal court

through Westminster, that they may [70] be ready at hand, within Call of a Question: All of them are received into Pension, and know their Pay day, which they never faile of: Insomuch that a great Officer was pleased to say, *That they came about him like so many Jack-daws*[409] *for Cheese, at the end of every Session.* If they be not in Parliament, they must be in Prison, and as they are Protected themselves by Priviledge, so they sell their Protections to others, to the obstructions so many years together of the Law of the Land, and the publick Justice; For these it is, that the long and frequent Adjournments are calculated, {78} but all whether the Court, or the Monopolizers of the Country Party, or these that profane the title of Old Cavaliers, do equally, though upon differing reasons, like Death apprehend a Dissolution. But notwithstanding these, there is an handfull of *Salt,* a sparkle of *Soul,* that hath hitherto preserved this gross Body from Putrefaction, some *Gentlemen* that are constant, invariable, indeed English men, such as are above *hopes,* or *fears,* or *dissimulation,* that can neither flatter, nor betray their King, or Country: But being conscious of their own Loyalty, and Integrity, proceed throw good and bad report, to acquit themselves in their Duty to God, their Prince, and their Nation; Although so small a Scantling[410] in number, that men can scarce reckon of them more then a *Quorum;*[411] Insomuch that it is less difficult to conceive, how Fire was first brought to light in the World, then how any good thing could ever be produced out of an House of Commons so constituted, unless as that is imagined to have come from the rushing of Trees, or battering of Rocks together, by accident,[412] so these by their clashing with one another, have struck out an useful effects from so unlikely causes. But whatsoever casual good hath been wrought at any time by the assimilation[413] of ambitious, factious, and disappointed Members, to the little, but solid, and unbyassed Party, the more frequent ill effects, and consequences of so unequal a mixture, so long continued, are demonstrable and apparent. For while scarce any man comes thither with respect to the publick service, but in design to [71] make and raise his fortune; it is not to be exprest, the Debauchery, and Lewdness, which upon occasion of Election to Parliaments, are now grown

---

[409] *Jack-daws:* small crows, easily tamed, and known for their craftiness and thieving. This was reputed the scornful comment of Danby himself.

[410] Scantling: small and insignificant amount.

[411] *Quorum:* Latin "of whom"; number of members needed for the proper conduct of business.

[412] Lucretius, *De rerum natura,* 1.897–900, 5.1096–1100, 6.161–2.

[413] assimilation *77b*].

habitual thorow the Nation, So that the Vice, and the Expence, are risen to such a prodigious height, that few sober men can indure to stand to be chosen on such conditions. From whence also arise Feuds, and perpetual Animosities, over most of the Countyes, and Corporations, while Gentlemen of Worth, {79} Spirit, and ancient Estates, and Dependances,[414] see themselves overpowered in their own neighbourhood by the Drunkness and Bribery of their Competitors. But if nevertheless, any worthy person chance to carry the Election, some mercenary or corrupt Sheriff makes a double Return,[415] and so the Cause is handed to the Committee of Elections, who ask no better, but are ready to adopt his Adversary into the House if he be not Legitimate. And if the Gentleman agrieved seek his Remedy against the Sheriff in Westminster-Hall, and the proofs be so palpable, that the Kings Bench cannot invent how to do him injustice, yet the major part of the twelve Judges, shall upon better consideration vacate the Sheriffs Fine, and reverse the Judgement; but those of them that dare dissent from their Brethren, are in danger to be turned off the Bench without any cause assigned. While men therefore care not thus, how they get into the House of Commons, neither can it be expected that they should make any conscience of what they do there, but they are only intent how to reimburse themselves (if their Elections were at their own charge) or how to bargine their Votes for a Place, or a Pension. They list themselves streightways into some Court faction, and it is as well known among them, to what Lord each of them retain, as when formerly they wore Coates, and Badges.[416] By this long haunting so together they are grown too so familiar among themselves, that all reverence of their own Assembly is lost, that they live together not like Parliament men, but like so many Good-fellows, met together in a Publick House to make merry. And which is yet worse, by being so thoroughly acquainted, they [72] understand their Number and Party, so that the use of so publick a Counsel is frustrated, there is no place for deliberation, no perswading by reason, but they can see one anothers Votes through both Throats and Cravats[417] before they hear them.

---

[414] Dependances: retinues.

[415] double Return: A return is the official report made by a returning officer (here the sheriff) as to the election of a member or members of Parliament; in a double return, two or more candidates were provisionally elected.

[416] Coates, and Badges: outdated sumptuary practice marking feudal allegiances.

[417] Cravats: scarves worn around the neck by men.

Where the Cards are so well known, they are only fit for {80} a Cheat, and no fair Gamster, but would throw them under the Table.

Hereby it is that their House hath lost all the antient weight and authority, and being conscious of their own guilt and weakness, dare not adventure, as heretofore, the Impeaching of any man before the Lords, for the most heinous Crimes of State, and the most publick misdemeanours; upon which confidence it is, that the Conspirators have so long presumed, and gone unpunished. For although the Conspirators have some times (that this House might appear still necessary to the People, and to make the money more glib) yielded that even their own Names should be tossed among them, and Grievances be talked of, yet at the same time they have been so prevalent as to hinder any effect, and if the House has Emancipated it self beyond Instructions, then by Chastizing them with *Prorogations*, frighting[418] them with *Dissolutions*, comforting them with long, frequent and seasonable *Adjournments*, now by suspending, or diminishing their pensions, then again by increasing them, sometimes by a scorn, and otherwhiles by a favour, there hath a way been found to reduce them again under discipline. All these things and more being considered and how doubtful a foot this Long Parliament now stood upon by this long *Prorogation*, there could not have been a more Legal, or however no more wise and honest a thing done, then for both the Lords and Commons to have separated themselves, or have besought his Majesty to that purpose; lest the Conspirators should any longer shelter and carry on their design against the Government and Religion, under this shadow of *Parliamentary Authority*. But it was otherwise ordered of which it is now time to relate the Consequences.

The four Lords having thus been committed, it cannot pro-[73]perly be said that the House of Peers was thence forward under the Government of the Lord Frechwel, and the Lord Arundel of Trerise, but those two noble Peers had of ne-{81}cessity no small Influence upon the Counsels of that House, (having hoped ere this to have made their way also into his Majesties Privy Council) and all things fell out as they could have wished, if under their own direction. For most of them, who had been the most active formerly in the Publick Interest, sate mute in the House, whether, as is probable out of reverence to their two Persons, and confidence in their wisdom, they left all to their Conduct, and gave them a general Proxey, or whether, as some would have it, they were sullen at the Commitment of the

---

[418] freighting *77b*].

four Lords, and by reason of that, or the *Prorogation,* began now to think the Parliament, or their House to be *Non Compos.*[419] But now therefore Doctor Cary, a Comoner, was brought to the Bar[420] before them, and questioned concerning a written Book which it seems he had carried to be printed, treating of the Illegality of this *Prorogation,* and because he satis-fyed them not in some Interrogatories, which no man would in Common honour to others, or in self preservation, as neither was he in Law bound to have answered, they therefore *Fined* him a thousand pound, under that new Notion of Contempt, when no other Crime would do it, and sentenced him to continue close Prisoner in the *Tower* until payment.[421] Yet the Commons were in so admirable good temper (having been conjured by the charming Eloquence of the Lord Chancellor, to avoid all misunderstand-ing between the two Houses) that their could no Member, or time be found in all the Session, to offer their House his Petition, much less would that breach upon the whole Parliament, by imprisoning the Lords, for using their liberty of speech, be entertained by them upon motion, for fear of entrenching upon the priviledge of the House of Peers, which it had been well for them if they had been as tender of formerly.

One further Instance of the Complexion of their House at that season, may be sufficient. One Master Harrington,[422] had [74] before the Session been Committed Close Prisoner (for {82} that was now the mode, as though the Earl of Northampton, would not otherwise have kept him Close enough) by Order of the King and Council, the Warrant being *for subornation of Perjury, tending to the Defamation of his Majesty, and his Government, and for Contemptuously Declaring, he would not answer his Majesty any Question, which his Majesty, or his Privy Council should ask him.* As this Gentleman was hurried along to the *Tower,* he was so dexterous as

---

[419] *Non Compos:* [*mentis*] not of sound mind, of no sound authority.

[420] brought to the Bar: The bar refers to the barrier marking off the precinct of the judge's seat, to which prisoners were brought for arraignment, trial, or sentencing.

[421] Cary . . . Prisoner . . . until payment: *JHL* 13:55, Mar. 1, 1676/7; *OPH* 4:837–42, Mar. 2, 1676/7. In constituency letters, Marvell noted the Lords' examination of Doctor Cary and his fine and imprisonment "for not having declared who was the Author of the Booke intitled the Grand Question Stated & discussed concerning the Prorogation, nor from what person he received it" (Feb. 27, Mar. 3, Mar. 10, 1676/7, *P & L,* 2:182, 183, 187).

[422] Master Harrington: John Harrington (ca. 1649–after 1696). Qv. introduction, pp. 193, 213; Lois Schwoerer, *"No Standing Armies!" The Antiarmy Ideology in Seventeenth-Century England* (Baltimore, 1974), p. 116.

to convey into a friends hand passing by, a Blank Paper only with his name, that a Petition might be written above it, to be presented to the House of Commons, without rejecting for want of his own hand in the subscription. His Case notwithstanding the Warrant was thus.

He had met with two Scotch souldiers in Town returned from Flanders, who complained that many of their Countrey men had in Scotland been seised by force, to be carried over into the French service, had been detained in the Publick prisons till an opportunity to transport them: were heaved on board fast tyed and bound like malefactors, some of them struggling and contesting it, were cast into the Sea, or maimed, in conclusion an intolerable violence and barbarity used to compell them, and this near the present Session of Parliament. Hereupon this Gentleman considering how oft the House of Commons had addressed to his Majesty and framed an Act for recalling his Majesties Subjects out of the French service,[423] as also that his Majesty had issued his Proclamation to the same purpose, thought he might do a good and acceptable thing in giving information of it to the House as time served. But withal knowing how witnesses might possibly be taken off,[424] he for his own greater security took them before a Master of Chancery, where they confirmed by Oath the same things they had told him. But hereupon he was brought before his Majesty, and the Privy Councill, where he declared this matter, but being here asked by the Lord Chancellour some insnaring and improper questions, {83} he modestly, as those that [75] were by affirmed, desired to be excused from answering him further, but after this, answered his Majesty with great humility and respect to divers questions. This was the subornation of Perjury,[425] and this the Contempt to his Majesty, for which he was made Close Prisoner. Upon his Petition to the House of Commons he was sent for, and called in, where he is reported to have given a very clear account of the whole matter, and of his behaviour at the Council board.[426] But of the two Scotch soldiers, the one made himself perjured without being suborned by Harrington, denying or misrepresenting to the House what he had sworn formerly. And the other, the honester fellow it seems of the two, only was absented. But however

[423] The Commons addressed the king on this subject in May 1675 and sharply debated his lukewarm response (*JHC* 9:319, 330, 333; *OPH* 4:678, 698–709); that the act was only "framed" resulted from the prorogation of that session.

[424] be taken off: be bought out through bribery.

[425] subornation of Perjury: procuring a witness on oath to commit perjury.

[426] *JHC* 9:401, March 16, 1676/7. Grey 4:261–67, 268–83; *OPH* 4:845–53; and *Mr Harringtons Case* (London, 1678).

divers honourable Members of that House attested voluntarily, that the souldiers had affirmed the same thing to them, and indeed the Truth of that matter is notorious, by several other soldiers that since came over, and by further account from Scotland. Master Harrington also carried himself toward the House with that modesty, that it seemed inseparable from him, and much more in his Majesties presence, so that their House was inclined, and ready to have concerned themselves for his Liberty. But Master Secretary Williamson stood up, having been a Principal Instrument in commiting him, and because the other crimes rather deserved Thanks and Commendation, and the Warrant would not Justify it self, he insisted upon his strange demeanour toward his Majesty, deciphered his very looks, how truly it matters not, and but that his Majesty and the House remained still living Flesh and Blood, it might have been imagined by his discourse that Master Harrington had the Head of a *Gorgon.*[427] But this story so wrought with, and amazed the Commons, that Mr. Harrington found no redress, but might thank God that he escaped again into Close Prison. It was thought notwithstanding by most men, that his looks might have past any where but with a man of Sir Josephs delicacy.[428] For neither indeed had Master Harrington ever the same opportunities {84} that others had of practising the *Hocus Pocus* of the Face, of Play-[76]ing the French *Scaramuccie,*[429] or of living abroad to learn how to make the Plenipotentiary *Grimass* for his Majesties service.

And now to proceed, rather according to the Coherence of the matters, then to the particular Date of every days action. By this good humour, and the House being so free of the Liberty of their fellow Commoners, it might be guessed that they would not be less liberal of their Mony this Session.

The Bill therefore for 600000 *l.* Tax for eighteen months[430] towards the building and furnishing of Ships, easily passed without once dreaming any more of appropriating the Customes. For the Nation being generally possessed by the Members with the defects of the Navy, and not considering at

---

[427] Head of a *Gorgon:* silenced, as when in Greek mythology those who looked upon the Gorgon's head were turned to stone.

[428] Sir Josephs delicacy: Williamson was noted for his courtliness and had had a plenipotentiary role in the negotiations at Cologne, 1673–74.

[429] the French *Scaramuccie:* "Scaramuccia" (little skirmisher) was a zany character in the Italian *Commedia dell'arte,* then the stock Scaramouche of French comedy, about which Marvell had complained to William Popple owing to its being acted "dayly in the Hall of Whitehall . . . as at a common Playhouse" (July 24, 1675, *P & L,* 2:342).

[430] month *77a*] months *1776*] 21 Feb. 1676/77, *JHC* 9:386.

all from what neglect it proceeded, the House of Commons were very willing, and glad to take this occasion, of confirming the Authority of their sitting, and to pay double the summe that in the former Sessions they had thought necessary towards the Fleet; thereby[431] to hedg in, and purchase their own continuance. And for the same purpose they ingrossed[432] the Act with so numerous a list of Commissioners, that it seemed rather a Register or Muster-roll[433] of the Nation, and that they raised the whole Kingdom to raise the mony. For who could doubt that they were still a lawful Parliament, when they saw so many Gentlemens names (though by the Clerks hand only) subscribed to an Act of their making? Only Mr. Seymour[434] the speaker, would have diminished their number in his own Country. For he had entred into a Combination,[435] that none should serve the King or their Country thorow Devonshire, in any capacity but under his approbation, and therefore he highly inveighed against many Gentlemen of the best rank there, that ought him no homage, as persons disaffected, opposing their names at a Committee of the whole House, before he heard them. But being checked in his careere, he let fall the contest, with as much judgment and modesty, as he had begun it with boldness and indiscretion. {85}

This Bill was not enough, but though the Nation had [77] hoped to be relieved from the Additional Excise upon Beer and Ale, which the Tripple League had foold them into, but was now of course to expire the 24th. of June, 1677. Yet a Bill for the continuing of it for three years more, passed

---

[431] hereby 77a].

[432] ingrossed: wrote up in full legal form.

[433] Muster-roll: an official list of officers or men, usually for military or nautical use.

[434] Mr. Seymour: Sir Edward Seymour (1633–1708) had been a very active MP in the 1660s and as a client of Buckingham had emerged as something of a leader in the parliamentary opposition. His defection to the Court in 1670 was precipitous (P & L, 2:318), and brought him much reward; he became speaker of the House of Commons (Feb. 18, 1673–April 11, 1678, May 6– Dec. 28, 1678). He remained an effective supporter of the Court while retaining at least some of the respect of the Country opposition, but in the storms of the winter session of 1678 he was forced to remove himself from the speaker's chair. His evident distance from Danby and his attacks on popery soon helped him recover the position for another session; in the first and second Exclusion parliaments he had to play a diminished role, but after prominently advising Charles in the third Exclusion parliament his political fortunes changed, in part owing to his dislike of France and Roman Catholicism (Henning, 3:411–20). For his role in Marvell's parliamentary discomfiture in the winter-spring session of 1677, see the introduction above (pp. 189–90, 192).

[435] Combination: conspiracy, illegal confederacy.

them likewise with little Difficulty. For the late fear of Dissolution was still so fresh upon them, that they would continue any thing to buy their own Continuance; and this Bill might considering their present want of Legality, have been properly intituled, *An Act for the Extraordinary Occasion of the House of Commons.* But that they might seem within this tenderness to themselves not to have cast of all toward the People, they sunk all former Grievances into a Bill of Chancery,[436] knowing well that a sute in that Court would be sooner ended, then a Reformation of it be effected; and that thereby they might gain work enough to direct the whole Session. And of their usual Bills for the Liberty of the Subjects, they sent up only that of *Habeas Corpus;* pretending, and perhaps truly, that they durst not adventure them either in their own or the Lords House as they were now governed, lest they should be further ensnared by strugling for freedom. But least they should trouble themselves too much with Religion, the Lords presented them with two Bills of a very good name, but of a strange and unheard of nature. The one intituled, *An Act for securing the Protestant Religion by educating the Children of the Royal Family, and providing for the continuance of a Protestant Clergy.* The other, *An Act for the more effectual Conviction and Prosecution of Popish Recusants.* And with these they sent down another for the further regulation of the Presses and suppressing all unlicensed Books, with clauses most severe and general upon the subject, whereof one for breaking all Houses whatsoever on suspicion of any such Pamphlets whereby Master L'Estranges[437] Authority was much amplifyed to {86} search any other House with the same liberty as he had Sir Thomas Dolemans.[438]

But as to those two Bills of Religion, although they were of the highest consequence that ever were offered in Parlia-[78]ment since *Protestancy* came in (and went out of fashion) yet it is not to be imagined, how indisputable and easie a passage they found through the House of Peers, to the House of *Commons:* which must be ascribed to the great unanimity among them, after the committing of the four Lords, and to the Power of those two noble Peers, their Adversaries, which was now so established, that their

---

[436] Bill of Chancery: also called a Bill of Equity, a petition for redress.

[437] Master L'Estranges: Roger L'Estrange (1616–1704), controversialist and surveyor of the press. He was a lively polemicist for the Crown at the Restoration and consolidated his position as licenser and "bloodhound of the press" in the early 1660s. His long war against oppositional printing included successive attempts to frustrate the publication of Marvell's tracts in the 1670s.

[438] Sir Thomas Dolemans: L'Estrange's father-in-law and an MP loyal to the court.

sence being once declared, the rest seemed to yield them an Implicite Faith and Obedience; and they were now in such Vogue, that whatsoever was spoken or done any where abroad in perfection, with great weight and Judgment, men said it was *A la Fraischeville.* But if gentily and acutely, *A la Trerise.*[439]

That Intituled, *An Act for the more effectual Conviction and Prosecution of Popish Recusants,*[440] is too long to be here inserted[441] and the Fate it met with, makes it unnecessary, for as soon as it was first read a Gentleman[442] of great worth and apprehension spake short but roundly and thorow against it.

A second[443] immediately moved that it might not only be thrown out, but with a particular mark of Infamy. And it being without any more ado ready to be put to the Question, a third[444] demanded that they should stay a while to see whether there were any one so hardy as to speak a word for it, which no man offering at, it was forthwith rejected with this censure added to the Journal.[445] {87}

---

[439] *A la Fraischeville . . . A la Trerise:* "in the manner of," with Gallic phrasing in order further to satirize their influence.

[440] *JHL* 13:56 and 57 (first and second readings in Lords, Mar. 1 and 2, 1676/7), 68 (to committee of Lords, Mar. 10, 1676/7), 71–89 passim (further reports from committee, and returns to committee, also of whole House, Mar. 13–28, 1676/7), and 92 (third reading, further proviso rejected, bill passed); *JHC* 9:414 (in the Commons, "Upon the reading the said Bill; and opening the Substance thereof to the House; it appeared to be much different from the Title: And thereupon the House, Nemine contradicente, rejected the same." Apr. 4, 1677); Grey, *Debates,* 4:334–39.

[441] The Commons was concerned that "the Bill has so good a Title, that it would be a reflection upon us to cast it out" (Grey 4:339), so Marvell scants its possibly misleading text—deemed "a Toleration of Popery" by some—and instead registers the formula the House settled on in dismissing it, which had been arrived at by Sir William Coventry and the speaker (*OPH* 4:863).

[442] William Sacheverell (c. 1638–91), Country MP who often spoke in the House (Henning 3:370–76), Grey, *Debates,* 4:335–36.

[443] William Garway (or Garroway, 1617–1701), outspoken Country MP—"great Garway" in "The Last Instructions," l. 298—noted for suspicions of France (Henning 2:373–80), Grey, *Debates,* 4:336.

[444] Either Sir Trevor Williams (ca. 1623–92), a Country MP who had been on the committee for the bill to ensure the Protestant education of the royal children (Henning 3:729), or the lawyer MP William Williams (ca. 1634–1700), a Country MP who had defended Joseph Browne in the prosecution of *The Long Parliament Dissolved* (*P & L,* 2:352). Grey, *Debates,* 4:336.

[445] Journal: the record of daily proceedings of the Houses of Parliament.

Because the Body of the Bill was contrary to the Title,[446] This unusual sentence of the *House of Commons,* though excusable by the Crimes of the Bill, yet was not to be justified by the *Rules* of entercourse between the two Houses. But because all men have hence taken[447] occasion to accuse the Lords Spiritual, as the Authors both of this Bill and the other, it is necessary to insert here the true Fact in their just vindication. It was above two years ago that a select Cabal[448] of great Ministers, had been consulting about Church matters, tho it seldom happens (nor did it in this instance) that the Statesmen are more fortunate in medling with Religion, than the Churchmen with Government, but each mars them with tamper-[79]ing out of their Provinces. This only difference, that what Ecclesiastical Persons may do by chance or consequence, that harm the others commit on set purpose. For it was by these Politicians, that these two *Cockatrice Eggs*[449] were laid, and by their assiduous incubation hatched. It is true indeed afterwards they took some few of the Bishops into Communication, and as it were for advice, upon what was before resolved. And to make this Bill go the better down, they flattered them with the other, as wholly calculated forsooth to the Churches Interest. And by this means possibly they prevailed so far, that the Bishops both there and in the *House* less vigorously opposed. But that the Bishops were either the Contrivers or Promoters of the Bill, is a scandalous falshood and devised by the Authors to throw the *Odium*[450] off from themselves upon the Clergy, and (the Bills that aimed at

---

[446] *And* because the Body of the Bill was contrary to the Title, This unusual sentence . . . *77a, 79, 89, 93, 1776*]. The text of the first edition (*77a,* pp. 87–88) presents this censure in a confused way, which is subject to manuscript correction in some copies (Bodleian Library, G. Pamph. 1359 (22); Newberry Library, Case J, 5454.55; Kingston open Hull Local Studies Library: Marvell Collection). This manuscript correction is then incorporated in the printing of *77b* (p. 79), which understands that the "Because" phrase is the censure entered into the Commons Journal, and that it should be distinguished as such by means of italics.

[447] taked *77b*].

[448] Cabal: a small group engaged in intrigue. Marvell had in his letters noted the consultation, *P & L,* 2:334 (Dec. 15, 1674 to Edward Thompson) and 338 (ca. Jan. 28, 1674/5 to Sir Henry Thompson).

[449] two *Cockatrice Eggs:* the cockatrice was a serpent, often identified with the basilisk, said to be hatched from a cock's egg and to kill with a glance. Isaiah 59:5: "They hatch cockatrice' eggs, and weave the spider's web: he that eateth of their eggs dieth, and that which is crushed breaketh out into a viper." The "two" refers to the two bills at issue.

[450] Odium: hatred.

the ruine of the Church of England having miscarried) to compass the same end by this defamation. A sufficient warning to the Clergy, how to be intreagued with the Statesmen for the future. *The second Bill follows.* {88}
An Act for further securing the Protestant Religion, by Educating the Children of the Royal Family therein; and for the providing for the continuance of a Protestant Clergy.[451]

To the Intent that the Protestant Religion, which through the blessing of God hath been happily Established in this Realm, and is at present sufficiently secured by his Majesties known Piety and Zeal for the preservation thereof, may remain secure in all future times.

Be it Enacted by the Kings most Excellent Majesty, by and with the advice and consent of the Lords Spiritual and Temporal, and Commons in this Parliament Assembled, and by the Authority of the same, That upon the demise of his Majesty that now is, to whom God grant a long and prosperous Reign, and upon the demise of any other King or Queen Regnant,[452] that shall hereafter bear the Imperial Crown of [80] this Realm, the Arch-Bishops, and all and every the Bishops of England and Wales, for the time being, as shall not be disabled by Sickness or other Infirmity, shall within fourty days next after such Demise, repaire to Lambeth House,[453] and being there assembled, to the number of nine at least, shall cause to be fairly ingrosed in Parchment the Oath and Declaration following.

I. *King or Queen of England, do declare and Swear, that I do believe that there is not any Transubstantiation*[454] *in the Sacrament of the Lords Supper, or in the Elements of Bread and Wine, at or after the Consecration, thereof by any person whatsoever. So help me God.*

Which blanck shall be filled up with the Christian Name of such King or

---

[451] *JHL* 13:56–92 passim (first reading in the Lords, Mar. 1, 1676/7; passed in the Lords Mar. 30, 1677), and sent to Commons, Mar. 15, 1676/7); *JHC* 9:400 (received in Commons, Mar. 15, 1676/7), 402 and 407 (first reading in Commons, Mar. 20, 1676/7), 407 (second reading in Commons, Marvell named to the committee, Mar. 27, 1676/7)—the bill died in committee according to Marvell (p. 000 below); *OPH* 4:853–57. Details of the House of Lords copy are reported in *Historical Manuscripts Commission, 9th Report,* Appendix II, pp. 81–82: the substantial variations are here noted between Marvell's and that text (as corroborated by another copy of the bill in the Wharton papers, Bodleian, MS Carte 81, ff. 352r–57r).

[452] Regnant: reigning.

[453] Lambeth House: the London residence of the archbishops of Canterbury.

[454] *Transubstantion 77b*].

Queen, And thereupon the Prelates[455] so {89} Assembled, shall without
delay repaire to the persons of such succeeding King or Queen Regnant,
and in humble manner tender the said Oath or Declaration, to be taken by
such succeeding King or Queen Regnant, which they are hereby Authorized to Administer, and shall abide in or near the Court by the space of
fourteen days, and at convenient time, as often as conveniently they may,
they shall appear in the presence of such King and Queen ready to receive
Commands for Administring the said Oath and Declaration, which if such
succeeding King and Queen shall make and subscribe in presence of them,
or any nine or more of them, they shall attest the doing thereof, by subscribing their Names to a Certificate, Indorsed upon the said Indorsment,[456] and
carry the same into the high Court of Chancery, there to be safely deposited
amongst the Records of the said Court. And if such King or Queen Regnant, shall refuse or omit to make and subscribe the said Oath and Declaration, for the space of fourteen days after such humble tender made in
manner aforesaid, the said Prelates may depart from the Court without any
further attendance on this occasion. But if at any time afterward such King
or Queen shall be pleased to take and subscribe the [81] said Oath and
Declaration, and shall signifie such pleasure to the Arch-Bishops and
Bishops or any nine or more of them, the said Arch-Bishops and Bishops,
or such nine or more of them, are hereby Authorised and required forthwith to Administer the same, and to attest and certify the same in manner
aforesaid.

And be it further Enacted by the Authority aforesaid, That if any succeeding King or Queen Regnant, shall refuse or Omit to make such Oath
and Declaration, within the time therefore limited, the same having been
tendered {90} in manner aforesaid, or there shall be any Let,[457] Obstruction, or hindrance whatsoever, to their making the said tender in manner
aforesaid, they are hereby enjoyned and required to endorse upon the said
Engrosement[458] such refusal or omission, or any obstruction, let or hin-
derance, that shall happen to them, whereby they are not able to make the
said tender, according to the Act, and attest the same by subscribing their
names thereunto, and carry the same into the high Court of Chancery,

[455] Prelates: bishops and archbishops.

[456] Indorsment] error for "Engrosment," as in the House of Lords text of the bill (and
Bodleian, MS Carte 81, f. 352v).

[457] Let: obstruction, hindrance.

[458] Engrosement: legal record.

there to be safely deposited in manner aforesaid. And if any the said persons, hereby appointed to make the said tender, shall neglect or refuse to do the same, or in case of any refusal, or omission of making the said Oath and Declaration, or in case of any Obstruction or hindrance to the making of the said tender, shall refuse or neglect to make certificate[459] thereof in manner aforesaid, that the Arch-Bishoprick or Bishoprick of the Person or Persons so refusing, shall be *Ipso Facto,*[460] voide, as if he or they were naturally Dead, and the said Person or Persons shall be incapable, during his or their Life or Lifes, of that, or any other Ecclesiastical preferment.

And be it further Enacted, That if any King or Queen Regnant, at the time when the Imperial Crown of this Realm shall devolve, shall be under the age of fourteen years,[461] and that upon his or her attaining the said age of fourteen years, the Arch-Bishops and Bishops shall, and are upon the like penalties hereby enjoyned, within fourteen[462] days next after such attaining to the said Age, to assemble at the said place, [82] and thereupon to do and perform all things in preparing and tendring the said Oath and Declaration, and making certificate of the taking or omission thereof, that are required by this Act to be done, upon the demise of any King or Queen Regnant.

And be it further Enacted by the Authority aforesaid, That until any succeeding King or Queen Regnant shall make the said Oath and Declaration, in manner aforesaid, such respective King or Queen shall not grant, confer, or dispose of any Arch-Bishoprick or any Bishoprick in {91} England or Wales, otherwise than in manner following, that is to say, within seven days after the Vacancy of any Bishoprick or See,[463] shall be known to the Arch-Bishop of Canterbury for the time being, he shall and is hereby required to send forth a Summons in Writing to all the Prelates in England and Wales, requiring them to meet at a certain convenient time and place, to be appointed by the summons, to consult concerning the nomination of

---

[459] make certificate: certify.

[460] *Ipso Facto:* by the fact itself.

[461] [] *77a, 77b, 79, 89, 93, 1776:* the gap in sense here should be filled with the missing House of Lords text: " . . . this said Oath and Declaration shall not be tendered unto him or her untill he or she shall attaine the said Age of 14 yeares, . . . " (also thus in MS Carte 81, f. 353r). There is no sign of this error (eye-slip) ever having troubled editors or readers of the *Account.*

[462] fourteen: should read "40" as in the House of Lords text (and MS Carte 81 353r).

[463] Bishoprick or See: a bishopric is a diocese, the district for which the bishop is responsible; a see is the official seat of a bishop, which usually is located in the cathedral of the diocese.

fit persons for the supply of that Vacancy. And in case of vacancy of the Arch-Bishoprick of Canterbury, the Arch-Bishop of York, for the time being. And if that See shall be also vacant, such Prelate of the Realm, as by the Statute of 31.H.8.[464] ought to have place before the rest in *Parliament,* shall and are hereby required to issue forth the said Summons, and at the said time and place, so appointed, in manner aforesaid, the Prelates then assembled, being seven at the least, or the major part of them, shall by writing under their Hands and Seals,[465] nominate three persons, natural born subjects of the King, and in holy Orders, for the supplying of the said Vacancy, and to be placed in such Order as the said Prelates so assembled or the major part of them shall think fit, without regard to dignity, antiquity, or any other form, which Writing shall be presented to the King, who may thereupon appoint one of the three persons so to be named, to succeed in the said Vacancy. And the person so appointed or chosen, shall by due form of Law, according to the course now used, be made Bishop of that See. But if in 30 [83] days after such presentment, of such Names, the King or Queen Regnant shall not Elect or appoint, which of the said three persons shall succeed in the said vacant See; or if after such Election or appointment there shall be any obstruction in pressing[466] of the usual Instruments and formalities of law in order to his Consecration,[467] then such person, whose Name shall be first written in the said Instrument of nomination, if there be no Election or appointment made by the King, within the time aforesaid, shall be the Bishop of the vacant See. And if there be an Electi-{92}on or appointment made, then the person so appointed shall be the Bishop of the vacant See. And the Arch-bishop of the Province wherein the said vacancy shall be, or such other person or persons, who ought by his Majesties Ecclesiastical Laws to Consecrate the said Bishop, shall upon reasonable demand, and are hereby required to make Consecration accordingly upon pain of forfeiting trebble damages and costs to the party grieved, to be recovered in any of his Majesties Courts at Westminster. And immediately after such Consecration, the person so consecrated, shall be, and is hereby Enacted[468] to be compleat Bishop of the said vacant See, and is hereby

---

[464] Statute of 31.H.8: an act for the king to make bishops, 1539 (St. 31 Henry VIII, c.9).

[465] writing under their Hands and Seals: authorized and legitimized by prelates' signatures and seals, which attest their promises and provide a guarantee.

[466] pressing: "passing" in the House of Lords text (and MS Carte 81, f. 354r).

[467] Consecration: being made bishop.

[468] Enacted: better "elected," as in MS Carte 81, 354r.

vested in the Temporalties[469] of the said Bishoprick, and in actual possession thereof, to all intents and purposes, and shall have a Seat and Place
in Parliament, as if he had by due forms[470] of Law been made Bishop,
and had the Temporalities restored unto him; And in case the person so
first named in the said Instrument of nomination, or the person so Elected
by the King or Queen Regnant, shall then be a Bishop, so that no Consecration be requisite, then immediately after default of Election or appointment by the King, or immediately after such Election or appointment, if any shall be made within the said time, and any Obstructions
in pressing[471] the Instruments and Formalities in Law, in such cases used,
the Bishop so first Named or Elected and appointed, shall thereupon,
ipso facto, be translated,[472] and become Bishop of that See, to which he
was so nominated and appointed, and shall be, and is hereby vested [84]
in the Temporalities and actual possession thereof to all intents and purposes, and shall have his Seat and Place in Parliament accordingly, and his
former See shall become vacant, as if he had been by due Forms[473] of Law
chosen and confirmed into the same, and had the Temporalities restored
unto him.

And be it further Enacted, That until the making the said Oath and
Declaration in manner aforesaid, the respective succeeding Kings and
Queens that shall not have made and subscribed the same, shall not grant
or dispose of any {93} Denary, or Arch Deconary,[474] Prebendary, Mastership of any Colledge, Parsonage, Viccarage or any Ecclesiastical Benefice
or Promotion whatsoever, to any other person, but such person as shall be
nominated for the same, until the said King or Queen Regnant, by the
Arch-bishop of Canterbury, or Guardians of the Spiritualities of the said
Arch-Bishoprick,[475] for the time being, if the same be within the Province
of Canterbury, and by the Arch Bishoprick[476] of York, or Guardians of the
spiritualities of the said Arch-Bishoprick for the time being, if the same be

[469] Temporalties: temporalities are the secular jurisdiction and business of the
bishopric.

[470] forms: "forme" in MS Carte 81, 354r.

[471] pressing of: "passing" in House of Lords text (and MS Carte 81, f. 354v).

[472] translated: transferred from one ecclesiastical office to another.

[473] Forms: "forme" in MS Carte 81, 354v (and elsewhere below).

[474] Arch Deconary: equivalent to "Arch deanary" in MS Carte 81, 354v.

[475] Arch-bishop-prick *77a*]; the mischievous spelling in the first edition seems to
reflect antiepiscopal feeling in the household of its Baptist printer, John Darby.

[476] Arch Bishoprick: "Archbishop" in MS Carte 81, 354v.

within the Province of York, by writing under their respective Hands and Seals, and in case any such[477] as shall be accordingly nominated, shall not be able to obtain Presentation or grant[478] thereof within 30 days, next after such nomination, then the said person shall and may, and is hereby enabled, by force of the said nomination, to require Institution and Induction from such person and persons unto whom it shall belong to grant the same, who shall accordingly make Institution and Induction, as if the said person were lawfully presented by the said *King* or *Queen Regnant,* upon pain to forfeit of the party grieved, trebble damages and costs, to be recovered in any of his Majesties Courts at Westminster; and in cases where no Institution or Induction is requisite the said person so nominated, from and after the end of the said 30 days, shall be and is hereby actually vested in the possession of such Denary, Arch-Deaconry,[479] Prebendary, Mastership, Rectory, Parsonage, or Vicarage, Donative,[480] or other Ecclesiastical Benefice or Promotion, and shall be full [85] and absolute proprietor and Incumbent thereof, to all Intents and Purposes as if he had obtained possession thereof upon a legal grant by the said King or Queen Regnant, and proceeding thereupon in due form of Law.

Provided always and be it Enacted by the Authority aforesaid, That it shall and may be lawful for the Lord High Chancellor of England, or the Lord Keeper of the great Seal of {94} England, for the time being, to pass presentations or grants, to any Ecclesiastical Benefice, under value in the Kings Gift, in such manner as hath been accustomed,[481] any thing in this present Act to the contrary notwithstanding.

And be it further Enacted, That during such time as any King or Queen Regnant, shall be under the said[482] fourteen years, no person that shall be Lord Protector,[483] or Regent of this Realm, during such minority, shall in

---

[477] []: "person" in MS Carte 81, f. 354v.

[478] Presentation or grant: a presentation is the action or right of presenting a clergyman to a benefice or to a bishop for institution; a grant is an authoritative bestowal of a right or possession.

[479] Arch-Deaconry: "archdeanary" in MS Carte 81, 355r.

[480] Donative: a benefice which the founder or patron can bestow without presentation to the ordinary of a diocese or province.

[481] accostumed *77b*].

[482] []: " . . . Age of . . . " in House of Lords text (and MS Carte 81, f. 355r).

[483] Lord Protector: the title adopted in situations of royal minorities, to avoid granting full royal powers. It was first exercised in England by Humphrey of Gloucester (1422–29); Oliver Cromwell also adopted the title from 1654 to 1658.

any wise, either in the name of the King or Queen Regnant, or in his own name grant, confer or dispose of any Arch-Bishoprick, Bishoprick, Deanary, Prebendary, Mastership of any Colledge, Personage, Vicarage, or other Ecclesiastical Benefice or Promotion whatsoever, but the same shall be disposed of in manner abovementioned, during such minority, until such Lord Protector or Regent, shall make and subscribe the said Oath and Declaration, (*mutatis mutandis*)[484] before such nine or more of the said Prelates, as he shall call to Administer the same unto him, which Oath and Declaration they are hereby Authorized and required to Administer, under the penalties aforesaid, when they shall be called thereunto, by such Lord Protector or Regent, for the time being.

And be it further Enacted, That the Children of such succeeding King or Queen Regnant, that shall not have made and subscribed the Oath and Declaration in manner aforesaid, shall from their respective Ages of seven years, until the respective Ages of fourteen years, to be under the care and government of the Arch-Bishops of Canterbury and York, and Bishop[485] of London, Durham and Winchester, for the time being, who are hereby enjoyned and required to take care, that [86] they be well instructed and Educated in the true Protestant Religion, as it is now Established by Law, and to the Intent that the Arch-Bishops and Bishops, for the time being, may effectually have the Care and Government of such Children, according to the true intent of this Law; Be it {95} Enacted, That after any such Children shall have attained their respective Ages of fourteen years, no person shall have, enjoy, bear and execute any office, service, imployment or place of attendment[486] relating to their persons, but such as shall be approved of in writing under the Hands and Seals of the said Arch-Bishops and Bishops in being, or the major part of such of them as are there[487] in being. And if any person shall take upon him to Execute any such Office, Service, Imployment or place of attendance, contrary to the true intent and meaning of this Act, he shall forfeit the sum of 100 *l.* for every moneth he shall so Execute the same, to be recovered by any person that will sue for the same, in any Action[488] of Debt, Bill, Plaint or Information, in any of his

---

[484] *mutatis mutandis:* after making the necessary changes.

[485] Bishop: "Bishops" in MS Carte 81, 355v.

[486] place of attendment: better "place of Attendance," as in next sentence and in House of Lords text (and MS Carte 81, f. 355v).

[487] there: better "then," as in House of Lords text (and MS Carte 81, f. 355v).

[488] Action: legal process.

Majesties Courts at Westminster, shall also suffer Imprisonment for the space of six moneths without Bayle or Maineprize.[489]

And be it further Enacted by the Authority aforesaid, That no Person born within this Realm or any other of his Majesties Dominions, being a Popish Priest, Deacon or Ecclesiastical Person, made or deemed,[490] or professed by any Authority or Jurisdiction derived, challenged, or pretended from the See of Rome, or any Jesuite whatsoever shall be allowed to attend the person of the Queens Majesty that now is, or any Queen Consort, or Queen Dowager,[491] that shall be hereafter, whilst they are within this Realm, or by pretence of such service, or any other matter, shall be Exempted from the penal Laws already made against such persons coming into being or remaining in this Kingdom, but shall be, and are hereby lyable to the utmost severity thereof.

Provided always, That it shall and may be lawfull for Master John Huddleston,[492] being one of the Queens Majesties Domestique servants, to attend her said Majesties service, [87] any thing in this Act or any other Law to the contrary notwithstanding. {96}

And be it further Enacted, That after the Death of the Queens Majesty, to whom God grant a long and happy life, all lay persons whatsoever, born within this Realm, or any other of his Majesties Dominions, that shall be of the Houshold, or in the service or Employment of any succeeding Queen Consort, or Queen Dowager, shall do and perform all things, in a late Act of this Parliament, Entituled, *An Act for preventing Dangers which may happen from Popish Recusants:*[493] required to be done and performed by any person, that shall be admitted into the service or Employment of his[494] Majesty, or his Royal Highness the Duke of York, which if they shall neglect or refuse to do and perform, and nevertheless, after such Refusal

---

[489] *77a* has "Manieprize"]: mainprize is to procure the release of a prisoner by guaranteeing his appearance in court.

[490] or deemed: "ordained" in MS Carte 81, 356r.

[491] Queen Consort, or Queen Dowager: A queen consort is the wife of the king; queen dowager a queen whose husband, the king, has died and who holds a "dower," the title or property which comes to a wife from her deceased husband's estate.

[492] John Huddleston (1608–98), a Benedictine monk who helped the king to escape after the battle of Worcester and at the Restoration took up residence at Somerset House. After the death of Henrietta Maria (1669), he was appointed chaplain to Queen Catherine of Braganza.

[493] *Act . . . Recusants:* the Test Act of 1673.

[494] his: "her" in MS Carte 81, 356r.

and execute[495] any Office, service, or Employment under any succeeding Queen Consort, or Queen Dowager, every person so offending, shall be lyable to the same penalties and disabilities, as by the said Act are or may be inflicted upon the breakers of that Law provided always. That all and every person or persons, that shall by vertue of this Act, have or claim any Arch-Bishoprick, Bishoprick, Deanry, Prebendary, Personage, Vicarage, or other Ecclesiastical Benefits,[496] with Cure[497] or without Cure, shall be and is hereby enjoyned, under the like penalties and disabilities, to do and perform all things whatsoever, which by Law they ought to have done if they had obtained the same, and by the usual course and form of Law, without the help and benefit of this Act.

And be it further Enacted, That all and every Arch-Bishops, Bishops,[498] appointed by this Act to Assemble upon the Demise of his Majesty, or any other King or Queen Regnant, in order to repaire and make humble tender of the Oath and Declaration aforementioned, to any succeeding King or Queen, be[499] bound by this Act to Administer the same, shall before such tender and Administration thereof, and are hereby required to Administer the same[500] Oath and Decla-[88]ration, to one another, with[501] such of the Arch-Bishops and Bishops, at any time assembled as by the statute 31.H.8. ought to have precedence of all the rest of them, {97} that shall be so assembled, is hereby authorized and required, to administer to the rest of them, and the next in order to such Prelates, is hereby authorized and required to administer the same to him, and the same Oath and Declaration being engrossed in other piece of Parchment, they and every of them are hereby enjoyned to subscribe their names to the same, and to return the same into the high Court of Chancery, hereafter with their Certificate, which they are before by this Act appointed to make. And if any of the said

---

[495] nevertheless, after such Refusal and execute] "nevertheless they shall after such neglect or refusall execute" in MS Carte 356r. To retrieve this error from *77a* and *77b*, the "and" is made into "shall" in *79* and *89*.

[496] Benefits: "Benefice or Promotion" in previous formulae and in MS Carte 81, f. 356 v.

[497] Cure: a parish or other domain of pastoral ministry.

[498] Arch-Bishops, Bishops: "Arch-Bishops & Bishops" in MS Carte 81, 356v.

[499] Queen, be: the House of Lords text and MS Carte 81, f. 356v, read more fully "Queen, or that shall at any time, upon signification of the pleasure of such succeeding King or Queen be."

[500] same: "said" in House of Lords text (and MS Carte 81, f. 356v).

[501] with: "w^{ch}" in MS Carte 81, f. 356v.

Arch-Bishops or Bishops, shall be under the same penalties, forfeiture, and disabilities, as are hereby appointed for such Arch-Bishops and Bishops, as neglect or refuse to make any tender of the said Oath and Declaration, to any succeeding King or Queen Regnant.

And be it further Enacted, That the Arch-Bishop of Canterbury, or Arch-Bishop of York, or such other Bishop to whom it shall belong to issue forth summons to all the Bishops of England and Wales, requiring to meet and consult concerning the Nomination of fit persons, for the supply of any Arch-Bishoprick, or Bishoprick, according to this Act, shall make the said summons in such manner that the time therein mentioned for the meet-ing[502] the said Arch-Bishops and Bishops, shall not be more then forty days, distinct from the time of the Date, and Issuing out of the said summons.

And be it further Enacted, That in case any person intituled by this Act, doth demand Consecration, in order to make him Bishop of any vacant See, in manner aforesaid, shall demand the same of the Arch-Bishop of the Province, and such Arch-Bishop that shall neglect or refuse to do the same, either by himself or by others Commissioned by him, by the space of thirty days, that then such Arch-Bishop shall over and besides the trebble Dam-mages, to the party before appointed, forfeit the summe of 1000 *l.* to any person that will sue for the same, in any of his Majesties Courts at [89] Westminster by Action of Debt, Bill, Plaint or {98} Information, wherein no Essoyn,[503] Protection, or Wager of Law shall be allowed: And being thereof lawfully convicted, his Arch-Bishoprick shall thereby become *Ipso Facto*, void as if he were naturally Dead, and he shall be and is hereby made uncapable and disabled to hold, have, receive[504] the same, or any other Bishoprick, or Ecclesiastical benefice whatsoever.

And be it further Enacted, That after such neglect or refusal by the space of thirty days after Demand, to make such Consecration, or in case of the vacancy of the Arch-Bishoprick, such Bishop of the said Province, for time being, who by the Statute of 31.H.8. ought to have presidents of all the rest, calling to his assistance a sufficient number of Bishops, who are likewise required to assist, at such time and place, as he shall thereunto appoint, shall and is hereby required, upon reasonable Demands, to make such

---

[502] meeting the: "meeting of the" in MS Carte 81, f. 356v.

[503] Essoyn: an excuse for not appearing in court at the appointed time.

[504] hold, have, receive: "have hold or receive" (cf. below, and MS Carte 81, 357r)

Consecration which shall be good[505] and effectual in Law, as if the said Bishops were thereunto authorized, and empowred by Commission from such Arch-Bishop, or any other person, or persons, having authority to grant Commission for the doing the same.

And be it further Enacted, That the said Bishops and every of them, are hereby enjoyned and required to perform the same, upon pain of forfeiting, upon any neglect or refusal trebble dammages to the party grieved, to be recovered with Costs in any of his Majesties Courts of Record[506] at West-minster, as also the sum of 1000 *l.* to any person that will sue for the same, in any of his Majesties Courts at Westminster, by any action of Debt, Bill, Plaint or Information, wherein no Essoyn, Protection, or Wager of Law shall be allowed; and being lawfully convicted of any such neglect or refusal, his or their Bishoprick that shall be so convicted, shall become *ipso facto,* void, as if he or they were naturally dead, and he or they are hereby made incapable, and disabled to have, hold, or receive the same, or any other {99} Bishoprick or any other Ecclesiastical benefice whatsoever.

Yet this Notorious Bill had not the same accident with the [90] first, but was read a second time, and committed; wherein their Houses curiosity seemes to have led them, rather than any satisfaction they had in the matter, or hope of amending it, For it dyed away, the Committee disdaining, or not daring publickly to enter upon it, some indeed having, as is said, once attempted it in private, and provided R. S. a fit Lawyer[507] for the Chair-man, but were discovered. And thus let these two Bills perish like un-seasonable and monstrous Births, but the Legitimate issue of the Conspira-tors, and upon the hopes of whose growth they had built the succession of their Projects.

---

[505] shall be good: "shall be as good" (MS Carte 81, 357r)

[506] his Majesties Courts of Record: courts whose judicial acts and proceedings are inscribed on parchment, for a perpetual memorial; those at Westminster are Superior Courts of Record.

[507] R.S. a fit Lawyer: Robert Sawyer (1633–92), an MP with strong links to the Court, hence "thrice vile" in Shaftesbury's list and "a lawyer of . . . ill reputation" in *A Season-able Argument,* though his stand against "popery" in later years might in some seasons make him more acceptable to Whigs (Henning 3:400–01). He helped prosecute John Harrington, as recorded in *Mr Harringtons Case* (1678), and though styled by Marvell as "the best at the Bar" he had in November 1677 failed Marvell in representing a case in the Exchequer for the Hull Trinity House (THL Dec. 30, 1676 and Nov. 15, 1677, *P & L,* 2:287, 295).

Hence-forward another Scene opens: The House of Commons thorow the whole remainder of this Session, falling in with some unanimity, and great Vigor against the French Counsels. Of which their Proceedings it were easy to assigne the more intimate Causes;[508] but they having therein also acted according to the Publick Interest, we will be glad to suppose it to have been their only Motive. That business having occasioned many weighty Debates in their House, and frequent Addresses to his Majesty, deserves a more particular account. Nor hath it been difficult to recover it, most of them being unwilling to forget any thing they have said to the purpose, but rather seeking to divulge what they think was bravely spoken; and that they may be thought some body, often arrogating where they cannot be disproved, another mans Conception to their own honour. {100} March the 6th, 1676,[509] the House being resolved into a Committee of the whole House to consider of Grievances, Resolved.

That a Committee[510] be appointed to prepare an Address, to represent unto his Majesty the danger of the Power of France, and to desire that his Majesty by such Alliances as he shall think fit, do secure his Kingdoms, and quiet the fears of his People, and for preservation of the Spanish Netherlands.[511] [91]

May it please your Majesty.

We your Majesties most Loyal Subjects, the Knights, Citizens and Burgesses, in Parliament Assembled, find our selves Obliged in duty and faithfulness to your Majesty, and in discharge of the Trust reposed in us, by those whom we repre-

---

[508] Owing to their fear of the electorate, or to raise their price in being bought off.

[509] Here begins the long passage only slightly abbreviated from a document for which there is separate witness in Add. MS 35865, ff. 135r–56v: "March 1676[/7]. A Journall touching the Engageing the King to joyne with the Confederates in a Warr against France." This Marvell follows down to the Commons' answer to the king's message of April 16 and their adjournment (April 19, 1677, p. 341 below = *77a*: pp. 100–19). The few changes tend to diminish the Lords' role in parliament.

[510] *Committee 77b*]

[511] *JHC* 9:393 and 396 (Mar. 6 and 10, 1676/7); *OPH* 4:845, Mar. 15, 1676/7); for the debate leading up to this, see also Grey, *Debates*, 4:188–204. Marvell omits from his source the heading "The Addresse to his Majestie aboute the growing power of France reported and agreed to be carryed upp to the Lords for their Concurrance" and his Commons' version addresses from "the Knights, Citizens and Burgesses" rather than "the Lords Spirituall and Temporall and Commons" (Add. MS 35865, ff. 136r–v). Otherwise, both Marvell and his source are close to the version in the Commons Journal (punctuation excepted), which they slightly soften: e.g., the version in the Commons Journal urges his "Majesties *serious* consideration" (cf. also Bodleian, MS Eng. hist. c. 170, f. 18r: "Majesties *most serious* consideration").

sent, Most humbly to Offer to your Majesties consideration, that the minds of
your People are much disquieted, with the Manifest dangers arising to your
Majesty, by the Growth and Power of the French *King; Especially by the*
acquisition already made, and the further progress like to be made by him, in the
Spanish Netherlands, in the preservation and security whereof, we humbly
conceive the Interest of your Majesty, and the safety of your People, are highly
concerned; and therefore we most humbly beseech your Majesty, to take the same
into your Royal care, and to strengthen your self with such stricter Alliances, as
may secure Your Majesties Kingdoms, and secure and preserve the said Spanish
Netherlands, and thereby quiet the Minds of your Majesties People.

This Address was presented to his Majesty the 16*th.* of March, and
his Majesties Answer was Reported to the House of Commons, by Mr.
Speaker, the 17*th.* of March, which was thus.[512] {101}

That his Majesty was of the Opinion of his two Houses of Parliament,
That the Preservation of Flanders was of great consequence; and that he
would use all means in his power for the Safety of his Kingdoms.

A motion was therefore made for a second Address upon the same
subject, on Monday March 26*th.* which here followeth.

May it please your Majesty,

We your Majesties most Loyal Subjects, the Knights, Citizens, and Burgesses in
Parliament Assembled, do with unspeakable joy and comfort, present our humble
thanks to your Majesty for your Majesties gratious acceptance of our late Address,
and that your Majesty was pleased in your Princely Wisdom to express your
Concurrance and Opinion with your two Houses in reference to the Preserva-
tion of the Spanish Netherlands. [92]

And we do with most earnest and repeated desires implore your Majesty,
That you would be pleased to take timely care to prevent those dangers that may
arise to these Kingdoms by the great Power of the French King, and the Progress
he daily makes in those Netherlands and other places.

And therefore that your Majesty would not defer the entring into such Al-
liances as may obtain those ends, and in case it shall happen, that in pursuance of
such Alliances, your Majesty should be engaged in a War with the French King,
we do hold ourselves obliged, and do with all humility and chearfulness assure
your Majesty, That we your most loyal Subjects shall always be ready upon your

---

[512] In his Commons emphasis, Marvell here remains closer to the Commons Journal
than to BL 35865, f. 137r, and he compresses his source by moving directly to the
Commons' next address as proposed on March 26, 1677/8, rather than presenting it
after the debate (cf. ff. 137v, 143r–44r).

signification thereof in Parliament, fully, and from time to time, to assist your Majesty with such Aydes and Supplies as by the Divine assistance, may enable your Majesty to prosecute the same with Success. {102}
All which we do most humbly offir to your Majesty as the unanimous sence and desire of the whole Kingdom.
March 30*th*. 1677.[513]

It was alledged[514] against this Address, that to press the King to make further Alliances with the Confederates against the French King, was in effect to press him to a War, that being the direct and unavoidable Consequence thereof.

That the Consideration of War was most proper for the King, who had the intelligence of Forraine Affairs, and knew the *Arcana Imperii.*[515]

That it was a dangerous thing hastily to Incite the King to a War.

That our Merchant-Ships and Effects would be presently seised by the French King within his Dominions, and thereby he would acquire the value of it, it may be near, a million to enable him to maintain the War against us.

That he would fall upon our Plantations[516] and take Plunder and annoy them.

That he would send[517] out abundance of Capers, and take and disturb all our Trading Ships in these Seas, and the Mediterranean. [93]

That we had not so many Ships of War as he, and those thirty which were to be built with the 600000 *l.* now given, could not be finished in two years.

[513] For copies in addition to BL, MS 35865, ff. 143r–44r; see BL, Add. MS 34339, f. 10r–v, 12r–v, 14r–v (the first hasty transcription and corrected; the latter two fair scribal copies); BL Egerton MS. 3345, f. 43r–v; Bodleian, MS Eng. hist. c. 710, f. 20. Note that the final word in all these additional MS versions is "Nation" rather than the more deferential "Kingdom."

[514] Following his source almost verbatim (qv. BL, Add. MS 35685, ff. 138r–43r), except for some paragraphing, Marvell supplies a useful text for these debates, since Grey omits those of Mar. 30 to Apr. 3, 1677. The point-by-point listing ("That . . . That . . . That") shows a partisan ordering of the summary that follows; it does not identify the speakers but summarizes the positions of the Court and then the Country MPs. For another almost verbatim version that numbers these "heads of the Arguments in the House of Commons against the last Addresse that House presented to his Majestie Aprill 16. 1677," see Middle Temple, Treby MSS, unnumbered volume (thick) including parliamentary proceedings, sub item 27.

[515] *Arcana Imperii:* state secrets.

[516] our Plantations: colonial ventures, especially in Ireland and the New World.

[517] sent 77*b*].

That we had not Naval Stores and Ammunition, &c. sufficient for such a purpose, and if we had, yet the season of the Year was too far advanced to set out a considerable Fleet: and we could not now lay in Beef, Pork, &c.

That when we were ingaged in a War, the Dutch would likely slip collar,[518] leave us in the War, and so Gain to themselves the singular advantage of sole trading in Peace, which {103} is the Priviledge we now injoy, and should not be weary of.

That it was next to Impossible, to make Alliances with the several parties as might be expected, such and so various were the severall Interests, and crosse-biasses, of and amongst the *Emperour,* the Spaniard, the Dane, the Dutch, the Brandenburgh,[519] and the several lesser Princes of Germany, *and others.*

That we might easily enter into a War, but it would be hard to find the way out of it, and a long War would be destructive to us; for though the *Emperour,* French, Spaniard, &c. use to maintain War for many years, yet a Trading Nation as England is, could not endure a long-winded War.

On the other side, it was said;

That they did not Address for making War but making Leagues, which might be a means to prevent War.

That the best way to preserve Peace, was to be in a preparation for War.[520]

That admitting a War should ensue thereupon, as was not unlikely, yet that would tend to our peace, and safety in conclusion; for it must be agreed, that if the Power of France were not reduced, and brought to a more equal Ballance with its neighbours, we must fight or submit, first or last.[521]

That it was Commonly the Fate of those that kept themselves Neutral, when their Neighbours were at War, to become a prey to the Conquerour.

That now or never was the Critical season to make War upon the French, whilst we may have so great auxiliary con-[94]junction; and if it

---

[518] slip Collar: escape from the undertaking. This point in debate is claimed for Sir John Ernle in a later pencil annotation in BL, Add. MS 35865, f. 139r.

[519] Brandenburgh: a domain in Germany, with the capital Berlin; at this time under the leadership of Friedrich Wilhelm, the "Great Elector."

[520] *Qui desiderat pacem praeparet bellum:* "who seeks peace should prepare for war," a common maxim, from Flavius Vegetius Renatus (fl. A.D. 380), *Epitoma rei militaris,* vol. 3, Prol. (the Lord Fairfax, Marvell's former employer, had translated Vegetius). The saying is incorporated into the previous paragraph in BL, Add. MS 35865, f. 139v.

[521] These successive points are presented in separate paragraphs in BL, Add. MS. 35865, ff. 139v–40r.

were a dangerous and formidable thing to Encounter him now, how much more would it be so when this Opportunity was lost, the Confederacy disbanded, a Peace made on the otherside the water, and we left alone to withstand him single. {104}

That as to his seizing our Merchants effects, the Case was (the same and) no other now than it would be three years hence, or at any time whenever the War should commence.

That as to our Plantations and our Traders, we must consider, though the French was Powerful, he was not Omnipotent, and we might as well defend them as the Dutch do theirs by Guards, Convoys, &c. and chiefly when the French have so many Enemies, and we shall have so many Friends, as no other time is like to afford.

That they were sorry to hear we had not Ships, Stores, &c. equal to the French, and to our Occasions, and hoped it would appear to be otherwise.[522]

That the season was not so far spent, but what a competent Fleet might be set out this Summer, and that however Deficient we might be in this kind, the Dutch were forward and ready to make an effectual Supplement in that behalf.

That howsoever ill and false some men might esteem the Dutch, yet *Interest will not lye,*[523] and it is so much their Interest to confine and bring down the French, that it is not to be apprehended, but they will steadily adhere to every Friend and every Alliance they shall joyn with for that purpose.

That however cross and divers the several Confederates and their Interests were, yet a common Allyance may be made with them against the French, and as well as they have Allyed themselves together, as well may the Allyance be extended to another, to be added to them, *viz.*[524] the King of England.

That a numerous and vigorous conjunction against him is the way to shorten the work, whereas if he should hereafter attaque us singly, he would continue the War on us as long as he pleased, till he pleased to make an end of it and us together, by our final destruction. {105} [95]

That if now we should neglect to make *Alliances,* we had no cause to expect to have one Friend, when the French should make Peace beyond

---

[522] This paragraph runs into the next in BL, Add. MS 35865, f. 140v.

[523] Proverbial, especially in interest politics (as in Marchamont Nedham's tract of this name, 1659).

[524] *viz.:* abbreviation of Latin *videlicet,* "one may see."

Sea, and single us out for Conquest; for all that are conjoyned against the French, are provoked and disobliged, by reason of the great number of English, Scotch and Irish, which have served, and do still serve the French, and it was proved at the Bar of this House within this fortnight, That 1000 men were levyed in Scotland, and sent to the French service in January last, and some of them by force and pressing.[525]

Also that it was understood and resented, that we had mainly contributed to this over grown Greatness of the French by selling Dunkirk,[526] that special Key[527] and Inlet of Flanders, by making War on the Dutch, in 1665. Whereupon the French joyned with the Dutch, under which shelter and opportunity the French King laid the Foundation of this Great Fleet he now hath, buying then many great Ships of the Dutch, and building many others: as to which, but for that occasion, the Dutch would have denyed and hindred him, by not observing the Tripple League, and by our making a Joynt War with the French against the Dutch, in which, the French yet proceeds and Tryumphs. So that in this respect we have much to redeem and retreive.

That enmity against the French, was the thing wherein this divided Nation did unite, and this occasion was to be laid hold on, as an opportunity of moment amongst our selves.

That the bent and weight of the Nation, did lean this way, and that was a strong Inducement and Argument to incline their Representatives.

That it had been made to appear, and that in *Parliament,* that upon the Ballance of the French Trade, this Nation was detrimented yearly 900000 *l.* Or a Million, the value of the Goods Imported from France, annually so much exceeding that of the Goods Exported hence thither, where-{106} by it is evident, that such a sum of the Treasure and money of the Nation was yearly Exhausted and carryed into France, and all [96] this by unnecessary Wines, Silks, Ribbons, Feathers, &c. The saving and retrenching of which Expence, and Exhaustion, will in a Great Degree serve to maintaine the Charge of a War.

That the present was the best time for the purpose, and that this would

---

[525] BL, Add. MS 35865, f. 141v, lacks this last subordinate clause.

[526] Dunkirk: a strategic port in northern France, on the Strait of Dover. England had sold it to France in 1662, which satirists of the day, perhaps including Marvell, very much held against the minister responsible, the earl of Clarendon.

[527] Key: or quay, a wharf, and by extension a harbor; and in this context also *key* in the usual sense, a means of entry.

give Reputation to the Confederates, and Comfort and Courage to our best friends Immediately, and safety to our selves in futurity, against the *Old perpetual Enemy of England.*

The second Address was presented to his Majesty, March the 30. and till the 11. of April, they received no Answer.[528] Insomuch that it became doubtful, whether the Money-Bill would be accepted or no, and if the Commons made any difficulty in passing them, unless they were first secured against the French Interest, it seemed that the supply would be rejected by the Conspirators good will; And that even the building of Ships, how necessary soever, might rather have been respited[529] again, as it had in former Sessions, and for the whole long *Prorogation.* But their House was far from such Obstinacy. And the news being come of the taking both of Valenciennes and St. Omer,[530] with the defeate of the Prince of Orange at Mont-Cassel,[531] so that now there was no further danger of preventing or Interrupting the successes of the French *King* this Campagn, at last therefore upon the 11 of April, this following answer was offered to their House, from his Majesty by Master Secretary Coventry.[532] {107}

C. R.[533]

His Majesty having considered your last Address, and finding some late alteration in affairs abroad, thinks it necessary to put you in mind, That the only way to prevent the dangers which may arise to these Kingdoms, must be by putting his Majesty timely in a Condition to make such fitting preparation, as may enable him to do what may be most for the security of them. And if for this reason you shall desire to sit any longer time, his Majesty is content you may Adjourn now before Easter, *and meet again suddenly* [97] *after, to ripen this matter, and to perfect some of the most necessary Bills now depending.*

---

[528] The rest of this paragraph is original to the *Account,* briefly intermitting its reproduction of its source.

[529] respited: delayed, postponed.

[530] Valenciennes and St. Omar: towns in the Spanish Netherlands. After a fortnight's seige, the former stronghold fell to a furious onslaught, Mar. 7/17, 1676/7; after a month's siege, the latter surrendered, Apr. 9/19, 1676/7.

[531] Prince of Orange at Mont-Cassel: The Dutch prince William of Orange (1650–1702), later William III of England, encountered a sharp defeat at Mont-Cassel (Apr. 1/11, 1677), as he sought to relieve Saint Omar.

[532] Master Secretary Coventry: Henry Coventry (1619–86) became secretary of state on July 8, 1672. Here the *Account* resumes its dependence on its source, qv. BL, Add. MS 35865, f. 144r.

[533] C.R.: Carolus Rex, "Charles R." in BL, Add. MS 35865, f. 144v.

Given at our Court at White-Hall, the 11. of April. 1677.[534]

Somewhat was said on both these matters, but the greater debate of them, was Adjourned till next day, and then reassumed.[535]

Then it was moved[536] that the House should Adjourn till after *Easter*, and then meet again, with a Resolution to enable the King to make such preparations as should be thought necessary, and also pass some necessary Bills for the Kingdom, which if they did not, the blame of the neglect must rest upon themselves, and it would be observed, they had not sat to any effect this four years; and that now they had a Session, and had given a Million, they did take little care to redress Grievances, or pass Good Laws, for the People, and that they should not be able to give any account of them-{108}selves to their Neighbours in the Country, unless they should face them down, that there was no Grievance or Mischief in the Nation to be Redressed, and that the King had stopped their mouths, and laid it to them by offering to them to sit longer.[537]

Others[538] said, they should perfect the two Money-Bills, and give the King Ease, and take another time to consider further of Religion, Liberty, and Property, especially seeing all Bills now depending, would be kept on foot, the Intended Recess, being to be but an Adjournment, that they had

---

[534] Cf. also the similar version communicated by Francis Benson in a newsletter to Sir Leoline Jenkins (Huntington MS 30314, no. 35, dated April 13, 1677), which Benson adds "because mention only is made of it in the Journall."

[535] Cf. Marvell's constituency letter of Apr. 12, 1677 (*P & L*, 2:196–7). A fuller summary of speeches on Apr. 11 is available in Grey, *Debates*, 4:343–51 (*OPH* 4:864–67). The debate that follows on Apr. 12 is missing from Grey (and thus from *OPH*), who left London at this point. Hence the value of Marvell's source in addition to Thomas Neale (Egerton MS 3345, ff. 49r–53r) and more generally Daniel Finch, Leicestershire RO, Finch Papers, P.P. 42, p. 34. Marvell's summary does not specify the speakers, however, and comparison with Neale shows that Secretary Henry Coventry's arguments for the Crown and Sir William Coventry's in opposition predominate in Marvell's account, with some reference to claims by secondary speakers (especially Sir John Ernle on behalf of the Court, and Sir Thomas Meres, Sir Thomas Clarges, William Lord Cavendish, Sir Thomas Lee, and Henry Powell on behalf of the Country).

[536] By Henry O'Brien, Lord Ibrackan (Grey, *Debates*, 4:343–44); these paragraphs follow the course of debate on Apr. 11–12, 1677—Marvell omits the dating of this motion to April 12, in BL, Add. MS 35865, f. 145r.

[537] With the Easter adjournment so near, the pressure now grew on the Court to gain further supply and on the Country to succeed with bills for redress of grievances and for measures against France.

[538] Especially Williamson and Arthur Stanhope (Grey, *Debates*, 4:343–44).

very good Laws already, and would give their shares in any new ones, they were making, to be in the Country at the present time, that it was necessary for them to be there the 10*th.* of May, to Execute the Act for 600000 *l. &c.* And some time was to be allowed for their Journeys, and rest after it, that *the passing some necessary Bills,* came in the end of the Kings Message, and by the by; For his Majesty saith, *That if for this Reason,* that is, for making of preparations, *&c. they should desire to sit longer,* and if so, then also take the opportunity of passing [98] such Bills.[539] So the sence and inclination of the House was to rise[540] before *Easter,* as had been before intimated and expected.

Then they fell upon the main consideration of the Message, and to make a present Answer.

The Secretary[541] and other Ministers of State, said, that the Alteration of Affairs which his Majesty took notice of, was the success of the French against the Prince of Orange, in the Battel, and their proceeding to take Cambray, and St. Omars.[542]

Thus by Inches or rather great measures they were taking in {109} Flanders, which was reckoned the Out-work[543] of England, as well as Holland; and they said plainly, nothing could put his Majesty in a condition to make fitting preparations to preserve the Kingdom, but ready money.

To this it was answered,[544] that it was not proper nor usual to ask money at the end of a Session, and it was fit that Alliances should be first made, and that they should Adjourn rather till that were done, for they ought not to give money till they knew for what, and it was clearly spoken and made

---

[539] Still following its source almost verbatim, the *Account* a few times (as here) slightly alters the paragraphing, although it is unclear whether this is owing to Marvell's or to compositorial changes or even to alterations between the source and our other witness to it (cf. BL, Add. MS 35865, f. 146r).

[540] rise: adjourn.

[541] Henry Coventry, seconded by Williamson and Sir John Ernle (Grey, *Debates,* 4:345).

[542] The town of Cambray, in the Spanish Netherlands, had been taken by the French on Mar. 25/Apr. 4, 1677. Grey 4:306, citing Burnet, notes that "these things happening during this Session of Parliament, made great impression on all people's minds," and Marvell, for example, makes sure to inform his constituency when "St Omar is taken" (Apr. 14, 1677, *PL* 2:198).

[543] Out-work: an outer defense or outlying fort.

[544] Especially by Sir William Coventry (Grey, *Debates,* 4:349–50); the complaints about introducing a request for an extra supply so late in the session are noted in Finch (Leicestershire RO, Finch papers, P.P. 42, p. 34).

out to them, that if there were no Summers War, there was money enough given already.

It was replyed,[545] That they had not direction from his Majesty as to what he had resolved, and it might be not convenient to discover and publish such things, but they would offer their Guesse and Ayme at some things, if there were any Approaches towards War, though they ought to consider and compute like him in the Gospel,[546] whether with such a force they could encounter a King that came against them with such a force, they should think of providing a Guard for the Isle of Wight, Jersey, Garnsey[547] and Ireland, and secure our Coasts, and be in a defensive posture on the Land, we might be Attaqued in a night.

Also there would be a necessity of an extraordinary Summer Guard at Sea, his Majesty did use to apply 400000 *l.* yearly out of the Customes upon his Fleets, (the very harbour Expence) which in Anchorage, Mooring, Docks, and Repaires, &c. was 110000 *l. per annum*,[548] and he was now setting forth [99] 40 Ships for the Summer Guard, but if there were a disposition towards War, there must be more Ships, or at least those must be more fully manned, and more strongly appointed, and furnished the more, especially if the Breach were sudden, for otherwise, our Trading Ships at Sea, as well as those Ships and Goods in the *French* Ports, would be exposed. Now it is reasonable that the remainder which was above and beyond the Kings ordinary Allowance, {110} should be supplyed by the Parliament, and the Extraordinary preparations of this kind for the present, could not amount to less than 200000 *l.*

It was answered,[549] that it was a Melancholy thing to think Jersey, &c.

---

[545] Especially by Secretary Henry Coventry (Grey, *Debates*, 4:345, 348–49).

[546] Jesus' parable of the wise virgins (Matthew 25:1–13) and his parable of the two servants (Matthew 24:45–51; Luke 12:42–46), the lesson being, "Watch therefore, for ye know neither the day nor the hour" (Matthew 25:13)—the implication is that the English army too should stand on guard.

[547] Garnsey: Guernsey.

[548] *per annum:* yearly expense. The debate over these temporary defenses turned in part on whether they should be funded out of the customs revenues, which the opposition proposed owing to the historical origins of the customs as a means of funding the navy; this proposal was designed to frustrate the Crown, which already had other purposes for those moneys, now expected as a matter of course. This paragraph reflects especially Sir John Ernle's position in debate (Egerton MS 3345, ff. 49r, 51r; Grey, *Debates*, 4:345).

[549] The Country positions are further summarized in the next three paragraphs.

Were not well enough secured, at least as well as in the year 1665. when we alone had War with the French and Dutch too, and yet the Kings Revenue was lesse then than now: That the Revenue of Ireland was 500000 *l. per annum*, beyond the Establishment (that is, the Civil, Military, and all payments of the Government) which if not sent over hither, but disposed there, would suffice to defend that Kingdom, and they remember that about a moneth ago, they were told by some of these Gentlemen, that the French King would not take more Towns in Flanders if he might have them, but was drawing off to meet the Germans, who would be in the field in May, and therefore it was strange, he should be represented now as ready to Invade us, and that we must have an Army raised and kept on our Islands and Land. No they would not have that, it would be a great matter in the Ballance, if the Kings Subjects were withdrawn from the French service, and applyed on the other side, and till that were done, that we did continue to be Contributary to the Greatness of France. But a Fleet would protect our whole. Ships are the defence of an Island, and thereby we may hope to keep at a distance, and not apprehend, or prepare to meet him at our Doors, he learns by Sicily[550] what it is to Invade an Island, he is not like to attempt an Invasion of us, till he hath some Masterie at Sea, which is Impossible for him to have so long as he is diverted and Imployed at Land in the Mediterranean, and in the West-Indies, as he is. [100]

And as to our Merchants Ships and Goods, they are in no more danger now then they were in any War whensoever. Nay, there was more expectation of this, then there was of the last War, for the first notice we or the Dutch {111} had of that Breach, was the Attempt upon their Smyrna Fleet.[551]

Also it is observed, that what was said a fortnight ago (that the season

---

[550] learns by Sicily: The revolt of Messina (1674) led those insurgents against Spanish rule to invite French protection. But even the French naval success against the Spanish and Dutch squadron at Palermo (June 12/22, 1676), which was thought by some to follow from the "English in the French ships" (Grey 4:132, 134), did not lead to much success on land, and by the time of this debate in 1677 the gazettes had for some months reported on the slow progress of the French in consolidating their gains in Sicily.

[551] Still following its source almost verbatim, the *Account* nonetheless presents this last argument as two paragraphs rather than one; and presents the next argument as one paragraph rather than three ("But still it was insisted that . . . ," "All they desired . . . "), cf. BL, Add. MS 35865, ff. 148v–49r. There are further such differences in the paragraphs following (not noted).

was too far advanced to lay in Beef,[552] and it would stink) was admitted to be a mistake, for that now it was urged, that a greater and better appointed Fleet must be furnished out, but still it was insisted on, that they were in the dark, his Majesty did not speak out, that he would make the desired Alliances against the growth of France, and resolve with his Parliament to maintain them, and so long as there was any coldness or reservedness of this kind, they had no clear grounds to grant money for preparations. His Majesty was a Prince of that Goodness and Care, towards his People, that none did distrust him, but there was a distrust of some of his Ministers, and a Jealousie that they were under French *Influences;* and Complaints and Addresses had been made against them; and upon the discourse of providing for the safety of the Nation, it being said we might be secured by the *Guarranty* of the General Peace, it was reflected on as a thing most pernitious to us, and that our money and endeavours could not be worse applied, than to procure that Peace. Articles are not to be relied on. All that they desired was, that his Majesty and his People Unanimously, Truly, Sincerely and Throughly declare and engage in this business, with a mutual confidence speaking out on both sides, and this, and nothing but this, would discharge and extinguish all jealousies.

But it was Objected,[553] It was not convenient to discover his Majesties secret purposes in a Publick Assembly, it might be too soon known abroad, and there was no reason to distrust his Majesty, but that being enabled, he would prepare and do all things expedient[554] for the Kingdom.

It was answered,[555] That it was usual for Forraine Ministers to get notice of the Councils of Princes, as the Earl of Bristol[556] [101] Ambassador in Spain, in the last part of King James's Reign, {112} procured Coppies, and often the sight of the Originals of Dispatches, and Cabinet papers of the King of Spain. But acknowledging that his Majesties Councels cannot be penetrated by the French, yet the things would in a short time discover themselves: besides they said, they did not much desire secresy, for let the King take a great Resolution, and put himself at the Head of his Parliament

[552] to lay in Beef: to put a stock of beef in storage.

[553] The Court rejoinder follows.

[554] expedient *77a*] convenient *77b*]; the error in *77b* follows from the repetition of the word from the beginning of the sentence.

[555] This paragraph reports a speech by Henry Powell (Egerton MS 3345, f. 51r), who was a consistent opponent of the Court.

[556] Earl of Bristol: John Digby, first earl of Bristol (1580–1654).

and People in this weighty and worthy Cause of England, and let a flying Post carry the news to Paris, and let the French King do his worst.

His Majesty never had nor never will have cause to distrust his People.[557] In 1667, in confidence of our Aid, he made a League without advice of Parliament (commonly called the *Tripple League*) which was for the Interest of England, and whereby his Majesty became the Arbiter[558] of *Christendom*, and in the Name and upon the account of that, the Parliament gave him several Supplies.

In 1672, He made War without the Advice of Parliament, which War the Parliament thought not for the Interest of England to continue, yet even therein they would not leave him but gave him 1200000 *l.* to carry himself on and out of it.

How much more are they concerned and obliged to supply and assist him in these Alliances (and War if it ensue) which are so much for the Interest of England, and entered into by the pressing Advice of Parliament.

We hope his Majesty will declare himself in earnest, and we are in earnest, having his Majesties heart with us, *Let his hand Rot off that is not stretcht out for this Affair,* we will not stick at this or that sum or thing, but we will go with his Majesty to all Extremities.

We are now afraid of the French King, because he has great force, and extraordinary thinking men about him, which mannage his affairs to a wonder, but we trust his Majesty will have his Business mannaged by thinking men, that will be provident and careful of his Interest, and not {113} suffer him to pay, *Cent. per Cent.*[559] more than the things are [102] worth, that are taken up and used, and if the work be entred upon in this manner, we hope England will have English success with France, as it is in Bowling, if your Bowl be well set out, you may wink, and it will go to the Mark.[560]

Were the thing clear and throughly undertaken, there would be less reason to dispute of time; there never was a Council but would sit on Sunday, or any day for such Publick Work.

[557] The ensuing paragraphs seem to report a speech by William Coventry (Egerton MS 3345, f. 52r–v), who advised this interim supply of £200,000 (Grey, *Debates,* 4:350).

[558] Arbiter: arbitrator, judge.

[559] *Cent. per Cent.:* a hundred for every hundred, payment in full.

[560] Bowling . . . Mark: In the next session, this is a favorite turn of phrase of the oppositional MP Colonel Birch, who twice uses it in Jan. 1678 (Grey, *Debates,* 5:4, 28); Birch very often seconded Sir William Coventry in debate, and this may be Birch being reported here.

In fine, they said, the business must lye at one door or another, and they would not for any thing that it should flat in their hands.

And although they should hope in an Exigence his Majesty would lend to his People, who had given so much to him, yet they said they could not leave him without providing him a sum of money, as much as he could use between this and some convenient time after *Easter*, when he might, if he please command their full attendance, by some publick Notification, and this was the mentioned sum of 200000 *l.* The expedient they provided for doing this, was adding a Borrowing Clause to the Bill for almost 600000 *l.* (such an one as was in the *Poll Bill*) the Effect of which is enable his Majesty presently to take up, on the Credit of this Bill 200000 *l.* ready money at 7*l. per Cent. per annum* Interest.

And this they said might now be done, though the Bill were passed by them, and also (save that they had made the above mentioned amendment) by the Lords, for that *Poll Bill*[561] was explained by another Act passed a few days after, in the same Session. But in Hackwells *Modus tenendi Parli. pag.* 173, was a more remarkable President, and exact in the Point.[562]

But after some Discourse of setting loose part of this 600000 *l. &c.* they reflected that this 600000 *l. &c.* was appropriate for the building of Ships, and they would not {114} have this appropriation unhinged by any means, and thereupon resolved to annex the borrowing Clause to the Bill for continuing the additional duty of Excise, for three years, which was not yet passed; against which it was Objected, [103] That it was given for other purposes, *viz.* to give the King ease to pay Interest for his Debts, *&c.* But on the contrary it was answered, that the Preamble speakes not of his Debts, but *His extraordinary Occasions;* But besides, they did not intend to withdraw so much of their Gift, but did resolve to re-emburse his Majesty the 200000 *l.* so much of it as he should lay out in extraordinary Preparations.

But then it was Objected, that this would be a kind of denouncing of War, and that 200000 *l.* was a miserable, mean and incompetent sum to defend us against those whom we should provoke.

---

[561] Poll Bill: Sir William Coventry similarly cited a proviso added to "25 Eliz. 31. March . . . a bill against Popish recusants" (Egerton MS 3345, f. 52v).

[562] Hackwells *Modus tenendi Parli. . . .* exact in the point: William Hakewill, *Modus tenendi Parliamentum: or, The Old Manner of holding Parliaments in England* (London, 1659), p. 173.

But it was Answered, That it was but an Earnest of what they intended, and that they were willing to meet again and give further Supplies: Besides the French King was not Formidable for any great hurt that he could do us during the Confederacy, there were several Princes of Germany, as the Arch-Bishop of Metz and Triers, the Palsgrave, the Duke of Newburgh, &c.[563] which are at War with him and are safe; and yet they are much more weak and inconsiderable than we; but they are defended not by their own strength, but by the whole Confederacy.

The Debate concluded, and the whole House Voting the following Answer, which was presented to his Majesty by the Speaker and the whole House, Friday April the 13th. {115}

May it Please your Majesty,

We your Majesties most dutiful and Loyal subjects the Commons in this present Parliament Assembled, do with Great Satisfaction of mind, Observe the regard your Majesty is pleased to Express to our former Addresses, by Intimating to us the late alterations of Affairs abroad, and do return our most humble thanks, for your Majesties most Gracious Offer made to us thereupon in your late message: and having taken a serious deliberation of the same, and of the preparations your Majesty hath therein Intimated to us were fitting to be made, in order to those publick ends, we have for the present provided a security in a Bill for the Addi-[104]tional duty of Excise, upon which your Majesty may raise the sum of 200000 l. And if your Majesty shall think fit to call us together again for this purpose, in some short time after Easter, by any publick signification of your pleasure, commanding our Attendance; we shall at our next meeting not only be ready to re-imburse your Majesty what Sums of money shall be expended upon such Extraordinary preparations as shall be made in pursuance of our former Addresses; but shall likewise with thankful hearts proceed then, and at all other times, to furnish your Majesty with so large proportion of assistance and supplies upon this Occasion, as may give your Majesty and the whole world, an ample Testimony of our Loyalty and affection to your Majesties service, and as may enable your Majesty by the help of Almighty God, to maintain such stricter Alliances as you shall have entred into against all Opposition whatsoever.[564]
{116}

---

[563] Princes of Germany . . . Newburgh &c.: allies against France.

[564] Here the *Account* omits a brief paragraph about parliament being unable to rise before Easter owing to the "difference betweene the two houses about the Amendment of the money Bill which the Lords have made" (BL, Add. MS 35865, f. 153v).

Easter Monday, April 19*th*.[565] Another Message in writing from his Majesty, was delivered by Secretary Williamson to the House of Commons (*Viz.*)

C. R.

"His Majesty having considered the Answer of this House, to the last message about enabling him to make fitting preparations for the security of these Kingdoms, finds by it that they have only enabled him to borrow 200000 *l.* upon a *Fond*[566] given him for other uses: His Majesty desires therefore this House should know, and he hopes they will always believe of him, that not only that *Fond,* but any other within his Power shall be engaged to the utmost of his power for the preservation of his Kingdoms; but as his Majesties condition is (which his Majesty doubts not but is as well known to this House as himself) he must tell them plainly, that without the sum of *Six hundred thousand pounds,* or Credit for such a sum, upon new *Fonds,* it will not be possible for him to speak, or act those things which should answer the ends of their severall Addresses, without exposing the Kingdom to much Greater danger: His Majesty doth further acquaint you that having [105] done his part, and laid the true state of things before you, he will not be wanting to use the best means for the safety of his People, which his present Condition is Capable off."

Given at our Court at White-Hall, April. 16. 1677.

Thereupon the House fell into present Consideration of an Answer, and in the first place, it was agreed to return Great thanks to his Majesty for his Zeal for the safety of the Kingdom, and the hopes he had given them that {117} he was convinced and satisfied, so as he would speak and act according to what they had desired, and they resolved to give him the utmost assurance that they would stand by him, and said no man could be unwilling to give a fourth or third part to save the residue. But they said they ought to consider that now they were a very thine House, many of their Members being gone home, and that upon such a Ground as they could not well blame them; for it was upon a presumption that the Parliament should rise before *Easter,* as had been intimated from his Majesty within this fortnight, and universally expected since, and it would be un-Parliamentary, and very ill taken by their Fellow-members, if in this their absence they should steal the Priviledge of granting money, and the Thanks which are given for it;

[565] 19th: should read 16th, as in Add MS 35865, f. 153v.
[566] *Fond:* a sum of money set aside for particular purposes.

That this was a National business if ever any were, and therefore fit to be handled in a full National Representative, and if it had hitherto seemed to go up-hill, there was a greater cause to put the whole shoulder[567] to it, and this would be assuring, animating, and satisfactory to the whole Nation. But they said it was not their mind to give or suffer any delay, they would desire a Recess but for three weeks or a moneth at most.

And the 200000 *l.* which they had provided for present use, was as much as could be laid out in the mean time, tho his Majesty had 600000 *l.* more ready told upon the Table.

And therefore they thought it most reasonable and advisable that his Majesty should suffer them to Adjourn for such a time; in the Interim of which his Majesty might if he pleased, make use of the 200000 *l.* and might also com-[106]pleat the desired Alliances, and give notice by Proclamation to all Members to attend at the time appointed.

The Answer is as followeth. {118}

                         May it please your Majesty.

We your Majesties most Loyal Subjects, the Commons in this present Parliament Assembled, having considered your Majesties last Message, and the gratious expressions therein contained, for imploying your Majesties whole Revenue at any time to raise money for the preservation of your Majesties Kingdoms; find great cause to return our most humble thanks to your Majesty for the same, and to desire your Majesty to rest assured, that you shall find as much duty and affection in us, as can be expected from a most Loyal People, to their most gratious Soveraign, and whereas your Majesty is pleased to signify to us, that the sum of 200000 l. is not sufficient without a further Supply, to enable your Majesty to Speak *or* Act *those things which are desired by your People; We humbly take leave to acquaint your Majesty, that many of our Members (being upon an expectation of an Adjournment before* Easter*) are gone into their several Countries, we cannot think it Parliamentary in their absence to take upon us the granting of money, but do therefore desire your Majesty to be pleased that this House may Adjourn it self for such short time, before the sum of 200000 l. can be expended, as your Majesty shall think fit, and by your Royal Proclamation to command the attendance of all our Members at the day of Meeting; by which time we hope your Majesty may have so formed your Affairs, and fixed your Alliances, in pursuance of our former Addresses, that your Majesty may be gratiously pleased to Impart them to us in Parliament; and we no ways doubt but at our next Assembling, your Majesty will not only meet with a Complyance*

---

[567] Whole shoulder: full effort.

in the Supply your Majesty desires, but withal such farther Assistance as the posture of your Majesties Affairs shall require; in confidence whereof we hope your Majesty will be encouraged in the mean time to Speak *and* Act *such things as your Majesty shall judge necessary for attaining those great ends, as we have formerly represented to your Majesty.*[568] {119} [107]

And now the money Bill being Passed both Houses, and the French having by the surrender of Cambray also to them, perfected the Conquest of this Campagne, as was projected, and the money for further preparations having been asked, onely to gain a pretence for refusing their Addresses, the Houses were adjourned April the 16*th*, till the 21. of May next. And the rather, because at the same moment of their rising, a Grand French *Embassade*[569] was coming over. For all things betwixt France and England moved with that punctual Regularity, that it was like the Harmony of the Spheres,[570] so Consonant with themselves, although we cannot hear the musick.

There landed immediately after the Recess, the Duke of Crequy, the Arch-Bishop of Rheims, Monsieur Barrillon,[571] and a Train of three or four hundred persons of all Qualities,[572] so that the Lords Spiritual and Temporal of France, with so many of their Commons, meeting the King at Newmarket, it looked like another Parliament, And that the English had been Adjourned, in order to their better Reception. But what Address they made to his Majesty, or what Acts they passed, hath not yet been Published. But those that have been in discourse were,

[568] Here with the adjournment ends "A Journall touching the Engageing the King to joyne with the Confederates in a Warr against France" (BL, Add. MS 35865, ff. 135–56), on which the *Account* has relied so minutely. Now four fuller paragraphs of Marvellian narrative are interpolated before he turns to his next source for the debates of May 1677.

[569] *Embassade*: a body of persons sent on a mission to or from a sovereign. As per errata in *77a*; correcting "Embassador" (retained in *77b*).

[570] Harmony of the Spheres: the mathematical movement of the heavenly bodies produces a music that is the harmony of the spheres, so perfect that it is inaudible to humans.

[571] Huntington MS 30314, no. 36: Francis Benson to Leoline Jenkins (April 17, 1677)—"The Duke of Crequi is shortly expected here, being sent by the K. of France to compliment his Majesty"; no. 37: same to same (April 20, 1677)—"On Tuesday night the Dukes de Crequi & Bouillon, together with the Archbishop of Rheims, & severall other of the Nobility of France, arrived here from the Camp"; no. 40: same to same (May 1, 1677)—" . . . Monsr Barillon, who came in [Crequi's] Company, is said to succeed Monsr Courtin here, in the quality of Ambr Extraordinary."

[572] Qualities: ranks or positions in society.

An Act for continuing his Majesties subjects in the service of France.

An Act of abolition of all Claims and demands from the subjects of France, on Account of all Prizes made of the English at Sea, since the year 1674. till that day, and for the future.

An Act for marrying the Children of the Royal Family to Protestant Princes.

An Act for a further supply of French money.

But because it appears not that all these, and many others of more secret nature, passed the Royal Assent, it sufficeth thus far to have mentioned them. Only it is most certain, that although the English Parliament was kept aloofe from {120} the business of War, Peace, and Alliance, as improper for their intermedling, & Presumptuous. Yet with these 3 Estates of France all these things were Negotiated and transacted in [108] the greatest confidence. And so they were Adjourned from New-Market to London, and there continued till the return of the English Parliament, when they were dismissed home with all the signs and demonstrations of mutual satisfaction.

And for better *Preparations* at home, before the Parliament met, there was Printed a Second Packet of Advice to the men of Shaftsbury,[573] the first had been sold up and down the Nation, and Transmitted to Scotland, where 300 of them were Printed at Edinburgh: and 40 Copyes sent from thence to England fairly bound up and Guilded, to shew in what great Estimation it was in that Kingdom; But this, the sale growing heavy, was dispersed as a Donative[574] all over England, and it was an Incivility to have enquired from whence they had it, but it was a Book though it came from Hell, that seemed as if it dropped from Heaven, among men, some imagined by the weight and the wit of it, that it proceeded from the Two Lords, the Black and the White, who when their care of the late Sitting was over, had given themselves *Carriere,*[575] and after the Triumphs of the *Tongue,* had Establisht those Trophies of the *Pen,* over their Imprisoned Adversaries. But that had been a thing unworthy of the *Frechwellian* Generosity, or *Trerisian* Magnanimity; And rather befits the mean malice of the same Vulgar Scribler, hired

573 Marchamont Nedham, *A Second Pacquet of Advices and Animadversions Sent to the men of Shaftsbury* (London, 1677).

574 Donative: gift, donation.

575 had given themselves *Carriere:* from the French "se donner carrière," which means to take liberty, make free with (Cotgrave, *Dictionary of the French and English Tongues,* 1611).

by the Conspirators at so much a sheet, or for day wages; and when that is spent, he shall for less money Blaspheme his God, Revile his Prince, and Belye[576] his Country, if his former Books have Omitted any thing of those Arguments; and shall Curse his own Father into the Bargain.[577] {121}

Monday, May 21. 1677.

The Parliament met according to their late Adjournment, on, and from April 16*th.* to May 21. 1677.[578]

There was no speech from the King to the Parliament, but in the House of Commons.

This Meeting was opened with a verbal message from his Majesty, delivered by Secretary Coventry, wherein his Majesty [109] acquainted the House, that having according to their desire in their Answer to his late Message April 16th. directed their Adjournment to this time, because they did alledge it to be unparliamentary to grant Supplyes when the House was so thin, in expectation of a speedy Adjournment; and having also Issued out his Proclamation of summons to the end there might be a full House, he did now expect they would forthwith enter upon the consideration of his last message, and the rather, because he did intend there should be a Recess very quickly.[579]

Upon this it was moved, That the Kings last Message (of April 16.) And the Answer thereto should be Read, and they were read accordingly.

Thereupon, after a long silence, a discourse began about their expectation, and necessity of Alliances.

And particularly, it was intimated that an Alliance with Holland was most expedient, for that we should deceive our selves if we thought we could be defended otherwise, we alone could not withstand the French, his

---

[576] Belye: belie, misrepresent.

[577] Curse his own Father into the Bargain: Marvell is particularly damning of this author, whom he may have known to be Nedham, his former colleague in the Protectorate.

[578] Here the *Account* begins its long extract from "Private Debates" (extant in BL, Add. MS 72603, ff. 48–59, and BL, Stowe MS 182, ff. 56–66), which was later published on the eve of the War of the Spanish Succession as *Private Debates in the House of Commons, In the Year 1677. In Relation to a War with France, and an Alliance with Holland, &c.* (London, 1702). Often different in details of wording—much more so than in the earlier debt of the *Account* to the "Journall" for March–April 1677—it continues to page 368 below.

[579] *JHC* 9:423 (*JHL* 13:121); *OPH* 4:870; Grey, *Debates*, 4:355.

purse and power was too great. Nor could the Dutch withstand him. But both together might.[580]

The general discourse was, that they came with an expectation to have Alliances declared, and if they were not made so as to be imparted, they were not called or come to that purpose they desired, and hoped to meet upon, and if {122} some few days might ripen them, they would be content to Adjorn for the mean time.[581]

The Secretary[582] and others said, these Alliances were things of great weight and difficulty, and the time had been short, but if they were finisht, yet it was not convenient to publish them, till the King was in a readiness and posture to prosecute and maintain them, till when his Majesty could not so much as speak out,[583] insisting on his words, *That without 600000 l. it would not be possible for him to speak or Act those things which should answer the ends of their several Addresses, without exposing the Kingdom to much greater dangers.* [110]

By others[584] it was observed and said, That they met now upon a publick notice by Proclamation, which Proclamation was in pursuance of their last Address, in which Address they desire the King they may Adjourn for such time, as with in which (they hoped) Alliances might be fixed, so as to be imparted, they mentioned not any particular day. If his Majesty had not thought this time long enough for the purpose, he might have appointed the Adjournment for a longer time; or he might have given notice

---

[580] This summarizes Sacheverell's position in that debate (Grey, *Debates*, 4:355–56; Egerton MS 3345, f. 60r).

[581] This summarizes Sir William Coventry, Sir Thomas Meres, and Sir Thomas Littleton's positions in debate that day (Grey, *Debates*, 4:357–8, 359–60; BL, Egerton MS 3345, f. 60r–v).

[582] Henry Coventry, and Sir Joseph Williamson, whose position in debate, seconded by Sir John Ernle, this summarizes (Grey, Debates, 4:359, 356–57).

[583] out] also thus in BL, Add. MS 72603, f. 48v; reads "on't" in BL, Stowe MS 182, f.56v, and in *Private Debates* (1702), p. 5.

[584] This and the following paragraph return more fully to the claim in debate of William Coventry (Grey, *Debates*, 4:357–8): "It has been said, 'The matter requires more time to finish, than this intermission of five weeks.' But our first Address was a longer time before than since the Recess. He has heard, that the Triple Alliance was made in five days, when Holland had Peace, and no more need of our Alliance than France had. Can any man think that Holland requires your Alliance less now, that when they were in Peace? He cannot imagine it hard, in time of War, to admit of a Confederate, the Triple Alliance being done in five days." See also BL, Egerton MS 3345, f. 60r.

by Proclamation that upon this account they should re-adjourn to a yet longer time.

But surely, the time has been sufficient, especially considering the readiness of the Parties to be Allyed with; it is five weeks since our Recess. He that was a Minister chiefly imployed in making the *Tripple League,* has since published in print that, that League was made in five days, and yet that might well be thought a matter more tedious and long then this; For when people are in profound peace (as the Dutch then were) it was not easy to embark them presently into Leagues. They had time and might take it for greater deliberation. But here the people are in the distress of War, and need our Alliance, and therefore it might be con-{123}tracted with ease and expedition, were we as forward as they.

Neither is five weeks the limit of the time, that has been for this purpose, for it is about ten weeks since we first Addressed for these Alliances.[585]

And as to the Objection, That it was not fit to make them known before preparation were made, they said, the force of that lay in this, that the French would be alarmed. But they answered[586] that the asking and giving money for this purpose would be no less an Allarm. For the French could not be ignorant of what Addresses and Answers have passed; and if money be granted to make warlike preparations, for the end therein specified, it is rather a greater discovery and denouncing of what we intended against the French.

Grotius (*de jure Belli & Pacis*)[587] sayes, If a Prince make [111] extraordinary preparations, a neighbour Prince who may be affected by them may expostulate, and demand an account of the purpose for which they are

---

[585] Not noted in Grey, but Sir Thomas Meres soon seems to be seconding this point (Grey, *Debates,* 4:359; Egerton MS 3345, f. 60v).

[586] Points made by William Coventry and Sir Thomas Littleton (Grey, *Debates,* 4:358, 360), the latter the "great Littleton" of "The last Instructions," l. 298.

[587] Grotius: Sir Thomas Littleton (Grey, *Debates,* 4:360; cf. BL, Egerton MS 3345, f. 60v) had thus quoted the Dutch theologian and jurist (1583–1645), drawing on *Hugonis Grotii de Iure Belli ac Pacis* (Paris, 1625), bk. 2, ch. 20, sect. 39. Littleton's diction conspicuously recalls that of the index to *The Most Excellent Hugo Grotius His Three Books Treating of the Rights of War & Peace,* trans. William Evats (London, 1632), sig. iiiirr, sv. "Preparations extraordinary for War a just Cause of War" (qv. pp. 383–84), in a way that suggests its consultation for present purposes. The manuscript and print versions of "Private Debates" also cite Bacon's essay "Of Empire" for the maxim that "a just Feare, of an Imminent danger, though there be no Blow given, is a lawfull Cause of a Warre" (Francis Bacon, *Essayes,* ed. Michael Kiernan [Oxford, 1985], p. 61).

intended, and if he receive not satisfaction, that they are not to be used against him, it is a cause of War on his part, so as that Neighbour may begin if he think fit, and is not bound to stay till the first preparer first begin actual Hostility, and this is agreeable to reason, and the nature of Government.[588]

Now the French King is a vigilant Prince, and has wise Ministers about him, upon which general account (tho we had not as we have seen an extraordinary French Embassy here during our Recess) we should suppose that the French King has demanded an account of our Kings purpose, and whether the extraordinary preparations that are begun and to be made are designed against him or not. In which case his Majesty could give but one of three answers,

1. To say, They are not designed against him, and then his Majesty may acquaint us with the same, and then there is no occasion of our giving money, {124}

2. To say, They are designed against him, in which case his Majesty may very well impart the same to us. For it were in vain to conceal it from us, to the end that the French might not be allarmed, when it is before expresly told the French, that the design was against him.

3. To give a doubtful answer. But that resolves into the second. For when a Prince out of an apprehension that extraordinary preparations may be used against him, desires a clear categorical and satisfactory answer concerning the matter (as the manner of Princes is) a dubious answer does not all satisfie his inquiry, nor allay his jealousy; But in that case it is, and is used, to be taken and understood, that the forces are designed against him.

And if his Majesty have given no answer at all (which is not probable) it is the same with the last.

So that this being so, by one meanes or other the French have the knowledge of the Kings purpose, and if it be known [112] to, or but guessed

---

[588] In the following paragraphs, "Private Debates" and Marvell seem to be drawing on a fuller text of Sir Thomas Littleton's speech, or some remarkably rapid notes of it. Compare Neale's report (BL, Egerton MS 3345, f. 6ov), and also that of Grey (*Debates*, 4:360) which summarizes Grotius more briefly, adding, "The use he makes of it is this; that the King of France has a vigilant Council, and a watchful eye upon the King, and our Messages to him, and his Answers, and on the King's demand of 600,000 *l*. When this was on foot, 'tis not to be imagined by that this expostulation being made, either the French Ministers are told, that this is not against France, or are left doubtful where it is intended. Why then is this darkness to the King's subjects, when the matter is clear to the King of France one way or the other? Would adjourn the debate and the House."

at by them, why is it concealed from his Parliament? Why this darkness towards us?

Besides we expect not so much good as we would, so long as we are afraid the French should know what we are adoing.[589]

In this state of uncertainty, and unripeness the House Adjourned to Wednesday morning nine a clock, having first ordered the Committee for the Bill for recalling his Majesties Subjects out of the service of the French King, to sit this after-noon, which did sit accordingly, and went thorough the Bill. {125}

Wednesday, May 23d. 1677.

His Majesty sent a Message for the House to attend him presently at the Banqueting House in White-Hall, where he made the following Speech to them.[590]

Gentlemen,

I Have sent for you hither, that I might prevent those mistakes and distrusts which I find some are ready to make, as if I had called you together, only to get money from you, for other uses than you would have it imployed. I do assure you on the Word of a King, that you shall not repent any trust you repose in me, for the safety of my Kingdoms; and I desire you to believe I would not break my Credit with you, but as I have already told you, that it will not be possible for me to Speak or Act *those things which should answer the ends of your several Addresses, without exposing my Kingdoms to much greater dangers, so I declare to you again, I will neither hazard my own safety; nor yours,[591] until I be in a better condition than I am able to put my self, both to defend my Subjects and offend my Enemies.*

I do further assure you, I have not lost one day since your last meeting, in doing all I could for your defence; and I tell you plainly, it shall be your fault and not mine if your Security be not sufficiently provided for.

The Commons returning to their House, and the Speech being there read, they presently resolved to consider it, and after a little while resolved into a Committee of the whole House,[592] for the more full, free, and regular debate. [113]

---

[589] Littleton's speech ends (Grey, *Debates*, 4:360).

[590] *JHC* 9:424 (May 23, 1677) and Grey, *Debates*, 4:361, showing minor variations in wording and punctuation. See also the transcript Marvell communicates to his constituency, LHC, May 24, 1677, *P & L*, 2:201–02.

[591] your *77b*].

[592] Henry Coventry, seconded by Williamson (Grey, *Debates*, 4:362) and Sir Heneage Finch had "sought to press the hous as if by their last address they were ingaged to

The Secretary and others[593] propounded the supplying the King, where-in they said they did not press the House, but they might do as they pleased. But if it be expected that Alliances be made, and made known, there must be 600000 *l.* {126} raised to make preparation before, for the King had declared that without it, it could not be possible for him to *Speak or Act;* he could not safely move a step further. The King had the right of making Peace, War, and Leagues, as this House has of giving money, he could not have money without them, nor they Alliance without him. The King had considered this matter, and this was his Judgment, That he ought by such a sum to be put into a posture to maintain and prosecute his Alliance, before they could or should be declared, and truly otherwise our nakedness and weakness would be exposed.[594]

'Tis true as has been Objected, the asking and giving money for this purpose, would allarm as much as the declaring Alliance, but then it would defend too. A Whip will allarm a wild Beast, but it will not defend the man, a Sword will allarm the Beast too, but then it will also defend the man.[595]

We know[596] the King would strip himself to his shirt rather then hazard the Nation. He has done much already, he has set out, and made ready to set out 44 Ships, but they must be distributed to several places for Convoys, &c. There would need, it may be 40 more in a body. And it is difficult to get Seamen, many are gone into the service of the French, Dutch, &c. The King is fain to presse now.

The King has not had any fruit of the 200000 *l.* credit provided him upon the three years Excise, he has tryed the City to borrow money of them, thereupon, and my Lord Mayor returned answer, that he had en-deavoured but could not encourage his Majesty to depend upon the City for it.

---

answer the kings desires as to the six hundred thousand pound" (BL, Egerton MS 3345, f. 62r), only for Sir Thomas Meres (BL, Egerton MS 3345, f. 62r; Grey, *Debates*, 4:363) and other Country speakers to demand successfully that supply be debated in a committee of the whole house.

[593] In the committee of the whole house, Williamson renewed the claim, followed by Sir Christopher Musgrave and Henry Coventry (Grey, *Debates* 364–65).

[594] BL, Add. MS 72603 and Stowe 182 cite Boccalini here.

[595] Henry Coventry still, who is reported as differentiating "betwixt allarums to provoke and defend and oppose," BL, Add. MS 28091, f. 107v.

[596] This and the following paragraph represent the speeches of Sir John Ernle, BL, Add. MS 28091, 107v, 108v, and concludes the present summary of the Court position.

Several others,[597] somewhat different, spake to this effect, We should consider in this case, as in the case of the Kings Letters, Pattents, Proclamations, &c. If any thing in them be against Law and Reason, Lawyers and Courts, Judge it[598] void, and reckon it not to be said or done by the King. *For* [114] *the King can do no wrong,* tho his Counsel may. So we {127} must look upon the Kings Speeches and Messages as the product of Counsel, and therefore if any mistake be therein, it must be imputed to the error of his Counsel, and it must be taken that the King never said it. Now to apply certainly[599] the treating and concluding of Alliances, requires not a previous sum of money, however the Kings Counsel may misinform. They may be propounded and accepted, by the means of the Forraign Ministers, even without an Embassy to be sent hence, and yet if that were requisite, it were not an extraordinary charg.

Alliances may be made forthwith, and then money would be granted forthwith; If they were declared to day, the 600000 *l.* should be given to morrow, and as occasion should require.

And there is no fear but money would be found for this purpose, our own Extravagancies would maintain a War.[600]

The money which has been provided the King already this Session, is sufficient for all Preparations that can possibly be made before these Alliances may be made.

Forty Ships of ours with the help of the Dutch, are a good Defence against the French at Sea, now he is so entangled with Sicily, the West-Indies, &c. In the *Tripple League* it was stipulated, that forty of our Ships, and forty of the Dutch, should be provided, and they were thought sufficient for the purpose.

If it were required that 40 more Ships should be set out, 600000 *l.* is enough to maintain and pay a whole year clear for the Carpenters work, and such like as should presently be required, for the fitting them to go out a little mony will serve.

And surely this is the only preparation that can be meant, for it should be

[597] The Country position, especially in speeches by William Williams and Lord Cavendish (Grey, *Debates,* 4:367–69; BL, Add. MS 28091, f. 108v).

[598] is *77b*].

[599] Stowe MS 182, f. 57v (*Private Debates,* p. 23) corrects this to "Now to apply: certainly . . . "; BL, Add. MS 72603, f. 50r lacks the punctuation, as usual.

[600] This sentence is drawn from Birch's much longer speech (Grey, *Debates,* 4:369–70).

meant, that we should fortifie the Land with Forts, Garrisons, walled Towns, &c. it is not 6 millions will do it. But our strength, force and defence, is our {128} Ships,[601] for the debate of this day it is as great and weighty as ever was any in England, it concerns our very being, and includes our Religion, Liberty and Property; *The door towards France* [115] *must be shut and Garded, for so long as it is open our Treasure and Trade will creep out and their Religion creep in at it,*[602] and this time is our season, some mischief will be done us, and so there will at any time when the War is begun, but now the least.

The French is not very dangerous to us, nor to be much feared by us at this present, but we ought to advise and act so now, as we may not fear or despair hereafter when the French shall make peace beyond Sea, and likely he will make Alliances with those People with whom we defer to make them; How ripe and great is our misery then?

 The power and policy of the French is extraordinary, and his money Influences round about him.

We[603] are glad to observe upon what is said by and of the King, that his Majesty agrees with us in the end, and we hope he will be convinced of the reasonableness of the means, which is to make and follow these Alliances, without which plainly we can give no account to our selves, or those we represent, of giving money.

We have made several Addresses about some of the Kings Ministers, their management, &c.[604] Of which we have seen little fruit, Their have continually almost to this hour gone out of England succours to France, of Men, Powder, Ammunition, Ordnance, &c. Not to rake[605] into the matter,

---

[601] Here the manuscripts and *Private Debates* mark a period, with a new paragraph for the more general point, and presumably new speech, that now follows.

[602] This sentence is Robert Sawyer's, and likely this and the ensuing paragraphs (Grey, *Debates*, 4:370–1).

[603] The Country position of Henry Powell (BL, Add. MS 28091, f. 107v]) and Sir William Coventry.

[604] The ensuing paragraphs seem to combine speeches by William Sacheverell (Grey, *Debates*, 4:366; BL, Add. MS 28091, f. 108r–v, see also BL, Egerton MS 3345, f. 63r) and especially Sir William Coventry, although with the latter Grey chiefly reports his interest argument about Holland (*Debates*, 4:371–72). Allowance again needs to be made for the vagaries of parliamentary reporting, and its omissions and additions; the present report may well have drawn on the text prepared for a fuller speech or on a summary of points for debate.

[605] rake: search or investigate.

how far the Ministers have been active or passive in this, nor to mention any other particulars, we must say that unless the Ministers, or their minds are altered, we have no reason to trust money in their hands, Though we declare we have no purpose to arraign or attempt upon them, but would rather propose to them an easy way how they might have Oblivion, nay, and the thanks of the People, *viz.* That they should en-{129}deavour and contend, who could do most to dispose the King to Comply with this advice of his Parliament.

We think the prosecuting these Alliances, the only good use for which our money can be imployed, and therefore before we give, we would be secure it should be applyed to [116] this purpose, and not by miscouncels be diverted to others.

This is the mature Counsel of the Parliament, and no Cross or other Counsel is to be received or Trusted, for attaining these great advices which the King and Parliament are agreed on.

To part with money before Alliances are made, is needless and to no purpose, at best it would be the way to spend that money before hand in vain, which we shall need hereafter, when we shall be forced to enter into this defence against France.

It would be like an errour committed in the late Kings time, and which looks as if men had given Counsel on purpose to destroy that Good King, he had by the care and faithfullness of Bishop Juxton[606] and others, Collected and preserved a good sum of money before the Scottish Rebellion,[607] in *One thousand Six hundred Thirty nine,* upon that Rebellion he was advised to raise an Army at Land, which indeed was necessary, But he was likewise advised to set out several of his great Rate Ships,[608] this appeared in the papers of Sir Robert Longs Office,[609] and may there be seen still, if

---

[606] Bishop Juxton: William Coventry is referring to William Juxon (1582–1663), archbishop of Canterbury and lord high treasurer of England; in January 1638–39, Juxon was added to the committee of the council of war, and he also served on other committees for administrative purposes during the king's absence in the north.

[607] the Scottish Rebellion: the concerted resistance to the Crown by Covenanters, Presbyterian adherents of the Scottish National Covenant of 1638 opposing Charles I's attempts to Anglicanize the Scottish Kirk. In the resulting Bishops' Wars (1639–40), Charles I mobilized an army to suppress the Covenanters' resistance, but after the failure of successive campaigns the king had been forced to ask for peace.

[608] Rate Ships: war vessels; navy ships were rated according to size and equipment.

[609] Sir Robert Longs Office: William Coventry thus refers to Sir Robert Long (d. 1673), formerly auditor of the exchequer.

the Papers are not scattered. A man cannot tell to what end this advise was given, unless to spend the Kings money, for the Admiralty of Scotland is not now, and much less then was so considerable, as to require any such force against it. And if the design were to hinder their Commerce and succours by Sea, the charge of one of those great Ships might have been divided and applied to the setting out five or six less Ships, each of which was capable of doing as much for that service, as such a great one, and could keep out at Sea longer. {130}

It is a plain case, unless the power of France be lowred we cannot be safe, without Conjunction with other Confederates, it cannot be done. The question is, whether the present be the proper time for the work. Certainly it is, there is a happy Confederation against the French, which we cannot so well hope to have continued without our coming into it, much less can we hope to recover or recruite it, if once broken. [117] The very season of the year favours the business. It is proper and safe to begin with the French in the summer, now he is engaged and not at Leisure, whereas in Winter when the Armies are drawn out of the Field he will be able to apply himself to us.

As to the Citizens not advancing mony upon the late credit, we[610] are informed they were never regularly or effectually asked, my Lord Mayor indeed was spoken to, and perhaps some of the Aldermen, but all they are not the City, he sent about curiously[611] to some of the Citizens, to know if they would lend, of which they took little or no notice, it being not agreeable to their way and usage, for the custom in such cases has always been, that some Lord of the Council did go down to the Common Counsel, which is the Representative body of the City, and there propound the matter.

Besides in this particular case the Citizens generally asked the same question we do: are the Alliances made, and said if they were made they would lend money, but if not, they saw no cause for it.

Philip the second of Spain[612] made an observation in his Will, or some

---

[610] Conflating Edward Vaughan, Sir Nicholas Carew, and especially Sir Thomas Clarges in debate (Grey, *Debates*, 4:372).

[611] Reads "cursorily" in BL, Stowe MS 182, f. 59v, *Private Debates*, p. 36.

[612] This abrupt shift seems to reflect the later turn in the debate toward consideration whether Spain should also be named in the request to the Crown for alliances; hence the appropriateness of the following Spanish maxim, and the comment that follows from it.

last Memorial, and 'tis since published in Print by Monsieur,[613] he observes the vanity of any Princes aspiring at the universal Monarchy, for that it naturally made the rest of the world joyntly his enemies, but ambition blinds men, suffers them not to look back on such Experiences. But this observation shews what is natural for others to do in such a case, and that the way to repel and break such a design, is by their universal confederation.[614] {131}

Philip the Second was most capable of making this Observation, for in his hands perished the *Spanish* Design of the Universal Monarchy, and that chiefly by reason of the Conjunction of the English and Dutch against him.

In the process of this debate, Gentlemen did more particularly explain themselves, and propound to Address their design to the King, for a League offensive and defensive, with the Dutch against the French power. [118]

Against which a specious *Objection* was made,[615] That the Dutch, were already treating with the French, and 'twas like they would slip Collar, make a separate Peace for themselves and leave us engaged in a War with France.

To which was Answered,[616] That there was no just fear of that, the Dutch were Interested in repressing the Power of France as well as we, and they knew their Interest; It was reasonable for them to say, If England, which is as much concerned in this danger, will not assist us, we will make the best terms we can for our selves, there is yet a Seam of Land between the French and us, we may Trade by or under them, &c.

But if England will joyn with the Dutch, they cannot find one syllable of reason to desert the Common Cause.

They have observed a propensity in the People of England to help them, but not in the Court of England. If they can find that the Court does heartily joyn, it will above all things oblige and confirm them.

In *One thousand six hundred sixty seven*, when the Dutch were in Peace

---

[613] BL, Add. MS 72603, f. 52r has "by Monsieur—": likewise "Monsieur***" in *Instructions de l'Empereur Charles V. A Philippe II, Roi D'Espagne, et de Philippe II. au Prince Philippe Sons Fils*, trans. Antoine Teissier (Berlin, 1699), f. *10r, of which copies had previously circulated, but in which example of such advice-literature neither emperor nor king proposes quite this maxim; cf. the earlier *The Advice of Charles the Fifth . . . To his Son Philip the Second* (London, 1670), pp. 14–15.

[614] Reads "mindfull consideracion" in Stowe MS 182, f. 59v, *Private Debates*, p. 38.

[615] Sir John Ernle (Grey, *Debates*, 4:367–68; Add. MS 28091, f. 108v).

[616] Sir William Coventry (Grey, *Debates*, 4:371).

and Plenty, when Flanders was a greater Bullwork[617] to them, for the French had not pierced so far into it, and when the direction of their affairs was in a hand of inveterate enmity[618] to the Crown of England (John de Witt) yet then their Interest did so far Govern him and them, as to enter into the *Tripple League,* against the growth and power of France, and keep it more, and most certainly therefore now they are exhausted and weakened by a War, and stand in {132} need of our help, now the French have approached nearer the brink of their Country, and are encreased in Naval force to the danger of their Trade and Navigation, and now their affairs are chiefly directed by a kinsman of the Crown of England, the Prince of Orange, they cannot deflect or start from a League they make with us against our Common Enemy.

It was moved, that there might be a League Offensive and Defensive with Spain and the Dutch, and other convenient Alliances with the rest of the Confederates, but the particular [119] concerning Spain, was retracted and laid aside by the general Discourse of the Members to this purpose. We do covet an Alliance with Spain above others, for that they are Owners of the Netherlands, for whose preservation we have Addressed, that it is with Spain that we have the most, if not the only profitable Trade, and the Spaniards are good, gallant and sure Friends. But they are remote, and we know not whether there are full powers here or at Brussels for this matter, and to wait for their coming from Madrid would make Church-work,[619] whereas we need the swiftest expedition.

Therefore they Voted their Address to be particular and expressly for such a League with the Dutch, and as to the Spaniards together with the other Confederates in general.

This passed with very general consent, there was an extraordinary full House, and upon putting the question, there were but two negative Voices to it.

There were more then ordinary particulars appointed to be in the Address, but no contest or debate about them.

---

[617] Bullwork: a defensive bulwark made of earth and trees; for this description of Flanders in relation to the Dutch, compare Sir William Coventry (Grey, *Debates,* 4:371).

[618] Enemy] "Enmity" in Stowe MS 182, f. 60v, *Private Debates,* 42.

[619] Church-work: work done at the edifice of a church, used to mean work which proceeds slowly. This seems the end of Sir William Coventry's speech, although it may catch a phrase used by another of the Country MPs seconding Coventry's reluctance to include Spain in the present arrangement.

The *Vote* was as followeth;

Resolved,

THat an Address be made to the King, That his Majesty would be pleased to enter into a League, offensive and defensive with the States General of the United Provinces, and to make such other Alliances with others of the Confeder-ate, {133} *as his Majesty shall think fit, against the growth and power of the French King, and for the preservation of the Spanish Netherlands, and that a Committee be appointed to draw up the Address, with reasons why this House cannot comply with his Majesties Speech, until such Alliances be entred into, and further shewing the necessity of the speedy making such Alliances, and when such Alliances are made, giving his Majesty Assurance of speedy and chearful sup-plyes, from time to time, for supporting and maintaining such Alliances.*

To which (the Speaker re-assuming the Chair, and this being reported) the House agreed, and appointed the Committee.

And Adjourned over *Ascension*-day[620] till Friday. [120]

In the Interim, the Committee appointed, met and drew the Address according to the above mentioned Order, a true Copy of which is here annexed.[621]

May it please your Most excellent Majesty.

"YOur Majesties most Loyal and Dutiful Subjects, the Commons in Parlia-ment Assembled, have taken into their serious consideration your Majesties gracious Speech, and do beseech your Majesty, to believe it is a great affliction to them, to find themselves obliged (at present) to decline the granting your Majesty the supply your Majesty is pleased to demand, con-ceiving it is not agreeable to the usage of Parliament, to grant Supplyes for maintenance of Wars, and Alliances, before they are signified in Parliament (which the two Wars against the States of the United Provinces, since your Majesties happy Restoration, and the League made in January 1668, for preservation of the Spanish Netherlands,[622] sufficiently proved, without {134} troubling your Majesty with Instances of greater antiquity) from which usage if we might depart, the president might be of dangerous consequence in future times, though your Majesties Goodness gives us great security during your Majesties Reign, which we beseech God long to continue.

"This Consideration prompted us in our last Address to your Majesty, before our last Recess, humbly to mention to your Majesty, our hopes, that

---

[620] *Ascension*-day: Thursday, May 24, 1677 (the church festival forty days after Easter).

[621] is here annexed: here follows.

[622] The League referred to is the Triple Alliance.

before our meeting again your Majesties Alliances might be so fixed, as that your Majesty might be graciously pleased to impart them to us in Parliament, that so our earnest desires of supplying your Majesty, for prosecuting those great ends, we had humbly laid before your Majesty, might meet with no impediment or obstruction; being highly sensible of the necessity of supporting, as well as making the Alliances, humbly desired in our former Addresses, and which we still conceive so important to the safety of your Majesty and your Kingdoms, That we cannot (without unfaithfulness to your Majesty [121] and those we Represent) omit upon all occasions, humbly to beseech your Majesty, as we now do, *To enter into a League offensive and defensive with the States General of the United Provinces, against the growth and power of the French King, and for the preservation of the Spanish Netherlands, and to make such other Alliances, with such other of the Confederates, as your Majesty shall think fit and useful to that end;* in doing which (That no time may be lost) we humbly offer to his Majesty these Reasons for the expediting of it.

"1. That if the entering into such Alliances, should draw on a War with the French King, it would be least detrimental to your Majesties Subjects at this time of the year, they having now fewest effects, within the Dominion of that King.

"2. That though we have great reason to believe the {135} power of the French King to be dangerous, to your *Majesty* and your Kingdoms, when he shall be at more leisure to molest us; yet we conceive the many enemies he has to deal with at present, together with the situation of your Majesties Kingdoms, the *Unanimity of the people in the Cause,* the care your Majesty hath been pleased to take of your ordinary Guards of the Sea, together with the Credit provided by the late Act for an additional Excise for three years make the entring into, and declaring Alliances very safe, until we may in a regular way give your Majesty such further supplies, as may enable your Majesty to support your Alliances; and defend your Kingdoms.

"And because of the great danger and charge which must necessarily fall upon your *Majesties* Kingdoms, if thro' want of that timely encouragement and assistance, which your *Majesties* Joyning with the States General of the United Provinces, and other the[623] Confederates would give them. The said States or any other considerable part of the Confederates, should this next Winter, or sooner, make a Peace or Truce with the French King (*the preven-*

---

[623] other the: other of the.

tion whereof must hi-[122]*ther to be acknowledged a singular effect of Gods goodness to us*) which if it should happen, your *Majesty* would be afterwards necessitated with fewer, perhaps with no Alliances or Assistance to withstand the power of the French King, which hath so long and so successfully contended with so many, and so potent Adversaries, and whilst he continues his over-ballancing greatness, must alwayes be dangerous to his Neighbours, since he would be able to oppress any one Confederate, before the rest could get together, and be in so good a posture of offending him as they now are, being Joyntly engaged in a War. And if he should be so successful as to make a Peace, or disunite the present Confederation against him, it is much to be feared, whether it would be possible ever to reunite it, at least it would be a Work of so much time and difficulty, as would leave {136} your Majesties [624] Kingdomes exposed to much misery and danger.

"Having thus discharged our duty, in laying before your *Majesty* the dangers threatning you and your Kingdomes, and the only remedies we can think of for the preventing securing and quieting the minds of your *Majesties* People; with some few of those Reasons which have moved us to this, and our former Addresses. On these Subjects; We most humbly beseech your Majesty to take the matter to your serious Consideration, and to take such Resolutions, as may not leave it in the power of any neighbouring Prince, to rob your People of that happiness which they enjoy, under your Majesties gracious Government, beseeching your Majesty to rest confident and assured, that when your Majesty shall be pleased to declare such alliances in Parliament, We shall hold our selves obliged, not only by our promises, and assurances given, and now with[625] great Unanimity revived in a full House, but by the Zeal and desires of those whom we represent, and by the Interests of all our safeties, most cheerfully to give your *Majesty* from time to time such speedy Supplies, and Assistances, as may fully and plentifully Answer the Occasions, and by Gods blessing [123] preserve your Majesties Honour, and the safety of the People.

All which is most humbly submitted to your *Majesties* great Wisdom.

Fryday May 25*th* 1677.

Sir John Trevor[626] reported from the said Committee the Address, as 'twas drawn by them, which was read.[627]

[624] *Majesty 77b*].

[625] "with" as per MS correction in *77a*, copy L] All print have "which," an easy mistranscription.

[626] Sir John Trevor (1637–1717) was later a judge and speaker of the House of Com-

Whereupon it was moved to agree with the Committee,[628] but before it was agreed to, there was a debate and division of the House. {137}

It was observed and objected[629] that there was but one reason given herein for declining the granting money and that is the Unpresidentedness, and as to one of the Instances to this purpose mentioned, *Viz.* the Kings first Dutch War, it was said to be mistaken for that the 2500000 *l.* was voted before the War declared.

But it was answered,[630] that if the Declaration was not before the grant of the money (which *Quere*)[631] yet 'twas certain that the War it self, and great Hostilities were before the money, and some said[632] there might be other reasons Assigned against giving money before the Alliances, but they rather desired to spare them, only in general said, 'twas not reasonable to grant money before there was a Change (they would not say of Counsellors but of Counsels) and an hearty undertaking these Alliances would be the best demonstration of that Change. For the swerving from this Interest and part, was the step by which we went awry, and the returning thereto would restore us to our right place and way.

---

mons. Trevor was chosen as chairman of a committee appointed to discuss with the lords the question of the growth of popery, the report of which he brought in on April 29, 1678.

[627] *JHC* 9:424–25. The address in question is reported in Add. MS 34729, ff. 208r–09r: "Your majesties most Loyall and dutifull Subjects the Commons in Parliament assembled having taken into their serious Consideration your Majesties Gracious Speech doe beseech your Majestie to beleeve it is a great Affliction to them to find themselves obliged (att present) to decline the granting your Majestie the supply your Majestie is pleased to demand Conceaving it not agreeable to the usage of Parliament to grant supplyes for maintenance of Warrs or Alliances before they are signified in Parliament which the few warrs against the States of the united Provinces since your Majesties happy restoration and the League made with them in Jan 1668 for preservation of the Spanish Netherlands sufficiently prove without troubling your Majestie with Instances of greater Antiquity."

[628] Moved by Sir John Mallet (Egerton MS 3345, f. 65r).

[629] By Secretary Henry Coventry, seconded by a number of Court MPs in concert (Grey, *Debates*, 377–81).

[630] By Sir William Coventry (Grey, *Debates*, 4:382–83; Egerton MS 3345, f. 66r).

[631] *Quere*] Quaere 77a]; "may be asked," or "is a question": hence "which remaynes a Query" (Stowe MS 182, f. 61v, also Add. MS 72603, f. 53v and *Private Debates*, 50).

[632] Especially Henry Powell (Grey, *Debates*, 4:386–87; Egerton MS 3345, f. 66r), seconded by William Williams; also Sir Nicholas Carew (Grey, *Debates*, 4:383–84).

And a Gentleman[633] produced and read the Kings Speech made Monday the 10. of February 1667. wherein he speak[634] chiefly of the League which afterwards when the Swede came into it, was called the *Tripple League*.

My Lords and Gentlemen.

"I Am glad to see you hear again to tell you what I have done in this Interval, which I am confident you will be [124] pleased with, since it is so much to the Honour and security of the Nation. I have made a League Offensive and Defensive with the States of the United Provinces, and likewise a League for an efficacious mediation of Peace between the two Crowns, into which League that of Sweden by its Ambassador hath offered to enter as a principal. I did not at our last Meeting move you for any Aid, {138} though I lye under great Debts contracted by the last War, but now the posture of our Neighbours abroad, and the consequence of this new Alliance will oblige me for our security to set out a considerable fleet to Sea this Summer, and besides I must build more great Ships, and tis as necessary that I do something in order to the fortifying some of our Ports. I have begun my self in order to these ends, but if I have not your speedy Assistance, I shall not be able to go thorow with it, wherefore I do earnestly desire you to take it into your speedy consideration, *&c.*

Which shews the proper course and practice, That Kings first communicate their Alliances made, before they demand Supplies upon the account of them.[635]

So the Exception was let fall.

But the grand *Objection* mannaged against it, was upon the main point of the Address, wherein they desired his Majesty to make a League Offensive and Defensive with the Dutch, and such other *Alliances* with the rest as he should think fit.

Those who were against this particular (or particularizing) in the Address,[636] spoke to this effect.

This is an Invasion upon his Majesties Prerogative of making Peace, War and Leagues, and it is the worse for the Distinction that is used; in respect

---

[633] Sir William Coventry (Grey, *Debates*, 4:382–83).

[634] "speakes" in Stowe MS 182, f. 61v, *Private Debates*, p. 51: but the form in *77a* and *77b* seems to represent the past tense, "spake."

[635] Sir William Coventry (Grey, *Debates*, 4:383).

[636] Summarizing especially the Secretaries Henry Coventry (Grey, *Debates*, 4:377–78, 385) and Joseph Williamson (Grey, *Debates*, 4:379–80).

of the Dutch and the rest; by which you giving him express directions as to the Dutch, and referring to his discretion as to the others, it looks and gives an *Umbrage*[637] as if what he was to do was by your leave.

The Antient Land-mark, the Boundaries between King and [125] People must not be removed: This power is one of the few things reserved entirely to the Crown. Parliaments are summoned to treat *de Arduis*, but He, *de quibusdam Arduis*,[638] this is unpresidented. {139}

The Marriages of the Royal Family is such a peculiar thing reserved to the King, and the matter of the Lady Arrabella[639] is an Instance. Queen Elizabeth resented it high,[640] that the Parliament should propound her marrying, and she said that however it is well they did not name the person, if they had named the person, it had been intollerable, now here you name the person whom you would have the King Ally.

If you may go so far, you may come to draw a Treaty, and propose to the King to sign it,[641] by this you would put a great *Indecorum* upon the King, he is now concerned as a Mediator at Nimmegen,[642] and it would be an indecent thing for him at the same time to declare himself a party. It is believed the House of Austria[643] (though they sent full powers to Nimmegen, for the purpose, yet) never intended to conclude a Peace. But it was an absurd thing for them to declare so in Publick: There must be publick decorum.

This is the way for the King to have the worse bargain with the Confed-

---

[637] *Umbrage:* appearance or semblance.

[638] *de Arduis:* taken from the writ of summons of Parliament, "concerning difficulties"; *de quibusdam Arduis:* "concerning certain difficulties." Picking up on Secretary Henry Coventry's introduction of the terms of that writ (Grey, *Debates,* 4:377).

[639] Lady Arabella: The secret marriage of Arabella Stuart (1575–1615) to William Seymour occasioned James I's imprisonment of them both, with Arabella finally locked in the Tower, where she soon lost her mind and died. This might also be cited as an example of proceedings against the presumptive heir to the throne, Add. MS 35865, 82v.

[640] high: with special indignation.

[641] Here Add. MS 72603 (also Stowe MS 182, f. 62v and *Private Debates,* p. 61) ends this sentence and adds a paragraph: "Lawyers can acquaint you with the president in Ri[chard the] 2d. time wherein the King nominated to the Commons a matter of peace and warr to bee treated on and they referred it backe to him as a thing not fitt for them to consult of"—to which claim the opposition soon responded (p. 362 below).

[642] Mediator at Nimmegen: The negotiations between Holland and France were now in progress at Nijmegen, with the English mediating; the Treaty of Nijmegen was signed in 1678.

[643] House of Austria: the House of Habsburg in the Holy Roman Empire.

erates, for they observing how he is importuned, and as it were driven to make these *Alliances,* will slacken and lessen those advantagious offers, which otherwise they would be forced to make.

And again and again, they said his Majesty did agree with this House in the end, and they did not doubt but he would prosecute it by the same means as was desired. But his Prerogative was not to be incroacht upon. This manner of proceeding would never obtain with the King, nay, it would make the Address miscarry with the King.[644]

On the other side, several spoke to this effect.

We ought to consider, we are upon the Question of agreeing an Address drawn by our Committee, by our Order.[645] [126]

If they have not in matter and manner corresponded with our direction or intention, we have cause to disagree. But here the exception taken, and cause pressed why we should not agree with them is, because they have observed the very {140} words and substance of our Order, which exactly justifyeth this Draught.

This passed on Wednesday,[646] upon a full Debate, in a very full House, two only contradicting, but not one speaking or thinking the *Kings Prerogative* was toucht: and therefore its[647] strange it should be made the great *Objection* and *Question of this day.*

But the *Prerogative* is not at all intrench'd upon, we do not, nor do pretend to treat or make Alliances, we only offer our advice about them, and leave it with the King, he may do as he pleaseth, either make or not make them. It is no more than other persons may do to the King, or doubtless the Privy Council may Advise him in this particular, and why not his Great Council? This rate of discourse would make the *Kings Prerogative* consist meerly in not being advised by his Parliament (of all People.)

There are manifold Presidents of such Advices:[648] Leagues have been

[644] Also Thomas Neale and Sir John Ernle (Grey, *Debates,* 4:380–81; Egerton MS 3345, f. 65r–v).

[645] Sir Thomas Meres, Sir Thomas Lee, and especially Sir William Coventry (Grey, *Debates,* 4:380–81, 382), seconded by Colonel Birch and William Sacheverell (Grey, *Debates,* 4:384–85).

[646] I.e., this had passed two days before, May 23, 1677.

[647] 'its *77b*].

[648] Henry Powell (Grey, *Debates,* 4:386): "Though he did not expect to meet with this opposition, yet, upon recollection, he can show Precedents wherein the King has been advised to particular Alliances. In the 18th of K. James, the Parliament advised him to break the Match with Spain, and to make a War, and they then advised stricter Al-

made by Advice of Parliament, and have been ratified in Parliament in Edw. 3. Rich. 2. and especially in Henry the Fifths time, and particularly with Sigismond the *Emperour* and King of the Romans, and Henry the fifth was a Magnanimous Prince and not to be imposed upon.

18 *Jac.*[649] The Parliament advised the *King* about making and mannaging a War, *Rushw. Coll.* 36, 41, 42, 45, 46.[650] And we may well remember our own advising the first Dutch War; and making Leagues is less than War.

But if there was no President in this particular Case, it was no *Objection*; for matter of advice is not to be circumscribed by President. If there be a new Case[651] that a Prince [127] should joyn in a War, together with another Prince, when that Prince was too potent before, and that when this was discerned, and a Peace made, yet Succors[652] should continually go out of the first Princes Dominions to the service of the other Prince (and that notwithstanding several Addresses and advices to the contrary).[653] {141}

Tis true (as *Objected*) that the Commons have sometimes declined advising in the matter of War, *&c.* proposed to them. But that shews not their want of right to meddle therewith but rather the contrary. The very Truth

---

liances with the States of Holland. In E. III, R. II, H. V, the Parliament advised to make a League with the Emperor, and it was signed and ratified in Parliament. He will not wave these Precedents, but he speaks these a little timourously, having not lately perused them. As for the argument of 'these Addresses being against the Prerogative,' Kings have always laboured to invite this House to Peace and War, because their judgment did import Supply, and they could not excuse giving money to support it, where they had advised." Compare also Egerton MS 3345, f. 66r.

[649] 18 *Jac.:* 19 James (1621) in Rushworth, *Historical Collections* (1659), p. 36.

[650] *Rushw. Coll.* 36, 41, 42, 45, 46: pagination of these precedents in John Rushworth, *Historical collections . . .* vol. 1 (London, 1659).

[651] Add. MS 72603, f. 55v (Stowe MS 182, f. 63r, and *Private Debates*, p. 68) has fuller phrasing, showing eye-slip in the *Account:* "If there be a new case there must be a new Councell[.] perhapps there is noe precedent of such a Case that a prince should joyne in a warr."

[652] Succors: military assistance in the form of supplies or men.

[653] Henry Powell, continued: "Our necessity of affairs brought us once to another course, but if there were new Precedents, new Dangers must create new Precedents, and a new way. But let any man show him a Precedent, that we ever assisted a neighbour too potent for us already. Would have a Precedent shown him, where, after a representation in Parliament of the greatness of the French King, still sending men to his assistance has been continued, and they were not ill received at Court, when they returned home" (Grey, *Debates*, 4:386). The ensuing paragraphs seem likely to have been drawn from a fuller text of Powell's speech.

is, it has been the desire and endeavour of kings in all Ages, to engage their Parliaments in advising War, &c. That so they might be obliged to supply the King to the utmost for and through it, but they out of prudent caution have sometimes waved the matter, lest they should engage further and[654] deeper than they were aware or willing.

Since his Majesty is treating as Mediator at Nimmegen, about the general Peace, it is a great reason why he should specifie the *Alliances* desired as we have done, that we might make it known, we are far from desiring such *Alliances* as might be made by and with a general Peace; but on the contrary coveting such as might prevent and secure us against that dangerous and formidable Peace.

Doubtless the Confederates will offer honourable and worthy terms; their necessity is too great to boggle or take advantages, nor will they think this League the less worth because we advise it, but rather value it the more, because it is done unanimously by the King with the Advice and applause of his People in Parliament. [128]

We cannot suppose that our proceeding thus[655] to his Majesty will prejudice our Address or endanger its miscarriage since it is *Rush Coll.* 171. for his Majesties advantage, in that it obliges us to sup-172, 177, 178.[656] ply him to all degrees through this Affair, and the more particular it is, the more still for the Kings advantage, for if it had been more general, and the King thereupon had made Alliances, whatever they were, men might have thought and said they were not the Alliances intended, and it might be used as an excuse or reason for their not giving money to supply his Majesty here-{142}after, but this as it is now, doth most expressly, strictly and particularly bind us up.

We reflect that a great deal of time (and precious time) has been spent since and in our Address on this Subject, and finding no effectual fruit, especially of our last Address, we have cause to apprehend we are not clearly understood in what we mean. Now it is the ordinary way of pursuing discourse in such case, and it is proper and natural for us to speak (out) more explicitly and particularly, and tell his Majesty, That what we have

---

[654] or 77a].

[655] proceeding thus 77a, 77b] "propounding this" in Add. MS 72603, f. 56r, Stowe MS 182, f. 63v, *Private Debates*, p. 72.

[656] *Rush Coll.* 171./172, 177, 178.: pagination in Rushworth, *Historical Collections* (1659), of precedents showing that James I and Charles I had taken parliamentary direction in foreign affairs, with a resulting obligation upon parliament then to vote supply to the Crown.

meant is a League offensive and defensive. And to perswade us again to Address on, in more general Terms, as before, is to perswade us, that as we have done nothing this ten weeks, so we should do nothing still.

And since[657] his Majesty in his late Message and last Speech, has been pleased to demand 600000 *l.* for answering the purpose of our Addresses, and assures us that the money shall not be imployed to other uses than we would have it imployed, it is most[658] seasonable for us to declare plainly the use and purpose we intend, that so it may be concerted and clearly understood of all hands, and therefore it is well done to mention to his Majesty these express Alliances, we thinking no other alliances, worth the said Sum, and we [129] withal promising and undertaking that his Majesty shall have this and more for these ends.

Nor have we any cause to apprehend that his Majesty will take amiss our advising Leagues in this manner. We have presented more than one Address for Alliances against the growth and power of the French King, and his Majesty has received, admitted and answered them without any exception, and if we may Address for Alliances against a particular Prince or State, Why not for Alliances with a particular Prince or State? It cannot be less regular or Parliamentary then the former.

And moreover (though we know that punctual presi-{143}dents are on our side, besides our Commissions by our Writs,[659] to treat *de arduis &* *urgentibus Regem, Statum, & Defensionem Regni, & Ecclesiae Anglicanae, concernentibus.*[660] And besides the Kings General intimations in his Printed Speech, yet) if it be said to be a decent and proper thing to have his Majesties leave and consent, before we proceed on such a matter, in such a manner as we now do, we say that that in effect is with us too; for consider all our former Addresses, and his Majesties Answers, and Messages thereupon, and it will appear that his Majesty has engaged and encouraged us too upon this Subject; and that which he expects and would have, is not to limit or check our advice, but to open and enlarge our gift. His Majesty appears content to be throughly advised, provided he be proportionably

---

[657] said *77a*].

[658] more *77b*].

[659] Writs: commands to MPs to join in parliamentary session.

[660] *de arduis & urgentibus Regem, Statum, & Defensionem Regni, & Ecclesiae Anglicanae, concernentibus:* "about difficult and pressing matters concerning the Crown, state, and defense of the kingdom and of the English Church."

furnished and enabled with money, which we being now ready to do, we clearly and conclusively present him our advice for the application of it. *To prevent those mistakes and distrusts which his Majesty says he finds some are so ready to make, as if he had called us together only to get money from us, for other uses then we would have it imployed.* [130]

And truly the advising these Alliances, together with assuring his Majesty thereupon to assist and supply him presently, and plentifully to prosecute the same, is our only way of complying and corresponding with his last speech, For those Leagues followed and supported by these Supplyes are the only means and methods to put his Majesty in the *best condition, both to defend his Subjects, and offend his Enemies:* and so there will be no fault in his Majesty nor Us, but His and Our security will sufficiently provide for.

Besides it will be worse, it will be a very bad thing indeed not to make the Address for this particular League, now since we have resolved it already. Our intention being to have the Dutch, *&c.* comforted, encouraged and assured, we did order this on Wednesday, and there is publick notice taken of it abroad, and beyond Sea. If we should now up-{144}on solemn debate set the same aside, it would beget a great doubt, discomfort, and discouragement to them; It is one thing never to have ordered it; another to retract it.

Also it was said,[661] that this was necessary, but was not all that was necessary, for suppose (which was not credible) that France should be prevailed with to deliver up all Lorrain, Flanders, Alsatia,[662] and other Conquered places; Are we safe? No, He has too many Hands, too much Money, and this Money is in great measure (a Million Sterling yearly at least) supplyed him from hence. We must depress him by force as far as may be, but further we must have Leagues and Laws to impoverish him, *We must destroy the French Trade.* This would quiet and secure us, this would make our Lands rise, and this would enable us to set the King at ease. [131]

After this long debate the House came to the Question, Whether this particular of a League *Offensive and Defensive with the Dutch* should be left out of the Address, upon which Question, the House divided,

Yeas 142, *Noes* 182.

So that it was carried by *Forty* that it should stand.

---

[661] William Harbord (Grey, *Debates,* 4:387–88; Egerton MS 3345, f. 66r).
[662] Alsatia: Latin for Alsace, one of France's German conquests.

Then the main Question was put for agreeing, with their Committee, this Address: which passed in the Affirmative without Division of the House.

Then it was ordered, That those *Members* of the House who were of his Majesties Privy Counsel, should move *His Majesty* to know his pleasure; when the House might wait upon him with their Address.

Mr. Powel reported from the Committee, *Amendments* to the Bill for Recalling his Majesties Subjects out of the French *Kings* Service, which were Read and agreed to by the House and the Bill with the *Amendments* Ordered to be Ingrossed.

And then the House Adjourned to the morrow. {145}

Saturday, May 26. *in the morn.*

The House being sate had notice by Secretary Coventry, That the King would receive their Address at three in the afternoon.

The Bill for Recalling his *Majesties Subjects, &c.* being then Ingrossed, was read the Third Time and Passed; The effect of the Bill in short was this.

That all and every of the Natural born Subjects of His *Majestie* who should continue or be, after the first of August next, in the military service of the French *King*, should be disabled to inherit any Lands, Tenements or Hereditaments,[663] and be uncapable of any Gift, Grant or Legacy, or to be Executor or Administrator; and being convicted, should be adjudged guilty of *Felony*, without benefit of the Clergy, [132] and not pardonable by *His Majestie*, his Heirs or Successors except only by Act of Parliament, wherein such Offenders should be particularly named.

The like appointment for such as should continue in the Sea-service, of the French King, after the first of May, 1678.

This Act as to the prohibiting the offence, and incurring[664] the penalties, to continue but for two years, but the executeing and proceeding upon it for Offences against the Act, might be at any time, as well after as within the two years.

Then it was Ordered, that Mr. Powel should carry up this Bill to the Lords, and withal should put the Lords in mind, of a Bill for *The better*

---

[663] Lands, Tenements or Hereditaments: The phrase "lands and tenements" usually means "lands and all other freehold interests," freeholds being lands which are not owned but held, by tenure. Hereditaments are inheritances.

[664] "inflicting" in Add. 72603, f. 58r (Stowe MS, f. 65r, *Private Debates*, p. 85).

suppressing the growth of Popery, which they had sent up to their Lordships before *Easter*, which was forthwith done accordingly.

As soon as this was ordered, several other Bills were moved for to be Read, &c. But the Members generally said, *No, They would proceed on nothing but the French and Popery*. So they adjourned to the afternoon, when they attended the King with their Address, at the Banqueting House in WhiteHall Which being presented, The King Answered, {146} That it was long and of great importance, that he would consider of it, and give them an Answer as soon as he could.

The House did nothing else but adjourn till Monday morn.

Monday, May 28. 1677.

The House being sate, they received notice by Secretary Coventry, that the King expected them immediately at the Banqueting House.

Whether being come, The King made a Speech to them on the Subject of their Address. Which Speech to prevent mistakes, his Majesty read out of his Paper,[665] and then delivered the same to the Speaker. And his Majesty added a few words about their *Adjournment*.[666] [133]

The Kings Speech is as followeth,

Gentlemen,

Could I have been silent, I would rather have chosen to be so, then to call to mind things so unfit for you to meddle with, as are contained in some parts of your last Addresses, wherein you have intrenched upon so undoubted a right of the Crown, that I am confident it will appear in no Age (when the Sword was not drawn) that the Prerogative of making Peace and War hath been so dangerously invaded.

You do not content your selves with desiring me to enter into such Leagues, as may be for the safety of the Kingdom, but you tell me what sort of Leagues they must be, and with whom, (and as your Address is worded) it is more liable to be understood to be by Your leave, then at Your Request, that I should make such other Alliances, as I please with other of the Confederates.

Should I suffer this fundamental Power of making Peace and War to be so far

---

[665] his Paper: comparison with other copies, including Grey, *Debates*, 4:389–90, and Egerton MS 3345, f. 67, shows Marvell working from the circulated text rather than just notes.

[666] At this point the narratives of the *Account* and Add. MS 72603, f. 58v (Stowe MS 182, f. 65v, *Private Debates*, p. 87) finally diverge, as Marvell supplies the king's speech and much fuller comment on the House's reaction, the confused adjournment, and subsequent events.

invaded (though but once) as to have the man-{147}ner and circumstances of
Leagues prescribed to Me by Parliament, *its plain that no Prince or State would*
any longer believe that the Soveraigntie of England rests in the Crown, Nor
could I think my self to signifie any more to Foreign Princes, than the empty
sound of a King. Wherefore You may rest assured, that no Condition shall make
me depart from, or lessen so essential a part of the Monarchy. *And I am willing*
to believe so well of this House of Commons, that I am confident these ill
Consequences are not intended by You. [134]

   These are in short the Reasons, why I can by no means approve of Your
Address, and yet though you have declined to grant Me that Supply which is
necessary to the ends of it, I do again declare to You, That as I have done all that
lay in my Power since Your last meeting; so I will still apply my self by all the
means I can, to let the World see my Care both for the Security and Satisfaction
of my People, although it may not be with those Advantages to them, which by
Your Assistances I might have procured.

   And having said this, he signified to them that they should Adjourn till
the 16*th.* of July.

   Upon hearing of this Speech read, their House is said to have been
greatly appalled, both in that they were so severely Checked[667] in his *Maj-*
esties name, from whom they had been used to receive so constant Testimonies of his Royal Bounty and Affection, which they thought they had
deserved, as also, because there are so many Old and fresh Presidents, of the
same Nature; and if there had not, yet they were led into this by all the steps
of Necessity, in duty to his Majesty and the Nation. And several of them
offering therefore modestly to have spoken, they were interrupted continually by the Speaker, contesting that after the Kings pleasure signified
for Adjournment, there was no further liberty of speaking.[668] And yet it is
certain, that at the same time in the Lords House, the Adjournment was in
the usual Form, and upon the Question first propounded to that {148}
House, and allowed by them; All Adjournments (unless made by special
Commission under his Majesties Broad Seal) being and having always been
so, an Act of the Houses by their own Authority. Nevertheless, several of
their Members requiring to be heard, the Speaker had the confidence,
without any Question put, and of his own motion, to pronounce the House

   [667] Checked: rebuked, reprimanded.
   [668] The confusions at the end of the session, May 28, 1677, are reported in brief in
Grey, *Debates,* 4:390–91.

Adjourned till the 16*th*. of July, and stept down in the middle of the floor, all the House [135] being astonished at so unheard of a violation of their inherent Privilege and Constitution. And that which more amazed them afterwards was, that while none of their own transactions or addresses for the Publick Good are suffered to be Printed, but even all Written Copies of them with the same care as Libels suppressed: Yet they found this severe Speech published in the next days News Book,[669] to mark them out to their own, and all other Nations, as refractory, disobedient Persons, that had lost all respect to his Majesty. Thus were they well rewarded for their *Itch of perpetual Sitting*, and of *Acting, the Parliament* being grown to that height of contempt, as to be *Gazetted*[670] among Run-away Servants, Lost Doggs, Strayed Horses, and High-way Robbers.[671]

In this manner was the second meeting of this, whether Convention[672] or

[669] News Book: a small newspaper.

[670] to be Gazetted: to be mentioned or advertised in newspapers.

[671] That Marvell's bitter jest did not fail of effect may be observed from the parliamentary debate in March 1678, when are reported "the sharp reflections that were made upon the King's Ministers upon this Subject, so farr as to call them Pensioners of France, they complained how their frequent Addresses to the King had been slighted, and of the sharp answer that had been given them in May last, which had been printed in the Gazette to lett all the world see the little regard the King had to the representations of his Parliament &c. This was the straine they ran in, and in that heat passed the Vote, to advise the King forthwith to declare warr against France as yr Exly will see in the Journalls, but that would not content them. They would have those Ministers, who were the cause that things were come into this State, and particularly that had adviced the King to that answer in May last, removed. And it was carried in the Negative only by 5 votes." Huntington MS 30314, Sir Leoline Jenkins, letters-in (1676–78), no. 107 (March 15, 1677/8), from Whitehall. Likewise Bodl. MS Carte 72, f. 361v (? to Ormond), March 16, 1677/8: "That his Majesties goodnes & love to his people was sufficiently acknowledged, but what could more industriouly [*sic*] have bin advised for the benefit of france then what has lately fallen out in the frequent adjournment of the parliament, when in that preceeding the very long one 300,000 li which was offered for the building of 20 ships which might have put us in a state of preparation & defence, but was rejected. Then, when in May last they addressed from obstructing the growth, and progresse of france, which seemes now insuperable, they were sent home with shame & reproaches for their boldnes, and put into the Gazet ignominiously, with run away servants, and lost Dogs."

[672] Convention: applied to certain extraordinary assemblies of the Houses of Parliament, without the summons of a sovereign, such as that of 1660, which restored Charles II.

Parliament, concluded: But by what Name soever it is lawful to call them, or how irregular they were in other things, yet it must be confessed, That this House or Barn of Commons, deserved commendations for haveing so far prevented the Establishment of Popery, by rejecting the Conspirators two Bills, intituled,

I. *An Act for further securing the Protestant Religion by Educating the Children of the Royal Familie therein; And for the Providing for the Continuance of a Protestant Clergy.*

II. *An Act for the more effectual conviction and Prosecution of Popish Recusants.* And for having in so many Addresses applyed against the French power and progresse; And their Debats before recited upon this latter subject, do {149} sufficently show, that there are men of great parts among them who understand the Interest of the Nation, and as long as it is for their purpose, can prosecute it. [136]

For who would not commend Chastity, and rail against Whoreing, while his Rival injoyes their Mistress?

But on the other side, that poor desire of perpetuating themselves those advantages which they have swallowed, or do yet gape for, renders them so abject, that they are become a meer property to the Conspiratours, and must, in order to their Continuance, do and suffer such things, so much below and contrary to the spirit of the Nation, that any honest man would swear that they were no more an English House of Parliament. And by this weakness of theirs it was, that the House of Peers also (as it is in contiguous buildings) yielded and gave way so far even to the shaking of the Government. For had the Commons stood firm, it had been impossible that ever two men, such as the black and white Lords, Trerise and Frechwel, though of so vast fortunes, extraordinary understanding, and so proportionable courage, should but for speaking against their sense have committed the Four Lords (not much their inferiors) and thereby brought the whole Peerage of England under their vassalage.

They met again at the Day appointed, the 16*th.* of July. The supposed House of Commons were so well appayed,[673] and found themselves at such ease, under the protection of these frequent Adjournments, which seemed also further to confirm their *Title*[674] to Parliament, that they quite forgot how they had been out-lawed in the *Gazette,* or if any sense of it remained, there was no opportunity to discover it. For his *Majestie* having signified by

[673] appalled *77b*] apaid, appeased or contented.
[674] *Title:* ground of right, recognized right (i.e., to be a member of Parliament).

Mr. Secretarie Coventrie his pleasure; that there should be a further *Adjournment,* their Mr. Seimour (the Speaker deceased) would not suffer any man to proceed: But an honourable member[675] requiring modestly to have the Order Read, by which they were be-{150}fore adjourned, he Interrupted him, and the Seconder of that motion. For he had at the last Meeting gained one President [137] of his own making for adjourning the House without question, by his own Authority, and was loath to have it discontinued, so that without more ado, like an infallible Judge, and who had the power over Counsels, he declared, *Ex Cathedra,*[676] that they were adjourned till the third of December next. And in the same moment stampt down on the floor, and went forth (trampling upon, and treading under foot, I had almost said, the Privileges and usage of Parliament, but however)[677] without shewing that decent respect, which is due to a multitude in Order,[678] and to whom he was a *menial Servant.*

In the mean time the four Lords lay all this while in the Tower, looking perhaps to have been set free, at least of Course by Prorogation. And there was the more reason to have expected one, because the Corn Clause which deducted *Communibus Annis,* 55000 *l.* out of the Kings Custome, was by the Act of Parliament to have expired.

But these frequent Adjournments left no Place for Divination, but that they must rather have been calculated to give the French more scope for perfecting their Conquests, or to keep the Lords closer, till the Conspirators Designs were accomplished; and it is less probable that one of these was false, than that both were the true Causes. So that the Lords, if they had been taken in War, might have been ransomed cheaper than they were Imprisoned. When therefore after so long patience, they saw no end of their Captivity, they begun to think that the procuring of their liberty deserved almost the same care which others took to continue them in Durance; and each of them chose the Method he thought most advisable.

The Earl of Shaftsbury having addressed in vain for his *Majesties* favor, resorted by *Habeas Corpus* to the *Kings* [138] *Bench,*[679] the constant

---

[675] honourable member: Lord Cavendish (Grey, *Debates,* 4:391), whose friendship with Marvell is attested in Thomas Cooke's dedication of *The Works of Andrew Marvell Esq.,* 2 vols. (London, 1726) to Cavendish's son, the second duke of Devonshire.

[676] *Ex Cathedra:* from the seat; a position of authority.

[677] however: signifying here "be that as it may."

[678] Order: the customary mode of procedure.

[679] the *Kings Bench:* one of the superior courts of common law, which heard cases

Residence of his Justice. But the {151} Judges were more true to their Pattents then their Jurisdiction[680] and remanded him, Sir Thomas Jones[681]
having done him double Justice, answering both for himself and his
Brother Twisden,[682] that was absent and had never heard any Argument in
the case.

The Duke of Buckingham, the Earl of Salisbury, and the Lord Wharton, had better Fortune then he in recurring to his Majesty by a Petition,
upon which they were enlarged, making use of an honourable Evasion,
where no Legal Reperation could be hoped for. Ingrateful Persons may
censure them for enduring no more, not considering how much they had
suffered. But it is Honour enough for them to have been Confessors, nor as
yet is the Earl of Shaftsbury a Martyr, for the English Liberties and the
Protestant Religion, but may still live to the Envy of those that maligne him
for his Constancy.

There remains now only to relate that before the meeting appointed for
the third of December his Majesties Proclamation was Issued, signifying
that he expected not the Members attendance, but that those of them about
Town may *Adjourn themselves* till the fourth of April, 1678. Wherein it
seemed not so strange, because often done before, as unfortunate that the
French should still have so much further leisure allowed him to compleat
his design upon Flanders, before the Nation should have the last[683] opportunity of interposing their Counsels with his Majesty (it cannot now be
said) to prevent it. But these words that the House may *Adjourn themselves,*
were very well received by those of the Commons who imagined them-

---

concerning the king and persons privileged to be tried before him: Marvell described
the press in the courtroom that day ("By foure in the morning there were no places
left . . . Several were carried out of Court for dead") in a letter to Sir Edward Harley,
June 30, 1677 (*P & L,* 2:353).

680 Patents . . . Jurisdiction: Patents are letters or documents given by the king to
authorize judges to carry out their office, whereas a jurisdiction is the actual exercise of
legal authority; the comparison here indicates that judges are not acting justly because
of their bias in favor of the king.

681 Sir Thomas Jones (d. 1692) became chief justice of the common pleas in 1683 and
judge of the king's bench in 1676.

682 his Brother Twisden: Sir Thomas Twisden (1602–83), judge, who "being absent
from court in June 1677 during the argument of the return to Shaftesbury's *habeas
corpus,* . . . sent his opinion in writing that the earl should be remanded" (DNB).

683 *77a*] "last" omitted *77b.*

selves thereby restored to their Right, after Master Seymours Invasion;
When in reversal of this, he probably desiring to retain a Jurisdiction, that
he had twice usurped, and to add this Flower to the Crown, of his own
[139] planting, Mr. Secretary Coventry delivered a written Message from
his *Majesty* on the third of December, of a contrary effect, though not of the
same vali-{152}dity with the Proclamation, to wit, That the Houses *should
be Adjourned* only to the 15. of January 1677. Which as soon as read, *Mr.*
Seymour would not give leave to a worthy Member offering to speak, but
abruptly, now the third time of his own authority, Adjourned them, without putting the Question, although Sir J. Finch,[684] for once doing so in
Tertio Caroli,[685] was accused of high Treason; This only can be said, perhaps
in his excuse. That whereas that in *Tertio Caroli* was a Parliament Legally
constituted, *Mr* Seymour did here do as a Sheriff that disperses a riotous
assembly. In this manner they are kickt from Adjournment to Adjournment, as from one stair down to another, and when they were at the bottom
kickt up again, having no mind yet to go out of Doors.

And here it is time to fix a period, if not to them, yet to this Narrative.
But if neither one Prorogation, against all the Laws in being, nor three
vitious[686] Adjournments, against all Presidents, can Dissolve them, this
Parliament then is immortal, they can subsist without his Majesties *Author-
itie*, and it is less dangerous to say with Captain Elsdon,[687] so lately, *Si
Rebellio evenerit in regno, & non accideret fore, contra omnes tres Status, Non
est Rebellio.*[688]

Thus far hath the Conspiracy against our Religion and Government

---

[684] Sir J. Finch: At the unruly adjournment of May 28, the egregious Seymour had in
escaping the House been assailed with cries "bidding him 'Remember Lord Finch's
case, of the like nature.'" Sir John Finch, Baron Finch of Fordwich (1584–1660),
speaker of House of Commons and lord keeper, was impeached in 1640.

[685] in *Tertio Caroli*: in the third year of Charles I's reign, (Feb. 25, 1628/9).

[686] vitious: vicious.

[687] Captain Elsdon: Elsdon was an informant used in the prosecution of Marvell's
associate John Harrington, newly tried in December 1677; that Elsdon had been suborned by the Court, and Danby in particular, is the burden of much of *Mr. Harringtons
Case*, pp. 3–6.

[688] *Si Rebellio evenerit in regno, & non accideret fore, contra omnes tres Status, Non est
Rebellio:* "if Rebellion be not against all three Estates its no Rebellion" (*Mr. Harringtons
Case*, p. 6), recalling a much-contested constitutional matter in the 1640s, the issue
being the scope for resistance to the Crown as separate from the Lords and Commons.

been laid open, which if true, it was more than time that it should be discovered, but if any thing therein have been falsly suggested the disproving of it in any particular will be a courtesy both to the Publick and to the Relator; who would be glad to have the World convinced of the contrary, though to the prejudice of his own reputation. But so far is it from this, that it is rather impossible [140] for any observing man to read without making his own farther remarks of the same nature, and adding a supplement of most passages which are here but imperfectly toucht. Yet some perhaps may *Object*, as if the Assistance given to France were all along *invidiously aggravated*, whereas there have been and are, considerable numbers likewise of his Majesties Subjects in the Service of Holland, which hath not been mentioned.

But in {153} answer to that, it is well known through what difficulty and hardship they passed thither, escaping hence over, like so many Malefactors; and since they are there, such care hath been taken to make them as serviceable as others to the Design, that of those three *Regiments*, two, if not the third also, have been new modelled under Popish Officers, and the Protestants displaced. Yet had the *Relator* made that voluntary Omission in partiality to his *Argument*, he hath abundantly recompensed in sparing so many Instances on the other side which made to his purpose; The abandoning his Majesties own *Nephew*[689] for so many years in complyance with His and our Nations Enemies, the further particulars of the French Depradations and Cruelties exercised at Sea upon his Majesties *Subjects*, and to this day continued and tollerated without reparation; Their notorious Treacheries and Insolencies, more especially relating to his Majesties affairs. These things abroad, which were capable of being illustrated by many former and fresh Examples. At home, the constant irregularities and injustice from Term to Term, of those that administer the Judicature betwixt his *Majesty* and his *People*.

The *Scrutinie* all over the Kingdom, to find out men of *Arbitrary Principles*, that will *Bow the knee to Baal*,[690] in order to their Promotion to all Publick Commissions and Imployments; and the disgracing on the con-

---

[689] his Majesties own *Nephew:* William of Orange, whose marriage to the Princess Mary, celebrated November 4, 1677, goes conspicuously unmentioned here.

[690] *Bow the knee to Baal:* Baal was a Canaanite god of fertility whose widespread cult became the focus of Israelite animosity (the phrase appears, among other places, at 1 Kings 19:18 and Romans 11:4).

trary and displacing of such as yet dare in so universal a depravation be honest [141] and faithful in their Trust and Offices. The defection of considerable persons both *Male* and *Female* to the *Popish Religion*, as if they entred by Couples clean and unclean into the *Ark*[691] of that Church, not more in order to their salvation, than for their temporal safety. The state of the Kingdom of Ireland, which would require a whole Volume to represent it. The tendency of all affairs and Councels in this Nation towards a *Revolution*. And (by the great Civility and Foresight of his Holiness) an English Cardinal now for several years prepared like Cardinal Poole[692] to give us *Absolution, Benediction,*[693] and receive us into *Apostolical Obedience.* {154}

It is now come to the fourth Act, and the next Scene that opens may be Rome or Paris, yet men sit by, like idle Spectators, and still give money towards their own *Tragedy*. It is true, that by his Majesty and the Churches care, under Gods special providence, the Conspiracy hath received frequent disappointments. But it is here as in Gaming,[694] where though the Cheat may lose for a while, to the Skill or good fortune of a fairer Player, and sometimes on purpose to draw him in deeper, yet the false Dice must at the long run Carry it,[695] unless discovered, and when it comes once to a great Stake, will Infallibly Sweep the Table.

If the Relator had extended all these Articles in their particular Instances, with several other Heads, which out of Respect he forbode to enumerate, it is evident there was matter sufficient to have further accused his Subjects. And nevertheless, he foresees that he shall on both hands be blamed for pursuing this method. Some on the one side will expect, that the very Persons should have been named, whereas he only gives evidence to the Fact, and leaves the malefactors to those who have the power of inquiry. It was his design indeed to give Information, but

---

[691] Couples . . . *Ark:* Genesis 6:19, 7:15–16.

[692] English Cardinal . . . Poole: Philip Howard was made cardinal in 1675. Reginald Pole (1500–58), having broken with Henry VIII over the divorce, became papal legate to England under Mary Tudor. As archbishop of Canterbury, he was infamous for his persecution of Protestants.

[693] *Absolution, Benediction:* Absolution is the forgiveness of sins in the Sacrament of Penance; Benediction of the Blessed Sacrament is a devotion involving the exposition of the Sacred Host on the altar, and a blessing of those present with the Sacred Host.

[694] Gaming: Gambling.

[695] Carry it: to gain the advantage, win the contest.

not to turn Informer. That these to whom he hath only [142] a publick enmity, no private animosity, might have the priviledge of Statesmen, to repent at the last hour, and by one signal Action to expiate all their former misdemeanours. But if any one delight in the Chase, he is an ill Woodman that knows not the size of the Beast by the proportion of his Excrement.[696]

On the other hand, some will represent this discourse (as they do all Books that tend to detect their Conspiracy) against his Majesty and the Kingdom, as if it too were written against the Government. For now of late, as soon as any man is gotten into publick imployment by ill Acts and by worse continues it, he if it please the Fates, is thenceforward the Government, and by being Criminal, pretends to be sacred. These are, themselves, the men who are the Living Libells against the Government, and who (whereas the {155} Law discharges the Prince upon his Ministers) do if in danger of being Questioned, plead or rather Impeach his Authority in their own Justification. Yea, so impudent is their ingratitude, that as they intitle him to their Crimes, so they arrogate to themselves his Virtues, challenging whatsoever is well done, and is the pure emanation of his *Royal Goodness,* to have proceeded from their Influence. Objecting thereby his Majesty, if it were possible, to the hatred and interposing as far as in them lies, betwixt the love of his People. For being conscious to themselves how inconsiderable they would be under any good Government, but for their notorious wickedness, they have no other way of subsisting, but by nourishing suspition betwixt a most loyal People, and most gratious Soveraign. [143] But this Book, though of an extraordinary nature, as the case required, and however it may be calumniated[697] by interested persons, was written with no other intent than of meer Fidelity and Service to his Majesty, and God forbid that it should have any other effect, than *That the mouth of all Iniquity and of Flatterers may be stopped,*[698] and that his *Majesty* having discerned the Disease, may with his Healing Touch apply the Remedy. For so far is the Relator himself from any Sinister surmise of his Majesty, or from suggesting it to others, that he acknowledges, if it were fit for Caesars

---

[696] Woodman . . . excrement: a woodman is a hunter; excrement: "This was much attended to, and rules laid down in books on venery. The excrement also of almost each animal had a different name" (Grosart, 4:431).

[697] calumniated: slandered.

[698] *That . . . stopped:* liturgical, drawing on Psalm 107.

Wife to be free, much more is Caesar himself from all Crime and Suspition.[699] Let us therefore conclude with our own Common Devotions, *From
all Privy Conspiracy,* &c.

Good Lord deliver us.[700]

FINIS.
{156} [144]

[699] Caesar's second wife, Pompeia, was implicated in an infidelity with Publius
Clodinus; the accusation was never proved, but Caesar divorced her because "Caesar's
wife must be above suspicion."

[700] *Good Lord deliver us:* from the Litany (General Supplication) in the Book of
Common Prayer.

REMARKS UPON A LATE
DISINGENUOUS DISCOURSE
WRIT BY ONE T.D. &c.

1678

Introduction

N. H. Keeble

THE CONTROVERSY OPENED: JOHN HOWE ON DIVINE PREDETERMINATION

In 1677 John Howe, formerly chaplain to both Oliver and Richard Cromwell and now a leading London nonconformist minister,[1] published anonymously,[2] but with the bishop of London's license,[3] a 154-page octavo

---

[1] For biographical accounts of Howe (1630–1705), in 1662 ejected from the living of Great Torrington, Devon, appointed chaplain to Sir John Skeffington, 2d Viscount Massarene in 1670, and from 1676 minister to a Presbyterian congregation meeting at Haberdashers' Hall, Staining Lane, London, see Henry Rogers, *The Life and Character of John Howe* (London, 1836), and Robert Horton, *John Howe* (London, 1895).

[2] On its final page the text is signed "H. W." (p. 154), for which Howe afterward gave this explanation: "For knowing my Name could not give the cause an advantage, I was not willing it should be in a possibility of making it incur any disadvantage. And therefore, as I have observed some, in such cases, to make use only of the *two last Letters*, I imitated some other, in the choice of the *penultimate*" (*Postscript*, pp. 2–3).

[3] The *imprimatur* is dated April 19, 1677, signed by Guil[lielmus] Sill, that is, William Sill (d. 1687), prebendary of St. Paul's and chaplain to Henry Compton, bishop of London. The copy was entered in the Stationers' Register under the hands of Sill and Richard Clark, warden of the company, on May 4, 1677 ([G. E. Briscoe Eyre, ed.], *A Transcript of the Registers of the Worshipful Company of Stationers, 1640–1708 A.D.*, 3 vols. [London, 1913], 3:36). The book was advertised in the Easter Term Catalogue, 1677, 1:272).

tract in the form of a letter to Robert Boyle[4] entitled *The Reconcileableness of God's Prescience of the Sins of Men, with the Wisdom and Sincerity of his Counsels, Exhortations, and Whatsoever Other Means He Uses to Prevent Them.* The dilemma Howe addresses is a perennial problem in Christian theology: how is divine foreknowledge of human impenitency and damnation compatible with biblical promises of salvation and exhortations to faith? This dilemma is posed particularly acutely by predestinarian theologies, and it had consequently engaged Calvin himself. There is no more dogmatic assertion of the doctrine of double predestination than his: "All are not created on equal terms, but some are preordained to eternal life, others to eternal damnation; and, accordingly, as each has been created for one or other of these ends, we say that he has been predestinated to life or to death."[5] What, then, of those apparently unlimited Gospel promises of salvation? For God to will humanity's salvation and to exhort his creatures to follow a life of godliness, in the full knowledge that many will persist in wickedness and be damned, appears a kind of perversity. In the course of his discussion of grace and soteriology in book 3 of the *Institutes of the Christian Religion*, Calvin acknowledged that it can be objected that God appears to be "inconsistent with himself, in inviting all without distinction while he elects only a few."[6] In Howe's words, God "seems intent upon an end, which indeed he intends not," for how can he seek to prevent what, "*to that all-seeing eye,*" is "*sure to come to pass*" (p. 3)? An end cannot be both sincerely intended and prevented. Prescience and sincerity hence appear to be in conflict: either the divine wisdom does not encompass all future contingents (which safeguards God's sincerity but at the cost of his omniscience) or the divine will does not truly intend men's happiness (which safeguards God's wisdom but at the cost of his sincerity).

Howe's approach to this old problem is refreshingly free from theological niceties, which he distrusts. He avoids detailed exposition of the Fathers

[4] Robert Boyle (1627–91), seventh son of Richard Boyle, first earl of Cork, was in his lifetime as renowned for his Christian witness and theological learning as for the work in the natural sciences that secured his enduring reputation. Like his brother Roger, Baron Broghill and first earl of Orrery, and his sister Catherine Jones, countess of Ranelagh (in whose house in Pall Mall he resided from 1668 till his death), he was an advocate of moderation in ecclesiastical affairs and a patron of nonconformist ministers. It was he who recommended the subject of the tract to Howe (*Letter*, sig. A3).

[5] John Calvin, *Institutes of the Christian Religion*, trans. Henry Beveridge, 2 vols. (London, 1962), 2:206 (book 3, chapter 21, section 5).

[6] Calvin, *Institutes*, 2:221 (3.22.10); the point is further discussed at 2:256–58 (3.24.17).

and Schoolmen, for whom he has little time. Those who "can satisfie themselves with what Thomas and Scotus have attempted" in exposition of the nature of the divine will and of divine foreknowledge, "let them enjoy their own satisfaction" (pp. 48–9). Rather than to such authorities, Howe's appeal is to the implied reasonableness of his reader. Though the case is teasing, Howe encourages his reader not to pursue its complexities but to rely upon what is known of the just and benign nature of God and to retain a due awareness of the inability of the human mind to encompass divine perfection. It is absurd to suppose that "all God's managements, and waies of procedure" can be comprehended by the "apprehension and capacity of our (now so muddied and distempered) Minds" (p. 151). Howe is ruefully aware that "'tis not hard for a good Wit to have somewhat to say for any thing. But to dispute against the common sense of Mankind . . . is but to trifle" (p. 38). Anticipating what would become an Enlightenment commonplace, he recommends trust in that common sense rather than in the partial, flawed, and idiosyncratic understanding of any one individual.

To appeal to common sense is to be persuaded that the divine desire of universal salvation (God "will have all men to be saved" [1 Titus 2:4]) constitutes neither a "universal Promise" of salvation nor a commitment to use such extraordinary means with the impenitent "as shall finally overcome their averse disaffected hearts" (p. 90). God's "respect to the congruity and order of things" and to his creatures will not compel his preferred end (pp. 94–96): human beings are not "meer machines" (p. 143). This is not to posit an ineffectual will in God: "imperfection were with no pretence imputable to the Divine Will, meerly for its not effecting every thing, whereto it may have a *real* propension" (p. 116),

> For tho, when God urges and incites men, by exhortations, promises, and threats, to the doing of their own part . . . he foresee[s], many will not be moved thereby; but persist in wilful neglect, and rebellions till they perish: He, at the same time, sees that they *might do* otherwise, and that, if they would comply with his methods, things would otherwise issue with them. His prescience, no way, imposing upon them a *necessity* to transgress. For they do it not because he foreknew it, but he only foreknew it because they would do so. And hence he had, as it was necessary he should have, not only *this* for the object of his foreknowledg, *that they would do amiss and perish*. But the whole case in its circumstances, *that they would do so, not thorough his omission, but their own.* (pp. 119–20)

Howe's discomfort with any suggestion that human beings are compelled to transgress touches on one of the key difficulties posed by Calvin's predestinarian theology: it appears to make God responsible for sin. Calvinist creeds, like Calvin himself in the *Institutes*, firmly rejected any such implication. The Calvinist *Belgic Confession* of 1561 (a version of the *Gallican Confession* of 1559, which was to be adopted by the Synod of Dort in 1619) affirmed that "nothing happens in this world without his appointment; nevertheless, God neither is the author of, nor can be charged with, the sins which are committed." In the English tradition, the Westminster Assembly's *Confession of Faith* (1647) similarly maintained that while "God from all eternity did, by the most wise and holy counsel of his own will, freely and unchangeably ordain whatsoever comes to pass; yet so as thereby neither is God the author of sin, nor is violence offered to the will of the creatures, nor is the liberty or contingency of second causes taken away, but rather established."[7]

Howe took a quite different view. While it is consonant with his disinclination to meddle with metaphysical divinity that he declines to be drawn into a sustained discussion of "God's *predeterminative* concourse unto sinful actions" as an "unfeasible, unnecessary, and unenjoyned task" (p. 50), he cannot pass by in silence what he takes to be the consequence of the doctrine of double predestination, "*That God doth . . . by an Efficacious Influence Universally move and determine men to all their Actions; even those that are most wicked.*"[8] "The horrour of so black a conception of God [that he should be supposed irresistibly to determine the will of a man to the hatred of his own most Blessed Self, and then to exact severest Punishments for the offence done]" (p. 40, square brackets in the original) fills him with such revulsion that he digresses from his main task to discountenance the notion (pp. 34–50). He finds a monstrous absurdity in the proposition that God should have "made Lawes for his reasonable Creatures, impossible, thorough his own irresistible counter-action, to be observed: and afterwards to express himself displeased, and adjudg his Creatures to eternal punishments, for not observing them" (pp. 37–38). While Howe concedes

---

[7] *Institutes*, 2:228–29 (3.23.4); *Belgic Confession*, art. 13 (cf. *Gallican Confession*, art. 8), and *Westminster Confession*, chap. 3, sect. 1, in Henry B. Smith and Philip Schaff, eds., *Creeds of the Evangelical Protestant Churches* (London, 1877), pp. 396, 364, 608.

[8] *Letter*, p. 52. Calvin disavowed this inference from his doctrine: to it he devoted chapter 1.18 of the *Institutes*, particularly its final section (1:198–205); see also 3.24.12–17 (2:251–58).

that "the Original and Fountain-Being" must needs be "the first Cause" of all things, it does not follow that this is the determining cause of everything, with "the dismal conclusion of God's concurring *by a predeterminative influence* unto wicked actions" (pp. 35–36). That is true of good actions: only grace can enable humanity to transcend its fallen state. However, "the influence and concurrence, the holy God hath to the worst of actions, is to be distinguisht from that which he affords to the best" (p. 32): *"in this temporary state of trial, the efficacious grace of God is necessary to actions sincerely good and holy . . . But . . . in reference to other actions, he doth only supply men with such a power, as whereby, they are enabled, either to act, or, in many instances (and especially when they attempt any thing that is evil) to suspend their own action"* (p. 44). For Howe, there was clearly scope for the human will to cooperate (or not) in the *ordo salutis*. To his mind, arguments which permit the inference that "the holy and good God should irresistibly determine the wills of men to, and punish, the same thing" amount to no more than "the efforts of a sophistical Wit against sense, and more against the sense of our Souls, and most of all against the entire summe and substance of all Morality, and Religion" (pp. 39–40).

THE CONTROVERSY'S CONTEXT: RICHARD BAXTER AND THE "MIDDLE WAY"

Howe's tract was only the latest addition to a huge Reformation corpus on this topic.[9] Although in book 3 of the *Institutes* Calvin had sought to silence debate on these issues, soteriological disputation, and especially contention over the scope, order, and effect of the divine decrees, was pursued by reformed divines with wonderful intellectual dexterity and subtlety for the next two centuries. High Calvinists, whose position was affirmed at the Synod of Dort (Dordrecht) convened in 1618–19 to settle these disputes, maintained the doctrines of double predestination (to salvation and to damnation), unconditional election, a limited atonement, the irresistibility of grace, and the inevitable perseverance of the elect. A necessary consequence of this stress upon the absolute supremacy of the divine will was an equal stress upon human incapacity and depravity.[10] The Synod

[9] The matter had of course exercised hardly less fascination over the minds of church fathers and medieval schoolmen: Reformation controversies repeatedly cite key antecedent texts by Augustine, Aquinas, Peter Lombard, Ockham, etc.

[10] For aspects of Calvinist thought and its development in England and abroad, see

of Dort was prompted by the challenge to these doctrines posed by the teaching of the Dutch theologian Jakob Hermandszoon (Arminius; 1560–1609), who held that Christ's sacrifice was for the salvation of all humanity and that eternal human destinies depended not upon divine predetermination but upon human choices.[11] The five articles reproduced from his *Declaratio sententiae* (1608) in the Remonstrance, a declaration of faith signed by forty-four of his followers in the year after his death, were unequivocally condemned at Dort.[12] Maintaining that divine omnipotence is compatible with the freedom of the human will, the Remonstrants repudiated both supralapsarian and sublapsarian predestination[13] and the consequent doctrines that Christ died only for the elect, that grace is irresistible, and that it is impossible the elect should ever fall away from faith. To Calvinists this was nonsense, for if justification and election are in any sense conditional not upon the divine decrees but upon human choice and obedience, then the divine will is no longer sovereign: "it is euery way . . . against common se[n]se," wrote the Elizabethan Puritan and "English Calvin," William

---

Alan C. Clifford, *Atonement and Justification: English Evangelical Theology, 1640–1790* (Oxford, 1990); R. T. Kendall, *Calvin and English Calvinism to 1649* (Oxford, 1979); Ernest Kevan, *The Grace of Law: A Study of Puritan Theology* (1964; rpt. Grand Rapids, 1976); John T. McNeill, *The History and Character of Calvinism* (New York, 1954); Richard A. Muller, *Christ and the Decrees: Christology and Predestination in Reformed Theology from Calvin to Perkins* (Grand Rapids, 1988); Menna Prestwich, ed., *International Calvinism, 1541–1715* (Oxford, 1985); Dewey D. Wallace, *Puritans and Predestination: Grace in English Protestant Theology 1525–1695* (Chapel Hill, N.C., 1982); John Von Ruhr, *The Covenant of Grace in Puritan Thought* (Atlanta, 1986).

[11] For some account of Arminianism and its development, see Carl Bangs, *Arminius: A Study in the Dutch Reformation* (Nashville, 1971); A. W. Harrison, *The Beginnings of Arminianism to the Synod of Dort* (London, 1926) and *Arminianism* (London, 1937). For a summary history of the dispute with Calvinism, see Alan Sell, *The Great Debate: Calvinism, Arminianism and Salvation* (Worthing, 1982).

[12] The Remonstrance and the ninety-two canons approved at Dort are published in P. Schaff, ed., *The Creeds of Christendom*, 3 vols. (London, 1877), 3:545–97.

[13] *Supralapsarianism*, the sterner version of the doctrine of predestination, holds that God decreed the election and reprobation of individuals before the Fall, *sublapsarianism* that he so decreed after the Fall. Calvin himself did not elaborate upon the working of the divine will, warning that those who "inquire into predestination, let them remember that they are penetrating into the recesses of the divine wisdom, where he who rushes forward securely and confidently instead of satisfying his curiosity will enter an inextricable labyrinth" (*Institutes*, 2:204 [3.21.1]), but his followers nevertheless analyzed the order and scope of the divine decrees with ever-increasing scholastic subtlety.

Perkins, for it is "flat to hang Gods will vpon mans wil, to make euery man an Emperour, and God his vnderling, and to change the order of nature by subordinating Gods will, which is the first cause, to the will of man, which is the second."[14] Nevertheless, and despite Dort, through the seventeenth century Arminian emphases increasingly qualified and often replaced Calvinism, especially among English episcopal divines. The "ever memorable" John Hales (1584–1656), an observer at Dort as chaplain to Sir Dudley Carleton, English ambassador to Holland, was led by the experience famously to *"bid John Calvin good night."*[15] From 1639 until 1642 Hales was chaplain to William Laud, and it was under Laud, successively bishop of London (1628) and archbishop of Canterbury (1633–45), that Arminianism came to prevail among the hierarchy of the established episcopalian church.[16] As a result of this association with the man commonly perceived to be both an enemy to the reformed character of the Church of England and a mainstay of Charles I's personal rule, "Arminianism" became in popular usage a catch-all term by which to stigmatize inclinations towards popery and absolutism.

There were Arminian Puritans (notably the Independent John Goodwin [1594?–1665] who defended universal redemption in *Redemption Redeemed* [1656]) but amongst Puritans dissatisfaction with Calvinism more usually appealed to the "middle way" associated with the French theologian Moise Amyraut (Amyraldus; 1596–1664) and the Protestant academy of Saumur, of which Amyraldus was principal from 1641 to his death.[17] The essential compromise of the teaching initiated by the Scot John Cameron (Camero; 1579?–1625), professor successively at the academies of Sedan (1602–04) and Saumur (1618), was to maintain election to salvation but not to damnation.

---

[14] William Perkins, *Of the Creede*, in *Workes*, 3 vols. (Cambridge, 1616–18), 1:295.

[15] John Hales, *Golden Remains* (1659), pref. letter from Anthony Farindon, sig. a4. Hales was a man Marvell admired; see below, p. 406 with n. 85.

[16] For Laud (1573–1645), see Charles Carleton, *Archbishop William Laud* (London, 1987), and H. R. Trevor-Roper, *Archbishop Laud, 1573–1645* (London, 1988). For the development of English Arminianism, see Nicholas Tyacke, *Anti-Calvinists: The Rise of English Arminianism, 1590–1640* (Oxford, 1987); Peter White, *Predestination, Policy and Polemic: Conflict and Consensus in the English Church from the Reformation of the Civil War* (Cambridge, 1992).

[17] For Moise Amyraut, his teaching, and that of other preceptors of the Saumur academy, see Brian G. Armstrong, *Calvinism and the Amyraut Heresy: Protestant Scholasticism and Humanism in Seventeenth-Century France* (Madison, 1969); F. P. Van Stam, *The Controversy over the Theology of Saumur, 1635–1650* (Amsterdam, 1988).

This "hypothetical universalism" rejected the limited atonement of Calvin-ism but, though holding that Christ died for all humanity, it maintained that those for whom God would efficaciously work salvation are predeter-mined by the decree of election. By attributing salvation to the beneficence of the divine will, damnation to the culpability of the reprobate, this view avoided both the Arminian pitfall of overreliance upon the human will and the Calvinist pitfall of implicating God in the moral turpitude of the wicked.[18] It is in just such terms that Milton's God explicates his divine purpose in *Paradise Lost:* some are "chosen of peculiar grace / Elect above the rest; so is my will," but those who "hear me call" in vain seal their own fate. A God who offers salvation yet predestines damnation is no more tolerable to Milton than to Howe. In *De doctrina christiana,* Milton holds that whenever predestination is mentioned in the Bible "specific reference is made only to election," that "reprobation . . . is no part of divine pre-destination," that "none are predestined to destruction except through their own fault," and that God "excludes no man from the way of penitence and eternal salvation."[19]

To its opponents this theological position led inevitably to Arminianism (and Milton's position is, indeed, often described as Arminian),[20] but for its advocates it answered the key objections to Calvinism: that it makes God the author of sin and dissociates Christianity from the moral life, encourag-ing antinomianism. In seventeenth-century England it was most influen-tially developed by the Puritan divine Richard Baxter (1615–91). For Amy-raldus and the theologians of Saumur he had an especially high regard: "*The middle way which Camero, Ludov. Crocius, Martinius, Amiraldus, Davenant,*[21] *&c. go, I think, is neerest the Truth.*"[22] Like them, he main-

---

[18] For the relationship of "hypothetical universalism" to Arminianism, see Harrison, *Arminianism,* esp. pp. 111–12, 160–61, and Sell, *Great Debate,* pp. 30–33.

[19] John Milton, *Paradise Lost,* 3:183–202, Milton, *De doctrina,* 1.4, in *CPW,* 6:168, 173, 190, 194.

[20] See e.g. Dennis Danielson, *Milton's Good God: A Study in Literary Theodicy* (Cam-bridge, 1982), pp. 58–91; Stephen M. Fallon, " 'Elect Above the Rest': Theology as Self-Representation in Milton," in *Milton and Heresy,* ed. Stephen B. Dobranski and John P. Rumrich (Cambridge, 1998), pp. 93–116.

[21] For the "most learned judicious" John Davenant (1576–1641), bishop of Salisbury, Baxter had "as high thoughts . . . for the solidity of his judgment . . . as of almost any that this Kingdom ever bred . . . as he studied to avoid extreams in Divinity, so was he admirably blest in the successe of those studies, God having opened to him (I think) the true middle way in many weighty points of Religion" (Baxter, *Plain Scripture Truth of*

[387
  388   Good fodder!

         [Have made notes of
              all this ?]

tained that "*Christ dyed for all men, so farr as to purchase them pardon and salvation on condition they would repent and believe; and for the Elect, so farr further as to procure them faith and repentance it self,*"[23] and, like them, he held that predetermination "is not necessary to all actions naturall or free; but predetermination gratious, or Grace that cometh with a prevailing intent is necessary to holy actions."[24] He was an inveterate foe of the antinomianism which he regarded as an inevitable consequence of high Calvinism, and throughout his life he was at work on a treatise of universal redemption.[25] Two years before Howe's tract, in *Richard Baxter's Catholick Theologie* (1675), he offered a "Summary of Catholick reconciling Theology" which sought to reconcile Arminians and Calvinists in Amyraldus's "middle way" and to "end our common Controversies, in Doctrinals, about Predestination, Redemption, justification, assurance, perseverance, and such like" by proving that "there is no considerable difference between the Arminians and Calvinists."[26] It takes the form of dialogues between A, C, and R: "Reconcilers" was Baxter's own preferred name for those moderate Presbyterians who, "of no Sect or Party, but abhorring the very Name of Parties," sought to heal both ecclesiastical and theological differences.[27]

Infants Church-Membership and Baptism ([1651], p. 332). The moderate divine Mathias Martini was rector of the academy at Bremen from 1611 until his death in 1630. Ludovicus Crocius was a professor at Bremen who represented Bremen at the Synod of Dort.

[22] *The Saints Everlasting Rest* (1650), ded. ep. of the whole work, sig. A4v. Baxter defends his high regard for Amyraldus in *Certain Disputations of Right to Sacraments* (1657), pref., sigs. b1v–c2v. For a defense of himself against the charge that he overvalues "Davenant & Amyraldus (& more Camero & Baronius [Robert Baron (1593?–1639)])," see N. H. Keeble and Geoffrey Nuttal, *Calendar of the Correspondence of Richard Baxter*, 2 vols. (Oxford, 1991), letter 148 (hereafter cited as *CCRB*).

[23] Baxter, *Certain Disputations*, pref., sig. c1.

[24] *CCRB*, letter 376. For further discussions of this topic in the correspondence, see N. H. Keeble, *A Subject Index to the Calendar of the Correspondence of Richard Baxter* (London, 1994), s.v. "Predetermination."

[25] His preoccupation with this subject and with this book can be traced through his correspondence from 1648; it was finally posthumously published in 1694 (*CCRB*, "Index of Printed Works" s.v.).

[26] *Reliquiae Baxterianae* (1696), 3.182, §16; 3.181, §13. For Baxter's own summary account of *Catholick Theologie*, see CCRB, letter 911.

[27] *Reliquiae*, 2.387, §285[2]. For Baxter's theology (and discussion of many of the issues raised by the predetermination controversy), see James I. Packer, "The Redemption and Restoration of Man in the Thought of Richard Baxter" (D.Phil. diss., Oxford, 1954); Tim Cooper, *Fear and Polemic in Seventeenth-Century England: Richard Baxter*

This was the intellectual and religious company kept by John Howe and this the line he followed in *The Reconcileableness of God's Prescience*.[28] As an undergraduate at Christ's College, Cambridge (1647–48), he had come under the influence of the Cambridge Platonist Henry More (1614–87), for whom he retained a lifelong friendship and respect. More spoke of Calvinism in just the appalled tones Howe himself was to employ in *The Reconcileableness of God's Prescience*: "*Antinomianism* and *Calvinism* (I mean that dark *Dogma* about Predestination) are such horrid Errours, that they seem the badges of the Kingdome of Darknesse, rather then of the Kingdome of God."[29] Howe received Presbyterian ordination, probably in 1652, and in 1654 became perpetual curate of Great Torrington in Devon. In 1656, however, he was persuaded to move to London as a private chaplain to Oliver Cromwell. It was now that his lifelong friendship, and extant correspondence, with Baxter began. Their letters disclose complete agreement on the desirability of reconciliation between ecclesiastical parties and of moderation in the formulation of theological opinions. Howe encouraged Baxter to pursue his work on universal redemption since, though "Davenant and Amyraldus may have spoken many of your thoughts, their bookes do not commonly fall into the hands of young schollars . . . as yours are like to do." Following his ejection from Great Torrington in 1662 Howe continued to work, like Baxter, for accommodation. Baxter described him as "a very Learned, judicious, godly man, of no Faction, but of Catholick, healing Principles, and of excellent ministerial Abilities."[30]

While the "Baxterians," "Reconcilers," "Middle-way Men,"[31] or "mod-

---

and Antinomianism (Aldershot, 2001); Hans Boersma, *A Hot Pepper Corn: Richard Baxter's Doctrine of Justification in Its Seventeenth-Century Context of Controversy* (Zoetermeer, 1993); Gavin J. McGrath, "Puritans and the Human Will: Voluntarism within Mid-Seventeenth Century English Puritanism as seen in the Works of Richard Baxter and John Owen" (Ph.D. diss., Durham, 1989).

28 For Howe's theology and his relation to this train of thought in English Protestantism, see David P. Field, "'Rigide Calvinisme in a Softer Dress': The Moderate Presbyterianism of John Howe (1630–1705)" (Ph.D. diss., Cambridge, 1994), esp. pp. 17–33, 112–58. Field discusses *The Reconcileableness of God's Prescience* on pp. 132–38.

29 Henry More, *Divine Dialogues* (1668), fourth dialogue, p. 68 (quoted in Field, "Rigide Calvinisme," p. 3).

30 *CCRB*, letter 436; *Reliquiae*, 3.97, §208(4).

31 Cf. the titles of tracts by Baxter's friend John Humfrey: *The Middle-Way in One Paper of Justification with Indifferency between Protestant and Papist* (1672); *The Middle-*

erate Presbyterians" formed a discernible and influential group in the Puritan, and subsequently nonconformist, tradition,[32] in the later decades of the seventeenth century Calvinism retained the committed allegiance of many dissenting divines.[33] Indeed, the debates in which Baxter had been engaged in the 1650s with such firmly Calvinist divines as the Independent leader John Owen[34] continued throughout his life. They were to be pursued with such virulence following the republication in 1689 of the sermons of the Calvinist and (in Baxter's view) antinomian divine Tobias Crisp (1600–43) that they wrecked the "Happy Union" of Congregationalists and Presbyterians.[35] It is no wonder, then, that strict Calvinists were not about to ignore Howe's discussion of predestination merely because he relegated it to an incidental digression. On the contrary, what he had endeavored to pass by as incidental they seized upon as central to reformed theology. Theophilus Gale, a London nonconformist minister and a contemporary of Howe when, in the early 1650s, both were fellows of Magdalen College, Oxford, but, unlike Howe, a Calvinist and Congregationalist,[36] had since

---

Way in One Paper of Election & Redemption, with Indifferency between the Arminian and Calvinist (1673); *The Middle-Way in One Paper of the Covenants, Law and Gospel, with Indifferency between the Legalist & Antinomian* (1674); *The Middle-Way of Perfection with Indifferency between the Orthodox and the Quaker* (1674).

[32] For a distinguishing of this group, see N. H. Keeble, *The Literary Culture of Nonconformity in Later Seventeenth-Century England* (Leicester, 1987), pp. 8–10, 33–37, and for a list of representative figures, with brief biographies, see Field, "Rigide Calvinisme," appendix 1.

[33] See Peter Toon, *Puritans and Calvinism* (Svengel, Penn., 1973) and *The Emergence of Hyper-Calvinism in English Nonconformity, 1689–1765* (London, 1967).

[34] For Owen (1616–83), during the Interregnum dean of Christ Church (1651–60) and vice chancellor of Oxford University (1652–57) and after the Restoration the leading Congregationalist among nonconformists, from 1673 ministering to a congregation meeting in Leadenhall Street, London, see Peter Toon, *God's Statesman: The Life and Work of John Owen* (Exeter, 1971), and for his theology in relation to and controversy with Baxter, see Boersma, *Hot Pepper Corn*, Cooper, *Fear and Polemic*, and McGrath, "Puritans and the Human Will," *passim*.

[35] On this controversy and its consequences for dissent, see Richard Thomas, "Parties in Nonconformity: Calvin Neat or Calvin Mild" and "Presbyterians in Transition: A Decade of Discord," in *The English Presbyterians*, ed. C. G. Bolam et al. (London, 1968), pp. 103–12, 113–25; J. T. Spivey, "Middle Way Men, Edmund Calamy and the Crisis of Moderate Nonconformity (1688–1732)" (D. Phil. diss., Oxford, 1986).

[36] For Gale (1628–79), ejected preacher at Winchester Cathedral, see A. G. Mat-

1669 been publishing the successive volumes of his monumental *The Court of the Gentiles* (1669–78). In 1677 he took the occasion of their imminent publication to add to the end of books 1 and 2 of part 4 of this work[37] animadversions upon Howe's book,[38] succinctly putting the essential Calvinist objection to any middle way: "Either the Human Will must depend on the Divine Independent Wil of God for al its natural motions and operations; or God must depend on the Human Wil in it self Independent, for al his Prescience, motives of Election, and all discrimination as to Grace and gratiose operations."[39] Howe's response, in *A Post-Script to the Letter of the Reconcileableness of Gods Prescience, &c* (1677),[40] only further incensed another defender of the Calvinist tradition, Thomas Danson.[41]

---

thews, ed., *Calamy Revised* (1934; rpt Oxford, 1988), *s.v.*

[37] It was advertised in the summer of 1677 in the Trinity term catalogue registered on July 5 (Term Catalogues, 1:283).

[38] There was another published reply to Howe: J. T., *A Letter to a Friend, Touching Gods Providence about Sinful Actions. In Answer to a Letter Entituled, The Reconcileableness of Gods Prescience, &c. And to the Postscript of that Letter* (1678), mentioned in the *Remarks* (p. 480 below). This was by John Troughton (1637?–81), ejected fellow of St. John's College, Oxford, whose theological distance from Howe is sufficiently indicated by the title of his *Lutherus Redivivus, or The Protestant Doctrine of Justification by Christ's Righteousness Imputed to Believers Explained and Vindicated* (part 1, 1678; part 2, 1679). Baxter's animadversions on this were later published in his *Scripture Gospel Defended* (1690). As Troughton's *Letter to a Friend* is dated July 27, 1677 on p. 1, it was presumably in the course of its composition that he saw Howe's *Postscript*. In *Postscript*, p. 10, Howe mentions also a manuscript reply, of which he takes no notice since he is unsure whether its reputed author would acknowledge it.

[39] Theophilus Gale, *The Court of the Gentiles,* part 4, books 1, 2 (1677), p. 523 (the concluding book 3 of part 4 of *The Court* was published separately in 1678). For some account of Gale's book, see Keeble, *Literary Culture,* pp. 167–70, 184–86.

[40] The *Postscript* has an imprimatur dated August 3, 1677, but it was not entered in the Stationers' Register (nor advertised in the Term Catalogues).

[41] These exchanges prompted Baxter to publish "an antidote against the poison" of Gale's arguments for predetermination, but "Mr. Gale fell sick, and I suppress my answer lest it should grieve him. (And he then died)" (*Reliquiae,* 3.182–83, §22). Baxter's unpublished reply, in two parts, the first "written twenty years ago" against Hobbes and the second consisting of animadversions on Gale's *Court of the Gentiles,* with a preface dated May 10, 1679, is still extant in the Baxter Treatises in Dr. Williams's Library (Roger Thomas, *The Baxter Treatises* [London, 1959], p. 17).

THE CONTROVERSY CONTINUED: THOMAS DANSON'S DEFENSE OF "THE CONSTANT SENSE OF PROTESTANTISM"

Danson was, like Howe and Gale, an ejected minister, and he too had been a fellow of Magdalen in the 1650s when the eminent Independent Thomas Goodwin was the college's president.[42] It was as a Presbyterian that in 1672 Danson was licensed at his house in Spitalfields under the Declaration of Indulgence, but the theological bias of his Presbyterianism was of a very different temper from Howe's, placing him with the Congregationalist Gale. In the prefatory epistle (dated October 31, 1677) to his *De Causa Dei: or, A Vindication of the Common Doctrine of Protestant Divines, concerning Predetermination: (i.e. the Interest of God as the first Cause in all the Actions, as such, of all Rational Creatures:) From the Invidious Consequences with which it is burdened by Mr. John Howe in a late Letter and Postscript, of God's Prescience* (1678),[43] "T.D." is outraged by what he takes to be denigration of the Protestant tradition in Howe's dismissal of predestinarian arguments as contrary to sense and to religion (sigs. A3^v, A5). To Danson, Howe's revisionism, and in particular his allowance of freedom to the human will, "borders as near upon Arminianism as Scotland does upon England" (p. 121). A commitment to predestination has hitherto been "the constant sense of Protestantism, till now of late that it grows weary of it self, if we may judg of its present humour by Mr. H. and Mr. B." (p. 44).[44]

Danson sets out to rebut Howe's assertion *"that God doth not by an Efficacious Influence Universally move and determine men to all their Actions; even those that are most wicked."*[45] He accuses Howe of inconsistency in allowing predetermination to actions which are good, but not to those

---

[42] For Danson (1629–94), ejected vicar of Sibton with Peasenhall, Suffolk, and from 1679 till 1692 minister to a congregation in Abingdon, Berkshire, see *Calamy Revised, s.v.*

[43] This was entered in the Stationers' Register by the licenser William Jane (1645–1707), chaplain to the bishop of London and from 1680 Regius Professor of Divinity at Oxford, and Thomas Vere, warden, on November 26, 1677 (*Registers*, 3:48).

[44] The identity of "H. W." (cf. above, n. 2) had been disclosed on the title page of the *Postscript*, though Danson was *"already aware of him"* (*TD*, pref. ep., sig. A2). "Mr. B." is presumably Richard Baxter.

[45] *Postscript*, p. 52.

which are bad, and of incoherence, for no actions are wholly good or evil (pp. 12–13, 77–96). With Calvinist consistency, Danson argues strenuously that only the predetermination of all human actions answers to the supreme power of the deity. For Howe, God's amiableness is what should most impress our minds and offer us reassurance when we are in theological difficulties: it "were a very unequal way of estimating what God can do . . . to consider him as a meer Being of Power."[46] Danson, however, has the true Calvinist's determination to maintain whatever doctrinal consequence may be required the most effectively to exalt absolute sovereign power as the deity's supreme attribute:[47]

> of Mr. H.'s Principles there are these desperate consequences, (which I have so much charity as to believe he does not see, and (so) nor own,) That God is justled out of his proper place; I mean, of being the first cause of all the Creatures actions, and the Creature put in his stead, as being represented able to use its powers, as it pleases. That one great Perfection of the Divine Nature, *viz.* Foreknowledg of future Contingencies, is separated from it, by denying the only true ground of such Foreknowledg, the Divine Decrees. And hence, the Providence of God in governing the actions of his Creatures is left in great danger of falling, because a Superstructure raised without a foundation. For how can God govern those actions which depend not immediately upon him in their production; nor are foreknown in his *Eternal Decree?* (pp. 121–22)

Danson, however, rejects the consequences which Howe draws from this doctrine—that it makes God the author of sin, relieves his creatures of moral responsibility, and constructs a monstrous God who compels human

---

[46] *Letter*, p. 124. The point is discussed in Field, "Rigide Calvinisme," pp. 121–31.

[47] In one of the more scornful and heated passages of the *Institutes*, Calvin insists that "God claims omnipotence to himself, and would have us to acknowledge it,—not the vain, indolent, slumbering omnipotence which sophists feign, but vigilant, efficacious, energetic, and ever active,—not an omnipotence which may only act as a general principle of confused motion, as in ordering a stream to keep within the channel once prescribed to it, but one which is intent on individual and special movements. God is deemed omnipotent . . . because . . . he so overrules all things that nothing happens without his counsel . . . there is no random power, or agency, or motion in the creatures, who are so governed by the secret counsel of God, that nothing happens but what he has knowingly and willingly decreed" (1:173–5 [1.16.3]).

beings to acts that will incur eternal punishment. His refutation of these positions is founded upon two distinctions commonly adduced in the Calvinist tradition. First, "though we own it a hard province to answer all objections that may be started against this partition made between the one and the other," he distinguishes between an act and its sinfulness. This allows him to assert God's predetermining influence over the former, without ascribing to him responsibility for the latter: "God is the Author, and consequently the Predeterminer of all the actions of rational creatures . . . yet . . . God is not the Author of the sinfulness, and so not the Predeterminer thereof;" "God affords a real influence upon the powers defiled with sin, and yet none upon the sin it self" (pp. 32, 34).[48] Danson consequently denies that "the Determinative Influence to all wicked actions we assert, does infer any coaction on the Will" (p. 77), and he rejects Howe's assertion that "our Doctrine represents God under the same character with the Devil, who induces men to sin, and then torments them for it" as "*an odious slander*. For we in no sense assert that God induces men to wicked actions, not *morally*, for we constantly affirm, that his commands, threats, are all against it; not *Physically*, for so he determines men to actions, not to the wickedness of them, nor does he ruine men for what he contributes by Predetermination" (p. 57). Responsibility for damnation is the sinner's, not God's.

Second, Danson appeals to the distinction traditional in metaphysical divinity between the secret (effective, efficacious, or absolute) and the revealed (permissive or disposing) will of God. By so doing, he claims to reconcile the apparently universal Gospel promises of salvation (God's revealed will) with the discriminatory decrees of election and reprobation (God's secret will). This distinction Howe had found wholly unhelpful. In one of the passages which most offended Danson, Howe had charged "the terms of that common distinction the *voluntas beneplaciti, et signi*"[49] with as much "impiety and wickedness" as "absurdity and folly" since they suggested that God "only intended to seem willing of what he really was not."[50]

---

[48] Cf. T[roughton], *Letter to a Friend*, p. 17: "When we say, God doth predetermine the Creature to sinful actions; we mean only, that he doth incline and guide them to the substance, and matter of the acts, not to the sinfulness which cleaves to them."

[49] "The absolute and revealed will [of God]," a staple distinction inherited from medieval scholastic theology.

[50] *Letter*, pp. 106–07.

Milton had similarly scorned "that academic distinction" which attributes to God "a will by which he wishes, and a will by which he contradicts that wish!."[51] On the authority of Davenant,[52] Danson attempts to resolve the contradiction by arguing that God's revealed will "*in effect is but a conditional will,*" conditional, that is, upon faith, but not upon any human decision, for "*there is in God an absolute will of permitting some to continue in their unbelief, and so perish*": "who seeth not these Propositions may well stand together? I will that if Judas repent and believe, he shall have remission and salvation. I will not to give to Judas the gift of repentance, of faith and of eternal life" (pp. 112–13; cf. pp. 114–15).

Danson's temper is quite unlike Howe's. He scorns Howe's willingness to remain ignorant of the manner of divine causation, for if of this, why not of all aspects of the divine nature (p. 33)? He mocks Howe's preference for "natural notions of Gods goodness" over reason and "our senses"[53] as offering a fine defense of the "Popish ridicule" of transubstantiation, which is quite contrary to sense (p. 35). Where Howe is content to trust in generalizations about God's benign disposition toward his creatures, Danson probes the workings of the divine decrees with pedantic exactitude. He spends pages worrying at Howe's indiscriminate use of such terms and phrases as *conservation, determinative influence, corroborating grace, predetermination, premonition, predeterminative concourse, mediate* and *immediate concurrence, efficacious influence.* For Danson, Howe's gratification of "his own unscholastick humour, in neglecting the strictness of Scholastick terms" merely muddies—indeed, "overthrows"—his argument (p. 76). Where Howe discusses, Danson casts every point into syllogistic form, systematically laying out and defending his major and minor premises, each defense and explication itself syllogistically managed. He can lecture Howe on the "Rules in Logick" (p. 63). Howe is unimpressed by authorities and regrets that "that which hath too apparently had greatest efficacy, with many" in persuading them of double predestination "hath been the authority and name of this or that man of reputation."[54] Danson is shocked by this slur upon those "*Heroick Souls*" of the earlier Protestant tradition (pref ep., sig. A3v). He himself refers to and cites not only "the *Incomparable Cal-*

---

[51] Milton, *CPW,* 6:177.
[52] For Davenant, see above, n. 21.
[53] *Letter,* p. 39.
[54] *Letter,* pp. 42–43.

vin,"[55] but also Augustine and a host of medieval and sixteenth- and seventeenth-century divines.

THE CONTROVERSY CONCLUDED: THE *REMARKS* ON DANSON'S "HECTORING DISCOURSE"

It was this cast of mind in Danson which provided the opening for the *Remarks upon a Late Disingenuous Discourse Writ by One T.D. under the Pretence De Causa Dei, and of Answering Mr. John Howe's Letter and Post-script of God's Prescience, &c. affirming, as the Protestant doctrine, that God doth by efficacious influence universally move and determine men to all their actions, even to those that are most wicked* (1678).[56] The tract is curiously uninterested in the points in dispute. Indeed, it begins by expressing its distaste for controversial divinity and its dismay that men called to the ministry should be tempted to succumb to the heated intemperance of disputation. Wrangling over "peevish questions" and the pursuit of "Enquiries too curious after those things which the Wisdom of God hath left impervious to Humane Understanding," to the neglect of pastoral care and the "obvious Truths of Faith, Repentance, and the New Creature" demonstrate the sad fact that "even the Theological Ground" is "under the Curse" of the Fall (p. 415):[57] "Endless Disputes concerning the unsearchable things of God . . . are agitated by men, for the most part, with such Virulence and Intricacy, as manifest the Subtilty and Malice of the Serpent that hath seduced them" (p. 416).

The tract's anonymous author (the title page reads "By a Protestant") accordingly presents himself as disinclined to dispute points of metaphysical divinity. In any case, he is an unskilled controversialist who "cannot boast of any extraordinary faculty for Disputation" (p. 442). His reticence, however, goes beyond what might be dictated by disinclination and incapacity. He is determined to keep his own counsel. He has nothing at all to say directly of the main points in dispute; he "intermeddles" "not as an Opinionist either way" (p. 433). He commits himself no further than to say

---

[55] *TD*, p. 42.

[56] The Imprimatur is dated April 17, 1678. The *Remarks* was entered in the Stationers' Register by Jane and John Macock, warden, on April 19, 1678 (*Registers*, 3:64) and advertised in the Easter term catalogue licensed on May 14, 1678 (Term Catalogues, 1:308), just one year after Howe's original *Letter* had been noticed there (see above, n. 3).

[57] References are to the following text of the *Remarks*.

that he is (like Howe) for taking the commonsensical line and for restraining intellectual speculation: Genesis "contains the plain History of Good and Evil, and . . . what other Comment needs there, for what belongs to God, than that, Jam. 1.17 that it is from God only, *That every Good Giving, and every Perfect Gift descendeth?* And, as to Evil, that also of St. James, is sufficient conviction, *cap.* 1 *v.* 13, 14. *Let no man say, when he is tempted, I was tempted of God; God cannot be tempted with Evil, neither tempteth he any man*" (p. 416).

About the manner, as distinct from the matter, of Danson's tract, however, he has very firm opinions indeed. Danson's appeal to the precedent of Peter's withstanding Paul (Gal. 2:11) to justify giving a "publick reproof" to one who is revered and highly esteemed[58] is contemptuously dismissed. What Danson presents as a disinterested service on behalf of the truth is arraigned as an "immodest and hectoring Discourse" (p. 420), arrogant, malicious, and mendacious, "so easy is it to patronize humane Passions under the pretence of the Cause of God, and Apostolical example" (p. 421). This disjunction between Danson's pious protestations and his intemperate manner is the *Remarks'* real target. Its business is to reveal the excesses and absurdities of Danson's "unruly Quill," that "as Mr. How's *Letter* may serve for a Pattern of what is to be imitated, so *The Discourse* may remain as a Mark (the best use it can be put to) of what ought to be avoided in all writing of Controversies, especially by Divines" (p. 421). The *Remarks* sets out to discredit Danson not by meeting him on the field of theological debate but through ridicule of his stylistic and methodological incompetencies, his infelicities of manner, his indecorums of tone. Rather than adopt the point-by-point refutation common in seventeenth-century controversy, the tract is structured around Danson's failings, grouped under eight heads.[59] From the *Remarks* it is consequently almost impossible to make out the main lines of Danson's argument; it is marginalized, reduced to an irrelevance.

For all his coyness about his own theological opinions there is consequently no mistaking where the sympathies of the author of the *Remarks* lie. He does not disguise the fact that for him "universal Predetermination" is a "Notion . . . altogether unrevealed" and "contrary if not to the whole scope and design of Divine Revelation, yet to all common understanding

---

[58] *TD*, p. 123.
[59] These fall on pp. 421, 428, 449, 456, 461, 464, 466, 470. A final section (pp. 471ff) discusses the prefatory epistle.

and genuine sense of right Reason" (p. 446). These are just Howe's terms, and the comic irony of the *Remarks'* initial repudiation of partiality (pp. 417–19) soon yields to explicit praise for Howe. Its author has "met with few manual Treatises" which equal Howe's in skill (pp. 419–20). He interprets Howe's business as practical, not polemical, "to rectifie mens apprehensions concerning God, and leave them without pretence for negligence in their Duties," and he finds Howe's manner exemplary:

> His Arguing . . . is plain and solid . . . nor does he either throw the Dust of antique Distinctions in the eyes of his Readers, to blind them; or yet raise the Spectres of ancient Authors, or conjure their venerable Names, to fright men out of their senses and understanding; but declares against all the Prejudice or Advantage by such proceeding, as unlawful Charms, and prohibited Weapons in the Controversie. His Method thereafter is direct and coherent, his Style perspicuous and elegant: So that it is in short, a Manly discourse, resembling much, and expressing the Humane Perfection; in the Harmony of Language, the Symmetry of Parts, the Strength of Reason, the Excellency of its End, which is so serious, that it is no defect in the similitude with Man, that the *Letter* contains nothing in it suitable to the property of Laughter. (p. 420)

Danson, by contrast, provokes laughter and derision at every turn. Where Howe is a plain dealer, reasonable, moderate, and modest, Danson is characterized as silly, intemperate, immoderate, arrogant, and inept:

> The Cause of God! Turn I beseech you [the] whole Book over, and show me any thing of that *Decorum* with which that should have been managed. What is there to be found of that Gravity, Humility, Meekness, Piety or Charity requisite to so glorious a pretence? (Graces wherewith God usually assists those that undertake his quarrel, and with which Mr. Howe on all occasions appears to be abundantly supplied.) But a perpetual eructation there is of humane Passions, a vain ostentation of mistaken Learning. (p. 474)

"BY A PROTESTANT": MARVELL AND THE AUTHORSHIP OF THE *REMARKS*

Who, then, was this urbane, unnamed mocker of Danson? The first known attribution of the *Remarks* to Marvell occurs in a "List of Famous Men and Women I have seen in my Travels" attached to the journal of

James Yonge (1647–1721), physician and surgeon in charge of the naval hospital at Plymouth, elected a Fellow of the Royal Society in 1702. Yonge visited London between February and March 1678, and again in 1681, 1686, 1687, 1692, and 1702. On his list Marvell is described as an "ingenious man" who "vindicated Mr. How, and the naked truthe, a man not well affected to the Church or Government of England." It is possible, though unlikely in view of his habitual reticence, that Marvell himself was Yonge's informant. It is more probable that his source was another of the virtuosi and writers whom he met on his visits to London. Buckingham appears on his list, and within the text of his journal Yonge records meetings with Boyle, Dryden, L'Estrange, and Samuel Parker. Each one of these could have known that Marvell defended Howe and so have been in a position to disclose his identity to Yonge.[60]

Powerful, if not quite conclusive, corroborative evidence is to be found in the library catalogues of two contemporaries. John Locke's catalogue includes a complete chronological listing of all Marvell's prose pieces. While Marvell's name is attached only to the first item in the list (the *Rehearsal Transpros'd*), the implication of the sequence is clear.[61] The *Remarks* appears also in very close proximity to the *Rehearsal Transpros'd* in John Owen's catalogue, published in 1684. Though correctly dated 1678, the "Remarques on a Discourse, de causa Dei" is here attributed to "Burthog." There was indeed a Richard Burthogge who had published *Causa Dei, or An Apology for God*, but in 1675. Despite the difference in the year of publication, the similarities of title appear to have misled the cataloguer into supposing this anonymous work must be Burthogge's. Its association with the *Rehearsal Transpros'd* (only two items before it in the listing and attributed to Marvell) might tell another story.[62]

The next person known to have attributed the tract to Marvell was

[60] F. N. L. Poynter, ed., *The Journal of James Yonge (1647–1721) Plymouth Surgeon* (London, 1963), pp. 21, 23 (the attribution to Marvell, cited in *P & L*, 1:348n), 156, 195, 200.

[61] John Harrison and Peter Laslett, *The Library of John Locke* (Oxford, 1965), pp. 185–6 (items 1931–36).

[62] *Bibliotheca Oweniana sive Catalogus Librorum Plurimis Facultatibus Insignium, Instructione Bibliothecae Rev. Doct. Vir. D. Ioan Oweni* (1684), p. 14, item 168. Owen also possessed Howe's *Reasonableness of God's Prescience* (p. 18, item 353). I am grateful to my fellow editors Annabel Patterson and Martin Dzelzainis for calling my attention to both Owen's and Locke's catalogues.

unequivocal and certainly knew what he was talking about. Edmund Cal-amy (1671–1732), the third seventeenth-century divine of that name and grandson of the Smectymnuan, was a close associate of Howe and, in his three-volume *A Defence of Moderate Nonconformity* (1703–05), an apologist for the Baxterian tradition in nonconformity. He was Baxter's successor as Matthew Sylvester's ministerial assistant, and he gave Sylvester some help with the editing of *Reliquiae Baxterianae* (1696).[63] He subsequently con-ceived the idea of revising and expanding the *Reliquiae* as a history of nonconformity. Work on the successive editions of this project gave him an unrivaled knowledge of nonconformist affairs and controversies.[64] This, and his familiarity with Howe, give authority to his attribution of the "very witty and entertaining" reply to Danson to "the ingenious Andrew Marvel Esq."[65] This is the sum of contemporary, or near contemporary, exter-nal evidence,[66] save that on the title page of the Yale copy of the *Remarks* there is an attribution to Marvell in what may be a late seventeenth-century italic hand.

A number of internal features of the tract are consistent with this attribu-tion, beginning with the title. Marvell's titles, in poetry as well as in prose, are carefully chosen, generically pointed, and often unexpected. The choice of *Remarks* is of this kind. The word was effectively never used in titles before 1660.[67] After the Restoration it gained currency, but almost always for essays on current affairs, biographies, and topographical works.[68] It

---

[63] For Calamy (1646–1721) and Sylvester (1636?–1708), see *Calamy Revised;* for Cal-amy's involvement with the *Reliquiae,* see his *Historical Account of My Own Life,* ed. J. T. Rutt, 2 vols. (London, 1829), 1:376–80.

[64] Edmund Calamy, *An Abridgment of Mr. Baxter's History of his Life and Times. With an Account of the Ministers . . . Ejected or Silenced after the Restoration . . . And a Continuation of their History, till the Year 1691* (1702); a second edition in two volumes continued the history to 1711 (1713); this was followed by a two-volume *Continuation of the Account of the Ministers* (1727).

[65] Edmund Calamy, *Memoirs of the Life of the Late Revd. Mr. Howe* (1724), p. 68.

[66] Wood, 4:594, is uncertain whether or not Howe wrote the *Remarks.* Wood does know that Troughton was the author of the *Letter to a Friend,* but he fails to associate this text with the controversy with Howe (4:11).

[67] The single exception appears to be Wing R935B, the broadside *Remarks on the Quakers Case* (for which Wing's conjectural date of 1648 is impossibly early).

[68] Notably close to the wording of the title of the *Remarks* is Henry More's *Remarks upon Two Late Ingenious Discourses* (1676) by Sir Matthew Hale. Though this particular

became more frequent in the 1680s and voguish in the 1690s, but even then there are no more than half a dozen cases in ecclesiastical or theological contexts. In 1678, *Remarks* is hence an unprecedented choice for animadversions. Its sensitivity to a recent addition to the English lexicon is typical of Marvell, who, interestingly, would have had the opportunity to pick it up from a contributor to the *Rehearsal Transpros'd* controversy.[69] The almost casual offhandedness of its refusal to announce a thorough and orderly trawl through Danson's work, such as might have been expected, is of a piece with its author's refusal to be drawn into the matters in debate.[70] By refusing Danson's work the dignity of *animadversions* it also contributes to that belittling of his efforts which is a key part of the tract's polemical strategy. This strategy is of a piece with Marvell's practice elsewhere. In *The Rehearsal Transpros'd* Marvell turns Parker's anonymity to his advantage through the mocking appellation Mr. Bayes which he bestows upon his opponent. Just so, the *Remarks* turns the opportunity offered by Danson's reticence to polemical advantage: observing that the author of *De Causa Dei* discloses only his initials,[71] the author of the *Remarks* goes on: "By which first Letters, seeing it appears that he desires to pass *Incognito*, I will so far observe good manners, as to interpret them only *The Discourse*, heartily wishing that there were some way of finding it Guilty, without reflecting upon the Author" (p. 421). Thereafter, "T.D." is pronominally neuter and its author is entirely obliterated.[72]

Marvell opens *Mr. Smirke* with ironic comment on the pretensions to wit and literary eloquence of the episcopal clergy and with discussion of the qualities to be expected in ecclesiastical controversy.[73] Likewise, the *Remarks* is an essay on "how the unruly Quill is to be managed" (p. 421),

---

tract is not on a religious subject, More was an author respected by Howe and one mentioned in the controversy, and Marvell had a high regard for Hale. See above, p. 291.

[69] For the sense of verbal or written comment or opinion *OED*'s first citation is [Richard Leigh], *The Transproser Rehears'd* (Oxford, 1673), p. 4. The word was clearly a recent import from the French, for the earliest citations for its other senses all fall between 1654 and 1675.

[70] See on this below, pp. 405–06.

[71] Wood, 4:594, explains that Danson set only his initials to his text "because it was written against his intimate friend and fellow collegiate." *TD*, p. 61 (quoted in *Remarks*, p. 440, alludes to this friendship.

[72] There is a single lapse into "he" on p. 468.

[73] See above, pp. 38–40.

structured around examples of "what ought to be avoided in all writing of Controversies, especially by Divines" (p. 421).[74] This preoccupation with manner and style, and the distinction which the *Remarks* draws between Howe and Danson, chime precisely with the cultural emphases of *The Rehearsal Transpros'd* and the distinction which that work draws between the manner of decent Protestant discourse and the histrionic and hectic stylistic posturing of Samuel Parker.[75] Howe writes "piously" and "modestly" (p. 446); he eschews "notional Terms or Distinctions, where he can make men comprehend him better without them" (p. 424); and, which "makes me like him the better," he "declares his own sense plainly" (p. 460). Herein he exemplifies that restrained Protestant style which in *The Rehearsal Transpros'd* is preferred before the rhetorical extravagance and emotional excesses of Parker. On the other hand, Parker's intemperance (or rather, Marvell's characterization of it) is reproduced in the *Remarks'* construction of Danson. Danson assumes a "magisterial" style (p. 437); his tract is "jovial . . . and bucksom, which is just the humour of Tyrants, bloodily cruel, and yet at the same time full of dissoluteness and laughter" (p. 440); it grows "perfectly wanton" but Danson has no facility of wit (p. 441); rather, he achieves "superlative Dullness" whenever he aspires to "Acuteness and Elegancy" (p. 471). While Howe exemplifies "Sobriety, Simplicity, and Equality of Temper; glorifying God rather in the exercise of Practical Christian Vertues, than affecting the honour of a speculative Question," Danson's tract deals in "Street-adages . . . odd ends of *Latine* . . . broken shreds of Poets" (p. 480); the "manliness" of the one commands attention (p. 420), while the other is no more to be heeded than "clamorous women" (p. 480). Just so, Marvell had scorned Parker's style as "luscious and effeminate."[76]

This effeminacy is detected as much in Danson's addiction to "Scholastick terms" as in his rhetorical extravagance. Logic, its terminology, techniques, and claims on truth, were much ridiculed in the later seventeenth century by advocates of moderation and reasonableness in religion and in public life as a relic of the superstitious Middle Ages whose ingenious fabrications they regarded as the merest sophistry. In a draft of the *Essay*

[74] This point is made in Annabel Patterson, *Marvell: The Writer in Public Life* (Harlow, 2000), pp. 130–31.

[75] For discussion of this distinction and these emphases, see N. H. Keeble, "Why Transprose *The Rehearsal?*" in *Marvell and Liberty*, ed. Martin Dzelzainis and Warren Chernaik (London, 1999), esp. pp. 257–9, 263–4.

[76] *RT*, p. 53.

concerning Education written in 1671 Locke, for example, inveighed against the "uselesse skill" of scholastic logic as a "learned ignorance" which deals in "unintelligible termes" and perpetuates the "mischiefe" of "wrangleing," keeping "even inquisitive men from true knowledge." He believed its "learned gibberish" was developed and perpetuated by "the interest & artifice of the church of Rome" to defend its "absurd doctrines." His contempt encompassed the system of disputations which enacted the convictions of logical method and upon which university education depended. In the published *Essay* (1693) he warned parents, "If the use and end of right Reasoning, be to have right Notions, and a right Judgment of things; to distinguish betwixt Truth and Falshood, Right and Wrong; and to act accordingly: be sure not to let your Son be bred up in the Art and Formality of Disputing, either practising it himself, or admiring it in others; unless instead of an able Man, you desire to have him an insignificant Wrangler, Opiniater[77] in Discourse, and priding himself in contradicting others."[78]

This was a bias Marvell shared. In the *Essay Touching General Councils* appended to *Mr. Smirke* (1676), their contentious readiness "to pick a Quarrel" by branding others "Hereticks" is a mark of how far the bishops of the early church had fallen away from the Apostolic ideal. In Marvell's view, the intemperance of abstruse theological controversy drove delegates to the early councils "from one to a second, from a second to a third, seeming absurdity . . . as is usual in the heat and wrangle of Disputation," especially when the disputants are "so speculative, acute, and refining in their conceptions." The result was the "Gibbrish" of creeds and doctrinal formulations, so unlike what is declared "articulately enough in the Scriptures."[79] Just so, the *Remarks* reproves Danson's "causeless Picking of Controversie" (p. 474) and it has no patience with what it calls his "musty lumber of Schoolmen" (p. 480). It mocks the "Phantastry" (p. 465) of his logical arguments "dreadfully accoutred" with syllogistic terms (p. 442), as so "much Powder . . . spent without doing the least execution" while Howe "is out of Gunshot" and Danson "starts meerly at the Report of his own Musquet" (p. 437).

[77] This unusual word is one that had already taken Marvell's fancy; see n. 81 below.

[78] John Locke, *Drafts for the "Essay concerning Understanding" and other Philosophical Writings*, ed. Peter H. Nidditch and G. A. J. Rogers (Oxford, 1990), pp. 194–96, and J. L. Axtell, ed., *The Educational Writings of John Locke* (Cambridge, 1968), pp. 296–97, quoted in part in Mordecai Feingold, "The Humanities," in *The History of the University of Oxford*, ed. Nicholas Tyacke, vol. 4: *The Seventeenth Century* (Oxford, 1997), pp. 279, 300, where see pp. 276–306 on this intellectual bias.

[79] See above, pp. 127, 136–37, 144.

University disputation it likens to horse races at Newmarket (p. 423). The "unscholastick humour" in Howe which so affronted Danson is commended by the *Remarks* precisely for preferring "Evidence" to "Dispute" (p. 420). And, as the Marvell of the *Essay* is dismayed by the early bishops "meddling with the mysteries of Religion, farther than humane apprehension, or divine revelation did or could lead them,"[80] so the *Remarks* deplores that "vain affectation of Learning" by which divines "have been tempted into Enquiries too curious after those things which the Wisdom of God hath left impervious to Humane Understanding, further than they are revealed" (p. 415). To this temptation, resisted by the manly Howe, the effeminate Danson succumbs.

As typically Marvellian as these opposed characterizations is the mockery to which the *Remarks* subjects Danson. His pretensions attract just the ironic tone bestowed on Parker: "Who would have thought that *T.D,* should become the Defender of the Faith, or that the Cause of God were so forlorn, as to be reduced to the necessity of such a Champion?" (p. 474). The ridicule of Parker as some absurd knight errant is paralleled by the image of Danson "dreadfully accoutred and armed *Cap-a-pe* in Logick" (p. 442) and the presentation of his polemic as a mock-heroic combat (p. 437). As Parker is presented as a writer of romances and stage plays, so to Danson is attributed the play *Amity a la Mode* (p. 440), a title recalling *Mr. Smirke*. Marvellian, too, is the deft citation in unexpected contexts of a range of classical and other sources, less frequently, perhaps, than in the *Rehearsal Transpros'd*, but quite as pointed: witness the curt dismissal of Danson's protestations of friendship toward Howe with the ironic exclamation, "Dear Damon, doubtless" (p. 440). There are, besides, occasional suggestive linguistic parallels,[81] and at least two explicit allusions to the *Rehearsal Transpros'd*.[82]

If the parodic and ironic strategies of the *Remarks* have convincingly Marvellian touches, so, too, the elusiveness and theological reticence of an author who is "no Opinionist" is exactly what would be expected from the

---

[80] *Essay*, p. 137.

[81] E.g., the occurrence of the unusual verb *opiniatre* in *Remarks*, p. 429, and of the noun *Opiniastry* in *Essay* (1676), p. 127; as the *Remarks*, p. 420, recognizes that even Howe's achievements "partake ... of Humane Imperfection," so *Mr. Smirke* allows that Croft's book "cannot be free from the imperfections incident to all humane indeavours," p. 41 above.

[82] See below, nn. 22 and 25 to the *Remarks*.

Marvell who, in all his prose pieces, "plays his religious cards, like his political ones, extremely close to his chest."[83] The religious bias of the *Remarks* is, however, no secret. It accords exactly with that of the Marvell who could express himself in thoroughly Baxterian terms: "Truth for the most part lies in the middle, but men ordinarily seek for it in the extremities."[84] It counsels restraint and moderation against extremism, preferring cooperation to divisiveness. The restrained "manliness" which the *Remarks* admires in Howe is in the *Rehearsal Transpros'd* admired in John Hales, a member of the Great Tew circle and author of the moderate and irenical *Of Schism* (1642).[85] The nonpartisan emphasis characteristic of moderate Presbyterianism which allowed Marvell to defend nonconformists against episcopalians in the *Rehearsal Transpros'd* and a bishop against episcopalians in *Mr. Smirke* might very well allow him to intervene in a controversy between two nonconformists. It might equally well allow him to refer sympathetically to Danson in his correspondence, as he does when Danson appears as the opponent of William Sherlock, an episcopalian of Parker's stamp, and yet to write against him when he controverts Howe.[86] It is true that, while his sympathies are with moderate nonconformity, there is no evidence that Marvell was a member of any nonconformist congregation or that he failed to attend his parish church.[87] Indeed, in the second part of the *Rehearsal Transpros'd* he explicitly denies that he is nonconformist.[88] In like manner, the persona of the *Remarks* refers to the Book of Common Prayer without reproach and as a text he is in the habit of consulting (p. 439). The *Remarks* thus shares with the *Rehearsal Transpros'd* the unusual distinction of being a nonconformist defense written (apparently) by a conformist.

Granted the tract's consistency with Marvellian practice and bias, we may yet ask why this rather minor theological exchange should have sufficiently interested Marvell to prompt him to intervene. The reply may be that Danson's Calvinist intransigency is the mirror image of Parker's episcopa-

---

[83] Patterson, *Marvell,* p. 62.

[84] See *Essay,* p. 137.

[85] *RT,* p. 134.

[86] *P & L,* 2:349, 350, with n. on p. 395.

[87] He was, of course, required to receive the sacrament according to the Prayer Book rite in order to sit as an M.P. It is possible that he was an occasional conformist in order to qualify, but evidence is wanting: see Douglas Lacey, *Dissent and Parliamentary Politics in England, 1661–1689* (Brunswick, N.J., 1969), pp. 15–21, 369–73.

[88] *RT2,* p. 267.

lian arrogance. The effects of the latter were all too evident in the legislation of the "Clarendon Code" and the persecution of nonconformists; but, to moderate Presbyterians, the former was as seriously damaging to the nonconformist cause for it prevented accommodation with the moderate, latitudinarian wing of the Church of England. Here, the *Remarks'* preference in theology chimes with the preference for moderation in ecclesiology of the *Rehearsal Transpros'd* and implies a similar political commitment to reconciliation. After the Restoration the political aspiration of Baxterianism remained the establishment of a comprehensive national church under a godly magistrate. This role now, of course, fell to Charles II, but Baxter, who had no time for the usurper Oliver Cromwell, had once, like Howe, had great hopes that Richard Cromwell might fulfill it.[89] Those hopes had been frustrated in 1659, so Baxter firmly believed, by the machinations of the Congregationalist leader John Owen,[90] the Owen who, in controversies over justification in the 1650s, had taken the Calvinist and, to Baxter's mind, antinomian position. After the return of Charles, Owen remained unsympathetic to proposals for an imposed national church order. For him and for others of Congregational persuasion (predominantly Calvinist in theology), separation of church and state, with toleration of gathered churches, was far preferable to comprehension, that is, incorporation within the established church. To Baxter's mind, Owen continued after the Restoration to present as much of an obstacle to church unity as he had been before 1660.[91]

To moderate Presbyterians, high Calvinists thus threatened not only to open the floodgates of antinomian license but to frustrate all hopes of good order in the commonwealth by their refusal to acknowledge the magistrate's authority in matters of religion or to promote a national church settlement. The kind of moderate accommodation which Baxter sought with John Wilkins, bishop of Chester, and John Tillotson, afterward archbishop of Canterbury, and which, in *Mr. Smirke*, Marvell had defended on behalf of Herbert Croft, bishop of Hereford, found no favor with Owen,

---

[89] *CCRB*, letters 509, 515 (with references to the *Reliquiae* there given); William Lamont, ed., *Baxter: A Holy Commonwealth* (Cambridge, 1994), pp. ix–xi (which describes the text as "a love poem to Richard Cromwell" [p. ix]).

[90] *CCRB*, letter 575 (with references to the *Reliquiae* there given); William Lamont, *Richard Baxter and the Millennium* (London, 1979), pp. 189, 220–21; Lamont, ed., *Holy Commonwealth*, pp. xvi–xviii.

[91] *CCRB*, letters 757, 760, 769, 771 (and references there given); Lamont, *Baxter and the Millennium*, pp. 220–23.

whose high Calvinist commitment Danson shared. Though a Presbyterian, not a Congregationalist, Danson shared little of the temper of the Baxter who, in *The Unreasonableness of Infidelity* (1655), had anticipated Locke's more famous title, *The Reasonableness of Christianity* (1695). In this respect, it was especially galling to have a dogmatist like Danson charge that the arguments against double predestination advanced by middle-way men such as Howe were indistinguishable from those of papists like Bellarmine.[92] The implication was that Howe was peddling popery and that the championing of a moderate national church order was no different from the "Arminian" and despotic Laudian aspirations of such episcopalians as Parker. The Marvell of the *Account of the Growth of Popery* would be no more willing to allow such misrepresentation to obscure the true threat posed by Rome than would the Marvell of the *Rehearsal Transpros'd* to countenance Danson's intemperance of thought and style, or the Marvell of *Mr. Smirke* to accept his intolerant partisanship.[93]

Early testimony to Marvell's authorship of the *Remarks* is, then, supported, if not confirmed, by the tract's polemical method, its religious bias, the congruity of its cultural emphases with those of Marvell's other prose pieces, and its consistency with Marvell's political commitments. The tract detects in Danson just that combination of disputatiousness, logical pedantry, rhetorical extravagance, and fanaticism which was so distasteful to late seventeenth-century liberal minds such as Marvell's, and it commends in Howe just that plain, reasonable, and moderate discourse they preferred. No rival author has ever been proposed, and there is nothing to disprove the attribution.

THE TEXT OF THE *REMARKS*

After Calamy's reference to the *Remarks* in his *Memoirs of Howe*, the text and its connection with Howe slipped from view for more than century: Edward Thompson did not include it in his 1776 edition of Marvell's *Works... Poetical, Controversial, and Political*. It was not recovered until, on Calamy's authority, in 1836 Henry Rogers devoted a chapter of his *Life and*

[92] *TD*, pref. ep., sigs A8–A8v.

[93] This paragraph draws on William Lamont, "The Religion of Andrew Marvell: Locating the 'Bloody Horse,'" in *The Political Identity of Andrew Marvell*, ed. Conal Condren and A. D. Cousins (Aldershot, 1990), pp. 135–56, where these points are more fully developed, with reference to the *Remarks* (esp. pp. 138, 141–44, 146, 147, 151).

Character of John Howe to extracts from "Andrew Marvell's Defence of Howe against Thomas Danson";[94] in 1844 a reviewer in the *Edinburgh Review* mentioned Marvell's authorship of the *Remarks*;[95] in 1854 it was reprinted, together with Howe's *Letter* and *Postscript*, in a series of theological tracts;[96] and finally Alexander Grosart included it in his edition of Marvells' *Complete Works*.[97]

Although Marvell maintained his habitual anonymity as its author, this text was not surreptitiously and illegally printed. It was duly licensed on April 17, 1678[98] and, in accordance with the requirements of the Licensing Act, the title page bears a full imprint: "Printed and are to be sold by Christopher Hussey, at the Flower-de-luce in Little-Brittain 1678." Hussey, who was at work from the mid 1670s until at least 1705, is a puzzling and unexpected choice of publisher. He is described by John Dunton as "a downright honest man" and "a man of moderation," and so may be thought to have had Marvellian sympathies, but, if he had, there is no further evidence for them in his business dealings.[99] The fourteen other seventeenth-century titles in which he is known to have had a hand are a mixed bag of broadsides, amatory works, and practical guides to such subjects as angling, surveying, "stereometry," geography, and domestic education.[100] There is no indication of that commitment to nonconformity and to oppositional politics characteristic of the printers and publishers who handled Marvell's other texts and of the booksellers who published such men as Howe, Baxter, Bunyan, and Owen.[101] On the contrary, Hussey produced no other title comparable to the *Remarks*. How or why it came to him is a mystery.

---

[94] Henry Rogers, *The Life and Character of John Howe* (London, 1836), pp. 220–46.

[95] *Edinburgh Review* 79, no. 159 (January 1844), 89. Unlike the reviewer, the book under review, John Dove's *The Life of Andrew Marvell* (London, 1832), did not have the benefit of Rogers's biography and consequently did not know of the *Remarks*.

[96] John Brown, ed., *Theological Tracts, Selected and Original,* 3 vols. (Edinburgh and London, 1853–54), 3:75–138.

[97] Grosart, 4:163–242.

[98] See above, n. 56.

[99] John Dunton, *The Life and Errors,* 2 vols. (London, 1818), 1:210. See also Henry R. Plomer, *A Dictionary of the Printers and Booksellers who were at work...from 1688 to 1725* (1922; rpt. Oxford, 1968), *s.v.*

[100] Titles are identified in Paul G. Morrison, *Index of Printers, Publishers and Booksellers in Donald Wing's Short-Title Catalogue* (Charlottesville, Va., 1955).

[101] For the very different commercial policy of such publishers, see Keeble, *Literary Culture,* pp. 120–26.

BIBLIOGRAPHICAL DETAILS

Title page

[within double rules] R E M A R K S / Upon a Late Disingenuous / DISCOURSE, / Writ by one *T. D.* / Under the pretence / DE CAVSA DEI, / And of Answering / Mr. *John Howe*'s Letter and Postscript / OF / GOD'S PRESCIENCE, &c. / Affirming, as the Protestant Doctrine, / That God doth by Efficacious Influ- / ence universally move and Deter- / mine Men to all their Actions, even / to those that are most Wicked. / [rule] / By a PROTESTANT. / [rule] / *LONDON,* / Printed and are to be sold by *Christopher Hussey,* at the / *Flower-de-luce in Little-Brittain.* 1678.

Collation

8^0: A-1^8, K^6, signed. Pages: 1–155, with unnumbered errata page following. Pages misnumbered are: 32 (as 33), 50 (as 52), 149 (as 146).

Contents

Title page, with imprimatur on verso; A1-K6 text, with *"FINIS"* between rules toward the foot of K6; K6v *"ERRATA'S."* A1 has a double rule at the head, followed by "REMARKS / Upon a Late / Disingenuous Discourse / *WRIT* / By one T.D. &c." I1v has only seven lines of text, followed by the catchwords 'I should' for I2 within spaced rules.

Running titles

None; pages are headed by page numbers within square brackets.

Catchwords (selected)

	A2 patr, [part,]	B4v (Cu-)riosity
C4 there- [therefore]	D4 *(ap-)pearance* [*pearanee*]	D5v mul- [multiply]
E6v (uni-)versal	F5v Ar- [Argument]	G3 a form- [a formed]
H1v *(con-)tinual* [*continual*]	I3 omit- [omitted]	K5v (li-)tigious

In 1836 Henry Rogers knew of only one copy of the *Remarks,* that held in Dr. Williams's Library. By the 1870s, Grosart knew of at least another four (including one in his own possession).[102] Wing M884 now lists nine copies,

[102] Rogers, *Life of Howe,* p. 221; Grosart, ed., *Works,* 4:164.

six in England and three in the United States.[103] The text which follows is based upon a hardcopy of the reproduction by University Microfilms Inc. of the Yale University Library copy (not listed in Wing). It has been compared with the copies held in the British Library; Dr. Williams's Library; Bodleian Library; Trinity College, Cambridge; Christ Church, Oxford; the Folger Library. Compositorial errors are common to these copies, indicating that there were no corrections to the text while in press and that the tract was issued in only one state.

As well as observing the editorial conventions described in the general introduction, the text which follows silently standardizes italicization of *The Discourse, Letter, Postscript, TD,* and *It* when the pronoun refers to *TD.* It is also consistent in giving initial capitals to *It* and to *The Discourse,* in rendering the possessive as *Its* and in printing the possessive "s" attached to *The Discourse* in roman type. In all these matters, the original follows a variety of procedures.

I am most grateful to the following friends and colleagues for generously answering queries on particular points in the annotation: Gordon Campbell of the University of Leicester; Karen Edwards of the University of Exeter; John Hale of the University of Otago; Stephen Penn, David Reid, and Robin Sowerby of the University of Stirling; and Geoffrey F. Nuttall. Above all, I am indebted to the extraordinary scholarly detective skills of our general editor, Annabel Patterson.

---

[103] Wing lists copies held at British Library, London; Bodleian Library, Oxford; Dr. Williams's Library, London; Christ Church, Oxford; Trinity College, Cambridge; Plume Library, Maldon; Princeton University, Princeton; University of Texas, Austin; Folger Library, Washington, D.C. I am most grateful to Jacqueline Tasioulas of Newnham College, Cambridge, and to James Knowles of the University of Stirling, for their help in checking copies.

REMARKS

Upon a Late Disingenuous

DISCOURSE,

Writ by one *T.D.*

Under the pretence

DE CAVSA DEI,

And of Answering

Mr. *John Howe*'s Letter and Postscript

OF

GOD'S PRESCIENCE, &c.

Affirming, as the Protestant Doctrine,

That God doth by Efficacious Influence universally move and Determine Men to all their Actions, even
to those that are most Wicked.

By a PROTESTANT.

LONDON,
Printed and are to be sold by *Christopher Hussey,* at the
Flower-de-luce in Little-Brittain. 1678.

REMARKS

Upon a Late Disingenuous

DISCOURSE,

Writ by one *T. D.*

R. H. Stoddard

Under the pretence

DE *CAVSA* DEI,

And of Answering
Mr. *John Howe's* Letter and Postscript

OF

GOD'S PRESCIENCE, &c.

Affirming, as the Protestant Doctrine,

That God doth by Efficacious Influence universally move and Determine Men to all their Actions, even
to those that are most Wicked.

BY a PROTESTANT. *And. Marvel*

LONDON,

Printed and are to be sold by *Christopher Hussey*, at the
Flower-de-luce in *Little-Brittain.* 1678.

Fig. 3. Title page from Remarks Upon a Late Disingenuous Discourse, *1678.*

REMARKS

Upon a Late

Disingenuous Discourse

WRIT

By one *T.D.* &c.

Of all Vocations to which men addict themselves, or are dedicated, I have alwaies esteemed that of the Ministry to be the most noble and happy Imployment; as being more peculiarly directed to those two great Ends, the advancement of God's Glory, and the promoting of Man's Salvation. It hath seemed to me as if they who have chosen, and are set apart for [2] that Work, did, by the continual opportunity of conversing with their Maker, enjoy a state like that of Paradise; and in this superiour, that they are not also, as Adam, put in *to dress and keep a Garden;*[1] but are, or ought to be, exempt from the necessity of all worldly avocations. Yet, upon nearer consideration, they likewise appear to partake of the common infelicities of Humane condition. For, although they do not, as others, eat their Bread, in the sweat of their brows (which some Divines account to be, though in the Pulpit, undecent,) yet the study of their brain is more than equivalent; and even the Theological Ground is so far under the Curse, that no Field runs out more in Thorns and Thistles, or requires more pains to disincumber it.[2] Such I understand to be those peevish questions which have overgrown Christianity; wherewith men's minds are only rent [3] and intangled, but from whence they can no more hope for any wholsom nourishment, than to *gather Grapes from Thorns,* or *Figgs from Thistles.*[3] And (if I may so far pursue the Allegory) this Curse upon Divinity, as that upon the Earth, seems to have proceeded also from tasting that forbidden Fruit, of *the Tree of Knowledge of Good and Evil.*[4] For, in general, many Divines, out of a vain affectation of Learning, have been tempted into Enquiries too curious after those things which the Wisdom of God hath left impervious to Humane Understanding, further than they are revealed. And hence, instead of those allowed and obvious Truths of Faith, Repentance, and the New Creature,

---

[1] Gen. 2:15.

[2] Gen. 3:18–19.

[3] Matt. 7:16.

[4] Gen. 2:17, 3:11–17.

(yet these too have their proper weeds that pester them,) there have sprung up endless Disputes concerning the unsearchable things of God, and which are agitated by men, for the most [4] part, with such Virulence and Intricacy, as manifest the Subtilty and Malice of the Serpent that hath seduced them.[5] But, more particularly, that very Knowledge of Good and Evil, the disquisition of the Causes from whence, and in what manner they are derived, hath been so grateful to the Controversial, Female,[6] Appetite, that even the Divines have taken of it as *a Fruit to be desired to make them Wise,*[7] and given to their people, and they have both eaten, at the peril of God's Displeasure and their own Happiness. Whereas that second Chapter of Genesis contains the plain History of Good and Evil, and (not to mention so many attestations to it of the Old and New Testament,) what other Comment needs there, for what belongs to Good, than that, Jam. 1.17. that it is from God only, *That every Good Giving, and every Perfect Gift descendeth?* And, as to Evil, that [5] also of St. James, is sufficient conviction, *cap.* 1. *v.*13, 14. *Let no man say, when he is tempted, I was tempted of God; God cannot be tempted with Evil, neither tempteth he any man: But every man is tempted, when he is drawn aside by his own lusts and enticed.* Or that of the same Apostle, *cap.* 4. *v.*1. *From whence come Wars and Fightings among you?* (and even that *Logomachia,*[8] I fear, with which this question is vexed,) *Come they not hence? even from your lusts that fight in your members.* And there is no examining[9] Christian but must find both these Truths evidently witnessed by his own Conscience.

Nevertheless, the Theologants[10] of former and later times, not content

---

[5] A common complaint: compare Baxter's view: "It was never the will of God that bare *speculation* should be the end of his *Revelation,* or of *our belief.* Divinity is an *Affective practical* Science" grounded in a few "Essential necessary Truths" which should never be neglected for controversial divinity or "*presumptious curiosity*" in prying into "the secret things of God" (Richard Baxter, *Directions for Weak Distempered Christians* [1673], pt. 1, pp. 97–98; *A Christian Directory* [1671], 1.2.40).

[6] Female: a common gendering of unruly desire, here underscored by the association of divines' inclination to controversy with Eve's inclination to eat the fruit offered by the serpent (contrast the *manly* discourse of p. 420, which expresses "Humane Perfection").

[7] Gen. 3:6.

[8] *Logomachia:* Latin original of *logomachy,* contention about words.

[9] examining: i.e., self-examining.

[10] Theologants: theologians (*OED* cites this instance as its only example).

with what is held forth in Scripture, have attempted to clamber and palm up[11] higher, by the Philosophy of that School where each of them hath first practised, and have drawn God's Prescience and Predetermination, upon [6] this occasion, into debate; arguing upon such points as no man, unless he were *Prior* and precedent to the First Cause, can have the Understanding to comprehend and judge of: and most of them do but say and unsay; and while in words they all deny God to be the Author of sin, yet in effect, and by the manner of their reasoning, they affirm it; I therefore, being both apprehensive of the danger in such Arguments, and more particularly conscious of mine own weakness, shall not presume to interpose my Opinion in the differences about this matter, further than to say; That if men by this fansied *opening of their Eyes,* have attained to see more clearly, and acknowledge the wickedness of their own Actions, it resembles the modesty of our First Parents, discerning their *Nakedness.*[12] But, if men shall also assert a *Predeterminative Concourse*[13] of God to our Evil, it seems to have [7] too much of Original Perverseness, and of that faln shortness of Reason, whereby they would have found a Nudity in the Creator, and did implicitely reject[14] their fault upon him, for the *Serpent that He had made,* and the *Woman that He had given.*

But, if any man there be that can reconcile this Controversie, and so many more that arise out of it; (for all the most important Doctrines of Christianity serve on the one side, and all the fiercest questions of Religion on the other, depending for Truth and Falshood upon the success of this Engagement,) if he can extinguish all those Ill Consequences, Dull Distinctions, and Inconsistent Notions, which have been levied in this quarrel, and reduce each Party within the due limits of Scripture and Saving Knowledge; such a person indeed deserves all commendation. And such an one I thought I had met with, nor yet see [8] reason, notwithstanding all the late attempts upon him, to alter my Opinion; in a Book intitled; *The Reconcileableness of God's Prescience of the sins of Men, with the Wisdom and Sincerity of his Counsels, Exhortations; and whatsoever other means He uses to*

---

[11] palm up: a usage not recorded in *OED*. It may suggest the manual dexterity of climbing, and there may be connotations of deviousness.

[12] Gen. 3:7.

[13] *Concourse:* concurrence, cooperation; the degree of divine causation this entails is the point in dispute.

[14] reject: return, cast.

prevent them. In a Letter to the Honourable Robert Boyl,[15] *Esquire; and in a Postscript to the late Letter of the Reconcileableness of God's Prescience, &c. by John Howe, the Author of that Letter.*

Yet there was one passage in the close of his *Letter, p.* 154. which seem'd, as I thought, to lye[16] open to censure; where he askt pardon, as *having hudled it up mostly in the intervals of a troublesome long Journey.* It seem'd a piece too well elaborate to have been perfected amidst the hurry of the Road, the noise of Inns, and the *Nausea* of the Packet-boat.[17] And how could he hope, after saying this, in so captious[18] an Age as we live, to escape some Reflexion? but that at least men [9] would inquire whether he went by Stage-coach, or on Horse-back; both which are professed enemies to Meditation and Judgment? (for it is probable[19] he had not that ancient accommodation of Horse-litters,[20] wherein, without any impediment to their thoughts, men travelled with all the privacy and equipage of a Closet,) whether he had not lost his way, or faln among Thieves, and how he found himself after his Journey? with all the questions that men are subject to at their arrival home, and which even when ask'd in civility, yet are troublesome. He might, had it not been for the jogging, have remembred how unfortunate most Writers have been in such excuses, and what advantage ill-natur'd men have taken to misinterpret them. So he that apologiz'd for using a Forein tongue, was told that no man had prohibited him his Native Language in his own Country.[21] [10] Others, alledging that they had at the same time a Fit of the Stone, Gout, or other Distemper, have been taxed, as lying under no obligation of publishing their Infirmities, but who might however, have cur'd themselves

[15] For Boyle, see introduction, p. 382, n. 4.

[16] lye] lay *R* (corrected in the list of errata).

[17] *Letter,* p. 154, does not identify the journey or include these details. The reference to the "Packet-boat" may suggest that the *Letter* was first drafted when, in December 1675, Howe moved from Ireland, where he had been chaplain to Sir John Skeffington, 2d Viscount Massarene, to become pastor to a congregation meeting in Haberdashers' Hall, Staining Lane, London.

[18] Cf. the prefatory epistle "To the Captious Reader" to *Mr. Smirke.*

[19] probable Ed.] propable *R.*

[20] Horse-litters: an enclosed litter carried on poles between two horses, one before and one behind. Despite Marvell's past tense they had not gone out of use at this time.

[21] The subject of this contemptuous remark has not been identified, but he would appear to have been a foreigner who published in English, such as Isaac Casaubon or Pierre du Moulin.

of that of Writing.[22] And he that pretended to treat at once of a Serious, while he was amused with *a more Comfortable Importance*,[23] was advertis'd,[24] that he ought therefore to have so long abstained either from the one or the other.[25] But, in earnest, this confession of Mr. How's, is so far from any such Arrogance, that it rather argues his modesty. For, if some can even in Riding name all the contrary motions,[26] till they have by memory plai'd out a Game at Chess, (which was first invented as an emblem of *Predetermination*)[27] why should it be more difficult, or less allowable, to one of Mr. How's abilities, in the interruptions of travel, to give a Mate also to that question? [11] The worst therefore that can be said of him, in allusion either to his *Letter* or his Journey, is—*at poterat tutior esse domi*.[28] Yet seeing this was the greatest fault that I remarked in reading him over, I would not pass it by without notice, lest I might have cause to suspect my self of a Partiality, which I desire not that others should exercise in mine own particular.

But for the rest, whereas the things considerable in all Discourses are the Subject, the End, the Reasoning, the Method, and the Style; I must profess that, as far as I understand, I have met with few manual[29] Treatises, that do

[22] This is an obvious reference back to Marvell's mockery of Parker's "distemper," *RT2*, pp. 223–35.

[23] *Importance:* subject.

[24] advertis'd: admonished.

[25] In his preface to John Bramhall's *Vindication . . .* (1672), Samuel Parker had referred to *"Matters of a closer and more comfortable importance to my self"* than the subject in hand (sig. A2). Wondering, in *RT,* p. 47, "what this thing should be of a closer importance; But being more comfortable too, I conclude it must be one of these three things; either his Salvation, or a Benefice, or a Female," Marvell decided that "it must be a Female." This recollection of that exchange is strongly suggestive of Marvell's authorship of the *Remarks,* though not conclusive, since the passage was of course available to any reader of *RT:* Rochester, for example, was sufficiently struck by it, and by the words "comfortable importance," to recall them in 1673 or 1674 in "Tunbridge Wells," ll. 64–71 (*The Complete Works,* ed. Frank H. Ellis [Harmondsworth, 1994], p. 45 with n. on p. 342).

[26] motions: moves.

[27] Whether or not this was Marvell's own idea has not been determined, but probably not: Cowley, for example, uses chess as an image of fate in "Destinie," in his *Pindarique Odes* (1656).

[28] "He would have been safer staying at home."

[29] manual: concise, summary.

in all these respects equal it. For the Subject, it appears in the Title, than which there was none of greater dignity to be handled, or of greater use, if rightly explain'd and comprehended. And no less is that of *Predetermination*, which he only treats of collaterally; and upon which there-[12]fore, in hope to find him less prepared, he hath been attaqued, as in the Flank, with most vigour. His End was most commendable, being to make the Paths streight,[30] and remove those stumbling-blocks which the asperity of others had laid in the way to Heaven; to rectifie mens apprehensions concerning God, and leave them without pretence for negligence in their Duties, or despair of performance; much less for despight against the Creatour. His Arguing then is plain and solid, for Evidence, rather than Dispute; nor does he either throw the Dust of antique Distinctions in the eyes of his Readers, to blind them; or yet raise the Spectres of ancient Authors, or conjure their venerable Names, to fright men out of their senses and understanding; but declares against all the Prejudice or Advantage by such proceeding, as unlawful Charms, and prohibited Wea-[13]pons in the Controversie. His Method thereafter is direct and coherent, his Style perspicuous and elegant: So that it is in short, a Manly discourse, resembling much, and expressing the Humane Perfection; in the Harmony of Language, the Symmetry of Parts, the Strength of Reason, the Excellency of its End, which is so serious, that it is no defect in the similitude with Man, that the *Letter* contains nothing in it suitable to the property of Laughter.

All which put together, and although it does, and must every where partake also of Humane Imperfection, it might have been hoped capable of[31] that civility which men, and especially Learned men, but most of all Divines do usually, or should allow, to one another. That it should not be made ridiculous, being writ in so good earnest; nor assaulted, being so inoffensive; much less that it should be [14] defaced, mutilated, stabb'd in so many places, and the Author through it, which is even in writing a kind of Felony. Yet this hath been its misfortune in a Rencounter[32] with an immodest and hectoring Discourse, pretending to the Title, *De Causa Dei; Or a Vindication of the Common Doctrine of Protestant Divines concerning* Predtermination, *viz. The Interest of God, as the First Cause, in all the Actions, as such, of Rational Creatures, from the Invidious Consequences with which it is*

---

[30] Matt. 3:3.

[31] capable of: entitled to, qualified to receive.

[32] Rencounter: hostile encounter.

burthened, by Mr. John How, in a late Letter and Postscript of God's Prescience; by *T. D.* By which first Letters, seeing it appears that he desires to pass *Incognito,* I will so far observe good manners, as to interpret them only *The Discourse,* heartily wishing that there were some way of finding it Guilty, without reflecting upon the Author; which I shall accordingly indeavour, that I may both preserve [15] his, whatsoever, former Reputation, and leave him a door open to Ingenuity[33] for the future. But *The Discourse* justifies it self, as if it had been typified by Paul's withstanding Peter to his face, when he came to Antioch,[34] (so easy is it to patronize humane Passions under the pretence of the Cause of God, and Apostolical example) *T.D.* p. 123.[35] whereas it rather resembles in the Bravery,[36] though not in the Occasion, that Exploit of Peter's Matth. 26.51, 52. for which our Saviour, though done in his defence, rebuked him, adding, *They that take the sword, shall perish by the sword:* And the taking the Pen hath seldom better success, if handled in the same manner. I therefore, having had the leisure to read it over, and thereby the opportunity of a second Caution, how the unruly Quill is to be managed, have thought that I could not at present render a better account of that time to my [16] self or others, than by publishing these Remarks; that, as Mr. How's *Letter* may serve for a Pattern of what is to be imitated, so *The Discourse* may remain as a Mark (the best use it can be put to) of what ought to be avoided in all writing of Controversies, especially by Divines, in those that concern Religion. The nature of this matter would admit of no better method, than that the Errours observable should be distinguished under several Heads, to each of which the particular Instances are referred. The first Article that I prefer against the *Discourse,* is;

Its *Trifling and Cavilling about Words,*
when they affect not the Cause.

First Instance. Mr. Howe, on purpose to prevent any such idle Practice, had in the last page of his *Postscript,* plainly summ'd up the constant sense [17] both of that and his *Letter* which he would abide by. *That God doth not by an Efficacious Influence universally move and determine Men to all their Actions, even those Actions which are most wicked.* Here was the Subject ready

---

[33] Ingenuity: a display of intellectual ability.
[34] Gal. 2:11.
[35] 123. Ed] 23.*R.*
[36] Bravery: bravado.

stated, against which, if any thing, *The Discourse* ought to have directly apply'd. But, instead of that *T. D.* p. 1. *It*[37] saith, *Mr. Howe gives us his sense in various terms, and such as seem repugnant to each other. One while that which he denies, is a* Predeterminative Concurrence, *and* Predeterminative Concourse; *another while, 'tis* Predetermining Influence, *and a* Determinative Influence, *and* Efficacious Influence. This is the same in *T. D.* as if *Its concurrent Wherry-men,*[38] p. 27. after they had taken in their Fare, should be long pulling off their Doublets, and then carry a man to another Stairs[39] than they were directed: The one shows that they had but little heart to their labour; the other, that [18] they know not the River, unless perhaps they have a design, if they can find a place convenient to rifle the Passenger. For Mr. Howe had expresly pitch'd upon that one term of Efficacious Influence. But, as for those other repeated by *The Discourse*, they were such as Mr. Howe found in the Controversie, not of his own making, nor therefore is he accountable for them: But, however, it was his Ingenuity to mention them; and having done so, to bind himself to a point, to one Word of the most certain signification, as a place where any adversary might alwaies be sure to speak with him. Yet *It*, to find out matter for Discourse, and to show *Its* great Reading, tells us, as if that were the business, what Strangius[40] saith, and what Doctor Twisse[41] concerning *Predetermination* and *Concourse;* and *again*, what Strangius of the Difference between *Concourse* and *Influence*, p. 2 and saith [19] that, *as for those two Phrases*, Predeterminative Concurrence, *and* Predeterminative Concourse, *they are in*

---

[37] *It:* here, and subsequently, *T.D.*, that is, Danson's initials interpreted as *The Discourse* (see p. 421, and introduction, p. 402).

[38] *Wherry:* rowing boat in service as a river ferry. *TD*, p. 27, speaking of the "concourse of God with Adam's will" in his eating of the apple, offers the elucidating analogy of "Two men lanching a wherry-boat" who "concur to the same effect; but the one does not determine the other, by lending common assistance to that act."

[39] Stairs: landing-stage (used most commonly of the Thames).

[40] John Strang (1584–1654), principal of Glasgow University, was a middle-way man theologically who was forced in 1650 to resign his principalship because of what were regarded as his heterodox opinions. *TD*, p. 102, describes Strangius as "Mr. H.'s friend, but my Adversary." Theophilus Gale, *The Court of the Gentiles* (1678), 4.3.8, similarly regards him as "our principal adversary."

[41] William Twisse (1578?–1646), rector of Newington Longueville, Bucks, was an exceptionally learned Puritan divine who enjoyed a high reputation as a defender of Calvinist orthodoxy against "Arminian" modifications, notably in his *Vindiciae Gratiae Potestatis, ac Providentiae Dei* (Amsterdam, 1632).

effect, Contradictio in Adjecto.[42] And so let them be, upon condition that not Mr. Howe, (as *The Discourse* would have it) but the first Inventer may[43] be bound to answer for it. For the truth is, the Brothers of Dispute do usually so handle their matter, and refine so far, till they want at last either words to express their meaning, or meaning to express in words. And so it hath faired with these Imaginers of the *Predeterminative Concourse* or *Concurrence.* 'Tis very well that this Scene of Debate lies in Oxford (or London)[44] for, upon these terms, it would be impossible at New-Market,[45] where *Pro*[46] and *Con*[47] run their heats, to decide any Match without sending for a Judge to the next University; and it is less difficult for *Pro* and *Con,* or for *Con,* and *Non-Con,* to set their Horses together. Yet sup-[20]pose, as *The Discourse* affirms, that this *Predeterminative Concourse* or *Concurrence* had been words of Mr. Howe's own choosing; whereas he on the contrary rejects them for that of *Efficacious Influence,* the Impropriety however therein had not been greater, than of that Phrase which *T.D.* p. 25. uses, and hath right to, *Simultaneous Concourse,* which is, if I mistake not, as much as to say, *Conconcourse.*[48]

The same (if greater be the same) *Trifling and Cavilling about Words that affect not the Cause,* it is to say, *T.D.* p.2. *As for that latter Phrase,* Influence, *which Mr. Howe makes equipollent with the former* Concourse *in the words,* Post. p. 29. I here affect not the Curiosity to distinguish these two Terms, as some do; *I had rather he should hear Strangius again* than me, *blaming his not* affecting that Curiosity of Distinction: and then *It* cites Strangius *de Vol.*

[42] "A contradiction in terms."

[43] may Ed.] my *R.*

[44] London: Both Danson and Howe were Oxford educated ministers to congregations in London.

[45] New-Market: Throughout the seventeenth century horse races had been run at Newmarket Health, Suffolk, patronized by courtiers and occasionally royalty. From 1666, Charles II regularly attended spring and autumn meetings there (J. P. Hore, *The History of Newmarket* [1886], 2:249–88).

[46] *Pro* Ed.] *Prae R.*

[47] *Pro and Con:* for and against, with reference to the scholastic disputations for and against a proposition or thesis which constituted the usual form of examination in seventeenth-century universities. See above, introduction, pp. 403–05.

[48] *Conconcourse:* Marvell plays on the prefix of *concourse,* from Latin *con* (together with) + *cursus* (traveling, journey), to make the point that *TD's simultaneous* is superfluous.

Dei, lib. I. *c.*II. *p.* 59. assigning the difference be-[21]tween them.[49] This is a trivial litigation about words, where the thing intended is sufficiently understood (or rather is intelligible) and, whether it be said *Influence* or *Concourse* makes no more to the business, than the Impropriety objected to *Predetermining,* or *previous Concourse,* which any indifferent Reader can see to have been spoken generally, of a priority of the supposed *Influence* on God's part, not in Time, but in Nature and Causality. Strangius, indeed, writing a large Treatise concerning that Subject, distinguished all the Terms more accurately: But Mr. Howe, it being there done to his hand, and writing on the by[50] only two or three pages, had not the space or the occasion to enlarge upon them. And it is an Infirmity which Mr. Howe, I observe, is much subject to, that he seldom useth any notional Terms or Distinctions, where he can make men comprehend [22] him better without them: And at that, indeed he hath a singular faculty. His very saying that he *affected not,* there, *the* Curiosity *to distinguish those two Terms, as some do,* shows it: But withall, that he was not ignorant of them, and that he also could distinguish when he saw reason, and in time and place convenient. *The Discourse* might with more cause have accused him of Ambiguity, and raised scruples about his *Curiosity:* for that is taken in many several significations. As for example; sometimes it is used for a commendable Exquisiteness in things considerable, and worth the labour. Otherwhiles it is described, *Quoties plus Diligentiae quam oportebat impendimus rebus, vel Nostris, vel Alienis. Nostris, quum minima quaeque disquirimus & nullius frugis: Alienis, quum de rebus caeterorum occultioribus non satis cum pudore perscrutamur aut interrogamus.*[51] So not Strangius, nor Doctor Twisse, but

---

[49] *TD*, p. 2–3, translates its citation from Strangius's *De Voluntate & Actionibus Dei circa Peccatum* (Amsterdam, 1637) thus: *"it seems worth our labour to distinguish between those two words* Concourse *and* Influence, *which in this matter are often conjoined and confounded. For first,* Influence *is of a larger extent than* Concourse. *For the causality of every Cause, especially the Efficient, is called* Influence. *And therefore in many instances there may be observed an* Influence *of God, when yet there is no concourse, as when he acts, not making use of any second cause. Again, although in the concourse of two Causes each of them are considered as having their* Influence, *yet the word* Influence *is absolute, and noting a respect to another cause; but the word* Concourse *is relative to another cause."*

[50] on the by: incidentally.

[51] The first sentence of this quotation (but not the second) is given as a definition of *curiosus* in Calepinus, *Dictionarivm* (Lyons, 1520), but it is dropped in the Basle 1584 and subsequent editions (save for the 1625 Venice reprint of the 1575 Venice edition). The dictionary entry attributes to Cicero, *Pro Appio pulchro,* not this sentence but another

Cicero. Which, [23] that I may do equal rights to *the Discourse* in translating Latine, is to say, *That is called Curiosity, when men use an impertinent Diligence in things relating to themselves or others: To themselves, when they are busie about every trifle, and what is of no moment: To others, when they exercise a scrutiny, or ask questions beyond modesty, concerning their private Affairs.* And I had rather *It* should hear Cicero again, than me blaming It for this latter sort of Curiosity. *Reperiam multos, vel innumerabiles potius, non tam curiosos, nec tam molestos quam Vos estis.*[52] That is, *I could find many, or rather innumerable men, neither so* Troublesome, *nor so* Curious *as* You are. And Quintillian explains it further. *Est etiam quae* Parergia *vocatur, supervacua, ut sic dixerim, Operositas: Ut a Diligente Curiosus, & a Religione superstitio distat,*[53] i.e. *There is also that which is called* Parergia, *a superfluous and laborious Nicety; as a* Curious *man differs from a Diligent, or Superstition* [24] *from Religion.* But besides all this, *Curiosus* signifies an Informer: in which sense, I suppose, both Mr. Howe, and *T.D.* would be loath to accept it. Yet perhaps I may gratifie them in the Authority of[54] Quotation. *Suet. Aug.* c. 27. *Nam & Pinarium, Equitem Romanum, quum Concionante se, admissa turba Paganorum, apud Milites, subscribere quaedam animadvertisset,* Curiosum *&* Speculatorem[55] *ratus, coram confodi imperavit.* Which Text, if a little help'd in the translating, might serve them to notable purpose: But however so it is, that, *taking the Knight to be a Spy and an Informer, he caused him forthwith to be slain in his presence.*[56] And lastly in the Code, *Tit. de Curiosus & Stationariis: Curiosus* is a Post-master, if Mr. Howe be dispos'd at any time to take another *long troublesome Journey,* and do not *disaffect also*

---

saying (not used by Marvell). In the 1584 and subsequent editions (again, with the exception of the 1625 Venice edition), this entry includes the quotation from the *Codex Theodosianus* to which Marvell refers toward the end of this paragraph; and in the Paris 1609 and subsequent editions, it also includes the citation from Suetonius which Marvell reproduces in this paragraph (see below, nn. 56, 57).

[52] Cicero, *De finibus bonorum et malorum,* 2.9.28.

[53] Quintilian, *Institutio oratoria,* 8.3.55.

[54] of Ed.] or *R.*

[55] *Speculatorem] Speculatorum R* (corrected in the list of errata).

[56] Suetonius, *De vita Caesarum,* 2: *Divus Augustus,* 27.3, which J. C. Rolfe (ed. and trans.), *The Lives of the Caesars,* Loeb ed. 2 vols. (London, 1914), 1:163, translates: "When he [Augustus] was addressing the soldiers and a throng of civilians had been admitted to the assembly, noticing that Pinarius, a Roman knight, was taking notes, he ordered that he be stabbed on the spot, thinking him an eavesdropper and a spy." For Marvell's sources, see nn. 51 and 57.

that Curiosity.[57] It had been much more to the purpose to have learnt these several acceptations of Cu-[25]riosity, than to have exercised it in the worst sense, in such needless disquisitions, when a question stated in other terms was in expectation every minute to be disputed.

But to say that in those words: *I here affect not the* Curiosity *to distinguish these two Terms of* Concourse *or* Influence, *as some do,* was to make the latter Phrase *Influence* equipollent *with the former Concourse* is *gratis*[58] or rather *ingratiis dictum,*[59] and ought not to have been but upon consultation first with Mr. Howe, to have had his concurrence; no nor then neither. For should Mr. Howe be never so much of opinion, as he seems otherwise, that they are *Equipollent,* yet it can never be true that these words do infer it. As suppose that I should say, I affect not *here* the *Curiosity* to distinguish betwixt the Candor and the Acuteness of *The Discourse* in this particular, do I therefore think them *Equipollent,* or [26] that one of them hath not the stronger ingredience?[60] though indeed there is little of either.

Another (for this hath been too pregnant to say a second) Instance to the same Head is where *The Discourse,* p. 26. tells us; *It is an unaccountable inadvertency, (for to salve his honour, so I will call it, rather than a slip of Judgment) to produce Cursing and Swearing for instances of Actions down-right, or for the substance of them Evil,* &c. This indeed is *Curiosity* in the highest degree of perfection, if (for I must be aware too of such exactness) there be degrees of Perfection. And an heavy Charge it is, which I know not whence it could light upon Mr. Howe, but that the Curious are likewise given for the most part to be Censorious, where they have no reason. For Mr. Howe *Post.* p.33, 34. examining an Argument used by some for God's *Predeterminative Concurrence* to *Wicked Actions,* because there are no [27] Actions of Man on Earth so good, which have not some mixture of sin in them &c. (see *Postscript,* p. 32.) saith, *This Argument must be thus conceived. That if God concur by* Determinative Influence *to the imperfectly good Actions of Faith, Repentance, Love to himself, Prayer, therefore to the Acts of* Enmity *against himself, Cursing, Idolatry, Blasphemy, &c. And is it not a*

---

[57] Thomas Cooper, *Thesaurus Linguae Romanae & Britanniae* (1565) includes among its instances under *curiosus:* "Curiosus dicitur. The maister of the poste horses or mulets [i.e., mules], to sende in haste aboute the Emperours affaires," referring to the *Codex Theodosianus,* 6.29. Cooper also refers to the Suetonius quotation Marvell has just reproduced (see n. 56).

[58] *gratis:* gratuitous.

[59] *ingratiis dictum:* a saying contrary to sense.

[60] ingredience: ingredients.

mighty consequence, if to Actions that are good quoad Substantiam,[61] *therefore to such as are in the Substance of them Evil? We our selves can in a remoter kind concur to the Actions of others. Because you may afford your self your leading concurrence to Actions imperfectly good, therefore may you to them that are downright evil? because to Prayer, therefore to Cursing and Swearing? and then ruine men for the Actions you induced them to? You'l say God may rather, but sure he can much less do so than you. How could you be serious in the proposal of this Question?* For this Argument had been proposed by [28] way of question, and I have on purpose set down Mr. Howe's answer at length, that it might be evident, without further brangling,[62] how little, I mean how no, cause there was for this Animadversion upon him, speaking expresly of such Cursing and Swearing only as is Evil *Quoad Substantiam.* For certainly those *Acts of Enmity against God himself,* which Mr. Howe there enumerates, *Cursing,* and then *Idolatry, Blasphemy,* &c. are, and were so understood by him, and by all but such as take care to the contrary, as much Evil in themselves as that *Adultery* which *The Discourse* it self owns to be so, p. 72, *because no end or circumstance can make it good.* So that this ado is made for Mr. Howe's not saying Prophane Cursing and Swearing: indeed a very hainous and notorious omission: even as it would be for a man, so often as he uses the words *And* or *The,* not to distinguish or tell his Reader, [29] that he intends *And* in an *Exegetical* sense, or *The* in an *Emphatical;* or whether in their ordinary capacity.[63] How *unaccountable* soever *this Inadvertency* were in Mr. Howe, it is well *The Discourse* did not call our Saviour to *account,* Matth, 5.34. for forbidding Swearing in general terms,[64] nor St. James, *cap.* 5. *v.* 12. for the same as to Swearing,[65] or *c.* 3, *v.* 9, 10. because the same Apostle does not there descant upon Cursing more distinctly, and add Prophane to its Character. But had *The Discourse* done so, it would have been obvious to every man, that the Pen deserv'd the same

[61] quoad Substantiam: as regards their substance, in their essence (see further below, nn. 241, 243.

[62] brangling: wrangling, contention.

[63] Marvell's point is that these are the "ordinary capacities," or senses, of these words. Just as there is no need to explain that the introduction of additional information by the conjunction *and* serves an expository purpose or that *the* is emphatic (in contrast to the indefinite article), so there was no need for Howe to explain the self-evident meaning of his phrase *Cursing and Swearing.*

[64] "But I say unto you, Swear not at all."

[65] "But above all things, my brethren, swear not, neither by heaven, neither by the earth, neither by any other oath."

Brand which is set upon the Tongue in that Chapter.[66] I wonder how in this *Lyncean*[67] perspicacity *It* oversaw a more remarkable errour of Mr. Howe's about *Actions in their Substance Evil;* where in the same pages, 33, 34. he writes it *Qoad Substantiam,* which could not be Mr. Howe's Inadvertency; for in that Paragraph he [30] also spells *Conseqence* and *Qestion* in the like manner, and therefore must by the same Consequence as that of Cursing and Swearing, have been a slip of his Judgment. But, had *It* continued to be so unmercifully accurate, Mr. Howe might perhaps have told *It Its* own; where p. 27. *It* mentions that *Evil Act of Adam's eating a Tree*[68] (for I see we are all mortal) which is a Phrase of very hard Digestion. Other proofs of this Head I reserve till further occasion, two or three instances upon each, being like so many Witnesses sufficient for *Its* Conviction. The second Article follows.

Its *Ignorance and Confusion about the*
Matter that is in Controversie.

First Instance. *The Discourse,* p.3. saith; *The Ambiguity of Mr. Howe's Phrases removed, and the sense of them being brought to a certainty, I assert the* [31] *Contradictory to his Proposition: the term* Efficacious *suiting well enough, if Mr. Howe intend by it an Infallibility of the Event, or the certain Production of those Actions which God hath an Influence upon.* Now, for the better understanding of this, it is fit to observe that Mr. Howe's Proposition is this; *God doth not by an Efficacious Influence universally move and determine Men to all their Actions, even those Actions that are most wicked.*[69] They that assert the Contradictory, must therefore affirm that God does: and much good may it do them. But *The Discourse* in the words before cited, capitulates that Mr. Howe should by *Efficacious* intend *Infallibility,* &c. *It* might almost as well have said *Transubstantiation,* which we shall meet with, p.35. hereafter.[70]

Now it is indeed fit that a Respondent should gratifie his Opponent as far as may consist with Civility and Safety. But here arises a Case of Con-

---

[66] "But the tongue can no man tame; it is an unruly evil, full of deadly poison. Therewith bless we God, even the Father; and therwith curse we men, which are made after the similitude of God. Out of the same mouth proceedeth blessing and cursing. My brethren, these things ought not to be so" (James 3:8–10).

[67] Lyncean: sharp-sighted.

[68] *TD*, p. 27, refers to "that act of Adam's will . . . of eating that tree."

[69] *Postscript*, p. 52.

[70] I.e., p. 35 of *TD*, cited later in *Remarks*, p. 470.

[32[71]]science; Whether a man may give another leave, that desires it, to speak Non-sense. I say no. For Non-sense and Idle words are of the same notion. But if he be one that I have no power over, and whom I can by no amicable means hinder from speaking Non-sense, I, after having used all good indeavours, am excused. But here the Case is stronger, where one shall not only take the Liberty himself, but oblige me too to speak Non-sense. To this I say, that to the best of my understanding, I never will, nor ought to do it in respect to any man. Yet no less a favour, or favours, doth *The Discourse* demand of Mr. Howe, in requiring that the term *Efficacious* may be expounded by *Infallibility,* that is, in effect, the most potent Influence by no Influence: For what Influence hath *Infallibility* upon the Actions of another, or upon anything? And this, if *It* should yet obtain it of Mr. Howe, [33] yet would consist as ill with his own following words, or *Certain Production;* wherein he more than implies that *Infallibility* and *Certain Production* are all one; whereas a man may certainly and infallibly know what he never produces, and some too, we see, produce what they never understand. But if *The Discourse* shall still opiniatre[72] in this matter, let *It,* to try how well it suits, strike *Efficacious,* for experiment, out of the Question, and insert instead of it, *Infallibility* and *Certain Production,* and then see if there be any sense in it or Grammar.

Second Instance. *The Discourse,* p.9. pretends to give a Definition of Predetermination. Predetermination, *It* saith, *is thus defin'd, A Transient Action of God, which excites every Creature to Act.* Now it is generally known, that the two most perfect Creatures in all Lo-[34]gick, are a Demonstration[73] and a Definition. How good *The Discourse* is at the first shall afterwards be remonstrated.[74] But as to a Definition, it alwaies consists, as being a Dialectick Animal,[75] of a Body which is the *Genus,* and a *Difference,* which is the Soul of the thing defined;[76] but this will in neither of these appear to be Perfect or Rational. For the *Genus* here is Action and yet a few lines

---

[71] 32 Ed] 33 R.

[72] opiniatre: persist in an opinion (see p. 405, n. 81, with p. 404, nn. 77, 79).

[73] Demonstration: logical argument, proof through deduction.

[74] remonstrated: demonstrated.

[75] I.e., a feature of logical argument.

[76] In classical logic, a *genus* is a class or group of concepts or things which includes a number of subordinate *species,* each sharing attributes with other species but each also distinguished by its distinctive characteristics, its *difference,* from other species in the same genus. For a contemporary account, see Milton, *Artis Logicae* (1673), in *CPW,* 8:301–07.

below *It* saith, that *Predetermination is to be conceived of* per Modum Principii, *under the Notion of a Principle, or Cause of the Creatures Acting, but Concourse only* per Modum Actionis. Predetermination was but even before under the *Genus* of Action, and now of Cause: so that *The Discourse* hath been very liberal indeed of Body to the Definition, having given it two rather than fail, though commonly we account such births [35] to be Errours of Nature, and monstrous.[77] Had *The Discourse* interposed some pages, it might have only argued a default of Memory; but this inconsistence at one sight, and before *Its* Pen could be taken off, shows that defect not to have been, as with some persons, recompensed in Judgment. And then for the Difference that is assigned in this Definition, it happens here as usually where there is most Body, that there is least Soul. For there is nothing else left to be the Difference, but, *whereby God excites every Creature to Act.* If this be all, *The Discourse* might indeed very well say, p.7. that Mr. Howe would be *forc'd to grant Predetermination;* for how could he possibly avoid it, when the Antagonist defines it in Mr. Howe's own words? who saith, *Postscript,* p.45. *In reference to sinful Actions; by this Influence God doth not only* [36] *sustain men who do them, and continue to them their natural faculties and powers whereby they are done; but also, as the first Mover, so far excites and actuates*[78] *those powers, as that they are apt and habile*[79] *for any congenerous*[80] *Action, to which they have a natural designation, and whereto they are not sinfully disinclin'd.* Whereby *God Excites* the Creature to Act, saith *The Discourse,* whereby *God Excites and Actuates those Powers to,* &c. saith Mr. Howe very fully here, and in all other places to the same sense; so that if *The Discourse* either understood Mr. Howe or it self, either *Its* own Definition, or the common Question, what place was there left for arguing, unless to debate for Debates sake? Usually when both parties say the same thing, there is an end of the discourse, but however of the Dispute: There is as [37] far as I see, no doubt to be made but Mr. Howe, as he hath, will grant this Predetermination even without *being forced,* but yet upon condition, and it is but reasonable that *The Discourse* will retract *Its* own foregoing words, p. 5. *This Act of God is called Predetermination, because it limits the*

---

[77] Nicholas Culpeper, *A Directory for Midwives* (1656), p. 109, includes the "double-bodied" among his examples of "monstrous Births." They were commonly supposed to result from the ill effects of the mother's imagination during pregnancy: see e.g. Culpeper, p. 109, and Jane Sharp, *The Midwives Book* (1671), pp. 116–20.

[78] *actuates*] *actuate* R (corrected in the list of errata).

[79] *habile:* suited.

[80] *congenerous:* of the same kind.

Creature to this Action rather than to that. This indeed will serve *The Discourse* for argument either of Discourse or Dispute with *It* self; being Definition in effect against Definition to prevent monstrosity, supplying hereby two Souls to the two Bodies. But till *It* be better agreed with it, and can come to a clearer understanding with *It* self, no third person needs or can be interested[81] in the Contest further than as a spectator of some strange sight for his money, like the double Child from Sussex.[82]

Third Instance. *The Discourse* [38] cites Mr. Howe, *Postscript*, p. 41. for having there said concerning *God's exciting Man to act* those foregoing words that I come last from mentioning. But those words are not p. 41. but p. 45. and the mistake in the citation is probably an errour[83] only of the Printer's. Though indeed in that page 41. Mr. Howe with much perspicuity declares the same Sense and Opinion which he gives in other expressions, p. 45. For p. 41. he saith, *It hath been the care and designment of the Divine Wisdom so to order the way of Dispensation towards the several sorts of Creatures, as not only, not ordinarily to impose upon them what they could not be patient of, but so as that their powers and faculties might be put upon the exercises whereof they were capable, and to provide that neither their Passive capacity should be overcharged, nor* [39] *their Active be unimployed.* But the words repeated and excepted against are to be found in his p. 45. and upon them it is that *The Discourse* fixes this unreasonable and ill interpretation and censure; *If by Exciting and Actuating the powers he means that God reduces them to Act, he hath taken a large jump from Durandus[84] to Twisse[85]*: and so goes on to prove that ill-favour'd and worse conceiv'd suggestion. It ought sufficiently to have prevented this usage that Mr. Howe's *Letter*, p. 43. hath said, *That which hath too apparently had greatest actual efficacy with many in asserting Predetermination, hath been*

---

[81] interested: concerned.

[82] "Monstrosities" such as Siamese twins were among the sights which might be viewed at fairgrounds for a fee (see Evelyn's diary under September 13, 1660 for an example); no other reference to this particular case has been located.

[83] an errour] any an errour *R* (corrected in the list of errata).

[84] Durandus of Saint-Pourçain (c. 1270–1332), a Dominican scholastic theologian, styled *Doctor modernus* and *Doctor resolutissmus*, bishop successively of Limoux (1317), Puy-en-Velay (1318), and Meaux (1326), whose principal work was a commentary on the *Sentences* of Peter Lombard. His criticism of Aquinas, his nominalist insistence that Platonic universals have no reality, and his stress on the limitations of rational inquiry led to his teaching being censured by his superiors and by the papacy.

[85] *from Durandus to Twisse:* i.e., from the moderation of Durandus to full-blown predestinarianism in Twisse, as Marvell goes on to explain.

the authority of this or that man of reputation, and the force of that Art of imput-
ing a Doctrine already under a prejudicial doom to some or other ill-reputed
former Writer, I profess not to be skill'd in the use of that sort of Weapons. And
[40] therefore, not being himself the Aggressor, but challenged and defied
by another, he ought to have had the choice of them. What signifies Durandus here, but to call a man ill names instead of coming to the Point? and what
Dr. Twisse, but to wear mail, or bring a second[86] when Mr. Howe comes
naked and single? It is not what this or that man, but what Truth saith that is
to be[87] regarded: what liberty soever *The Discourse* here takes to the contrary.
It can by no means be made true, that Mr. Howe by these words, *God as the*
first Mover so far excites and actuates those powers, as that they are apt and habile
for any congenerous Action; professes himself of Doctor Twisse's opinion, no
more than that he is of Durandus's after having thus declared his own as
clearly as it is possible for any man's meaning to be minuted or explain'd. [41]
For Durandus holds only a meer Conservation of the Faculty, Doctor Twisse
a Predetermination. But Mr. Howe, to avoid Durandus on the one hand,
saith, *that in reference to sinful actions (for of these is the Question) God doth not*
only sustain men who do them, and continue to them their natural faculties and
*powers (*which was all Durandus pretended to*) but also so far Excites and*
actuates those powers, as that they are apt and habile for any congenerous[88] *action,*
&c. whereas, if he would have spoke with Doctor Twisse, he must have said,
but also excites and actuates those powers *determinately* to this or that action,
which would have differ'd the whole breadth of Heaven from Mr. Howe's
Hypothesis. And certainly such an actual influence as Mr. Howe describes,
added to the Natural Faculty, is, if men look near, very distinguishable [42]
from meer *Conservation* of that Faculty on the one, and *Predetermination* on
the other side. For a Faculty conserved, as a Faculty, in *Actu Primo,*[89] (as men
call it) includes no such hability and present promptitude in it self to Action,
as Mr. Howe proposes; since then it could never suffer a Privation of it but
what were irrecoverable. Whereas common experience shews Faculties may
be sometimes unapt for Action, and may be supposed alwaies so, if every
moment when they act they be not rendred apt by a superadded Influence,
which may habilitate them for Action, without Determining them to This
or That. So that all the Confusion herein objected to Mr. Howe, is to be

[86] second: representative and supporter of a participant in a duel.
[87] be Ed.] he *R.*
[88] *congenerous* Ed.] *congeeruous R.*
[89] in *Actu Primo:* in the first impulse.

referred to that Head upon which I have charged it; and the great *Jump* is no more than what brain-sick Passengers, being carried [43] alongst by the Wind and Sea, in the heaving of their Vessel imagine of the Trees and Steeples. For he is still in the same place, but no man knows whither away *The Discourse* may be driven, or what port[90] *It* is bound to, and whether it do not fail without Steerage, Compass, or Anchor.

A Fourth Instance of *Its* Ignorance and Confusion about the matter in Controversie, is *Its* varying, and that so often and so materially, the Terms of the Question. First of all, *It* told us that *It* asserted the Contradictory of Mr. Howe's Proposition; which must be therefore by undertaking to prove (as was said formerly) *That God doth by Efficacious Influence universally Move and Determine Men to all their Actions, even those Actions that are most Wicked.* T.D. p. 3. yet immediately after having [44] joyn'd Issue upon this, *It* hath a second device, p. 4. and *better likes Strangius his state of the Question*, viz. *Whether God does Determine or Predetermine all Creatures to all and each of their Actions.*[91] And then Thirdly, p.5. *It* tells us more fully what the Question is, and how *Its* Predetermination is to be understood, explaining it thus (though not fully enough) *viz. an Act of God's by which he limits the Creature to this Action rather than to that.* Such an Act *The Discourse* hath granted at last, and 'twere to be reasonably expected, that, after having transformed the Question thus oft to *Its* own understanding and convenience, this Contradictory at least to Mr. Howe's Proposal should be adhered to as far as it goes, and maintained: For otherwise what occasion was there, or what imployment is there left for this [45] Spirit of Contradiction? unless to rattle through the Air, make vain Apparitions, or in a calm day on a sudden to stir up a Tempest. But if this be *The Discourses* Antiproposition, I that intermeddle not as an Opinionist either way, but endeavour only to comprehend as far as I can *Its* meaning, shall for that purpose put a Case in *Its* own terms.

Suppose a man to meet with some afflicting calamity which tends to provoke, among other his Passions, that of Aversion or Hatred. He considers this or that man may have contributed to his calamity: He considers also that God may have had an hand in bringing it upon him: He considers, perhaps, (and is yet Undetermined, till God at least Determine him) whether to put forth one Act of Hatred toward this man, or another, toward that [46] man, or another, toward God, or whether only to hate the

---

[90] port] part *R* (corrected in the list of errata).
[91] Strangius, *De Voluntate . . . Dei*, 2.4.155.

Evil it self that afflicts him. (For it cannot be that he should Hate this man by the same Act of Hatred with which he Hates another man, nor can he Hate God by the same Act whereby he Hates either of them, or the afflicting Evil that hath befaln him.) At last he is limited to this rather than another Action, and apprehending with that prophane person,[92] 2 *King.* 6.33. *Behold this Evil is from the Lord, what should I wait for the Lord any longer?* He pours out his Hatred against God himself. The Question now is, who limits him to this Action rather than to another? shall we say it is God? *The Discourse,* holding the Affirmative, must say it is God. This is indeed a dreadful representation of the Case, but a true one. [47]

Nor is it therefore to be wondred, the Question being so frightful, that *The Discourse* starts and runs away from it so often; and after all this, p. 9. would forget that *Predetermination is an Act by which God limits the Creature to this Action rather than that,* and undertakes to define it, exclusively to those words, (for the Definition includes the whole nature of the thing defined) no more but *a Transient Action of God which excites every Creature to Act.* And yet Fourthly, Considering that the Cause required no less; after taking breath, and comforting *Its* spirits, *The Discourse* returns again in part to the Question, telling us in the bottome of the same page, 9. *That it is in plain words whether God does Move men to all their natural Actions, and so to one rather than another.* And thus now we have a fourth State of the Question, but [48] yet very different from the First; the Affirmative of which was undertaken to be defended. In short, the main Controversie is about *Determining;* but this Fourth Question does not so much as mention it either in word or in sense. For the *Determining* in Mr. Howe's Proposition imports and is so express'd, not only a *Moving* men, but an *Efficacious Moving* them. (There are many Motions which may be Ineffectual.) Nor only a moving them to *This* Action rather than to *That,* but also to do *this Wicked* Action (for of such is the Controversie) *rather* than *forbear it.* What kind of practice is this? It is a worse thing to adulterate Truth than Mony. The Terms of the Question are the Standard. But at this rate no man can know what is *Meum* or *Tuum,*[93] which is his own Hypothesis, and which his Adversaries, while what he issued in [49] currant sense and weight is return'd him Clipp'd or Counterfeit. But the observation of this manner of dealing hath

[92] Jehoram, king of Israel.

[93] *Meum* or *Tuum:* mine or yours; in legal discourse, a summary way of defining individual property rights.

put me upon another thought much differing, and which at first perhaps may seem something extravagant.

The Camel is a beast admirably shap'd for Burthen, but so lumpish withall, that nothing can be more inept for feats of Activity. Yet men have therefore invented how to make it danse, that, by how much unnatural the spectacle might appear more absurd and ridiculous. Its Keeper leads it upon a Pavement so throughly warmed, that the Creature, not able to escape nor abide it, shifts first one foot, and then another to relieve it self, and would, if possible, tread the Air on all four, the ground being too hot for it to stand upon. He in the mean time traverses and trips about it at a [50[94]] cooler distance, striking some volunteer Notes on his Egyptian Kit,[95] like a French Dancing-Master. But, knowing that his Scholar is both in too much pain, and too dull to learn his measures, he therefore upon frequent observation accords a tune to its Figure and Footing, which comes to the same account. So that, after daily repeating the Lesson in private, they seem both at last to be agreed upon a new Arabick Saraband.[96] Having thus far succeeded, he tries next whether what he taught by torture be not confirm'd by custom, and if a cool Hearth may not have the like effect. The Camel no sooner hears his Fiddle, but, as if it's ears burned with the musick, and it's memory were in it's feet, the Animal bestirs forthwith it's long legs, and with many an Antick[97] Motion, and ill-favour'd *Coupe*,[98] gratifies the Masters [51] patience and expectations.[99] When he finds, upon constant experiment, that it never fails him, he thenceforward makes it publick, and having

[94] 50 Ed.] 52 *R.*

[95] Kit: small fiddle.

[96] Saraband: formal Spanish dance known in England from the early seventeenth century.

[97] Antick: grotesque, bizarre.

[98] *Coupe:* i.e., coupee, a dance step.

[99] This account of how a camel may be taught to dance derives from a passage entitled "The Camel Dromedary" in Edward Topsell, *The History of Four-Footed Beasts, Serpents, and Insects,* 2 vols. (1658), 1:78, which tells how a camel, repeatedly brought into a stable with a heated floor while a musician played, "not for the love of the musick, but for the heat under his feet, lifted up first one foot, and then another, as they do which dance . . . so that at last, use framed Nature to such a strain, that hearing a Timbrel, he instantly rembred the fire that was wont to punish his feet, and so presently would leap to and fro like a dancer in publick spectacle, to the admiration of all beholders."

compounded with the Master of the Revels,[100] shows it, with great satisfaction to the Vulgar,[101] every Bartholomew-Fair[102] in Grand-Cairo. I would not too much vex the similitude, but was run upon this by a resemblance it hath with some, who, not being fram'd at all for Controversie, and finding the Question too hot for them, do, by their flinching and shuffling from it, represent a Disputation, till it is grown habitual to them, and they change ground as often, and have the same apprehension of the sound of an Argument, as the Camel of an Instrument.

And yet *The Discourse* hath a Fifth loose Foot to clap on at need, as if Four had not sufficed to praevaricate with, p. 11. where *It* exercise *Its* [52] uncouth nimbleness in syllogizing: but never was any thing more ridiculously aukward. Mr. Howe had, *Letter* p.35. mentioned an argument used by those who hold the Affirmative of Predetermination; *That it necessarily belongs to the Original and Fountain-Being to be the First Cause of whatsoever Being, and consequently that what there is of Positive Being in any the most Wicked Actions, must principally owe it self to the Determinative Productive Influence of this First and Soveraign Cause, otherwise it would seem that there were some Being that were neither* Primum *nor a* Primo.[103] This was as plain and distinctly laid out as possible, but must forsooth be cast into a Logical Figure, where the officiousness argues the fraud, as of those who make false Plate imbezilling part of the Metal, and yet make the Owner pay moreover for the Fashion. This is *The Discourse*s Syllogism. *All Positive Beings are Effects of the First Cause. All sin-*[53]*full Actions* (for, *It* adds, *this is our limitation*) *are Positive Beings;* Ergo *All sinfull Actions, as Actions, are Effects of the First Cause.* So that here, by a Syllogistical Legerdemain,[104] that term so essential in their Argument, as cited by Mr. Howe, the *Determinative Productive Influence of the First and Soveraign Cause,* is cleanly conveyed away out of sight; the Proposition undertaken to be maintained, that *God doth by an Efficacious Influence universally Move and Determine Men to all their Actions, even those Actions that are most Wicked;* or, as *It* lately varied, *Limits Men to This Action rather than to That,* is turned out of doors by it's

---

[100] Master of the Revels: specifically, the title of a member of the royal household appointed to supervise court entertainments, and, more generally, any person in charge of a fair or festivity.

[101] Vulgar: common people.

[102] Bartholomew-Fair: fair held annually at Smithfield on August 24 (St. Bartholomew Day) from the twelfth to the nineteenth centuries.

[103] *neither* Primum *nor a* Primo: neither first nor from the beginning.

[104] Legerdemain: sleight of hand, trickery.

own foster-father, the keeping of it being grown it seems too chargeable; and all now that is inferred is only that *all sinfull Actions, as Actions are Effects of the First Cause.* And what is that to the purpose? If Mr. Howe must neither be allowed the use of his own Weapons, nor upon the Ground which [54] they both were agreed on, it appears that his Challenger, notwithstanding all *Its* bravades,[105] had no design or but little disposition to meet him. The whole of this may in a just sense be granted without prejudice to Mr. Howe's Cause. For it matters not that they are *Effects,* unless it be also said and proved that they are *Effects produced by God's Determinative Influence.* Yet how much Powder is spent without doing the least execution! First a Categorical, then an Hypothetical Syllogism fired at him,[106] then forces him to distinguish, which is among Disputants next to crying quarter, but will not give it him; runs him thorough with three Replies to his Distinction, and leaves him dead upon the place. While the Proposition is all this while untoucht, Mr. Howe is out of Gunshot, and his Adversary (if one that only skirmishes with himself, deserves to be called so) is afraid to take aim, and [55] starts meerly at the Report of his own Musquet. Thus hath *The Discourse* Five several times altered the Property[107] of the Question; which is my Fourth Instance of *Its* Ignorance and Confusion about the matter in Controversie; unless it ought to be interpreted as an argument rather of a strong brain, after so many times, and suddenly turning round, not to have faln down sensless.

A Fifth Instance to the same Head, Mr. Howe, *Letter,* p.36, 37. had said, *It seems infinitely to detract from the Perfection of the Ever Blessed God, to affirm that he was not able to make a Creature of such a Nature, as being continually sustained by him, and supplied with power every moment suitable to it's Nature, should be capable of acting, unless what he thus inables he* determine (*that is, for it can mean no less thing,* impel) *it to do it also.* To this *The Discourse* replies p. 15. *If we should take liberty of judging things by their* ap-[56]*pearance*[108] *at first sight, without giving our selves the trouble of a strict Disquisition* (take whether you will, the Liberty or the Trouble, only talk not so magisterially) *we might easily be seduced into an imagination that it does no less infinitely detract from the Divine Perfection to affirm; that God was*

---

[105] bravades: bravados.

[106] In a *categorical syllogism* the premises are unqualified and absolute; in a *hypothetical syllogism* one of the premises is conditional or speculative.

[107] Property: form, nature.

[108] *appearance* Ed.] *appearanee* R.

not able to make a Creature of such a Nature, as that it might continually sustain *it self, without a supply of power every moment from God. For that opinion seems to tye God to a shorter Tedder*[109] (how trivial and irreverently spoken!) *than an ingenious Artificer who can raise an Edifice that shall last many years without any need of his help for reparations.*[110] Compare now these two together, and mark what this Reasoning of *The Discourse* amounts to. Mr Howe conceives (else it were very hard) that a Creature may *Act*, being inabled by a continual supply of power from God every moment. Therefore quoth *It*, A Creature may *Be*, without being sustained [57] or supplied from God any moment. But this perhaps[111] was only to show how ingenious *Its* first apprehensions, and how candid are *Its* first inclinations; and whether *It* were *easily seduced* it self, or had a mind to seduce others, *It* likes this conceit so well that *It* cannot yet let it go, but subjoyns immediately; *And this I the rather take notice of, because I find it the sentiment of the most acute Suarez,* &c. But, whereas others find their second Thoughts to be the more judicious, *Its* judging thus *at First Sight*, seems more accurate than *Its* Second *Seeming:* They, *ib. who deny God's immediate operation in every action of the Creature, (which Mr. Howe seems to do in his Answer now under discussion) will doubtless be compelled to deny that the Creature does depend immediately upon the Actual Influence of God.* So *It* quotes the most acute Suarez. Met. Disp. 20.[112] This is a most exemplary and Primitive Charity, whereby *The* [58] *Discourse* hath sold all *Its* own acuteness to give it to the poor Suarez; so that it hath reduced it self to that desperate and utmost dulness, as herein to

---

[109] Tedder: tether.

[110] *reparations:* repairs.

[111] perhaps Ed.] parhaps *R.*

[112] Francisco de Suarez (1548–1617), Spanish Jesuit theologian whose *Disputationes metaphysicae* (1597) was hugely influential and cited with respect in the Reformed as well as the Roman Catholic tradition. In a series of writings on grace he developed the ideas of his Jesuit compatriot Luis de Molina (1535–1600) to argue that, rather than predetermining human actions, God effects the salvation of the elect by conferring grace upon those through whom he foresees it will be most beneficial. This grounding of salvation not in predestination but in divine foreknowledge of human cooperation with grace was by its opponents (Roman Catholic as well as Protestant) charged with giving priority to human works over the divine will. By Pope Pius V (reigned 1605–21) Suarez was styled *Doctor eximius*, that is, "exceptionally skilled" or "most distinguished," not unlike *TD*'s description of him as "most acute." Marvell is quoting the translation of Suarez given by *TD*, p. 15.

say,[113] *They who deny what Mr. Howe* seems *by this Answer to do,* that is as much as to say, They who suppose with Mr. Howe that a Creature may act being inabled by God every moment, without being impelled, (which he above, and alwaies modestly asserts) will doubtless be *compell'd to deny* that the Creature depends immediately upon the Actual Influence of God, which is tantamount in sense, which useth to be the meaning, as to say, It seems to be denied that the Creature does depend, because it is affirmed to depend. Ought not Bills[114] to be put up for men affected with so peculiar a distemper? I cannot in the whole Common Prayer find any that is proper for this occasion.

Another Instance (for they do so [59] multiply on me in reading, that I forget to number them, and yet they are so signal in their kind, that they are not to be omitted) is p. 96. and onward: the vain attempt to reconcile God's Predetermining by Efficacious Influence to Wicked Actions with his Wisdom and Sincerity by the same *Mediums* that were used by Mr. Howe to reconcile his Prescience of them, yet this is undertaken to be done from p. 96. for several pages forward, and with the same confidence which is alwaies necessary to such as promise impossibilities. But it is in the mean time an high contempt of all other men, and presumption of ones own Understanding that can imbolden to such an Argument. Who is there, unless Adam gave him his Name,[115] but sees the difference between having an Influence upon Men's Wicked Actions, and having no Influence, which Prescience, as such, cannot signifie him to have [60] that foreknows? But nevertheless Mr. Howe hath expresly enough asserted and explained the Influence God hath on all Humane Actions.

For further Instance, see what *The Discourse* saith, p.61. and so along, struggling to bring the immediate Concourse, which Mr. Howe speaks of and avows, under the same prejudice with Predetermination, which he disclaims and argues against: For all that idle indeavour might have been saved and prevented by a small supplement of Understanding or Memory. For Mr. Howe alwaies distinguishes (and so might any ordinary capacity for him, should he have trusted either that or men's common Ingenuity) between Concurring, though never so Immediately, by an Influence which doth *but Inable* to an Action, and by that which doth *Determine* to it, or

---

[113] What follows is made up largely of phrases from *TD,* p. 15.

[114] Bills: prayers, petitions.

[115] I.e., unless in a state of prelapsarian innocence (Gen. 2:20).

impell. If any man do but carry this about with him, as Mr. Howe does thorow his [61] whole troublesome Journey, it is a certain remedy against all Gauling,[116] at least by this Argumentation.

One thing I could not but remark here, p.61. of *The Discourse* in passing, how jovial *It* is and bucksom,[117] which is just the humour of Tyrants, bloodily cruel, and yet at the same time full of dissoluteness and laughter. *I will pause a little with the Readers leave, and try my skill what answer I can excogitate for Mr. Howe which will not be a common friend to us both* (pleasant) *as we have been hitherto one to another, and I hope shall remain notwithstanding this Publick Contest.* Dear Damon, doubtless.[118] But I perceive not that Mr. Howe hath yet had any Contest with you, nor, if I can perswade him, is he likely to have for the future, but will avoid you for several reasons. Is this your friendship? what then and how terrible [62] is your Malice? The Ancient Contests of Friendship, and which made some pairs so illustrious, were which of them should die for the other, not which should cut the others throat. The utmost that I have observed upon such Publick Contests, or that I think a man is bound to in Christianity, hath been to pardon such a Friend, and bid him do his office. Here is to be seen or play'd *T.D.* indeed, or *Amity a la Mode.* But go on, *This Distinction is an open Friend to us, and to which therefore upon all fit occasions we pay our respects.*[119] This is prity, and most softly said, as if it were by the Great Mogul[120] lying upon a silken-bed, and leaning upon Cushions. And besides, 'tis a new Invention, being the first time this that ever I heard of a man that contracted Friendship with a Distinction; but most wise men, (and so I think should Mr. Howe), [63] have been used to distinguish with whom they contract it. To

---

[116] Gauling: galling, rubbing till sore.

[117] bucksom: i.e., buxom, amiable, good-tempered.

[118] An ironic allusion to the description in Cicero, *De Officiis,* 3.10.45, of the perfect friendship between Damon and Phintias.

[119] *TD*, p. 61: The first of the three "answers" which Danson "excogitates" to Howe's allowance of predestination to good but not to evil acts is that "immediate concurrence, as to sinful actions, divides between the action and the sinfulness; so that 'tis only the action as such, which is Gods and mans at once: the sinfulness of it is to be attributed to man only. And this distinction is an open friend to us, and to which therefore upon all fit occasions we pay our respects."

[120] Great Mogul: although *Mogul* is from *Mongol* and from the early seventeenth century was used in this sense, and of followers of Genghis Khan and of Tamberlaine in particular, the title *Great Mogul* referred to the emperors of Delhi who ruled northern India (Hindustan or "Cambaya"), thought of as types of luxury and despotism.

proceed, speaking of Determination and Concurrence, these are the words; *But that it waits a fitter time to speak out* Her *mind,* She *could say that* She *conceives not how* She *can compel the Will,* &c.[121] (of this compelling the Will, I shall have occasion also to speak out my mind hereafter.) What use was to be made of a *She* in this place, I cannot well Imagine. At last *The Discourse* grows perfectly wanton. *If* immediate Concurrence *thinks* Her self *disobliged to satisfie an inquisitive Curiosity as to the* Modus[122] *or manner how* She *joyns with the Creature in an Action to which Sin does necessarily adhere,* &c.[123] What would a man think of this? A Female! *An immediate Concurrence!* What sport were here prepar'd for that which is by our Moderns called Wit, but [64] is no more than the luxuriant sterility of Land, nor broken up or manured! In the mean time, if *The Discourse* be really at so much ease, as *It* would seem by this way of talking, 'tis but a security of understanding, like that of Conscience wherewith guilty persons confirm and deceive themselves for the present.

I shall now come to the last Instance of this Article. Not that I want abundance of more, or might not produce the whole Book in evidence, but because it were time that I came to some period: And lest *The Discourse* should think I avoided *Its* main strength, I shall there examine *It,* where *It* pretends to no less than Demonstration. For never was there thing so

---

[121] *TD*, pp. 61–62: The second of the "answers" Danson "excogitates" is that "if it be granted divine concurrence is as immediate to evil, as to good actions . . . yet that does not necessitate or compel the will to any elicite act, [i.e., inward acts of willing or nilling]: neither does Predetermination judg it self guilty, as to any such crime; for that does but put the creature upon that action, which is produced by Gods immediate concurrence with it. And but that it wants a fitter time to speak out her mind, she could say, That she conceives not how she can compel the will to any act, without compelling God himself: seeing one and the same act thereof, is as truly Gods as the creatures."

[122] Modus: mode (perhaps in the particular philosophical sense denoting the way in which attributes or qualities combine, of which *OED*'s first illustrative citation is from Howe in 1675 and, in its English form *mode,* from Gale's *Court of the Gentiles* in 1677).

[123] *TD*, p. 62: The third "answer," of which Marvell here quotes the opening words, continues: "Seeing the thing it self is plain, that so strict is the dependence of the creature upon the Creator, that it cannot act without Gods immediate concurrence: Predetermination claims the same priviledg upon the like ground, that the creature cannot exert its natural powers, till they be applied to action, nor determine it self to action, till it be determined; which determination cannot include a compulsion of the will (which is the main, if not the only controversie), for if the will act spontaneously, and from precedent deliberation, how is it forced? if it do not, how is it a will, *i.e.,* a rational appetite?"

dreadfully accoutred and armed *Cap-a-pe*[124] in Logick, Categorical and Hypothetical Syllogisms, Majors, Minors, Enthymems, Antecedents, Consequents, [65] Distinctions, Definitions,[125] and now at last *Demonstration*, to pin the basket:[126] Terms that good Mr. Howe as a meer novice is presum'd to be unacquainted with, and so far from being able to endure the ratling of *The Discourses* Armour, that as those Roman Legions once bragg'd, even the sweaty smell of *It*'s Arm-pits would be sufficient to rout him.[127] But some Creatures are as safe by their weaknesse, as others by their strength, from being medled with by a considerable Adversary. I that cannot boast of any extraordinary faculty for Disputation, nor yet confess my self void of common understanding, am therefore the most proper perhaps to try the force of this Demonstration; and whether *The Discourse* be not therein as feeble, as it was lately short in Definition. *It* p.25. quotes Mr. Howe, *Postsc.* p.28. that he does *really be-*[66]*lieve God's* Immediate Concourse *to all* Actions *of his Creatures both* Immediatione Virtutis & Suppositi,[128] *yet not* Determinative to Wicked Actions; then *The Discourse* proceeds: *We shall adventure*[129] *a Demonstration that it implies a Contradiction for God to make a Creature that can Act without Predetermination*, i.e.

---

[124] *Cap-a-pe:* i.e., *cap-à-pie*, from head to foot.

[125] In the terminology of logic, the premises are unconditional in a *categorical syllogism* but in a *hypothetical syllogism* at least one of them is conditional or speculative; of the three parts of a syllogism, the *major premise* contains the predicate of the conclusion (the major term), the *minor premise* contains its subject (the minor term), and the middle term occurs in both premises but not in the conclusion; an *enthymeme* is a syllogism in which one of the premises is implied but not stated; an *antecedent* is the conditional premise of a hypothetical syllogism and a *consequent* is the conclusion of a hypothetical syllogism. For guidance to contemporary usage, see e.g. the seventh part ("Of the Art of Logick") of John Newton, *The English Academy* (1677), pp. 171–204, and Milton's definitions in his *Artis Logicae* (1672) in *CPW*, 8:350–89, though Marvell's rhetorical effect here depends rather upon the rebarbative accumulation of logical terms than upon their precise meanings.

[126] to pin the basket: to conclude the matter.

[127] A source for this pun on Latin *ala* ("armpit" and "cavalry wing of an army") has not been traced.

[128] Immediatione . . . Suppositi: "By the directness of its power and the circumstances through which it operates." This common distinction in medieval theology between the intrinsic power (*virtus*) of an action, thought, or utterance, and its context, reference, or field of operation (*suppositum*) is adduced by *Postscript*, p. 28, "that I may more comply with his [Gale's] Scholastic humour, in the use of such terms, than gratifie my own."

[129] *adventure* Ed.] *adveuture* R.

applying it to Action and to one rather than to another Action. And 'tis this, That such a Creature would be but Ens Secundarium, *a Second Being, not* Causa[130] Secunda *a Second Cause, or (which is all one) God should be but* Ens Primum, *not* Causa Prima, *The First Being, not the First Cause,* which it proves thus: 1. *If God does concur only by* Simultaneous (an elegant term of *The Discourse*'s own production) *Concourse, and not by* Predetermination, *or Previous Motion, then God cannot be the Cause of the Actions of the Creatures, as they* [67] *proceed from them: But the Consequent is absurd, and it presumes Mr. Howe will not own it.* What Mr. Howe may do, being thus hard put to it, I will not undertake: but surely there was never any thing affirm'd with less truth or sense than *The Discourse* here doth, that *God should be the Cause of the Actions of the Creatures, as those Actions proceed from them.* One would think the Creatures themselves should be the Cause of the Actions as they *proceed from them;* (for how otherwise are they Causes at all of those Actions?) and God the Cause of those Actions as they *proceed from him.* Now how they proceed from him Mr. Howe hath sufficiently shown his own conception of it, *viz; as they are done by a sufficient Influence, which God Immediately affords to inable the Creature to do them, not to Determine it thereto.* And is not [68] God to be entitled a *Causa Prima* as well as *Ens Primum,* in reference to what is done by his influence in the way before expressed? Whereas, if God be the Cause of the Action of the Creatures, as those Actions proceed from *Them,* the Action must be done by his Influence alone, and then he should not be *Causa Prima,* because then there were no *Causa Secunda.* But this was only sure *The Discourse*'s Demon—and the next that follows it—stration.

Mr. Howe had, as before cited, *Postsc.* p.28. avowed God's Immediate Concourse to all Actions of his Creatures, both *Immediatione Virtutis & Suppositi.* Upon which Concession of his *It* argues thus (with this prelusory[131] vaunt, p.26. *He is twice killed that is killed with his own Weapon,*[132] so that no less than sudden Death is to be expected in the case.) *If there be an Immediate Concourse,* [69] *then there is a Predetermination or putting the Creature upon Action before it Acts: or else the Creature is the First Mover of it self to Action.* This is so unimaginably dull an argument, that really it

---

[130] Causa Ed.] (Causa *R.*

[131] prelusory: preliminary.

[132] Why *TD,* p. 26, should style this "the English Proverb" is not clear. It was not included in John Ray, *A Collection of English Proverbs* (1670) and is not known to Morris Palmer Tilley, ed., *A Dictionary of Proverbs in England in the Sixteenth and Seventeenth Centuries* (Ann Arbor, 1950).

requires a proportionable dulness in the Reader, or an extraordinary acuteness to comprehend it, and how it should be deduced from Mr. Howe's Concession of Immediate Concourse. For the argument so put receives not the least strength, not any, from that Concession of Mr. Howe's, but rather from his Non-concession, and that he hath not yielded enough, and as much as *The Discourse* would have him, which pretends that Immediate Concourse alone is not sufficient to exclude the Creature from being the First Mover of it's own Actions. For, whether Immediate Concourse be granted, or not granted, the case is all one as to this ar-[70]gument while so much is not granted whereby *an account may be given how God and the Creature joyn in one individual Action rather than another* as *The Discourse* would have it, p. 27.[133] if Mr. Howe could have been perswaded to be thus Demonstrated out of his Reason.

The Illustration of *Its plausible Consequence*, as 'tis called p. 27.[134] may perhaps be noted, and shall hereafter in it's due place, but the Demonstration carries the Bell away,[135] and I must yet follow it's tinkling. And thus *It* goes on p. 27, 28. *An account how the particular Actions of any rational Creatures Will come to be Determined, upon the exclusion of Predetermination, I know none can be given.* And how is this[136] proved? for sure to affirm it is not Demonstration. Why, thus. *Not by Chance:* (unless this saying so be an Instance that it may in some cases) no body [71] dream'd of any such thing, but this was put in, I suppose, only for more harmony, & to run Division.[137] A good slight[138] it is, by proving first a thing which no man denies to make it more credible that the argument upon the Subject in Controversie will be as cogent. For the Question is upon *Its* Second Member, *Not by the Creatures Self-determining Power,* and here *The Discourse*s main strength comes upon trial. *For that, as such, is indeterminate as to the Acts to which we conceive it must be some way or other Determined.* Admirably good! so it is indeed till the Creature, as Mr. Howe conceives, have Determined it self: and so it will be too if God be to Determine it, Indeterminate till he have Determined it. But if the Creature do Determine it self (which if it never do, how does *The Discourse* call it *a Self-determining Power?*) then I hope it is not Indetermi-

---

[133] *Recte TD,* pp. 26–27.

[134] *Recte TD,* p. 26.

[135] carries the Bell away: wanders on (as a cow or sheep with a bell around its neck).

[136] this Ed.] thus *R.*

[137] to run Division: to execute a variation on a melody.

[138] slight: i.e., sleight, ruse.

nate. So [72] that the whole stress of the Cause which was to prove that the Creature (*so Influenced and Actuated by God Immediately for any congenerous Action,* as Mr. Howe hath exprest it) cannot Determine it self, is left in the lurch, and no Demonstration hath been given hitherto, but of that Confusion and Ignorance with which I have charged *The Discourse* in this Article, about the matter in Controversie.

But *It* argues further, p. 28, 29. and, with the same Demonstration, from a second Concession (it were methinks more ingenuous, to call it a Declaration or Assertion) of Mr. Howe's of God's Immediate Concourse and Predetermination to the Production of Good Actions, and the necessity thereof, pretends to infer the Necessity of God's Immediate Concourse and Predetermination likewise to all (that is, even to the most Wicked) Actions. But this [73] beside the ridiculousness, is so odious an undertaking, that any pious man, should he be superiour in the contention, would repent of his Victory; I shall here wave[139] it; but if *The Discourse* pride it self herein, I give *It* the Joy as *It* deserveth.

This Demonstration I had assigned as the last Instance of this Head; but I think I may be dispensed with[140] to add another, it being an Act of Charity. For there are yet behind six Articles[141] more, some of them of a more criminal and hainous[142] nature than those two that hitherto I have insisted upon.

1. Its *Falsifications and Fictions of what Mr. How hath not said.*
2. Its *Injurious Perverting of what he hath said.*
3. Its *Odious Insinuations concerning what there is no colour to object against.*
4. Its *Insolent Boasting and* [74] *Self-applause upon no occasion.*
5. Its *Gross Absurdities, Inconsistencies, Self-contradictions, and Unsafe Expressions.*
6. *The Wrath and Virulence of* Its *Spirit.*

And oftentimes it chances that one and the same Instance is applicable, and may be reduced to several of these Heads. But therefore, as oft as I can impute any thing which might receive an higher accusation to *Its* Ignorance, Confusion or Dulness (which it is left in any man's self-determining power to remedy) I rather chuse to state it upon this more innocent account. And that hath been the Cause which hath swell'd this Head beyond equality: my

---

[139] wave: i.e., waive.
[140] be dispensed with: be excused, receive a dispensation.
[141] articles Ed.] Aricles R.
[142] hainous: heinous.

intention, being to be briefer on those that follow. I say therefore, that it is out of Charity that I here attribute *Its* Indifference between the *Modus* of God's Prescience, and God's supposed Prede-[75]termination to Wicked Actions to *Its* stupidity rather than any other Article, or make a new one for it on purpose. The thing is thus.

Mr. Howe *Letter,* p. 47, 48, 49, 50. had, taking notice of an Argument which some use from God's Prescience for his Predetermination, said, among other things, very piously; *This supposed Indetermination of the Humane Will, in reference especially to Wicked Actions, is far from being culpable of inferring that God cannot therefore foreknow them,* &c. And after, upon consideration what others had endeavoured towards explaining or perplexing this matter, modestly adds, *For my own part, I can more easily be satisfied to be ignorant of the* Modus *or* Medium *of his Knowledge, while I am sure of the thing,* &c. *It cannot therefore be so affrightful a thing to suppose God's Foreknowledge of the most Contingent* [76] *Future Actions well to consist with our Ignorance how he foreknows them, as that we should think it necessary to overturn and mingle Heaven and Earth rather than admit it.* But *The Discourse,* p.32, 33. signifies, and then by quoting some of these words would confirm it, that we need not be more sollicitous, and are no more concerned to satisfie our selves of the *Modus* of Predetermination to sinful Actions, so as to separate them from the sinfulness of them, (for to hold the conclusion is with *It* Demonstration) than about the *Modus* of God's Prescience of them. Which must argue (whatever else) a palpable shortness of discourse to think there is no odds betwixt a thing so plainly reveal'd in the Word of God as his Prescience is, and so agreeable to all rational apprehension, and a Notion so altogether unrevealed as this uni-[77]versal Predetermination yet appears, and so contrary if not to the whole scope and design of Divine Revelation, yet to all common understanding and genuine sense of right Reason. But whensoever there shall be so clear proof made that there is such a thing as *The Discourses* Predetermination, as may soon be brought of Prescience, when it shall be as duly stated among the Divine Attributes, then, and not till then ought men to practise the same devout resignation of their reasoning about it, as Mr. How hath laudably done in that of Prescience: but in the mean time it may be handled not as *Causa Dei,* but *Causa Hominis,*[143] it is lawful to plead against it, and not to pay mens belief, but to afford their Charity to its abetters.

[143] not as *Causa Dei,* but *Causa hominis:* not as the cause of God but as the cause of men (that is, not a matter of revelation but a legitimate subject of dispute).

There was one called Antipheron, whose name therefore seems rather to have been given him by the [78] people from a natural defect they observed in him than by his Godfathers:[144] He had a peculiar shortness of sight, but which turned him to account, and saved him the expence of sending to Malamocco[145] or Lambeth to the Glass-house.[146] He needed not so much as contemplate himself in Polyphemus his mirrour, the water.[147] He carried his Looking-glass alwaies with him, the next Air supplied all, and serv'd him not only to breath, but to see his face in, without any danger of staining or breaking it. A great convenience thus to be able every minute to blow himself a new Looking-glass. But how happy were it, if, what the shortness of his sight, the dulness of mens minds could have the same effect, to object to them[148] continually their own Image, and make it unnecessary for others to represent them. Then might *The Discourse* also have excused me [79] from this labour, and upon reflexion with it self, have discern'd *Its* own unfitness and ignorance to manage this or any other Controversie.

For want of such an immediate inspection on *Its* own defects, *Its* natural undistinctness seems to perceive faults in others, and to find a mote in their eye, neglects the Beam in *Its* own.[149] *It* overlooks so gross a practice as in *Its* p. 47. to translate out of Strangius into English Doctor Twisse's Argumentation about the same Prescience of God of future Contingencies, undertaking still to demonstrate, p.46 (that is the word) that this Foreknowledge depends upon the Divine Decree, while in the meantime *It* never gives us,

---

[144] Antipheron is apparently a coinage, from the Greek ἀυτιφέρω, "to set against, oppose," perhaps with reference to his having to stand intimidatingly close before he can recognize anyone, or to his being cross-eyed.

[145] Malamocco: one of the original lagoon settlements which make up Venice, famed for glasswork (including the making of mirrors).

[146] About 1670, under the patronage of the duke of Buckingham, a number of Venetian glassmakers were established at Lambeth, in Vauxhall Square, to manufacture looking glasses by the then new method of flint glassmaking (introducing lead into the glass's composition). On September 19, 1676 Evelyn visited "the *Duke of Bouckingams Glasse worke,* where they made huge *Vasas* of mettal as cleare & pondrous & thick as Chrystal, also *Looking-glasses* far larger & better than any that come from Venice." There is still a street in Lambeth named Glasshouse Walk (Alexander Nesbitt, *Glass* [1875], p. 131; Walter Thornbury, *Old & New London,* ed. Edward Walford, 6 vols. [1873–78], 6:424).

[147] The Cyclops Polyphemus uses a pool as a mirror by which to groom himself in preparation for the wooing of Galatea in Ovid's *Metamorphoses,* 13.767.

[148] to object to them: to present to their sight.

[149] Matt. 7:3.

though the Book was in *Its* hand, Strangius his full and articulate answer to it in the same place, lest any man should know of it; but, to conceal *Its* own disability for any reply to it, challenges Mr. Howe to [80] answer Doctor Twisse's irrefragable Argument over again.[150] But p. 16. in Mr. Howe *It* can find two *unpardonable faults in a man of Learning and Ingenuity.*

First, Anticipation, For, he having *Letter,* p.36, 37, said, *unless he*[151] *Determine (that is to say, for it can mean no less thing,* Impel,) that is the word accused, *the Creature*[152] *to do it;* this is made so hainous, that I thought at first it had been the Anticipation of the Revenue,[153] but, when all comes to all, I see it is nothing but the explaining a word of less obvious import by another more obvious: and nothing is more usual in *The Discourse* it self, and among men of Learning. And *The Discourse* it self adds here in the same minute *Impelling,* i.e. *Compelling (for that is Mr. Howe's sense of the term,* as *will appear ere long)* which is methinks as early, and a more perverse Anticipation than Mr. Howe is unpardonable for, by how much *It* [81] does by these last words own that Impel, unless it signifie Compel, is allowable, but affirms that in Mr. Howe's sense it is Compel, as will appear ere long, which is moreover false, and therefore I will be so subtile as to take out my pardon in time for calling this Anticipation; for indeed that which neither is, nor ever can appear, *ere long or short* (as for Mr. Howe, to mean Compel) cannot be Anticipated.

---

[150] *TD,* pp. 46–47, does at least acknowledge that the "learned Strangius" opposes Twisse's argument, "but not with strength enough to overthrow it" (with a reference *De Voluntate . . . Dei,* 3.9.626). Later, Danson acknowledges one of Strangius's objections to Twisse's argument has "some probability" (p. 50), that he does not "wholly dislike" Strangius's modifications of Twisse's syllogisms (p. 50), and that he has not "had time to examine Strangius throughly since he came to my hands, (which was long after Mr. H.'s *Letter and Postscript* came out" (p. 51).

[151] I.e., God. Howe is arguing against divine concurrence with, and predetermination of, evil actions in a passage which is again cited, again in part, on p. 449 below: "it may well be thought sufficiently to salve the rights and priviledg of the first Cause, to assert that no action can be done but *by a power derived from it;* which, in reference to forbidden actions, intelligent Creatures may use or not use as they please . . . Besides, that it seems infinitely to detract from the Perfection of the ever Blessed God, to affirm he was not able to make a Creature, of such a nature, as, being continually sustained by him . . . should [not] be capable of acting, unless whatsoever he thus *enables,* he *determines* (that is, for it can mean no less thing, *impel*) it to do also."

[152] *Creature* Ed.] *Creatuue* R.

[153] Anticipation of the Revenue: expenditure of national income before it has been received.

But the second unpardonable fault of Mr. Howe's is his *immodest begging the Question:* And wherein? *I may well call it so* (quoth *The Discourse*) *because he knows we neither can nor will grant his Argument without ruining our Hypothesis.* This is all the proof assigned of his begging the Question. I do indeed confess that Mr. Howe was much to blame in urging an Argument to the ruine of their precious Hypothesis; but I think it falls not under that Predicament[154] of [82] begging, though this does of robbing the Question: and however his crime is more excusable, because, in common probability, Mr. Howe, having writ his *Letter* and *Postscript* before *The Discourse* replied to him, might be ignorant that it was *Its* dear Hypothesis. For my part I take the very first Title of the Book, *de Causa Dei,* to be more notoriously guilty both of Anticipation and Begging the Question, than that Mr. Howe could have any thing upon either account herein justly imputed or objected to him.

The third Article[155] of which I shall Catalogue some, it being endless to enumerate all the Instances.

> Its *many strange Falsifications & Fictions of*
> *what Mr. Howe hath not said, and then*
> *discoursing of them as if they were said.*

As for a first Instance. In *Its* Epistle,[156] p. 10,[157] Mr. Howe is accused of [83] having *denyed God's Immediate Concurrence to all Actions,* because *Letter* p.36. he saies (not, as *The Discourse* cites it, *it sufficiently salves,* but) *it may well be thought sufficiently to salve the rights (and priviledges,* omitted) *of the first Cause that no Action can be done but by a power derived from it, which, in reference to forbidden Actions, intelligent Creatures may use or not use as they please.* Is anything said here that implies any denial of Immediate Concurrence? Why may not that Power derived be Immediate to the Action? Is any thing said to the contrary, or which accords not well with what is pretended to be said *ex opposito?* But, to make this Accusation good, *It* conceals another passage in the very same Paragraph. *Besides that it seems infinitely to detract from the perfection of the Ever Blessed God, to affirm he was not able to make a Creature of such a nature, as, being continually sustained by him, and supplied with power every moment* [84] *suitable to its nature, should*

---

[154] Predicament: assertion, charge.

[155] Article] Artice *R* (corrected in the list of errata).

[156] Epistle] Epistles *R* (corrected in the list of errata).

[157] I.e., *TD,* sig. A6v (the prefatory epistle to Howe is unpaginated).

be capable of Acting, unless whatsoever he thus Inables he Determine it to do also.[158] So that the charge is founded meerly upon Mr. Howe's not having used the express word Immediate Concurrence in that sentence, and in concealing disingenuously what he had expressed, and what fully includes Immediate Concurrence in the sense that he afterwards asserts and explains it, *Postsc.* p. 28. to be both *Immediatione Virtutis,* and *Suppositi* to *all Actions, though not Determinative to Wicked Actions.* Although it would be something ridiculous to say, that *The Discourse* read one part of this with *Its* eyes shut, and the other part with *Its* eyes open; yet 'tis more false that Mr. Howe did there, or any where else deny God's Immediate Concurrence; and 'tis the best excuse of which this (otherwise Forgery) is capable.

Second Instance. It feigns in the same p. 10 that Mr. Howe hath *Postsc.* [85] p. 39. affirm'd *Predetermination to all Actions.* It were strange if he should, but pretended to be proved by these his words, *The Active Providence of God above all the Actions of Men, consists not meerly in giving them the natural powers, whereby they can work of themselves, but in a real Influence upon those powers.* This is (to speak the most softly, and indeed more softly than the thing will admit) an unkind Interpretation, after what Mr. Howe hath been quoted to say in my former Instance: but especially, if *The Discourse* can or would be pleased to consider (after *Its* invidious and deceitful generality in citing *Letter,* from p. 32, to 50. and the *Postscript,* without assigning one word)[159] that Mr. Howe's asserting here of God's real Influence upon mens natural powers does not at all imply that Predetermination, which he there all along opposes. For can there be no Influence but such as is Determining? He hath [86] shown there both may be and is. How often is there such Influence by the operation of Common Grace[160] as doth not Determine?

Third Instance. In the same p. 10.[161] Because Mr. Howe hath *Letter,* p. 32. said, *Some Actions of the Creatures are in themselves most malignantly wicked,* and *Letter,* p.46. *Intrinsecally Evil;* therefore *It,* falsly enough, reproaches him to have by these words *denied that all Actions have in them a Natural Goodness:* Whereas Mr. Howe here speaks of Actions as they are

---

[158] *Letter,* pp. 36–37 (quoted in full above, n. 151).

[159] *TD,* pref. ep. sig. A7v: "This is the design of all your *Letter,* from p. 32 to 50. and of the *Postscript.*"

[160] Christian discussion of soteriological issues commonly distinguished between *common* (or *sufficient*) grace, which sustains and inspires all human beings, and *special* (or *efficacious*) grace, reserved for the regeneration of the elect.

[161] I.e., *TD,* pref. ep. sig A6v.

Morally Evil or Wicked, that is, as specified by direction to an undue Object. Is not such a specifying Direction *Intrinsecal?* Is not the specification of every thing Intrinsecal to it? And so are not such Actions truly said to be Evil in themselves which so specified can by no Circumstances be made good. But *Postsc.* p. 36. (which is produced[162] to argue him of Inconsistence) he owns that *there is* [87] *not any Action so sinful, but hath some natural good as the substrate*[163] *matter thereof,* abstractly and physically considered, (and yet so they can never be produced by God or Man, but concreted with their Individuating Circumstances[)]; nor doth the Affirming the one, infer the Denial of the other. If it did, *The Discourse* it self hath done the same thing, p. 72. *Thus some Actions are said to be in themselves Evil, when they are Evil in regard of their Object,* &c. *Thus the Hatred of God and Adultery are in themselves Evil,* &c.[164] But I suppose 'twould judge it hard dealing to say that hereby *It* denies (though it be an hard saying to affirm) that natural good which is the substrate[165] matter thereof, and which alwaies at a dead lift[166] *It* hath recourse to.

Fourth Instance. From Mr. Howe's having *Letter,* p. 33. said, *Nothing is more apparently a simple and most strictly natural impossibility, than not to do an Action where-*[88]*to the Agent is Determined by an Infinite Power. It Epist.* p. 11[167] hath the ridiculous grosness to charge Mr. Howe with there affirming that Predetermination forces the Will; as if nothing could make a thing naturally impossible to a man but force: he cannot make a new Sun: but what force hinders him? This is indeed Force, or rather Fraud; for

---

[162] is produced Ed.] isproduced *R.*

[163] *substrate*] *substract R* (corrected in the list of errata); see n. 163.

[164] Discussing the phrase "in themselves most malignantly wicked," *TD,* pp. 71–72 says, "Those actions are said to be in themselves evil which are a breach of the Law of nature, and so are opposed to those which are evil only by a positive law . . . Thus the hatred of God, and Adultery, are in themselves evil, because no end or circumstance can make them good; but giving alms out of vain glory is not in it self evil, because changing the end, the action is good, that before was bad."

[165] substrate: underlying. *OED's* earliest citations is from part 4, book 3 of Theophilus Gale, *The Court of the Gentiles* (1678), p. 5: "Sin, as to its *material constitution,* has for its substrate matter or subject some natural good." Gale had used the word a year earlier in book 2 of part 4 (1677), p. 523, in a passage to which *Postscript,* p. 32, citing Gale's usage, replies.

[166] at a dead lift: when at an impasse, when nothing else can be done (used of the predicament of a horse harnessed to a weight beyond its power to move). Cf. *Essay,* p. 138.

[167] I.e., *TD,* pref. ep., sig. A7.

otherwise it is impossible to deduce it. But whether [either] of them be used against a chosen adversary, makes it seems no scruple in a Conscience diverted with Disputation.

Another Instance. *It* calumniates Mr. Howe, p. 87, to have *asserted the Positivity*[168] *of Sin,* and there calls it, *the foundation of his Hypothesis,* proceeding with great pains to disprove it *borrows one Argument,* to load[169] him with, *from the most Learned Dr. Barlow, the now renowned Bishop of Lincoln,*[170] urges the *Minor,* then the *Major,* and draws up a [89] whole Process, as if it were in the Spiritual Court, against him, and *T. D.* were become his Chancellour.[171] There is none in England, nor especially Mr. Howe, as I imagine, but would reverence the Authority of that Excellent Person in all points of Learning or Controversy.[172] But *The Discourse* is too bold to make use of his Power without his Commission, in a Case where Mr. Howe hath not said one word to affirm such Positivity.

A further Instance. With the same Truth that is Falshood *It* feigns, and that often, that Mr. Howe by God's having Irresistible Influence upon the Will means *God's Forcing of the Will unto the most Wicked Actions.* As for

---

[168] *Positivity:* having positive identity. *OED* again cites Theophilus Gale, *The Court of the Gentiles* (1678), 4.3.8: "We grant . . . that sin is not a *mere nothing,* but has some kind *of logic positivitie* or *notional entitie,* so far as to render it capable of being the terme of a Proposition."

[169] load] lead *R* (corrected in the list of errata).

[170] *TD,* pp. 87–88: "We shall now proceed to raze the foundation of his Hypothesis, by proving, that there are no actions of free agents evil in themselves; or that no moral evil is positive, but only privative . . . And I shall borrow one Argument, which will be instead of all, from the most learned Dr. Barlow, the now Renowned Bishop of Lincoln. Arg. *Every real and positive Being is from God the author and first cause of all Being. But moral evil [formally] taken, is not from God the author and first cause of all Being.* Ergo, *moral evil [formally taken] is not a real and positive Being."* The point is developed on pp. 88–89.

[171] Chancellour: here, an officer responsible for conducting cases in ecclesiastical courts on behalf of a bishop.

[172] Thomas Barlow (1607–91), formerly fellow and provost of Queen's College, Bodley's librarian, and Lady Margaret Professor of Divinity at Oxford, and since 1675 bishop of Lincoln, was a moderate Calvinist sympathetic to nonconformists (in 1667–68 he was involved in negotiations to comprehend them within the established church, as was Howe in 1680). Barlow was a friend of Boyle and, as Howe wrote his *Letter* at Boyle's prompting, so at Boyle's request Barlow wrote *The Case of Toleration* (posthumously published in his *Several Weighty and Miscellaneous Cases of Conscience* [1692], with a dedication to Boyle).

example, p. 39. from Mr. Howe's, p. 40. *Irresistibly, that is in his sense Forcibly.*[173] Whereas Mr. Howe there objects to his Adversaries, their holding such an Irre-[90]sistible Determination of the Will, but Forcing of it no where. Yet at what expence of Learning, amd with how much loss of Ink and Ingenuity does *The Discourse* argue that the Will cannot be forc'd! which Mr. Howe, having denied that Irresistible Influence must of necessity disown for it's further absurdity, had he thought his Adversaries guilty of it. But he appears to have been far from imagining it of them, nor could any but *The Discourse* have imputed it to him as his sense, that God does by Force whatsoever he does Irresistibly. What Law of Reason is there, or how can *The Discourse* justifie such a Falsification but by Custom?

If that shall be a sufficient Plea, *It* will never want Instances further to warrant the Practice. As in this following (Forgery I may not call it, having to do with such exactness, but) Rasure.[174] Mr. Howe, having been upon the [91] Argument of the Will of God concerning those that perish, had *Letter* p. 112.[175] said, *The Resolve of the Divine Will in this matter,*[176] *was not concerning the Event,* what he[177] shall do (*i.e.* abstractly and singly, as these next following words shew) *but concerning his Duty what he should, and concerning the connexion between his Duty and his Happiness.* Hereupon what does mean *The Discourse?* p. 116. *It* refers to those words of his, p. 112. and recites a further passage of his *Letter,* p. 115, 116.[178] to argue them of

---

[173] *Letter,* p. 40, exclaims at the "horrour of so black a conception of God [that he should be supposed irresistibly to determine the will of a man to the hatred of his own most Blessed Self, and then to exact severest Punishments for the offence done," which, says *TD,* p. 39, "tragically, but *falsely* represents our opinion. I say *falsely,* for God does not punish that natural passion we call hatred . . . nor does God determine the will to that natural passion, its elicite act, *irresistibly,* in his sense *forcibly.* But as Austin [i.e., Augustine] long ago, of Gods influence upon good actions; [so say we of bad] God acts *Omnipotenter pro te, suaviter pro me, Omnipotently according to his own nature, but sweetly according to ours*" (square brackets in the originals).

[174] Rasure: erasure.

[175] 112. Ed.] 12 R.

[176] I.e., humanity's salvation.

[177] I.e., man.

[178] *Letter,* pp. 115–16: "And if yet it should be insisted, that in asserting God to will what by his Lawes he hath made become Man's duty, even where it is not done, we shall herein ascribe to him, at least, an *ineffectual* and an *imperfect Will,* as which doth not bring to pass the thing willed. It is answered, that imperfection were with no pretence imputable to the Divine Will, meerly for its not effecting every thing, whereto it may have a *real* propension."

repugnancy these[179] to the former, but to that purpose conceals Mr. Howe's last Clause, *but concerning his* Duty *what he should, and concerning the* Connexion *between his Duty and his Happiness,*[180] which being taken in, as it ought, there could have been no pretence of Inconsistency. And it adds[181] that Mr. Howe's Answer *Letter,* p. 116. *that Imperfection is no way imputable to the Divine Will meerly for not Effecting every-*[92]*thing whereto it may have a Real Propension,*[182] is no Answer to the Objection: upon this strange pretence, that, *a Real Propension of Will is no Will,* as if it were a thing impossible that Propension should be either Habitual or Actual.

So also for continual Instance. *The Discourse* p. 118, 119. feigns a Question to have been proposed by Mr. Howe, *Whether it be fitting for God efficaciously to overpower all men into a compliance with the overtures he makes to them in Common:* and then *It* creates also an Answer for him; *It is not fit for God to overpower men without making any overtures to them at all;* and, to make a song of three parts,[183] judicially decides: *the Answer is not fitted to the Question.* I must confess that upon some former experiments I doubted of the Rectitude of *Its* Judgment, but I was not wary enough to suspect a Falshood, which must be so notorious, as that there should be no such Question or Answer. [93] But in good truth none there is that I can find of Mr. Howe's mark. The Question no where in Terms, but the Answer neither in terms nor sense, nor any thing like it. So that *The Discourse* is not to be allowed in any Court either as a Competent Judge, or a Legal Witness, but may deserve to be tryed for this as a Criminal before any Logick-tribunal. Nor needs there any other Evidence against it for Conviction, than those very words of Mr. Howe, that *It* there hath cited. *Grace sometimes shows it self in preventing exertions, and in working so heroically as none have beforehand [in the neglect of it's ordinary method] any reason to expect. Letter* p. 138. Now look back upon the supposititious Answer, *to whom God makes no overtures at all:* Then compare Mr. Howe's words *in the neglect of it's ordinary methods:* And now let any man judge of the Honesty of such an Adversary. For can they be said to neg-[94]lect God's ordinary methods to whom he makes no overtures at all? Nor is the second scheme of *Its* Ques-

---

[179] I.e., these words.

[180] In fact *TD,* p. 115, had included these words in its citation of *Letter,* p. 112.

[181] *TD,* p. 117.

[182] *Propension:* propensity, inclination.

[183] song of three parts: part-song had three or more voice-parts, usually unaccompanied and, unlike madrigal, in simple harmony.

tion and Answer which immediately follows any whit better, but guilty of as perfect Forgery as the first, and so ill contriv'd, that it neither agrees with the former, nor with the Book, though pretending to be a true Copy.

And an Instance it is of the same Fraud to feign, p. 119, 120. that Mr. Howe in his *Letter* hath, abstractly from the more fit course that God hath taken, *determin'd the unfitness of God's giving grace and salvation to all men.*[184]

All that Mr. *Howe* hath said therein amounts only to assert the course which is not taken to be less fit, and that God doth from the perfect rectitude of his own nature, take that course which was to be taken most wisely, and do that which was most congruous and fit to be done, *Letter* p. 149. What can better become us than to judge so of [95] the waies that God hath pitched upon, and wherein we have God's own choice to precede and be a guide to our judgment?

I shall conclude this Article with *Its* quotation, p. 44. out of Dr. Manton's Comment on James 1. 13. p. 101.[185] as if that Learned Divine had affirmed the disputed Predetermination by the[186] words. *Many who grant Prescience, deny Preordination,* (viz. quoth *The Discourse,* the Decree whereof Predetermination is the execution, so I understand him) *lest they should make God the Author of sin;*[187] and *It* forsooth understands him so, but I hope without any obligation to better and sincerer judgments. For what one word is there here that can imply that Preordination to be executed by the way of Predetermination? It is no wonder if Mr. Howe be not secure while

---

[184] *TD*, p. 119: "I am at a loss for a Reason, why it should be unfit for God efficaciously to overpower all men into a compliance with the means . . . unless it be this, that it is unfit for God to bestow grace, and salvation on all men (which would be a very hard saying)."

[185] Thomas Manton, *A Practical Commentary or an Exposition with Notes on James* (1651), p. 101.

[186] the] those *R* (corrected in the list of errata).

[187] Seeking to prove that "God foreknows sinful actions in his own Decree," *TD*, pp. 43–44, "especially recommend[s] to Mr. H. for the friendship sake between the Doctor and him" "a notable gloss" from "the Learned Dr. Manton (now newly deceased, to the great grief of Pious & Learned Men)": "*Many who grant Prescience, deny Preordination,* [viz. the Decree, whereof Predetermination is the execution; so I understand him] *lest they should make God the Author of sin: but these fear where no fear is. The Scripture speaketh roundly, ascribing both to God,* Act 2.23 . . . So far he: and for ought I know consonantly to the constant sense of Protestantism, till now of late that it grows weary of it self, if we may judg of its present humour by Mr. H. and Mr. B." Mr. B. is Baxter; see introduction, p. 393, and below, n. 190.

yet living, when those that are at rest[188] cannot escape so notorious a practice. [96] This is the same as to cut off a dead man's hand to subscribe with it to a Forgery. There needed no less it seems than Doctor Manton's good name, which is like a precious ointment, to give a better odour to those putid[189] suggestions and expressions of *Protestantism grown of late weary of it self,* &c. bestowed on Mr. Howe on this occasion. And yet (for it made me curious) there are Witnesses above exception that also Dr. Manton consented with Mr. Howe in this point, and exprest a great sense of the danger of the contrary Opinion.[190] And whensoever *The Discourse* signifies *Its* doubt of it, I will undertake to make out their Evidence. [97]

The Fourth Article that naturally succeeds the former Falsifications.

> Its *vain, but most injurious Attempts to*
> *pervert what Mr. Howe hath said.*

As for a First Instance, where p. 45. *It* represents Mr. Howe's words; *Letter* p. 29, 30. to imply *an affirmation of a Foreknowledge of Christ's Death antecedent to God's Decree concerning it.*[191] The words are these (which *It* ushers in with *Let*[192] *us hear if our patience can bear this exercise, whether Mr. Howe's gloss upon* Act. 4. 28[193] *doth not corrupt the Text*).[194] If they had known

---

[188] Manton died on October 18, 1677.

[189] putid: rotten, putrid, and so used to express contempt for the morally worthless.

[190] It was, as William Lamont, "The Religion of Andrew Marvell: Locating the 'Bloody Horse,'" in *The Political Identity of Andrew Marvell,* ed. Conal Condren and A. D. Cousins (Aldershot, 1990), pp. 143–44, notes, a bold stroke of Danson to enlist Manton in his support because Manton was, like Howe, in the moderate Baxterian camp and a divine who, wary of the excesses to which rigid Calvinism such as Danson's could lead, like Howe, attracted the charge of being "half Arminian" (Richard Baxter, *Reliquiae Baxterianae* [1696], 3.182, §17).

[191] *TD,* p. 45: "These words plainly imply a denial of Gods foreknowledge of the Death of Christ, as consequent to his Decree of that event . . . and they imply an affirmation of a foreknowledge of Christs Death antecedent to Gods Decree; and so make a confusion (where a distinction ought to be kept) between Gods foreknowledge of *possibles* and *futures;* or of what *may,* and what *shall* come to pass; and run Mr. H. into this absurdity, to deny that any Decree passed upon the Death of Christ at all. For to what end should he pass a Decree, if he foreknew it would come to pass without it?" The "words" from *Letter,* p. 29, to which *TD* refers are accurately reproduced by Marvell in what follows.

[192] *Let* Ed.] (*Let R.*

[193] *Recte* 1 Cor. 2:8, as given in *Letter,* p. 29; *R* takes the incorrect reference from *TD,* p. 44.

[194] *Text*) Ed.] *Text R.*

they would not have crucified the Lord of Glory.[195] That is, *God foreseeing wicked hands would be prompt and ready for this tragick enterprize, his soveraign Power, and wise Counsel concurred with his Foreknowledge, so only and not with less latitude, to define or determine the bounds and limits of that malignity than to let it proceed unto this execution.* [98] What common sense or ordinary ingenuity could have found less in these words than that Mr. Howe doth therein at least profess the Foreknowledge and the Decree to have been *simul & semel,*[196] which is far from affirming the Foreknowledge to be antecedent? But Mr. Howe had moreover, immediately before these words cited, said; *It was a thing which God's Hand and Counsel had determined before to be done.* But this *The Discourse* conceals, lest *It* self should be detected of such a wilful perversion, and the better to make Doctor Twisse's censure (which otherwise had been nothing to the business) take place upon Mr. Howe p. 46. *Those Jesuitical dictates of the foreseen Determination of the Humane Will before God's Decree, are not the Dictates of Divines Disputing but Dreaming.*[197] There was not any colour in Mr. Howe's words for any such imputation; though I doubt not that Mr. Howe believes God's [99] Decree in this case to be but suitable to that Agency which he every where supposes him to have in things of that nature.

A Second Instance of the same dealing is upon Mr. Howe's Assertion, *Postsc.* p.28. of God's Immediate Concourse to all Actions of his Creatures. For p. 55. thence *It* pretends that it follows, and that Mr. Howe implies that *God affords men a leading Concurrence to Actions downright Evil.* And yet Mr. Howe had but *Postsc* p.29. explain'd and limited that concession, saying, *The Concourse or Influence, which I deny not to be Immediate to any Actions, I only deny to be Determinative as to those which are Wicked.* Agreeably to what he saith also *Postsc.* p.45. n.9. But that limitation *The Discourse* takes not any notice of, pretending not to understand a difference between inducing men to [100] Actions which God will reward, and to those for which he will ruine them. And upon this presumption it falls into the usual fit of boasting vain-gloriously over Mr. Howe. For where Perversion may go for Ingenuity, Insolence may also pass for Reason.

I cannot but observe also how in pursuit of this Subject, because Mr. Howe *Postsc.* p.35. cited Luk. 6.9. with Hosea 13.9. to shew the difference,

---

[195] Glory. Ed.] Glory.) *R.*

[196] *simul & semel:* simultaneous and once for all.

[197] *TD,* p. 46, refers to William Twisse, *Vindiciae Gratiae Potestatis, ac Providentiae Dei* (Amsterdam, 1632), book 2, digression 2, chap. 1, p. 31.

and how much more agreeable it was to the Nature of God to induce men by Determinative Influence to Imperfectly good Actions which yet lead to Salvation and Blessedness, then[198] to such as are downright Evil, and tend to their ruine: *It* hereupon p. 58. frames a Chain of Syllogistical Argumentations, all of *Its* own devising, which yet *It* hath the face to father upon Mr. Howe. I call it the rather a [101] *Chain,* because I remember to have read of one who had so singular a faculty of linking one Lye artificially upon another, that they called him at Rome by a new Nickname *Catena:*[199] and the dexterity of *The Discourse,* in almost as sinister a quality, might pretend to the same denomination. The Samoiedes wear Guts about their necks, but swallow them at last down their throats.[200] The same natural Links serving them first for ornament, and then for nutriment: and were *The Discourse* obliged to eat *Its* own words, and feed upon *Its* own Chain of Syllogisms, 'twere a diet, though slender and unclean, yet fit enough for a *Barbarian.* There is nothing can be more savage and inhumane, than to personate[201] Mr. Howe here arguing, *If it be unlawful for Man to destroy Life, then it is unlawful to God.* And then, as if it were [102] a formed Dispute, and wherein Mr. Howe maintain'd the Affirmative, *It* denies the Antecedent, the Consequent, and the Connexion of *Its* own (not, as is pretended Mr. Howe's) Enthymeme,[202] and laboriously proceeds to disprove the whole Argument thorow the several members. Let but any man have recourse to that place of the *Postsc.* p.35. and consider whether there be

---

[198] then] taen *R* (corrected in the list of errata).

[199] Ammianus Marcellinus, *Res Gestae,* 15.3.4 tells (in John C. Rolfe's Loeb translation [1935]) of the fourth-century notary to the imperial *consistorium* Paulus who "was nicknamed 'the Chain,' because he was invincible in weaving coils of calumny" (cf. 14.5.8).

[200] Samoiedes . . . throats: Samoyeds, pagan nomadic inhabitants of Samoedia, in east Siberia. The third volume of Samuel Purchas, *Purchas His Pilgrimes,* 4 vols. (1625), was the standard account in the seventeenth century, upon which Milton drew in chapter 2 of his *Brief History of Moscovia* (1682), "Of Samoedia, Siberia . . . " (*CPW,* 8:497–502; cf. *Paradise Lost,* 10:696), where he tells that they "live on the Flesh of . . . Wild Beasts" and "carry Provision of Meat with them" (8:501). Their name was commonly interpreted to mean *self-eaters,* that is, cannibals. Marvell had had the opportunity to meet Samoyeds when in 1663–64 he accompanied the earl of Carlisle's embassy to Russia: see Guy de Miège, *A Relation of Three Embassies from . . . Charles II to the Great Duke of Muscovie . . .* (1669), pp. 83–85, which says of the "very barbarous" Samoyeds that they "eat the bodies of their dead friends with Venison."

[201] personate: falsely represent.

[202] Enthymeme: argument, syllogism (see above, n. 125).

any colour thence to suppose that Mr. Howe intended there, or gave any occasion for such arguing; and whether all the Blasphemies or Heresies that ever were invented, might not be imputed to him with as much reason. I find my self so concern'd hereat (not in behalf of Mr. Howe, but of all common morality among mankind) that I think fit to repress my self, and rather leave the Crime to any Readers, or to *The Discourses* own Censure; for notwithstanding [103] this and all *Its* other Errours, I conceive *It* yet to have some intervals both of Understanding and Conscience.

But a most undecent thing it was for *It* to trifle in a matter so serious, and it had been far more becoming to have given a clear account of *Its*[203] own Belief in this point, than to have forged arguments for others, create shadows for *It* self to sport with, and to act in one personage, the Cause, the Judge, the Witness, the Plaintiff, and the Defendant. After all those To and Fro's, Up and Downs of so many tedious pages that *It* obliges us to, if we will go along with it thorow this particular, might I not in recompence crave leave to be solemnly and soberly answered upon two or three Questions arising upon this debate for my own better information? First, whether *It* do not con-[104]scientiously believe that God doth punish men for doing Actions which in such and such circumstances he hath forbidden them to do? Next, whether it be not manifest that according to *Its* opinion God must Determine men to those Actions in those circumstances, that is in the same circumstances wherein they are done? And lastly, whether that Determining Influence can be withstood? If *It* once affirm all these, as I see no tolerable evasion indeavour'd, but that *It* holds them all *pro confessio*,[204] how can *It* with all *Its* Logick and Metaphysicks extricate *It* self from maintaining that absurdity that God ruines men for what he hath induc'd them to, that is not simply to destroy life (as *It* vainly strives to shift off the business) but to destroy it upon such terms? And then how frivolous will all those Answers, p. 55. and so forward appear [105] to Mr. Howe's argument mention'd on a former occasion, *Postsc.* p.33, 34. *We our selves can in a remoter kind concur to the Actions of others: Yet it doth not follow that because we may afford our Leading Concurrence to Actions imperfectly good, that therefore*[205] *we may afford them to those*[206] *that are downright Evil; because to Prayer, therefore*

---

[203] Here, and for the next page (and occasionally thereafter), "*It'* " is printed for "*It*"; such cases are silently rendered *It*.

[204] *pro confessio* Ed.] *pro confesso R.*: as certain, as a matter of faith.

[205] *therefore* Ed.] *thereore R.*

[206] *afford them to those* Ed.] *afford them to afford to those R.*

to Cursing and Swearing, and then ruine men for the Actions we have induced them to: You'l say, God may rather, but sure he can much less do so than you. Now *The Discourse* calls this (and would blame it upon that account, as comparing God and the Creature) Mr. Howe's argument *a Pari:*[207] But it is methinks *a Fortiori,*[208] and therefore more reverent. If a well-natur'd man would not do so, it is much more disagreeable to God's Nature.

In all these things Mr. Howe (and 'tis that makes me like him the bet-[106]ter) declares his own sense plainly however, while the other never speaks out, unless to give ill words, and seems to search not for the Truth, but meerly for Contention.

The last Evidence of this Article shall be where *It* p. III. takes occasion to say Mr. Howe p. 106. *professes his dislike of the common distinction of* Voluntas Beneplaciti & Signi,[209] *in this present Case* [*viz.* to explain how God Wills the Salvation of all, and yet only of some] *under which such as coined, and those that have much used it, have only rather (I doubt not) concealed a good meaning, than expressed an ill one.* Thus far *It* quotes Mr. Howe, but there stops and saith, *the rest is not worth the trouble of transcribing;*[210] but I therefore suspect the more that it is[211] worth it, and out of some cunning fetch omitted, and shall the rather take that trouble upon me. *It seems,* [107] *I confess, by it's more obvious aspect, too much to countenance that ignominious slander, which prophane and atheistical dispositions would fasten upon God and the course of his procedure toward men, &c. as though he only intended to seem willing of what he really was not; That there was an appearance to which nothing did* subesse.[212] *And then why is the latter call'd* Voluntas, *unless the meaning be, he did only Will the Sign, which is false and impious?* &c.[213] But upon the former quotation out of Mr. Howe, wherein he only excepts against the Distinction *in the present Case,* and signifies that a good meaning was intended by it; *The Discourse* p. 116. represents him as meaning the same thing with Dr. Twisse (who also notes the impropriety of the latter

---

[207] *a Pari:* from what is weaker or insufficient. *TD,* p. 55: "In general 'tis unsafe arguing *a pari,* from the creature to God; that what the former may not do, neither may the latter."

[208] *a Fortiori:* from what is stronger or greater.

[209] Voluntas Beneplaciti & Signi: the absolute and revealed will [of God] (on this distinction, see introduction, p. 395 with n. 49).

[210] *TD,* p. 114.

[211] that it is Ed.] that that it *R.*

[212] subesse: exist beneath, hide behind.

[213] *Letter,* pp. 106–07, following on from the previously cited passage.

member *Voluntas Signi,* as improperly called a Will, and only signifying Man's Duty) [108] and *blaming himself yet in blaming him:* When Mr. Howe had in plain words approved the meaning of the Distinction. The gentlest imagination a man can frame to himself hereof, is that *Its* own brain was perverted before Mr. Howe's intention.

The Fifth Article is,

> Its *Odious Insinuations concerning*
> *what* It *hath no colour to object or*
> *except against.*

Of this I shall give three Instances in one Paragraph. *T.D.* p. 103, 104. where *It* pretends first to be *at a strange loss for an Antecedent to a Relative*[214] in Mr. Howe's *Letter,* p. 67. *Neither yet was it necessary that effectual care should be taken* they *should actually reach all, and be applied to every individual person.* The loss is indeed a strange one, and I condole [109] it. For *It* hath herein suffered great damage of Eye-sight, Understanding, Memory and Ingenuity, very sensible disasters, and with great difficulty to be repaired. Mr. Howe's immediate words in the foregoing period[215] were *that the Divine Edicts should be of an Universal tenour as they are, the matter of them being of Universal concernment, and equally suitable to the common case of all men.* Now add to these words as it follows in that place, *Neither yet was it necessary they should actually reach all,* and then say whether any man else would not have seen that the *They* here was Relative to the *Divine Edicts:* beside that the whole Tract[216] of the foregoing Argument leads and refers continually to them. But then, when after a long loss *It* hath, casting about even to *Postsc.* p. 35. and 40. *out of love to Mr. Howe's person and the Truth,*[217] hit it at last to [110] be the Divine Edicts *of which possibly Mr. Howe meant it,* yet then *It* suggests from those words of his, *Neither yet was it necessary* (that is to the purpose Mr. Howe was speaking of, the Vindicating of God's Wisdom and Sincerity, as any sober Reader will easily see) as if they were thought not at all necessary. If this be candour, what is blackness?[218] It is as

[214] I.e., in this case, a personal pronoun.

[215] I.e., the period preceding the sentence just quoted from p. 67.

[216] Tract: course, drift.

[217] *TD*'s own phrase (p. 104) in explanation of his desire "to do Mr. H. all the right I can" by adopting the reading Marvell here presents as obvious.

[218] A pun is involved. *Candour* is from Latin *candor* meaning "brilliant whiteness," its original sense in Middle English, still current in the seventeenth century when the sense which Marvell here uses ("honest," "frank," or "fair") developed.

much as to say, that, unless it be necessary for the Vindication of God's Wisdom and Sincerity to provide that every man should have a Bible and read it, it is no way necessary for man's salvation.

The Second Instance in the same Paragraph is to quote Mr. Howe *Letter,* p. 69. *And thus how easily and even* naturally (*by Messengers running from Nation to Nation, some to communicate, others to enquire after the tidings of the Gospel*) *would the* [111] *Gospel soon have spread it self through the World?* and hereupon to suggest as if Mr. Howe thought *the seeds of the Gospel were in men by nature.*[219] Unless Understanding and Wilful Ignorance be the same thing, no man could have avoided the sense of the word *Naturally* here, to be, easily, and of course. But if that term had been intended in the strict sense (though the mollifying of it by that particle, *even,* shows it was not) how could the Inquiry after a thing new, and said to be of common concernment, be Natural, although the thing it self were not?

And the Third is; Whereas Mr. Howe had, *Letter,* p. 75, 76, 77. enumerated many Instances of God's Clemency and Bounty to Men in general, and added that, *they might by these understand God to have favourable propensions towards them; and that though they have offended* [112] *him, he is not their implacable enemy, and might by his Goodness be led to Repentance,* that hereupon *The Discourse* p. 104. having nothing to alledge against any particular of what is there said, brings in Mr. John Goodwin to have writ somewhat of the like import in his *Pagans Debt and Dowry;*[220] and the like

[219] In *Letter,* pp. 68–71, this passage is conditional: if men had "behaved themselves sutably to the exigencie of their case, and as did become reasonable Creatures" when the Gospel was first proclaimed, it "would have been entertained with so great a transport of joy, and so ready and universal acceptance, as very soon to have made a great noise in the World" so that "It could not but be, that Messengers would interchangeably have run from Nation, to Nation . . . And thus how easily, and *even naturally,* would the Gospel soon have spread it self thorough the World?"; but, in historical fact, men's "sensual terrene inclination" ensured that the Gospel made only "little, slow progress." Upon this, *TD,* pp. 103–04 comments, "I confess that term *naturally* will not down with me: for I have always seen cause to own Dr. Sibs's weighty observation, in his *Souls Conflict* [(1636)], *That though there are seeds of the Law, yet there are none of the Gospel in man by nature.*" Sibbes writes on this theme (though without this form of words) in chap. 12, pp. 153–75.

[220] The republican Independent John Goodwin (1594?–1665), vicar of St. Stephen's in Coleman Street, London (where he ministered to a gathered church), and a nonconformist minister after the Restoration, was notorious among Calvinist divines for the avowed Arminianism of his *Redemption Redeemed* (1651) and other writings. It is *TD*'s purpose to discredit Howe by associating his views with those of Goodwin in his *The*

quotations *It* cites afterwards from Mr. Hoard,[221] which is all for spight, but nothing to the purpose. Could *It* have laid down an *Antithesis* to any thing that Mr. Howe here said, 'tis probable *It* would have gone that way to work, and not have used this *Pagan* invention of baiting Mr. Howe in the skins of others; or daubing him over with pitch to serve for Torch-light, and put out the light of the Gospel. But 'tis more probable *It* would have proceeded both waies; for *Its* Zeal for the Truth seems not greater than *Its* Animo-[113]sity against Mr. Howe, whencesoever it arises. But *It* durst not adventure to say that Mr. Howe hath made Mr. John Goodwin's ill use of this notion. Had there been any such thing, *The Discourse* seems not in humour to have past it over, and that calumnious figure of *Meliora Spero*,[222] hoping the best of him, but suggesting the worst, would have been changed to a plain accusation. If *It* would have dealt fairly, here was the proper place to have spoken out, and have told us distinctly *Its* own opinion in so weighty a matter. Does it know what God (though most unobliged) might do to furnish such with what might be sufficient, if they seriously desired such mercy at his hands? Will *It* think it self bound to tear Rom. 2.4. out of *Its* Bible, because John Goodwin hath cited it? Or, will *It* adventure to be the Heathens Comp-[114]urgator[223] at the day of Judgment, that they have no more considered the tendency of the Divine Goodness?

These indeed would have been worthy Atchievements, and proper to one of so great enterprize; but to throw upon Mr. Howe an undeserved obloquy of other mens names in this manner, how base a thing was it? considering besides how *Its* own name (though hitherto studiously concealed,) might in the vicissitude of humane affairs, serve men hereafter for a more infamous quotation.

Pagans Debt and Dowry (1651), whose bold claim that heathens, "by the light of Nature," might come to repentance and salvation ran directly counter to prevailing thought, as represented by the remark from Sibbes approvingly quoted by *TD* (see n. 219).

[221] *TD*, pp. 109–10, claims Howe's views are "the same" as those of Samuel Hoard (1599–1658) in his anonymous *Gods Love to Mankind Manifested by Disproving his Absolute Decree for their Damnation* (1636), which *TD* quotes from Davenant's *Animadversions* (1641) upon it (for Davenant, see introduction, n. 21). *TD* is again seeking to discredit Howe by identifying his stress on the mercy, rather than the justice, of God with the views of another convinced Arminian.

[222] *Meliora Spero*: "I hope for better things" (Cicero, *Epistolae ad Atticum*, 14.15, written following the assassination of Caesar).

[223] Compurgator: witness to the good character of innocency of another.

I shall add no more than p. 108. *Its* citing Mr. Howe's *Letter,* p. 89, 90. *That which God's declarations do amount to is,* &c. *that, if they which finally perish, neglect to attend to those external discoveries of the Word,* &c. *they are not to expect he should overpower them by a strong hand, and save them against the con-*[115]*tinual*[224] *disinclination of their own Wills;*[225] upon which *It* saith, *I am not able to make sense of the last words, for I understand not what overcoming by a strong hand (in a sinner's case) God can make use of that leaves the Will under disinclination to Salvation.* What reason or occasion do Mr. Howe's words give for making this puzzle? Could it not understand that some men are so unreasonable as to expect Salvation, while yet at the same time they are disaffected to the means of it? And that some, because they dislike the ordinary means, please themselves with an hope that God will at last cast[226] use some extraordinary, to overcome that disaffection?

The Sixth Article.

Its *most unseemly and insolent boastings and*
self-applauses upon no occasion.

Yet therefore the more frequent, as his *killing Mr. Howe with his own* [116] *weapon,* p.26. in *Its* Argument about Mr. Howe's two Concessions, the vanity whereof as to the first I have before noted:[227] And now as to what he brags of against the second as a *Triumphant Evidence,* I shall no less shew *Its* impertinency. The Argument is *Its* own, p. 30.[228] *If it be the Indetermination of the Powers to Individual Actions that makes an Excitation of them, to one rather than to another, necessary.* Stay here: *It* takes this for granted, and as it is in it self destitute of strength, so *It* leaves it very unkindly without any proof or assistance to shift as well as it can. Whereas *It* knows that 'tis said on the opposite part, *That it is not Indetermination meerly (which the Self-determining power of the Will can remove) but aversion to good Actions (which gracious Habits do lessen, but not remove) that makes*

---

[224] *continual* Ed.] *con-* [p. 114] *continual* [p. 115] R.

[225] Marvell quotes *TD*'s summary, with his reference to *Letter,* which should read pp. 87–90.

[226] at last cast: at the last cast, in the end, as a last resort.

[227] See above, p. 443 with n. 132.

[228] *TD,* p. 30, takes the phrase "triumphant evidence," which it calls "one of Mr. Howe's lofty epithets," from *Letter,* p. 62, where, in fact, it refers not to Howe's own argument at all but to the inevitability with which God's unqualified dominion is to be inferred from his being "the Original and Root of all Being." Marvell notes the misapplication on p. 465.

God's holy Determining Influence necessary. Now let *It* go on,—*and the pos-sibility of Action contained in the Powers that makes* [117] *the reducing of that possibility to Action no less necessary to good Actions:* If there be any sense in this, it is very recondite, and would require a spirit that can discover hidden treasure; Can Possibility of Action make Action necessary? It must be as false as it is true, that an Argument can be drawn from Power to Act, affirmatively. Indeed, should *It* have said, where there is only a possibility of Action, that possibility must be reduced to Action, before there can be any Action, it were true, but then it is one of these things that are *Nimis vera,*[229] and which it is ridiculous to put into any proposition, much more where it is to no purpose. As here it is manifestly to none; for we are still left as uncertain, as if no such thing had been said, what it is that must reduce that possibility to Action. But that it should be added *no less necessary to good Actions,* is beyond the power of Witchcraft to understand what *It* [118] should mean here. Doth *It* pretend to be discoursing with any one that thought Determination to good Actions less necessary? I thought *Its* pres-ent part was to oppose one that said it was more necessary. And yet this most insignificant Scheme of Discourse is shut up with a *Quod erat Demon-strandum,*[230] and with the Phantastry[231] of claiming to it evidence equal to what the Apostles words carry, Rom. 11.36. For it was to those words that Mr. Howe's *Letter,* p. 62. gave those *lofty Epithets* of *Triumphant Evidence,* which *The Discourse* cavils at, and borrows, with no mind to restore them, to adorn the street-pageantry of this pitiful Argument.

Another Instance may be *Its* Jovial rant, p. 37. *What is now become of Mr. Howe's thin Sophistry, and collusive Ambiguity?* &c. It is necessary to read upon this occasion from *Its* p. 32. 1. 12. at least to p. 37. 1. 14. for it is too [119] long to insert here such a parcel of stuff, but there you may have it. *Its* business here is to defend the Predeterminers[232] Opinion against the charge of God's necessitating men to sin, and of attempting to alleviate it by God's being above Law, but Man under it. Let me conjure any Reader by the most potent charms of perswasion, by all that is ridiculous in *Its* whole Book, or in mine, but to peruse at leisure how miserably those points are there along

---

229 *Nimis vera:* too obviously true.

230 *Quod erat Demonstrandum:* which was to be proved, the traditional conclusion to a geometrical proof (*QED*).

231 Phantastry: delusion, with a suggestion also of absurdity and of arrogant ostentation.

232 Predeterminers: believers in predestination (this is the only example of the word's use known to *OED,* which observes that "properly" the form should be *predeterminist.*

managed. *It* owns at first that it is *an hard Province to answer to all the Objections,*[233] then softens it, as fire mollifies clay, and at last, after having confessed and begged, comes off with that glorious exaltation over Mr. Howe's thin Sophistry. It were needless to exemplifie all the like passages, where *It* arrogates Commendation to *It* self beyond what any friend, and vilifies Mr. Howe below what any other enemy would offer at,[234] both equally undeserved. [120]

The Seventh Article

> Its *very gross Absurdities, Self-contradi-*
> *ctions, and Inconsistencies, to which may*
> *be added divers unsafe Expressions, not*
> *a little reflecting on God and Religion.*

As first p. 18. *It* discourses concerning the security of good Angels by God's determining Influence, which no man that I know will quarrel for, and by which I doubt not it supposes their Immutability, but p. 20. speaking of Man, *It* saith, that *God made him Mutable* (and *how could he do otherwise, unless he should have made him a God?*) what then, doth it conceive that the good Angels are Gods? Such like was *Its* absurdity, p. 27. of the necessity of Predetermination, because God's Immediate Concourse could not determine Adam's Will. Than which, what can be more notorious? the Controversie being, Whether God [121] doth determine Men to Wicked Actions, but *Its* Argument to this Effect; That, if God do not determine Men to such Wicked Actions by Concourse, he doth it, as elsewhere *It* calls it, by Precourse.[235] Whereas it should have known the thing denied by Mr. Howe to be, that God doth by Efficacious Influence determine to them at all. And so *Its* Argumentation there signifies only that if God do not determine to them, he doth determine to them.

---

[233] *TD*, p. 32, with reference to the difficulty of maintaining its argument that, while "God is the Author, and consequently the Predeterminer of all the actions of rational creatures," yet "God is not the Author of the sinfulness" of any predetermined action.

[234] at, Ed.] at R.

[235] Precourse: anticipatory action. *OED*'s first citation for the noun *Precourse* is this example, but without any reference to *TD*, p. 5, whose coinage it apparently is: "The grand term then to be explained is *Predetermination,* or (as some Divines and Metaphysicians sometimes call it) *Praecurse* and *Praemotion* . . . this act of Gods is called *Predetermination,* because it limits the creature to this action rather than to that; and 'tis called a *Precourse,* or *Premotion,* i.e. a *running before,* or *fore motion,* (as I may so speak), because in order of nature it is before the action of the creature."

A third Instance is where p. 40. Mr. Howe having *Letter* p.17.47. said that the *Argument from the pretended Impossibility of God's foreknowing Sinful Actions, if he did not determine the Agent to them, will not infer, that if he determine not to them, he cannot foreknow them, but only that we are left ignorant of the way.*[236] It collects thence p. 41. (and *thinks Mr. Howe hath much overshot himself*) that he *universally denies our knowledge of* [122] the *way how God foretells future*[237] *Contingencies.* Whereas Mr. Howe *Letter* p. 35. stated their Argument in express words, *that it were otherwise impossible God should foreknow the Sinful Actions of men,* and here 47. only saith, *the Argument infers so much and no more,* as to *Wicked Actions,* yet *It* makes this an universal denial as to all Actions: Hereby it is easie to judge, which of the two is the better Archer, or came nearer the mark, which shot home,[238] and which over.

That for a Fourth is what you please for to call it, p. 70. but a pretty innocent thing of the like nature *Irresistible Imports, It* saith, *A Relation of the Action of the Agent to some resistance,*[239] which is pleasant, by how much impossible to imagine how that which cannot be resisted imports that which is resisted.

But this p. 76. is a most refined absurdity, while in the same place *It* [123] taunts Mr Howe for *gratifying his own unscholastick humour.* Something *is said to be Impossible respectively, as if a man will fly* that *he should have wings.*[240] But this among duller men hath hitherto been thought an

---

[236] I.e., the way in which God foreknows them.

[237] *future* Ed.] *futnre* R.

[238] shot home: hit the mark or target.

[239] *TD*, pp. 70–71: "irresistible, imports a relation of the action of the agent, to some resistance or counteraction of the patient; as when the water endeavours to put out the fire, which would lick it up; or in free agents, when a man with all his strength resists him that by force would carry him away Prisoner."

[240] From the distinction between *absolute necessity* ("a connexion of those things which cannot be sever'd without a contradiction; *i.e.* destroying the nature of their subject. So justice to God, reason to man, agree so necessarily to their subjects, that if you deny either, you do in effect deny them to be what they are") and *respective necessity* ("a necessity whereby those things that are not in their own nature conjoined, are yet upon supposition of something antecedent conjoined for this or that time"), *TD*, pp. 75–77, infers that similarly "something is said to be impossible either *absolutely,* which involves a contradiction, as for a stone to be a man; or *respectively,* as if a man will fly that he should have wings. And here we may stop a while and observe how Mr. H. hath *gratified his own unscholastick humour,* in neglecting the strictness of Scholastick terms, to the overthrow of his own assertion. For I am much mistaken if it is not plain

instance of what is quite contrary, to wit, of Hypothetical Necessity. And if *It* should find it self hereafter obliged to fly from *Its* adversary, I suppose that *It* would think a pair of wings to be pertinent and highly convenient, if not necessary.

I have before upon occasion, and in passing, noted how he undertakes to prove that there are no Actions of free Agents Evil in themselves, when nevertheless *It* had p. 72. affirmed the hatred of God and Adultery to be in themselves Evil.

Such is that too elsewhere touched, p. 63. where it cites Mr. Howe, *Postsc.* p. 36. intimating that some Actions are Evil *quoad Substantiam*,[241] that is, morally Evil or Wicked; and *It* [124] would have it to be a Contradiction to own that any such have natural good in them. How wisely? As if it were not possible for the same Action to be morally Evil, and naturally Good. Or did *It* never hear of the Substance of an Act in the moral sense? And doth not a forbidden Action use to be called Evil in the Substance of it? When, if the Action be not forbidden, but commanded, and only the undue manner or end forbidden, as in *Its* own Instance of Alms-giving for vain-glory, it is said to be Good, *quoad Substantiam?* It is to be wondred that it summoned not here *Its Logick* to prove than an Action hath no Substance; but that would have spoiled *Its* Learned Note that follows, where Mr. Howe, *Postsc.* p. 36, to the Question, *Is there any Action so sinful, that hath not*[242] *some natural Good as the substrate matter thereof?* Answers, *True, and what, shall it therefore be inferr'd, that* [125] *God must by a Determinative Influence produce every such Action whatsoever reason there be against it? One might better argue thence the necessity of his producing every hour a new World, in which there would be a great deal more of Positive Entity, and natural Goodness. It* hereupon undertakes p. 65. to prove that there is *as much Entity and natural Goodness in a sinful Action, as there would be in Myriads of Worlds, should God create every hour a new World;* and saith, that

---

enough that Mr. H. confounds the distinction of *necessity* or *impossibility*, into *absolute* and *respective.*"

[241] *quoad Substantiam:* as regards their substance, essentially or fundamentally (Howe had used the phrase in *Postscript*, p. 33, cited above, p. 427). In late medieval and Renaissance philosophical and theological discourse *substantia* denoted the inherent nature or distinctive character which confers identity, as distinct from accidental or circumstantial qualities (cf. n. 243 below).

[242] *not* Ed.] *not not* R.

to deny this were unworthy a Philosopher: and *Its* proof is, If *Substantia non recipit magis & minus,*[243] or if *Ens & bonum sit convertible,*[244] then *an Action hath as much Entity as a World.*

But how much doth *It* reflect upon God and that Religious sense which we ought to cherish of him, p. 27. when *It* makes God to have determined Innocent Adam's Will to the choice of eating the fruit that was forbidden him? This seem'd so horrid at first, [126] that *It* self startles a little at it, interposing in a Parenthesis (*suppose before the Prohibition past upon it*) and yet, because *Its* cause required no less, and appetite gathers with eating, *It* takes courage afterward[245] to assert God's Predetermination of Adam's Will to the Act of eating, which was not till after the Prohibition: and to *Illustrate* (as *It* pretends) so black a thing, *It* parallels God's moving him to that Act rather than to another, *with a Writing-Master's directing his Scholars hand.*[246] If the Cause be not to be defended upon better terms than so, what Christian but would rather wish he had never known Writing-Master, than to subscribe such an Opinion; and that God should make an innocent Creature in this manner to do a forbidden Act, for which so dreadful a vengeance was to issue upon him and his posterity?

No less pregnant with impious ab-[127]surdity is it to assert p. 29, 30. the equal necessity of Predetermining Influence to Wicked Actions as to Good; and that dangerous Insinuation, p. 19. that God's promises convey

---

[243] *Substantia non recipit magis & minus:* an essence cannot take on greater or lesser (that is, it is immutable; cf. n. 241 above).

[244] *Ens & bonum sit convertible:* entity (or being) and goodness are interchangeable. *Ens* denotes the essence of a being or entity distinct from its attributes, qualities, or accidental features, or the abstract notion of *being* as distinct from context or circumstance.

[245] afterward Ed.] afteward R.

[246] *TD*, p. 27: "The concourse of God with Adam's will in the election of one [tree] (suppose that in the midst of the Garden, before the prohibition passed upon it) could not determine it to that rather than to any of the rest, as is plain in external actions. Two men lanching a wherry-boat concur to the same effect; but the one does not determine the other, by lending common assistance to that act. There must be therefore a Predetermination in order of nature, though not of time, to that act of Adam's will *supposed* of eating that tree instanced in, to which God concurred. This may be illustrated by the example of a Writing-Master and his Scholar, wherein there is a concurrence to the action of writing, and its effect the letter written; and also a Predetermination, a putting the Scholar upon the action of writing."

no right to them to whom they are made. For, *'tis a ruled case,*[247] *It* says, *in the Schools,*[248] *that God cannot properly be said a Debter to his Creatures;* and then adds of *Its* own, *no not when he hath passed a Promise to them,* and pursues this so far as to say, *if he should (to suppose an Impossibility)* which, considering what follows had been therefore better omitted, *break his word,* he would be but Mendax, non Injustus, and puts it too in English, a Lyer, not Unjust. What dispensation have some men to speak at this rate, or what dangerous points do they run themselves upon, and their Readers? I remember there is a Picture before that *Ruler* [128] *of the Case* his Book with this Addition, *bene scripsisti de me Dive Thoma.*[249] But let God be True and *Just* to his word, and every man (that saith otherwise) a Lyer.

For the last I shall only transcribe a few lines of *Its* idle Harangue, p. 35. in which I know not whether the malice against Mr. Howe, or irreverence towards our Saviour do predominate thorow the whole absurdity. *We might also observe upon his Rhetorical Amplifications of his Argument, that he seems to be no ill-willer to Transubstantiation: for if the natural notions of God's Goodness should be infinitely dearer to us than our senses, I see not why the notion of God's sincerity that he means as he speaks, should not challenge a share in our Indearments, and so why* hoc est corpus meum, *should not assure us that the bread is transubstantiated, though our sen-*[129]*ses,* &c. *joyn in a Common Testimony against it.* Viciously and wantonly said, as if God, wheresoever he speaks in a figure,[250] were guilty of Insincerity.

The Eighth and last Article against *The Discourse,* shall be *The Virulence of* Its *Spirit.*

Whereof one Instance, may suffice, p. 122. where, closing the Book, *It* saith, *that Mr.* Howe's *Doctrine opens a wide door for Atheism, and reckons*

---

[247] *ruled case:* established view, accepted dogma which is beyond dispute.

[248] *Schools:* strictly, the faculties of a university; more generally, academic discourse, the world of learning.

[249] Marvell discredits Danson by associating him with the Roman Catholic Thomas Aquinas ("the ruler of the case," or moderator, traditionally appealed to in the schools) as one who has reputedly written well of God ("you have written well of me, divine Thomas") but who in fact has only written with misleading ingenuity (in Danson's case, calling God a liar). Marvell may have had in mind a particular engraved frontispiece to an edition of Aquinas.

[250] God is said to speak figuratively because, in contrast to the doctrine of transubstantiation in the Roman tradition, the Protestant tradition does not take literally Jesus' words at the Last Supper, "This is my body" (Luke 21:19).

him by strong Implication, *among those who acknowledge God in Words, but deny him in Deed:* Whereas, what is it that Mr. Howe hath denied, but *that God doth determine men by Efficacious Influence to those very Actions which he forbids, and for which he will punish them?*

But I spare my hand, *The Discourse* all along boiling over, foaming, frothing and casting forth the [130] like expressions, which I refrain to enumerate, that I may not incur the fate of him that stirs the Indians Poison-pot, who when he falls down dead with the steam and stench, they then throw the doors open, and dip their Arrows.[251] [131][252]

I should now therefore have concluded, were there not something yet in *Its* Prefatory Epistle so sordid, that I reserved it for behind, as the most proper place it could be applied to. Nor shall I therein only have marshall'd it according to *Its* dignity, but do hope moreover, as the Head of the Viper is a specifick[253] against It's Venom;[254] so to find out a Remedy against the Book in the Preface; wherein *It* shows so peculiar a malice and despight to Mr. Howe, and insinuates the same to the Reader, as requires a particular Preservative. And, had I not already been at the pains of the foregoing Remarks, here was, I see, a more compendious occasion, but sufficient to have administered me the same observations. For all the other faults that I have objected against the bulk of *The Discourse* might as easily have been discovered [132] in *Its* Preface, as a good Physiognomist can by the Moles in the face assign all those that are upon any other part of the body: But among them all *Its* superlative Dulness is here especially the more manifest (as usually happens in such cases) by how much *It* endeavours most at Acuteness and Elegancy; so palpable, that even it self could not be wholly insensible of it: but p. 3, 4.[255] feelingly confesses both in Latine and English, that in reading Mr. Howe's *Letter* and *Postscript, Obstupuit steteruntque Comae;*[256]

---

[251] Accounts of voyages to and discoveries in the New World frequently refer to the Indians' use of boiling pots or cauldrons, often in the context of alleged cannibalistic practices; but no source for this "Poison-pot" has been traced.

[252] P. 130 carries only seven lines of text, followed by the catchwords for p. 131 ("I should") within spaced ruled lines.

[253] specifick: remedy for a particular condition (in this case, a snake bite). *OED's* earliest citations in this sense are 1677 for the adjective and 1661 for the substantive.

[254] Pliny, *Natural History*, 29:21: "The head of a viper, placed on the bite, even though the same viper did not inflict it, is infinitely beneficial." Loeb translation, 8.229.

[255] *TD*, pref. ep., sigs. A3–A3v.

[256] "He was astonished and his hair stood on end": a third-person version of Aeneas's

and a double *Astonishment* under which *It* laboured: This doubtless it was, like the disaffections[257] derived from the Head to the Nerves, which propagated that horrid stupidity that I have already noted thorow *Its* whole Treatise. But that Quality is here so exalted, (Nature[258] it seems, having given *It* that Torpor for a Defence) that in [133] touching it thus lightly, I perceive a numness to strike up thorow my Pen into my Faculties, and shall therefore point at some particulars, rather than adventure to handle them.

Mr. Howe had in passing, *Postsc.* p.22. glanced upon an improper redundance of words used by a former Adversary.[259] *The Divine Independent Will of God;* as he might with good reason take notice of it, being as much sense as to have said the Humane Dependent Will of Man. But hereupon *The Discourse* p.9.[260] having for revenge turn'd over his whole *Letter* and *Postscript* to find out the like absurdities, highly gratulates[261] it self in three Instances, but all of them curtaild from the coherence[262] to make for the purpose. One *Letter* p. 42. *In which sense how manifest it is that the perfect* (all this omitted) *Rectitude of God's own holy gracious Nature is*[263] *an eternal Law to him* [134] (omitted.)[264] The second; *Letter* p.59. *God satisfies himself in himself, and takes highest complacency in the perfect Goodness, Congruity, and* (all this omitted) *Rectitude of his own most holy Will and Way;* and for these Mr. Howe arraigned upon a Crime, by a Greek word of Law called *Pleonasme.*[265] The third is *actions Malignantly Wicked* (which *The Discourse* saith is the same as *Wickedly Wicked*) *Postscript* p. 22. and 32. as *It* quotes, but is in *Letter;* p. 32.[266] and here, *It* leaves out also the word *most*, which would have spoiled the exception taken against it; for what Mr. Howe there saith is, *even those Actions that are in themselves* most *malignantly wicked.* Are there not some Actions, some Men, more malignantly wicked than

---

first-person account of his reaction to the appearance of the ghost of his wife, Creusa, in Virgil, *Aeneid,* 2.773.

[257] disaffections: disorders, disabilities.

[258] (Nature Ed.] Nature *R.*

[259] I.e., Theophilus Gale; see introduction, pp. 391–92.

[260] TD, pref. ep., sig. A6.

[261] gratulates: compliments, congratulates.

[262] curtaild from the coherence: deprived of their sense (by incomplete quotation).

[263] *is* Ed.] (*is* R.

[264] (omitted.) Ed.] omitted.) *R.*

[265] *Pleonasm,* the rhetorical term for linguistic superfluity or redundancy, is from the Greek πλεοναζειν, to be superfluous.

[266] p. 32. Ed.] 32. *R.*

others? Or will *The Discourse* apply *Its* old end of Latine here—*aliquando bonus dormitat Homerus*[267] to Paulus,[268] Rom. [135] 7. 13. *sin, exceedingly sinful?* It was time therefore in all reason to conclude this exercise with saying; *But these are childish Criminations, unfit to be bandied from hand to hand by sober persons;* owning it self at once to have been guilty herein of an Intemperate, Inept, and Unmanly kind of procedure.

Neither can I pass by unregarded that new Invention of rearing up Pillars to mens Infamy; but which have sometimes, and may now also, turned[269] to the disgrace of the Architect. *It* cuts out p. 10, 11. several Lines here and there, out of the whole *Letter* and *Postscript*, to post them up in Columns,[270] and Mr. Howe upon them as a common notorious Self-contradicter: Whereas, if any man will take the pains to restore those sentences to their first situation and coherence, (as I have formerly done) there will not be found [136] the least Inconsistency in them: But if this Practice be allowable, there is not any Chapter in the Bible out of which *It* may not with the same integrity extract either Blasphemy or Nonsense; though I am far from suspecting *The Discourse* of such an undertaking. For indeed *It* assigns the True Reason, (and fit to be inscribed over the *Portico*) *non est ingenii mei hosce nodos*[271] *dissolvere*, and as faithfully translates it; I *have not the wit to untie these knots*,[272] which is now the third publick Confession of *Its* stupidity, in the Preface. Yet will I not do *It* the affront to ascribe it either to *Its* Modesty, Ingenuity, or Self-Conviction; for *It* intended them doubtless all to the contrary. Only the same Dulness, that first occasioned *Its* errours and mistakes, did likewise lead *It* to these ominous expressions, and like those that discern not the Back from the [137] Edge,[273] to wound it self in cutting at the Adversary.

Its Dulness therefore, or as it is expressed p. 8. *the consciousness of* Its *own*

---

[267] "Even the good Homer sometimes dozes": Defending Gale's use of the "*innocent Pleonasm*, The Divine Independent Will of God" from Howe's strictures, *TD*, pref. ep., sig. A6, appeals to this "*old saw*," which derives ultimately from Horace, *Ars poetica*, l. 359.

[268] Paulus: i.e., the apostle Paul.

[269] turn Ed.] turned *R*.

[270] *TD*, pref. ep., sigs. A6v–A7, prints in two columns apparently contradictory quotations from Howe.

[271] *nodos* Ed.] *nudos R*.

[272] No source for this Latin tag has been traced.

[273] Edge: i.e., of a knife-blade.

disabilities,[274] being so oft attested under *Its* own hand, and to which, if necessary, *It* might have another Thousand Witnesses, I shall not further pall[275] my Reader on this Subject, but return rather from this digression to my first design of obviating that in the Preface, which hath all the marks upon it of Malice, except the Wit wherewith that vice is more usually accompanied. Of that the very Title is an Argument. *De Causa Dei, or a Vindication of the Common Doctrine of Protestant Divines concerning Pre-determination, &c. from the Invidious Consequences with which it is burthened by Mr.* John Howe, *in a late* Letter *and* Postscript *of God's Prescience. By T.D.* Who would have [138] thought that *T.D.* should have become the Defender of the Faith, or that the Cause of God were so forlorn, as to be reduced to the necessity of such a Champion. It seems much rather to be the Fallacy of *Non Causa pro Causa,*[276] and usurped only the better to prepossess against Mr. Howe such Readers as would be amused by the Frontispiece.[277] The Cause of God! Turn I beseech you *Its* whole Book over, and show me any thing of that *Decorum* with which that should have been managed. What is there to be found of that Gravity, Humility, Meek-ness, Piety or Charity requisite to so glorious a pretence? (Graces where-with God usually assists those that undertake his quarrel, and with which Mr. Howe on all occasions appears to be abundantly supplied.) But a perpetual eructation[278] there is of humane Passions, a vain ostentation [139] of mistaken Learning, and a causeless Picking of Controversie.

To that Title, under which Mr. Howe is so injuriously proscribed, suc-ceeds forsooth an Epistle Dedicatory,[279] *To the Reverend Mr. John Howe, Author of the late* Letter *and* Postscript *of God's Prescience.* An additional Civility and Compellation[280] invented by *The Discourse* only for greater mockery. And many a fine word[281] *It* bestows upon him at first, to miscall him presently with the more Emphasis, praises the Author, and then the Book; but no otherwise then, as a person to be degraded is brought forth in

---

[274] *TD,* pref. ep., sig. A5v.

[275] pall: satiate, deaden interest through excess.

[276] *Non Causa pro Causa:* no cause for a cause.

[277] Frontispiece: title page.

[278] eructation: belching.

[279] In fact, a prefatory rather than a dedicatory epistle.

[280] Compellation: style of address.

[281] And many a fine word Ed.] And a many fine words *R.*

publick attired in all his Formalities, to be stripped of them again with further Ignominy.[282]

Nay, even Mr. Boyle[283] himself cannot wholly escape *Its* Commendation: which I do not object as if any thing could be well said of him that [140] is not due to his merit. But there are a kind of Sorcerers that praise where they intend to do most mischief. And the Occasion, the Place, the Manner, the Person that gives the Commendation make alwaies a difference, and cause a great alteration in that matter. Nor is it less here. For, Mr. Howe having taken the Pen on this Subject, as *The Discourse* also observes, upon that honourable Gentleman's command, the officious mentioning of Mr. Boyle p. 1. seems as if *It* had a mind too to try his mettle; or at least would reproach him for having imployed one so unfit for the service, and that was to be so shamefully (or rather shamelessly) treated for his performance.

But the summe of all *Its* Malice, whereby *It* endeavours to outlaw Mr. Howe, not only from Mr. Boyle's patronage, but from all Protestant [141] protection, is to represent him under a Popish Vizard.[284] As p. 2.[285] *Old Popish Arguments drest up* A-la-mode. *An averment of the Old Popish Calumny. An* Affidavit *of a Pontificial Accusation. Trampling* p.4. *on the Venerable Dust, which was sometimes animated by truly heroick souls, and bore the names of Zuinglius, Calvin, Beza, Perkins,*[286] *Pemble, Twisse, Davenant, Ames,* &c.[287] Then p. 12. still objects to him the opinion of Durandus,[288]

---

[282] In the ritual of degradation a priest to be deprived of his orders is formally stripped of his clerical vestments.

[283] For Boyle, see above introduction, n. 4.

[284] Vizard: mask, disguise.

[285] This and the following citations are from *TD*, pref. ep., sigs. A2v, A3v, A7v–A8v.

[286] Perkins Ed.] Penkins R.

[287] These divines represent what *TD* regards as the orthodox Protestant theological tradition slighted by Howe: the Swiss reformer Ulrich Zwingli (1484–1531); Theodore Beza (1519–1605), Calvin's successor at Geneva; William Perkins (1558–1602), the preeminent English Puritan theologian of the Elizabethan period; William Pemble (1592?–1623), a renowned Puritan preacher and writer; William Ames (1576–1633), a Calvinist Puritan divine who, to avoid persecution, emigrated to the Low Countries. For Davenant and Twisse, see above, introduction, n. 21, and above nn. 41, 84.

[288] For Durandus, see above n. 84. The point at issue has to do with God's immediate responsibility for sinful actions. Denying that it "necessarily belongs to the Original and Fountain-Being to be the first Cause" of all human actions, Howe had argued that "it may well be thought sufficiently to salve the rights and priviledg of the first Cause, to assert that no action can be done, but *by a power derived from it;* which, in reference to forbidden actions, intelligent Creatures may use or not use as they please" (*Letter*, pp. 35,

though Mr. Howe had in his *Postscript* so fully vindicated himself against it, that his first Accuser hath let it fall out of perfect ingenuity.[289] Draws *a parallel between his and the Papists Arguments against Predetermination.* And p. 13 erects another pair of Columns to that purpose, betwixt which Mr. Howe is to look out as thorow a Pillary.[290] After[291] this p. 14. saith, *the point under debate between* It *and Mr. Howe, is a* [142] *stated Controversie between the Papists and Protestants. Gives it self a little pleasure mixed with disdain, that* because there was no Smith to be found throughout al the Land of Israel, he[292] was fain to go down to the Philistines to sharpen his Ax and his Mattock, 1 Sam. 13. 19, 20. *Imitates Bradwardins Piety, therefore intituling* Its Book de Causa Dei,[293] *the Cause of God being that which* It *designs to secure*

---

36). This *TD*, p. 12, presumed was the occasion of Gale's charging Howe "with Durandus his Opinion, which was, That God concurs remotely and mediately with second Causes, (*viz.*) no otherwise than as he confers and conserves their Essence and Power of action, by which they themselves act nextly and immediately" (see further next note).

[289] The "first Accuser" is Theophilus Gale, for whom see introduction, pp. 391–92. Gale had charged Howe with "espousing" the "Hypothesis" of Durandus in arguing against divine predetermination of all human acts (*The Court of the Gentiles,* part 4, books 1, 2 [1677], p. 523), to which Howe replied that "when I wrote that *Letter,* I had never seen Durandus." Having been prompted by Gale's charge to do so, he is led in his *Postscript* to distinguish his position from Durandus's with some vehemence, insisting that whereas Durandus "denies God's *immediate concourse* to the actions of the creatures," he "never said nor thought" any such thing, denying only that this concourse is "*determinative unto wicked actions*" (*Postscript,* pp. 20, 27–28). Although *TD* continues to insist that Howe is as heterodox as Durandus, Gale did not repeat his charge (or mention Howe) in book 3 of part 4 ("Of Divine Predetermination") of the *Court of the Gentiles* (1678), which prompts Marvell's comment here that he let it fall out of "perfect ingenuity."

[290] Pillary: pillory. In *TD*, pref. ep., sig. A8, Danson had printed two columns, paralleling Howe's arguments against predetermination with citations from the Jesuit Robert Bellarmine (1542–1621), the preeminent Roman Catholic apologist of his time, and from the Dominican Diego Alvarez (c. 1550–1635), who was one of those who opposed de Molina (see n. 297).

[291] After Ed.] Af *R.*

[292] I.e., Howe.

[293] *TD*, pref. ep., sig. A8v: "*I have intitled my Answer* De Causa Dei [About the Cause of God], *rather than* De Causa Deo [About Cause from (or in relation to) God]; *which latter might be proper enough for the subject, a Defence of Gods interest as the first cause in all the actions of his Creatures. But herein I have imitated Bradwardine's Piety, who would signifie thereby that it was the Cause of God he designed to secure from the impetuous assaults of its Adversaries, among whom I am heartily sorry you should be numbred, as to this instance.*" The *De Causa Dei contra Pelagium* of Thomas Bradwardine (c. 1290–1349)

from the impetuous Assaults of Its *Adversaries, among which* It *is heartily sory Mr. Howe should be numbred as to this instance.* This kind of proceeding does argue rather the strength of Malice, than of the Cause. For although we live under a rationall jealousie alwaies of Popery, yet whatsoever is said by any author of that perswasion, is not forthwith therefore to be clamorously rejected. Have not there constantly been among them, men [143] fit to be owned for Holy Life, Good Sense, Great Learning?[294] And in many points we agree with them, and shall in all, whensoever Our Eyes shall be shut, or Theirs shall be opened.[295] *The Discourse* had indeed done something to the purpose, could *It* have shown the Doctrine of Predetermination to be one of those Discriminating Causes upon which we have made a separation from that Church, that it is an Article of Faith in which our Creeds differ, and that it were a fit Test to be imposed upon them in order to their more speedy Conviction.

Which last, if *It* can bring about for them, so that they may be acquitted upon Renouncing this Doctrine imputed to them, (instead of the Transubstantiation, (which Mr. Howe too escaped so narrowly.)[)] I presume they would, notwithstanding all the Popery, take it for an high obligation. For indeed, whereas *The* [144] *Discourse* affirms this of Predetermination to be *a stated Controversie betwixt the Papists and the Protestants;* the Papists against, the Protestants for it; there is not through *Its*[296] whole Book a more notorious Falshood. For this Debate arose first among the Papists, some of them being of one, others of the contrary Opinion; so that the Controversie was stated betwixt themselves. But that which is now *T.D's* was first the Dominican Doctrine;[297] and I wonder therefore the less if *It* continue

---

developed a predestinarian line of thought stressing the irresistibility of divine grace. It was first printed in 1618, edited by Sir Henry Savile, with the assistance of William Twisse (for whom see above, n. 41).

[294] The generosity and catholicity of this distinguishes Marvell from the Milton of *Of True Religion* and sets him in the company of Baxter, who wrote of the papists, "I doubt not but that God hath many sanctified Ones among them" (*Reliquiae Baxterianae* [1696], 1.131, §213 (25).

[295] I.e., when we Protestants enjoy illumination after death ("Our Eyes shall be shut"), or when Roman Catholics recognize the truth ("Theirs shall be opened").

[296] *Its* Ed.] I*t't R.*

[297] The "congruist" teaching of the Jesuits Luis de Molina and Francisco de Suarez (for whom see above, n. 112) that salvation depends not upon predetermination but upon divine foreknowledge of human cooperation with grace (that is, upon the congruity between the gift of grace and its recipient), led to controversy with Dominican

herein the Dominican Spirit. Since, and from that original, the same Argument hath indeed been also diffused among the Protestants, and they likewise have differ'd about it with one another; but it was never taken, in holding it either way, to be the Protestant Character. The Predeterminative Concourse is not to be found in any Confession of the several Re-[145]formed Churches; But this matter hath been left entire to every man's best Judgment, and one Party is as much Papist in it as the others. What two men of equal Capacity can argue against Predetermination, but they must have the same Apprehensions in some measure, in matters so obvious? and it ought not to be improved to eithers prejudice, no more than for two to speak the same words in discoursing of one subject. Charron,[298] whose Wisdom, p. 1. Bradwardine,[299] whose Piety, p. 14. and especially, Caesar Borgia, whose Chalk, p.15. *T.D.* makes use of,[300] were none of the best Protestants: And yet I am far from taxing *It* therefore of Popery, *or giving my self a little pleasure mixed with disdain,* that it was fain to go down to them to sharpen *Its* Howe or *Its* Mattock.[301] Let *It* rather solace *It* self in that Lordly posture of mind; nor will I envy *It;* especially, seeing to take [146] that satisfaction in a thing which *It* makes so Criminous,[302] is the only Joy of which I think the Evil Spirits are capable.

And as to *Its* saying, p. 2. *that Mr. Howe avers the Old Popish Calumny, that by the Protestant Doctrine God is made the Author of Sin.* And p. 4. *that he trambles upon the venerable dust,* &c. *of Zuinglius, Calvin, Beza, Perkins,*

---

theologians, notaly Domingo Banez (1528–1604), who stressed the divine role in effecting salvation in ways which their critics identified with Calvinism. When a resolution of the dispute proved impossible, Pope Paul V in 1607 decreed that neither party was heretical and that the Dominicans were not to be charged with Calvinism, nor the Jesuits with Pelagianism (an undue stress on the human role in effecting salvation).

[298] An unexpected person for *TD,* pref. ep., sig. A2, to refer to uncritically since Pierre Charron (1541–1603) was a Roman Catholic apologist whose three-volume *De la sagesse* (1601) developed a distinction between worldly, human, and spiritual wisdom often thought to have contributed to the development of moralism and Deism.

[299] For Bradwardine, see above, n. 293.

[300] *TD,* pref. ep., sig. B1: "I have been as brief and I could in my Answer . . . and have come (as Caesar Borgia said of the French in their Expedition into Italy) rather with Chalk in my hands to mark out the Inns, than with Arms to break through and take possession." Machiavelli says this of Charles VIII of France in his own voice (not that of Caesar Borgia) in chapter xii of *The Prince.*

[301] 1 Sam. 13:20, cited above p. 476, but here with "Howe" naughtily substituted for "Ax."

[302] Criminous: criminal.

Pemble, Davenant, Twisse, Ames, &c. it proceeds from the same malice, and may therefore receive the same answer: For I have shown, first, that this Predetermination is not the stated Doctrine of Protestants, nor hath there yet any General Council of them been held, where *T. D.* hath presided: but if there should at any time hereafter, *It* is so unhappy and singular in expressing *Its* sense, in this matter, that I much fear lest the Plurality of Votes should affix the dangerous Greek name to *Its* Religion.[303] [147] And as to those Worthies whom *It* cites by rote, *It* draws them indeed within the reach of both Old and New Calumny, by pretending they were of *Its* Opinion; whereas one may safely affirm at adventure,[304] that they were all of them too well inlightned to have ever thought or spoken after *Its* manner. What it may have extorted from them by Necromancy, I know not; but they had not the happiness to have read *Its De Causa Dei* in their life-time: Nor do I think that Death corrupts mens Minds as their Bodies. Of these, whom *The Discourse* enumerates, Calvin and Beza, have been reproachfully charged by Bellarmine and other Romanists, as making God the Author of Sin: but yet there is not to be found in all their works an assertion of God's Determinative Concurrence. How far some of the rest of them have taken scope on this subject, I have no obligation here [148] more than *The Discourse,* to particularize: neither did Mr. Howe name any man, as being the fairer way by much, arguing only against the Opinion. But seeing *T.D.* hath made bold with Bishop Davenant, I will ask no better. For that truly venerable, dust, which *It* hath stirred will flie in *T.Ds.* eyes; if I be not mistaken. *Dissert de Predestinatione & Reprobatione,* it is thus, *Deus, Agens ex Praedestinationis, operatur haec priora* (scil. *Fidem, Sanctitatem, Perseverantiam) per Influxum Gratiae Efficacis, At ex Decreto Reprobationis nihil agit quo Deterior efficiatur Reprobatus—*That is, for it is well worth the translating: *God; acting according to his Decree of Predestination, works these things in the first place,* (to wit, *Faith, Holiness, and Perseverance) by the Influence of Efficacious Grace; but, according to his Decree of Reprobation he acts nothing by which the Reprobate should be made worse.*[305] Methinks, [149[306]] as *T.D.* will have the Bishop to be of *Its,* so, in all reason, *It* should be also of

---

[303] Presumably the "Greek name" is *heresy,* or perhaps *anathema.*

[304] at adventure: at a hazard, without more ado (i.e., "one may safely take the risk of affirming . . . ").

[305] John Davenant, *Dissertationes Duae: Prima de Morte Christi . . . Altera de Praedestinatione & Reprobatione* (Cambridge, 1650), p. 114. For Davenant, see introduction, n. 21.

[306] 149 Ed.] 146 R.

the Bishop's Opinion; and if *It* intends no more, as Mr. Howe no less than is here said, I cannot see why there might not be an end of *The Discourse,* and of this Controversie.

But however, I hope that I may have done a good work, if upon sight of these unexpected Remarques, Mr. Howe, though fitted doubtless for a much better and fuller Reply, would deliberate before he makes this Adversary so considerable as to blot Paper on *Its* occasion. Let *It* in the mean time, venditate[307] all *Its* Street-adages, *Its* odd ends of *Latine, Its* broken shreds of Poets, and *Its* musty lumber of Schoolmen. Let *It* enjoy the ingenuity of having unprovoked fallen upon a person, *whose parts* It *acknowledged,* for whom It *hath such an Affection,* with whom It *had so many* [150] *years Academical Society,*[308] and so *long friendship:* but whom *It* now *must number among God's Adversaries.*[309] Let *It* value it self upon these things: for all these considerations do heighten the Price of an Assassinate.[310] But may Mr. Howe still continue his Sobriety, Simplicity, and Equality of Temper: glorifying God rather in the exercise of Practical Christian Vertues, than affecting the honour of a speculative Question. But if he had a mind to be Vindictive, there is no way to despight the Adversary more sensibly, than, as clamorous women, by giving them no answer. Till men grow into a better humour, and learn to treat of Divinity more civilly, they are unfit for conversation.

Another, I see, who is now his Third Aggressor, hath already assaulted him, though less barbarously, in a *Letter to a Friend,* &c.[311] Yet even [151] he introduces his Book with Job 13.7. *Wilt thou speak wickedly for God, and talk deceitfully for him?* What shall Mr. Howe do in this Case? Is the Bible therefore to be turned into a Libel? And shall he *search the Scriptures* to find out a test equally cutting? He need not go far, were he of that mind, to retaliate. How easie were the parallel betwixt Job's three Friends (to whom those words were spoken) and three such comfortable Gentlemen! And why may not Mr. Howe nick them as well out of Job, *c.* 12. *v.* 3, 4. *But I have understanding as well as you; I am not inferiour to you; yea who knoweth not such things as these? I am as one mocked of his neighbour, who calleth upon God,*

---

[307] venditate: display or exhibit, as for sale.

[308] At Oxford, where Howe and Danson were both fellows of Magdalen College in the 1650s (1652–55 and 1652–57, respectively).

[309] These phrases are from *TD*, pref. ep., sigs. A2, A4v, A8v.

[310] Assassinate: either murder or assassin, the deed or the role on which *TD* is here ironically recommended to congratulate itself.

[311] For this work by John Troughton, see introduction, p. 392, n. 38.

and he answereth him. The just upright man is laughed to scorn. Or, if he
would be yet severer, the same, *chap.* 13. *v.*4, 5. will hit them home. *But ye are
For-*[152]*gers of Lyes; ye are all Physicians of no value. O that you would
altogether hold your peace, and it should be your Wisdom.* And then at last, to
determine the whole Dispute, He might conclude with *Job* 42.7. The Lord
*said to Eliphaz the Temanite, My wrath is kindled against thee, and against thy
two Friends; for ye have not spoken of me the thing that is right as my servant
Job hath.* After all which, what more reasonable, in order to Reconciliation,
than the *verse* following? *Go to my servant Job, and offer up for your selves a
burnt offering, and my servant Job shall pray for you (for him will I accept) lest I
deal with you after your folly, in that you have not spoken of me the thing that is
right, as my servant Job hath.* But the Word of God is not so to be turned
into the Reproach of Man, though the Allusion may seem never so happy;
nor have I instanced thus far, otherwise than [153] to show the frivolousness,
though too usual of that Practice.

But therefore I would advise Mr. Howe, though not to that excusable
sullenness and silence, with which some have chastised the World for
having used them unworthily; nor to that tacite contempt of his Adversaries, in which he were hitherto justifiable; yet, that, having made a laudable Attempt, of which several good men are it seems not capable, he
would, for peace sake, either wholly surcease this contest; or forbear at least
till they have all done. For it is more easie to deal with them all than single;
and, were they once imbodied, come to a consistence among themselves, or
had agreed who should speak for them, they had right to his Answer. But
until then, Mr. Howe is no more obliged in whatsoever is called Honour,
Reason, or Conscience, than if [154] every hair of *T.Ds.* that stands on[312]
end, should demand particular satisfaction. It is the same for a Divine, as
he, to turn Common Disputant, as for an Architect to saw Timber, or
cleave Loggs; which, though he may sometimes do for health or exercise,
yet to be constant at it, were to debase and neglect his Vocation. Mr. Howe
hath work enough cut out of a nobler nature, in his *Living Temple,*[313] in
which, like that of Solomon, there is *neither Hammer, nor Axe, nor any Tool
of Iron to be heard,* I King. 6. 7.[314] nothing that can offend, all to edifie. And
this I heartily wish that he may accomplish: But therefore, as he hath not
hitherto sought, so that he would avoid all Contention; lest, as David, for

---

[312] on Ed.] an *R.*
[313] I.e., Howe's *The Living Temple* (1675).
[314] 7. Ed.] 8. *R.*

having been a man of blood, was forbid to build the Temple, I Chron. 22.8. so he, as being a man of Controversie.

As for my self, I expect in this li-[155]tigious Age, that some or other will Sue me for having Trespassed thus far on Theological Ground: But I have this for my plea, that I stepped over on no other Reason than (which any man legally may do) to hinder one Divine from offering violence to another. And, if I should be molested on that account, I doubt not but some of the *Protestant* Clergy will be ready therefore to give me the like Assistance.

FINIS

Index